INDUSTRIAL RELATIONS
IN SOUTH AFRICA

INDUSTRIAL RELATIONS IN SOUTH AFRICA

by

SONIA BENDIX

THIRD EDITION

**Foreword to the First Edition
by
Prof. S P Cilliers**

JUTA & CO, LTD
1996

First published 1989
Third edition 1996
Second impression 1997

© Juta and Co, Ltd
PO Box 14373, Kenwyn 7790

ISBN 0 7021 3453 8

Cover illustration used with kind permission of the South African
International Trade Exhibition, SAITEX. The illustration was originally
commissioned as a "mini-mural" by the organisers of SAITEX for the
promotion of the exhibition. Three professional South African public
artists, Nicky Blumenfeld, Dumisano Mabaso and Eve Dumont, part
of a group intent on renewing city landscapes and linking issues of
culture and economy, produced the work. Titled "The Art of Doing
Business in Africa", the original hangs at SAITEX headquarters at
the National Exhibition Centre in Johannesburg—as testimony to the
powerful potential contribution that art can make to a developing
nation.

Subediting and typesetting: Sarah-Jane Galbraith, Greyton
Cover design: Joy Wrench, Cape Town

Printed and bound in South Africa by
Creda Press, Eliot Avenue, Eppindust II, Cape Town

To

My Parents, whose many sacrifices empowered me.

For

My Children and all my Students, both past and present.

PREFACE TO THE THIRD EDITION

Whenever a revision of *Industrial Relations in South Africa* becomes imminent, a critical decision has to be made — 'Update or rewrite?' — and, inevitably, what starts off as an update or new edition evolves into a more comprehensive rewrite. This is particularly true of this, the latest version of the text: not only because the sequence of chapters has been drastically altered, but also because of the numerous changes and additions to the content. It is now seven years and a few days since the first edition was published, and perhaps the magical figure had some influence on the magnitude of the reshuffle. Be that as it may, the reader will find much which is still familiar, together with a great deal of new material.

The change in sequence was regarded as necessary, firstly to create a more even flow from the macro view of Industrial Relations and of different systems in their societal setting to the more micro perspective on structure, processes and practices within a system; secondly, to integrate general theory with the South African reality; and, thirdly, to travel the road from traditional Industrial Relations thinking to the more modern, more progressive mode of developing organisations and, therewith, relationships within those organisations.

Because of the dynamic nature of Industrial Relations, the content of text on this subject *must* be continually revised and adapted — even more so in the South African context where, over the past five years, radical sociopolitical changes have occurred. At the time of writing the expansion of these changes into legislation, labour relations practices and relationships within the system has only just commenced. The industrial relations arena remains volatile and numerous changes (or, even, entirely new developments) may be expected within the next five years. It is to be hoped that, on all sides, rationality and reasonableness will prevail; that the parties involved will rapidly grow in sophistication so that we may, eventually, achieve the ideal of general labour peace and constructive relationship building so necessary for continued prosperity.

Once again it remains merely to thank those without whom the completion of this text would have been well nigh impossible. First and foremost, I wish to convey a special word of thanks to Sarah-Jane Galbraith — typist, typesetter and editor — whose Christmas and New Year have passed her by (due mainly to our joint underestimation of our job) but who continued resolutely and expertly to the end. Then, too, there are my publishers — in particular Adèle Levitan — for her admirable patience and for displaying sufficient faith in me to know that I would eventually deliver, albeit at the very last moment! My thanks also go to my children and to my mother, whose patience with me was, as always, never ending; and, lastly, to those special colleagues and friends who, paradoxically, provided distraction from my work but who may, in the process, have helped to preserve the faculties necessary to complete the task ahead.

SONIA BENDIX

Cape Town
Monday 1 January 1996

FOREWORD TO THE FIRST EDITION

The extension of the right to collective bargaining to the majority of South Africa's labour force at the beginning of the Eighties followed shortly upon the transformation of the South African economy from being based on agriculture and mining to being fully diversified in the modern sense.

These developments have heralded a completely new era for industrial relations, characterised by the rapid growth of trade unions and an escalation in the potential for labour conflict. This is evidenced by the upward trend in the incidence of work stoppages and strikes, which dramatically underscores the need for industrial relations skill for both labour and management representatives.

Under these circumstances the demand for the services of skilled industrial relations practitioners has increased significantly in South Africa. The skills required are, however, not limited to those pertaining to negotiation and the settlement of disputes. Industrial relations practitioners, in order to be effective, need to have an understanding of the framework within which negotiations occur.

Given these needs, Sonia Bendix's text offers a useful contribution to the literature on the subject available to students and practitioners. It deals with both the broader context as well as the technical aspects of industrial relations issues.

S P CILLIERS
Stellenbosch
December 1988

AUTHOR'S NOTE: FIRST EDITION

This book is not intended as an academic treatise. It was written to fulfil a need among industrial relations practitioners and students for a comprehensive reference work in industrial relations, with particular emphasis on the South African situation. It can, therefore, be regarded as a practical guide to South African Industrial Relations and, where theoretical concepts or historical facts are introduced, they have been supplied to enhance our understanding of the day-to-day practice.

Because of the non-academic intentions of the book, it has been regarded as unnecessary to use the scientific method of referencing and quotation. Footnotes and numerical references tend to cause discomfort among readers not intent upon strictly academic pursuits and to disturb their train of thought and understanding. Instead, sources are listed at the end of each chapter. To some of these authors (such as Salamon and Friedman) I am greatly indebted, as their writings underscored by own perceptions. The others, in general, contributed much to my understanding of specific topics. Nevertheless, I take full responsibility for all ideas and proposals put forward within the text.

The field of industrial relations is so wide, so diverse and so interesting that the greatest problem encountered was the question of what should be omitted. In making my selection, I have attempted to keep in mind the needs of the student and practitioner but, at the same time, to supply them with the necessary background material. Even so, further reading would be required for a more intensive study of particular topics.

It remains only to thank the many persons who assisted and supported me in the writing of this text. Firstly to Fred Jacobs and Colman Foods, who so readily offered me the necessary word-processing facilities, thus relieving me of what to some writers is a greater problem than the actual compilation of a text. I sincerely hope that the book will contribute towards improved workplace practices and to a better understanding between management and employees so that, for Colman Foods, it will prove to have been a fruitful exercise in social responsibility. In particular, I should like to express my thanks to Veronica Twynam who, under considerable time pressure and in often difficult circumstances, so expertly and professionally executed her task in typing (and retyping) the manuscript.

This book would also not have been written in the time allowed had I not received the unqualified support of my Department Head, Mr Cyprian Martin. I know that he fought many battles on my behalf and I sincerely appreciate the faith he displayed in my efforts. Then there are my other colleagues at the Peninsula and other technikons and in business, from whom I received both moral and practical support, especially Bernie Pick, who acted as my mentor and advisor during the writing of the chapters on Labour Economics and the South African Labour Market, and Philip Greybe, with whom the idea of writing the book originated.

Finally, I should like to thank my family and all my very good friends, who may have had no direct input but whose love and forbearance encouraged me to continue with my task.

16 August 1988

CONTENTS

1

THE LABOUR RELATIONSHIP — A CONCEPTUAL ANALYSIS

OVERVIEW

Industrial Relations cannot be studied before some background to the subject has been obtained and some basis for analysis and interpretation established. This necessitates, in the first place, an analysis of the concept 'industrial relations' and an identification of its principal elements. Thereafter, the logical step is to analyse the relationship itself and to see what sets it apart from other relationships.

The labour relationship arises from work in industrial society and is marked by certain negative attitudes, a great degree of depersonalisation and feelings of powerlessness amongst employees. Much of this has its roots in the Industrial Revolution, in the type of work which evolved from this and in traditional attitudes to work and the work situation.

Having analysed the basic characteristics of the relationship, it is necessary to identify the parties and the roles adopted by each, and to discover not only how they interact but why they interact in that manner. Commonality and conflict constitute the two poles of interaction within the labour relationship. The parties can either cooperate and engage in participative processes or rely on the use of power and collective bargaining, although these are not mutually exclusive. In fact, often parties move continually between the two poles established by commonality and conflict. Also, attention may shift continually between the individual and the collective. Essentially, a party may adopt one of three approaches, depending on whether he favours bargaining or cooperation — or, perhaps, neither of these. The mode of interaction will be largely determined by the interactive effect of custom and tradition, legal determination, mutual agreement and ethical considerations, among the most important of which are integrity, trust and concepts of fairness.

Finally, there are numerous external factors which will influence the manner in which the parties behave towards each other. These include sociopolitical and economic factors and the role of trade unions, as well as demographic and technological developments.

DEFINITIONS

The term 'labour relations' refers to the relationships between people who work and those for whom they work; as such, labour or work relationships have, therefore, existed since the first individual approached another to perform a task for him against the promise of payment. On the other hand, Industrial Relations as a specific area of study is comparatively new, having had its origins in the Industrial Revolution and in subsequent attempts to regulate the interactions between the new breed of employer and employee which evolved within modern industrialised society. Because this new work relationship, centring in mass employment and mass production and marked by a growing polarisation between those who owned and those who laboured, revealed a heightened potential for conflict, Industrial Relations as a field of study placed emphasis on the institutionalisation of conflict by way of collective representation, collective bargaining, joint regulation and legislative constraints. This emphasis is evident in most traditional definitions of the term 'industrial relations'. Thus the British Commission on Industrial Relations defines the term as including '... any policy action, pay condition or agreement within a given concern which enables the workforce to continue in a cooperative way', while Clegg sees it as encompassing '... the rules governing employment, together with the ways these rules are made and changed and their interpretation and administration'. Flanders, too, emphasises the institutionalised aspects of the relationship when he says that '... a system of industrial relations is a system of rules ... in other words, the subject deals with certain regulated, institutionalised relationships in industry. Personal or (in the language of sociology) 'unstructured' relationships have their importance for management and workers, but they lie outside the scope of a system of industrial relations. ... The study of Industrial Relations may therefore be described as a study of the institution of job regulation.'

While these definitions do point to the need for regulation of the modern labour relationship and to the fact that this is often done on a collective basis, they do not sufficiently stress that we are, in essence, dealing with a relationship, on both an individual and a group basis, and that the nature of the rules and regulations, even the manner in which they are made, will largely depend on the nature of the relationship itself. If the labour relationship, whether formal or informal, individual or collective, undergoes radical change, new and different industrial relations processes, rules and institutions will evolve. Equally, significant changes within society or within the institutions and laws which govern the labour relationship will impact on labour relations, causing the parties to adopt new roles and to interact in new and different ways. There is, thus, a great deal of reciprocity between the labour relationship and the institutions and laws which govern it. Any definition of 'industrial relations' or 'labour relations' should take cognizance of this fact.

What, then, is meant by the term 'industrial relations'? When answering this question it is, in the first place, necessary to deal with the existent confusion as regards the distinction between 'industrial relations' and 'labour relations'. Literature on this subject contains numerous highly technical and semantically sophisticated distinctions between the two concepts, yet it could be contended that no such differentiation should be made and that the term 'industrial (labour) relations' — or, better still, 'work relations' — should be used. The subject deals with labour in that the relationship is established in and arises from the work situation. However, the nature of the work performed — and, therefore, of the relationship — is particular to modern industrialised or industrialising society. If it is accepted that the epithet 'industrial' refers not only to industry but to a type of society based on sophisticated economic activity, then all relationships arising from work which contributes to, supports or promotes the economy and economic society will resort under the term 'industrial (labour) relations'.

Having dealt with the semantic aspects of the concept, we turn to its meaning. From previous discussions it has become clear that, in our study of industrial (labour) relations, we are dealing with relationships between people within a work situation; that these relationships may be of an individual or collective nature; that they are particular to modern industrialised society and that they give rise to actions, reactions, processes, rules, institutions and regulations which in turn will affect the relationship itself. On the basis of this analysis, Industrial Relations may be described as encompassing a study of:

- relationships,
- the work situation and working man,
- the problems and issues of modern industrialised and industrialising society

and of certain

- processes,
- structures,
- institutions and
- regulations,

all of which are placed or occur within a specific social, political, economic and historical context and none of which can or should be studied in isolation.

ANALYSIS OF THE LABOUR RELATIONSHIP

The Labour Relationship as a Human Relationship

In Labour Relations we deal essentially with people who, because of their mutual involvement in the work situation, have been placed in a specific relationship with one another. The relationship formed is a human one and, as such, will contain elements common to all other relationships such as friendship, marriage, business partnerships, social, religious and political liaisons. What makes these relationships work should also promote a sound labour relationship. Consequently, it could be postulated that, like all other relationships, the labour relationship will be nurtured by mutuality of interest, reciprocity of support, understanding, trust, facilitative communication, shared goals and shared values; and that it will falter should one or more of these qualities be absent. Also, as in the case of all other relationships, the labour relationship is multi-layered and dynamic, such change being dependent on the evolving status, needs, attitudes and perceptions of the parties concerned.

Uniqueness of the Relationship

Just as the institution of marriage is unique in that it centres in two persons committing to each other and raising a family, so the labour relationship has its unique characteristics and problems. The major distinguishing feature of this relationship is that it arises from the need for economic activity within society and from man's need to work and to earn a living, but its uniqueness is to be found in the societal and individual importance of the relationship, the often negative attitude of the parties involved and in the depersonalised and mostly collective nature of the relationship itself.

The society in which we live is economically based. The greater part of our activities and institutions centre in the economy. Within this context, adult man's identity is derived from the type of economic activity in which he is engaged. Who you are depends on what you do. If this is accepted and if we consider that at least one half of man's waking hours is devoted to work, then work and the relationships established within the work situation are amongst the most important aspects of modern human life. In today's world, work is central to man's existence; yet those who employ labour, working man himself and society at large place too little emphasis on the work relationship and man's attitude to work remains, at best, ambivalent and, at worst, predominantly negative.

The negativism prevalent in the labour relationship derives mainly from traditional attitudes to work and to workers and from the problems engendered by industrialisation and mass production, both of which are discussed in greater detail below; but it also arises from the almost involuntary and impersonal nature of the relationship. An employee does not seek work with a particular employer because he likes that employer or because he is in any way committed to the undertaking, although this may later occur. Essentially he takes a job and enters the relationship merely to fulfil other, more personal, needs. Thus, from the beginning, there is not that sense of partnership, closeness and mutual commitment which is found in many other relationships. This is further aggravated by the fact that an employee may feel that he is coerced into the work situation; that he is, because of circumstances, his lack of education or personal limitations, forced to work or to do a certain type of work while he might prefer to be engaged in another, more attractive, pastime or occupation. Thus, more often than not, the relationship has from the outset a negative valence. This negativism increases if there is a markedly uneven distribution of wealth, if employees cannot perceive themselves as being advantaged by the increased profitability of the undertaking, if too much power resides with some of the participants and if, in the extreme, employees regard the situation as an 'unfair' deal brought about by an 'unfair' system.

Equally, from his side the employer or the manager who represents him has no personal interest in the relationship or, for that matter, in the employee. He is not interested in the individuality of the worker or in his unique characteristics as a human being different from all other human beings, but merely in his ability to perform the work required. At worst, he sees the worker as just another factor of production and, at best, as another, replaceable, member of the labour force. Thus, traditionally, the labour relationship is defined not as a relationship between an employer and an employee, but as one between employers and employees. Both parties, and particularly the employee, are placed in a group context, leading to further depersonalisation. This perception of collectivism is exacerbated by societal divisions between those who work for others and those who own or manage, leading ultimately to the concept of a working class, where the word 'work' connotes not an action in itself but the act of working for others.

From the above it becomes apparent that the labour relationship is both complex and paradoxical by nature. The relationship itself and the manner in which it is conducted are of immense importance to the individual and to society, yet both parties approach the relationship and each other with a certain amount of negativity and indifference. It is also a relationship in which perceptions of collectivity, from both sides, play an important role, with the result that personal identities become submerged in the anonymity of the collectivity but where, in the final analysis, only the assertion of and respect for individuality can lead to personal satisfaction and meaningful relationships. It is these paradoxes which the Industrial Relations student and practitioner will ultimately be required to resolve.

CONTEXTUAL BACKGROUND

History plays an important role in the shaping of individual attitudes and societal norms and institutions. Thus the labour relationship needs to be placed within the context of the most important occurrence in economic history, the Industrial Revolution, and within the context of traditional attitudes to work.

The Industrial Revolution

The Industrial Revolution was a social and economic convulsion which commenced in the fourteenth century, or even earlier, but which displayed its full impact only towards the middle of the eighteenth century. Because it changed the economic order, it had an immense impact on existing social structures, on the perceptions of individual men and society at large and on man's working life. Together with the French Revolution, it played a major role in shaping the type of society we know today.

In pre-industrial society man's work was traditionally or mandatorily determined. Furthermore, his working life was closely aligned to his political and religious life. Working man, with the exception of merchants and those in service, was engaged either in agriculture or in an established craft. An accepted, even if not acceptable, order and pattern of relationships existed, such as that between the landowner and his tenants or between the craftsman and his apprentice. Small communities were formed, in which the worker saw himself not as being in employment but as fulfilling a particular function in society. The idea of earning a living, if consciously formulated, was secondary to his fulfilment of this traditional or functional role. Also, until the eighteenth century, the striving for gain or excess profit, as we know it, was generally regarded as highly immoral. Heilbroner quotes the example of a sermon delivered in a Boston church in the year 1644. The minister, referring to a certain Keayne charged with the crime of making more than sixpence profit in a shilling, goes on to expand on the following 'false' principles of trade.

- That a man buys low and sells high
- That a man raises prices to make up for losses suffered
- That a man sells expensively because he bought expensively

As Heilbroner states, 'The early capitalists were not the pillars of society, but often its outcasts and deracines'. This does not mean that capital did not exist. It did, in the form of private wealth, but there was little or no attempt to put it to aggressive use — that is, to risk it in order to accumulate more capital. Even at a later stage, when the first efforts at mass production were initiated, the longest and most labour-intensive process was favoured above the shortest and most efficient.

By the year 1700 the old order was already on the decline. In contrast to the sermon referred to above, society now began to accept that man was necessarily greedy for gain, that gain was the centre of commercial activity and that no law should exist against gain. This change in mores had not occurred overnight and was a consequence of a number of interrelating factors, among which were colonial expansionism, the rise of nationalism and internationalism and increased scientific curiosity, the latter having as a result the marketing of new inventions, leading to greater mechanisation of the manufacturing process.

Thus the industrial era was born. It brought with it the uprooting of working man from his traditional way of life and the birth of a disorientated class of people known as the Proletariat. Large factories were established where a mass of workers performed relatively humdrum tasks to the dictates of a single employer or owner. Man was obliged by economic necessity to sell his labour, to perform tasks within prescribed limits and to assist in producing goods, the end product of which he often did not see, much less own. It stands to reason that work lost much of its meaning and that the working man had to search for a new identity. This he later found in the working class and in membership of workers' trade unions, which differed greatly from the guilds previously established for craftsmen.

New relationship patterns had to be established. The depersonalisation of work and the work situation caused a division between the employer and his employees, bringing about a further polarisation between those who laboured and those who owned or managed. Particularly during the early years of industrialisation, workers suffered great hardships. Many saw capitalist activity as based on the principle of keeping the poor poor, since any increase in wages would signify a concomitant cut in profits. The idea took root that the capitalist, through his control of economic activity, had forced the ordinary man into a situation where he had to abandon his traditional role in society and sell his labour for a wage which was often below subsistence level, all to the benefit of the employer. This is a perception which, sometimes unjustifiably so, is still held by many employees today. It greatly contributes to the negative attitude many workers hold towards their employment and to the basic conflict between employer and employee.

Much has been said of the negative effects of the Industrial Revolution and little of the positive results, such as greater progress and development in all spheres and, later, a general improvement in the standard of living of all people. In the Industrial Relations context our concern is mainly with the fact that the Industrial Revolution gave rise to a new type of society, centred in sophisticated economic activity, and thus to economic man. Industrial Relations, as a human science, concentrates on the latter, namely economic man. For the Industrial Relations student, the greatest impact of the Industrial Revolution is, therefore, to be found in the following.

- The removal of man's economic activity from his personal and social life
- The depersonalisation of work and, consequently, of the employment relationship
- The polarisation between the mass of employed on the one hand and the owners or managers on the other, resulting in the rise of a working class consciousness and providing the necessary impetus for the growth of trade unionism
- The negative attitudes engendered by the new dispensation
- The central role now played by economic activity, causing it to become the main aspect of man's life and one which impacts greatly on his personal, social and political life
- The predominance of capitalism, being the ownership by one person of the 'tools' of production
- The consequential concept of 'selling labour', leading to the disempowerment of the producers of such labour

By the beginning of the twentieth century the Industrial Revolution was full blown in that all its major consequences were already evident. In fact, what is often termed the Second Industrial Revolution had already begun. The world was now faced with even more sophisticated technology and systems; yet the major problems caused by industrialisation are still prevalent within the work situation today. Even within what is perhaps incorrectly called 'post-industrial society', no significant reconciliation has occurred between man's working life and his personal and social life. Work and the employment relationship are still by and large of a depersonalised nature. Polarisation, although perhaps not as great as before, continues to exist and the role of trade unions is essentially antagonistic. Thus negative attitudes remain and man continues to negate or resist the importance of work and economic activity, seeking instead to promote his personal and social life — often at the expense or in defiance of the work relationship.

Traditional Attitudes to Work

Individual perceptions of work differ, being dependent, inter alia, on the type of work performed. However, a generally negative attitude to work does exist. As explained earlier, this attitude is engendered firstly by the nature of the labour relationship as such, and secondly by the presumed ills of industrial society, but they are also rooted in traditional perceptions and attitudes.

Traditionally, work to most men is no more than a necessary evil. Biblically this is supported by the fact that work was the form of punishment meted out for man's original sin. The Israelites, too, viewed work as a means of atonement for disobeying the word of God. In ancient Greece, work was viewed as degrading, a drudgery and a curse. This led, according to Biesheuwel, to the institution of slavery, which constituted an attempt by man to exclude labour from the conditions of his life. In more recent times the feudal system perpetuated the distinction between the idle rich and those who laboured.

Although these views may be ascribed to a pre-industrial society, they continue to influence modern man's attitude towards his work. More importantly, they established a division between those who were either so privileged, so good or so rich that they could afford not to work and those who were obliged to labour. This resulted in a desire on the part of the working man also to achieve that state of idleness enjoyed by his perceived superiors.

The negative attitude previously held towards work was to some extent ameliorated by the rise of Christianity and later by the teachings of Calvin and the acceptance of the so-called Protestant Work Ethic. Calvin taught that those living a pious life, devoted to hard work, would be earmarked for eternal salvation. Work was held out as ennobling and a fulfilment of man's purpose in life. Idleness and self-indulgence, on the other hand, came to be regarded as deadly sins. This did not mean that man found any greater pleasure in work, but merely that he now regarded hard work as necessary for achieving his place in heaven.

It was the Protestant Work Ethic which partly carried working man through the Industrial Revolution and well into the twentieth century. With the onset of industrialisation, man was faced by an entirely new work situation and, naturally, his attitude to work also changed. Prior to the Industrial Revolution man might have held a negative attitude to work, but his place in society — that is, whether he worked or not and the type of work he was required to perform — had been established by tradition or command. He accepted it as part of the social order and, therefore, his destiny. Also, his working life was integrated with his personal and social life. Industrialisation, underscored by the principles of individual freedom established by the French Revolution, brought a change in the existing order. Although man now had greater personal freedom, he became estranged from his work and was obliged to sell his labour, often for a mere pittance. It can be conjectured that work became an even greater burden than before and that, for many such workers, the only consolation was to be found in the thought that they would eventually receive their reward in heaven.

The twentieth century brought with it a change in values, a greater emphasis on individualism and the rise of the so-called permissive society. As a result, the Protestant Work Ethic was gradually, but not totally, eroded. In a society which stressed the rights of the individual, democratic structures and social consciousness, man no longer accepted his work or what happened to him in the workplace as punishment for his sins, his predestined lot, or a duty within a prescribed moral code. Instead, he now emphasised his individual rights, including his right to fair treatment, to meaningfulness and growth and to some satisfaction from the tasks performed. Yet strains of traditional and Calvinist perceptions remained. To many, work still had a negative valence, particularly in that it still separated the 'haves' from the 'have nots' and in the perception that man was forced to sell his labour to an employer or owner in order to survive. On the other hand, most individuals regarded work as an obligation and a status symbol, frowning upon dilettantes who did not earn their own living. Yet the modern worker is prepared to fulfil his obligation to work only under certain conditions. It is these conditions which so far have formed the subject of both individual and collective bargaining.

Now, as the end of the twentieth century approaches, the work relationship and man's attitude to work are again undergoing significant change. In post-modern society, dominated by technological innovation and the population explosion, working man is becoming increasingly better educated and better equipped to handle tasks of an advanced nature. Yet, as Thompson states, it has to be acknowledged that 'Behind the glossy advertisements showing futuristic electronic equipment lies the reality of more routine tasks and less skilled jobs'. Within this context the search for meaning in the work situation is accorded still greater emphasis and man himself is hard pressed to assert his essential identity and humanity in the face of the technological onslaught. At the same time, positive changes have taken place: improved education and training, as well as the growing tendency to flatten and decentralise organisational structures, are beginning to blur the distinctions between different groups of employees and between employers or managers on the one hand and 'workers' on the other; gigantic projects have emphasised the need for a team approach, while all around there is an increased awareness not only of the need to humanise work but also of the value of human resources as one of the only remaining competitive advantages. Thus new meaning may be achieved by greater personal ownership of one's work and by the recognition of individual and collective value, while equalisation and team activity will enhance identification and social interaction. This may, in time, eradicate much of the negativism created by the traditional work situation and may breed in man a completely new attitude to his work. On the other hand, escalating automation renders man and his labour increasingly dispensable. The alarming growth in unemployment around the globe is sufficient proof of this. The question to be asked is whether work, as we know it, will not eventually disappear. This would point to an entirely new social and economic order, and one of which most of us cannot as yet conceive.

THE PARTIES TO THE RELATIONSHIP

**Employers,
Employees and
the State**

The labour relationship is usually described as a tripartite relationship between employers, employees and the State. This, however, places undue emphasis on the institutionalised aspects of the relationship and places the State in the position of permanent and equal partner and regulator. Because the conduct of the labour relationship is of such importance to society at large, the State most certainly has a role to play in this relationship; nevertheless, the degree to which the State interferes or is allowed to interfere in the relationship will vary from one country to the next and will be dependent not only on the nature of the relationship itself but also on the predominant ideological and political orientation of the society in which the relationship is conducted. In most societies the State will, at the very least, provide minimum legal protection to the parties in the relationship and, if necessary, establish a framework for the peaceful conduct of the relationship. This does not, however, render it a full and permanent partner in the relationship. Thus the labour relationship is best described as a relationship between an employer and an employee or employers and employees as the main partners, with the State, to a greater or lesser extent, playing a regulatory and protectionist role as it does in numerous other relationships, albeit to a less noticeable degree.

There is one instance in which the State becomes a full partner in the labour relationship. Because it administers a vast public sector, the State is in itself an employer, a role which may conflict with its other roles of legislator, conciliator and regulator. Traditionally the State is regarded as a different type of employer from the private sector employer. The argument for differentiation rests on the fact that the State is a non-profit organisation and that it gains its income from society at large, including its own employees. Simplistically put, the more such employees demand by way of wages, the more might they themselves have to pay in taxes. Also, managers in public service are not viewed as representatives of employers, but rather as administrators. In the past this has led to the adoption of different labour relations policies in the public sector and often to the curtailment of collective bargaining and the freedom to strike in this sector.

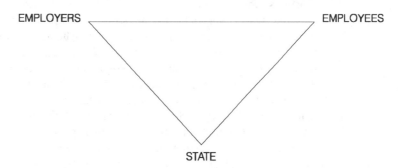

Figure 1: THE PARTIES TO THE LABOUR RELATIONSHIP

Of late, this trend has been reversed. The public sector is being encouraged to operate along business lines. Consequently, an argument can be made also for adequate representation of public sector employee interests. This argument does not apply only to the wage- or salary-related interests of these employees, but extends also to their rights regarding participation in decisions at their place of work. If the employees (as taxpayers) so to speak pay themselves, then certainly there should be more participative decisionmaking in State organisations and not the strict, hierarchical structures that so often exist.

There are governments which have divorced their role as agent of the people from their role as employer. This they have done by allowing the same or similar rules to apply in the public as in the private sector. In South Africa, the most recent move to include under the same legislation all employees —whether from the private or public sector — is a case in point.

The Union as a Party to the Relationship   The labour relationship is also, at times, described as a management–union relationship, but this would negate the existence of the relationship in circumstances where no union exists. Moreover, the term 'union' is an abstraction for a collectivity of employees. A union does not have a separate, independent existence; it is merely the representative of employees and although — within the context of traditional, antagonistic labour relationships — unions have played an important role, they are not essential to the existence or conduct of the labour relationship *per se*.

Roles Adopted by the Parties   As in many other relationships, the roles and status of the parties to the labour relationship are, to a large extent, assigned by custom and tradition. Traditionally the employer, owner or entrepreneur plans, decides, directs and controls, while the employee executes the orders of the owner, takes no part in decisionmaking or planning and is not concerned with the results of his actions. These roles are still accepted and upheld by most participants in the labour relationship, resulting in a more or less willing acceptance of what may loosely be termed 'employer prerogative'. Although it could be said that the challenge to employer prerogative has of late gained impetus, the mere fact that it needs to be challenged proves its existence, the tacit acceptance thereof and the lack of agreement on changes in traditional perspectives. Thus, despite phenomenal changes in societal values and systems, individual beliefs and goals and organisational and ownership structures, the perception of the roles to be adopted by the employer and employee respectively remains, in essence, the same as that held at the turn of the century. Managers of large corporations, who are themselves employees but who view themselves as representatives of the employer, have unquestioningly accepted the traditional role of the employer and assumed for themselves the previously held employer prerogative. There is no doubt that the most significant changes in the employment relationship within the next ten to twenty years will evolve from changes in the role definition of the participants and from the erosion or redefinition of employer or management prerogative. The right of employers or managers unilaterally to plan, decide, direct and control will be increasingly challenged. This does not signify that no coordination will be required, but rather that the word 'management' will take on an entirely different meaning. Within this context, managers will need to resolve the conflict inherent in their positions and will, perhaps, have to relinquish claims to status based on the assumption of employer representation, in exchange for respect earned as persons with particular and necessary skills.

INTERACTIONS AND PROCESSES WITHIN THE RELATIONSHIP

Commonality Cooperation and Cooperative Processes

Basic to any relationship is a certain commonality of interest. In the labour relationship, such commonality is to be found in the fact that both the employer and the employee — and the State, for that matter — have a vested interest in the continued profitable existence of the undertaking. The employer, in order to produce certain goods or services and to reap the intended profits, creates work for the employee who, in turn, accepts the work in order to gain remuneration, status and/or personal satisfaction. Consequently, both are interdependent and both should be interested in advancing the work process to the highest possible level of efficiency since both will (or should), in the long run, reap the benefits of continued profitability.

Where commonality of interest exists, a certain measure of cooperation becomes essential. In the labour relationship, each party needs the other to achieve his own ends. Therefore, willingly or unwillingly, he cooperates in order to achieve his individual goals. Contrary to common belief, such cooperation still forms the basis of the relationship. Were this not so, very little economic activity would occur. Rationally, therefore, we could assume that the relationship should be conducted in a spirit of harmony and mutual support. Unfortunately, a number of factors militate against this assumption.

Firstly, the said commonality of interests is not perceived because of its abstraction from day-to-day realities. Because of their traditionally assigned roles and behaviour within these roles, the negativity permeating the relationship, the polarisation between the parties and the perception of unequal rewards, employees in particular do not perceive themselves as having anything in common with the employer or manager. Secondly, the commonality of interest is often overshadowed by conflict in personal and group goals, values, interests and ideologies and the position is exacerbated by social and political conflicts which intrude on the work situation. Thirdly, the employer does not view himself as dependent on a particular employee, but on his labour — which, from his perspective, he buys and relinquishes at will. Finally, and most importantly, there has hitherto been a lack of emphasis on processes and structures which promote cooperation within the workplace. Instead, Industrial Relations and those involved in the labour relationship have concentrated on the institutionalisation of conflict. Consequently it is in the arena of conflict, rather than cooperation, that the emphasis has traditionally been placed. This is true of both traditional Industrial Relations theory and its implementation in practice.

Thus, despite the underlying commonality in the relationship and the resultant interdependence between the parties, the labour relationship remains at best one of unwilling cooperation and, at worst, antagonistic by nature.

Fortunately also this trend is seen to be reversing. New insights into the relationship have brought the realisation that mere containment of conflict does not develop the relationship and that, if such development is desired, greater attention will have to be focused on the commonality in the relationship and, therefore, on cooperative or participative processes. Thus, also in South Africa, there has been an attempt to balance conflict and its concomitant process of collective bargaining with cooperation and greater worker participation.

Conflict and Collective Bargaining

The potential for conflict within the labour relationship is infinite. At its most basic level, conflict is evidenced by disagreement about the division of profits and benefits. Employees will want as much as possible in the form of wages, benefits and leisure, whereas the employer wishes to maximise profits for payouts to shareholders, expansion and reinvestment. On a more sophisticated level, conflict centres in such matters as role and status definition, decisionmaking powers, accountability structures, flexibility and control, and in a conflict of personal values and goals, beliefs and ideologies.

Studies in conflict prove that conflict in itself is not undesirable; in effect, that a certain level of conflict is functional, since it prevents stagnation. Thus the presence of conflict in a relationship is not at issue. Such conflict will become dysfunctional only if it reaches destructive proportions, is not balanced by cooperation and is not handled in the proper manner. In the labour relationship it has long been accepted that conflict is endemic; consequently, processes have been devised to handle and contain conflict. This has led to the institutionalisation of collective bargaining as a predominant process within the relationship. Although the process of collective bargaining does prevent one party to the relationship from pursuing his own interest at all costs and consequently prevents conflict from reaching unmanageable proportions, experts in the field are now questioning the overriding emphasis placed on this process, its viability as a method of resolving conflict and the quality of the outcomes. Collective bargaining, particularly if it is distributive by nature, results in compromise solutions and very often in a win–lose or lose–lose result. By contrast, it is generally accepted that integrative problem-solving, relying also on a large measure of cooperation, is a far superior method of resolving conflict, since it usually results in a win–win and a more universally acceptable solution.

The Power Dynamic

Because it is based on win–lose outcomes, the process of collective bargaining as practised in contemporary labour relations relies greatly on the use of power. In fact, collective bargaining commences only when there is a mutual perception of power and the process centres in continual attempts to balance or equalise power. The amount of power wielded by either party at any particular time is dependent on certain power variables. Of these the most important are dependence, importance, scarcity and non-substitutability. The more dependent an employer is on an employee, the more power will that employee wield over him and *vice versa*. The more important an employee or group of employees is to an organisation, the more power will be wielded by those employees. When jobs are scarce, employers wield more power. When an employee cannot be replaced, he finds himself in a position of power.

Power is never constant or attributable to only one party; it is of a reciprocal and continuously shifting nature. In the past it was believed that the more balanced the power, the better would be the outcome. This was highlighted by the studies of Magenau and Pruitt who concluded that, when power is balanced, there is usually an easy agreement of high value and the parties will more readily concede and reach an agreement. Unfortunately, a balance of power is often unachievable since, as soon as one party perceives the other as having equal power, the former will strive towards greater power. This results in continuing power competition. It is important to note this phenomenon as most traditional industrial relations and collective bargaining theories rest on the unrealistic assumption of a power balance between the parties which may, in practice, not be achieved.

Much also depends on the one party's perception of the other's power. Power, if it exists, must be seen to exist. This is why it is sometimes necessary for one of the parties to the labour relationship to engage in an overt display of power, since only then will the other party agree to engage in meaningful bargaining with him.

In the labour relationship, as in so many other relationships, the source of power on both sides is, unfortunately, usually coercive by nature. Employers start from a basis of power *vis-à-vis* the employee, and organisational structures, systems and processes are designed with a view to the continued exercise of coercive power or, at best, to the use of what might be termed negative rewards. Managers gain their legitimacy from their ability to punish or reward employees, and most work processes are established within these parameters. The most extreme form of coercive power utilised by management rests in the ability to withhold the opportunity to work — and, therefore, to earning a living — from the employee. This manifests itself in dismissals, retrenchments and lockouts. Dismissals and retrenchment are claimed as managerial prerogatives and it would seem that, on the face of it, employees hold very little power. Indeed, the individual employee — particularly if he is easily replaceable — will not possess sufficient power to counter that held by the employer or manager. His power would rest with his ability to withhold his labour from the employer, but very few employees are indispensable. It is for this reason that employees, and particularly those in the ranks of the semiskilled and unskilled, have been obliged to resort to the power of the collective, usually manifested in union membership. Only by a joint withholding of labour can they hope to match the power of management. Nevertheless, there are those who contend that this is but an illusion of power, since the very nature of organisational design and the processes emanating therefrom ensure the retention of managerial power. This notwithstanding, the threat by either side that it will resort to the use of extreme coercive power in the form of lockouts or strikes forms the basis for the collective bargaining process.

French and Raven, having identified five forms of power — coercive, reward, legitimate, expert and referent — explain that, of the five, coercive power is the least desirable and, it might be added, the most primitive. Reward power is closely related to coercive power, since the threat of not bestowing a reward becomes coercive. Also, legitimate power, which rests on authority structures, relies heavily on the use of punishment and reward. This leaves expert power, derived from knowledge and experience in a particular field and referent power, obtained through the process of identification with another person or party or with a system of beliefs and values. It would seem that, to gain really legitimate power, managers should rely not on the authority bestowed by their positions but on that gained from their expertise and that, at the same time, each employee should gain power through his expertise; furthermore that, in the labour relationship, we should be striving to substitute the overuse of one-sided coercive power with 'interactive' referent power, resting in a system of shared goals, values and beliefs. In short, we should be substituting 'power over ...' with 'power to ...', since only if we empower each individual will the organisation itself become powerful. This would again point to the establishment of joint structures and processes, not necessarily to the exclusion of those designed for collective bargaining (which, ironically, also occurs because there is mutual interest) but alongside them. However, it should be mentioned that, for this to occur, the stances, perspectives and behaviours of both parties need to undergo substantial, if not radical, change.

The Freedom of the Individual versus Allegiance to the Collective

Nowadays, most work is performed on a collective basis. Consequently, enterprises are structured as collectives. We speak of a company in which there are departments, sections, management boards, production workers and administrative staff. From the perspective of the enterprise, people are viewed not as individuals but as members of a particular group. On the employee side, this collectivity is further emphasised by the need to identify with fellow employees in order to match the power of the employer. Within this context, it becomes extremely difficult for the employee to assert his individuality. Thus a certain amount of tension is created between the employee's need for personal recognition, advancement and satisfaction and his need to form part of the collective. Equally, tension exists between employers and unions since the former, in spite of their own collective emphasis, wish at times to treat employees on a differentiated basis as individuals, while unions, being the representatives of the collective, will in all probability counter such attempts.

In Labour Relations we deal, therefore, with both individual and collective interactions and the tensions created between these two. Even if it is accepted that individual freedom is to some extent curtailed as soon as a particular individual voluntarily associates with another person or collective, points of controversy still remain. Can an employer award differentiated increases on the basis of merit, or in any way treat one employee differently from another? Has he the right to demand of an employee that he take an individual decision contrary to that of the union, and can he establish direct representation by employees even where collective representation by a union is the norm? Conversely, does the union have the right to demand that all employees abide by a majority decision, that no differentiation be made by employers, that all employees become union members and that the employer communicate only through a representative body? These are the questions that need to be answered, and the answer lies in the achievement of a balance between the interests of the collective and those of the individual, with due respect for the allegiance owed by the individual to a particular collective. As long as the matter is handled with sensitivity and acknowledgement of both individual and collective rights, there is no reason why due recognition cannot be given to both the collective and individual interests of employees. It should, however, also be remembered that the employee may owe allegiance to two collectives, namely the company and the union, and care should be exercised that demands from the one do not clash with the interests of or erode his allegiance to the other.

The Interaction Continuum   From the above it becomes evident that, in the labour relationship, we move (or can move) on a continuum between conflict and cooperation, each dynamic being underscored by its own power relations and processes (see Figure 2). Also there is continued tension between the needs and demands of the individual and those of the collective, as regards the individual's relationship both to the organisation and to the employee collective.

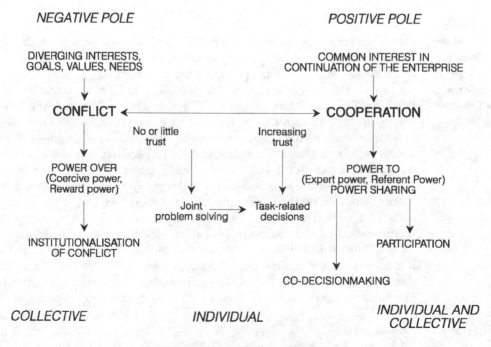

Figure 2: THE INTERACTION CONTINUUM

FACTORS REGULATING THE INTERACTION

Custom and Tradition

The manner in which the parties to a relationship behave towards each other, as well as their status and roles within the relationship, is often determined by custom and tradition. This is also the case with the labour relationship, where custom has not only determined the roles of the parties but has also accorded certain rights and duties to each party. Thus, as stated earlier, managers have assumed a traditional prerogative and employees have traditionally obeyed without question. The influence of custom and tradition within societal structures is strong, and any attempt to change traditional perspectives or hierarchies is vehemently resisted. Yet custom and tradition are not always correct or rational, particularly from the perspective of ever-changing realities. Consequently, too great a reliance on custom as a regulator of the labour relationship results in stagnation and in a relationship which is out of touch with the world in which it exists.

Legislation

Because we cannot rely solely on custom and tradition to regulate the work relationship, because the relationship itself is often unequal and because the parties might engage in destructive practices to the detriment of society at large, it is necessary to establish a legal framework within which the labour relationship can be conducted. Consequently, the law may establish machinery for the peaceful resolution of conflict between the parties, delimit the rights of both parties and even attempt to correct perceived power imbalances which exist. Yet the State, as legislator, can never within a free society presume to control all aspects of the labour relationship and experience has shown that, notwithstanding the law, the parties will eventually regulate the relationship in the way they deem fit.

Mutual Agreement

Since custom and tradition and the imposition of legislation have proved to be deficient, the parties to the labour relationship have increasingly resorted to mutually agreed rules and regulations as a basis for their interactions with each other. Agreement is achieved either by the process of collective bargaining or, in more sophisticated systems, by joint structures established for this purpose. The more the parties to a relationship are able to agree on rules, processes and substantive issues, the less they will have to rely on the assistance or jurisdiction of external instances.

Ethical Considerations: Trust, Integrity and Fairness

Unfortunately, too little attention is paid to a system of ethics as regulator of the labour relationship. Of late there has been a gradual realisation by businessmen of the need to conduct business along more ethical lines, but little is said regarding an ethical framework for the conduct of the labour relationship.

The lack of an ethical code to which both parties subscribe is best evidenced by the lack of trust which permeates the labour relationship. Like any other relationship, a labour relationship not founded on trust will inevitably experience difficulties. Despite the conflict which admittedly exists and the continued battles of will in which the parties may be engaged, some measure of trust has to be established. This cannot be achieved if there is no respect for the other party and no faith in his integrity. The value, power, ability and legitimacy of the other party has to be recognised and each participant should be assured that the other will not abuse his position, that he will view situations from a balanced perspective, will not attempt any form of subversion, that he will keep his word and that he will act consistently in the light of his own beliefs and values — all of which may seem a tall order, but is achievable if both parties operate within a mutual ethical framework and, also, if a common work ethic does exist.

Further proof that ethical considerations do not predominate in the labour relationship is to be found in the lack of appreciation of the concept of fairness and in the necessity to legislate fair labour practices. It is admitted that concepts of fairness do differ from person to person and that perceptions of fairness need to be placed within the context of particular circumstances; yet certain neutral and universally accepted standards of fairness can be postulated. The most commonly used is the test of the 'reasonable man', although this in itself may require a common definition of the word 'reasonable'. Ultimately the question has to be asked as to whether others in the relationship or an impartial judge would regard the interaction as reasonable and whether the party committing the action would deem it reasonable were it committed against himself.

Further criteria for fairness are suggested by Salamon, who states, firstly, that there should be reciprocity and balance between the parties concerned, that one party should not obtain all the benefits to the detriment of the other and that there should be equitable exchange of both substance and behaviours; and, secondly, that both parties should receive equal treatment and equal consideration in that the same criteria and judgments should apply to each and the treatment of persons should, as a whole, be consistent. Finally, our own Industrial (Labour) Court has repeatedly indicated that the parties should be 'perceived to be acting fairly'; in other words, that 'fair' is not 'fair' unless others perceive this fairness in action. This would entail, at the least, the explanation of behaviours and decisions and, at the most, the actual involvement of those concerned when decisions are being made.

The question of ethics, and particularly of fairness, is complex and the subject of much debate, but it is of considerable importance to the conduct of the labour relationship and will require more in-depth discussion in the future.

EXTERNAL INFLUENCES ON THE LABOUR RELATIONSHIP

The Sociopolitical System

No relationship functions in a vacuum. It is a product of time and place and, as such, it will be subject to influences from the wider society in which it exists. Conversely, the type of labour relationships established and the processes emanating from those relationships will impact on society at large.

In the political sphere this interaction is demonstrated by the fact that the political dispensation, reflective of a particular ideology, will largely determine the type of industrial relations system, as well as the power balance between the employer and employees. On the other hand, individual employers and employees, as voters within the political system, are able to influence the policies of government and will have a say in the type of industrial relations system established. Also, specific public policy — not necessarily connected to the labour relationship — will impact on the relationship. In South Africa the policy of 'apartheid', with its concomitants such as influx control, has greatly influenced labour relations in this country. It has led to unequal bargaining power, the immobility of labour, divisions in and the politicisation of the trade union movement.

Societal Influences

In the social sphere there is continual interaction between social relationships and labour relationships. Employees bring to the workplace perceptions established in their subsocieties. If, for example, there are large divides of class and race in society itself, this will be reflected in the workplace. Similarly, tensions arising in the workplace will be carried outwards to the wider society, either by individuals or by organised groups such as trade unions and employers' organisations. If goodwill and cooperation predominate at the workplace, this may spread to society at large. On the micro-level, problems experienced by the employee in his community — such as lack of housing, inadequate facilities, lack of transport and defective education — impact on the labour relationship or become issues in the process of collective bargaining.

The Economic Dispensation

Most obviously, the economic dispensation, on both a macro- and a micro-level, will directly influence the conduct of labour relations. The predominant economic philosophy of a particular society — that is, whether it favours free enterprise or planned economy — will largely determine the type of labour relationship and the role of collective bargaining in the system, while other factors such as fiscal policy, economic growth and unemployment also exercise a strong influence.

The Influence of Trade Unions

Labour organisations are the direct result of worker dissatisfaction with the capitalist enterprise. Thus, although they arise from this system, they are essentially antagonistic to it. Initially, owner–managers and the government of the time attempted to subvert these organisations but, particularly during the nineteenth and early twentieth centuries, the labour unions grew in strength. Many established their own political parties or affiliations, thereby extending their power also to society at large. As such, they served to curb the previously unfettered prerogative of the entrepreneur or owner, and influenced governmental recognition of the labour relationship. Consequently, attitudes to and behaviour within the relationship have been and continue to be greatly affected by trade unions. A particular employer may in theory favour a certain style and approach to the labour relationship, but the style he eventually adopts will to a large extent be circumscribed by the amount of influence a trade union has in the enterprise. Equally, a government may tend to favour the employer party and the capitalist economic system but, within a democratic system, it cannot enact legislation without due reference to a strong trade union movement. This, eventually, will impact also on the relationship at enterprise level.

Additional Influences

A number of other interactive factors such as technological development, business structure, industry concentration and labour demography further influence developments in labour relations and particularly the collective bargaining process, but the subject matter of this chapter does not justify a detailed discussion of these forces. It is important merely to note that the labour relationship and the processes emanating from it cannot be studied in isolation, once again illustrating the necessity of adopting an interdisciplinary approach to the subject.

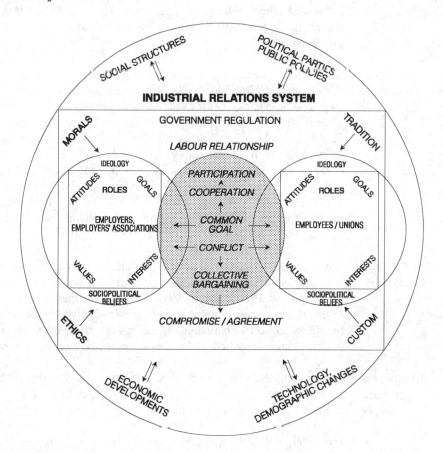

Figure 3: SCHEMATIC REPRESENTATION OF THE LABOUR RELATIONSHIP

APPROACHES TO THE LABOUR RELATIONSHIP

Depending on their view of the most desired interactions and processes, employers and employees, and now the State, may adopt different approaches to the labour relationship. These approaches evolved largely in response to the growing power of workers and unions within the enterprise and the resultant more overt conflict between the participants to the relationship.

Fox, in 1966, initially identified two basic approaches to the relationship — the unitary and the pluralist — but it is now accepted that a third, radical perspective is to be found in the approach of fundamentalist unions and their members.

The Unitary Approach From the unitary approach the organisation is viewed as a coherent group or team with a single, common aim: the continued, profitable existence of the enterprise. Employers and employees are thought to share the same set of values; that is, general support for the free enterprise system, a respect for the authority of management and an emphasis on loyalty and diligence. All participants are supposed to strive for higher profits through greater productivity in order that all can share the rewards. The prerogative of management is accepted and managers who adhere to this approach do not regard challenges to their authority as legitimate. Conflict is viewed as irrational and antisocial. When it does arise, it is attributed either to interpersonal friction and a lack of understanding or to aberrants who enjoy causing conflict for conflict's sake. It is believed that conflict can be resolved either by promoting better human relations, usually in a somewhat paternalist fashion, or by the use of authority and coercion. The law and established rules of conduct usually constitute the last resort.

Trade unions are not seen as necessary. They are, in fact, regarded as an intrusion in that they compete with management for the loyalty of employees and engender distrust between the parties. Managements who favour this approach may go so far as to bargain with unions on issues such as wages and general conditions of employment, but they resent any challenge to their managerial prerogative and will resist bargaining on matters such as retrenchment, technological change and relocation, since they regard these as the responsibility of management.

The unitary approach is one still adopted by numerous managements and accepted by some employees. In South Africa it was almost universally held until the so-called 'new' trade union movement, as well as judgments emanating from the Industrial (Labour) Court, began to challenge the absolutism of managerial prerogative and to promote a more pluralist approach.

The Pluralist Approach

The pluralist approach is based on an acceptance of the conflict of goals and interests between employer and employee, but with the presupposition that it is possible to achieve some balance of both interest and power between the participants to the labour relationship. This does not imply an inevitable compromise in all cases, but merely that conflict can be contained and effectively managed.

From this approach, conflict is viewed as unavoidable and as arising from the organisational structure or the very nature of the employment relationship. However, such conflict occurs within the framework of a limited common purpose — that is, the continued profitable existence of the enterprise — since, if this were destroyed, both parties would suffer. Because of this common interest, the parties are usually willing to reach a compromise and jointly to establish rules for their conduct towards each other. By this means they ensure that the conflict inherent in the relationship does not assume destructive proportions. The freedom of association principle, the process of collective bargaining and some measure of joint decisionmaking are accepted as means by which to achieve a balance of power between the various participants. Furthermore, the law is not regarded as the final and absolute authority and is usually balanced by considerations of interests, fairness and equity.

Adherents to the pluralist approach see trade unions not as a threat but as necessary to balance the power between employer and employee and to give expression to the demands of employees. More importantly, the trade union's right to existence is acknowledged not merely because of its power base, but within the framework of a set of societal values which accepts the right of employees to give expression to their demands on a communal basis.

The pluralist view is the one most widely held in Western democratic societies, although it also cannot be supported without, at the least, a consideration of the unitary and radical approaches. The most common criticism of pluralism is that it still accords no real power to employees and trade unions.

The Radical Approach

The radical approach, also known as the Marxist approach, denies that any balance of power can be achieved within a capitalist system. In terms of this approach the root cause of the conflict between employer and employee is to be found not in the narrow confines of the employment relationship but in the wider society which supports a capitalist economic system and establishes social, political and legal structures which favour the employer. The latter's power is, consequently, always greater than that of the employee, although collective bargaining procedures may establish the illusion of equality. Proponents of this approach regard collective bargaining as an employer strategy aimed at coaxing the working class into compliance, and even regard workers' participation in the decisionmaking process as an attempt at cooption. Trade unions are supported, but only if they also play a political role; that is, if they act as agencies toward total change.

Adherents to this approach believe that there can be no point of common interest between employer and employee since, in working towards increased profits and great surplus value, employees would, in effect, be supporting their own exploitation. The solution is that proposed by Marx, namely the supplanting of the capitalist system with a system of shared ownership and communal control.

Neo 'Unitary/ Pluralist' Approach

Although the three approaches outlined above constitute a basis for theoretical differentiation, a particular party may amalgamate two or more of these approaches. Thus many unionists whose approach may be essentially radical tend to live with and even promulgate a pluralist approach to the relationship. Also, there is a tendency amongst management and employees to accept pluralism but, at the same time, to move towards a new kind of unitarism. The latter would emphasise commonality and cooperation but, in all likelihood, would not be paternalist in nature. The extremes of traditional unitarism would also be tempered by the acceptance of trade unions and the collective bargaining function. This is in line with the move backwards and forwards along the continuum, as already depicted in Figure 2.

CONCLUSION

To explain the intricacies of any relationship within the scope of a single chapter is a daunting undertaking. This is more so in the case of the labour relationship, with its unique and often paradoxical characteristics and its extremely dynamic nature. The intention was merely to introduce the reader to the vast panorama of actions, interactions and processes which constitutes the labour relationship.

Specific aspects will be discussed in greater detail in ensuing chapters, but it is hoped that this introduction has provided an overall perspective and understanding and that it will facilitate insights into these aspects of Industrial Relations.

SOURCES

Biesheuwel, S *Work Motivation and Compensation*, McGraw-Hill, 1984.

Clegg, H *The System of Industrial Relations in Great Britain*, Blackwell, 1972.

Flanders, A *Management and Unions*, Faber, 1970.

French, W L and S Raven 'The Basis of Social Power' in Cartwright, D (Ed) *Studies in Social Power*, Michigan, 1959.

Heilbroner, R *The Worldly Philosophers*, Penguin, 1980.

Hyman, R and I Borough *Social Values and Industrial Relations*, Blackwell, 1975.

Magenau, J M and D G Pruitt 'The Social Psychology of Bargaining' in Stephenson, G M and C J Brotherton (Eds) *Industrial Relations: A Social Psychological Approach*, John Wiley & Sons, 1979.

Salamon, Michael *Industrial Relations Theory and Practice*, Prentice Hall, 1987.

Thompson, Paul *The Nature of Work*, Macmillan Education Limited, 1986.

2

INDUSTRIAL RELATIONS SYSTEMS

OVERVIEW

Labour Relations systems are societal structures. This means that they will be shaped by the societies in which they occur. A system itself comprises the various participants, the processes employed in the labour relationship and the legislative framework.

The most important variable shaping societies — and therefore, their industrial relations systems — is the dominant ideology. In this respect we differentiate between the two ideological precepts of individualism and communitarianism. As modern society centres in economic activity, these precepts are transferred also into economic ideologies, resting mainly on the philosophies of Adam Smith at the one extreme and Karl Marx at the other. However, modern society displays a tendency to convergence between these extremes, so that very few societies or their industrial relations systems reflect extreme ideological stances.

The government of the day will, in its formulation of policy in the industrial relations sphere, be guided largely (but not exclusively) by the dominant ideology. Other factors influencing the type and extent of government interference include the economic situation, trade union strength and the government's labour capital bias.

Although ideology (and particularly economic ideology), together with the type of State interference, constitute the primary variables shaping industrial relations systems, there are other variables such as the degree of democratisation, public policy, economic developments, trade union and employer organisation and historic events which also have to be taken into account. In fact, in any particular industrial relations system, all the variables mentioned interact in a complex manner to produce a system unique to that society.

THE LABOUR RELATIONS SYSTEM AS A SOCIETAL STRUCTURE

The labour relations system operating in a particular society is a product of and is structured by that society. It follows that a country's labour relations system will be shaped by all the different forces prevailing in that society and, because all societies are unique, that no two labour relations systems will be exactly the same.

THE COMPOSITION OF AN INDUSTRIAL RELATIONS SYSTEM

Major Components

The term 'industrial relations system' embraces the totality of actors, actions, processes, rules and regulations involved in or pertaining to the labour relationship in a particular society. The main components of an industrial relations system are, therefore, the parties to the labour relationship, the processes (such as collective bargaining and workers' participation) emanating from it, and the legal system governing the relationship. These components are common to all systems but, depending on the interaction of a number of societal variables, they are contained to different degrees and interact in different ways in various industrial relations systems.

Variations in the Composition of Different Systems

The Parties to the Relationship

Employers, employees and the State are, in all industrial relations systems, the major participants in the labour relationship, but one system will differ from the other in terms of the importance attached to and the role of each participant. In certain systems the State dominates the labour relationship, while in others it adopts the role of junior partner. Similarly, some societies will emphasise the interests of the employer, while in others the employee is regarded as the most important participant. The power relationship between employer and employee and the amount of influence each can bring to bear will greatly depend on the society in which they function.

Usually the two parties directly involved in the relationship, and particularly the employee party, will act through representative bodies. These organisations will differ from country to country. In one society the functioning of trade unions may be facilitated, while in another efforts at organisation are hampered by legislation and social circumstances. Trade union members may be an integral part of one society, while in another they may be relegated to second-rate citizenship. Consequently, trade union actions and goals will vary from one to another.

Processes and Procedures

The predominant processes in industrial relations systems are collective bargaining and, in recent years, the practice of workers' participation. According to their different orientations, the participants in different societies will place varying emphasis on these processes. Furthermore, in some social systems the use or implementation of one or both of these by the major participants is compulsory, whereas in others it is completely voluntary. Equally, collective bargaining, where it does occur, may be conducted at a highly centralised or a highly decentralised level, and it may take place in orderly or random fashion.

Subordinate to the two major processes are other processes such as dispute settlement procedures, communication structures and systems for the conclusion of agreements, as well as in-plant disciplinary and grievance procedures. As in the case of collective bargaining and workers' participation, the nature of these procedures and the relative emphasis placed on them will differ in terms of societal constraints.

The Legislative Framework

Most obviously, the legislation governing the establishment and conduct of the labour relationship will vary from country to country. Yet there are definite similarities in labour legislation, particularly in societies resting on the same ideological base. The most pertinent differences in the legislative framework are to be found in the varying degrees of compulsion, in the different forms of protection granted to employers and employees and in the applications of the principles of freedom of association and the right to bargain collectively. Societies also differ in their concepts of fairness and in legislation pertaining to such practices. Finally, certain societies may establish other laws which do not pertain directly to the labour relationship but nevertheless impact upon the industrial relations system.

IDEOLOGICAL BASIS

All societies rest on an ideological base. Since industrial relations systems are structured by society, the dominant ideology of a particular society will largely determine the basic framework for the industrial relations system in that society. Equally, as the ideology of a society changes, so will the industrial relations system undergo similar change.

Definition Hunt and Sherman define ideology as '... a set of beliefs that tend to justify morally a society's social and economic relationships'. Alternatively, it may be described as a set of common feelings or values about how relationships in society should be conducted. Whether ideology arises from social and economic processes or is responsible for the establishment of such processes is open to debate, but it would seem that radical societal changes wrought by various historical forces, sometimes based on philosophic teachings, bring about a new socioeconomic order and that this order is then rationalised, or continues to be rationalised, by a new ideology. The perpetuation of a societal system and of individual beliefs and values is, therefore, dependent on the perpetuation of a particular ideology.

Individualism versus Communitarianism The greatest divergence in ideology between different societies exists between the belief in individual freedom on the one hand and communitarianism on the other. Individualism, in its absolute sense, implies that individual persons or groups in society are free to make their own choices and pursue their own goals, that they have little or no responsibility towards society and that society has little or no obligation towards them; at best, that society is secondary to the individual. Supporters of individualism view society as being shaped by and composed of individual beings; whereas, by contrast, communitarianism holds that individuals are shaped by society. The proponents of a communitarian ideology do not agree that the choice and self-interest of the individual should predominate. It is believed that man's first duty is towards the society from which he emanates, that individual interests should always be subordinate to those of a society as a whole. Consequently, the communitarianist will regard it as the duty of a government also to attempt to shape and control society. Whereas the individualist will propose minimum government interference in all spheres, the communitarianist will support bigger government, even though this holds the danger of increased bureaucracy. Although he may support the democratic institution of majority government, the individualist will emphasise the necessity of minority representation. In the communitarian system, minority interests are not usually taken into account. This stems from different attitudes to conflict. Whereas the individualist sees conflict as unavoidable and, consequently institutionalises its accommodation within the system of government, the communitarianist believes that conflict and individual interests should be superseded by cooperative effort.

Transferred to the economic sphere, these ideologies lead to the promotion of private property and capitalism in one instance and to the endorsement of a socialist system of common ownership on the other. Also, the individualist will actively promote a free market economy, based on competition between individuals, whereas the communitarianist will advise the institution of a more planned economic system.

The implications of these differing ideologies in the industrial relations sphere are self-evident. A society which supports individualism recognises the right of employers to pursue their own self-interest, limited only by the power of the other side. It accepts conflict within industrial relations and provides institutions for its containment. Such society will not place an onus on the employer to share in his profits or decisions with his employees. In general, he will not be expected to display any extraordinary concern for the material and spiritual wellbeing of his employees. A society of this kind endorses the right to private property and promotes the regulation of business and labour by the market principle. In the sphere of industrial regulation it opts for a system of self-government by employers and employees. In each case the opposite would be true of a society subscribing to a communitarian ideology.

Individualism and communitarianism have been described in their most extreme forms. Nowadays pure individualism is rarely practised in Western society. Equally, communitarian ideologies are, in many socialistic countries, being tempered by increased consideration of the individual and allowance for the operation of the market principle. In Western Europe in particular, the integration of individualist and communitarian ideologies has resulted in the adoption of mixed sociopolitical and economic policies. Although the rights of the individual, including individual property rights, are recognised and although economies operate mostly (but not exclusively) on free market principles, the interests of all members of society are taken into account and their wellbeing is ensured. The individual is free to pursue his own development, but within the parameters of the wider societal interests. Similarly, in many Eastern bloc countries the emphasis shifted from absolute collectivism to a type of socialism based on individual community interests. This system allowed for the free association of different groups of workers, competition in the market place and a certain amount of self-government. Nevertheless, individual and group interests were still balanced by the duty of all towards society at large.

This mixture of ideologies is reflected in the industrial relations systems of both types of society. For example, in Europe, collective bargaining is balanced by participatory systems, while a system of worker management in competitive undertakings and of payment according to contribution made was previously introduced in Yugoslavia. The tempering of extreme ideological stances on both sides of the spectrum supports the belief that the direction for the future lies in a convergence of individualism and communitarianism and the establishment of a new ideological framework in developed societies.

ECONOMIC IDEOLOGY AS A BASIS FOR SOCIETAL STRUCTURING

As mentioned in the previous chapter, the roots of modern industrial society, centring in sophisticated economic activity, are to be found in the Industrial Revolution. Because a new pattern of relationships was established, it also became necessary to develop a new philosophy or new philosophies which would explain why the society functioned as it did and would provide man with a set of values and beliefs by which he could live and judge the activities of those around him. These philosophies were readily found in the writings of a new breed of economic thinkers, most of whose writings related to the ownership of working capital by individuals and to the consequences, whether beneficial or otherwise, of such private ownership of capital and of the labour process.

Capitalism   In preindustrial society the Church held great powers and the predominant ideology was thus determined by, particularly, the Roman Catholic Church which, although it did not condemn wealth, taught that the wealthy should care for their less fortunate brothers. With the advent of industrialisation the concept of working capital, and thus of capitalism, replaced the notion of private wealth.

Hunt and Sherman, in their book *Economics: An Introduction to Traditional and Radical Views*, provide an excellent description of the transition from the 'Christian–paternalist ethic' (in itself exploitative) of preindustrial society to a general acceptance of capitalism. They describe capitalism as referring to '... the materials that are necessary for production, trade and commerce. It consists of all tools, equipment, factories, raw materials and goods in process, means of transporting goods and money'. The essence of the capitalist system is said to be '... the existence of a class of capitalists who own the capitalist stock'.

As far as labour is concerned, capitalism commenced with the 'putting out' system, which replaced the system of owner–craftsmen. In the textile industry, for example, the merchant–capitalist would supply the craftsman with the raw materials and pay him for producing the finished product. In reality, what the craftsman then sold back to the merchant was not the product as such (since he had not supplied the raw materials) but only his labour power. With the passage of time, this kind of work became more and more specialised and, with the invention of new machinery, the steam engine as a source of power and better systems of transportation, it shifted from individual craftsmen to workers in large factories. Unlike the craftsmen, these workers no longer owned even their tools or machinery, nor could they claim complete identification with the end product. Thus the age of 'industrial capitalism' was born.

The Mercantilists Mercantilism has its origins in the thirteenth century, when it became obvious that trade and commerce were growing in importance and needed to be promoted but that — in terms of the Christian–paternalist ethic still dominant at the time — merchants could not be allowed to pursue their interests to the detriment of society at large. Consequently the State, which was gradually taking over the role of the Catholic Church in this respect, began on the one hand to promote commerce and industry and, on the other, to impose certain laws and regulations in an attempt to balance the interests of the various participants. This is best exemplified by the economic controls instituted by Edward III who, as an incentive for dedication to work, tried to give labourers a more favourable deal by fixing both prices and wages. His efforts were later antiposed by the Statute of Artificers, passed in 1563, which regulated such aspects as employment conditions, apprenticeships and **maximum** rates paid to workers, and by monopoly patents granted to individuals to promote certain industries.

An important consideration at that stage was also the growing problem of unemployment, which led to the institution of the Poor Laws and the gradual acceptance of responsibility for the indigent, firstly by individual parishes and later by the State. As Hunt and Sherman put it, 'They acknowledged that those who were the victims of the deficiencies of the economic system should be cared for by those who benefited from the system'. There was thus, during this time, also a strong communitarian trend. However, despite these initial noble intentions, the Poor Laws were later used to control the supply of labour to the market and to promote the payment of subsistence wages.

This kind of welfare ethic, supported by Christian paternalism, often came into conflict with the interests of the growing cadre of capitalist–owners and, by the late seventeenth century, most theorists (including those professing to be mercantilists) had begun to adopt a more individualist approach and to protest against internal forms of State interference in or control of the marketplace.

Adam Smith and the Rise of Classical Liberalism During the eighteenth century, trade and manufacturing increased significantly. It was during this time that classical liberalism, bolstered by the individualist ethic which had evolved during the mercantilist period, took root. Classical liberalists, among whom were such eminent thinkers as Thomas Hobbes, John Locke and Bernard Mandeville, regarded human nature as essentially egotist in its striving for pleasure and avoidance of pain. Furthermore, the individual was seen as the fundamental component of society. Consequently, he needed to be freed to pursue his own interests — which, in terms of the liberal ideology, would eventually benefit society as a whole. It was within this setting that **Adam Smith** in 1776 published his work entitled *The Wealth of Nations*.

Although not intended for this purpose, Adam Smith's *Wealth of Nations* came to be adopted as the basis of and justification for a capitalist system. Smith's main interest was to prove that a freely operating market was the best regulator of economic activity and that a *laissez-faire* approach should therefore, be adopted. It may be borne in mind that Smith wrote at a time when industrialisation had not yet reached full bloom and that he regarded a factory employing a few people, manufacturing pins by the use of machinery and the division of labour, as the prime example of this new type of economic activity.

In Smith's view the developments which he saw around him, where an entrepreneur brought workers together and divided their labour in order to produce more efficiently and more competitively, would eventually be to the benefit of society as a whole. As long as the market mechanism operated freely, the desire of individual entrepreneurs to accumulate profits would result in healthy competition. This, together with the rationalism of the consumer, would lead to a regulation of profits and prices which would ultimately benefit the consumer, and the employee as one such consumer. Too much profit-taking, resulting in increased prices, would give rise to undercutting by competitors or to consumer resistance, which would either push the profit-taker out of the market or oblige him to lower his prices. In his Law of Accumulation, Smith supported the amassing of profits within limits dictated by the market. He saw it as leading to investment in new ventures, new job opportunities and the development of society as a whole.

Wages, according to Smith, could also be regulated by the law of supply and demand. Thus he advised the removal of all restraints and all forms of interference in order to give price, wage and labour market competition free rein. Smith's theories were based on the supposition that, in a perfectly competitive labour and consumer market, all wage rates would tend towards an average rate. He nevertheless realised that various factors would interfere with the establishment of an average wage rate and that this would result in higher wages for some employees and lower wage rates for others. According to Smith, factors such as skill (or a scarcity of skills), the amount of training needed for a certain job, the degree of responsibility involved and the seasonal or unpleasant nature of certain jobs would serve as additional criteria in the establishment of wage levels. Also, wages would be affected by government interference in the operation of the labour market. (It is interesting to note that Smith's criterion of the degree of responsibility entailed in a job is one which is still used in the establishment of various remuneration scales.)

The theories of Adam Smith regarding the determination of wage levels are still supported by proponents of the market system. Market theorists believe that wages should basically be determined by demand and supply on the labour market, but reality dictates that allowances be made for the imperfections of the market, for government interference in the market process and for the counter-demands of trade unions.

Smith promoted economic individualism in its most extreme form. He was opposed to any form of government interference in the free play of the market forces. He warned against the establishment of monopolies and the effects of mass production on the creativity and morale of employees. Moreover, he maintained that no society could flourish if the majority of its citizens were poor and miserable: *the total wealth of nations was equal to the sum of individual wealth*. Adam Smith did not live to see the rise of large factories and later, the monopolistic corporations; nor could he have envisaged large-scale economic interference and manipulation by various governments. His was essentially a Utopian system. It presupposed a perfect market, operating within an allowed legal and moral code; one in which the economy responded to market demands, where there was universal and fully effective competition, as well as a complete absence of any form of political interference.

The interest of the Industrial Relations student centres mainly on Smith's individualistic economic ideology and his view of the employment relationship. His approach is that of an economist, who is concerned with the employee mainly as another factor of production. This does not mean that he had no sympathy with employees as individuals, as evidenced by his warnings on the negative effects of mass production, but merely that, in his explanation of economic activity, he did not see the employee as being in need of special protection or having a particular or more important place in this activity different from the other factors of production — land, capital and entrepreneurship. At one stage Smith did remark rather wryly that, whenever tradesmen gathered, it was to scheme for higher wages. Evidently his sympathies lay more with the entrepreneur who, he believed, provided the impetus for economic activity and who, in pursuing his own gain, benefited his employees and society at large. Therefore there would be no conflict of interest between employer and employee, since both would (or should) be interested in the continued profitability of the undertaking: the employer because it would lead to the accumulation of profits and further development, and the employee because it would provide work and a continued, assured income. In Smith's opinion, the State had no role at all in this relationship.

This view of the employment relationship is still widely held today. However, since Smith's day industrialisation has progressed to full bloom and beyond. Factories have increased in size and large, often monopolistic, conglomerates and public companies have supplanted the single entrepreneur or owner. Governments have increasingly been obliged to interfere in all spheres of economic activity, and employees as a class have realised that they can greatly influence the conditions of their working life. Thus, although some of Smith's views still hold, they can no longer be applied from a simplistic or unidimensional perspective.

Thomas Malthus

The optimistic views of Smith regarding the function of the labour market were succeeded by the gloomy predictions of **Thomas Malthus**. Malthus wrote in an era when modern technological development was not envisaged. He was concerned primarily with the population explosion and the state of the world in the future, should this explosion continue. In order to solve what to him was the main problem, Malthus proposed a theory of wage determination based on a very cynical view of the working man. In his *Essay on Population* he advanced the concept of a Wage Fund, established by capital for the payment of labour. Such a fund remained fixed and an increase in wages, therefore, could be achieved only by cost saving or by reducing the number of persons benefiting from the fund. Malthus accepted the argument that, if wage rates increased, the poor would procreate more prolifically, thus increasing the supply of labour to the market and bring down wage levels once again. Lower wage levels would lead to a decrease in the population and a subsequent rise in wages. However, unlike Smith who stuck doggedly to individualism and to the free play of market forces, Malthus built on this theory for his own purposes: to control a growth in population. He suggested that the best wage rate was a subsistence rate, as this would keep a steady supply of labour to the market and would prevent workers from producing too many children.

Malthus, therefore, did not promote a purely individualist approach. The very fact that he suggested an artificially low wage rate speaks of interference, brought about by his concern for the future of society as a whole — albeit at the cost, unfortunately, of the worker's wellbeing.

In the extreme, Malthus's views regarding the working class are still propounded by those who suggest that employees should not seek higher wages, but should consider the wellbeing of society in total and rather improve their standard of living by family planning. Generally, his views are most often reflected in the argument that there is a fixed wage pool, that increases will have to be accompanied by cost cutting in other spheres or by a reduction in the workforce. This view overlooks the possibility of capital growth, of technological development and of a cut in employer profit margins to satisfy employee demands or to pay market-related wages.

Perpetuation of the Individualist Ideology

The classical–liberal ideology was later refined by economists such as **David Ricardo** and **I.B. Say**. There is no doubt that this philosophy helped to entrench the capitalist system, thereby endorsing mechanisation, specialisation, division of labour and the notion of market-related wages. Because of the vast supply of unskilled workers, these wages at best allowed for a bare subsistence level. Moreover, as indicated in the previous chapter, economic problems were accompanied by the social and psychological effects of industrialisation such as the new class distinction between owners and labourers, estrangement from work, loss of identity and monotony, all within the context of rapidly increasing urbanisation; with the result that, from the mid-eighteenth to the mid-nineteenth century, there were numerous social, political and economic upheavals, best exemplified by the Luddite Revolts in the early 1800s, where workers displayed their dissatisfaction with the new system by smashing and destroying the machines and factories which they regarded as the source of their newfound misery.

The Rise of Socialism and the Writings of Karl Marx

As can be expected, the capitalist system evoked reaction and criticism not only from the workers but also from eminent thinkers. Among the first of these was **Robert Owen**, himself a capitalist–owner, who nevertheless criticised the class divisions and oppression emanating from private ownership of capital and who suggested that private ownership should be abolished in favour of a system of cooperation and joint ownership. Most early socialists, such as **Gracchus Baboeuf**, **Henri Saint-Simon**, **Charles Fournier** and **Pierre Joseph Proudhon**, rejected private ownership of the capital means of production and espoused a philosophy of universal equality. (Ironically, the latter has its roots in the principle of individualism and was propounded, but not often practised, by the classical liberalists.) The first socialist philosophers differed greatly as regards the role of the State. The question was whether the State should be the instrument by which individualism should be subdued and the welfare of the whole of society ensured. On the other hand, if the State did not adopt this role, who would? Many saw the State (meaning systems of government) as the entrencher of the system of private property and capitalist production; thus they argued against any form of State or government. This, in the extreme, would favour an anarchical system. Others such as Saint-Simon saw the State playing an active role by intervening in the production process and in the distribution of wealth.

Most of these theorists were labelled 'Utopian socialists' by **Karl Marx** since, according to him, they relied too much on rationality and morality as the basis for change. Because he commenced by analysing the ills of the capitalist system and concluding from this that it would eventually destroy itself, Marx's brand of socialism is often described as 'scientific' socialism. Marx also introduced the concept of historical or **dialectic materialism**. This principle of dialectic materialism is based firstly on Hegel's theory of dialectic change, namely that every idea or force will automatically breed its opponent and that the two will merge into a new force, making history nothing more than a continuous flow of forces, counterforces and mergers of such forces. To this Marx added the concept of materialism: that societies will structure their laws, government, religion and politics in the light of the type of productive activity practised in each society. Arguing from this basis, he proposed that the capitalist system was essentially self-destructive in that its superstructure, which entrenched private property and private control of the means of production, was incompatible with its economic base, namely industrial production, which is an interrelated and interdependent process. Industrial production, according to Marx, demanded social planning, not generally favoured by the supporters of private ownership. The result was planless production, leading to a constant disorganisation of economic activity. Because of the disruption caused by this, capitalism would unwittingly breed its own successor, namely a rationally planned economy. This, in Marx's view, could be achieved only in a system in which the individual did not operate freely but was subject to planning which benefited the entire society.

Marx's main criticism of the capitalist system was that it reduced workers to the level of automatons who could not develop their full potential as human beings. In the words of Hunt and Sherman, 'Money replaced the relationship with things and other human beings'. The worker became a commodity, measured only in terms of the exchange value of his labour. Marx, on the other hand, saw labour as the most important instrument in the welfare of society, since it was the only factor creating value. In the capitalist society, man was not only alienated from his labour but was also obliged to produce surplus value, in the form of profits for the employer. The market-related wage paid to a labourer was sufficient to maintain him, but was not proportionate to his input. Using the analogy of a person living off the land, Marx postulated that a labourer need work only a certain number of hours per day for the purpose of providing food, shelter and clothing for himself and his family. Any excess time worked would produce excess value. In applying the analogy to the capitalist system, he argued that employees provided value in excess of the amount needed to maintain themselves. However, since they were paid only the equivalent of such maintenance, the surplus value created was being pocketed by the employer. Moreover, according to Marx, the capitalist system ensured a supply of labour which was always in excess of the market demand, thus guaranteeing continued low wage levels. This could be counteracted by the power of the working class to withhold its labour and, eventually, by a system of common ownership, which would lead to a more equitable distribution of surplus value or profits or, at the least, would allow the employee to work only long enough to supply his basic needs.

Marx's theory is based on the payment of 'maintenance level' wages and does not take into account the possibility of increased wages by competition, government interference or the moral conviction of employers. His theory of surplus value is often supported from the employee side and is reflected in demands for a greater share of the total profit: that is, wage rates related not to market factors but to the profitability of the enterprise and based on concepts of fairness.

In terms of Marxist philosophy it would be this 'alienated' and exploited working class, bred by the capitalist system, which would eventually become a social force for change towards a new order, based on common ownership of the mode of production and rational planning of production. For Marx this was the only solution — a sociopolitical revolution which would bring the superstructure of society into line with its economic base.

In the Industrial Relations context it is important that Marx emphasised the dichotomy between employer and employee in the modern industrial relationship. In his view the root cause was to be found in the misalignment between the interdependent, interrelated production process and the individualism of private property and of systems of government resulting from the latter. Marx offered a solution in the form of social (and, therefore, political) change, a view still expressed in the radical approach to Industrial Relations. He did not believe that the conflict arising from the dichotomy could be confined purely to the work situation or that a compromise could be found in the development of trade unionism and collective bargaining. If his view is accepted, trade unions are useful for conscientising and organising the working class, but the very reason for their existence is to be found in the capitalist system. If the working class were to gain momentum as a social and not merely an economic force, trade unions as we know them might become increasingly irrelevant.

Thus Marx emphasised the necessity to change society and the system of government to a communitarian base rather than to attempt the containment of employer–employee conflict within the capitalist or private property system. Although his predicted solution has not generally materialised, it is necessary to take Marx's principles into account in any study of Industrial Relations, particularly since some form of communitarianism is supported by most trade unions in our society today.

The Reformist and Institutional Economists

During the latter half of the nineteenth century workers not only made political gains through parties formed to represent their interests, but also experienced an increase in real wages. This resulted in the amelioration of revolutionary thinking and in proposals that peaceful change could be achieved by using the government as an instrument of social reform. Even the socialists of that period, such as George Bernard Shaw, believed that other objectives could be achieved by evolution rather than revolution. Furthermore, the emphasis of their criticism shifted from capitalist ownership of the means of production to the unequal distribution of wealth resulting from inequitable division of the fruits of production.

Among the most prominent of these so-called Fabian socialists were the British researchers **Beatrix and Sidney Webb**. As socialists the Webbs agreed with Marx that there was, between the participants in modern industrial society, a basic conflict of interest centring in control of the mode of production and, therefore, an ongoing conflict between the 'haves' and the 'have nots'. This needed to be resolved if society were to function optimally. In their view this conflict could be solved by a process of gradual accommodation rather than a complete and immediate change of the existing order. Such accommodation would entail the adoption of legal safeguards to ensure that the freedom and rights of both parties to the relationship were maintained, and also of special strategies which would increase the negotiating or bargaining power of the 'have nots'. For the Webbs the solution was initially to be found in **combination**: the development of trade unions as an economic and political force, and in the entrenchment of a system of collective bargaining — a term which was, in fact, coined by them. In their major works, *The History of Trade Unionism* and *Industrial Democracy*, they emphasised the importance of a mass trade union movement and the use of collective bargaining, by which they meant a shelving of individual differences between employees, as a means of correcting the imbalance between the owners of capital and those who labour. The Webbs also rejected the idea that, within a socialist society, workers might democratically manage their own industries. They proposed instead the idea of professional managers, accountable to the general population.

The Webbs were the first to put trade unionism and collective bargaining on the map. Their theories were later used by institutional economises such as **Commons**, who rejected both Marx's class struggle theory and the classical economic view of labour as a mere factor of production. Commons emphasised the fact that labour was not an inanimate commodity, that work was too central to man's life to be separated from the totality of his goals and needs, and that workers needed special rights and treatment not accorded to the other factors of production. Like the Webbs before him, he accepted that there was a conflict of interest between employer and employee and unequal bargaining power between the parties. In Commons's view the best method of handling such conflict was by organised negotiation. Key decisions should be negotiated, organised groups of workers accorded the right to join trade unions and industrial legislation promulgated to protect rights on both sides. The theories of the Reformists and the Institutionalists were, to some extent, supported by the Revisionists, who saw the potential in a system of universal franchise and shared ownership of the means of production.

It may well be said that the world of the reformist and institutional economists gave rise to the pluralist approach to industrial relations although, particularly in the case of the Webbs, their originators were essentially communitarian-orientated. They differed from Marx only in that they did not promote revolution as the means of achieving communal ownership. Rather, they saw this as being attainable through the systematic erosion of employer prerogative and private ownership. They also saw unions as playing an important role in this process. It is a view which, particularly in union circles, is still widely held today.

The Twentieth Century   The late nineteenth and early twentieth centuries saw the partial rejection of detrimental competition between enterprises and the amalgamation of large corporations; thus the birth of what is now termed *monopoly capitalism*.

However, no new economic philosophy has yet been propounded to explain or meet this development. The economic theories which do exist have all evolved from classical liberalism, Marxism, the reformists and even the Christian–paternalist ethic. **Neo-classical theory**, popular at the start of the twentieth century, totally ignored the tendency towards monopolies and bound its precepts on the concept of small, relatively powerless enterprises which would, like consumers and the providers of labour, be subject solely to the invisible hand of the market, the rationality of man in making his choices and the marginal utility of inputs and outputs. Later proponents of this theory did admit that the government might be obliged to intervene in order to right the social ills occasioned by this absolutely *laissez-faire* approach to the economy. Others who approved of the capitalist system but recognised its ills began to promote the new industrial magnates as benefactors of society, to emphasise their social responsibility and to point the way to more humane corporate cultures, this to some extent reviving the Christian–paternalist ethic. In the socialist field, there were those who continued to advocate redistribution of income and wealth within the capitalist framework, and others who saw (and still see) the only resolution in the total revolutionary overthrow of the capitalist system.

The Convergence Theory

It is now increasingly accepted that, between the poles of individualism and communitarianism and between the extreme theories of Adam Smith and Karl Marx (both of which have independent merit but which equally are beset by practical problems), a middle road can be negotiated, promoting individual endeavour and competition but with due reference to the needs of society at large. This would necessarily indicate continued but not undue State intervention. Also, it would require new interpretations of and distinction between:

- the free market as it pertains to the production and sale of goods and services,
- capitalism as it refers to private ownership of the means of production, and
- capitalism as it is often interpreted —
- that is, sole ownership of the fruits of production or the accumulation of wealth at the expense of those who produce.

THE ROLE OF THE STATE

Government and the State

The State may be said to be the abstraction of all the individuals in a society. It thus represents society at large. However, it is extremely difficult to picture or conceptualise the State in such abstract terms. Thus the State is commonly perceived as being embodied in systems of government, causing the words 'State' and 'government' to be used interchangeably. In democratic systems governments are elected by the people; but, because democracy is based on the principle of majority rule, governments so elected are not necessarily representative of all those who constitute the State. A particular government, as representative of the majority in society, will adhere to a greater or lesser degree to a communitarian or individualist ideology.

In practice, the State (in the form of its main instrument, the government) will have a political bias which, in modern, economically based society, manifests itself in a pro-capital or pro-labour orientation. This bias is of importance in industrial relations since it, with other factors, will determine the degree of State interference in the conduct of the labour relationship.

Voluntarism and Mandatorism

Whether or not the State interferes in the labour relationship will, in the broadest terms, depend on its adherence to the principle of voluntarism on the one hand or mandatorism on the other — which, in turn, depends on its ideological base. Adherence to the principle of voluntarism presupposes minimal or no interference in the conduct of the labour relationship. Conversely, the principle of mandatorism rests on absolute or maximal government control of all aspects of the labour relationship. This would occur only in a society where government also exercises or attempts to exercise control over economic and social forces and where labour relations, in the Western sense, do not exist.

In general, most Western societies operating to a greater or lesser degree on the free market principle support voluntarism as the basis of their industrial relations systems. Yet, in practice, absolute or pure voluntarism exists nowhere in the world. In all so-called voluntary systems there are mandatory elements, the degree varying from country to country and, even in one country, from government to government or from year to year. This is so for the following reasons.

- The government, in establishing a legal framework for society at large, necessarily impinges on the sphere of industrial relations.
- Labour relationships, if left solely to the main participants (that is, employers and employees or unions) may be inequitable and it becomes necessary for the State to step in to restore the power balance.
- The conduct of industrial relations will impact on society and the economy. Where either is adversely affected, the State is bound to interfere.
- Industrial relations also involves politics. The government, being a political instrument, necessarily interests itself in developments in this sphere.

Consequently governments will, at the very least, provide the legal framework for the conduct of industrial relations, give maximum protection to employees and employers, attempt to preserve labour peace and attempt to safeguard society against extreme behaviour by either party.

Forms of State Interference

The degree and type of interference in the labour relationship practised by a particular government will depend, interactively, on its ideological base, its political objectives, on the sociopolitical and economic circumstances and on the strength of the union movement. This results in different forms of interaction between the State and the other roleplayers in the labour relations sphere.

Market Individualism
Where a government supports an individualist ideology, is biased towards capital and adopts a *laissez-faire* approach to the economy, where the union movement

is weak and the economy relatively healthy, a government will tend to adopt a completely *laissez-faire* attitude to the conduct of industrial relations. It will take the view that the conduct of the labour relationship is the affair of the employer and the employee, that the contract of employment is the ultimate regulator of the relationship and that the operation of a free market principle will sufficiently regulate industrial relations practices. This is the approach which Crouch has described as 'market individualism'. It may appear to embody voluntarism in its absolute form, but it could also be a biased approach. In reality, the government could indirectly intervene on behalf of the employer. This is so because the institutions and laws of the government may favour capital and entrench property rights. Also, nothing would be done to correct the inherent imbalance in the employer–employee relationship and the unions themselves might not be strong enough to redress the situation. Nowadays the increased power of trade unions and general sociopolitical developments have led to the demise of market individualism in most Western societies.

Institutionalised Voluntarism

In the case where the government is individualist-orientated, is biased towards capital and supports the free market system but where trade unions are strong, it becomes necessary for the government also to accommodate, or at least to acknowledge, the interests of the latter group. In essence, the government may still adopt a *laissez-faire* approach to the conduct of labour relations, but it accepts the trade unions' right to existence and it may entrench this right in legislation. Collective bargaining becomes an accepted, if not obligatory, practice and the government may go so far as to establish or endorse machinery for this purpose. Since collective bargaining may not always end in agreement, disputes are accepted as part of the process. This leads to acknowledgment of the freedom to strike and lock out and the government, in its efforts to maintain industrial peace, may establish itself in the role of conciliator and peacemaker. The acknowledgment of the interests of employees leads to the institution of safeguards in the form of minimum conditions of service regulations, health and safety legislation and regulations pertaining to workmen's compensation and unemployment. A government which has adopted this approach may set the framework for the conduct of industrial relations by regulating the registration of employers' associations and unions, establishing the machinery for collective bargaining and conciliation, setting minimum standards and providing guidelines for the parties concerned; but it will usually not interfere too much in the actual conduct of the labour relationship and will not oblige employers or employees to enter into a formal relationship by making recognition of trade unions compulsory. A governmental policy of this kind constitutes what is generally regarded as a voluntary approach, but it is better described as a policy of 'institutionalised voluntarism'.

Pro-Capital Interventionism

It could happen that a trade union movement becomes so strong that it poses a political or economic threat or causes a power imbalance between unions and employers. If this occurs, the government may abandon institutionalised voluntarism for a policy of greater interference. Such interference will be aimed at curtailing the power of unions by, for example, limiting their freedom to strike or restricting their activities in other spheres. This policy of pro-capital interventionism may also be adopted where a previous, labour-orientated government has, in the opinion of a new government, intervened too much on behalf of labour — for example, by nationalising industries and allowing employees too much power at the workplace. The new government will denationalise industries, encourage capital accumulation and place stronger restrictions on trade union action. This happened in Britain under the Conservative government.

Corporatism
Economic or political developments in themselves may oblige a government to intervene in labour relations. In times of reconstruction or economic recession, a government may request cooperation from employers and employees in bringing about economic improvement. This would entail that they do not engage in aggressive collective bargaining, that unions limit their wage demands and employers limit price increases. This is what Crouch calls corporatism. Such a policy may be adopted with the voluntary cooperation of unions and employers, or an incomes policy may be imposed by the government. Also, within a certain ideological framework or for the sake of political expediency, all parties may voluntarily cooperate to formulate labour relations and economic policies; they enter into a social contract, aimed at achieving maximum benefit for all. This approach usually hovers between individualism and communitarianism, as it is meant to curtail the individual power of both capital and labour in the interests of society as a whole.

Pro-Labour Interventionism
If labour gains dominance in the government or the changed objectives of government bring about a bias towards labour, a government may seek to intervene on behalf of labour. This happens particularly where economic ideology shifts to a more communitarian approach and seeks to incorporate social welfare principles or a social market policy. The government, by its economic policy, engages in a redistribution of wealth and thereby partly alleviates the need for aggressive collective bargaining and strike action by unions. A policy of pro-labour interventionism will also lead to greater protection and promotion of employee interests and to an extension of their rights at the workplace. Typical outflows of such a policy are compulsory employee profit-sharing schemes, workers' participation schemes and regulations regarding employee or union codetermination on boards of directors.

It is ironic that government, taking up the cause of the employee, renders the union less relevant in its basic role as collective bargainer and protector of employee rights. Added to this is the fact that provisions for worker participation and codetermination necessitate cooperation with the employer, which unions may find hard to reconcile with their role as antagonists of the employer. Thus greater intervention by government on behalf of labour does not promote unions, but might instead render them irrelevant.

Pro-Labour Mandatorism
The decreasing relevance of trade unions is obvious in a society where absolute communitarianism and pro-labour mandatorism prevails. In this instance the

government has an absolute bias towards labour, the free market principle is not accepted and capital accumulation is not encouraged. The government will regulate the labour relationship in its totality and there is no perceived need for union action in the form of collective bargaining or protection of employee rights. Whether the government in this case does not itself become the employer is a question which could be debated.

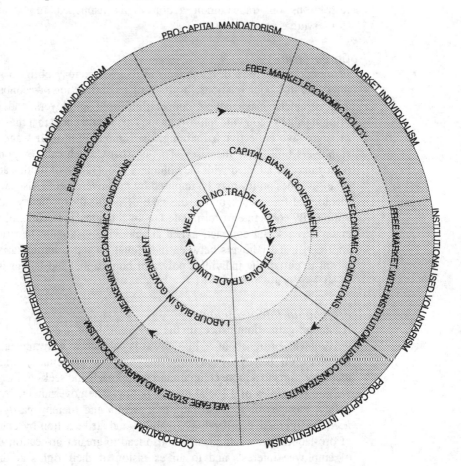

Figure 4: THE CYCLE OF STATE INTERFERENCE

Pro-Capital Mandatorism

Absolute mandatorism could also prevail where a totally individualist government favours capital to the exclusion of labour. Since labour, which usually constitutes a majority of the national population, will have a vote in government, this is unlikely to happen in a democratic society, nor will it be possible where there is a strong trade union movement. In theory, a policy of pro-capital mandatorism will be marked by government intervention to curtail employee rights. This would manifest itself in the non-recognition of unions, in government curtailment of the right to strike, in laws promoting the cause of the employer and in control of labour relations to promote the free enterprise and capitalist systems.

With this policy the circle of government intervention is closed, as the next step would be the adoption of a policy of market individualism.

The compartmentalisation of levels of government intervention into seven basic types is an oversimplification of the real situation. It has been done merely to provide a framework for understanding different governmental policies and actions. In practice there are not only exceptions to the rule, but also many fine differences of degree and numerous interacting variables. So, for example, economic circumstances or a change in objectives may lead a government to abandon one particular policy for another, despite its basic ideology, its capital or labour orientation and the strength or weakness of the trade union movement. Furthermore, labour itself may become disenchanted with a labour-orientated government and may vote a capital-orientated government into power. This would lead to the adoption of a completely new policy. Figure 4 attempts a schematic representation of some of the factors influencing the degree of government intervention and tries to take into account their dynamic interaction.

The non-arrowed circles in Figure 4 represent changing government bias and economic policy and, in the outer circle, the interventionist policies which result. The arrowed circles are dynamic forces which represent, firstly, the growth of the union movement and, secondly fluctuations in the economy. It will be perceived that, as trade unions grow in strength, government is gradually obliged to adapt its policy. Equally, as governments increase their intervention, unions become weaker. Finally, the weaker the economy becomes, the more will government be obliged to intervene.

Roles Adopted by the State

Salamon divides the roles adopted by the State into four categories. The State, according to Salamon, can act as employer, legislator, conciliator and regulator. Whether the State as employer intervenes in industrial relations is debatable. This aspect is, therefore, omitted and another method of intervention will be added to those of Salamon: the role of the State as advisor to the other two parties. In addition, the role of State agencies such as the judiciary and the police deserve consideration.

The State as Legislator

The legislative role of the State is its most important in the sphere of industrial relations. The State may legislate on individual rights and on collective rights; it may by legislation establish collective bargaining machinery and may prescribe statutory procedures to be followed by the other participants in the labour relationship.

Government legislation on **individual rights** supplements the rights granted by common law. Common law, under which is included the contract of employment, does not necessarily protect an employee against exploitation or poor treatment by an employer. Consequently, the government is obliged to intervene and, by its labour legislation, to protect mainly the employee, although it may also make provision for the protection of the employer. The most common form of individual legislation is that regulating basic employment conditions and health and safety and that protecting employees from victimisation by an employer, but a government may go further and also establish protection against unfair labour practices and, in particular, against the unfair dismissal of an employee.

In the sphere of **collective rights**, governments will most commonly protect the freedom of association principle and will establish rules for the formation and registration of trade unions and employers' associations. A government may or may not protect the freedom to strike and lock out. Similarly, it may or may not grant unions immunity from the actions of their members and shop stewards. Certain governments may make collective agreements enforceable by law and others may compel an employer to bargain with a representative trade union. Recently, some governments have also entrenched in law the collective right of employees to participate in decisionmaking at their place of work and to elect representatives to management boards. In the extreme, a government may act totally on behalf of the collective. In this instance it becomes difficult to discern collective rights from individual rights.

A government may also decide to establish a statutory **collective bargaining machinery**, but the use of such machinery by employers and unions may not be obligatory. In establishing such machinery it may prescribe or suggest procedures for the settlement of disputes and may provide general guidance for the conduct of grievance, disciplinary and retrenchment procedures. Where collective bargaining between employers and employees is weak or nonexistent, the government may itself bargain with both parties and legislate on minimum wage rates.

Generally, the type and amount of legislation will depend on a government's overall policy regarding intervention in the labour relationship, which in turn is dependent on the numerous interacting factors mentioned in the previous section.

The State as Conciliator

The State may not only provide processes for conciliation and mediation by its legislation, but it may itself act as conciliator and mediator. In pursuing its objective of maintaining industrial peace, a government may establish conciliation, mediation and arbitration services. The use of such facilities may or may not be made compulsory by the government. The government may, in certain stances, itself interfere in disputes.

The State as Regulator

If the State wishes to regulate the conduct of industrial relations, it will be obliged to intervene more directly in the labour relationship and particularly in the conduct of collective bargaining. The most common form of regulation is to be found in the establishment of an incomes policy or a complete freeze on wages and prices, but the State also regulates the labour relationship when it provides for compulsory recognition and bargaining and when it compels workers' participation at plant level.

The State as Advisor

The State may set itself up as watchdog and advisor in the sphere of industrial relations. In this instance the State will establish various bodies to monitor developments in industrial relations, to produce guidelines on the conduct of the labour relationship and to suggest innovations to the participants. If its advisory status is accepted, a government can indirectly influence the development of industrial relations in a particular society.

The Role of the Judiciary

Despite its theoretical independence from the government, the judiciary remains an instrument of the State. The function of the judiciary is to determine common law pertaining to the employment relationship and also to interpret and apply the statutes passed by government to regulate the labour relationship.

Problems with the normal judicial process are experienced where the judiciary is not acquainted with the intricacies of the labour relationship or with the law pertaining to it. Such problems increase when the judiciary is required to interpret concepts of fairness, as pertaining to the labour relationship. For this reason, certain governments have seen fit to introduce labour courts dealing specifically with labour matters, and tribunals or industrial courts to adjudicate in industrial disputes.

The Role of the Police

Essentially the police force has no role to play in industrial relations in that it is not supposed to side with either party. However, it does have a duty to protect the public and to prevent public disturbances. Therefore, whether either of the major parties poses a threat to the public or causes a public disturbance, the police, as the law enforcement arm of the State, may be asked to intervene. Unfortunately, it is usually employees and their unions who are seen as causing a disturbance or infringing upon the rights of other individuals. Consequently the police are viewed as siding with the employers. For this reason and various others, police intervention should be allowed or requested only in extreme circumstances — and then only for the purpose of public protection or to prevent individuals from harming one another.

The Future Role of the State in Industrial Relations

The State, with its instruments of government, represents a permanent institution, which may change in nature and policy but will not change in essence. As explained throughout this section, the role of the State in industrial relations will largely be determined by circumstances. Nevertheless, with the shift from absolute free market principles to a support for mixed economies or a social market system, it would appear that the State may be required to play an increasingly interventionist role in the conduct of the labour relationship.

OTHER VARIABLES INFLUENCING THE COMPOSITION OF A SYSTEM

As explained earlier, ideology is the basis from which an individual or group adopts a certain perspective or approach to the labour relationship. Equally, the type of labour relations system established within a particular society will depend on the dominant or prevalent sociopolitical and economic ideology. Therefore, the primary variable in the composition of different industrial relations systems and that around which all the other variables will hinge is the divergence of ideologies between societies. This divergence is best illustrated by the polarisation between societies or social subgroups which support an individualist ideology and those which believe in absolute communitarianism, with the concomitant support for capitalism, the free market and voluntary industrial relations systems on the one hand and for socialism, a planned economy and a mandatory system of industrial government on the other. Although ideology will determine the basic orientation of the State within the system, there are, as outlined in the previous section, other factors which will influence the eventual role of the State. Thus the form of intervention adopted by the State becomes, in itself, an important variable in the establishment of an industrial relations system.

Besides these two, there are a number of other variables shaping particular systems. These are discussed below.

**Democrat-
isation of
Political
Systems**
In Western societies it may happen that the majority of employers support the principles of individualism, while most employees favour a communitarian ideology. In these circumstances it could be expected that the ideological principles of the ruling party will always prevail and that the industrial relations system will be fashioned solely in terms of the dominant ideology. However, owing to the operation of a democratic political process, neither side is usually permitted to prevail. This further strengthens the possibility of 'mixed' sociopolitical and economic systems being established.

In a society where all individuals have an equal and free vote, the combined political vote of the employing or owning class is balanced by that of the employees or working class. A government which is voted into power will, irrespective of its ideological orientation, be obliged to take into consideration the interests of all its citizens and especially those of employees, because they constitute a large bloc of voters. Where differences in ideology exist, a sensible government will finely balance conflicting interests in order not to antagonise any section of the voting public. For this reason even governments which are essentially employer-supportive will protect the interests of employees and will provide for power-balancing institutions in the industrial relations system. Equally, many governments may be biased towards labour, but will not be able to favour only labour in their policies since this may lead to the withdrawal of capital or may act as a deterrent to investment.

Furthermore, although workers constitute the majority of the voting public in all societies and it could be argued that they will also predominate in the political sphere, this is not always the case: not all employees necessarily subscribe to the same ideologies, nor do all employees identify with each other or perceive themselves as members of the 'working class'. Added to this are social differences in the form of race, religion or geographical affiliation, and circumstantial factors relating to the economy and governmental actions which may lead to a split vote among employees. As a result, a balance of interests may be maintained.

The power balancing which occurs in the political systems is reflected in the industrial relations systems of Western societies. Yet complete balance in the political sphere is rarely achieved. The fulcrum of power continually shifts from one side to the other and, at any one time, one of the parties to the labour relationship will wield more power in the political sphere. This leads also to an adjustment of the industrial relations system in favour of that party. Should it happen that this creates too great an imbalance of power in the industrial relations system, or should one party view the political system as antagonistic to his interests in the industrial relations system, it is more than likely that he will vote, in the next election, for a government which will restore the balance, if not favour him outright. Thus the fulcrum will shift, for the time being, to the other side.

This balancing of interests in the industrial relations system, occasioned by a balance of power in the political system, can be achieved only if all participants to the labour relationship also have a vote in a multiparty political system. Where this is not the case, the party which holds power in the political sphere will enforce the establishment of an industrial relations system geared to the predomination of his particular interests. The other party, provided that it has the power to do so, will turn to alternative methods of addressing the imbalance — an event which may place unnecessary strain on the industrial relations system. To a large extent, this happened in South Africa during the previous dispensation.

Sociopolitical Forces

Sociopolitical forces emanate from the dominant sociopolitical ideology or the conflict in ideologies between different groups. These forces will, in the same way as the prevailing ideologies, impact directly on the industrial relations system.

In the light of its ideology a government will adopt a particular public policy. This may lead to the promotion or otherwise of certain groups, to the encouragement or otherwise of education and training and to restrictions on certain practices. Moreover, the policy adopted could give rise to factionalisation and divisions in society. Obviously all of these will have an influence on the labour relations system and on the nature of the trade union movement. A lack of education, for example, results in a proliferation of unskilled workers and a shortage of skilled employees. The latter will wield great power in the system, while the former will have to gain power by other means. Equally, restrictions on labour mobility will interfere with the operation of a balanced industrial relations system.

Economic Forces

Economic circumstances also play a part in determining the type of overall system established. Unemployment, arising from economic adversity, may necessitate the review of processes and practices in an existing industrial relations system. Furthermore, continued economic adversity may promote solidarity among the working class, resulting in their achieving greater political power. This may be used to bring about changes in both the sociopolitical and industrial relations systems. Alternatively, shared economic adversity could result in greater cooperation between employers, employees and the State and to a de-emphasis on collective bargaining in favour of more participative structures.

Economic forces are numerous and variable. As such, they constitute one of the most dynamic factors in the establishment of industrial relations systems.

History and Nature of the Trade Union Movement

The origins and development of trade unions, their primary goals, methods of organisation and place within society will, more so than in the case of employer organisations, help to shape the industrial relations systems in which they exist. The reason for this is that trade unions are proactive within the industrial relations system, while employers are, more often than not, reactive.

Trade unions which recruit on an *ad hoc* and geographically spread basis may take a long time to establish a unified front. This could lead to a factionalised system and to the fragmentation of the collective bargaining process. It may also prevent the trade union movement from wielding sufficient influence, resulting in a neglect of employee interests in the establishment of the industrial relations system.

In certain societies trade unions subscribe to the same ideology as employers. This leads to a greater acceptance by both sides of the systems and processes introduced and even to greater cooperation. Conversely, where the ideology of a trade union movement differs from that prevalent in the rest of society, it may attempt to achieve political power in order to promote its beliefs and values. This trend is particularly noticeable in societies where there are marked class differences, where wealth is unequally distributed and where trade union members are less privileged in one way or another.

Trade unions in themselves are dynamic organisations. Principles and practices within the trade union movement change continually, resulting in concomitant changes in the industrial relations system.

Employer Organisations

The manner in which and extent to which employers organise themselves will also have a significant effect on the industrial relations system, albeit less overtly than that of trade unions. Employers, in both trade and bargaining organisations, usually engage in lobbying government and politicians, seeking in this way to influence developments within the system.

Interaction of Variables

Industrial relations systems are the complex product of numerous dynamic and interacting forces. Not one of the variables mentioned functions on its own, and each will have an effect on the other. Thus the relationship between societal variables and industrial relations systems is never straightforward. The existence of a particular variable does not signify that an industrial relations system will necessarily function in a certain manner. The totality of variables, their interaction with each other and other prevalent circumstances have always to be taken into account. Together they will shape the roles of participants within the system, their actions and attitudes, the processes adopted and the legislative framework.

EFFECT OF THE INDUSTRIAL RELATIONS SYSTEM ON SOCIETY

The interaction between the society at large and the industrial relations system is not a one-way process. Developments and events in the industrial relations system will affect the wider society, particularly in societies where progress has been retarded.

At its most basic level, this interaction is seen in the effect that strike action has on the community. Not only do such actions impede economic activity, but they cause a general upheaval in society which may have further repercussions. Also on the micro-level is the case of the employee who is poorly treated and robbed of his human dignity. This leads to the situation where he is unable to fulfil his rightful role in society. Equally, polarisation in the workplace will be reflected in similar societal divisions, while collective organisation in the industrial sphere leads to greater influence in the outside world. Both trade unions and employers' organisations play significant roles in the societies in which they function.

Participation and cooperation in the workplace may lead to similar cooperation between different groups in society. Training provided by the employer and the practice of social responsibility uplifts society as a whole. In many respects the industrial relations system can take the lead and show those in power the route to follow.

CONCLUSION

It is important to achieve an understanding of the variables shaping different systems, since only then can effective comparisons between different systems be conducted. Moreover, it is only when similar variables exist that a transfer of practices and structures from one system to another can be considered.

SOURCES

Anthony, P D *The Conduct of Industrial Relations*, Institute of Personnel Management, London, 1977.

Heilbroner, R *The Worldly Philosophers*, Penguin, 1980.

Hunt, E and Howard J Sherman *Economics: An Introduction to Traditional and Radical Views*, Harper & Rowe, 1978.

Hyman, R *Industrial Relations: A Marxist Introduction*, Macmillan, 1975.

Hyman, R and I Brough *Social Values and Industrial Relations*, Blackwell, 1975.

Salamon, Michael *Industrial Relations Theory and Practice*, Prentice Hall, 1987.

Thompson, Paul *The Nature of Work*, Macmillan Education Limited, 1986.

3

COMPARATIVE INDUSTRIAL RELATIONS SYSTEMS

As mentioned in the previous chapter, industrial relations systems have three major components: the participants in the labour relationship, the processes and procedures established by the participants, and the rules and laws regulating the relationship. These in turn will depend on the societal variables influencing the system, the most important being the dominant ideology, the role of the State, public policy, historical forces, economic circumstances, trade union activity and history and, finally, the degree of democratisation in a particular country.

A study of the industrial relations systems operative in a cross-section of countries reveals the strong interaction between these systems and the societies in which they function. At the one extreme is the United States of America with its strong belief in individualism and the free market system. Despite certain mandatory elements, occasioned mostly by historical forces, the industrial relations system is mostly a voluntary system where tough collective bargaining has hitherto predominated and where no noteworthy attempts at industrial democracy have been instituted. In counterposition to this system we find that which prevailed in Yugoslavia, dominated by a communitarian ideology, but with State control of economic activity supplemented by a form of market competition together with a system of worker management of competitive enterprises.

Ranging between Yugoslavia and America is the British system with its ambivalent liberal individualist and communitarian ideology. This system was until recently the most voluntary, with greatly decentralised collective bargaining being the most prevalent, yet major industries have in the past been nationalised. Experiments in worker management have been conducted, but on all sides there has been a notable reluctance to introduce full worker participation, particularly in the decisionmaking sphere.

The final system is that of Germany, where an evidently beneficial mix of sociopolitical and economic ideologies has let to the coincidence of collecting bargaining and workers' participation. Yet there is evidence of tensions within the system which may give rise to increased conflict.

SYSTEMS AS REFLECTIVE OF SOCIETIES

The influence of societal factors on an industrial relations system is best illustrated by studying the systems of different countries against the backdrop of ideologies, policies and developments in those societies. At present, the most distinct societal differences are to be found between countries with a liberal–capitalist orientation and those still propounding a Marxist/socialist view. Between these extremes are those countries which have, to a greater or lesser extent, adopted a more pragmatic and less ideologically extreme position.

It will be noted that, as we move through the spectrum from individualism to communitarianism, State interference and regulation increases. Similarly, the emphasis shifts from free collective bargaining to worker participation or control and, at the same time, unions become less relevant or undergo a change in role.

For the purpose of illustration, the United States, Britain, Germany and Yugoslavia have been used as prototypes — although it should be borne in mind that the establishment of prototypes necessarily involves oversimplification. Also, Yugoslavia has for the past few years been in turmoil, so that its inclusion is more as an illustration of a type of system, rather than an absolute reflection of reality.

UNITED STATES OF AMERICA

Societal Background

The United States has traditionally given unqualified support to the ideology of individualism. This is best illustrated by the American tenet that 'the sky is the limit' and that the cabin boy can, by his own efforts and enterprise, become a millionaire. The emphasis on individualism is reflected in America's strongly capitalist orientation, its promotion of the free market system and its encouragement of intense, sometimes aggressive, competition. Furthermore, it would appear that this ideology is shared by most Americans, that there is no marked difference between the beliefs and values of employers and employees. This commonality of belief is underscored by a strong sense of national pride and by the fact that the United States does not suffer from a historical class dichotomy. Class differences certainly do exist, but these arise from wealth accrued by the pioneers and through individual effort and not from preindustrial societal structures. There are, admittedly, certain groups in America which, because of the previous practice of slavery and the use of cheap imported labour, may regard themselves as less privileged as a class; yet the equality of all persons is entrenched in law. While over the past years there has been a tendency in America to place greater emphasis on social welfare and the upliftment of communities, there appears at present to be a reversal of this trend, typified by the Republican takeover of Congress and the strong individualist stance now being adopted by numerous politicians.

The Principle of Voluntarism

In the light of the above it seems logical that the American industrial relations system will be based on the principles of voluntarism and freedom of association and that free and unfettered collective bargaining will prevail; equally that the government will not concern itself too greatly with adjusting the power balance between the parties, with the promotion and protection of employee interests and with participative practices. This expectation increases if it is considered that the origin of American unionism lies in craft unions, which found protection in their skill and had little need of protection from government or society.

A system of almost complete voluntarism did exist in America up to the 1920s. Until that time business was conducted in a spirit of aggressive capitalist endeavour and few restraints were imposed, as far as the conduct of both business and the labour relationship was concerned. Employers and employees were allowed to pursue their own interests in whatever manner they saw fit.

Historic and Economic Influences

This early voluntaristic trend might have continued for some time were it not for the stock market crash of 1929, the ensuing economic disaster and Roosevelt's promise of a 'New Deal' to the American people. The economic recession led to the realisation that employers and employees could not be allowed to pursue their goals without any interference whatsoever and that checks and balances were required. This resulted also in changes in the labour relations sphere, in the form of minimum protection for employees and the institutionalisation of collective bargaining. Consequently, the American industrial relations system now contains numerous mandatory elements, such as the compulsion on employers to recognise representative unions within legally prescribed bargaining units, the obligation to bargain in good faith, the wide-ranging prohibitions on unfair labour practices, the circumscription of the freedom to strike and presidential powers to intervene in certain types of dispute. Also, various governments have, from time to time, attempted to bring the economy back on its feet by introducing wage and price freezes and even by interfering in the bargaining process.

Collective Bargaining Practices

Despite these restrictions, the American industrial relations system remains essentially a voluntary system, its main purpose being the promotion of collective bargaining which is usually of an aggressive and antagonistic nature. No concerted attempt has yet been made to introduce industrial democracy or a Western European type of workers' participation. Although such innovations have been discussed at various levels, communitarianism has not advanced to the extent that it has influenced industrial relations developments. This may be partly due to the fact that the trade union movement is relatively weak numerically, in terms of the total population. Moreover, there is the trade unions' protection of their roles as tough bargainers. Alternatively, the ideologies of American trade unions may not support the principle of joint decisionmaking.

Employees and Employee Organisations

American employees and unions in general have never proved themselves overintent on achieving political goals; nor have they been particularly supportive of socialist principles. Traditionally, greater emphasis has always been placed on the achievement of economic, rather than sociopolitical, objectives. For this reason American unions have been typified as business unions. Unions in the United States are run along very much the same lines as business enterprises and they gain members mostly by their ability to achieve financial rewards for their members. Furthermore, they place themselves continually into competition with non-unionised enterprises, whose managements are intent on proving to employees that unions do not bring better rewards for employees.

Although unions are structured on a centralised level and act under the auspices of the American Federation of Labour and the Confederation of Industrial Organisations (AFL–CIO), unions in America are highly factionalised. Regional bodies are given almost complete independence and possess their own resources. Bargaining is mostly localised and, within the prescriptions of the law, employers and local unions establish their own structures and procedures. This decentralisation of power in the trade union movement is in line with the principle of individualism and runs parallel to the decentralisation of power in the political system.

Workers' Participation

American unions have traditionally emphasised their collective bargaining role *vis-à-vis* the employer and are intent on not blurring the distinctions between the role of unions and that of management. Unions feared that any sign of cooperation with management would lead to loss of membership and that, if such cooperation should take place, unions would, as one writer has put it, be the junior partners in success and the senior partners in failure. Managements, too, have in the past been openly hostile to unions, resisting unionisation by all means possible. Nevertheless, they did, if obliged, settle into quite comfortable relations with recognised unions. In the light of the above it is not surprising that very little interest was shown by either side in any form of joint decisionmaking at plant or board level. Even in non-unionised enterprises, few initiatives towards shared decisionmaking were undertaken until very recently.

Where cooperation between unions and employers does take place in the United States, it has so far been spurred mainly by the need for survival of the enterprise in the light of weakening economic conditions and competition from countries such as Japan. This is exemplified by the Experimental Negotiation Agreement in the iron and steel industry, the objectives of which were to improve productivity, to promote orderly and peaceful relations, to promote the use of domestic steel, to achieve the desired prosperity for the company and its employees and to review matters of common concern. Yet another example is to be found in the case of the United Auto Workers which, in 1973, because of a marked increase in absenteeism and a noticeable lack of motivation on the part of employees, entered into an agreement with employers. The agreement was aimed at improving the quality of working life and the plant-level liaison committees established as a result concentrated on such problems as alcoholism, drug abuse, orientation of employees, administration of benefits, health and safety, selection and training and equal opportunity. In both these instances the union maintained its role as adversary of the employer and, although there was greater cooperation on certain issues, it did not share in any major managerial decisions.

Most Recent Developments

There are theorists who believe that the sociopolitical and economic ideology of American society is undergoing change; alternatively, that it will have to change in the light of modern developments. They believe that the traditional American emphasis on individualism, property rights, competition and limited State interference will gradually give way to a new spirit of communitarianism and that the government will be obliged to engage in more extensive socioeconomic planning. This may be the direction for the future, but as yet there is little evidence of such a change in the industrial relations sphere. Individual companies may be moving towards greater cooperation, but such cooperation is usually based either on a renewed belief in individualism or on guarded and limited coordination between management and unions. There is no marked general trend towards the implementation of participatory systems similar to those established in Western Europe.

Over the past two decades, union membership has declined and employers have actively contributed to this by adopting new management styles which would make the employee identify more with the enterprise than with the worker movement. This is evidenced by the spate of American 'recipes' aimed at gaining employee involvement and commitment — and, of course, higher productivity.

The two main precepts on which the American system has so far been based are the principles of individuality and equality. Pure individualism has to some extent been tempered with notions of social justice but, by and large, economic activity still centres in capitalism and the free market and the most dominant practice in the labour relationship is to be found in the conduct of tough negotiations. In fact, as noted earlier, it would seem that there are those who contend that the individualist approach is again gaining ground and that this accounts for the decline in trade union membership as well as for the increasing popularity of direct representation and fragmentation into smaller groups at the workplace. Also, Power submits that, even though the American trade union movement from the outset showed no interest in gaining control of the productive process, American management has never really accepted unionism, that cooperation is reluctant and that the eventual aim of most American employers is to manage without unions if possible.

GREAT BRITAIN

As in America, the spirit of individualism has long been entrenched in British society and even today marks what is generally described as Britain's own brand of liberalism. Yet, unlike America, the principle of social equality was not always enshrined in Britain. Modern British society arose in and from the feudal system and, even up to the present, British people still possess a strong sense of class, which gives rise to an ongoing, if now diluted, class struggle. Also, Britain was the seat of the Industrial Revolution which, in its turn, resulted in the formation of the British trade union movement and to a pervasive collective consciousness among the working class. Thus, since the beginnings of industrialisation, two conflicting yet intermingled ideologies have been prevalent in Britain. On the one hand, there is the traditional liberal–individualist ideology of the country and, on the other, the communitarianism of the working masses. Yet even in the 'working class' there has, together with an awareness of collective interests, always been a strong sense of individualism, reflected in the fact that both individual employees and unions still claim the right to independent action.

Trade Union History In the light of the class struggle and the opposing ideologies existing in society, British unions were established with the purpose not only of achieving economic gains but also of forming a 'more humanitarian and egalitarian society'. Consequently, British unionism has always contained strong socialist, even

Marxist, elements, counterposed by those of a more liberal bent. The emphasis of unions also on political goals led to the establishment of the Labour Party as the political wing of the British trade union movement. Reflecting the strong belief in democracy, the main purpose of the Labour Party was to achieve greater consideration of working class interests, either by forming an opposition in Parliament or by itself achieving political dominance.

The Principle of Voluntarism

The traditional and still continuing existence of a liberal–individualist ideology in Britain resulted in an almost completely voluntary system of industrial relations. Until the late 1960s there were few prescriptions regarding the conduct of the labour relationship. The prescriptions that did exist were aimed, initially, at curbing trade union power and, later, at more rational organisation of trade unions and at the settlement of industrial disputes. The first half of the Twentieth Century was the age of the capitalist and of free economic activity. The power of the employer was matched only by the growing strength of the trade union movement and frequent disputes were the order of the day. In the political sphere, the Conservative government held sway for most of this period and employees gained rights and protection mainly by agreements with management. Although the 1918 Trade Boards Act had provided for the establishment of trade boards to regulate wages in industries where there was no adequate wage regulation machinery, other employee rights received attention for the first time only after the Labour Party came to power again in the early 1960s. Soon afterwards the 1963 Contracts of Employment Act was passed. This laid down minimum notice periods and provided that a written statement of terms and conditions of employment should be issued to employees.

The previous absence of legislation regarding conditions of work does not mean that employees in Britain had no rights, merely that the government of the time, in keeping with the principle of voluntarism, left it to the unions and employees to reach agreements governing these matters. A policy of the greatest possible non-interference was followed, although the State had set up machinery, in the form of an industrial court and boards of arbitration, to facilitate the settlement of disputes. Also, the government was willing to endorse agreements once they had been reached. This is proved by the 1959 Terms and Conditions of Employment Act, which provided that an industrial court could order compliance with voluntary agreements reached between unions and employers.

In essence the parties to the employment relationship in Britain were, for the most part, left to muddle their own way through. Very few rights were denied to them, but they also had no special rights or particular legislation to govern their relationship. The continuance of this practice over so long a period may be attributed either to the fact that employees and unions were quite satisfied with the *status quo* or to workers having insufficient collective and political power. In all likelihood both reasons pertain. It should also be remembered that, during that period, Britain had been engaged in two world wars. This nurtured a sense of nationalism and solidarity amongst the British citizenry as a whole.

Greater Government Interference

The coming to power of the Labour Party in the early Sixties led to the increased representation of working class interests in the seats of government, and legislation passed at the time (such as the Redundancy Payment Act, the Race Relations Act, the Equal Pay Act and the Trade Disputes Act) furnishes proof that a greater balance of employer and employee interests was being sought. However, the Labour Party also expected cooperation from unions in its efforts to regulate the economy. The establishment of the National Board for Prices & Incomes which resulted from this policy was partially responsible for this party's political downfall at the end of that decade. The Conservative government which followed introduced a statutory wage freeze. It also passed the 1971 Industrial Relations Act. This Act was the first to attempt the provision of a comprehensive framework for industrial relations practice, but the unions saw it as restricting their freedom and it proved to be vastly unpopular. Mainly because of its industrial relations policies, the Conservative Party was defeated in the next general election. One of the first actions of the new Labour government was to repeal the 1971 Industrial Relations Act and to restore the position as it had previously existed. In the following year the Employment Protection Act introduced a number of additional employee rights in the form of guaranteed payments, maternity rights and procedures for handling redundancy. The government also set up the Arbitration, Conciliation & Advisory Service (ACAS) to investigate recognition disputes and to assist employers and employees in the conduct of their relationship. For a while it seemed that employee interests were gaining ground. The Bullock Commission gave full support to the extension of industrial democracy by employee representation on boards of directors. During this time the Labour government was, however, once again faced by the need to curb inflation and reduce unemployment. To these ends it entered into a social contract with unions, whereby wage demands would be kept within limits, on condition that the government managed to reduce price increases and inflation, as well as the level of unemployment. Inflation was eventually reduced to less than ten per cent, but unemployment figures continued to rise and employees became increasingly impatient with their lack of real wage increases. The result was a wave of strikes and general discontent with the Labour government which culminated in its being voted out of office. The Conservative Party, which has been in power since that time, has adopted a policy of promoting free enterprise and individual ownership. Although it has maintained the protection previously granted to employees, it has passed a number of laws obviously aimed at curbing trade union militancy and power. The right to picket has been limited, certain secondary industrial actions have been declared unlawful, closed shop rights have been diluted, regulations pertaining to the holding of secret ballots prior to industrial action have been introduced and unions are no longer indemnified if they encourage an unlawful action. The curbs stem from the perception that the ills suffered by the British economy during the Seventies can be attributed mainly to the 'irresponsible' actions of trade unions and to overemphasis on employee interests. The Thatcher government attempted to counter this by a renewed promotion of individualism, unqualified support for the free market system, privatisation, decentralised collective bargaining and the encouragement of employee involvement and share ownership.

Trade Unions and Collective Bargaining

The collective bargaining structure in Britain is reflective of the same voluntarism which marked the industrial relations system. British unions initially attempted to establish industry-wide agreements and to centralise organisation structures. Yet, since World War II, individualism has again prevailed. In the period of increased industrial activity which followed the war, employees and individual unions saw their power *vis-à-vis* the individual employer growing significantly. It became more profitable for individuals or plant-level representatives to negotiate direct with the employer than to rely on industry-wide agreements. The result was an increased emphasis on the role of the shop steward and a proliferation of plant-level agreements.

As previously noted, British unions have always displayed a strong individualism and a resistance to losing their identity or independence. Although most unions fall under the umbrella of the Trades Union Council and a small number of large unions predominate, there are numerous smaller unions, many of which represent the same interests. Consequently, multiunionism is prevalent and a single employer may be faced by a number of plant-level agreements, as well as a regional and national agreement, covering the same employee. While the Eighties have seen a number of union mergers and employers are now promoting single union agreements, problems and controversies still beset the system, not the least of these being the union problem of declining membership (from 54 per cent in 1979 to 42 per cent in 1987).

Workers' Participation

Britain has a tradition of strong trade unionism, backed politically by the Labour Party, and of tough collective bargaining. After World War II there was a proliferation of plant-level agreements and shop stewards came to play an increasingly important role in the conduct of the labour relationship. In many instances shop stewards acted independently and national or regional agreements were supplemented by additional agreements at plant level. Because of this active representation of employees at their place of work, the need for plant-level committees might not have been as urgent in Britain as in other countries with more centralised systems. Furthermore, it would have been difficult in Britain to functionally separate trade union activity from workers' participation schemes. It could, in effect, be said that the extension of plant bargaining and the involvement of shop stewards in all matters affecting employees already constituted a form of employee participation. (Compare to the situation in South Africa.)

For the reasons mentioned above, participatory schemes were initially consistently rejected by British trade unions. As early as 1949 the Whitley Committee attempted to place greater responsibility for the prosperity of the enterprise on employees and unions by its proposal for the establishment of joint industrial councils. These councils were not intended to usurp the functions of collective bargaining, but rather to '... promote industrial efficiency by employer and worker cooperation'. The plan did not meet with much success. Similarly, worker committees, which had been established during the Second World War for the purpose of increasing output and minimising friction, were later merely taken over by shop stewards, who turned them into collective bargaining bodies and thereby defeated their initial purpose.

The first substantial indication of trade union support for extended participation came with the evidence of the Trades Union Council to the Royal Commission on Trade Unionism and Employers' Associations. The TUC recommended that trade unions should be represented on all management boards, a suggestion which was rejected by the Commission, but the TUC followed up its evidence with its own independent report on industrial democracy, published in 1973. The report emphasised the necessity to continue and extend the practice of collective bargaining but, at the same time, also took note of the need to have trade union representatives on the policy boards of industries. At the same time the Labour Party entered into an agreement with the TUC that, if it came to power, it would enable trade unions to be appointed to policymaking boards at enterprises.

One of the problems related to the implementation of codetermination in Britain was the fact that British companies did not have a two-tier board system. A British board of directors was more involved in the actual management of the undertaking than a supervisory board in Germany. Both British management and unions had reservations about this type of direct involvement by employee representatives. Consequently, repeated suggestions were made for the adoption of a two-tier board structure, as in Germany. The Bullock Commission, appointed in 1975 to investigate the possible enforcement of codetermination, rejected the idea of a two-tier board structure for the very reason that it would exclude trade unions from participation in direct decisionmaking. The Commission suggested that a joint representative council of all trade unions recognised by a company should be entitled to elect a number of directors. Such number would be equal to that elected by the shareholders and both sets of directors would then jointly elect a third group of directors, which would be smaller than the individual shareholder and employee groups. These proposals were rejected by the minority employer group on the Commission, who suggested that supervisory boards should be created and that one third of these should consist of shareholder representatives, one third trade of union representatives and one third of neutral directors. The general view of employers was that the Bullock proposals would extend collective bargaining to the boardroom and lead to greater conflict rather than cooperation. A number of unions also rejected the proposals, stating that they would under no circumstances agree to this type of involvement in organisational decisions.

In a subsequent White Paper the Labour government adopted the strategy of encouraging employers and joint representative councils to set up their own schemes, subject to the approval of the majority of employees in the enterprise. The White Paper favoured a two-tier system, but one where the supervisory board would have greater control over management than in Germany, with the proviso that management would still have reasonable freedom to make decisions.

With the coming into power of the Conservative government, pressure for the institution of compulsory codetermination lifted and the emphasis shifted to the individual participation of employees in financial rewards and the encouragement of share ownership. Pressure was placed on employers to involve workers and to obtain their commitment by sharing information, consultation and share ownership. Thus the Employment Act of 1982 made it compulsory for companies with more than 250 employees to report annually on:

- arrangements made for providing information to employees,
- consultation with employees and their representatives,
- efforts made to encourage participation through profit sharing, and
- efforts made to achieve common awareness of financial and economic factors affecting the organisation.

Despite protracted debates and investigations, there is as yet no statutory form of codetermination in Britain, although it may be practised in individual undertakings and in national enterprises. There is also no provision for the institution of works councils. The Bullock Commission did investigate this aspect and reached the conclusion that works councils, if established, should function through the trade union or shop steward structure. This was rejected by the employer minority on the commission, who wanted works councils to be elected jointly by all employees. By and large the question of works councils has not received much attention in Britain, mainly because of the strong union presence on the shop floor. Since Britain's entry into the European Economic Community, trade unions have become more amenable to the idea of participation, especially at the higher organisational levels, but they still see it as inextricably linked to trade unionism. Moreover, their policy is one of demanding influence in organisational decisions, but of not accepting coresponsibility with management for such decisions.

In general, the concept of employee participation in decisionmaking, either at boardroom or plant level, has not yet been entrenched in British industrial relations. This may be attributed to a number of factors, among which are the fierce protection of its collective bargaining role by the trade union movement, divisions among unions on the method of participation, the proliferation of plant-level bargaining, the active opposition of employers and, more recently, the more individualist ideological leanings of the Conservative government.

Political Democracy   Because of the previous dearth of statutory industrial relations functions and institutions and its ambivalent ideological base, the British system is extremely difficult to describe. Nevertheless it illustrates, more than any other system, the strong interaction between the industrial relations system and political structures, as well as the continual fluctuation and balancing of power and interests which, in a democratic society, occurs in both the industrial and political spheres. Moreover, it contains very strong similarities with the South African system, also in the stance adopted by trade unions.

GERMANY

Societal Background   The German system is not rooted as strongly in the past as the British system. The decisive defeat suffered by Germany in World War II led to an almost complete reorganisation of German society. Although the new society had its origins in previous values and systems, such as the Weimar Republic, there was a general desire to wipe the slate clean, to learn from the past and to avoid extreme ideological posturing. Historical class differences had been virtually eliminated by the war and common adversity had engendered a spirit of cooperation between all concerned. This meant that employers, employees and the State largely worked together deliberately to shape a new social system. Furthermore, in keeping with German tradition, it was accepted that the State would play a decisive role in the establishment of the new order.

Germany had been given the opportunity of learning from its own past and the experience of other countries. By the end of World War II, the glow of rapid industrialisation and the practice of pure capitalism had receded and the flaws had become apparent. It was realised that capitalism, where it led to social injustice, had to be contained and modified, that economic freedom should be balanced by social security and social justice. Yet it was perceived also that economic growth would establish the basis for social security and that such growth could be achieved mainly by the operation of the market principle. Consequently, Germany developed a social market economy in which private property, capital accumulation and the operation of the free market are still protected, but where the government promotes social security, security at the workplace, the economic security of certain groups, the achievement of qualifications by the workforce and the protection of employees.

The constructive interaction which existed in the shaping of society found its reflection in the industrial relations system, where employers accepted the fundamental role of trade unions, their right to collective bargaining and, later, to participation in decisionmaking.

Trade Union History

The German trade union movement has played a decisive role in the shaping of the social and industrial relations systems. It has, since shortly after the war, been a highly unified body, with eighty per cent of all unions resorting under the Deutsche Gewertschäftsbund. From the beginning the unions had, according to Hetzler and Schienstock, a twofold task. The union movement regarded itself firstly as a cooperative enterprise, the duty of which was to protect members from economic and social inequality by bargaining and participation at the workplace. Secondly, it saw itself as a political movement, aimed at abolishing the sociopolitical conditions which created dependence and underprivilege among the working class. The trade unions were among the first to propose a plan for a new form of economic democracy. To these ends they demanded nationalisation of basic industries, centralised planning of the economy and comprehensive codetermination. A compromise was eventually achieved in that the free market continued to operate, but unions could use their bargaining power to promote worker interests and could ensure protection of employees by participation and joint decisionmaking.

Collective Bargaining

In line with the high degree of centralisation in the trade union movement and the practice of workers' participation at the workplace, collective bargaining occurs at a centralised level. Industries are divided into sectors, and bargaining occurs at either national or regional level. The result has been a more ordered system than in many other societies and less industrial unrest than in countries such as Britain and the United States of America.

Workers' Participation

In what was previously known as West Germany, the government legally entrenched joint decisionmaking at the highest level of the enterprise, as well as participation by employees at their place of work. This system of worker codetermination and participation exists hand in hand with the constitutional protection of the right to bargain collectively and with a strong, though highly centralised, trade union movement. The juxtaposition of these two practices conforms with the balance being sought in society between the limited protection of private property and the operation of the free market on the one hand and principles of social justice, community interest and egalitarianism on the other.

All German employees, except those employed in very small undertakings, are entitled to representation by works councils at their place of work while, in all major enterprises, one half of the seats on the supervisory board must be held by worker–directors. This two-tier system has led to a differentiation between participation (plant-level representation) and codetermination (representation on supervisory boards).

Plant-Level Representation

The German Industrial Consolidation Law of 1952 provided for the establishment of works councils, which were at that stage already granted the right to codetermination in social welfare and personnel matters and the right to make representations as regards business policy decisions. The 1952 Act also placed the obligation on works councils to cooperate with management and to maintain confidentiality. In 1972, works councils' rights were extended and today include the right to participation in manpower planning, dismissals, work procedures, economic matters, organisational change and the protection of labour, as well as the right to joint determination of working hours, methods of payment, social facilities, training, hiring, transfers and health and safety regulations.

The 1972 Act specifically stated that the structure of the organisation and matters relating to production, development and planning were the preserve of management and not subject to codetermination by works councils although, as stated, works councils do have a right to be heard on business policy decisions. Also, by the design of the system, worker–directors on supervisory boards do have some say in these matters.

In essence works councils at plant level serve a strong representational and advisory function. Failure by management to consult with and to heed the advice of Works councils on any matter within their jurisdiction may lead to legal action against the employer. Works councils may also, by agreement with the employer, regulate any other aspect of the employment relationship not specifically mentioned in legislation, except matters dealt with by an industrial agreement. They may enter into commitments with the employer and engage in negotiation, but they may not institute strike action.

Works councils are elected by all employees. They are independent of trade unions, but Works council members may also be members of trade unions and, where there is a strong trade union presence, councils may be dominated by union members. Generally, they supplement the trade union function and work together with the trade union in a relationship of mutual trust and support. Because it allows for representation at plant level, the works council system serves to diffuse tensions which may be created by the highly centralised collective bargaining system prevalent in Germany. They ensure that, within this system, the interests of all employees are adequately represented, but, since works councils are primarily cooperative institutions, the incidence of strike action in Germany is markedly lower than in most other Western countries. As such, the Works council system, balanced by centralised collective bargaining, has greatly contributed to the orderliness which characterises the German industrial relations system.

Codetermination on supervisory boards

Supervisory boards in Germany usually establish general company policy and oversee the management of the enterprise by executives. They approve financial statements and receive reports from the Board of Management regarding organisational policy, profitability and sales. In addition, the Supervisory Board may exercise control over management in such areas as capital investment, acquisition and the sale of property, the introduction of social policies, loans and credits, relocations and the acquisition and disposal of subsidiaries. Codetermination on supervisory boards was first introduced in Germany in 1951. At that stage the regulation relating to codetermination applied only to the coalmining and iron and steel industries. The regulations made it compulsory for all undertakings in these sectors which employed more than 1 000 persons to allocate at least half the seats on their supervisory boards to employee representatives, the rest of the board being made up of shareholder–directors. Supervisory boards were also required to appoint a neutral chairman who could, however, be nominated by the shareholders. A further provision was that a Labour Director be appointed to the board of management, with the specific requirement that such appointment could not be made without the approval of the majority of employee–directors on the supervisory board.

In 1952 the practice of codetermination was extended to other industries by the requirement that all joint stock and limited liability companies employing more than 500 persons should restructure their supervisory boards to provide for one third representation by employee–directors. Unions and employees remained dissatisfied with the lack of parity representation and their continued lobbying led to the passage of the Codetermination Act of 1976. This Act provided for parity representation by employee–directors on the supervisory boards of joint stock companies which employed in excess of 2 000 persons. The majority of employee–directors on supervisory boards have to be actual employees in the enterprise, while a minority may be appointed by the trade union. There is a further stipulation that at least one employee–director has to be a blue-collar worker, one has to be a white-collar worker and another must function at a managerial level. There is no provision for an additional neutral chairman, as in the iron and steel and coalmining industries, but the chairman is always elected from the ranks of the shareholder representatives and has a casting vote.

When parity codetermination was first introduced in the coalmining and iron and steel industries, it was feared that the new dispensation was a recipe for deadlock, that efficiency would decrease and that wages would rise. Subsequent studies proved these fears to be mainly unfounded. Nevertheless, many employers remained opposed to parity codetermination on functional and constitutional grounds and, in 1977, a legal action was brought against the State, based on the contention that the Codetermination Act of 1976 had violated the constitutional rights of employers. Employers argued that the law brought about a situation of disparity in favour of employees and unions, that it restricted the employer's right of property and disposal of property, that it endangered decisionmaking and infringed upon the rights of shareholders. Unions, on the other hand, argued that parity codetermination had not yet been achieved, since the chairman of the supervisory board had a double vote. However, it is unlikely that the principle of codetermination will be abandoned, unless a significant change in the overall economic and sociopolitical ideology of German society occurs. At present employers and unions both agree on the principle of codetermination. Their differences are differences mainly of degree and practical implementation.

The German system of participation and codetermination provides a balance between participation at the lower and higher levels of the organisation. Yet, with the exception of the Labour Director in the coalmining and iron and steel industries, there is no participation at management board level. Even the regulations pertaining to the appointment of a Labour Director elicited serious opposition. It was argued that, when collective bargaining occurred, labour would be bargaining with itself, in the person of the Labour Director, and that such a person would suffer a great deal of conflict. This proved not to be the case, but participation at management level remains limited, probably for fear that it will dilute the role of collective bargaining. Already collective bargaining in Germany has been described as lacking in depth. Management-level participation might further detract from the need to bargain collectively. Unions would gain power in the participatory sphere, but might lose ground on the bargaining front. At present they still succeed in achieving a fine, perhaps ideal, balance between their cooperative and antagonistic roles.

Spokesmen's Committees

In January 1989 the system of participation in Germany was further extended by the provision that all companies with more than ten managers must, where a majority of such managers vote in favour, establish a body to represent the interests of managerial employees. This committee will regulate the employment contracts of executives and generally oversee the conditions of service and treatment of this interest group. The law did not clearly specify who would be designated as managers, and some complications were foreseen in this respect. Also, it was feared that the establishment of such committees might lead to further divisions in the workforce and to clashes with works council members.

Shareholding and Profit-sharing Schemes

Besides workplace and decisionmaking participation, attempts have also been made in Germany to establish schemes by which employees can share in productive property. It is argued that, despite the social equality of German citizens, income is still unequally distributed; that it is impossible to bring about a fairer distribution by the wage mechanism; also that, since property originates with social production, employees are entitled to a share of productive income. The position in Germany at the beginning of the last decade was that one per cent of all industrial enterprises provided for equity participation of employees in the profits of the enterprise, six per cent of joint stock companies had a system of staff bonds and the ten largest companies were all profit-sharing. In total, 62 percent of all employees were included in profit-sharing schemes of one kind or another, but employers and unions have remained divided on the method of profit sharing which should be adopted. A number of unions do not agree that payouts to employees should be linked to the profits of a particular company. They would prefer a fixed proportion of all company profits to be paid into a mutual fund for all employees. Certain unions have also raised the possibility of a tax-free investment wage being paid to employees, over and above their normal wages. Yet others believe that greater economic equity can best be achieved by codetermination and collective bargaining, with priority being given to wages and collective security. So far, profit-sharing schemes are not compulsory, but the principle of a fairer distribution of income may well receive greater attention in the future.

Recent Develop-ments

The German system of industrial relations has long been regarded as a model system. In times of economic prosperity it certainly functioned well. However, the rise in unemployment, the problem of maintaining extended social security for all and the inability of the present system to bring about a more equitable distribution of wealth have led to a questioning of the system by employers and unions and to a certain amount of conflict. This is best illustrated by the disagreement as regards parity codetermination. Employers argue that increased State intervention and emphasis on employee rights will subvert the principle of economic freedom and detrimentally affect economic growth. Unions, on the other hand, maintain that present policies favour the concentration of capital, do not sufficiently satisfy collective needs and prevent the democratisation of the economy. It may happen that German unions, employers and the State, having commenced from a position of relative consensus, will move increasingly to positions of conflict. This does not signify a reversal of the present system but, rather, its modification.

YUGOSLAVIA

Societal Background

Yugoslavia could best be described as a socialist state in which communism, as it was originally instituted, was partially reformed. The basic ideology remained one of communitarianism. The needs of society took priority over the individual and the acquisition of private property, in the form of capital accumulation, was not encouraged, although in the agricultural sector private ownership existed and small private enterprises, employing up to seven persons, were allowed. This ideology is common to all communist states. Where Yugoslavia differed was in its devolution of power from the State machinery to communities and worker groups and in the encouragement of competitive enterprise. Whereas in a purely communist system enterprise, labour and finances are controlled by bureaucrats and technocrats, the Yugoslavian system allowed for the free association of work groups, for worker control of the enterprise and its finances and for competition between different associations of labour. In the industrial relations sphere, democratic decisionmaking processes were introduced through the system of workers' committees. Trade unions had no collective bargaining function, as there was no employer with whom bargaining could be conducted, but they did act as watchdogs over the interests of members.

Workers' Participation

The practice of industrial democracy in Yugoslavia was based on an extremely complicated system of labour associations, divided into basic organisations of associated labour, work organisations and composite organisations of associated labour. These embraced entire communities but relied on the free association of basic work groups, which cooperated with the community to establish their own social infrastructures and which played a competitive role in the marketplace. In labour relations terms, the core structure was the system of worker management centring in the establishment of workers' councils which, in essence, controlled all these organisations.

Workers' Councils

The concept of workers' councils was first formulated in 1950 by the Basic Law on the Management of the Enterprise by Worker Collectives. The law provided that rank-and-file workers of all grades in a particular enterprise might elect a council from among their own ranks with real power to decide on the management, production, investment and allocation policies of their undertaking. In enterprises where there were less than thirty employees, the entire staff constituted the workers' council. In others the size varied from fifteen to 120 members, depending on the size of the undertaking. It was common practice to elect members equally from various staff categories. Council members were elected for a term of office not exceeding two years, and could not be elected for more than two consecutive terms. This prevented council members from becoming entrenched in positions of power, which would be contrary to the socialist system. In practice the majority of council members were elected from among the more experienced or more highly educated employees, and reliable employees were usually re-elected after their layoff term had expired. Experience proved that councils renewed themselves by one third with every election.

Management of the Enterprise

In the Yugoslavian model, the elected representatives on the Workers' Council were accountable to their constituents and might be removed by the latter if their performance were not satisfactory. Fundamental decisions were taken at workers' meetings or tested by referendum, and it was the duty of the Workers' Council to execute these decisions. Normal operational decisions were taken by the workers' council, which also made senior appointments and selected a manager or management board. Selection of management took place on the basis of a public competition and was effected by the workers' council, in conjunction with trade unions and community representatives. Managers or management bodies were appointed for a term of four years, but might be reappointed after the expiry of each term. Such management was responsible for the day-to-day conduct of business and could make proposals regarding policies and their implementation to the workers' council, but managers remained subject and accountable to the workers' council and were obliged to implement decisions made by the worker body.

Supervisory Commissions

The workers' council elected its own executive and could decide to establish various committees to execute specialised functions, subject to guidelines set by, or the approval of, the members of the workers' council. The functioning of the workers' council was itself overseen by supervisory commissions. These commissions were elected by workers and could not contain members of the workers' council, its executive or management. In production enterprises at least three quarters of the commission had to be productive workers. The supervisory commission ensured that rules and agreements were implemented, that the decisions made by workers were executed by management, that social resources were responsibly utilised, that income was distributed according to work done and that both workers and management performed their work obligations. The supervisory commission was not a decisionmaking body. It functioned as watchdog, reporting any irregularities to the general meeting of workers or to the bodies capable of instituting action.

Modus Operandi

Enterprises competed with one another and with foreign undertakings, and — within the parameters of minimum wages and price controls established by government — had power to decide on these aspects. Furthermore, Yugoslavian law provided that basic associations of labour might decide on the disposal of the income produced by them, but only after they had discharged their responsibilities towards other workers and to the community in general. A portion of nett income could be allocated to workers in terms of work done or as joint 'non-productive' income, while the rest was reinvested in expansionary or renewal programmes. This was done according to scales adopted in the self-management rules of the organisation, with due regard to other basic organisations in the same work organisation to which they belonged. Scales for the distribution of personal income were also set by basic organisations, but tended to conform with principles established by the Associated Labour Law. Employees usually received remuneration in accordance with the work done and their contribution, either as labourers or managers, to the total income of the undertaking. Special awards could also be made to employees who, by an innovative process, rationalisation or any other creative means, made a particular contribution to overall income.

Trade Unionism and Collective Bargaining

There was no collective bargaining in Yugoslavia, as workers jointly decided on wages, hiring and firing and disciplinary practices. The term 'labour relationship' was used to refer to the contract and tenure of employment of an individual employee. Despite the absence of collective bargaining, strike action did occur as a result of the temporary dissatisfaction of workers with particular practices, but it was usually of short duration. Trade unions played an ancillary role to the Workers' Councils and an official of a trade union could not be elected to such a council, although this did not preclude council members from belonging to trade unions. The trade union acted mainly as educator and opinion shaper. Its duty was to interest workers in the functions of the enterprise, to liaise between the enterprise and the community and to take care of housing and other social needs. In essence, it represented interests wider than those of the Workers' Councils.

Problems Experienced with the System

According to Pasic et al, the Yugoslavian system was not problem-free. One of the primary problems encountered was the fact that employees, although supportive of the system, were often not capable of grasping its mechanics or were afraid to assume responsibilities within the system. In many instances, workers were not properly prepared for decisionmaking and consequently preferred to retain the previous system of domination by bureaucrats and technocrats. Many employees also experienced difficulties in expressing their views at worker meetings. As a result Yugoslavia engaged in an ongoing programme aimed at training employees in decisionmaking and self-management. It was also found that some employees were inclined to act in accordance with their own self-interest to the detriment of the undertaking and the community, that differing interests were sometimes difficult to reconcile, that some workers' council representatives did not consult with all their constituents and that, very often, rights and duties were not clearly defined. All these problems, as well as the problem of monopolisation resulting from State limitations on the number of enterprises, continued to be addressed. Pasic and his co-authors summed up the situation by concluding that: 'Contemporary Yugoslavia is certainly not free from disputes and conflicts of interest, whether in its basic organisations or at the level of society as a whole. However, the country's worker management system appears to have demonstrated its vitality, resistance and capacity to overcome serious conflict in a democratic way.' It is impossible to foresee, however, whether it will survive the present disruptions in Yugoslavia.

Evaluation   The Yugoslavian system as it existed was still a prescriptive and controlled system. Numerous regulations governed the establishment and functioning of worker enterprises and community organisations. Also, as pointed out in the previous section, it was not without its problems in the form of delayed decisionmaking, lack of interest of employees, lack of ability on the part of workers' representatives and the conflict of sectoral interests. Nevertheless, the country made a noteworthy effort to amalgamate its concept of social justice and egalitarianism with a more freely functioning market. The system highlighted the fact that capitalism and the operation of the market did not necessarily go hand in hand, as is commonly supposed. The antithesis of capitalism is socialism, while the market principle is antiposed by the concept of a controlled economy. These four practices may occur in various combinations.

CONCLUSION

Any attempt to explain as complex a topic as the interaction between society and the industrial relations system within the confines of one chapter must necessarily be superficial. The variables are so numerous and of so interactive a nature that only a detailed study would do justice to the topic. For the present purposes, it is sufficient to be aware of the forces at play within an industrial relations system. An understanding of these forces leads to greater insight into particular developments and to greater foresight when planning structures and practices.

SOURCES

Bendix, D W F *Labour and Society in Comparative Socioeconomic Systems*, Industrial Relations Texts, 1984.

Bendix, D W F *Limits to Codetermination*, Lex Patria, 1980.

Board of Trade *Report on the Committee of Enquiry on Industrial Democracy (Bullock Committee)*, HMSO Britain, 1977.

Dunlop, John T *Industrial Relations Systems*, Southern Illinois University Press, 1958.

Pasic N, Giozdavic S and Radevic M *Workers' Management in Yugoslavia*, International Labour Office, 1982.

Power, Don 'Employee involvement in the USA' in Anstey, Mike *Worker Participation*, Juta, 1990.

Roberts, Benjamin C (Ed) *Towards Industrial Democracy*, Croom Helm, 1976.

Salamon, Michael *Industrial Relations Theory and Practice*, Prentice-Hall, 1987.

4

THE SOUTH AFRICAN INDUSTRIAL RELATIONS SYSTEM IN SOCIETAL AND HISTORICAL CONTEXT

Prior to the first democratic elections in 1994, South Africa was essentially a dualistic society. This dualism was reflected in its paradoxical ideological basis and in the separation of people of different race groups. The dominant ideology rested on a belief in individual freedom and the operation of the free market principle. Yet, because of the apartheid policy, certain groups had been denied individual freedom and, as a result, the market never operated freely. In fact, the maintenance of white dominance necessitated the ever-increasing use of controls and the introduction of systems of distribution which would not exist in other societies subscribing to an individualist ideology. Besides the basic paradox, there is also the fact that, owing mainly to previous policies, different sections of South African society may now subscribe to different ideologies. While one group still supports individualist and free market principles, the other group may have become increasingly supportive of socialist ideals.

The dichotomy in society was necessarily transferred to the industrial relations system. Even in the early years of industrialisation white workers, fearing that they would be replaced by cheaper black labour, adopted a protectionist stance. This protectionism was entrenched in law when the Industrial Conciliation Act of 1924 excluded black African males from the definition of 'employee' and thereby debarred them from participating in the official industrial relations system.

The result of white worker protectionism and the Industrial Conciliation Act was that black (African) employee movements developed independently from the then mainstream of the union movement, which consisted of unions representing those persons who were entitled to use legally established structures and procedures. Even in the latter movement, divisions arose between those bodies which adopted a protectionist stance and the nonracial or multiracial organisations.

During the 1930s and 1940s, when unionists of all races were very active and when many unions acted on behalf of all workers, it seemed possible that black (African) employees might be accommodated in the system. This possibility became less likely when, in 1948, the National Party came to power. Labour and other legislation introduced created further polarisation. In 1953 the government attempted to create a separate system for Blacks by the introduction of Workers' Committees. These were hardly used. The black trade union movement arising at that time became overpoliticised and, with the bannings in 1960, it disintegrated. In the meantime, the rest of the trade union movement had adapted to the status quo. Between 1950 and 1970, strike action decreased and bargaining occurred mainly in statutory bodies. South African industrial relations appeared to have settled into a comfortable mould.

The illusion that all was well in the industrial relations system was shattered with the reawakening of black worker consciousness in the 1970s. Early in that decade various bodies were established to promote black employee interests, but the real impetus towards a new dispensation was furnished by the Natal strikes of 1973. The government reacted by allowing for the establishment of liaison committees to improve communication between employers and black (African) employees. Despite these measures, new black trade unions now came into existence. They concentrated on strong shop floor representation and, in 1974, the first plant-level recognition agreement was concluded. In 1977 the Wiehahn Commission was appointed to investigate means of adapting the existing industrial relations system to meet changing circumstances. Its most revolutionary proposal was that freedom of association be granted to all employees and that black trade unions be permitted to register. It was believed that black trade unions could be better controlled if they were part of the system and that they might be absorbed into the established labour movement. The government accepted most of the Commission's recommendations. The Industrial Conciliation Amendment Act of 1979 and subsequent Amendment Acts in 1980, 1981 and 1982 radically changed the South African industrial relations system. The most significant change was that all employees now had equal status in terms of labour legislation.

The newer unions did not become coopted into the existing system; instead they helped to establish a new type of system, in which the conclusion of recognition agreements at plant level became accepted practice. After 1980 these unions gradually gained dominance in the labour relations arena and, although many of these bodies were nonracial, black employee interests now formed the focal point of industrial relations. In the process, the multiracial movement existing before 1970 disintegrated.

The government, though perhaps not expecting its 1979 legislation to have the results that it did, reacted by adopting a principle of non-interference in the labour relationship. Developments were thus, in the main, left to run their course.

By 1985, the South African industrial relations system had outstripped the sociopolitical system. This misalignment created pressure in the industrial relations system, particularly since unions, as the only legitimate voice of Blacks in society, saw it as their role also to bring about political change.

Such sociopolitical change has now occurred and, although labour legislation had already been deracialised, the new government, adopting essentially a social market policy and having a strong constituency among Blacks and trade unionists, has brought about further changes in the system by way of both policy and legislation. Also, the labour movement, seeing 'its' government to be in power, and pressurised by rising worker expectations, continues to exert pressure aimed at gaining increased rights and the complete deracialisation of the workplace. On the other hand, in the spirit of reconstruction and having a legitimate government in place, the union movement may also be willing to play a more constructive role in labour relations.

IDEOLOGICAL BASIS AND SOCIETAL COMPOSITION

South Africa finds itself in a unique position among Western countries in that it was for long marked by historically, politically and legally entrenched racial divisions. This led to the establishment of two distinct societal groups which, because one group perceived itself as being politically, socially and economically underprivileged, often had conflicting interests. The most obvious distinctions were to be found between the group which believed in white exclusivity and dominance and that which subscribed to a policy of black nationalism. Ranging between these were those who supported a policy of 'separate but equal' multiracialism and others who were strongly nonracist. Distinctions also existed and still exist in economic ideology. While the white class is, in general, supportive of a capitalist free enterprise system, there are many Blacks who see their future as secured in a more socialist, though not necessarily Marxist, dispensation. This is supported by the fact that the black people of South Africa arose from more communitarian societies and still are more closely knit as communities than Whites, owing partly to their previous segregation from the privileged white class. By contrast, the Whites brought to South Africa a strong sense of individualism, engendered by the French Revolution, the birth of capitalism in Europe and the pioneering spirit. This was underscored by a firm belief in competitive, individual effort and the right to private ownership. Even the skilled European workers, who were imported to work on the mines and who were initially more socialist in their ideals, later embraced the capitalist ideal because of their privileged positions in South African society.

The distinctions made are necessarily an oversimplification of the real situation. Despite efforts directed at racial separation, much intermingling occurred, particularly in the economic sphere and also in the sociopolitical sphere. This served to dilute extreme ideologies on both sides but, because Whites had always been in a position of political dominance, the overriding ideology was until very recently the support of white supremacy, capitalism and the free market system. Yet the sociopolitical and economic effects of this ideology largely applied only to Whites. Moreover, the protectionism required to maintain the supremacy of the white population necessarily led to the imposition of greater restrictions on other groups, to greater planning by government and to certain totalitarian practices. Thus South Africa had, not by consent or consensus but by political expediency, an unusual mixture of raw capitalism and the free market enterprise on the one hand and of socialism, targeted at white Afrikaners, as well as a large number of institutionalised controls, on the other. A final, important societal aspect is the fact that, until 1990, South Africa was subjected to increased criticism, both from within the country and from the outside world. This did lead to some modification of extreme ideological stances on the part of the ruling party, and to subsequent sociopolitical changes which also impacted on labour relations.

In 1994 South Africa made a relatively peaceful transition to a new, nonracial, democratic dispensation. For the next few years the country will be ruled by the Government of National Unity, comprising all the major political parties. However, within this new sociopolitical dispensation, the ANC, together with its alliance partners, the SACP and COSATU, has the strongest foothold. Both the SACP and COSATU, as well as many other members of government, hold strong communitarian views. In line with this, the government has undertaken a programme of reconstruction and upliftment encapsulated in the Reconstruction and Development Programme (RDP). Nevertheless, no marked attempts have yet been made at nationalisation or enforced redistribution. It would appear that, at present, the government intends to promote investment and enterprise while, at the same time, helping to alleviate the ills of the past by a strong social welfare programme concentrating on housing, health, education and training. Thus it seems to favour a mixed economic system or a social market system similar to that existing in Germany and other Western European societies.

THE INDUSTRIAL RELATIONS SYSTEM AS REFLECTION OF THE SOCIOPOLITICAL SYSTEM

The divisions which previously existed in the sociopolitical system necessarily found their reflection in the industrial relations system. Even before the onset of industrialisation, the supremacy of Whites in society and in the economic sphere had been established. This trend was to continue and intensify after industrialisation had commenced. Although black and white employees initially worked side by side and shared common interests, particularly in the manufacturing industry, the need for protection of Whites from competition by cheaper black labour and the rise of Afrikaner nationalism gradually led to ever-strengthening divisions in the sphere of labour relations.

The first comprehensive labour legislation to be introduced, in the form of the Industrial Conciliation Act of 1924, reflected an individualist orientation in that it entrenched a voluntary system of free collective bargaining. Yet it concretised racial divisions by the exclusion of 'pass-bearing natives' from the ambits of the legislation. Black Africans, who had no legitimised power in the political sphere, were now also denied the right to legitimate exercise of power in the labour relationship. It was believed that black employees were not sufficiently responsible to engage in collective bargaining. Instead, the 1953 Black Labour Relations Regulation Act, passed after the ascent to power of the National Party, created a separate industrial relations machinery for black African workers, in the form of workers' committees. These could be regarded, but were not in reality, a form of workers' participation. A situation of imbalance was created between white employers and black workers and, because Blacks had no vote in the political system, they had no legitimised means of redressing the situation. This did not prevent protest action and by the mid-1970s internal pressures, in the form of political and industrial unrest among Blacks, had mounted to such an extent that an adjustment to the system became imperative. These internal pressures were underscored by mounting pressure from the outside world and the gradual isolation of South Africa. The result was the appointment of the Wiehahn Commission and the passage of the Industrial Conciliation Amendment Act of 1979. The major impact of this Act and subsequent amendments was that it no longer excluded black African workers from the definition of employee, thereby granting all South African employees equal rights in the industrial relations sphere. This led to a rapid growth in trade union membership among black employees and to the institution of plant-level bargaining systems. However, whereas prior to 1979 the South African industrial relations system was a true reflection of the sociopolitical dispensation, an anomaly then existed in that all South African employees had, at least in law, an equal say in the industrial relations system, but a large number still had no say in the political sphere. This resulted in extraordinary pressures being placed on the industrial relations system and on the increasing politicisation of the trade union movement. Furthermore, government action against protest movements, in the form of measures under the State of Emergency and the restriction of trade union activities, necessarily impacted on the relationship between trade unions and employers.

The development of the trade union movement was closely linked to the political dispensation. Despite the fact that the black trade union movement originated at the beginning of the century, their lack of political and industrial legitimacy and their necessary interest in political objectives for a long time prevented effective organisation. Also, the historical composition of the trade union movement largely, but not totally, reflected the divisions existent in the political sphere. The political situation was not reflected in its totality because Coloureds and Asians who, after 1948, had no political vote, were never excluded from the industrial relations machinery. This led to the establishment of multiracial and nonracial trade unions, along with those representing only white or black African employees. Notwithstanding the new labour dispensation introduced in 1979 and the fact that many of the major trade unions were now nonracial, these divisions remained in essence, except for the fact that many predominantly black African nonracial unions now also represented coloured and Asian employees. Similarly, overall trade union ideology ranged from a support of the free enterprise system on the one hand to a widely held support of socialist principles on the other. Furthermore, because capital had historically been held by the white ruling class, trade unions of the latter persuasion tended to regard racism and capitalism as synonymous; thus their opposition not only to capitalism, but to 'racial capitalism'. Employers were now in the position where they had to prove that the two were not necessarily coincidental and that a market system could operate without the extremes of 'raw' capitalism.

It was generally believed that, with the advent of the new sociopolitical dispensation, radical changes would occur also in the industrial relations sphere, particularly since COSATU, as the largest trade union movement, had played a decisive role in mobilising support for the ANC. Although the present government definitely displays greater concern for labour and there are more open lines of communication between government and labour, there has been no marked attempt to favour labour to the absolute or almost total exclusion of business. Unions have not lost their militancy, nor do they seem prepared to enter into a limiting social contract with the government.

However, in contrast to the past, unions are now more willing to heed the government's pleas and there have been occasions when union leaders have ameliorated demands in view of the poor economic situation in the country. For its part, the government has attempted to strengthen cooperation between the State, labour and business and to achieve some form of balance between the interests of the major parties, together with a balance between collective bargaining and workers' participation. This is most clearly illustrated by the provisions of the Labour Relations Act of 1995, but there are many who contend (and not, perhaps, without reason) that the balance has now tilted in favour of the larger trade unions and their federations.

Perhaps because of the country's distinctive characteristics, the interaction between the industrial relations system and the wider society is more apparent in South Africa than in most other countries, although, during the 1980s, the industrial relations system had certainly overtaken the sociopolitical system. As South African society becomes more 'normalised', a closer integration between the sociopolitical system and the industrial relations system is certain to exist.

THE PREINDUSTRIAL ERA

Industrialisation in South Africa commenced with the discovery of diamonds in 1870 and of gold in 1872. Prior to these events, South Africa was a mainly agrarian society. There were, of course, merchants and craftsmen to supply the services needed by various communities, but there was no actual industrial activity although machinery, in the form of printing presses, was used by the newspapers established at the time. In terms of the definition given in Chapter 1, no industrial relations *per se* existed. Employment relationships which did exist were governed by the Master and Servants Act of 1841. This Act was amended in 1856 to provide for harsh punishment of black servants who defaulted in their work. The Master & Servants Act governed the rules of work, particularly as regards black African employees. There were no collective labour relations and no concerted attempts at organisation by workers. Some workers, such as those employed in the printing industry in the Cape, did show an interest in establishing forms of collective representation; but these were random attempts, as were the occasional strikes which occurred before 1870.

Of importance about this period is the fact that the unskilled position of the black African employee was already entrenched. Blacks, meaning the indigenous Africans, were employed mainly as servants and labourers on the farms and in the towns. Skilled work was undertaken by Whites, many of whom were immigrants, or by the slaves who came from the East. The result was a coincidence of race and skill, with the majority of black Africans constituting the unskilled labour force and the skilled workforce being made up of Whites, Coloureds, and Asians. This situation still prevails today although, of late, the position is gradually improving.

THE EARLY YEARS OF INDUSTRIALISATION (THE PERIOD FROM 1880 TO 1924)

The discovery of gold and diamonds led to the influx of labour to the Witwatersrand and to the establishment of other industries to support the mining community. Industrialisation was slowly commencing in the rest of the country, but the focus of this period falls on the diamond and gold mines and on the industries, such as the railways and the engineering and building industries, established around them.

As South Africa did not have a sufficiently skilled labour force, European (mostly British) immigrants were employed to do much of the work in this category. These workers brought with them the European, and especially the British, brand of trade unionism, based at that time on the ideal of a universal worker movement but balanced by the British sense of individualism. The first real unions established, therefore, were skilled unions. Because the services of these workers were in high demand, they occupied a privileged position in a labour force which otherwise consisted of unskilled migrant Blacks and those local Whites who had been obliged to leave the land. Traditionally, black employees, who had been specifically imported to work on the mines, were paid far less than the rest of the labour force. With increased mechanisation it was discovered that many skilled jobs could be broken down and done by cheaper black unskilled or semiskilled labour. This posed an enormous threat to the skilled workforce. Unions which previously might have held universally socialist beliefs began to insist on guarantees of white job security. As a result the first regulation instituting an industrial colour bar, even if indirectly, was introduced in 1897. This regulation effectively prevented black African employees from becoming engine drivers. It was followed by the 1911 Mines & Works Act which, in essence, reserved thirty-two jobs for white mineworkers.

In the meantime the Anglo–Boer War had come to an end. After the war many white Afrikaans families were obliged to seek work in the industrial areas. They too posed a threat to skilled workers and, in 1907, a strike by white mineworkers was effectively crushed by the use of unskilled white persons. In order to widen their power base and to prevent this kind of scabbing in the future, the traditional skilled mine unions expanded into industrial unions, which could include also semiskilled and unskilled workers, most of them white. Although these unions became increasingly militant, the danger of members losing their jobs to cheaper black labour persisted. Realising that they would have to gain power by other means, many of these workers joined the newly formed South African Labour Party and, later, the Afrikaner National Party.

From the early 1900s onwards strike action by white employees — and also by black employees, who had learnt from their white counterparts — had continued to increase. The situation came to a head with a large-scale strike by white mineworkers in 1913. In the same year black mineworkers went on strike. These actions were followed by strikes at the railways and power stations and by a general strike of white workers in 1914. The government, which until then had adopted a completely *laissez-faire* approach to labour relations and had interfered in industrial unrest by the use of martial law and other measures only when security was threatened, realised that certain controls had to be introduced. It appears that the government was particularly afraid that the heightened militancy of black African employees would lead also to their increased politicisation. Thus, in essence, it approved of the separatism of white trade unions. After the 1913 strikes the government passed the Act of Indemnity and the Riotous Assemblies Act, curtailing certain industrial actions. A commission of inquiry was also appointed to make recommendations on the containment of industrial unrest. It recommended the recognition of white unions and the establishment of a conciliation body. The 1914 Industrial Disputes & Trades Bill which followed basically curtailed the right to strike until conciliation procedures had been used. Significantly, it excluded 'pass-bearing natives'. The bill, opposed by the Labour Party, was never passed and the onset of the First World War partly stabilised the situation.

In the meantime, unions had been established also in the secondary industries and services such as the engineering and building trade, the leather, clothing, chemical and sweet industries and in the glass and laundry services. Furthermore, industries in the rest of the country were now expanding. Except in those trades where crafts were required, work in these industries and services was mostly of a semiskilled or unskilled nature. Employees of all races worked side by side and the protectionist tendencies evident in the mining and craft unions were not present, although Whites played a dominant role in most of these unions. This multiracial and nonracial situation was most evident in the Cape, where the majority of the labour force was coloured.

The proliferation of unions on the mines and in the manufacturing sector led to the establishment of federations. In the Transvaal most of the existing unions, including those on the mines, established the National Industrial Federation, while in the Cape employees formed the Cape Federation of Labour.

In 1915 the Transvaal Chamber of Mines agreed to recognise white unions. Partly as a result of the First World War, a period of relative stability followed, both in the mines and in the manufacturing and service sectors. As a result the government in 1919 called a national conference of employers and employees, at which it was resolved that 'recognition of employees by employers of labour would alleviate industrial unrest'. Various agreements had in the meantime been reached between the white unions and the Chamber of Mines, the most significant being the Standstill Agreement whereby employers agreed that the ratio of Whites to Blacks employed would never be less than two Whites for every seventeen Blacks in employment.

This cooperative spirit between employers and employees was not to last. In 1920 the price of gold began to fall. General prosperity declined and a number of strikes occurred, also in the industrial and service sectors. The mineowners started looking towards the deskilling of jobs by the introduction of new machinery. Soon afterwards it was announced by mine employers that a new type of machine would be introduced. Later the Standstill Agreement was dropped, and white employees were informed that wages might have to be cut and that certain marginal mines in the Transvaal and the Cape might close, the result of which would be the retrenchment of about ten per cent of the white workforce. Old insecurities reared their heads. White mineworkers viewed the announcement as yet another attempt to replace them with cheaper black labour. In January 1922, 25 000 white miners went on strike. Because the miners later took up arms, this strike became known as the Rand Rebellion. The Smuts government sent in the Army and the strike was effectively crushed. By the end of the strike, 153 miners had been killed and 500 were wounded. Five thousand strikers had been arrested, of whom four were later hanged for treason. Hundreds of white miners were subsequently laid off. Those who did return had to be satisfied with lower wages and the deskilling of certain jobs.

This strike and those which occurred in allied industries and services, as well as in other parts of the country after 1915, had one important result in that the government, having realised the strength of workers and fearful of another surge of industrial unrest, decided that it needed to establish statutory machinery for collective bargaining and the settlement of disputes between employers and employees. The result was the drafting of the Industrial Conciliation Act of 1924. This effort at institutionalising labour relations did not save the Smuts government. In the next election the white workers, who felt that the government had sided with the mineowners, voted the South African Party out of power. The actual legislation was passed by the Pact government which followed. This government had been established by a coalition of the Labour Party and the National Party. Both parties had been brought to power by the white worker vote. It followed that, in the years to come, there would be closer cooperation between government and those workers who had the vote.

THE RISE OF THE BLACK TRADE UNION MOVEMENT

For the sake of clarity and because of the impact of the non-African worker on initial labour legislation, the emphasis so far has been placed on this group of employees. As indicated, action also occurred amongst black African workers on the mines. This later spread to allied industries and services. The first recorded strike among black mineworkers took place in 1896, in reaction to a decision by mine managers to reduce wages. This was followed by more strikes after the Anglo–Boer War and by other protest actions, such as boycotts of the mines, desertion and non-cooperation. Following the black mineworkers' strike of 1913 a number of improvements were introduced in the mine compounds where black African employees lived, but protest action continued. As prices rose in comparison with wages, dissatisfaction among black workers spread to other industries and this led to the formation, in 1918, of the Industrial Workers of Africa, generally believed to be the first union for black workers. The IWA worked closely with the Transvaal Native Congress and the African People's Organisation and, after the mineworkers' boycott of compound shops in 1918 and the black municipal workers' strike of the same year, a joint meeting of these three bodies called for a general strike to launch a 'shilling a day' campaign on behalf of all black employees. The proposed action was called off when the then Prime Minister, Louis Botha, agreed to look into the complaints of black workers. Not much came of this promise and in 1919 workers decided to take action against the pass laws. This and the subsequent strike by mineworkers led to some improvements. However, a massive strike by black mineworkers in 1920 resulted in a tightening up of the pass laws and in the curtailment of black mineworker resistance for some time to come. The 1920 mineworkers' strike had coincided with numerous actions by black employees in other industries and services.

In the meantime the IWA had been overtaken by the Industrial & Commercial Workers' Union of South Africa (ICU), born from the organisation of dockworkers of all races in the Cape, under the leadership of Clements Kadalie. In 1919 this organisation staged a successful strike at the Cape Town docks. Subsequent to this Kadalie spread his activities to other parts of the country, concentrating on the organisation of black employees. The ICU as such was established at a meeting of various black organisations held in Bloemfontein in 1920, and by 1924 its membership had risen to 30 000, higher than that of any other worker federation in the country. The ICU covered a wide range of black interests but, perhaps because of the diversity of its membership, the various factions influencing the movement and (later) government antagonism, it began to disintegrate in the late 1920s. It is still remembered as the first real black worker body, but even more as the first mass movement among the black working class. As the then Prime Minister, Barry Hertzog, whom the ICU had at one stage supported, put it: 'The ICU, to my mind, was not a trade union. It was really a political organisation with members recruited from every walk of life.'

THE INDUSTRIAL CONCILIATION ACT OF 1924 AND SUBSEQUENT LEGISLATION

The primary purpose of the Industrial Conciliation Act was to prevent industrial unrest, by providing the machinery for collective bargaining and for conciliation in the event of dispute. The Act and the subsequent amendments provided for conciliation boards and industrial councils and placed a criminal sanction on strike action which occurred without prior negotiation in these bodies. It also provided for mediation and arbitration, the latter being compulsory in essential services. Trade unions and employers' associations, established on a voluntary basis, could register under the Act and together establish and register industrial councils. These industrial councils became the recognised bargaining bodies and agreements reached by them were, if gazetted, legally enforceable. Since they provided for associations of employers to bargain with one union or more, bargaining tended to be more centralised, a trend which was to continue and intensify during the next fifty years.

Although the use of this system was completely voluntary, the fact that it was sanctioned by the government lent a certain legitimacy to those who bargained on the councils. Furthermore, the legal enforceability of agreements and the fact that legal strike action could be undertaken if the statutory machinery were used made the system acceptable to both employer and employee parties — or at least to those of the latter who were allowed to use it. As a result the industrial council system (or, where no council existed, the negotiation of disputes on conciliation boards) became the accepted and officially sanctioned system for the conduct of the labour relationship. Ironically, the mining industry, which provided the major impetus for the new legislation, has never established an industrial council and has preferred to bargain in its own independent bodies.

The Industrial Conciliation Act provided a very sound basis for the more orderly conduct of the labour relationship. However, no union representing black African males could register under the Act, since the definition of 'employee' specifically excluded 'pass-bearing natives'. (Black females were at that time not obliged to carry passes and were thus included under the legislation, as were certain black males in the Cape.) The exclusion had the effect that black unions, not being allowed to register, were also not allowed to join industrial councils or apply for conciliation boards and could not, therefore, institute legal strike action. It is significant that, 25 years before the apartheid policy was legally entrenched by the National Party, it had already been embedded in the industrial relations system.

The Industrial Conciliation Act was followed by the 1925 Wage Act which, with later amendments, allowed for the establishment of minimum wage rates for all employees, irrespective of race, in industries where collective bargaining structures were not sufficiently developed. Some observers view this as a progressive step, while others see it merely as a ploy to prevent black employees from undercutting white wages. Nevertheless, organisations such as the ICU and black unions formed afterwards did use this Act to improve the wage rates of black African employees. The Wage Act was followed by the 1926 Mines & Works Act, which further entrenched job reservation on the mines and by the Native Administration Act of 1927 which made it an offence to promote 'hostility' between the races. This Act was effectively used against black unionists such as Clements Kadalie.

The Pact government also introduced what is generally known as the Civilised Labour Policy. This policy arose from the concern of the government at the fact that the living and moral standards of Poor Whites in the industrial areas had deteriorated. It led to the active promotion of the white employee, through the provision of more opportunities at higher wages, a policy which had already been in practice on the railways and was now extended to other industries, despite the opposition of numerous employers. Whereas, previously, discrimination had occurred only through the favouritism shown to Whites in employment structures, the Civilised Labour Policy marked the beginning of an active campaign to promote the use of white, and especially Afrikaner, employees in preference to those of other race groups.

THE GROWTH OF THE MANUFACTURING AND SERVICE INDUSTRIES (THE PERIOD 1925–1948)

The White and Multiracial Trade Union Movements

The prosperity engendered by the goldmining industry had resulted in rapid growth in the manufacturing and service sectors, a process which was to accelerate during the next decades and especially during the Second World War.

Unionisation of employees in these industries had already occurred during the previous decade. These unions, lacking the protectionism of the mining unions, often organised across colour lines and among the organisers were many members of the Communist Party. Even in the mining industry, active communists had stood side by side with white Afrikaners in 1922. As a result of these developments, the South African Labour Movement in the 1920s was composed of various heterogeneous groups. Not only were the most active members white Afrikaners and immigrant workers, some of them Communists, but the composition of individual unions varied from those which were exclusively white, to the mixed unions, the exclusively coloured and Indian and then the exclusively black African bodies. The exclusion of Blacks from the Industrial Conciliation Act would increasingly polarise black unions, but some worked with other unions and a number of Blacks, especially females, remained members of the mixed unions. Various interests were represented by the union movement. Individual unions started to grow and to mushroom, and alignments were broken and re-established. In the light of this, it is little wonder that developments during this period are difficult to trace.

Soon after the Pact government had come to power the then Minister of Labour, in line with the new policy of active involvement with and promotion of labour relations, convened a conference in Cape Town at which a representative body of employers and another for trade unions was established. The idea was that the government should be able to consult with these bodies on labour matters. The union body formed was the South African Trade Union

Congress (TUC), later to become the South African Trades & Labour Council (TLC). The Trades & Labour Council, established in 1930, consisted of unions and federations across the spectrum and from the various provinces. Most of the unions were registered and could participate in the official bargaining machinery. They were thus more favourably placed than the exclusively black unions. Yet the TLC was greatly influenced by more liberal elements. This is proved by the fact that, soon after its inception, it called for the abolition of racist labour legislation. In the years that followed many of the TLC unions continued, under the leadership of organisers such as Solly Sachs of the Garment Workers' Union and Ray Alexander, founder of the Food & Canning Workers' Union, to institute militant action on behalf of the entire working class. The most lowly paid employees in this class were black African men and white women. In some instances black interests were represented in the same union, while in others separate unions for black African males were established. By contrast, there were other unions in the TLC which wished to promote only white interests and some which were concerned at the influence of Communists and militants in their ranks.

The Influence of Afrikaner Nationalism

During the 1930s other divisions began to arise. Afrikaners had for long resented the dominance in industry of the English-speaking section, and especially the immigrant workers. This, among other things, had led to the establishment in 1918 of the Afrikanerbond, now known as the Broederbond. One of the specific aims of this body was to capture a share of the wealth of the country for the Afrikaner nation. By the 1930s the Labour Party, which had previously been supported by many Afrikaners, had declined and in 1933 Hertzog's National Party and Smuts's South African Party joined to establish a new party, the South African National Party. This caused Malan and Strijdom to leave the National Party and to establish the Purified National Party, later supported by many white Afrikaans workers. The 1929 depression and the resulting Poor White problem had intensified the need for greater protection and promotion of white, and especially Afrikaner, workers. Soon after its inception the Purified National Party began a campaign to organise white Afrikaners into trade unions, establishing, in the process, the 'Blankewerkersbeskermingsbond'. In the meantime, Hertzog had reconciled with Malan and in 1938 he established the 'Hervormingsorganisasie', which was backed by the Afrikanerbond. This organisation was intent on eradicating communism in trade unions and on wooing white Afrikaner workers. It did not meet with much success in those manufacturing industries where most of the Whites employed were poorly paid females, but many white workers in the service sector and in the male-dominated mining, building and iron and steel industries heeded the call and in 1948 the Mineworkers' Union was eventually taken over by the Hervormers.

The result of these developments was a greater division in labour ranks, yet most of the unions operating in the official system still resorted under the Trades & Labour Council. By 1947 the TLC consisted of 100 unions of very diverse types. The most prominent unions differed particularly in their attitude to other race groups, and it was this issue which eventually caused the withdrawal of some unions from the TLC. In 1945 the Executive Committee of the TLC had recommended that those black trade unions without a political bias be allowed to register and to elect representatives on industrial councils. This had led to further polarisation in the TLC and in 1948 the South African Iron, Steel & Allied Trades Association left the TLC to establish the Coordinating Council of South African Iron & Steel Trade Unions, the policy of which was to admit only all-white unions to membership. The withdrawal of the Iron & Steel union was followed by that of the Mineworkers' Union and various railway staff associations. With this development the ideal of a unified South African labour movement was finally abolished.

Developments in Collective Bargaining

The unions belonging to the Trades & Labour Council had all been active in the official collective bargaining system. Numerous industrial councils had been established and labour relations had become more rationalised. Yet, because these unions were in a growth stage and also because of the militancy of many leaders and their involvement with political and shop floor issues, the system had not yet become as staid as it did after 1950. Numerous strike and protest actions occurred, and unions campaigned vigorously for better working conditions. Between 1924 and 1948 there was a vitality in South African labour relations which was surpassed only during the 1980s.

The Independent Black Trade Unions

During this period of heightened union activity black African employees, often under the leadership of militant Whites, increasingly flexed their industrial muscle. Despite the provisions of the 1924 Act, the government was initially not unsympathetic to the interests of black employees, who were supported by many Whites in industry. For a while it appeared that black unions might eventually be included in the system but, after 1948, this possibility became more remote.

The fact that black employees were not allowed to belong to registered organisations did not prevent them from continuing to establish unions. With the disintegration of the ICU, it was realised that organisation on a sectorial basis was more effective than general unionism and numerous smaller union bodies were established. In 1928 these unions amalgamated to form the Federation of Non-European Trade Unions (FNETU). Some of the FNETU unions worked together with registered unions. FNETU was initially quite active, but the depression of 1929 diluted union power and in 1933 FNETU disbanded. However, one of its leaders, Max Gordon, went on to organise no less than 31 black unions, later coordinated under the Joint Committee of African Trade Unions. Gordon did much to improve the lot of black employees by actively using the wage board system to increase minimum rates and conditions of employment. Nevertheless, some union officials resented the leadership of a White. In 1940 Gordon was imprisoned and, because he had trained no successor, the Joint Committee began to disintegrate. A Coordinating Committee of African Trade Unions (CCATU) had been established earlier, to coordinate the activities of Gordon's unions and those organised by Makabeni of the Black Clothing Workers' Union. Also, a fast-growing African Mineworkers' Union had been established. Finally, in 1942, all the existing unions and federations came together to form the Council of Non-European Trade Unions (CNETU). This body was to dominate the black trade union movement for the next decade. The outbreak of the Second World War brought many more Blacks to the industrial areas. Because they were now sorely needed by employers, they began to wield more power. Numerous strike actions were initiated and employers made various concessions to black employees.

By the end of the war, CNETU could boast a membership of 158 000 in its 119 affiliated unions. The organisation had made notable advances during the war but, after peace had been declared, black African workers again became dispensable and CNETU's power declined. The failed mineworkers' strike in 1946 had also dealt the organisation a hard blow. Furthermore, government action against members of the Communist Party was robbing the organisation of much of its leadership. Despite the fact that CNETU had established more efficient structures than its predecessors, there was a lack of grassroots involvement. The result was that, by 1950, CNETU was no longer able to wield the same influence as before. It had, however, provided a base for the establishment of more coordinated union structures. With the bodies which went before it, CNETU had shown Blacks that they could wield some influence in the economic sphere. This had resulted in greater political awareness of their position in South African society.

All these bodies were necessarily not only economic organisations, but also people's bodies, representative as much of a mass movement as of specific employee interests. The same could, in fact, be said of the all-white, Afrikaner-orientated trade unions of the time.

Government Actions

The militancy of many of the nonracial and multiracial unions and of the unions representing black African employees had focused government attention on the problem of continuing unrest among black workers. Some government officials tried to encourage black unionists to use the wage board system in order to improve conditions for their members, while others advocated the establishment of a collective bargaining system for Blacks. As early as 1928 the then Under Secretary for Labour had recommended the recognition of black employees to create '... legitimate channels for the ventilation of grievances and the settlement of disputes by conciliatory methods similar to those approved by the State for Europeans'. He went on to say that: 'By these measures the activities of those Communists who see in the large masses of South African natives fertile ground for revolutionary action would be circumvented'. In 1930 the amendment of the Industrial Conciliation Act provided for the extension of industrial council agreements to Blacks.

The 1937 Industrial Conciliation Amendment Act added to this provision, allowing for representation of black African employee interests on industrial councils by representatives of the Department of Labour. These measures were effectively used by unionists, who worked through industrial councils to establish better wages for black employees. Nevertheless, the general feeling in official circles was still that black employees were not sufficiently 'developed' for direct representation in official bargaining bodies.

Some good had come of the new provisions, but representation of black employee interests remained poor and most negotiations were conducted with the Wage Board. As the power of black employees continued to grow, it became increasingly important to establish some formal representation channels for this section of the workforce. The government's concern with this issue is proved by the Industrial Conciliation (Natives) Bill of 1947. This Bill proposed the formal recognition of black employee representatives, but in bodies separate from the industrial council. The Bill was never enacted. Shortly after it had been tabled the National Party came to power.

THE ASCENT TO POWER OF THE NATIONALIST GOVERNMENT
(THE PERIOD 1948–1970)

The Appointment of the Botha Commission

The National Party came to power during the postwar slump in the late 1940s. It was a period of general dissatisfaction amongst people of all races. Jobs were scarce and the influx of black Africans to the urban areas had led to unrest in the townships. This, in turn, had resulted in demands for stricter influx control. Polarisation between race groups and between English and Afrikaans speakers had increased, setting the scene for the policies which were to follow.

The new government immediately appointed a commission, generally known as the Botha Commission, to institute an investigation into the existing labour legislation. The Botha Commission argued that, if parity representation were granted to black employees in the industrial situation, it would lead to equality between races. This would put white supremacy at stake. Nevertheless, the Commission did recommend that separate bargaining bodies should be established for Blacks, but it emphasised that recognition of black unions should be subject to stringent conditions and that strike action should be outlawed. The government did not agree that trade unions should be encouraged. It accepted some, but not all, of the Commission's recommendations and in 1953 passed the Bantu Labour (Settlement of Disputes) Act, later known as the Black Labour Relations Regulation Act.

The Bantu Labour (Settlement of Disputes) Act of 1953

The main thrust of the Bantu Labour Act was an attempt to avert trade unionism among Blacks, by allowing for the establishment of workers' committees for black employees. These committees were to be established on the initiative of the employees themselves. Complaints were to be taken to the regional workers' committees, consisting of Blacks appointed by the Minister of Labour, under a white chairman. The regional committees were also to act as watchdogs over conditions of work pertaining to black employees and had to report to the Black Labour Board, which had an all-white membership.

According to one observer, the workers' committees were intended to 'bleed black trade unions white'. This is supported by a statement made by the then Minister of Labour that, if other channels were presented for the lodging of black worker grievances, black trade unions would probably die a natural death. The system did not prove to be very popular. Very few employees had the initiative to form committees and, even where they did, they lacked the necessary expertise to represent themselves effectively. By 1973 only 24 committees had been formally registered under the Act, although another 110 were said to exist.

Besides employee shortcomings, there was the additional problem that only one workers' committee, consisting of five members, was allowed per plant, preventing effective representation. Also, where committees did exist, they merely raised grievances and did not interact on a regular basis with management. Nevertheless, until 1979 the committee system, with later modifications, remained the only legitimised form of black worker representation. In 1955 the government also amended the Wage Act to provide that only the Minister could order wage investigations. This largely closed this form of representation to Blacks.

The Industrial Conciliation Act of 1956

Three years after the passage of the Black Labour Relations Regulation Act, the government passed the Industrial Conciliation Act of 1956 (now known as the Labour Relations Act of 1956). This Act became the new basis for labour legislation relating to collective bargaining. It caused further polarisation in that it excluded all 'Bantu' (including black African women), prohibited the further registration of mixed unions, except with ministerial permission, placed restrictions on the registration of already mixed race unions and provided that such unions could not have mixed executives. It also introduced a system of job reservation whereby a particular occupation could be legally reserved for a certain race group. Contrary to common belief, jobs were not necessarily reserved for Whites, but for members of a single race group. This notwithstanding, the Job Reservation clause became one of the most notorious provisions in South African labour legislation.

The passage of the abovementioned Acts more effectively than ever before entrenched racial division in the conduct of the labour relationship. They were underscored by separatist legislation in other spheres, such as the Group Areas Act introduced in 1950 and the new Influx Control Act.

The Multiracial Union Movement

From 1950 onwards the labour movement, including those unions using the official system, began to reflect to an ever-increasing degree the divisions which had already begun to develop in the previous era. Soon after the Nationalists had come to power the consideration given by the Trades & Labour Council to the establishment of parallel black unions caused small craft unions to split off to form the South African Federation of Trade Unions (SAFTU). The Suppression of Communism Act, passed in 1950, also robbed many of the more militant unions in the Trades & Labour Council of their officials and leaders. Numerous known Communists and even individuals like Solly Sachs, who had resigned from the Communist Party in 1931, were banned and no person listed as a Communist could hold a public office. Remembering that the National Party had never favoured a free collective bargaining system, trade unionists began to fear that additional controls might be introduced. In 1954 the TLC, SAFTU and the Amalgamated Engineering Union established a joint committee, known as the Trade Union Unity Committee, the purpose of which was to consolidate the position of the trade union movement. The outcome was the establishment of the South African Trade Union Council (SATUC) which in 1962 changed its name to the Trade Union Council of South Africa (TUCSA). The TLC and the Western Province Federation of Labour Unions thereafter disbanded, but the South African Federation of Trade Unions continued to exist, despite the fact that many of its member unions had joined TUCSA. The latter body now decided to admit only registered unions, but to work closely with black union bodies. In 1962 it changed this decision and readmitted black unions. The decision not to admit black (African) unions immediately caused a number of the coloured and Indian unions to leave the federation with their black counterparts.

TUCSA continued to maintain that it represented workers of all race groups and in one of his first speeches TUCSA's new president strongly emphasised this policy. He also stated categorically that leadership, and not protectionism, would ensure the future of the white man and that job reservation could never be effectively applied. The Trade Union Council of South Africa became, with the conservative white unions, the major union representative on official bargaining bodies. The organisation remained multiracial and even had in its ranks a number of African, parallel unions. However, the 1956 Act prohibiting mixed executives resulted in the establishment of separate coloured and Indian unions in some cases and the establishment of racially separate branches in others.

Although TUCSA arose from militant union roots, by accommodation to the existent system it developed a new type of trade unionist. The system of collective bargaining established by the Industrial Conciliation Act had led to ever-increasing centralisation of bargaining structure. Registered trade unions bargained through the machinery, the aim of which was to avoid industrial disputes. Since agreements were legally enforceable, unionists began to spend more and more time guarding against breaches. Also, benefit funds were

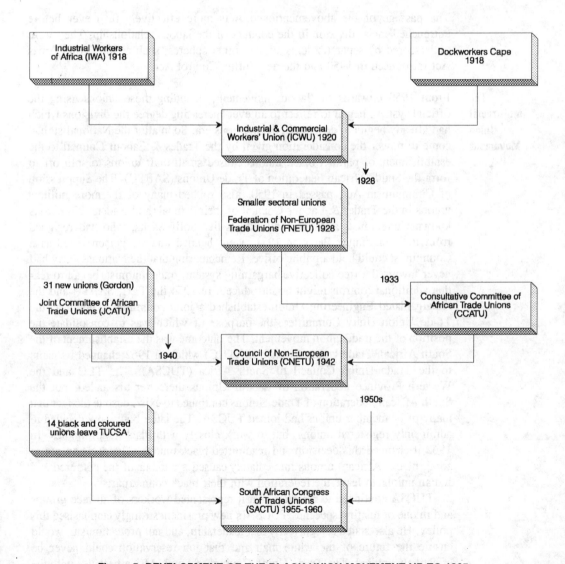

Figure 5: DEVELOPMENT OF THE BLACK UNION MOVEMENT UP TO 1965

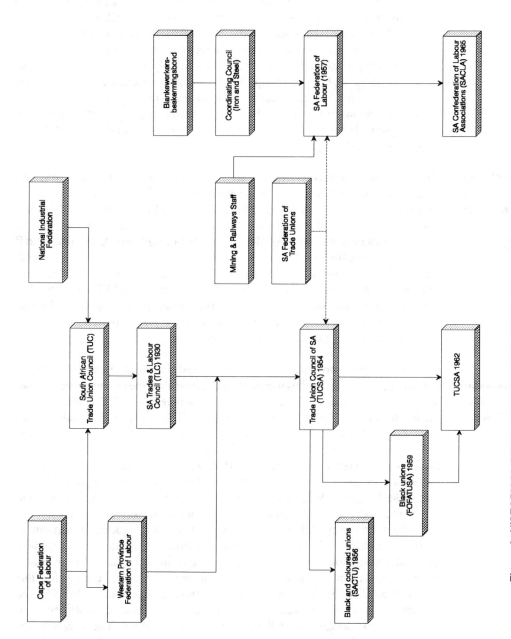

Figure 6: HISTORICAL DEVELOPMENT OF THE WHITE AND MULTIRACIAL MOVEMENT UP TO 1965

established and many unionists found themselves overburdened by their administrative functions. In the process a large number of unions lost touch with their grassroots organisation and took on the role of bureaucrats. Added to this was an increasing acceptance of, or at least abidance by, the sociopolitical *status quo*, so much so that in later years TUCSA unionists were called upon to sit on government advisory bodies. This does not signify that TUCSA did not play a major role in the development of the South African trade union movement. TUCSA did keep the worker movement alive at a stage when it was in danger of disappearing altogether. It did try, at least overtly, to represent the interests of all workers, and, by participation in industrial councils, maintained the tradition of collective bargaining. Nevertheless, in the period until 1970 industrial relations in South Africa developed mainly along prescribed lines. No major upheavals occurred and the 1960–1970 era is generally known for its unprecedented labour peace.

The All-White Labour Movement

The all-white Coordinating Council which had been started in the late 1940s also continued to grow. Soon after its inception the Iron & Steel Union was joined by the Mineworkers' Union and several railway staff associations. In 1957 this body, together with the South African Federation of Trade Unions and the Federal Consultative Council of the South African Railways & Harbours Staff Associations, established the Confederation of Labour, now known as the South African Confederation of Labour Associations (SACLA). TUCSA also joined the Federation initially but withdrew a year later, as did the SAFTU unions. The Confederation continued to promote exclusively white unions and was at the time a firm supporter of government policies. In later years divisions arose over policy issues and a number of unions withdrew.

The Independent Black Movement

The black union movement in the 1950s had its roots in the Council of Non European Trade Unions which, despite setbacks in the previous decade, had remained in existence. In 1955 the unions remaining in CNETU combined with the fourteen unions which had split off from TUCSA to form the South African Congress of Trade Unions (SACTU). Friedman calls this body '... the first formal alliance between independent African unions and those representing other races. It even boasted a few hundred white workers, although they were never more than one per cent of its membership'. Shortly after its inception SACTU joined the Congress Alliance and from then onwards was to play a prominent role in this body. SACTU's initial policy was one of grassroots organisation and shop floor militancy. Initially it did make noteworthy gains. According to Friedman, it succeeded in obtaining a general increase in the metal industry, won informal recognition from some employers and in 1957 staged a successful stayaway to support its 'pound a day' campaign. However, shortly after this stayaway SACTU began to decline as a workplace organisation. In 1958 the Congress movement persuaded SACTU to participate in another stayaway, in which workers' demands were linked to the general election. The stayaway was a failure, but SACTU leaders began to work even more closely with the Alliance. Shop floor committees were organised in support of the anti-pass campaign and, instead of progressively establishing itself as a worker movement able to make shop floor gains, SACTU attempted to grow too fast in order to meet the political objectives of the alliance. Friedman sums it up by saying that:

'Because the Congress needed a mass worker movement, SACTU tried to become one before it was ready. It threw its meagre resources into a campaign to build numbers, not strength'. Added to this lack of systematic organisation was the fact that SACTU suffered from government action more than other movements before it. Numerous officials were banned and, in some unions, no organisers remained.

In 1960 the African National Congress was finally banned and in the ensuing years more than a hundred SACTU leaders were arrested. Of those remaining many went underground and with this the black worker movement, at least in its overt form, disintegrated.

One other non-white worker movement had arisen during this period. In 1959 the black unions which had previously decided to continue their relationship with TUCSA established the Federation of Free African Trade Unions of South Africa (FOFATUSA). It remained a moderate movement and in 1961 had 18 000 members, compared to SACTU's 39 000. In 1962, after TUCSA had decided to readmit black unions, FOFATUSA disbanded.

The years 1950 to 1970 saw a shift on the South African labour scene from a time of heightened action by unions across the colour and political spectrum in the 1930s and 1940s to a phase of relative, perhaps imposed, peace. It also marked a greater polarisation between workers of different races and the virtual disappearance of the black labour movement.

THE NEW LABOUR DISPENSATION (THE PERIOD 1970–1990)

The Start of a New Era   The relative labour peace experienced during the late 1950s and throughout the next decade was not to last. Despite (or perhaps as a result of) the bannings and stricter pass laws imposed by the Nationalist government, black Africans in general, and black workers in particular, gradually became more conscientised to their rights. Furthermore, with the economy still growing, the position of the black employee in industrial society became more firmly entrenched. As Whites moved up in the occupational hierarchy, Blacks came in to take their places. Since this section of the population now constituted the majority of the economically active population, it was unlikely that the position of Blacks in industry and in the labour relationship as decreed by the 1956 Industrial Conciliation Act could be maintained.

The Revival of Black Employee Interests   During the 1960s the only bodies representing black Africans which were prominent on the labour scene were those working under the auspices of or in conjunction with TUCSA, but the beginning of the 1970s saw renewed attempts to organise Blacks into independent unions. In the Transvaal, two unionists dismissed by TUCSA in 1969 established the Urban Training Project (UTP), with the purpose of promoting trade unionism among Blacks. In Natal a number of politically aware students, assisted by an official of the registered Textile Workers' Industrial Union, established the Wages & Economics Commission which attempted to assist black workers by arguing their case before the Wage Board and by trying to persuade employers to raise minimum wage rates. Wages Commissions were later established at other university campuses and, in Durban, the first Wages Commission subsequently formed the General Factory Workers'

Benefit Fund (GFWBF) to provide benefits to black employees and, more importantly, to investigate worker grievances. Students were also active in the Cape where, together with former SACTU unionists, they established the Western Province Workers' Advice Bureau (WPWAB). Another body, of completely different origin, was formed in the Transvaal. Under the impetus of a call from the South African Students' Association for Blacks to form their own leadership cadre, Drake Koka, a prominent member of the Black People's Convention, in 1972 established the Black Allied Workers' Union (BAWU).

Some of the bodies mentioned were not really unions, but together they established the basis from which an entirely new trade union movement, representative of mainly black African employees, would emerge.

The 1972–1973 Strike Wave By the beginning of the 1970s black workers were no longer prepared to accept their secondary status in industry. This was marked by the fact that, in 1972, altogether 9 000 black employees engaged in strike actions, of which the most noteworthy were the Putco bus drivers' strike and the strikes at the Durban and Cape Town docks. Yet the 1972 strikes were insignificant compared with those which occurred in 1973 when, in Natal alone, an estimated 61 000 black employees came out on strike over a very short period. The strike wave started at Coronation Brick, but later spread to the textile and other industries and to the Durban Municipality. Even after the strikes had ended, stoppages occurred intermittently and action was also initiated in other areas, such as the Eastern Cape and the Transvaal.

The strikes had no immediate or obvious cause and the strikers made no fixed demands, but the actions were indicative of general dissatisfaction among black employees. More importantly, they highlighted the joint power of those employees and the necessity to accommodate their interests within the industrial relations system.

Although the strikes were all illegal, no arrests were made — perhaps because it was impossible to imprison all strikers and no ringleaders had emerged, or because the government was at that time being subjected to heightened criticism both from the outside world and from opposition groups inside the country. Employers, on their part, reacted in various ways. Some threatened dismissal, others granted increases, while a few attempted to talk to their workers. All became aware that they had no effective channels by which they could communicate with their black employees. Contrary to the common misconception, the new era in South African industrial relations began here, and not with the Wiehahn reforms.

New Unions Emerge The 1973 strikes added impetus to the reawakened black worker consciousness. In Natal several new unions were established under the auspices of the GFWBF. These unions later founded the Trade Union Advisory & Coordinating Council (TUACC). A number of unions also emerged from the efforts of the Urban Training Project which, by utilising workers' committees, made steady gains. The new unions initially concentrated on enlisting as many members as possible, but soon realised that they would have to consolidate their organisation at each plant by building up strong shop steward representation. For some time they had no notion of how to establish relationships with employers, and toyed with the idea of somehow gaining entry to industrial councils. However, a notable breakthrough occurred when the National Union of Textile Workers and the Textile Workers' Industrial Union managed, in 1974, to conclude a recognition agreement with the British-owned company, Smith & Nephew. It was the first agreement of its kind since the passage of the Industrial Conciliation Act in 1924, which had provided only for industrial council agreements. Until 1980, only four recognition agreements were concluded, but the Smith & Nephew agreement precipitated a new development in collective bargaining.

The new wave of black worker militancy prompted the Trade Union Council of South Africa (TUCSA) to increase its efforts to establish parallel black unions. According to observers like Friedman, TUCSA's concern was not so much for the promotion of black worker interests, but rather arose from its fear of competition from the new union movement. There seems little doubt that TUCSA adopted a 'dog in the manger' attitude towards the new unions and that their emergence posed a threat to TUCSA's dominance in the existing industrial relations system.

Despite its initial gains, the emerging union movement soon ran into difficulties. From 1974 onwards, the government commenced banning many of the persons involved in the organisation and promotion of black trade unions. The bannings increased after the Soweto Riots of 1976 and, together with the recession which followed, caused a decline in the momentum of trade union development. Nevertheless, the total impetus was not lost and in 1979 a number of the bodies and unions involved established the Federation of South African Trade Unions (FOSATU). Another federation, the Council of Unions of South Africa (CUSA), was founded in 1980. Together these bodies, and especially FOSATU, would dominate the South African labour scene during the next five years.

The 1973 Black Labour Relations Regulation Act

The government reacted extremely rapidly to the 1973 strike wave. In the same year it passed the Black Labour Relations Regulation Act. This Act provided for the establishment of liaison committees at plant level, as an alternative to the already existent workers' committees. Liaison committees were to consist of representatives of employers and employees, elected on a parity basis. Their main purpose was to improve communication between the employer and his black employees. Although these committees could consult on any matter of mutual interest, the liaison committees subsequently established often confined themselves to matters of physical hygiene or other paltry issues. Yet the government appears to have seen these committees as a panacea for all the problems which had developed, and obviously favoured them over workers' committees. This is proved by the fact that, where a liaison committee was in existence, a workers' committee could not be established; and by the provision that liaison committees, but not workers' committees, could send representatives to industrial councils.

The Black Labour Relations Regulation Act also gave black employees a limited freedom to strike. This it did by setting up a disputes machinery similar to that provided for in the Industrial Conciliation Act. Disputes arising between employers and black employees had to be channelled via the Black Labour Officer responsible for that area, thereafter to the regional Labour Committee, from there to the Divisional Inspector and from him to the Black Labour Board. Only once these channels had been exhausted were workers entitled to engage in legal strike action. Yet a few unions representative of Blacks did make use of these procedures.

The provisions of the Act met with an enthusiastic response from employers and in the following years numerous liaison committees were established, mostly upon the initiative of the employer parties. Many employers, like the government, saw the liaison committees as a method of dealing with growing black worker militancy, while others founded liaison committees merely to avert unionism or the establishment of worker committees by employees. By contrast, response from the unions was negative. Black unions saw the Act as a renewed attempt to break the power of unionism among black employees. Workers were advised by bodies promoting black unionism to establish workers' committees rather than liaison bodies. Also, organisations such as the UTP and the WPWAB began to use the workers' committee system to gain entry to enterprises through the back door. The aims and methods of these two bodies were different. While the UTP encouraged the establishment of workers' committees as a basis for plant-level organisation and the formation of unions, the WPWAB believed that committee members should be trained to negotiate on their own behalf, eventually rendering the union officials unnecessary.

In 1977, in a last attempt to promote the committee system as an alternative to unionism, the government drafted a Bill allowing workers' committees to negotiate 'binding wage agreements'. It did not say how these agreements were to become binding, and the Bill was never passed.

The committee system for black employees was introduced in South Africa not to supplement the process of collective bargaining, as has happened elsewhere in the Western world, but to replace it. Its introduction can be ascribed partly to the belief that Blacks were not able to engage in 'responsible' collective bargaining at official level, but perhaps more to the fear of black union power and the fear of dominance by these bodies in the industrial relations and collective bargaining systems. The irony is that the very structure intended to destroy unionism could equally promote it.

The Wiehahn Commission

By 1976 it had become obvious that the provisions of the Black Labour Relations Regulation Act of 1973 had not solved the problem of black worker militancy. Also, South Africa's major trading partners had, partly because of representations made to overseas bodies by local unions and partly because of the 1976 riots, become more aware of the position of the black worker. The threat of sanctions and disinvestment had increased and various codes of employment practice (notably the EEC Code, the Sullivan Code and the British Code of Employment Practice) had been issued to multinational companies in South Africa. An improved image was sorely needed, and it was in this climate that the government in 1977 appointed the Commission of Inquiry into Labour Legislation, commonly known as the Wiehahn Commission.

Friedman comments most perceptively on the circumstances surrounding the appointment of the Commission, the role of Wiehahn and the reaction to the Commission's first report. The original brief of the Commission was to rationalise the then existent labour legislation, to seek possible means of adapting the industrial relations system to 'changing needs' and to '... eliminate bottlenecks and other problems experienced in the labour sphere'. This was the stated brief but, in retrospect, it appears highly probable that the Commission was specifically instructed to consider a method by which black trade unions could be controlled and incorporated into the industrial relations system without creating too great a disruption.

The findings of the Commission were reported in six parts, the last report appearing some time after legislation implementing previous recommendations had been passed. Part I of the report dealt mainly with the labour relationship and the then Industrial Conciliation Act. Many of the recommendations made were theoretically backed up or elaborated upon in Part V, which appeared much later. Part II of the report pertained mainly to training and manpower utilisation, while Parts III and IV concerned themselves with job and social security, health and safety issues and conditions of employment.

Many of the recommendations of the Commission were accepted and implemented by the government, thus substantially changing South African labour legislation. By the time all the recommendations had been implemented the Industrial Conciliation Act, later to become the Labour Relations Act, had been subjected to significant amendments; the Black Labour Relations Regulation Act had been repealed; all previous legislation pertaining to training and manpower development had been consolidated into the Manpower Training Act; and, finally, the Shops & Offices Act and the Factory, Machinery & Building Works Act had been put together and divided into the Basic Conditions of Employment Act and the Machinery & Occupational Safety Act (now known as the Occupational Health & Safety Act).

The Wiehahn Commission's first report was certainly the most momentous and the legislation which followed would bring about the most radical changes in labour relations. The report recommended, *inter alia*, that:

- full freedom of association be granted to all employees regardless of race, sex or creed;
- trade unions, irrespective of composition in terms of colour, race or sex, be allowed to register;
- stricter criteria be adopted for trade union registration;
- a system of financial inspection of trade unions be introduced;
- prohibitions on political activity by unions be extended;
- liaison committees be renamed as works councils;
- where no industrial council had jurisdiction, works councils and workers' committees be granted full collective bargaining rights;
- statutory job reservation be phased out;
- safeguards be introduced to protect minorities previously protected by job reservation;
- the Industrial Tribunal be replaced by the Industrial Court;
- fair employment practices be developed by the Industrial Court;
- job reservation be phased out, with the consent of those concerned;
- allowance for a closed shop be maintained; and
- a tripartite National Manpower Commission be established.

The first and second recommendations mentioned were, in the light of past history, the most revolutionary. The granting of registered trade union rights to black Africans, which would give them access to the collective bargaining machinery, was something which had previously been avoided at all costs. Yet the intentions of the Commission were not as progressive as they would at first appear. In reading the report it becomes apparent that the Commission's point of departure was that the cooption of black trade unions into the existing system would make them more controllable and would prevent the flourishing of the system of plant-level recognition agreements, which had reared its head in the previous three years. It was believed that the new trade union movement (at that stage relatively small) would, by cooption into the system and by bargaining with other established unions on industrial councils, lose much of its impact; that it would become more 'responsible' and perhaps even be absorbed into the established movement. The proposal for the establishment of multiracial plant-level works councils, with full bargaining powers, further reflects the fear that plant-level bargaining by unions representing black employees would get out of control. The Commission in effect proposed that this system be replaced by one where representatives of all employees at a plant could bargain with the employer. This was an illogical suggestion. While it hoped on the one hand that new unions would be encouraged to use the centralised, industrial council system, the Commission itself proposed that a two-tier system, which would include plant-level bargaining, should be established.

It was, furthermore, obvious that the Commission was concerned about the future welfare of minority groups. The concept of the Industrial Court was, it is believed, originally introduced for the specific purpose of protecting minority groups from unfair practices by other, supposedly majority, groups. The purport of this is underscored by the proposal that minorities previously protected by job reservation should be further safeguarded.

Despite these supposed intentions, the proposals represented a step forward in South African labour relations, by the very fact of their admission that black employees could not be excluded from the machinery pertaining to all other race groups. In the White Paper published shortly thereafter, the government accepted most of the Commission's recommendations. However, the Amendment Bill drafted to implement them did not meet with expectations. In the first place it allowed for the inclusion of only Section 10(1) Blacks (i.e. those with permanent residence in urban areas) under the new definition of 'employee'. Secondly, it proposed that unions should be fined R500 for each migrant or commuter who was a member of the union. Other sections to which there were objections included the proposal that new unions should initially be given 'provisional registration', and the clause granting existent members of industrial councils the right to veto entry by a new party. The reaction was so great that the provision for the R500 fine was immediately dropped. The other controversial provisions, except that relating to veto rights, were modified at a later stage.

The Industrial Conciliation Amendment Act

The Industrial Conciliation Amendment Act (later known as the Labour Relations Amendment Act) of 1979 did, notwithstanding misgivings on many sides, introduce a new era in South African labour relations. Not all the recommended innovations were introduced forthwith, and important amendments to the Act were made in 1980, 1981 and 1982; but, by 1983, the following major changes had been made.

- The term 'employee' had been redefined to include all persons working for an employer.

- Previous provisions for racially mixed unions to have separate branches and all-white executives had been withdrawn.
- The provision for ministerial approval prior to the registration of mixed unions had been cancelled.
- Previous provisions regarding submission of financial statements and membership records had been extended to non-registered unions.
- Unions were more explicitly prohibited from influencing members in order to assist the activities of a political party.
- Stop orders on behalf of non-registered unions could be deducted only with the permission of the Minister.
- Unregistered unions had been granted the right to apply for conciliation boards.
- The job reservation clause (Section 77) had been repealed.
- A definition of an 'unfair labour practice' had been added.
- Provision had been made for the establishment of the Industrial Court and the Manpower Commission.
- The provision for workers' committees had been taken over from the Black Labour Relations Regulation Act. The Works Councils, as they were now called, could '... perform such functions as may be agreed upon between the employer and employees concerned'.
- The name of the basic Act had been changed to the Labour Relations Act of 1956.

The Reaction of the Newer Trade Unions

The trade unions established to represent black employees during the previous decade did not display much enthusiasm at the fact that they were now permitted to participate in the official system. Initially most of these unions refused to register, either as a matter of principle and in protest at their previous exclusion or because they believed that registration would entail greater government control. Also, the newer unions stayed out of the industrial councils, partly because they resented these bodies and partly because their power base would be diluted by centralised bargaining. Instead they pursued their previous strategy of organising a strong shop floor presence and demanding recognition from individual employers. Although unions representing black African employees had now gained greater legitimacy, employers in the early stages of the new dispensation offered strong resistance to demands for plant-level bargaining. The most prevalent excuse was that the employers were not prepared to deal with unregistered unions — that unions should register and join the industrial councils. The result was a significant increase in strike actions, all of them illegal, culminating in the strike wave on the East Rand early in 1982. By then, some employers had relented and had concluded recognition agreements with representative unions at plant level. This trend continued — so much so that plant-level bargaining soon became entrenched in the South African industrial relations system.

The resistance of unions to registration began to wane as it became apparent that the advantages gained might outweigh the disadvantages and that registration was not necessarily synonymous with control. Problems were experienced, however, when a number of the newer unions — significantly those in the Federation of South African Trade Unions — applied for registration on a nonracial basis. The Industrial Registrar initially decided that they should be registered to represent black workers only, but this decision was later overruled by the Supreme Court. (It is important that many of these major new unions subscribed to a policy of nonracialism, while others followed the black consciousness line.) Once they had acquired registered status and as their power base expanded to cover a substantial number of employees in a particular industry, certain of these unions applied for admission to industrial councils. Again problems were experienced when unions already on councils exercised their veto right. Court cases followed, and this issue soon became something of the past. In fact, many of the major unions which were established after 1975 now played a significant, even dominant, role on industrial councils.

As was to be expected, the new union movement grew significantly. According to the Department of Manpower's report for 1990, actual black membership of registered trade unions amounted to 967 619, while black and coloured membership amounted to 1 288 619 out of a total registered membership of 2 458 712. This did not include those registered unions whose membership was not specified, nor did it include membership of non-registered unions, of which there were still quite a number. Total union membership, discounting the unregistered unions, had increased by one and a half million since 1980. Almost all the additional members came from the ranks of black African and coloured African employees, and it can be safely estimated that most of them belonged to the newer unions. Although the majority of the more prominent newer unions were nonracial, these unions — because they concentrated on organising unskilled and semiskilled workers — represented mainly Blacks, Coloureds and Asians, and a very small sprinkling of Whites.

The unions emerging in the 1980s displayed the militancy to be expected of a new movement and particularly of one attempting to establish itself in an entrenched system. Working in close cooperation with shop stewards, they took up every issue affecting their members. Many actions were hard fought, and strike frequency increased from 101 strikes in 1979 to 1 148 in 1987 and 1 025 in 1988. In 1989 and 1990 there was a slight drop, to 855 and 948 respectively. At the beginning of the 1980s, nearly all strikes which occurred were illegal in that no attempt had been made to use the statutory dispute settlement machinery. After 1985 this trend was reversed, owing to greater sophistication on the part of the unions, a greater willingness to use the system and more firmly establishedrelationships. Towards the end of 1983 the newer unions also began to use the unfair labour practice legislation and the Status Quo Order provision to bring Industrial Court actions against employers. This proved a viable alternative to strike action, and the activities of the Industrial Court expanded accordingly. Ironically, contrary to the expectations of the Wiehahn Commission, it was the black employees and not the white minority who would prove the viability of the unfair labour practice legislation. All in all, the newer unions tended to dominate the industrial relations arena. In contrast to previous era, the interests of black employees gained prominence and, as some would have it, may have led to the neglect of their white counterparts.

The newer trade unions were from the outset intensely aware of the mistakes which had been made by black trade union movements in the past. Consequently, they concentrated on worker organisation and the achievement of gains on the shop floor, rather than on mass mobilisation. However, trade union growth coincided with the mushrooming of protest movements and trade unions, as the major representatives of the black working class, increasingly found themselves in a politically prominent position. This was to be expected since, until 1990, the trade union movement constituted the only legitimate public forum for disenfranchised employees. Even after the De Klerk reforms of that year and the unbanning of all political parties, the trade union movement — and particularly COSATU — remained established as a formidable political power bloc.

White Opposition

The new dispensation in labour relations was not without its opponents. Even before the first Wiehahn report was published, white mineworkers, who had evidently been informed of its content, went out on strike to protest the inclusion of Blacks in the official industrial relations system. The strike was unsuccessful, but the opposition remained. Many white employees, fearful of their position, found their political home in the Conservative Party, proved by the fact that the former general secretary of the all-white Mineworkers' Union was afterwards elected as a Member of Parliament for that party. The South African Confederation of Labour Associations, now taking a position to the right of the government, still existed. By 1983 this Association, having lost more than half of its previous membership, appeared to be on the decline but it stood its ground and, as white reactionism increased, again began to grow.

TUCSA Disintegrates

The Trade Union Council of South Africa was, despite its active participation in the Wiehahn Commission, the worst hit by the new dispensation. During the first three years after the passage of the Labour Relations Act of 1979, TUCSA grew at a significant rate but most observers attribute this to the fact that, with the new legislation, previous closed shop agreements were automatically extended to black African employees. Therefore TUCSA unions gained, without their own initiative, a mass of new members. A number of TUCSA unions did open up their ranks and most of the unions did try to service the new members by representation on industrial councils, but they lacked the grassroots organisation of the newer unions. They were slower to take up issues and, as the major multiracial organisation in existence before 1980, TUCSA was the first to feel the pinch when black and coloured members started defecting to the newer unions. Because of this decrease in established union membership, a number of industrial councils became unrepresentative and the government became more reluctant to extend the agreements of these councils to other parties. This served to diminish further the influence exerted by TUCSA unions. Also within the councils the position of these unions became less relevant, partly because many employers were dealing with other unions at plant level and partly because the newer unions which did join councils soon began to play a dominant role. Another reason for TUCSA's decline was the fact that many unions belonging to this body had mainly coloured and, later, black members. Not only did they have to compete for membership with the newer unions, but they also had to prove that, ideologically, they represented the interests and values of their members. This proved difficult in view of TUCSA's past history and the cooperation of coloured and black TUCSA unions with white unions. The result of this and TUCSA's non-involved image in the collective bargaining sphere was that, from 1984 onwards, individual unions, finding their position in the movement unviable, began to withdraw from TUCSA. TUCSA's attempt to adapt had come too late and, at the end of 1986, the organisation officially disbanded.

The Collective Bargaining System

Whereas collective bargaining in South Africa previously occurred mainly at industrial council level, a dualistic bargaining system established itself during the 1980s. Industrial council agreements were still concluded at industry, regional or area level, but there was also a proliferation of recognition agreements between individual employers and unions representing black employees. Therefore, the same group of employers could be covered by two agreements. Even where newer unions joined industrial councils, they continued to bargain at plant level and insisted that shop stewards be allowed to participate in industrial council negotiations. Others established centralised forums outside of the industrial council system. The duplication of bargaining did not find favour with employers, many of whom threatened to withdraw from centralised bargaining. This led to extensive friction between major employers and the unions.

Government Reaction

The previous government, having set the new system in motion, appeared initially to have been taken aback by it but thereafter became increasingly inclined to take a back seat and to let developments run their course. During the first two or three years after the passage of the Industrial Conciliation Amendment Act of 1979, Department of Manpower officials actively assisted employers when problems arose and in some instances intervened in disputes between employers and their employees or unions. A few abortive attempts were also made to 'put the system on the right track', but this initiative did not last. In 1982 the Director General of Manpower repeatedly declared that the government believed in the principle of self-government in industry and that employers and employees should attempt to regulate their own relationship in the best possible manner. Gradually official sources also began subtly to encourage employers to negotiate with recognised unions. The government was letting the system sort itself out, taking the role mainly of observer and adviser. This policy persisted until 1988, when the government — obviously pressurised by employers and perhaps of the opinion that unions were gaining too much power — passed controversial amendments to the Labour Relations Act. The amendments included certain codifications of unfair labour practices, some of which seemed to be directed against union actions. Also, unions could now be sued for illegal strikes undertaken by their members. The 1988 Labour Relations Amendment Act was widely opposed by the union movement. Stayaways demonstrating protest against the Act followed, and employers came under pressure to 'contract out' of the Labour Relations Act as a totality — which some, in fact, did. Instead of rationalising and improving labour relations, the amendments had caused increased conflict. Realising this, the South African Consultative Committee on Labour Affairs (SACCOLA) initiated discussions between themselves as employer representatives and the two major trade union federations, COSATU and NACTU. The talks culminated in an accord, the contents of which were presented to the Manpower Commission and the Minister of Labour. As a result, most of the 1988 amendments were withdrawn by the Labour Relations Amendment Act of 1991. This move towards a more corporatist approach of consultation between unions, employers and the State was a significant landmark.

DEVELOPMENTS WITHIN THE NEW SOCIOPOLITICAL DISPENSATION (THE PERIOD FROM 1990 ONWARDS)

The Period of Transition   With the unbanning of previously banned political organisations and the release of Nelson Mandela, it was evident that a new sociopolitical era had begun and that the process towards the institution of a democratically elected government was irreversible. The government of the time, having already adopted a more corporatist approach (see above), increasingly opened itself up to the major stakeholders in the labour sphere as well as that of other community interests. This led, in 1993 and 1994, to the inclusion of agricultural and domestic employees under the Basic Conditions of Employment Act and, in the same year, to the Agricultural Labour Act, which effectively incorporated farmworkers under the Labour Relations Act. Also as regards the public sector, a change of heart occurred, proved by the passage of the Education Labour Act of 1993 and the Public Service Labour Act of 1994. For the first time the scope of labour relations was expanding to include hitherto unrepresented and often exploited workers and to acknowledge the role of the State as yet another employer.

The New Dispensation   In April 1994 the ANC, supported and bolstered by COSATU and the SACP, took over as the majority party in the Government of National Unity. Having come to power by the vote of the poor and previously oppressed, and having in its ranks many former trade unionists, the new government faced expectations from that section of society which were (and still are) great, to the point of being unrealistic. Workers now expect the government to serve mainly their interests, forgetting that it has a far wider constituency (including also the forty percent or more unemployed persons) and that its concerns do not only centre in the workplace but also embrace the economy in general, the need for job creation and investment and the dire need for mammoth improvements in training, education and health services. The fact is also overlooked that the former trade unionists are just that: they are no longer trade unionists but politicians, burdened with serving the wider constituency and balancing the interests of all stakeholders.

Conversely, the oft-expressed fears of other sectors of society, including the business sector — that a government with 'socialist' partners would inevitably attempt to destroy capital and engage in an 'irresponsible' programme of nationalisation and redistribution — have also not been realised. Already during the CODESA negotiations the major players adopted an increasingly pragmatic stance. With a few exceptions, this approach has been maintained, often to the ire of some COSATU unionists. The new government continues to express its encouragement of investment and its belief in the free market principle as the main route to economic growth. In fact, it appears to be going further than its predecessors in stimulating competition, as proved by the intention to reduce import tariffs as far as possible. On the other hand it is attempting, through the RDP and by way of new education and training, housing and health policies, to uplift previously disadvantaged communities and persons, reflected on the micro-level by the emphasis on affirmative action and social responsibility. Also, it is the government's stated intention to unbundle the large conglomerates and to provide opportunities for black business.

In its efforts to satisfy all sectors of society and at the same time to reconcile and reconstruct an economically and socially devastated country, while remaining as democratic and inclusive as possible, the government is straddling numerous divides. The tension caused by this precarious position may well stretch its capacity to breaking point. Moreover, the ever-increasing crime rate and continued labour unrest serve only to exacerbate an already problematic position.

Labour Relations Policy and Legislation

After the 1994 elections the reconstituted Department of Manpower, now renamed the Department of Labour, commenced putting its own stamp on the labour relations system. A task team was established to draft a new Labour Relations Act and, in February 1995, the first 'Draft Negotiation Document' was published for comment.

Furthermore, early in 1995 the National Manpower Commission (NMC) and the National Economic Forum (NEF) disbanded, to be replaced by the National Economic Development & Labour Council (NEDLAC), intended to represent all major stakeholders and to consult on economic, industrial relations and labour market policy. The government revealed its intention to continue adopting a corporatist approach by recognising NEDLAC in the proposed legislation and making the final acceptance of the draft Bill subject to consensual approval from NEDLAC. This proved to be more easily said than done and it was only after prolonged negotiations, with the unions in NEDLAC threatening repeated mass action if they did not get agreement from the employer parties on certain controversial sections, and after the Minister of Labour had intervened, that an uneasy truce was eventually reached and the proposed legislation could be passed through Parliament. Essentially, employers saw the proposed legislation as stifling business, while unions felt that it did not 'go far enough'. Also in Parliament the legislation caused divisions, with most of the minority parties voting against its passage.

The above reflects the problems involved in adopting a corporatist approach in a society which is, in essence, still divided and where participants, although prepared eventually to compromise, still adopt different ideological positions.

The Labour Relations Act of 1995

This Act is discussed in detail in Chapter 5 and in other parts of this text. To prove that it heralds a new dispensation, the Act repeals the Labour Relations Act of 1956 and subsequent amendments although many of the procedures and structures contained in that Act are retained, albeit often with a change of name. The most significant changes are the provision for legislated organisational rights, the granting of the right to strike without fear of dismissal once prescribed procedures have been followed, the limitations placed on the use of scab labour, the provision for the establishment of agency shops and closed shops, the codification of unfair dismissals and the provisions relating to workplace forums.

While there appears to be a genuine desire on the part of the government to balance power, create more certainty and promote cooperation between the parties, most of the changes favour the unions rather than business. Also, while bargaining and the choice of bargaining structure remain mostly voluntary, the

Act unashamedly promotes centralised bargaining, which would favour the position of certain larger unions rather than that of employers. This has led various commentators to opine that, in its attempt to balance power and please the unions, the government has perhaps created a new power imbalance.

Labour Action

Contrary to expectations, labour action has not decreased to any significant extent (from 904 strikes in 1990 to 804 in 1994). In fact, while the sectors with more established labour relations have negotiated relatively peaceful settlements, major actions have occurred and are still occurring in the health services, the police services, the municipal services and the fishing and transport industries. The continuance of labour action may be ascribed to the perception of employees that, at grassroots, no significant changes have occurred; to a new (perhaps exaggerated) awareness of rights; and to the lack of effective processes in certain sectors, notably the public and municipal services.

As mentioned previously, the continuation of labour unrest places both the government and the unions supporting it in a predicament. While the government may wish to curb labour unrest in the interests of promoting the economy and while some unions may wish to cooperate in this respect, neither the government nor these unions can really afford to take a stand against grassroots sentiment for fear of losing the support of their constituents to other political parties and unions.

The Union Movement

COSATU remains the major union federation, although the unions affiliated to NACTU and the recently formed Federation of South African Labour, as well as other grassroots-centred bodies, appear to be gaining ground. Also, it could be speculated that there are numerous other political factions battling for the hearts and minds of the workers.

It would seem that COSATU, by opting for centralised bargaining and closed shop agreements, is attempting to entrench itself in a central position, although this could eventually lead to its demise (as happened with TUCSA).

In general, unions of all persuasions are re-aligning themselves and attempting to establish a foothold within the new dispensation (see Chapter 7), with the notable exception of SACLA which, its members threatened by affirmative action initiatives, continues to adopt a reactionary (albeit relatively low-key) stance.

Assessment of Developments

It is obvious that we are at present merely at the beginning of the new dispensation, and that various realignments and changes of stance are bound to take place.

CONCLUSION

The South African industrial relations system, because of its unique societal setting, remains beset by divisions. Despite the fact that discrimination on the basis of race, sex or creed has been eliminated from labour and other legislation, the composition of the trade union movement still reflects racial and political divisions and there is as yet no unified or dominant bargaining system. The industrial relations system had to adapt and develop very rapidly over the past decade, and was beset by problems in the political sphere. Although past problems are gradually disappearing, new ones have arisen and new adaptations will be required of both employers and unions. The industrial relations system consequently remains dynamic and subject to rapid change necessitated by developments in the labour, economic and sociopolitical arenas. (For further reading in this respect see Chapters 5, 7 and 9.)

SOURCES

Callinicos, Luli *Gold and the Workers 1886–1924*, Ravan Press, 1981.

Callinicos, Luli *Working Life 1886–1940*, Ravan Press, 1987.

Department of Labour *Annual Report 1994*, Government Printer, Pretoria, 1995.

Department of Manpower *Report of the Director General* (for the year ended December 1990), Government Printer, Pretoria, 1991.

Du Toit, M A *South African Trade Unions*, McGraw-Hill, 1976.

Friedman, Steven *Building Tomorrow Today*, Ravan Press, 1987.

Gray, Coetzee J A *Industrial Relations in South Africa*, Juta & Co, 1976.

Labour Relations Act, 1995. *Government Gazette* Vol.366 no.16861, December 1995.

Maree, Johann (Ed) *The Independent Trade Unions 1974–1984*, Ravan Press, 1987.

Ncube, Don *Black Trade Unions in South Africa*, Skotaville, 1985.

Webster, Eddie (Ed) *Southern African Labour History*, Ravan Press, 1978.

5

THE LEGISLATIVE FRAMEWORK GOVERNING THE EMPLOYMENT RELATIONSHIP

The legislative framework governing the employment relationship reflects the degree of State involvement in the conduct of and conditions pertaining in this relationship. In a completely voluntary system no labour legislation would exist but, as has by now become evident, no purely voluntary system can or does exist. The market principle is influenced by too many sociological, political and administrative factors to be able to operate freely, and even its free operation might lead to unfavourable employment conditions; nor can the parties to the labour relationship be left entirely to their own devices, particularly where power is unequally distributed.

Labour legislation, if it is to be deemed acceptable, should conform to universal standards. The best guidelines to such standards are to be found in the various conventions and recommendations of the International Labour Organisation. Moreover, any legislation passed in this country cannot deviate from the principles established by the Constitution. As far as labour legislation is concerned, the most relevant section of the Constitution is that outlining fundamental rights, including labour relations rights.

In South Africa the employment relationship is governed, in the first instance, by the contract of employment which, in turn, is subject to common law. Parties who agree that one will work for another and be paid a certain amount have entered into a contract and, at common law, will thereafter have certain rights and duties which are enforced by the civil courts. Equally, a written contract will influence the decision of the courts or, in the absence of a written contract, practice, custom and tradition. The common law does not take into account the fairness of the contract, but merely the fact that a contract has been concluded.

The common law is superseded by statute which will in future be developed in consultation with the National Economic Development & Labour Council (NEDLAC), as will government policy on labour affairs. The new Labour Relations Act (which is in itself not wholly prescriptive) provides for delegated legislation in the form of bargaining council agreements, unfair labour practice determinations and arbitration awards. These may establish conditions and rules more favourable than those obtaining under a contract at common law. The Labour Relations Act further establishes the parameters for the collective labour relationship. It provides for organisational rights, the registration of unions and employers' associations and the formation of bargaining and statutory councils. Provision has been made for workplace forums in an attempt to encourage consultation and codetermination on certain issues between employers and employee representatives. The Act also attempts to promote labour peace, by providing a dispute settlement process aimed at conciliation and third party intervention, and by not permitting a legal or protected strike or lockout unless the prescribed procedures have been followed. Furthermore, the Act has introduced a new dispute settlement body in the form of the Commission for Conciliation, Mediation & Arbitration and has replaced the Industrial Court with a Labour Court which has higher status and more extended functions. Finally, the Act prohibits victimisation and any interference with the freedom of association.

In industries or areas where collective bargaining is not established, employees are protected by the Basic Conditions of Employment Act and by determinations made under the Wage Act. The Basic Conditions of Employment Act provides for maximum working hours, payment for overtime and for work on Sunday and public holidays, minimum notice periods, minimum annual leave and sick leave, the regulation of overtime and the prohibition of certain deductions. Wage determinations are issued on an ad hoc *basis by the Wage Board and deal with substantive conditions of employment in particular industries, occupations, areas or trades where there is no bargaining council. All employees are further protected by the Occupational Health & Safety Act, which provides for the appointment of safety representatives and safety committees.*

The Unemployment Insurance Act and the Compensation for Occupational Injuries & Diseases Act are, basically, insurance schemes for employees. The firstmentioned Act provides for compulsory deduction of unemployment contributions from employers and employees who earn R69 000 per annum and less. This entitles employees to certain benefits in the event of unemployment. The Workmen's Compensation Fund relies on compulsory levies on employers and provides for payment of compensation to employees who suffer disability as a result of an accident or an illness which has befallen them in the course of their employment.

The last Act is the Manpower Training Act, which is reflective of government policy in the sphere of manpower development. This Act provides for the training of apprentices and the establishment of industry training boards, regional and private training centres, a training fund for the unemployed and a training development fund.

RATIONALE OF THE LEGISLATIVE FRAMEWORK

Labour legislation is introduced for the specific purpose of establishing parameters for the conduct of the labour relationship and to provide minimum regulations pertaining to substantive conditions of employment. Where no labour legislation exists, the employment relationship is governed by the contract of employment, enforceable at common law, but it is generally agreed that this does not provide sufficient protection for employees; nor does the common law adjudicate on the concept of fairness or equity, which is crucial in the labour relationship.

Labour law has, in the first place, to ensure the protection of employees. Early industrialisation taught that the operation of the market principle is not a guarantee against exploitation and that an individual may, by force of circumstances, enter into an unfavourable contract. For this reason it is regarded as the duty of the State of legislate on minimum terms and conditions of employment and to protect the health and safety of the workforce.

Secondly, labour law in a voluntary system will provide the framework for the conduct of the collective labour relationship. Legislation will provide for freedom of association, freedom from victimisation and the right to engage in industrial action. To promote labour peace, dispute settlement procedures may also be provided. Furthermore, it may happen that each party is protected from unfair practices by the other and that collective bargaining is promoted by the body of labour law.

Principles of social justice and the protection of society's members have led to the institution of welfare schemes in the form of unemployment funds and, in some countries, State pension and medical schemes, while the promotion of more efficient economic activity necessitates the State's involvement in training and manpower planning programmes.

INTERNATIONAL LABOUR STANDARDS

In establishing labour legislation, governments need to be guided by universally accepted standards. These are best supplied by the various conventions and recommendations of the International Labour Organisation.

The International Labour Organisation was founded in 1919 and by 1984 could boast 150 member countries, all of which had equity representation by employers, employees and the State. The ILO has as one of its main tasks the setting of international labour standards by way of conventions and recommendations. These are subsequently ratified and implemented by member countries. Although the ILO has no punitive power, it does act as watchdog and expresses censure on those countries which do not adhere to ratified conventions and also on non-member countries who transgress the bounds of acceptability in the sphere of labour relations. South Africa was expelled from the ILO during the apartheid era, but has now again been admitted as a member. Its body of labour law, as well as labour relations policies and practices, should therefore be measured by the standards established by this organisation.

By 1985 the International Labour Code consisted of no fewer than 159 Conventions and 169 Recommendations dealing with a wide range of subjects in the labour and social spheres. Recommendations and Conventions have been passed concerning almost every aspect of industrial relations. Some of these are discussed in the relevant chapters, but for the present purpose we are concerned only with those which set the basic principles for the conduct of a labour relationship. These are to be found in the Declaration of Philadelphia, the Convention concerning the freedom of association and protection of the right to organise, and the Convention concerning the application of the principles of the right to organise and to bargain collectively.

The Declaration of Philadelphia The Declaration of Philadelphia reaffirms the main principles on which the ILO is based and, although it was passed only in 1944 and thereafter appended to the ILO constitution, it is generally regarded as the founding document of the International Labour Organisation.

Part I of the Declaration makes the following statements.

- That 'labour is not a commodity'
- That 'freedom of expression and association are essential to sustained progress'
- That 'poverty anywhere constitutes a danger to prosperity everywhere'
- That the war against poverty should be carried on unrelentingly by all concerned in an atmosphere of 'free discussion and democratic decisionmaking'

Part II affirms the ideological premise of the ILO, namely that 'all human beings, irrespective of race, creed or sex, have the right to pursue both their material wellbeing and their spiritual development in conditions of freedom and dignity, of economic security and equal opportunity'. The Declaration goes on to state that the attainment of such conditions will be the main purpose of the organisation and that all national and international policies, particularly those of an economic nature, will be judged in the light of this fundamental objective.

The third part is more specific in that it sets as the ILO's duty the task of promoting full employment and raising the standard of living of all people, and sees as means of achieving this the promotion of training, the provision of facilities for the transfer of labour, the setting of policies regarding wages and conditions of service, the recognition of the right to collective bargaining, the promotion of cooperation between management and labour to improve productive efficiency, collaboration between workers and employers in deciding on social and economic measures, the promotion of social security measures, the institution of comprehensive medical care, protection of the life and health of workers, provision for child welfare and maternity protection and the provision of adequate cultural facilities for all employees.

The Declaration of Philadelphia, and especially Parts I and II thereof, is still regarded as the blueprint for the establishment of an equitable industrial relations system and indeed for the conduct of individual labour relationships. The aims contained in Part III might appear idealistic; yet the ILO has translated these into concrete objectives which are well worth the attention of all parties engaged in the labour relationship.

Convention (No. 87) Concerning the Freedom of Association and Protection of the Right to Organise (1948)

This Convention enlarges on one of the founding statements of the Declaration of Philadelphia, namely that '... freedom of association and expression are essential for sustained progress'.

The most important statements contained in Convention no. 87 are the following.

- 'Workers and employers, without distinction whatsoever, shall have the right to establish and, subject only to the rules of the organisations concerned, to join organisations of their own choosing without previous authorisation.'
- 'Workers' and employers' organisations shall have the right to draw up their constitutions and rules, to elect their representatives in full freedom, to organise their administration and activities and to formulate their programmes.'

- 'The public authorities shall refrain from any interference which would restrict this right or impede the lawful exercise thereof.'
- 'Workers' and employers' organisations shall not be liable to be dissolved or suspended by administrative authority.'
- 'In exercising the rights provided for in this Convention workers and employers and their respective organisations, like other persons or organised collectives, shall respect the law of the land.'
- 'The law shall not be such as to impair, nor shall it be so implied as to impair, the guarantees provided for in this Convention.'
- 'Each member of the International Labour Organisation for which this Convention is in force undertakes to take all necessary and appropriate measures to ensure that workers and employers may exercise freely the right to organise.'

The Convention speaks for itself. Essentially it safeguards the most basic freedom in the labour relationship — the freedom to associate (or, for that matter, to disassociate) — on condition that any organisation so established does not break the law, but with the added proviso that the law should not be such as to impair the freedom of association and the right to organise.

Convention (No. 98) Concerning the Application of the Principles of the Right to Organise and to Bargain Collectively (1949)

As is evident from its title, this Convention deals in more concrete terms with measures to be taken to ensure freedom of association and free collective bargaining in a particular society. To these ends the Convention firstly recommends safeguards against anti-union discrimination in the form of protection against acts calculated to —

- '... make the employment of a worker subject to the condition that he shall not join a union or shall relinquish trade union membership',
- '... cause the dismissal of or otherwise prejudice a worker by reason of union membership or because of participation in union activities outside working hours or, with the consent of the employer, within working hours', or
- '... promote the establishment of workers' organisations under the domination of employers or employers' organisations, or to support workers' organisations by financial or other means, with the object of placing such an organisation under the control of employers or employers' organisations'.

The Convention goes on to suggest that —

- 'Machinery appropriate to national conditions shall be established, wherever necessary, for the purpose of ensuring respect for the right to organise ...', and
- 'Measures appropriate to national conditions shall be taken, where necessary, to encourage and promote the full development and utilisation of machinery for voluntary negotiation between employers or employers' organisations and workers'

organisations, with a view to the regulation of terms and conditions of employment by collective agreement.'

According to this Convention, labour legislation, if it is to be acceptable, should protect employees from victimisation for trade union membership or activity, should create the machinery for the establishment of employee and employer organisations and should provide the machinery for collective bargaining; while the State should encourage this process as far as possible. It is interesting to note that the Convention mentions that negotiation should occur on a voluntary basis and that the machinery established should be '... appropriate to national conditions'. There is no prescription as to the type of machinery, nor that employers and employees should be obliged by law to bargain with each other.

The Declaration and Conventions outlined underscore the tenets of the labour relationship. A labour relations system or a labour relationship established without reference to these three documents is more than likely to be insufficient, if not outrightly inequitable.

CONSTITUTIONAL FRAMEWORK

Chapter Three of the Interim Constitution sets out certain fundamental rights of all persons and makes the content of this Chapter binding on 'all legislative and executive organs of State at all levels of government'. This means that no law may contain provisions which rob individuals of these fundamental rights, although the Constitution does provide that the rights may be limited by law provided that the limitation is '... reasonable and justifiable in an open and democratic society based on freedom and equality' and that the limitation does not '... negate the essential content of the right in question'. No rights are limitless, as the exercise of individual rights may impinge on the rights of others. Thus the law may limit these rights, but cannot remove them altogether.

Section 27 of this Chapter relates specifically to labour relations and provides that —

- 'Every person shall have the right to fair labour practices',
- 'Workers shall have the right to form and join trade unions, and employers shall have the right to form and join employers' organisations',
- 'Workers and employers shall have the right to organise and bargain collectively',
- 'Workers shall have the right to strike for the purpose of collective bargaining', and
- 'Employers' recourse to a lockout for the purpose of collective bargaining shall not be impaired'. (It is specifically stated, however, that this last right may be subject to limitations.)

Besides the section dealing specifically with labour relations, there are other sections in the 'Bill of Rights' which will affect labour relations and labour legislation. The following are examples.

- Clause 8, dealing with equality, provides that 'No person shall be unfairly discriminated against, directly or indirectly, ...'. However, the clause does state that this provision does not preclude '... measures designed to achieve the adequate protection and advancement of persons or groups or categories of persons disadvantaged by unfair discrimination ...'. Thus affirmative action initiatives will not be regarded as unfair discrimination.
- Clause 10 entitles every person to '... respect for and protection of his or her dignity'.
- Clause 13, dealing with the right to privacy, spells out the right of persons '... not to be subject to searches of his or her person, home or property, the seizure of private possessions or the violation of private communication'.
- Clause 15 details the right to freedom of speech and expression.
- Clause 16 grants every person the right '... to assemble and demonstrate with others peacefully and unarmed, and to present petitions'.
- Clause 26 provides that everyone '... shall have the right freely to engage in economic activity and to pursue a livelihood anywhere in the national territory'.
- Clause 29 entitles all persons to '... an environment which is not detrimental to his or her health and wellbeing'.

As a result of the entrenchment of these rights in the Constitution, all labour legislation (and, in fact, actions and processes in labour relations) should in future be evaluated in this context. Should a law or a provision in a law negate any of these rights, it may be challenged in the Constitutional Court.

GOVERNMENT POLICY AND LABOUR AFFAIRS

This and other chapters dealing with South African labour relations sufficiently illustrate the decisive impact that government policy has on industrial relations. Separatist policies, the exclusion of black African employees from the ambit of labour legislation from the start and attempts to establish alternative structures for Blacks led to a divided system. On the other hand, the government's reform initiatives of the late 1970s gave impetus to the 'new' system, which had been born of employee unrest at the beginning of that decade.

Since then other dramatic reforms, commencing with the unbanning of previously outlawed political parties at the beginning of 1990 and culminating in the elections of 1994, have significantly affected industrial relations policy and legislation.

Official Labour Relations Policy

The government's official labour relations policy has in the past been based broadly on the principles of voluntarism and maximum self-government by employers and employee bodies. Although mandatory elements were introduced into the 1988 Labour Relations Amendment Act, these were later withdrawn and, in general, the system still functions in terms of the following principles, as issued by the then Department of Manpower.

The Right to Work — *All workers in the Republic of South Africa have the right to provide for themselves and their families through taking part in the productive activities of the country. This right, however, places an obligation on everybody to make themselves available for work, to offer their talents and skills, and to accept such employment opportunities as are available.*

The Right to Fair Remuneration and Conditions of Service — *Every worker in South Africa has a right to fair remuneration in accordance with his skills and the effort and loyalty he devotes to his employer. This right includes a limitation on the hours he may work in a normal day and week, and entitles him to overtime pay, vacation and sick leave.*

The Right of Access to Training and Retraining — *It is the worker's right to receive training and retraining, so that he may increase his productivity and earning capacity. It is his right to be fully utilised in the work for which he has been trained. The State, employers and employees are co-partners in the national training effort.*

The Right to Organise and to Belong to a Trade Union — *All employees have the right at all times to organise themselves into trade unions, to register those unions and to utilise the bargaining and conciliation machinery created by legislation. In this way a labour climate is created which promotes favourable relationships between employer and employee.*

The Right to Negotiate and Bargain Collectively — *Collective bargaining and negotiation, in accordance with legally recognised rules, are the golden steps to the settlement of disputes between employers and employees. A spirit of mutual understanding and fairness is thereby engendered which individual or overhasty action cannot achieve.*

The Right to Protection of Safety and Health — *Certain occupations hold inherent dangers to safety and health, and it is the worker's right to work in the safest working environment that the employer can reasonably provide and to enjoy reasonable facilities for personal hygiene.*

The Right to Security Against Unemployment and the Payment of Amounts to Dependants of Deceased Contributors — *Certain workers are compelled to contribute to the Unemployment Insurance Fund and to receive compensation for loss of earnings arising from unemployment due to termination of employment, illness or maternity. Dependants of deceased contributors can also receive compensation. The rate of compensation is 45 percent of the insured's earnings as a contributor.*

The Right to Security in the Event of Injury on Duty — *Workers are entitled to compensation against loss of earnings due to accidents or industrial diseases contracted in the course of their employment, free medical treatment and lump sums or pensions for permanent disablement. In fatal cases pensions and an allowance for funeral expenses are paid to dependants. The onus rests on employers so submit the prescribed accident and medical reports, as well as medical accounts, to the Workmen's Compensation Commissioner.*

The Right to Job Security and Protection Against Unfair Labour Practices — *A worker's job security lies largely in his own hands, through the dedicated performance of his duties. But he also has a right to job security, which is entrenched in our labour legislation. Employers may not arbitrarily change labour practices and workers have a right to protection under the Act if their security is thus jeopardised.*

Official Policy of the New Department of Labour

In 1994 the Department of Labour broadly stated its policy in the following terms.

That it is the policy of the Department —

- *To, as far as possible, leave the regulation of labour relations to employers and employees*
- *To legislate only as regards minimum conditions of employment 'in circumstances under which they are not determined by statutorily recognised agreements or other statutory measures'*
- *To provide for procedures to regulate collective negotiation and the application of industrial democracy*
- *To provide for collective agreements and dispute settlement*
- *To ensure the negotiating balance between employers and employees, so as to ensure that the principle of supply and demand functions as far as possible*
- *To consult employers and employees wherever changes to legislation are considered*

This last the government does through NEDLAC.

THE NATIONAL ECONOMIC DEVELOPMENT & LABOUR COUNCIL

NEDLAC, formed early in 1995, arose from an amalgamation of the National Manpower Commission and the National Economic Forum. The founding document of this body cites its purpose as the bringing together of labour, business, government and development actors in order to 'ensure consensus on all matters relating to economic policy' and to 'consider all proposed labour legislation'. Thus the idea is that all relevant stakeholders should have some input into proposed policies and legislation before these are formally adopted by government agencies and Parliament.

NEDLAC consists of four chambers: the Labour Market Chamber, the Trade & Industry Chamber, the Public Finance & Monetary Policy Chamber and the Development Chamber. The three major union federations — COSATU, NACTU and FEDSAL — are represented in NEDLAC on a proportionate basis, while business is represented by Business South Africa (including the National African Federation of Chambers of Commerce, NAFCOC). Other roleplayers include government officials, politicians and community delegates representing, for example, women, civic organisations, rural bodies and disabled persons.

It is clearly the government's intention to consult on as inclusive a basis as possible before passing new labour legislation— although, eventually, Parliament will have the final say.

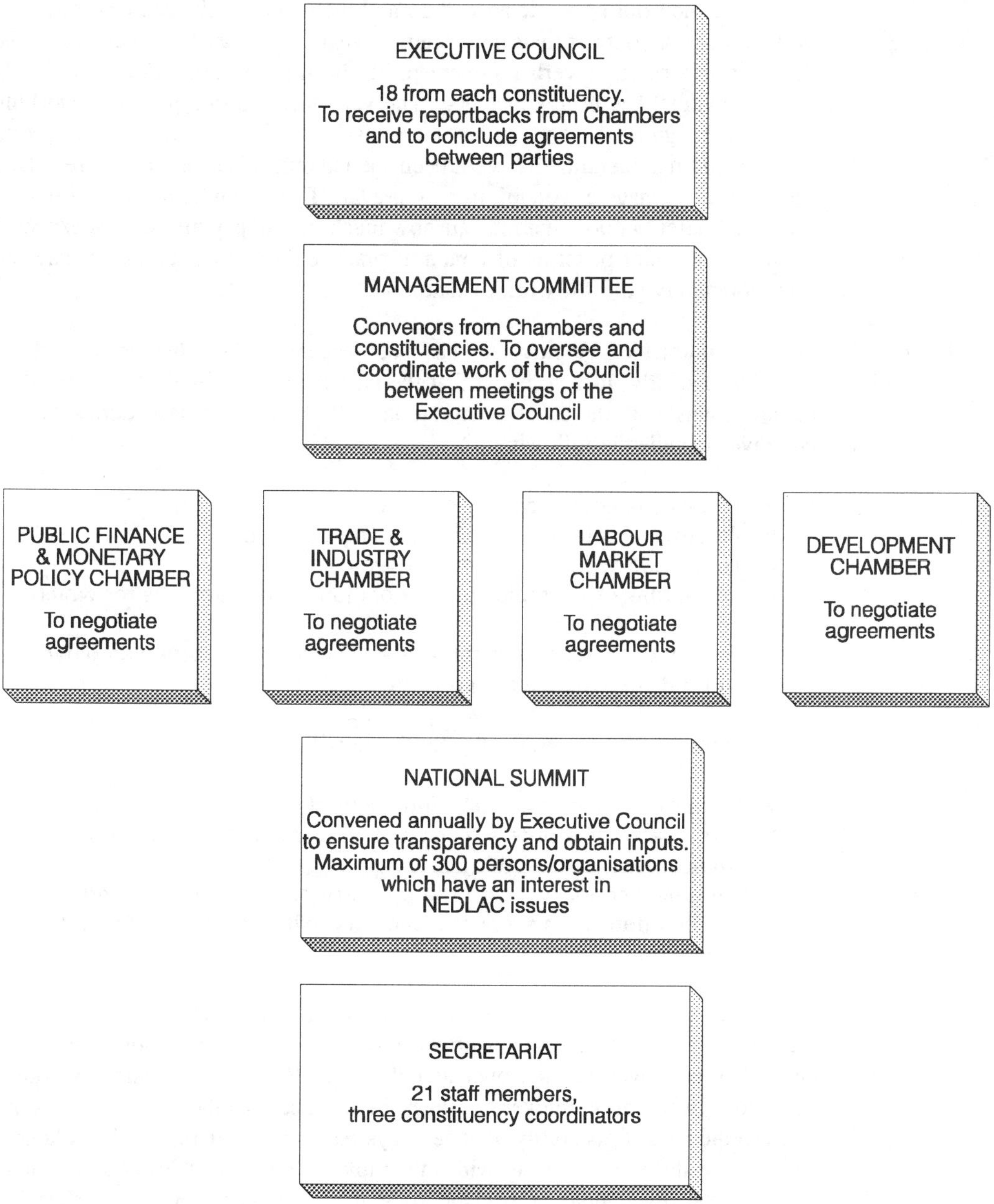

EXECUTIVE COUNCIL

18 from each constituency.
To receive reportbacks from Chambers
and to conclude agreements
between parties

MANAGEMENT COMMITTEE

Convenors from Chambers and
constituencies. To oversee and
coordinate work of the Council
between meetings of the
Executive Council

PUBLIC FINANCE
& MONETARY
POLICY CHAMBER

To negotiate
agreements

TRADE &
INDUSTRY
CHAMBER

To negotiate
agreements

LABOUR
MARKET
CHAMBER

To negotiate
agreements

DEVELOPMENT
CHAMBER

To negotiate
agreements

NATIONAL SUMMIT

Convened annually by Executive Council
to ensure transparency and obtain inputs.
Maximum of 300 persons/organisations
which have an interest in
NEDLAC issues

SECRETARIAT

21 staff members,
three constituency coordinators

Figure 7: NEDLAC STRUCTURE

THE CONTRACT OF EMPLOYMENT

The Law of Contract   The basis of the employment relationship is the contract of employment. A contract of employment comes into existence when both parties agree that the employee will enter into employment with the employer. This presupposes agreement on the **period** for which the employee will perform work for the employer, the **kind of work** he will do and the nature of the **remuneration** he will receive. A contract may be written, verbal, or it may be understood. The fact that no written or verbal agreement has been entered into does not signify that no contract has been concluded. The very fact that one person is working for another signifies that a contract does exist. Even if the period of work, kind of work and remuneration have not been spelled out, it is taken that there is tacit acceptance of whatever conditions may prevail. For example, an employer who hires a labourer but does not indicate how much he will pay him will be expected to remunerate him in terms of common practice — that is, he should pay the rates commonly paid for work of that kind.

Rights and Duties

Once a contract of employment has been entered into, whether in writing, verbally or tacitly, it is accepted that the parties have by implication agreed to certain rights and duties at common law. The common law duties of the employer include the following.

- To pay the employee
- To provide safe and healthy working conditions
- To provide work for the employee
- Not to make the employee do work junior to the status for which he was employed
- Not to contract the employee's services to another employer without the employee's consent

It is understood that, in return, the employee will:

- perform his work faithfully and diligently,
- obey reasonable orders given to him in the normal course of his employment,
- not deal dishonestly with the property of the employer, and
- not compete in his private capacity with the business of the employer.

The duties of one party constitute the rights of the other. Thus the employee has the right to remuneration, to perform work, not to be demoted, not to work for any other employer but his own and the right to safe and healthy working conditions, while the employer has the right to expect that the employee does his work to the best of his ability, that he obeys reasonable orders, that he is honest and that he does not compete with the employer's business. In addition, it is accepted that the employer has the right to select whomever he wishes for employment, that he can stipulate the method by which the work should be done and that he has the right to dismiss the employee. The employee implies by accepting the job that he is competent to perform it and that he has an obligation to work for the employer for a certain period. In most cases this period is indefinite and will be limited only by the termination or breach of the contract.

Private Contracts

The parties may decide to enter into a verbal or written contract which sets out the duties and rights of each in greater detail. A specific contract may contain any provision agreed to by the parties, but with the proviso that no conditions established may be illegal, immoral or contrary to public policy. A contract would be illegal if it contained a provision which would entail a breach of a statute or of the common law. Thus a contract in which the employee agrees to steal for an employer is illegal, as is an agreement on conditions of employment (including wages) which are less favourable than those prescribed in an industrial council agreement or a wage determination. An agreement to engage in prostitution would be both illegal and immoral. Contracts which contravene these rules will be declared null and void. Contracts are also voidable where the consent of one party has been improperly obtained by misrepresentation, coercion or undue influence, or where one of the parties does not have contractual capacity.

If a contract does not contain any of the irregularities described, it will be regarded as sacrosanct by the court. This is the case even if the position of one party to the contract might be unfavourable in relation to that of the other. It is regarded as basic to the judicial process that persons above the age of consent should be free to enter into any contract they please. As long as it can be established that both parties concluded the contract of their own free will and that it is not immoral, illegal or against public policy, the court will uphold the terms of the contract, whether it is grossly unfair to one party or not.

The Written Contract

Because implied and verbal contracts create uncertainty, it has become customary for new employees to receive a letter of appointment or to conclude a full contract of employment. The letter of appointment or contract will, at the very least, specify the type of work which the employee will be required to perform, the remuneration he will receive, the date of commencement of duties and, if it is a fixed term contract, the period for which he will be employed. A contract may also state the following.

- Hours of work, including maximum and minimum number of hours per week
- The duration of annual leave
- Provisions for sick leave
- Provision for compulsory contributions to a pension fund or medical scheme
- Notice periods on either side
- Intervals of payment
- Overtime provisions
- Restrictions on the employee
- A provision that the employee adheres to the rules of the company
- Any other matter agreed to by the parties

If a matter is not specifically dealt with in the contract of employment it is subject to common law or, where applicable, to the relevant statutory provisions. Thus, if a letter of appointment does not state the period of notice, it will be taken to be the period specified in the industrial council agreement or wage determination governing that industry or, in the absence of either, the period specified in the Basic Conditions of Employment Act. It is important to keep in mind that a statute which specifies more favourable conditions supersedes the common law contract, and that any determination in terms of the Labour Relations Act or the Wage Act — such as a gazetted industrial council agreement, a wage determination and a conciliation board agreement or arbitration award which has been made legally enforceable — supersedes the Basic Conditions of Employment Act, even where the provisions of such agreement contain terms which are less favourable than the terms of the Act. Furthermore, where there is no specific provision by statute and no common law precedent, the common law will refer to custom or established practice. Consequently, an employer who has for five years paid his employees on the 15th of each month and who unilaterally decides to pay them on the 25th may be held to be in breach of contract, even if there is no specific provision for payment on the 15th.

Termination of the Contract

A contract of service which does not specify otherwise can be terminated upon reasonable notice by either party, upon the consent of both parties, upon the death or incapacity of the employee or upon the insolvency of the employer.

A reasonable notice period is, at common law, taken to be a month in the case of a monthly-paid employee, a week for a weekly-paid employee, one day if the employee is paid on a daily basis and three months where there is a fixed-term contract. It is important that the common law does not oblige an employer or an employee to supply a reason for the dismissal or resignation, but merely to give reasonable notice of the intention to dismiss or resign. Furthermore, the common law provision for reasonable notice is waived if the continuance of the contract has been made impossible or intolerable, or if either side is in material breach of contract. A contract would have been breached if either side failed to perform the duties or to adhere to the obligations set out above. Thus an employee may terminate his contract without notice if the employer fails to pay him or demotes him, or if working conditions become unsafe. Equally, the employer would, at common law, be able to terminate the employee's service forthwith if he committed any of the serious transgressions listed in Chapter 10.

Common Law Remedies

A party which has suffered breach of contract may, at common law, sue for damages or specific performance of the contract. Damages will be awarded only for the actual material loss suffered. Thus, an employee who has been subjected to wrongful summary dismissal may claim only his wages in lieu of notice. Equally, an employee who has deserted his employer may be sued for the amount of pay which would have been due to him had he worked out his notice period. An order for specific performance means that the party who is in breach is ordered to reinstate the terms of the contract. Where an employer has wrongfully dismissed an employee without notice he may be ordered to reinstate that employee; but, once the employee returns, in terms of common law the employer may give him reasonable notice. Moreover, despite the Stag Packaging case (where it was ruled that an Order for specific performance could be applied to the contract of employment), the general opinion of the courts has been that such an Order is not suitable for the employment relationship.

It is obvious that, because common law allows for the lawful termination of a contract subject only to reasonable notice, the remedies of both parties to the employment relationship are, at common law, very limited. Since civil proceedings are both costly and lengthy, it is usually not worth the effort to obtain a remedy through the ordinary courts.

Common Law and the Employment Relationship

The common law treats the contract of employment by the same measures as any other contract. Yet, unlike other contracts (such as a lease or a hire purchase agreement), the contract of employment leads to the establishment of a special relationship. Because in most instances no date of termination is established beforehand in the contract of employment it is expected that, if each party performs his duty, the term of contract will be indefinite. It follows that, if termination of contract occurs, there should be a sound reason for such termination. As Brassey states: 'Ordinarily, what they expect of their relationship, whatever the terms of the contract, is that it will continue until one or other of them has some good reason for terminating it'. Moreover, the employment relationship is more often than not an unequal relationship in which the employer holds more power than the employee. In these circumstances it can

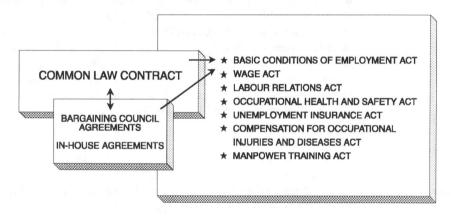

Figure 8: THE LEGAL REGULATION OF WORK RELATIONS

be construed that an employee might enter into a contract which will lead to his exploitation. This problem is not addressed by common law; nor is the fact that breach of an employment contract does not cause only material damage. An employee who is dismissed may suffer loss of future prospects, loss of reputation or status and actual emotional damage.

Finally, there is the problem that the contract of employment relates only to the individual employment relationship. It has been held that the individual employment relationship differs from the collective relationship between a group of employees and a single employer, and that a different measure should apply.

All the above considerations have led to the establishment of labour statutes intended, in the main, to safeguard the employee against blatant exploitation by the employer, to provide for a more equal distribution of power between employer and employee, to guard against unreasonable behaviour by either party and to allow for the establishment of collective relationships. As illustrated in Figure 8 the employment relationship is, therefore, governed not only by the contract of employment but also by the various labour statutes which, where they refer to similar matters, may supersede the conditions of the contract.

THE LABOUR RELATIONS ACT, 1995

Until very recently the framework for the practice of industrial relations in South Africa was provided by the Labour Relations Act, no. 28 of 1956, and numerous subsequent amendments, the most significant being the Labour Relations Amendment Act of 1979. The stated objectives of the 1956 Act were the 'prevention and settlement of disputes between employers and employees' and provision for 'the regulation of terms and conditions of employment by agreement and arbitration'.

The 1956 Act has now been replaced by an entirely new Act known as the Labour Relations Act of 1995. Like the Labour Relations Act of 1956, the new Act provides for the registration of trade unions and employers' associations and for the establishment of centralised bargaining bodies (previously known as industrial councils and now to be called bargaining councils). It provides also for dispute settlement procedures and facilities, for certain procedures to be followed in order to engage in a legal strike or lockout, for the declaration of unfair labour practice disputes and for certain disputes to be heard by the Labour Court. However, the 1995 Act states that the overall purpose of the legislation is the advancement of '... economic development, social justice, labour peace and the democratisation of the workplace'. This it intends to achieve via the following objectives.

- To give effect to and to regulate the fundamental rights contained in Section 27 of the Constitution
- To give effect to the duties of the Republic as a member state of the International Labour Organisation
- To provide a framework in which employees and their unions, employers and employer associations can —
  - bargain collectively to determine wages, terms and conditions of employment and other matters of mutual interest, and
  - formulate industry policy
- To promote —
  - orderly collective bargaining,
  - collective bargaining at sectoral level,
  - workers' participation and decisionmaking at the workplace and
  - the effective resolution of disputes

Furthermore, the Act replaces the old conciliation boards with a permanent Commission for Conciliation, Mediation & Arbitration; it rules out some of the processes of the old Industrial Court (now to be known as the Labour Court); and it makes an entirely new provision for the establishment of workplace forums. Unfair dismissals, as opposed to other unfair labour practices, are codified and most will be dealt with by the Commission rather than by the Labour Court.

It is apparent that, by the passage of the Act within the context of the new sociopolitical dispensation, the government is attempting to give further protection to employees and unions (*cf.* new trade union rights to access, etc.) and yet to maintain, as far as possible, the principles of voluntarism and free collective bargaining. (The Act contains no compulsion to bargain, but does provide that disputes relating to a refusal to bargain should first be submitted to advisory arbitration.) On the whole, however, the Act does reveal greater government interference in the relationship, best exemplified by the compulsion to form workplace forums upon the request of a majority union, the onus to engage in consultation and co-decisionmaking with workplace forums on certain prescribed matters and the onus to disclose information required for the purpose of collective bargaining, for shop stewards to perform their functions effectively and for workplace representatives to engage in effective consultation and co-decisionmaking. Obviously the legislators believe that, by promoting this kind of cooperation and information sharing, they will promote the maintenance of industrial peace. It remains to be seen whether these expectations will be realised within the context of South Africa's labour relations history and the particular nature of its industrial relations system.

Besides the compulsions mentioned above, other existing mandatory elements — such as the prohibition on interference with the freedom of association, the sanction on victimisation, the prohibition on strike action in essential services and the compulsion to follow prescribed procedures in the event of a strike or lockout — remain.

Finally, one of the most significant new provisions in the 1995 Act is that which protects employees engaged in a legal strike from dismissal by the employer, thus effectively granting the right to strike. Certain new provisions regarding the employment of scabs and the right to picket are also included. Although controversial, the insertion of these provisions constitutes a significant victory for the unions which have long been engaged in a battle to achieve these rights.

Exclusions Certain categories of employees — and employers, for that matter — were previously excluded from the ambit of the Labour Relations Act. The 1956 Act did not until very recently apply to agricultural workers or domestic servants, nor did it apply to students whose employment at a place of business or at an educational institution was part of their education or training. Persons working without payment for a charitable institution and State employees were also excluded. 'State', in this sense, was taken to refer only to central State departments, and not to provincially administered bodies or to corporations such as the SABC. In terms of the 1988 amendments to the Labour Relations Act, persons employed in a teaching capacity at universities, technikons, colleges, schools or other educational institutions which were wholly or partly funded by the State were also excluded from the Act. The exclusion of certain employees from the ambit of the Labour Relations Act was a hotly debated issue, particularly among unionists who maintained that all employees should have access to the bargaining and dispute settlement mechanisms of the Labour Relations Act.

In 1993 the government passed the Agricultural Labour Act, which effectively incorporated agricultural employees under the Labour Relations Act but provided for certain particular processes and institutions in this sector. The same was done for the education sector by the Education Labour Relations Act of 1993, and for the public sector by the Public Service Labour Relations Act of 1994. The Labour Relations Act of 1995 repeals all these Acts except Chapter Two of the Agricultural Labour Act of 1993. Since that chapter deals with basic conditions of employment, all labour relations in the agricultural sector are now covered by the Labour Relations Act of 1995.

All previous exclusions of employees from the ambit of the Labour Relations Act have been removed, but the national Defence Force, the National Intelligence Agency and the South African Secret Service are now specifically excluded. This brings an entirely new dimension to the Labour Relations Act as the public service, the South African Police, the nursing and teaching professions, as well as agricultural and domestic employees now have virtually the same rights as other employees. However, in certain instances, specific procedures are established for these sectors.

Status of the Act In the case of any conflict between the provisions of the Labour Relations Act and any other Act (except the Constitution), priority will be given to the provisions of this Act. Also, the Labour Relations Act automatically supersedes the Basic Conditions of Employment Act. This is effected by the exclusion from the latter Act of the Labour Relations Act and 'any matter regulated thereunder'. This exclusion explains why there are industrial council (now bargaining council) agreements which contain conditions of employment less favourable than those provided for in the Basic Conditions of Employment Act.

MAJOR PROVISIONS

The major provisions of the Labour Relations Act of 1995 are outlined hereunder, in the order in which they appear in the Act. Since many of the provisions are covered in chapters in this book which relate specifically to their implementation in practice, all sections will not be discussed in equal detail.

Chapter One: Purpose, Application and Interpretation The purpose of the legislation, as stated in the Act, has already been outlined in a previous section. However, with a view to understanding the new directions taken by the Labour Relations Act of 1995, it is useful to look at the brief given to the task group responsible for drafting the new Act. This brief stipulated that proposed legislation should:

- give effect to government policy as reflected in the RDP;
- give effect, *inter alia*, to Conventions nos. 87, 98 and 111 (dealing with discrimination) of the International Labour Organisation and the outcome of the ILO's Factfinding and Conciliation Commission;
- comply with the Constitution;
- be explicit and, where possible, spell out the rights and obligations of workers, trade unions, employers and employers'

associations so as to avoid a case-by-case determination of what constitutes an unfair labour practice;

- recognise fundamental organisational rights of trade unions;
- provide a simple procedure for the registration of trade unions and employers' associations, and for regulating certain aspects of these organisations in order to ensure democracy and proper financial control;
- promote and facilitate collective bargaining, both at the workplace and at industry level;
- provide simple procedures for the resolution of disputes by statutory conciliation, mediation and arbitration;
- provide for the licensing of independent alternative dispute resolution services;
- provide for a system of labour courts to determine disputes of right in a manner which would be accessible, speedy and inexpensive and where there would be only one level of appeal;
- entrench the Constitutional right to strike, subject to limitations which are reasonable and justifiable in an open and democratic society based on the values of freedom and equality;
- regulate lockouts in a similar manner; and
- decriminalise labour legislation.

A study of the particular provisions of the Act will reveal that all the above objectives have, wholly or partially, been met. Nevertheless it remains to be seen whether, in bringing out these changes, the legislators have achieved their overall purpose of establishing a more orderly collective bargaining system, facilitating the resolution of disputes, maintaining labour peace and promoting greater cooperation at the place of work (see previous section).

The extended sphere of application of the Act has also been discussed in a previous section. As mentioned there, the more inclusive approach greatly changes the ambit of labour relations in this country and heavily involves the State as an employer subject to the same provisions as all other employers.

The last part of this very short first Chapter deals with the bases for any interpretation of the Act. This specifies that all interpretations should have a view to the main objectives of the Act, the relevant provisions of the Constitution and the question of conformity with the Republic's obligations in public international law.

Chapter Two: Freedom of Association and General Protection

The sections contained in this Chapter grant employees the right to participate in the formation of a union or federation and, subject to the constitution of that union, to join any union. Union members have the right to take part in the lawful activities of that union, to participate in the election of office bearers, officials and shop stewards and, subject to the terms of a collective agreement, to stand for election to any of the above positions and, if elected, to hold office or to carry out the functions of a shop steward (trade union representative) in terms of the Act or a collective agreement. The same provisions apply to members of a union which forms part of a federation in respect of the election of office bearers and officials to that federation. The protection of the right to freedom of association is carried further by the provision that nobody may compel or threaten to compel an employee to become or not to become a member of a union or workplace forum or to relinquish membership of a union or workplace forum. Also, nobody may prohibit an employee or a prospective employee from exercising any rights or from participating in any activities to which he is entitled in terms of the Act.

Freedom from victimisation is ensured by the clause which stipulates that no one may prejudice an employee because of his previous, existing or prospective membership of a union or workplace forum, for his participation in the establishment of a union, federation or workplace forum, for his omission or failure to do anything which the employer by law may not compel or allow him to do, for the publicising of information which an employee may lawfully give to another person, for the employee's assertion of any rights in terms of the Act or for his participation in any activities of the Act. Furthermore, no one may offer or promise an employee favourable treatment if he waives any rights granted to him or desists from any activities in terms of the Act.

Contracts which directly or indirectly interfere with the freedom of association are automatically void, unless the Act itself allows for the establishment of such a contract. (The latter is very important as it allows a loophole for the conclusion of closed shop agreements — see relevant section.)

In the remainder of this Chapter, employers are granted essentially the same rights in respect of freedom of association and freedom from victimisation. Trade unions and employers' associations likewise have the right to establish independently constituted bodies, to organise their own administration and activities, to take part in the establishment of federations and to affiliate to other bodies, both locally and internationally.

With regard to an allegation regarding victimisation or interference with the freedom of association, the complainant merely has to prove that he has been compelled, threatened, prohibited or detrimentally affected in any manner and it is then up to the defendant to prove that his action was not contrary to any of the provisions of the Act.

Disputes arising from any allegations regarding victimisation or interference with the freedom of association may first be referred for mediation to the Commission for Conciliation, Mediation & Arbitration or to a bargaining council which has jurisdiction, and thereafter, should the dispute not be resolved, to the Labour Court for a final determination.

The freedom of association and the freedom from victimisation have always been protected by South African labour legislation (bearing in mind that, between 1924 and 1979, a large section of the population was excluded from such legislation). The new Labour Relations Act, however, emphasises the importance of these rights by placing them at the commencement of the Act. It also expands on these rights by including, in specific terms, the right to join and form trade unions, employers' organisations and federations, and the right of unions to establish themselves independently and to affiliate with other bodies.

Chapter Three:
Collective
Bargaining

Part A: Organisational Rights

This part accords to unions which are 'sufficiently representative' certain rights, such as the right to access, to hold meetings with employees outside working hours, to conduct an election at the workplace and to be granted stop order facilities. A majority union, or two or more unions which together represent a majority of employees at the workplace, may also appoint shop stewards, may be given information necessary for the purpose of representation or collective bargaining and, in consultation with the employer, establish thresholds for representivity. Registered unions which are party to a bargaining council will automatically have the right to access and to demand stop order facilities at all workplaces within the registered scope of the council, regardless of the union's representivity at that particular workplace. A bargaining council may also establish thresholds of representivity.

The Act further sets out procedures for the exercise of these rights and for the processing of disputes in this respect. Disputes involving organisational rights may (except for disputes regarding representivity) be submitted for conciliation to the Commission for Conciliation, Mediation & Arbitration and thereafter to arbitration by the Commission.

Further details regarding organisational rights, the exercise of these rights and the processing of disputes may be obtained from Chapters 9 and 14.

Most of the rights accorded to unions in this section were previously subject to negotiation during the recognition process. The new Act provides a large degree of direction which should greatly simplify and facilitate this process.

Part B: Collective Agreements

This section deals with the enforceability of collective agreements, provides for agency shop and closed shop agreements and outlines disputes procedures in respect of agreements.

For the first time the Labour Relations Act makes all collective agreements, whether concluded at centralised or decentralised level, enforceable in terms of the Act. It further makes agreements relating to substantive issues and to conduct at the workplace applicable to all members of unions as well as employers who are party to such collective agreements, as well as to members of the bargaining unit and to persons identified in or connected with the agreement. Finally, collective agreements will in future be binding on all party members for the duration of the agreement, regardless of whether or not such party remains a member of the union or employers' association. A collective agreement automatically changes the employment contract of an employee covered by such agreement. Unless otherwise specified, an agreement may be terminated by giving the required notice.

Procedures for settlement of disputes regarding the interpretation or application of a collective agreement must be specified in such agreement and must provide for conciliation as a first resort and thereafter for arbitration. (For further details regarding the implementation of collective agreements and the dispute settlement procedure to be followed, see Chapters 9 and 14.)

An entirely new development is the provision for the establishment of an agency shop, whereby non-members who would qualify for union membership are obliged to pay an amount equal to or less than the prescribed union dues into a fund to be administered by the representative union and to be used to advance the socioeconomic interests of employees. The agency shop agreement differs from a closed shop agreement in that there is no onus on non-members to join the representative union, but at the same time it addresses the oft-voiced union complaint regarding 'free riders' who benefit from union agreements without paying union dues (see Chapter 9).

In the light of the above, it is surprising that the Act provides also for the conclusion of closed shop agreements, particularly since the original Draft Bill suggested that only existent statutory closed shops should be allowed to remain until such time as the new Constitution is finalised. Extensive arrangements for closed shops are now outlined in the Act (see Chapter 9). The entire issue of the closed shop is extremely controversial. Despite the *caveat* provided in the Act, the closed shop directly contradicts the freedom of association principle as contained in the Bill of Rights. Consequently, it appears highly likely that this provision may, in future, be challenged in the Constitutional Court.

Part C: Bargaining Councils

Industrial councils will now be called bargaining councils but will, essentially, perform the same functions as before (see Chapter 9). However, it is foreseen that these bodies will in future play a greater role in shaping policy and legislation for their particular industries, as the Act specifically allows them to present to NEDLAC or 'any other appropriate forum' proposals for policies and legislation affecting their industries. Bargaining councils will also be able to determine which additional matters should be dealt with by workplace forums and which matters are not to be regarded as issues in dispute for the purposes of a strike or lockout. Bargaining councils may register by sector or area. As before, an application for registration still has to be published in the *Gazette* to allow for objections. Not only the Registrar but also NEDLAC will play a role in deciding whether or not a bargaining council should be registered.

The constitution of a bargaining council has to make provision for representation by small to medium enterprises and for the procedure to be used in applying for exemptions from collective agreements. Such exemptions must be undertaken by an independent body, and not by the bargaining councils themselves.

The functions of bargaining councils are, briefly, as follows.

- To conclude collective agreements
- To enforce such agreements
- To prevent and settle labour disputes
- To establish and administer funds for the settlement of disputes
- To promote and institute training and education programmes
- To establish and administer pension, provident, medical aid, sick pay, leave, unemployment and training schemes or funds, or any similar schemes or funds, for the benefit of one or more of the parties to the council
- To develop proposals as regards policy and legislation which may affect their sector or area for submission to NEDLAC or any other relevant forum
- To determine by collective agreement which matters should not, for the purposes of a strike or a lockout, constitute an issue in dispute
- To delegate to workplace forums additional matters for consultation

Part D: Public Service Bargaining Councils

The Act has already provided, in Part C, that the State may be a party to a bargaining council should it be an employer in a sector or area in respect of which a council is being established. Part D provides for a Coordinating Public Service Bargaining Council to cover the public service as a whole, and further outlines particular provisions for bargaining councils in this sector.

Part E: Statutory Councils

This is an entirely new provision which allows for the establishment of what may be termed 'trainee' bargaining councils. In terms of this section, any employers' association or any union which represents at least thirty percent of the employers or employees in a sector or area may apply for the establishment of a statutory council. The Registrar will then issue an invitation to all registered employers' organisations and registered unions in that particular sector or area to attend a meeting the purpose of which is to conclude an agreement regarding the parties to and the establishment of a statutory council. Should no such agreement be reached, the Commission for Conciliation, Mediation & Arbitration will attempt to facilitate the process. However, if the Commissioner still fails to bring about an agreement as to who should constitute the parties, the Minister must allow any applicant and any other registered union or employers' organisation to become party to the council.

Statutory councils may also apply to have their agreements regarding training and education schemes, pension, provident, unemployment and other funds promulgated as determinations in terms of the Wage Act. The Minister may levy all employers and employees within the registered scope of a statutory council in order to cover the cost of such council.

The provisions outlined above thus provide for an essentially unrepresentative body to set up schemes and funds and to engage in dispute resolution for an entire sector or area.

Part F: General Provisions Regarding Councils

This part stipulates firstly that, in assessing the representativeness of a council, the Registrar must take the council as representing an entire sector or area, irrespective of whether the union or employers' association has no members in a particular part of that area (see Chapter 9).

Other provisions include an annual review of representativeness, a detailed procedure for the settlement of disputes by bargaining councils and the stipulation that bargaining councils must either become accredited as mediators and arbitrators or appoint an accredited agency to fulfil these functions (see Chapter 15). Section 56 allows a union or employers' association which has been refused membership by a council to appeal to the Labour Court, and grants the Court the power to admit such union or employers' association as a party to the council and, if necessary, to amend the council's constitution accordingly.

A final section in this part of the Chapter provides that, unless stipulated otherwise, any dispute regarding the interpretation of organisational rights and the sections relating to bargaining and statutory councils should be referred firstly to the Commission for Conciliation, Mediation & Arbitration and, failing settlement, to the Labour Court.

Chapter Four:
Strikes and
Lockouts

Strikes and lockouts are circumscribed in the Definitions (see discussion relating to this section). Chapter Four provides firstly that, subject to certain procedures and time limits (see Chapter 14), every employee has the right to strike and every employer the right to lock out. An employer may not dismiss employees engaged in a legal strike, but may dismiss individual employees for reasons of misconduct or operational requirements. (For a full discussion of these aspects, see Chapter 14.)

Statutory procedures do not have to be followed if the strike or lockout is in reaction to an unprocedural strike or lockout, if the employer has failed to comply with a request to reinstate terms and conditions of employment which had been unilaterally changed by him or if the parties have followed a disputes procedure contained in a collective agreement or a council constitution. A strike or lockout regarding the refusal to bargain may not be undertaken before the dispute has been submitted to advisory arbitration. (For a definition of the refusal to bargain, see Chapter 9.)

Strikes or lockouts are not allowed where the party is subject to a collective agreement which prohibits a strike or lockout over the issue in dispute or when the issue may be submitted to arbitration or the Labour Court, or where the issue is the subject of an arbitration award or other determination. Persons involved in essential or maintenance services are prohibited from engaging in a strike or lockout. Strikes which conform with the provisions of the Act are regarded as 'protected' strikes, and the protection accorded to such strikers is not extended to employees who engage in an unprocedural or spontaneous strike, although certain provisions are also outlined for such strikes.

Secondary or 'sympathy' strikes are allowed subject to certain conditions, as is the formation of picket lines. (For further details, see Chapter 14.)

This chapter of the Act further deals with the designation of essential and maintenance services and the conditions and procedures pertaining to such services, as well as with the allowance for protest action to protect the socioeconomic interests of employees and the use of scab labour during strike action (see Chapter 14). In this respect it is noteworthy that an employer may not employ substitute labour if the whole or part of his service has been designated as a maintenance service; nor may he use scab labour to perform the work of any employee who has been locked out, unless the lockout was a reaction to a strike.

Chapter Six of the Act stipulates that unions and employers' associations have to include in their constitutions a provision relating to the holding of strike ballots. However, Chapter Four explicitly states that failure to hold such ballot should not give rise to litigation regarding the legality of the strike or lockout or the protection afforded under the Act (see Chapter 14).

Chapter Five:
Workplace
Forums

The most innovative — and perhaps the most controversial — aspects of the Labour Relations Act of 1995 are contained in this chapter, which provides for the establishment of workplace forums, upon the request of a majority union or unions, in any workplace employing more than 100 persons (see Chapter 10). There is, however, some confusion as regards the exact nature of the 'workplace', since the definition as contained in the Act can be very widely or very narrowly interpreted. In terms of this definition, a 'workplace' is, in areas other than the public service, '... *the place or places where the employees of an employer work*'. To this is added the provision that, where '... *an employer conducts two or more operations which are independent by reason of their size, function or organisation the place or places where employees work in connection with each independent operation constitutes the workplace for that operation*'. The problem will lie firstly in the definition of 'operation', and secondly in the criteria to be applied in establishing whether an operation is independent or not (see Chapter 10).

Workplace forums are intended to promote the interests of *all* employees at the workplace, to increase the efficiency of the workplace, to engage in consultation on certain matters stipulated in the Act and in joint decisionmaking on issues such as disciplinary codes and procedures, rules regarding conduct and behaviour, measures to protect individuals against discrimination and changes to the rules applicable to social benefits.

The forums must be representative of all employees, with 'employee' being defined in this Chapter as *'any person employed in a workplace'* except a 'senior managerial employee' whose status and contract of service grant him the authority to represent the employer in interactions with the workplace forum or, on behalf of the employer, to determine policy or make decisions which might conflict with the representation of workers at the place of work.

As in the case of collective bargaining, workplace forums are entitled to all relevant information necessary to perform their functions effectively, excluding information which is legally privileged, information which cannot be made public in terms of a court order, information which is confidential and, if publicised, could cause substantial damage to the employer and information of a confidential nature regarding an employee (unless such employee agrees to the information being made public). An onus is also placed on the employer to report annually to the workplace forum on such matters as the financial and employment situation of the organisation, overall achievements, future plans and prospects.

(A detailed account of the establishment and functioning of workplace forums, as well as a discussion as to their efficacy, is provided in Chapter 10.)

Disputes regarding the interpretation of the provisions relating to workplace forums will, unless a collective agreement determines otherwise, be referred for mediation to the Commission and, should mediation fail, to arbitration.

**Chapter Six:
Unions and
Employers'
Associations**

Part A: Registration and Regulation

A new, simplified procedure, which makes registration of unions and employers' associations meeting the stipulated requirements almost automatic and obviates the need to call for objections, as was the case previously, is provided for in this part of the Act. (See Chapter 7 for a detailed discussion of the relevant provisions.)

It should be noted that all rights in terms of the Labour Relations Act are granted only to *registered* unions and employers' associations. It is to be inferred that a body which remains unregistered will have no status within the statutory labour relations system.

Part B: Regulation of Federations of Unions or Employers' Associations

For the first time federations too are required to furnish the Registrar with regular information regarding their membership, the names and addresses of their office bearers, their constitutions and their addresses in the Republic.

Parts C and D: Labour Relations Registrar and Appeals against Decisions of the Registrar

These parts relate to the appointment of a Registrar by the Minister. There is an onus on the Registrar to maintain up-to-date records relating to unions, employers' associations and federations, and to allow the public access to such records.

Any party aggrieved by a decision of the Registrar may request a written explanation as to the reasons for such decision and/or may, within sixty days of the decision or of the reasons furnished, appeal to the Labour Court against such decision.

Chapter Seven: Dispute Settlement

Part A: Commission for Conciliation, Mediation & Arbitration (CCMA)

In an entirely new development, this part makes provision for the appointment of a Commission which is to be independent of the State and of any political party, union, employers' association or federation of unions or employers' associations, and which will have jurisdiction in all the provinces to perform the functions outlined hereunder.

The Commission should —

- attempt to settle, by conciliation, any dispute referred to it in terms of the Act;
- where conciliation has not achieved the desired agreement, conduct arbitration should the Act require such or should any of the parties to a dispute within the jurisdiction of the Labour Court request that the Commission conduct such arbitration;
- provide assistance with the establishment of workplace forums; and
- compile and publish information and statistics regarding its activities.

Other than the above, the Commission *may* also —

- if so requested, advise a party to a dispute on the procedures to be followed in terms of the Act;
- if so requested, assist a party to a dispute in obtaining legal advice and/or representation;
- offer to settle a dispute which was not referred to it;
- accredit councils or private agencies;
- subsidise accredited councils and agencies;
- conduct, oversee or scrutinise an election by ballot for a registered union or employers' association, or supervise or check such ballot if requested to do so by the union or employers' association;

- publish guidelines as to any matter regulated by the Labour Relations Act; and
- conduct and publish research into matters relevant to its functions.

Furthermore the Commission may, if so requested by a registered union, employers' association or federation of unions or employers' associations, provide advice and training regarding any matter related to the main objectives of the Act, including (but not limited to) the following.

- The establishment of collective bargaining structures
- The design, establishment and election of workplace forums and the provision of mechanisms to resolve deadlock
- The functioning of workplace forums
- The prevention and settlement of disputes and employee grievances
- Disciplinary procedures
- Procedures relating to dismissal
- The process relating to workplace restructuring
- Programmes relating to affirmative action, equal opportunity and sexual harassment at the workplace

The Commission must also perform any other duties assigned to it, and may perform any other function assigned by any other law.

Detailed information regarding the composition, appointment and functioning of the Commission is provided in Chapter 14.

Since most disputes should be processed for conciliation or mediation through either the Commission or a bargaining council, these bodies will serve as catalysts for labour relations conflicts. Furthermore the Commission is obliged, if so requested or determined, to arbitrate in numerous disputes and particularly on unfair dismissals. Much of the previous burden of the Industrial Court will therefore devolve upon the Commission.

Part B: Accreditation and Subsidisation of Councils and Private Agencies

The provisions contained in this part empower the Commission to accredit and subsidise bargaining councils and private agencies as mediators and arbitrators, and further set out the conditions and procedures for such accreditation (see Chapter 14).

Part C: Dispute Settlement under the Auspices of the Commission

Detailed procedures for mediation and arbitration of different types of dispute have been outlined in this part of the Act, which also describes the power of Commissioners in arbitration proceedings and the effect of arbitration awards, and allows for a review by the Labour Court of an arbitration award where it is alleged that the arbitrator has been guilty of corruption or misconduct, that he has committed a gross irregularity, that he has exceeded his terms of reference or that an award was improperly obtained. (For further details on these aspects, see Chapter 14.)

Part D: Labour Court

To replace the Industrial Court, the Act makes provision for a Labour Court to be constituted as a court of law. It will also be a court of record and will, as regards matters within its jurisdiction, have the same powers and status as a provincial division of the Supreme Court.

The Labour Court will be presided over by a Judge President, a Deputy Judge President and as many judges as the State President, on the advice of NEDLAC and in consultation with the Minister of Justice and the Judge President, may decide.

The Labour Court may make any appropriate order, including the following.

- The granting of urgent interim relief
- The granting of an interdict
- An order determining a certain action which, when executed, will correct an injustice and give effect to the primary objectives of the Act
- A declaratory order
- A compensatory award
- An order for damages relating to any circumstance covered by the Act
- An order as to costs

Moreover, the Court may —

- order adherence to any provision of the Act;
- declare any arbitration award or any settlement (except a collective agreement) to be an Order of the Court;
- request the Commission to conduct an investigation which will assist the Court or to report to the Court;
- determine a dispute between a registered union and a registered employers' association regarding the constitution of one of the parties;
- condone (subject to the conditions of the Act) the late filing of documents or a late referral of a dispute;
- review, on legally justifiable grounds, any actions by a person or body where such actions are provided for in the Act;
- review any decision or action by the State in its capacity as an employer; and
- hear and determine appeals brought under the Occupational Health & Safety Act.

(Further details regarding the rules, constitution and functioning of the Labour Court are provided in Chapter 14.)

Part E: Labour Appeal Court

The two-tier appeal procedure, to the Labour Appeal Court and to the Appellate Division of the Supreme Court, has been removed and the Act now provides only for appeals to the Labour Appeal Court. This Court is constituted as a court of law and equity. It too will be a court of record and, in relation to matters within its jurisdiction, will have the same status as the Appellate Division of the Supreme Court.

For further details regarding the constitution and function of the Labour Appeal Court, see Chapter 14.

Chapter Eight: Unfair Dismissal

In this chapter, unfair dismissals have been codified and separated from other unfair labour practices, as have the processes to be employed as regards the settlement of disputes centring in such dismissals.

The chapter commences by providing that every employee has the right not to be unfairly dismissed, and continues to define dismissal in the following terms.

- Termination of contract, with or without notice
- Refusal to renew (or the offer to renew under less favourable conditions) a fixed-term contract where the employee could reasonably expect the contract to be renewed on the same terms and conditions as before
- Refusal to allow an employee who has been on maternity leave, or who has been absent for four weeks before and eight weeks after her confinement, to resume her duties
- Selective re-employment of employees who were dismissed for the same or similar reasons
- Constructive dismissal of an employee by making the continuation of his employment intolerable

Dismissals will be unfair if the employer fails to prove that there is a fair reason for the dismissal related either to the employee's conduct, capacity or competence or to the operational requirements of the employer, and that the dismissal was effected in terms of a fair procedure.

Any agency charged with deciding whether a dismissal was fair will be required to take into account the Code of Good Practice appended in the Schedules. This Code contains detailed guidelines for the different types of dismissal (see *Schedules* below, and Chapter 10).

Certain dismissals will be regarded as automatically unfair. These include the dismissal of an employee for any of the following reasons.

- Victimisation or interference with the freedom of association
- The employee took part in, supported or declared his intention to participate in a strike or protest action in terms of the Act.
- He refused or declared his intention to refuse to perform work normally done by an employee who is engaged in a legal strike or who has been locked out by the employer (except where such work is necessary to prevent the endangering of the life, health or safety of individuals).
- The employer wanted to oblige the employee to comply with a demand related to any matter of mutual interest.
- The employee took steps or declared his intention to take steps against the employer by exercising any rights or engaging in any action to which he is entitled in terms of the Act.
- The employee is pregnant or intends to become pregnant (or any other reason related to her pregnancy).

- The employer directly or indirectly discriminated unfairly against the employee on any arbitrary ground, including (but not limited to) race, gender, sex, ethnic or social origin, colour, sexual orientation, age, disability, religion, conscience, faith, political opinion, culture, language, marital status or family responsibility.

However, despite the above, the Act states that a dismissal which appears discriminatory can be fair if it is based on the inherent requirements of a particular job or if the employee has reached the stipulated retirement age for that position.

Chapter Eight of the Act goes on to set out procedures to be followed in disputes surrounding dismissals, and outlines the legal remedies to be applied by arbitrators or the Labour Court (see Chapters 10 and 14). It also outlines procedures for retrenchment and redundancies (see Chapter 10) and stipulates that retrenchment pay of at least one week's wages per year of service is obligatory. Furthermore, where a contract of service is transferred as a going concern (or as part of one) to another employer, the rights and duties of employees and the employer are automatically transferred to the new owner — except where the first employer was declared insolvent, in which case the contracts are automatically transferred but the rights and duties remain those of the employees and the ex-employer. (For further details, see Chapter 10.)

Chapter Nine: General Provisions

The most important provisions in this chapter of the Labour Relations Act are those pertaining to the following.

Labour Brokers

Labour brokers (now called temporary employment services) are defined as persons who, for reward, provide persons to perform work for a client where such persons are remunerated by the labour broker. In terms of the Act the persons so remunerated are regarded as employees of the labour broker, unless such persons are independent contractors. Labour brokers and their clients are jointly and severally liable if the labour broker fails to abide by a substantive agreement concluded by a bargaining council, a binding arbitration award related to terms and conditions of service, the Basic Conditions of Employment Act or a determination in terms of the Wage Act.

Two or more bargaining councils can agree that a labour broker, someone in the service of a labour broker and the client of such labour broker will be covered by an agreement concluded by one of the bargaining councils or within the combined registered scope of such bargaining councils, provided that the agreement has been extended to non-parties.

Confidentiality

Any person who makes public any information regarding the financial and business affairs of any other person is guilty of an offence and subject to a maximum fine of R1 000, or a sentence to be determined by the Court, where such information has been obtained in any capacity by or on behalf of a council, an independent body intended to grant exemptions from collective agreements, the Registrar, the Commission or any accredited agent. This provision is not applicable where the information was made public in order to enable the person who received the information to perform his duties or act in a capacity as determined by the Act.

Defects and Irregularities

Defects and irregularities — such as an omission in the constitution of a registered body, a vacancy in the membership of a council, any irregularity in the appointment of a representative, a substitute or a chairman of a council or in the appointment of a director or Commissioner — will not render invalid the constitution of a registered body, a collective agreement or an arbitration award, any action of the council or any action of a director or Commissioner.

Definitions

As regards the interpretation of the Act, the following definitions are of importance.

- **Employee** — Any person (except an independent contractor) working for another person or the State and who receives or is entitled to receive remuneration; or any person who in any manner assists in carrying on or conducting the business of an employer
- **Essential service** — A service the interruption of which will endanger the life, personal safety or health of the entire population or part thereof (Parliament and the Police will also be regarded as essential services)
- **Issue in dispute** — In relation to a strike or lockout, the demand, grievance or dispute which forms the subject matter of the strike or lockout
- **Legal practitioner** — Any person who is admitted to practise as an advocate or attorney within the Republic
- **Lockout** — The exclusion by an employer of employees from the workplace of the employer for the purpose of compelling the employees to accept a demand in respect of any matter of mutual interest between employer and employees, irrespective of whether or not in the course or purpose of such exclusion the employer breaches the contracts of employment of its employees
- **Operational requirements** — Requirements based on the economic, technological structural or similar needs of the employer
- **Protest action** — The partial or complete concerted refusal to work, whether or not the refusal is partial or complete; or the retardation or obstruction of work for the purpose (other than for the purpose referred to in the definition of a 'strike') of promoting or defending the socioeconomic interests of workers
- **Remuneration** — Any payment, in money or in kind or both, owed to a person in exchange for which that person works for another person, including the State
- **Strike** — The concerted refusal to work, whether or not the refusal is partial or complete, or the retardation or obstruction of work by persons who are or have been employed by the same employer or by different employers, for the purpose of remedying

a grievance or resolving a dispute in respect of any matter of mutual interest between employer and employee ('Work', in this definition, includes overtime work, whether voluntary or compulsory.)

- **Workplace** — The rather confusing definition of 'workplace' has already been discussed, under *Workplace Forums*.

Schedules

Schedule 1: Establishment of Bargaining Councils in the Public Service

This section provides for the establishment of a bargaining council for the public service, for the departmental and provincial chambers of the existing Public Service Bargaining Council, the Education Labour Relations Council and the National Negotiation Forum to be constituted as bargaining councils in terms of the Act, and for sectors to be defined by the State President as sectors requiring a bargaining council.

Schedule 2: Guidelines for the Constitution of Workplace Forums

Detailed guidelines regarding the establishment of workplace forums are contained in this Schedule, and are discussed in detail in Chapter 10 of this text.

Schedule 3: Commission for Conciliation, Mediation & Arbitration

Certain aspects concerning the regulations pertaining to the CCMA as contained in this Schedule will be discussed in Chapter 14.

Schedule 4: Dispute Settlement: Flow Diagrams

See Chapter 14 for a reproduction and discussion of the procedures depicted by these flow diagrams.

Schedule 5: Amendment of Laws

This Schedule provides for certain minor amendments to the Basic Conditions of Employment Act and to the Occupational Health & Safety Act.

Schedule 6: Repeal of Laws

All previous Labour Relations Acts are repealed, as well as Section 9 of the General Law Amendment Act (no. 9 of 1991), the Education Labour Act (no. 146 of 1993), Chapter One of the Agricultural Labour Act (no. 147 of 1993), Section One of the Agricultural Labour Amendment Act (no. 50 of 1994), the Public Service Labour Act (Proclamation no. 105 of 1994), all but Section 6 of the Education Labour Act: Amendment Proclamation (no. 28 of 1994) and Sections One and Two of Proclamation no. 134 of 1994.

Schedule 7: Transitional Arrangements: Residual Unfair Labour Practices

Various transitional arrangements are made, the most important being that related to unfair labour practices.

This Schedule allows, *inter alia*, for the settlement of disputes regarding 'residual unfair labour practices'. Evidently the intention is that, eventually, such practices will resort under civil rights or similar legislation.

An unfair labour practice is defined in this Schedule as any unfair practice or omission which arises between an employer and employee and which involves any of the following.

- Unfair discrimination
- Unreasonable behaviour on the part of the employer as regards the promotion, demotion, grading or training of an employee or the granting of benefits to an employee
- The unfair suspension of an employee or any other disciplinary measure (other than dismissal)
- The refusal of an employer to re-employ or reinstate a previous employee in terms of an existing agreement

It is interesting to note that, for the purposes of unfair discrimination, an applicant for a position may be regarded as an employee. Also, an employer is not prevented from adopting a policy or practice aimed at the protection and advancement of employees previously disadvantaged by unfair discrimination or from appointing persons in terms of the inherent requirements of a job.

The Schedule further provides regulations regarding the Education Labour Relations Council, for other matters relating to the Public Service Bargaining Council and for negotiating forums in the South African Police Services.

SUBJECT	REFERENCE
Freedom of association Freedom from victimisation	Chapter 2 and Chapter 7 (Disputes)
Trade unions Employers' associations Federations of trade unions or employers' associations	Chapter 6
Collective rights Collective agreements Bargaining structures	Chapter 3 Schedule 1 and Schedule 7, Parts C and D
Consultation Co-decisionmaking Workplace forums	Chapter 5 Schedule 2
Strikes Lockouts	Chapter 4 Definitions Schedule 8: Code of Good Practice
Dispute settlement	Chapter 7
Unfair dismissals Unfair labour practices	Chapter 8 Schedule 7 (Part B) and Schedule 8 Chapter 7 (Disputes)

Table 1: THE MAJOR PROVISIONS OF THE LABOUR RELATIONS ACT

Schedule 8: Code of Good Practice: Dismissal

This is an important section, as it contains detailed guidelines for dismissals in general and sets out specific procedures for dismissals regarding such matters as misconduct, illegal strikes, poor performance, ill health or injury. The law acknowledges only three valid reasons for dismissal: the conduct of the employee, the capacity or competence of the employee, and the operational requirements of the employer. (For a detailed discussion of all these aspects, see Chapter 10.)

In designing the new Labour Relations Act, the legislators were evidently intent on achieving some measure of certainty in previously disputed areas — particularly those relating to organisational rights, unfair labour practices and retrenchments. However, in the process new doubts have been raised, such as the question about the differentiation between bargaining units and workplaces. Also, although the Explanatory Memorandum states the intention that only a majority union or majority unions should be able to request the establishment of a workplace forum, the wording of the Act itself is ambiguous (see Chapter 10). It is expected that amendments will be needed to clarify these uncertainties.

THE BASIC CONDITIONS OF EMPLOYMENT ACT, 1982

Rationale Before the Basic Conditions of Employment Act was promulgated, certain provisions pertaining to minimum conditions of employment were contained in both the Shops & Offices Act and the Factory, Machinery & Building Works Act. This division was rectified by the Basic Conditions of Employment Act, which lays down general minimum conditions for persons in employment, whether in an office, at a factory, on a farm or in a private household.

The Act is prescriptive in that the transgression of any of its provisions is a criminal offence. Thus an employer who, for example, obliges his employees to work more than the maximum number of hours per week prescribed in the Act or does not grant employees the requisite annual sick leave may be prosecuted in terms of the Act.

The fact that the legislature has seen fit to impose minimum conditions of employment reflects the perceived need for protection of employees from malpractice by the employer. It could be argued that this is contrary to the principle of voluntarism and that it should be left to the market or to negotiations by employees to determine minimum conditions. However, most Western systems accept the fact that the market is imperfect and that collective bargaining is not sufficiently pervasive to establish favourable conditions for all. Consequently, legislation aimed at minimum protection for employees is almost universal.

Status of the Act The Basic Conditions of Employment Act is generally applicable to all employees, but Section 1(3) of the Act does specifically state that the provisions of the Act will not affect any matter regulated by the Labour Relations Act, the Wage Act, the Mines & Works Act or the Manpower Training Act. Thus these Acts — or agreements or determinations made thereunder, such as a wage determination or a bargaining council agreement — supersede the Basic Conditions of Employment Act in instances where the former stipulate conditions of employment, irrespective of whether the conditions established by those Acts are more or less favourable than those of the Basic Conditions of Employment Act.

By contrast, Section 35 of the Act states that no provision of the Basic Conditions of Employment Act will '... be affected by any term or condition of any agreement'. This does not refer to bargaining council agreements, but to contracts of employment and to substantive agreements concluded at plant level. Agreements of this kind may not (unless an exemption has been granted) provide for terms and conditions of employment which are less favourable than those in the Act.

Exclusions The following employees are thus far excluded from the ambit of the Act.

- State employees
- Those employed by State bodies such as the SABC and HSRC
- Persons employed by a university, technikon, college or other educational institution maintained wholly or partly by the State
- Control board employees
- Persons working without remuneration for a charitable institution
- Employees of organisations registered in terms of the Children's Act
- Employees of cultural and welfare organisations
- Those employed at sea (who fall under the Merchant Shipping Act)
- Persons temporarily employed for an agricultural or other show

Furthermore, demonstrators and property salesmen, travellers, travellers' assistants, insurance agents and outside sales assistants, as well as persons in shops and offices, managers, submanagers, senior managerial and administrative personnel, technicall and professional personnel and foremen who earn more than R40 500 in Area A, R37 500 in Area B and R34 000 in area C (the areas being delimited by regulation) are excluded from the provisions relating to hours of work, meal intervals, overtime, work on Sundays and public holidays and the clocking of work hours. In specific instances certain other employees, such as casual and seasonal workers, are also excluded.

In 1993 agricultural employees and thereafter domestic employees were included under the Act. However, these employees are subject also to a number of separate conditions aimed at their particular sector.

Definitions Of the definitions, those pertaining to 'shop', 'office' and 'factory' are the most important. It should be noted that an office established 'in or in connection with' a factory is deemed to be a part of the factory. A shop is described as any place which displays articles for sale or which packs, despatches or stores such articles, including hairdressers and restaurants. An office is any place where bookkeeping, typing, writing or other clerical work is done; and a factory is any place which produces, assembles, disassembles and finishes off articles or goods, or which packs or stores goods and articles produced, as well as a place where gas is produced, livestock is slaughtered, electricity is generated, photographs are developed, or where any other similar process occurs.

The definitions of 'employer' and 'employee' and a number of other definitions are the same as those in the Labour Relations Act. In terms of the 1993 Amendment Act, 'farm' includes 'fresh water and sea water as far as farming activities are carried on therein or thereon', and 'farming activity' means 'any activity on a farm in connection with agriculture, including stockbreeding, horticulture and forestry', while 'farmworker' means 'an employee who is employed mainly in or in connection with farming activities and includes an employee who wholly or mainly performs domestic work on dwelling premises on a farm'. 'Domestic worker' is defined as 'an employee charged wholly or mainly with the performance of domestic work on dwelling premises' and includes gardeners, drivers and those who take care of children, the aged or the sick. The Act now also provides for a 'regular day worker', who is defined as a domestic worker employed by the same employer for not more than three days a week and for not less than four consecutive weeks.

MAJOR PROVISIONS

Maximum Hours of Work (Sections 2–6)

Maximum hours of work per day, per week and during spreadovers, as stipulated in the Act, are reflected in Table 2.

Meal Intervals (Section 7)

The Act provides that an employee may not work for more than five hours without a meal interval of one hour, during which he may perform no work; except that a driver may, during the meal interval, remain in charge of his vehicle. The time of the meal interval may, by agreement with the employee and upon notification to an inspector, be shortened to 30 minutes. If an employee who has not agreed to this is granted an interval which is shorter than the prescribed time, the interval will be calculated as working time. If the employee has an interval which is longer than 1¼ hours, the time by which the interval exceeds this period is taken as working time, except in the case of farmworkers.

Security guards, continuous shift workers and employees unloading or loading ships and aircraft or any vehicle of Transnet, as also employees involved in the arrival and departure of ships and aircraft, are excluded from the provisions relating to meal intervals.

Overtime (Sections 8 and 9)

An employee may not be required or permitted to work overtime unless there is an agreement to that effect between him and the employer. Such agreement may be contained in the contract of employment (compulsory overtime), or may be obtained from the employee from time to time (voluntary overtime).

Overtime may not exceed three hours on any single day and may not total more than ten hours per week, but an inspector appointed in terms of the Act may, if application is made to him, grant permission for additional overtime to be worked for a specified period.

Overtime, excluding that worked on a Sunday or public holiday, must be paid at a rate equal to at least 1⅓ times the normal hourly wage. The recent amendments do allow farmworkers to work an additional eight hours per week

Type of Employee	Maximum hours	Meal Intervals and Overtime	Exclusions
All employees falling under the Act	46 hours per week	Not calculated as part of working time except for continuous shift workers	Security guards Farmworkers Domestic servants
Farm- and domestic workers	48 hours per week		
Domestics minding children or the sick		Meal intervals included in calculation of working hours	
Security guards	60 hours per week		
Ordinary employees working a 5-day week	9 hours 15 minutes per day	Not included in calculation	Security guards and shift workers
Ordinary employees working a 6- or 7-day week	8 hours per day		
Shift workers employed for 5 shifts a week	9 hours 15 minutes per day	Not included, except where continuous shift is worked	
Shift workers employed for 6 shifts a week	8 hours per day but, if one shift is not more than 5 hours, the rest may be extended to 9¼ hours		
Security guards (shift or ordinary) working 5 days or shifts per week	12 hours per day	Included in calculation	
Security guards working 6 days or shifts per week	10 hours per day		
Employees whose work is spread at different intervals during a day	12 hours per day	Not included in calculation	Emergency services and employees engaged in unloading or provisioning of ships and aircraft, or involved in the arrival and departure of these, as well as employees unloading a truck or other vehicle for Transnet
Farmworkers whose work is spread	14 hours per day		
Domestic workers whose work is spread	16 hours per day		

Table 2: MAXIMUM HOURS OF WORK

over and above the normal working hours and normal working time without any additional pay for a period not exceeding four months in a year, provided that the employee does not work for more than ten hours on any day and that, during the rest of the year, the working hours are reduced in such a way that, on average, they do not exceed the maximum of 48 hours per week over the entire 12-month period; and provided further that the written agreement of the employee has been obtained.

A similar arrangement is made for domestic employees, but here the hours may not be extended for more than four hours per week for a maximum period of 26 days, and the employee may not work more than ten hours per day during this time. Hours should be shortened for the equivalent period during the rest of the year.

Overtime for farmworkers and domestic employees may not exceed ten hours per week — except where a domestic employee cares for children, the sick or the aged, in which case a maximum of fourteen hours per week is stipulated. Domestic employees may also not work overtime on days when extended hours are worked.

Overtime payment for domestic and agricultural employees is calculated on the total wage, i.e. the cash wage plus the value of payment in kind.

Those employees excluded from the minimum hours as regards hours of work (see previous section) and continuous shift employees whose conditions of service have been regulated by the Minister of Labour are excluded from this provision.

Work on Sundays (Section 10)

No employee may perform work connected with a factory or office on a Sunday unless written permission has been obtained from an inspector. This clause does not apply to persons who earn more than the prescribed amount or to continuous shift workers, employees engaged in emergency services and those at airports, harbours and Transnet.

Payment for work on Sundays is usually calculated in the following way.

- If an employee works for less than four hours, he is paid at the normal daily rate — that is, he is paid as if he had worked a normal day.
- If he has worked for longer than four hours, he will be paid at double the daily rate or double the hourly rate for the time he has worked, whichever is the greater.
- The employer may choose to pay the employee at the normal overtime rate, but will then be obliged to grant the employee one day off at full pay within the following week.

Shift workers will be regarded as having worked on a Sunday if more than half of their shift falls on that day.

The following employees are excluded from these provisions.

- Employees loading and unloading at harbours, airports or for Transnet
- Continuous shift workers subject to a determination by the Minister

- Employees working in a shop which is permitted to open on Sundays, provided that such employees are given one day off in the following week

In the case of farmworkers a distinction is made between work which is normally done on Sunday (e.g. milking) and work which is not normally done on a Sunday. In the latter instance the provisions are the same as for employees in industry or shops and offices, but in the former case an employee who works for up to two hours is paid for a minimum of two hours. If he works for more than two but less than five hours he is paid as if he worked a normal working day; and if he works for longer than five hours he is paid at double the daily rate or double the hourly rate for the hours he actually works, whichever is the greater. An employee who works for longer than two hours at a job which is normally done on a Sunday must be given an ordinary day off (at no remuneration) during the following week.

Public Holidays (Definition and Section 11)   An employee who does not work on a prescribed public holiday is still paid his normal daily wage. If an employee works on a paid public holiday, he is paid a normal day's wage *plus* another day's wage, *or plus* the rate for the hours worked, whichever is the greater. Alternatively, he can be paid at normal overtime rates and be given a paid day off in the following week.

The following are statutory public holidays.

- New Year's Day (1 January)
- Good Friday
- Family Day
- Human Rights Day (21 March)
- Freedom Day (27 April)
- Workers' Day (1 May)
- Youth Day (16 June)
- National Women's Day (9 August)
- Heritage Day (24 September)
- Day of Reconciliation (16 December)
- Christmas Day (25 December)
- Day of Goodwill (26 December)

A public holiday which falls on a Sunday is observed as a holiday on the Monday immediately thereafter.

The provisions of this section do not apply to the employees mentioned on page 139.

Annual Leave   All ordinary employees are entitled to two consecutive weeks' (ten or twelve working days') leave for every twelve consecutive months of service. Outside sales assistants, travellers, travellers' assistants, demonstrator salesmen, insurance agents, guards and security guards are entitled to 21 consecutive days. Regular day workers (domestic) must be granted one day's paid leave for every 26 days worked for a particular employer.

As regards the granting of leave, the following rules apply.

- An employer may determine the date on which leave will commence but this may not be later than four months (or, with the employee's permission, six months) after the time when leave becomes due to the employee.
- No leave may run concurrently with sick leave or a notice period; nor may military service be taken as leave, unless the employee requests this
- Public holidays to which the employee would normally have been entitled and which fall during the employee's absence are not counted as leave.
- No employee may work during his period of leave.

If the services of an employee are terminated, whether by him or by the employer, he (the employee) must be paid for outstanding leave. This payment is calculated as follows.

- In respect of outstanding leave for a completed year of service, the employee is paid at the daily rate for the number of days outstanding.
- Where the payment of leave relates to leave accrued in a new leave cycle, he is paid at one sixth of the weekly rate for every completed month of service if he is entitled to 14 days' leave per year, and at one quarter of the weekly rate for each completed month of service if he is entitled to 21 days' leave per year.

No employee who has not given the necessary notice will, unless he has acted within his rights, be entitled to payment in lieu of outstanding leave.

Sick Leave (Section 13)

Employees who work a five-day week may be granted 30 days' sick leave at full pay in every three-year employment cycle and those who work a six day week 36 days for the same cycle. However, an employee who has been in employ for less than a year is granted sick leave calculated at the rate of one day per five weeks of service (in the case of a five-day week employee), or one day per month of service if he is a six-day week employee. Regular day workers are to be granted one day's paid sick leave for every 26 days worked for the same employer.

An employer is not obliged to pay the employee during his sick leave if the employee is a member of a sick fund which pays him the same benefits or if another law obliges the employer to pay the same benefits.

Termination of Contract (Sections 14 and 15)

Both employers and employees who intend terminating a contract of service are, unless they have lawful cause for summary termination, subject to the following notice periods.

- Persons employed for less than four weeks — one day
- Employees paid on a weekly basis — one week, but notice must be given on the normal payday or the day before, and becomes effective on the normal payday

- Employees paid on a monthly basis — two weeks, with the proviso that notice may be given only on the 1st or 15th of the month
- Any employment contract which provides for longer notice periods supersedes these provisions.
- Either party may waive the notice period if he pays the other the amount equal to that which the employee would have earned during his notice period.

Unless an employee is illiterate, notice must be given in writing. Furthermore, all employees who leave their place of employ (except casual employees and deserters) must be furnished with a certificate of service stating the following.

- The full name of the employer
- The full name of the employee
- The occupation of the employee
- The date on which he commenced service
- The date of termination
- The employee's wages at the date of termination

Farmworkers and those domestic employees who are not paid on a weekly basis and who have been employed for longer than four weeks must be given a month's notice; and, where farmworkers have been dismissed without notice or paid out in lieu of notice, they are entitled to retain their accommodation for the time that they would have been able to do so had they been given proper notice. They must also be allowed to keep livestock on the land for the same period, and to tend and harvest standing crops intended as payment in kind, unless the employer compensates them for those crops.

The Act is mute on notice periods during fixed-term contracts, but by common law a fixed-term contract may be terminated before the stipulated time only by giving three months' notice.

Prohibitions on Deductions and Fines (Section 19)

Except for Section 16, which sets out the manner in which wages should be calculated, this is the only part of the Act relating to remuneration. It specifically provides that an employer has to pay the employee on the agreed date and prohibits the employer from levying a fine on employees or from deducting any money from the remuneration of an employee, except on authority from the employee or in terms of a law of a court order. Furthermore, an employer may not allow or require an employee to repay any part of his salary to him or to agree to any act which will rob the employee of his benefits.

Prohibitions on Employment

An employer may not take into his employ a person under the age of 15, nor may he oblige a female to work during the four weeks preceding her confinement or the eight weeks thereafter. (This does not mean that he may dismiss such an employee — see Chapter 10.)

Victimisation

The Act contains basically the same victimisation clause as that in the Labour Relations Act of 1956.

Keeping of Records Employers are obliged by the Act to record the time worked by each employee, the wage paid to each employee and any other particulars prescribed by regulation or by an inspector.

Other Provisions The rest of the Act, about 21 sections in all, is mostly of an implementational and administrative nature. It contains, *inter alia*, provisions regarding the appointment of inspectors, the declaration of certain omissions as offences, the recovery of monies owed to an employer or employee and exemption from certain conditions, on application to the Minister of Labour. A number of regulations are also appended to the Act.

At the time of writing, the Minister of Labour has indicated that the Basic Conditions of Employment Act will be amended in 1996. Controversy has already arisen regarding his expressed intention to reduce maximum working hours to 40 hours per week. Also, it appears likely that many employees still excluded from this Act will then be covered as regards their terms and conditions of employment.

THE WAGE ACT, 1957

Rationale The first Wage Act was passed in 1925 and although, as discussed in Chapter 4, the reasons for its application to all race groups may not have been altruistic, it conforms with one of the early conventions of the International Labour Organisation. This Convention prescribes that all ratifying countries should implement a wage machinery to ensure that, in industries or occupations where collective bargaining is not prevalent, a reasonable minimum wage rate and acceptable minimum standards are maintained. The Wage Act therefore supplements the Labour Relations Act in that it covers those areas where the collective bargaining machinery of the Labour Relations Act is not used and where there are no bargaining councils having jurisdiction. In addition, the Labour Relations Act of 1995 now stipulates that a statutory council, which may not be sufficiently representative of employers and employees in an industry, may apply to the Minister to have its agreement gazetted and extended as a determination in terms of the Wage Act.

Upon application by an interested party or upon a directive of the Minister, the Wage Board (appointed by the Minister of Labour) will make a determination on wages and conditions of service which will then become binding on the parties concerned, but the Act does allow for representations to be made to the Wage Board by employer and employee parties. Thus the decision of the Board is not purely discretionary.

While the Wage Act does provide protection for employees who would otherwise not be covered by an agreement, it may also be of use to employers. A wage determination, like a centralised agreement, is a means of ensuring that other employers in the same industry, occupation, trade or area do not pay lower wages, enabling them to cut costs and to sell their products at lower prices. Also, there are certain industries or trades where the conditions stipulated in the Basic Conditions of Employment Act are not suitable and where it is more feasible to apply for the implementation of a wage determination relating to that particular industry than to seek numerous exemptions from the Basic Conditions of Employment Act.

Before 1979 the Wage Act fulfilled an important function, but the proliferation of plant-level agreements and the passage of the Basic Conditions of Employment Act gradually rendered it less relevant. With the inclusion in the Labour Relations Act of the abovementioned provision regarding the agreements of statutory councils, the Wage Act again becomes significant.

Status of the Act

Determinations made in terms of the Wage Act supersede the Basic Conditions of Employment Act, but do not override any determination made under the Labour Relations Act or the Manpower Training Act.

Exclusions

The general exclusions are basically the same as those contained in the Basic Conditions of Employment Act, but the inclusion of domestic and agricultural workers under the Wage Act is still being considered.

MAJOR PROVISIONS

Appointment of a Wage Board

The Board consists of a minimum of three members, appointed by the Minster of Labour (now the Minister of Manpower) for a period specified by him. The Minister designates the chairman, and may at any time appoint additional members if he so wishes.

Investigations and Reports by the Board

The Minister may at any time request an investigation by the Board. He determines the terms of reference as regards the industry, trade or class of employees to be covered, provided that he may not distinguish on the basis of race, sex or colour. The Board reports back to the Minister, and he may direct that it make a recommendation.

Matters for Consideration by the Board

The Board must consider any representations made to it, and all information and reports received. It also has to take into account the cost of living in the area, the value of board, rations or other benefits received by employees and the effect a determination would have on the business of employers.

Matters on Which the Board May Make Recommendations

These are similar to the matters which may be regulated by bargaining councils, and include any of the following.

- Minimum wage rates and minimum average wage rates
- Increases in wage rates over specific periods
- Methods of calculating minimum rates, time and method of payment
- Piecework rates
- Prohibitions or restrictions on deductions, setoff debts, piecework, task work or the granting of other forms of remuneration
- Overtime provisions
- Any other matter related to remuneration or terms or conditions of employment (including leave, sick leave and public holidays)

**Represent-
ations and
Information
Gathering**

The Board is obliged to publish notice of its investigation in the *Government Gazette* and to allow time for representations to be made by interested parties. Any person connected with the trade may also be directed by the Board to supply information on request, and the Board may subpoena any person to appear before it. Once it has all the necessary information, the Board will make a recommendation to the Minister.

**Implement-
ation of a
Determination**

On receiving the recommendations of the Board, the Minister will make a determination, which is published in the *Government Gazette*. Non-compliance with the provisions of a determination constitutes an offence. Provision is also made for amendments to determinations, exemptions from certain conditions and for the appointment of inspectors to police the implementation of determinations by employers in that industry or area.

INCLUSION OF DOMESTIC AND AGRICULTURAL WORKERS

During their deliberations on the position of domestic and agricultural workers, the then NMC and the two specialist committees appointed in 1991 for this purpose also considered the inclusion of domestic and agricultural workers under the Wage Act. In both instances, opinion was divided.

In the Farmworkers Committee there were basically three schools of thought. One group favoured immediate inclusion, arguing that many agricultural workers were exploited that it was unlikely that the bulk of labour in this sector would be unionised. Another group contended that minimum wages in this sector would exert upward pressure on inflation, that there was great diversity in profitability, that the minimum wage might become the maximum wage and that the rules of supply and demand would be disturbed; while yet a third group declared itself of the opinion that the time was not yet ripe for inclusion, that the matter should be reconsidered in two years' time and that in the interim certain wage guidelines should be established.

The NMC eventually decided to put forward all three points of view, with modifications, and also to include in its report the original majority view of the committee: that the extension of the Wage Act to agriculture should be reconsidered within two years and that, in the interim, the Wage Board should make recommendations regarding acceptable wages in the various agricultural regions and sectors. The purpose of this would be to 'orientate' the farming community towards the concept of minimum wages.

In the case of domestic workers, two views were held. The one was that these employees should not be included under the Act, but that non-binding wage guidelines should be established by the Wage Board or a similar institution; while the other group argued for the immediate inclusion of domestic workers, pointing to the fact that the Wage Board was a 'forum for debate, argument and presentation of evidence' and that it could take into account relevant aspects or even make different determinations for different regions.

No finality has yet been reached as regards either agricultural or domestic employees, and it remains to be seen whether particularly domestic employees will eventually be governed by minimum wage legislation or whether the provision for statutory councils will be used to this effect.

THE OCCUPATIONAL HEALTH & SAFETY ACT, 1993

Rationale This Act replaces the Machinery & Occupational Safety Act (no. 6 of 1983), which was intended to consolidate and extend all previous health and safety legislation — particularly that of the Factory, Machinery & Building Works Act and its voluminous regulations. The Act and regulations imposed stringent health and safety conditions although, as a Chief Inspector of Health & Safety once said, no workplace can be made a hundred percent safe and accidents still do occur. Nevertheless, employers who are found by inspectors to have been negligent face heavy fines or prison sentences. This conforms to the common law principle that it is the employer's duty to provide healthy and safe working conditions. The State has taken it upon itself to ensure that the employer performs this duty.

The Act itself was very short. Particular health and safety conditions were contained in the regulations appended to the Act. With its passage in 1983 only the General Administrative Regulations, referring mostly to the duties of employers as regards safety representatives and to general safety matters, were published. Where no specific regulations were passed in terms of the new Act, those pertaining under the Factory, Machinery & Building Works Act still applied. From 1983 onwards a number of new regulations were published.

The Occupational Health & Safety Act (no. 85 of 1993) extends the terms of its predecessor in many respects. It also includes numerous provisions previously contained in the General Administrative Regulations. For example, employers are now responsible for the health and safety not only of their employees but also of anyone who might be affected by their activities — in other words, the general public. Other changes include increases in fines and prison sentences where negligence has been proved, and more specific provision for the appointment of health and safety representatives.

Status of the Act The Occupational Health & Safety Act supersedes all agreements, which means that no parties can agree that work will be conducted in unsafe conditions. Since the Labour Relations Act is not mentioned, it is taken that the same applies to bargaining council agreements or to any regulation under the latter Act.

The definitions of 'employer' and 'employee' are the same as those contained in the Labour Relations Act and in the Basic Conditions of Employment Act. Unlike the other Acts, however, no specific category of employees is excluded: the Occupational Health & Safety Act applies to agricultural workers, domestic servants, public servants and students — in effect, to almost all persons in employ, including those in private households.

Exclusions The only exclusions are labour brokers, mines, mining areas or any works defined in the Minerals Act (no. 50 of 1991), except where the Act provides otherwise, and any load-line ship, fishing boat, sealing and whaling boat as defined in the Merchant Shipping Act (no. 57 of 1951), or any floating crane.

MAJOR PROVISIONS

Advisory Council on Occupational Safety

This Council is composed of representatives from the Department of Labour, persons nominated by the Minister of Health & Welfare and the Minister of Mineral & Energy Affairs, the Chief Inspector, the Workmen's Compensation Commissioner or his nominee, six employee and six employer representatives and various experts nominated by the Minister. The Council advises the Minister on policy matters and may conduct research, advise the Department on the formulation of standards, the promotion of training and education in the area of health and safety, and the collection and dissemination of information regarding these matters.

Duties of Employer

The final responsibility for the health and safety of employees and other affected persons rests with the employer. The Act states that it is the duty of the chief executive officer to ensure that the employer's obligations are discharged, and that the CEO may assign this duty to any person under his control. (In the case of the State, a head of department is regarded as the CEO.) However, the assignation of duties to another person does not relieve the employer from any responsibility or liability in terms of the Act.

Overall, it is the employer's duty to ensure that, as far as is reasonably practicable, a working environment which is safe and without health risks is maintained. In terms of the definition, 'reasonably practicable' means that it is practicable with due regard to the severity and scope of the danger, the knowledge available concerning that hazard or risk, the availability of suitable means to remove or mitigate the danger or risk, and the cost of such removal in relation to the benefits derived.

In particular, it is the employer's duty —

- to ensure that systems of work, plant and machinery are reasonably safe and without health risks;
- to initiate steps to eliminate possible health and safety hazards or risks before resorting to the use of protective equipment;
- to ensure, as far as is reasonably practicable, that the production, use, handling, storage or transport of articles and substances does not endanger health and safety;
- to establish which hazards or risks are involved in any type of work and in the handling of any substance, and what precautionary measures should be taken;
- to provide the necessary information, instruction, training and supervision;
- to ensure that precautionary measures and the requirements of the Act are implemented;
- to ensure that work is performed and plant or machinery is used under the supervision of a trained person with sufficient authority to ensure that safety measures are implemented;
- in the area of 'listed' work (so declared by the Minister), to ensure not only that all safety measures are taken but also that occupational hygiene and biological monitoring programmes are undertaken;

- to inform safety representatives of the steps taken to identify the hazards and evaluate the risks entailed in 'listed' work, and of the monitoring and occupational hygiene programmes and their results;
- to inform all employees of the danger involved in their work;
- to provide facilities, assistance and training to health and safety representatives;
- to inform health and safety representatives beforehand of inspections, investigations, formal inquiries and applications for exemption;
- to inform representatives of any incident which occurs at the workplace ('incident' is defined as an occurrence as a result of which a person dies, becomes unconscious, loses a limb or part of a limb, becomes so ill that he is likely to die or be disabled, or will not be able to work for a period of more than 14 days); and
- to see that the safety committee performs its functions.

Duties of Employees

Employees themselves have a duty to care for their own health and safety, to obey the safety regulations, to cooperate with the employer in this regard, to report any unsafe situation to the safety representative or the employer and to report to the employer, his mandatary or a safety representative any incident which has caused an injury to himself. Thus the maintenance of safety is the joint responsibility of the employer, the safety representative, the employees and (if one exists) the safety committee. Nevertheless, the greater responsibility still falls on the employer.

Safety Represent- atives

Within four months of commencing business, any employer who employs more than twenty people must appoint, in writing, safety representatives for a particular workplace or part thereof. The employer must consult with employees or their representatives regarding the nomination and selection of safety representatives and, should no agreement be reached, the dispute must be submitted to an arbitrator agreed to by both parties. Failing such agreement, the Labour Court will appoint an arbitrator.

Safety representatives must be fulltime employees who have knowledge of conditions and activities in that workplace. In shops and offices the number of safety representatives is one for every 100 employees, and in all other workplaces one to every 50 employees. However, the Inspector may declare that the number of representatives is inadequate and may also order an employer with fewer than twenty employees to appoint a safety representative if he (the Inspector) deems this to be necessary.

The training and all activities of safety representatives must take place during normal working hours. The functions of these representatives are as follows.

- To review the effectiveness of health and safety regulations
- To identify potential hazards and potential major incidents
- Together with the employer, to examine the causes of incidents
- To investigate employee complaints
- To make representations regarding health and safety to the employer or to the health and safety committee or, if this fails, to the Inspector

- To inspect the workplace at agreed intervals, and to give the employer reasonable notice of the intended inspection
- To consult with inspectors and to accompany the latter during inspections
- To receive information from the Inspector
- To attend meetings of the health and safety committee

A health and safety representative is further entitled to visit the site of an incident or attend an inspection at that site, to attend any investigation or formal inquiry, to inspect any document the inspection of which is necessary to perform his functions, and to participate in an internal health and safety audit. He may, with the permission of the employer (which should not be unreasonably withheld), be accompanied on his inspections by a technical advisor.

Safety Committees

In terms of the Act, a safety committee must be established wherever two or more safety representatives have been appointed. All safety representatives must be members of a committee, but the employer may appoint additional members to the committee (provided that the number of such members does not exceed the number of safety representatives on the committee), and the committee itself may coopt advisory members. The members of a safety committee are designated in writing by the employer, who may decide to establish more than one committee in the undertaking.

The following are the functions of the safety committee.

- To perform any prescribed function
- To discuss any incident which occurred and report in writing to an inspector
- To keep records of recommendations and reports made to inspectors (to be retained for three years by the employer)
- To meet on a regular basis (the committee may determine how often, but meetings must take place at least once every three months or, if ten percent of the workforce requests a meeting, whenever so requested)

The employer has the duty to ensure that a safety committee is established, that regular meetings are held and that the committee performs the functions specified in the Act.

Reporting of Incidents

Serious incidents (described above under the duties of employers), if not reported by the representative, must be reported by the employer or by the user of the machinery. The same applies in the case of any 'major' incident (an incident of 'catastrophic proportions') or where a dangerous substance was spilled or a substance under pressure was uncontrollably released, where the failure or fracturing of machinery resulted in 'flying, falling or uncontrolled moving objects' or where machinery ran out of control. If the incident results in death, the Inspector must be notified immediately and, where death occurred on the premises, the surroundings are to be left undisturbed unless some action is necessary to prevent further damage or loss of life.

Prohibitions The Occupational Health & Safety Act contains prohibitions on the deduction of monies from employees for safety equipment issued or for damage to equipment or clothing issued, unless it is proved that such damage was wilfully committed. Furthermore, in terms of the Act, the Minister may by declaration in the *Government Gazette* prohibit the employment of certain categories of workers — for example, pregnant women — in certain workplaces. In the same manner he may prohibit the employment of any person in certain specified processes or in connection with certain substances, and he may ban smoking, drinking or eating on designated premises. The Minister may also prohibit the sale of machinery which has been found to be unsafe.

Doctors Any doctor who treats a disease subject to Workmen's Compensation or a disease which he believes arose from his patient's employment is obliged to report this to the employer and to the Chief Inspector.

Inspectors The Act provides for the appointment of inspectors and a Chief Inspector, and bestows wide-ranging powers on these officials. An inspector has the right to enter premises, seize books, conduct inquiries into serious incidents, bar or fence off an unsafe workplace and order the discontinuance of any operation regarded as unsafe. Appeals may be lodged against the decisions of inspectors. Such appeals are lodged with the Chief Inspector and, if the complainant is still dissatisfied, with the Labour Court.

Formal Inquiries The Chief Inspector may at any time order an inspector to hold a formal inquiry. The inspector may then subpoena any person to appear before him, and may designate any person to lead evidence. Interested parties (such as the employer, the injured or maimed person, the person said to have been responsible and the owner of the premises or the machinery) are allowed to attend and question the witnesses at an inquiry. Once an inquiry is completed, the inspector must submit a copy of his report to the Attorney General, who will deal with it in terms of the Inquests Act and/or the Criminal Procedures Act.

Victimisation The victimisation of an employee for committing any act or supplying any information which, in terms of the law, he is required to do is forbidden.

Offences and Penalties The Act stipulates that the employer will be held responsible whenever an employee or a mandatary of the employer commits or fails to commit an act which, in terms of the law, he is required to do or not to do, unless it can be proved that an employee acted without the connivance or permission of the employer, or that he acted outside his authority; or that the employer took every precaution to prevent an act or omission of this kind; or that, in the case of a mandatary, there was a written agreement between them to ensure that the mandatary complied with the provisions of the Act. Moreover, the fact that an employer issued instructions to prevent an act or omission of the kind envisaged will not be regarded as 'reasonable steps' to prevention, and will not free him from blame. This notwithstanding, an employee or mandatary who commits or omits an action which would constitute an offence on the part of the employer may be sentenced together with the employer or, in the case of a State employee or mandatary, on his own.

Any failure to comply with the provisions relating to the maintenance of health and safety or the provisions of an exemption, as well as the wilful furnishing of false information, the obstruction of an inspector in the performance of his functions, the failure or refusal to comply with requirements or requests made by an inspector, refusal to answer questions put by him, failure to heed a subpoena, refusal to appear before an inspector or in any way to comply with the requirements of an inquiry constitutes an offence. Furthermore, no one may tamper with, discourage, deceive or unduly influence somebody who is to give evidence; and no one may prejudice or precipitate proceedings, tamper with or misuse safety equipment or wilfully or recklessly do anything which endangers health or safety. These offences are subject to fines of up to R50 000 or one year's imprisonment, or both. Finally, anyone who commits or omits to do an act and thereby injures another person in such a way that, if he were to die, the perpetrator would have been guilty of culpable homicide, can (irrespective of whether or not the person dies) be subject to a fine of up to R100 000 or two years' imprisonment, or both.

Although the Act attempts to ensure that all premises on which work is conducted are as safe as possible, it is difficult to provide by law for all eventualities. Furthermore, inspectors are not able to police every undertaking and often act only when unsafe conditions are reported to them. For this reason the newer unions have raised the issue of health and safety during plant-level negotiations, in some cases demanding the conclusion of health and safety agreements. Health and safety campaigns have also been undertaken by many unions. In the textile industry the high incidence of 'brown lung' disease amongst employees was publicised by unions. The dangers of asbestos received much attention and, in the mining industry, safety concerns continue to predominate as an issue between management and unions.

THE COMPENSATION FOR OCCUPATIONAL INJURIES & DISEASES ACT, 1993

Rationale This Act replaced the Workmen's Compensation Act (no. 30 of 1941) and allows for compensation to be paid to an employee who, as a result of his activities in the work situation, is partially or totally disabled or contracts an occupational disease. In the event that the employee dies as a result of the accident, injury or disease, the compensation will be paid to his dependants.

Ambit The Act covers all employees, including casual and seasonal workers, and directors who have a contract of employment.

MAJOR PROVISIONS

Duties of Employers Every employer must register with the Compensation Commissioner and supply him with the necessary particulars regarding his business and employees, as well as with any other information which the Commissioner may request. Should the address of the employer change, the Commissioner must be notified immediately.

Employers are obliged to keep records of wages, time worked and payment for piecework and overtime, and to retain these records for at least four years. Furthermore they must, by 31 March each year or within a month of starting up a business, fill in a prescribed form indicating the total amount of salaries or wages paid during the preceding financial year.

The Act obliges employers to keep the necessary first aid equipment, to provide injured employees with the necessary medical attention or to transport them to a place where they can receive such attention, and to pay the medical expenses (which can be reclaimed from the Commissioner).

As regards actual accidents or diseases, the onus is on the employer, within seven days of an accident being brought to his attention (or, in the case of an illness, within fourteen days), to notify the Commissioner of the accident or illness. He must also submit to the Commissioner any claims for compensation brought by employees, and must pay assessments within 30 days of receiving them.

Assessments   Assessments are made at the discretion of the Commissioner, who will consider the position of the Compensation Fund and levy an assessment based on a percentage of total wages or salaries paid by a particular employer. The Commissioner may determine that different percentages should apply to different groups of employers, or that a minimum assessment be imposed on a particular employer class. Also, the Commissioner may limit the maximum amount of earnings on which an employer may be assessed. The amount of the assessment may further depend on whether the operation is organised in such a way that there will be few serious accidents, and on the safety record of a particular employer.

Employers may apply to pay assessments in instalments instead of one large lump sum. Should an employer fail to pay within the prescribed period of 30 days, the Commissioner may levy a fine equal to a percentage of the assessment. However, should an employee meet with an accident during a period for which the employer has not paid, the Commissioner may levy a fine equal to the total amount of compensation paid to that employee. No money may be raised from the employees themselves to pay for assessments.

Claims for   Any employee or the dependants of an employee who is injured, contracts a
Compensation   listed disease or dies as a result of an accident or circumstances at work is entitled to claim compensation. An employee who is being transported to or from work by a person appointed by the employer is also regarded as being at work.

Once the employer has been notified or has learnt in some way of the accident injury of disease he must, within seven days (if it is an accident or injury) or fourteen days (if it is a disease), notify the Compensation Commissioner on the prescribed form. The Commissioner will then make enquiries and request further information from the employee. He will also request that the employee submit to a medical examination by an appointed medical officer. However, the employee may at his own expense have another doctor of his own choice present at the examination.

Claims for compensation must be lodged within a period of twelve months after the accident or illness occurred or after the employee died. The Commissioner may hold a formal hearing and thereafter decide on the compensation to be paid. Payment may be effected in instalments, as a pension or in a lump sum and may be paid to the employee, a trustee or his dependants. In certain instances the Commissioner may request that the employer pay compensation for the first three months, but this money will later be refunded to the employer.

No compensation will be paid if it is proved that the employee lied by saying that he had not previously suffered from an injury or disease and if that injury or disease caused or aggravated the present condition; nor will it be paid if the accident was the result of wilful misconduct of the employee, unless it led to serious disablement or unless the employee dies and leaves a dependant. Even when the employee acted against his employer's instructions or contravened a law, compensation will be paid if the Commissioner is convinced that the employee was acting in the interests of the employer or in connection with the employer's business.

Dependants Any person who was totally or partially dependent on a deceased employee may be considered as a dependant. Such dependants could include a widow or a widower; a person who, at the time of death, was living with the deceased as husband or wife; any child, stepchild, adopted, illegitimate or as yet unborn child of the deceased or his/her spouse if such child is younger than 18; a child over the age of 18 who is a child of the deceased or his/her spouse; and a brother, sister, half-brother or -sister, grandparent, grandchild or parent of the deceased, or a third party acting in the place of such person.

Appeals Any person affected by a decision of the Commissioner may appeal to him against such decision. The Commissioner is then obliged to review the case, together with two assessors. If unanimity is not achieved or the complainant remains dissatisfied, the matter may be submitted to the Supreme Court for a final decision.

THE UNEMPLOYMENT INSURANCE ACT, 1966

Rationale This Act provides for contributions by employers and employees to the Unemployment Insurance Fund and for payment of unemployment benefits to persons who become unemployed, who are ill for lengthy periods or, in the case of females, who give birth to or adopt a child. The Fund also provides for payments to dependants of deceased employees.

Ambit All employees who earn less than R69 000 per year are covered by the Act except for seasonal workers, workers who are employed for less than one day or less than eight hours per week, domestic employees, persons employed casually and not for the purpose of the employer's business, persons who enter the country on contract, the husband or wife of the employer, persons to whom work is put out, officers in the public service, officers on the fixed establishment of Parliament, provincial administration employees who contribute to the Government Services Pension Fund and certain persons in the educational sector.

MAJOR PROVISIONS

Duties of Employer

Employers are obliged —

- to register with the Department of Labour on the prescribed form;
- to supply the Director-General of Manpower with particulars regarding employees who qualify as contributors; and
- to obtain and keep an Unemployment Insurance Fund card for every such contributor.

Where an employee who already has a card comes to work for an employer, that employer must obtain the UIF card from such employee.

The employer should deduct monthly contributions from all employees, submit these (together with his own contributions) to the Unemployment Insurance Commissioner and, upon the termination of contract, complete the necessary details (including the reason for leaving) on the card, which is then returned to the employee.

Other than this, the employer should keep records of the paid earnings, time worked, payment for overtime and payment for piecework in respect of all employees, and should retain these records for at least three years. He is also obliged to keep UIF records reflecting the name of the employee, date of commencement, date of termination of service, weekly or monthly earnings during the last thirteen weeks of service, the date on which the UIF card was issued, the date on which the card was filled in and, finally, a note of what was done with the card.

Contributions

Contributions are calculated at one percent of the employee's real monthly earnings, excluding overtime, payment for work on Sundays or public holidays and special bonuses. The employer and the employee each make a contribution of one percent; the total contribution is thus two percent of the employee's earnings.

Where an employee is paid on a weekly basis, contributions must be deducted from every wage packet but should be paid over only once a month. In terms of the Act, all Unemployment Insurance Fund contributions must be paid over within ten days after the end of each month.

If a weekly-paid employee is absent from work for longer than four or five days (depending on whether he works a five-or six-day week respectively) and is unpaid for that time, no contribution is paid on his behalf. The same applies to a monthly-paid employee who is absent for a full month. In all other cases, contributions are paid in full.

An employer who fails to pay over contributions to the Fund may be fined an amount of ten percent of the total contribution or R20, whichever is the greater. However, if he fails to pay contributions at all, does not furnish the necessary particulars, fails to keep records, gives false information or does not comply with any other obligation in terms of the Act, he may be fined a maximum of R500 or be given one year's imprisonment, or both.

Benefits An employee who wishes to claim benefits in terms of the Act should apply to the Claims Office in his area and produce his UIF card. The Claims Officer will investigate his circumstances, check the employee's records and see whether it is possible for the employee to find work. If not, he will decide how much and for how long the employee should be paid in terms of benefits.

Normally, employees are paid benefits at a rate of 45 percent of the total weekly or monthly earnings, based on the average wage at the time they became unemployed. The employee receives one week's benefits for every six weeks that he was employed, usually to a maximum of 26 weeks in any 52-week period. However, an appeal for extension of benefits may be made to the Unemployment Benefit Committee.

An employee will not be granted benefits if he worked for less than thirteen weeks in any period of a year, if he was dismissed as a result of a strike or a work stoppage, or if he refuses to be trained for another job. He also will receive no benefit during the first week that he is unemployed, unless his last job was for less than nine weeks and he was unemployed before that. No persons earning a third or more of their last salary will receive benefits, nor will benefits be paid during the first two weeks of an illness.

Where a contributor dies, the widow, widower, children under 17 or any other dependant may claim benefits for a maximum of 26 weeks.

THE MANPOWER TRAINING ACT, 1981

Rationale The Manpower Training Act (no. 56 of 1981) replaced the Apprenticeship Act, the Training of Artisans Act, the Black Employees' In-Service Training Act and the In-Service Training Act. Its purpose was to consolidate into one Act all previous legislation related to training, to continue to regulate the training of apprentices, to coordinate training activities and to allow for and encourage the establishment of training facilities suitable to the needs of industry and the country as a whole.

MAJOR PROVISIONS

The following are provided for in the Manpower Training Act.

Establishment of a National Training Board This board is appointed by the Minister of Labour, to advise him on matters of policy related to the Act and on any other matter related to training. The board also conducts research into training needs and takes steps to establish uniform standards of training. Of late it has been particularly concerned with schemes for training the unemployed, as well as with a new national education and training strategy and the establishment of a national qualification framework.

Industry Training Boards

The Manpower Training Amendment Act of 1990 provides for the establishment of industry training boards to replace the training committees which were formerly established by the National Training Board. Industry training boards may be established by a group of employers, an employers' association, a bargaining council, a union or a group of employees and, once constituted, may apply to the Registrar for accreditation. A trade union may also negotiate with employers for the establishment of a board.

Once it has been constituted, an industry training board must (even if a trade union is not involved in its establishment) invite a trade union to appoint a representative as a member or, if there is no trade union, invite an employee representative. Before accrediting a board, the Registrar must satisfy himself that there is no other board in that industry or area, and that the main objective of the applicant board is to promote training.

Specific regulations are laid down as regards the constitution of a training board, and it is stipulated that the board must, within three months of its financial year end, furnish the Registrar with copies of accounts, financial statements and auditor's reports. Investments may be made only in certain stipulated securities.

The industry training boards are mainly responsible for the regulation of apprenticeships in their particular industries and for industry training in terms of the national qualifications framework. Furthermore, they have to provide vocational guidance and career advice, and keep the Department informed of technical, professional and career opportunities in their industries. They must foster cooperation between formal educational and training institutes, promote training (especially during downturns in the economy), initiate training programmes and monitor their progress. Together with the Minister, they advise on standards of professional and technical training in their industries, the time required to complete certain training modules and the amount of actual on-the-job or practical training required. In collaboration with the Minister, they make provision for the training of persons other than apprentices and evaluate qualifications obtained in other countries. The onus for general training initiatives has thus been shifted from the Department of Labour to employer and/or employee representatives in particular industries.

Training of Apprentices

A vast number of provisions relate to the indenture, employment and training of apprentices, as well as to the achievement of artisan status by such apprentices; but the 1990 amendments to the Act replaced many of the uniform regulations as regards the training of apprentices and have provided the opportunity for more flexible programmes. Apprenticeship training can now be conducted along modular and competency-based lines.

Training of Trainees

The Minister may, at his discretion, provide for the establishment of schemes whereby trainees other than apprentices qualify for certain jobs in a particular trade or occupation.

Regional and Private Training Centres

The previous provision for group training centres was replaced in the 1990 amendments with regional training centres, which also need to be properly constituted. The regional training centres may be established by a group or association of employers in a particular area, and are regulated by an advisory board consisting of one representative from each regional training centre, one person nominated by the National Training Board and one nominated by the Department of Labour. The Minister may, at his discretion, grant monies appropriated by Parliament to assist these centres.

A single employer who establishes a training centre where his employees (and others) are trained may apply for registration of a private training centre.

Grants-In-Aid These can be approved by the Minister and may be given to a registered trade union, employers' association or federation conducting training in labour relations.

Training Allowances The Minister may, at his discretion, grant allowances to any regional or industry training centre from monies appropriated by Parliament for this purpose.

Fund for the Training of the Unemployed Provision for this fund was made by the 1990 Manpower Training Amendment Act. It was envisaged that the fund would be financed by monies appropriated by Parliament, money appropriated by interest groups in the private sector, any other money which might accrue and interest on investments. The fund was controlled by the Director General and a committee which, other than the Director General, consisted of seven persons from the private sector, two officers from the Department and the chairman of the National Training Board.

Manpower Development Fund This fund receives monies accruing to Parliament from various sources. It is used to provide loans for regional and industry training centres.

CONCLUSION

South African labour legislation has been revamped and rationalised during the past ten years. The legislation as it stands is extensive and effective. It does provide the necessary protection for employees, and attempts to preserve the rights of both parties to the employment relationship.

SOURCES

Brassey, Cameron, Cheadle and Olivier *The New Labour Law*, Juta, 1987.

Gladstone, A *The Manager's Guide to International Labour Standards*, ILO, Geneva, 1986.

Hickman, Craig R and Michael A Silva *The Future 500*, Unwin Hyman Limited, 1989.

Ringrose, H G *The Law and Practice of Employment*, Juta, 1983.

Thompson, Clive and Paul Benjamin (Eds) *De Kock's Industrial Laws of South Africa*, Juta, 1991.

Thompson, Clive and Paul Benjamin *South African Labour Law*, Juta Revision Service 33, June 1995.

Basic Conditions of Employment Amendment Bill, Government Printer, Pretoria, 1993.

Labour Relations Act (No. 66 of 1995), *Government Gazette* Vol.366 no.16861, Government Printer, Pretoria, December 1995

Unemployment Insurance Amendment Bill, Government Printer, Pretoria, 1991.

Department of Labour *Annual Report 1994*, Government Printer, Pretoria, 1995.

'Recommendations on Labour Relations and Minimum Wage System for Farmworkers' in *Government Gazette*, Vol. 311 no. 13273, Pretoria, 30 May 1991.

'Recommendations of the National Manpower Commission regarding the Extension of Labour Legislation to Domestic Workers' in *Government Gazette*, Vol. 315 no. 13511, Pretoria, 13 September 1991.

6

TRADE UNIONS AND EMPLOYER ORGANISATIONS – THEORETICAL BASIS

In Industrial Relations we deal mostly with collectives. Consequently the two main participants in the relationship — employees and employers — should be described in their collective forms.

The collective with the highest profile is the union. Unions are both the reactive and the proactive participants in the relationship. Often as a result of employer behaviour, they initiate the action to which the employers or employers' associations, and sometimes also the State, react. Any attempt to understand industrial relations processes, therefore, necessitates and understanding of unions, of what they are, what they try to achieve, what methods and strategies they use and of how they are organised.

Unions initially arose out of the desire on the part of employees to counter the power of employers, particularly on the economic front; but nowadays unions have far wider objectives and employ a diversity of strategies. Also, although unions may be democratically founded and structured, the very real danger exists that they may eventually be dominated by a few individuals. Equally shop stewards, as representative of the union at the place of work, may at times assert their independence from such union.

Unions are not all the same. According to their orientation and the priority placed on certain goals, they may range from business unions to community, welfare and political unions. The style adopted by the union will, in turn, influence their managerial and organisational style. A union need not necessarily be constituted of outside agencies. Employees within an enterprise can form a bargaining committee or an in-plant union. Such bodies have their advantages and disadvantages. For employees who belong to these bodies, the most notable disadvantage is the fact that they have no sociopolitical clout. On the other hand, this could be obtained through political bodies. In other instances, workers' councils are established as participative or consultative bodies, independent or irrespective of union representation. This could result in conflict or overlap of interests between the different bodies.

Unions do not act alone. They are antiposed by employers, who need not form collectives to deal with the union but who, for various reasons, may prefer to do so. Employers' associations may not hold as high a profile as unions, but they do play an important role in industrial relations, both in the sphere of collective bargaining and as mouthpiece for employers in an industry. Their organisational structure and management resembles that of a union, although they do not have to engage in the same concerted recruitment as unions. Their aims, and methods of achieving such aims, may also be more limited than those of a union. While some employers may readily accept unions, others will fight to the last to counter any form of unionisation.

The collectivisation of the labour relationship remains controversial. However, where conflict and the use of coercive power are the order of the day, collectivisation is bound to remain.

TRADE UNIONS

TRADE UNIONS AS COLLECTIVE ORGANISATIONS

The analysis of the traditional labour relationship revealed that the power of an employer is best matched by a combination of workers who, by collective action, obtain concessions which would not otherwise have been granted and, in doing so, attempt to improve their position, both at the workplace and in society as a whole. It is this collective organisation which forms the basis of trade unionism.

There are, admittedly, numerous informal ways in which employees or groups of employees can express perceptions and interests conflicting with those of management or resist controls imposed by management, but their resistance becomes all the more effective once they have established or joined some type of formal organisation and have appointed an effectual spokesman. Employees have found that it is not sufficient merely to come together and appoint spokesmen on an *ad hoc* basis. If they are to regulate their relationship with management on an ongoing basis, they need a permanent organisation to represent them at all times and on all issues. Furthermore, such an organisation should, preferably, wield wider power than that which could be exercised by the employees alone. It should also have the necessary expertise to meet and deal with management on an equal basis. Thus employees form or join trade unions. In essence, trade unions are coalitions of workers but, because they rely on formal organisation and attempt to extend this organisation over as wide a range as possible, they have become societal institutions whose identity arises from, but is not synonymous with, a coalition of employees.

One of the first definitions of a trade union was that of Sidney and Beatrix Webb, who described a union as '... a continuous association of wage earners for the purpose of maintaining or improving their working lives'. In South Africa the Labour Relations Act of 1956 defined a union as 'any number of workers in a particular enterprise, industry, trade or profession who are united for the purpose, either alone or with other objectives, of organising relations between them or some of them and their employers or some of their employers in that enterprise, industry, trade or profession'. Neither of these definitions allows for a distinction between unions and certain associations which may also seek to represent the interest of their members, but which do so on a cooperative or consultative basis. The element missing from the definitions is that unions establish a position of equality with the employer and engage in bargaining with the employer, as opposed to associations which do not bargain but merely talk and which have to rely mostly on the goodwill of the employer because they do not have the power base or position to elicit concessions from him. Therefore a better definition of a union is that given by Salamon, namely that a union is

> '... any organisation, whose membership consists of employees, which
> seeks to organise and represent their interests both in the workplace and
> society, and, in particular, seeks to regulate their employment relationship
> through the direct process of collective bargaining with management.'

Salamon's definition highlights two other aspects of unionism. Firstly, trade
unionism requires organisation. A union does not merely happen, It may be
established by a few employees or interested persons, but thereafter it has
actively to recruit members in order to strengthen its power base. To these ends
a union may employ fulltime organisers who need not necessarily come from the
ranks of the employees themselves. Secondly, a union also seeks to improve the
position of its members in society at large. This may be done by the
improvement of their general economic position, but may mean that the union
has to play a social and political role.

One other assumption concerning unionism requires clarification: a union
constitutes more than the some of its parts. Although the members *are* the union
and, in a democratically organised union, the decisions executed are those of the
majority, a union as a body also gains a life of its own which is larger than the
sum of its constituent or individual members and which becomes a force within
the society. Individual members may come and go but the union, as a body with
its own character, policy and functions, may remain.

THE HISTORICAL DEVELOPMENT OF TRADE UNIONISM

As Salamon states, 'Trade unionism may be seen as a social response to the
advent of industrialisation and capitalism'. Prior to the Industrial Revolution
there had been in Britain trade guilds which, to a limited extent, protected the
interests of craftsmen and their apprentices, but these guilds really represented
the interests of so-called employers and did not engage in bargaining. The
Industrial Revolution brought with it a loss of independence and extremely poor
working conditions, as well as a belief in the freedom of contract, the operation
of the market forces and the pursuit of self-interest. Although these beliefs might
seem harmless or even advantageous, they could and did engender the
exploitation of the workforce. This necessitated some form of protection for the
workers and, at the same time, led to the birth of the 'working class'.

The achievement of the necessary protection was not easy as society was
geared mainly to increased production and to the attainment of economic goals,
usually at the expense of employees. So, for example, the British Combinations
Act of 1799/1800 prohibited the coalition of employees for the purpose of
promoting their interests. Strike action was outlawed and was subject to criminal
prosecution. Nevertheless the need to protect their joint interests did bring groups
of workers together, despite the obstacles encountered.

The actual beginnings of trade unionism in Britain are to be found in the so-
called Friendly Societies of the late 18th century. These were established by
craftsmen, who contributed a small amount each week and were then entitled to
receive benefits in case of sickness, retirement, unemployment or death. This
benefit function is still to be found in many unions today. The Friendly Societies
were very localised and, after the passage of the Combinations Act, had to

operate in secret. Thus they lacked power and failed to make an impression on employers.

In 1824 the Combinations Act was repealed and a new act, passed shortly afterwards, allowed workers to combine to protect their interests and even provided for a limited freedom to strike. At this stage the State took its first steps towards instituting some form of protection for workers, commencing with certain prohibitions on the use of child labour and later extending these to the employment of women on the mines. A number of unions were established in this era, mostly by skilled workers; but, like the Friendly Societies before them, the unions were localised, lacked effective organisation on a wider basis and did not engage in collective bargaining. At a later stage attempts were made to organise non-craftsmen and the working class in general. In 1824 the General Union of Operative Spinners of Great Britain was established, and in 1834 Robert Owen founded the shortlived Grand National Consolidated Trade Union, which was intended to be a union of workers in all industries. Many of the unions formed did not last long, firstly because of poor organisation and secondly because unionism was still generally resisted by the State and by employers. It was only after 1850 that the first real trade unions, as we know them, were established, and those mainly among craftsmen.

Salamon points out that the 'new' unions, as they were called, had a number of characteristics in common with modern trade unions. They were organised on a centralised, national level; they had a national executive as well as branch structures; they employed fulltime organisers, provided benefits and controlled entrance to their crafts by the apprenticeship system. They engaged in collective bargaining with employers, emerging with agreements on specific issues. Furthermore, they formulated joint policies, leading to their involvement in social and political matters and to the first Trade Union Congress in 1868.

Organisation among non-craft workers commenced only in the 1880s when the first unions for unskilled and semiskilled workers were established, as well as the first real general unions. The same period saw the emergence of white-collar unions representing, for example, the interests of teachers, clerks and municipal employees. Still later, the dilution of certain crafts by technology and the necessity for unions to organise on a wider scale led to the establishment of industrial unions.

Broadly speaking, this was the picture at the beginning of the 20th century. Trade unions of various kinds had established themselves as a permanent feature on the industrial scene. The next twenty years, marked by accelerated industrialisation, saw trade unionism proliferate in most economically advanced Western societies.

TRADE UNION CLASSIFICATION

As has been seen, trade unions historically organised themselves according to the type of interest they represented; that is, unions were established to represent employees in certain occupations, employees who did not resort under a specific occupation or, later still, employees who worked in a particular industry. Although trade unions are dynamic institutions and each may have individual reasons for recruiting a particular type of membership, they are still broadly classified into **occupational unions**, **industrial unions** and **general unions**.

Occupational
Unions

Occupational unions are so called because their membership derives from employees in a certain occupation. Because they organise across industries, these unions may be described as 'horizontal' in character.

The first occupational unions established were the **craft unions**. The main characteristic of these unions is their concern for and protection of the skilled status of their membership. For this reason they concentrate on recruiting apprentices to their trade, controlling the number of apprentices indentured and regulating the training of apprentices. Craft unions find their power in the skill of their members and in their ability to restrict entrance to the occupation which they represent. Their strength lies not in numbers, but in the fact that their members occupy strategic positions in an undertaking and are not easily replaceable. The dilution of skills by the introduction of technology has had the result that very few pure craft unions still exist. Most craft unions now also recruit among so-called 'allied occupations' and some have amalgamated with other unions in particular industries to form industrial unions; but, even in such bodies, those representing workers with specific skills may still occupy special positions.

A variation of the craft union is the **promotion union**. This type of union also recruits amongst workers with a particular skill, but the skill is one which is achieved by on-the-job training and promotion rather than by an apprenticeship, as in the case of an established craft. An example of a promotion union is the Footplate Workers' Association on the Railways. Because these unions often recruit workers in a certain occupation in a particular industry, they are similar in many respects to industrial unions. However, their power base is the same as that of a craft union, namely the strategic importance and skill of the workers they represent. By organising the various grades of workers in a particular occupation, they ensure that production cannot continue, should they decide to strike.

In order to fill the void left by craft and promotion unions, unions were established to represent **unskilled** and **semiskilled** workers in certain industries. These unions restricted their membership to so-called 'lower level employees', who then represented a specific occupational interest. This has happened particularly in South Africa, where skill and race are historically coincidental and where the interests of African workers were not represented by craft and promotion or even industrial unions. It is obvious that unions representing semiskilled and unskilled workers do not have the strategic power of craft and promotion unions. Their power base lies in mass organisation and in preventing the incidence of 'scabbing'. Sometimes these unions organise across industries and become similar to general unions. Others restrict themselves to certain industries and may, therefore, be termed industrial unions. As union organisation and the fragmentation of skills increase, these unions may amalgamate with craft and promotion unions to form larger industrial unions.

The last type of occupational union is that established to represent the interests of **non-manual** or **white-collar** workers. Traditionally there has always been a difference in interests between these and so-called blue-collar workers.

Non-manual workers have also been slower to organise. This may be ascribed to the fact that white-collar workers often perceive themselves as being closer to management, or see themselves as 'professionals'. Lately, with the shift to service industries in the economies of many Western countries, there has been a marked increase in white-collar unionism. Most of these unions will organise only workers in a particular industry but some, especially those representing certain professions, may organise across industries. There have been instances where white-collar workers have been recruited into traditionally manual unions or where white-collar unions have amalgamated with manual unions to form industry unions, but they have continued to represent specific interests within that union.

General Unions

General unions originated both from the politically inspired ideal of organising the entire working class into one body and from the need to represent non-skilled workers without reference to industries, or to form amalgamations of unions operating in different industries. Although their membership is, in theory, open to any employee, many general unions have tended to adopt a particular industrial pattern, as proved by a name such as Transport & General Workers' Union. Often they will concentrate on workers in a particular industry or industries and otherwise act as a 'clearing house' for other unions. They will recruit all workers, but some will later be passed on to unions in specific industries. The ideal of one union to represent all workers has proved over the years to be a Utopian dream, since sectoral interests continue to predominate. This idea seems to have been replaced by a policy of directing organisation towards a federation of like-minded unions. Consequently, and owing also to the establishment of industrial unions, the concept of a general union has become less popular. This may further be attributed to the fact that general unions often find their manpower thinly spread, have a relatively low power base and, in certain countries, encounter difficulties in the registration of their unions.

Industrial Unions

The purpose of an industrial union is to represent all the workers in a certain industry or, at least, as many workers as possible in a particular industry. According to its orientation, an industrial union may either seek to be a **monopoly union**, in which case it will try to be the only union for all workers in an industry, or be merely a **single-industry union**, which is a union confining its efforts to organising workers in one industry only. Because sectorisation of interests still exists, most industrial unions are of the latter type. They will organise only workers in a certain industry, but this does not mean that they represent all classes of workers in that industry.

Industrial unions arose as a reaction to occupational stratification of unions and as a direct result of the dilution and fragmentation of crafts and skills, but they may also have a sociopolitical purpose. According to Salamon,

> '... the original concept of industrial unionism was ... seen as a means, together with a general strike, whereby the working classes could take control of both their workplace and society. If workers are to control their workplace and industry, including the election of those who manage it, it

is axiomatic that trade unions should adopt similar boundaries for their organisational pattern.'

Industrial unionism has definite advantages in that it leads to stronger unions, helps to eliminate inter-union competition, reduces the number of unions with which an employer has to bargain, brings correspondence between union organisation and employer organisation and leads to improved industrial planning. For the union it has the added advantages that officials can gain expertise in the intricacies of a particular industry and that the union's power base, through its ability to strike an entire industry, is greatly enhanced. On the other hand, a number of factors militate against industrial unionism as the only form of unionism. Very often, sectoral interests will predominate. Furthermore, it is sometimes difficult to establish absolute boundaries between industries. This leads to accusations of 'poaching' between unions. Finally, in many countries it has proved difficult to break down historically diverse unions and to reamalgamate them into industrial unions.

In South Africa the Congress of South African Trade Unions has adopted the concept of one union per industry as a definite objective, for both organisational and sociopolitical reasons. COSATU itself was founded only after years of planning, and it is understandable that problems were experienced in achieving the 'one union per industry' ideal.

Representation of Sociopolitical, Racial and Religious Interests

So far, the discussion on trade union classification has centred in the union's representation of workplace interests. In some countries different trade unions representing the same workplace interests are established to represent varying interests outside the workplace. So, for example, unions in the Netherlands have traditionally been divided along religious lines, while in France union organisation reflects the political divisions in society. In South Africa, historical divisions, underscored by the policy of 'apartheid', have led to the formation of white, black consciousness, multiracial and nonracial unions. It is obvious that strong divisions in society, carried into union organisation, lead to greater diversification of unionism and to more complicated labour relations.

The Problem of Multiunionism

Despite the ideal of a united working class, there is still a tendency in most countries for groups of employees to organise in such a manner as to promote their particular interests, be these of a personal, occupational, industrial, religious, racial or sociopolitical nature. Consequently, even though the formation of monopolistic industrial unions would lead to more rational labour relations, the problem of multiunionism remains. This is particularly so in societies with strong ideological or other divisions. The best to be hoped for, in the interim, is that unions representing the same workplace interests will realise that inter-union rivalry may eventually lead to self-destruction. Employers, on their part, will be obliged to accept the fact that, however much this may complicate their labour relations, they cannot deal only with one union if there are conflicting interests within the enterprise. Acceptance of this principle would preclude the conclusion of closed-shop agreements and of agreements granting sole collective bargaining rights to a particular union.

REGISTRATION OF TRADE UNIONS

Usually provision is made for trade unions to register or to become certified in terms of industrial legislation. Requirements for registration differ from country to country. Generally a union is required to demarcate its area of operation, to prove representativeness by submitting a membership register and to submit annual audited accounts to the Industrial Registrar or similar official. The union is given the status of a legal person which, in broad terms, means that it can acquire and dispose of property, can sue and be sued. Furthermore, in certain countries unions are allowed to participate in the collective bargaining and dispute settlement machinery established by law only if they are properly registered or certificated.

Non-registration of a union does not signify its non-existence. A union, like any club, can be constituted by a number of persons with common aims who adopt a constitution and declare themselves members of that organisation. Yet the process of registration does bestow a certain 'legitimacy' on a union. Besides the advantage of 'legitimacy', registration can safeguard members against misappropriation of funds and malpractice by officials.

In a voluntary system the decision to register or not rests with the union and its members. Unless unacceptable controls are instituted by registration, unions may find that the advantages of registration outweigh the trouble involved in applying for and maintaining registered status. This has occurred in South Africa, where the unions emerging in the Seventies initially opposed registration, mostly as a matter of principle, but where the majority of those unions are now registered bodies.

TRADE UNION OBJECTIVES

Simplistically, the overall objective of a trade union is to represent the interests of its members; but, because these interests range widely, both within the enterprise and outside, the objectives of trade unions become multiple and complex.

This multiplicity is best illustrated by studying the objectives of the British Trade Union Council, as set out in its evidence to the Donovan Commission. According to this, the aims of the TUC are as follows.

- To improve the terms of employment
- To improve the physical environment at work
- To achieve full employment and national prosperity
- To achieve security of employment and income
- To improve social security
- To achieve fair shares in national income and wealth
- To achieve industrial democracy
- To achieve a voice in government
- To improve public and social services
- To achieve public control and planning of industry

As can be seen, these objectives range from the individual through the economic to the sociopolitical. Very few trade unions manage to achieve all these objectives, and the degree to which any objective is pursued will vary from union to union.

Also, the emphasis which a trade union places on particular objectives will depend on the type of society in which the union operates, the position of its members within society and their attitude towards that society. In a society where trade union members share the same ideology with employers and government, their emphasis will fall on individual and economic objectives. Alternatively, in a society where trade union members perceive themselves as repressed, or where they are not satisfied with the sociopolitical *status quo*, emphasis will necessarily also be placed on their sociopolitical objectives.

Broadly speaking, the objectives of trade unions can be classified as follows.

Economic Objectives

Maintenance or improvement of the economic status of its members remains one of the major functions of a trade union, if not its primary reason for being. Employees join trade unions mainly in the hope that they will increase their bargaining power *vis-à-vis* the employer. Since the most concrete manifestation of such bargaining power is the union's ability to gain economic concessions in the form of increased wages or improved benefits from the employer, a union which does not produce economic results may soon lose its members. There are instances in which members of a union may not be overly concerned with their economic position, or where other objectives override economic issues, but this usually happens when the primary economic need has been fulfilled, or when circumstances make the fulfilment of this economic need impossible, as in a society where the system of government supports a grossly inequitable distribution of wealth, or where free collective bargaining is prohibited.

It is important to note that a union which attempts to improve the economic position of its members at all costs could, in the long term, bring about a decline in general economic conditions. It could thereby jeopardise the very economic position which it seeks to protect. This is so because unrealistic wage demands from unions may result in a wage–price spiral, which inevitably has inflationary effects on the economy. For this reason unions may sometimes temper their demands or even cooperate with government and other agencies by temporarily freezing wage demands, for the purpose of improving the general economy. Closely related to this is the union dilemma of achieving maximum wages while, at the same time, maintaining or maximising employment levels. At the enterprise level a union which demands ever-increasing wages may do so at the cost of staff reductions. This is reflected on the macro-level, where the rising cost of wages may adversely affect the economy and result in general unemployment.

A union cannot pursue its economic objectives without reference to the total situation. Yet unions tend to be reactive rather than proactive in this respect. They will continue to demand until they become aware of adverse effects. Only then will they modify their demands or shift the emphasis to other objectives.

Job Security

It is almost as important for a union to maintain the job security of its members as it is to achieve economic benefits. For this reason a union may, both in individual bargaining situations and in general, waive increased economic benefits for some of its members so that all members may keep their jobs. The concern of unions with job security is further displayed by their involvement with dismissals and retrenchments and their attempts to prevent these from occurring. This desire of unions to protect the jobs of members leads to ongoing conflict with management about rationalisation and the introduction of new technology.

In respect of employment, unions see themselves as having a further function, namely the promotion of full employment throughout a particular society. This may lead to disgruntlement with the economic and other policies of government, particularly in a capitalist system, where the free market principle of demand and supply still predominates and where a certain level of unemployment is usually viewed as inevitable.

Social Welfare Allied to its economic function is the union function of ensuring the welfare of its members. Its first concern in this respect is with sickness, accident, death and pension benefits. These benefits may be provided by the union itself, or the union may ensure that an employer or the State establishes funds and offers the necessary protection to workers. The union's welfare function further embraces such aspects as health and safety, and may extend into areas such as housing and education.

Job Regulation A union does not attempt merely to regulate the wages of its members at their place of employment, but also to influence as many other aspects of their working lives as possible. Therefore, joint agreement on such matters as working hours, overtime, work on public holidays, vacation leave, sick leave and notice periods are regarded as basic to any union–management agreement. In more sophisticated systems the union will demand joint regulation of dispute settlement procedures, dismissal procedures, grievance handling, retrenchment, technological innovation and health and safety matters. In its extreme, joint regulation extends to joint planning of the work process, and to joint decisionmaking in the management of the enterprise.

Some of the aspects mentioned, especially minimum conditions of work, may be regulated by the State. The State may, furthermore, lay down rules obliging management to engage in joint regulation with unions on certain aspects of work. Consequently, unions can achieve their objective of joint regulation by lobbying with or placing political pressure on the government.

Individual Development A union consists of individuals and one of its functions is to promote the moral, physical and intellectual wellbeing of each member. This is partially achieved by the very fact that someone belongs to a union, that his dignity is respected, that he does not feel himself to be alone in his struggles or with his problems, that he fulfils a role in the organisation and that he can count on the support of other members of the group. Yet the union's function does not end here and most organisations will offer other facilities for the individual, such as social gatherings, lessons in practical affairs and opportunities for education and training. This happens especially in underdeveloped or developing societies. In economically developed societies the individual is usually presented with other avenues for self-fulfilment and the role of the union in this respect has, consequently, diminished. However, even when unions themselves no longer fulfil the developmental function, they may still oversee the development of workers by employers or the State.

Because a union is a collective which is representative of a large number of people, it needs constantly to reassess its objectives and ensure that it is adequately representing all the interests of its members.

Sociopolitical Aims

The last objective of the British Trade Union Council was 'to achieve public control and planning of industry'. This, in a society which supports the capitalist system and the free market principle, would entail political action directed at overthrowing the system of government and replacing it with one which would support socialist principles and would be willing to institute a planned economy. Numerous unions throughout the world subscribe to this broadly socialist objective. Yet the very reason for the existence of trade unions is rooted in the capitalist system. Anderson puts it this way:

> *'As institutions, trade unions do not challenge the existence of a society based on a division of classes, they merely express it. Thus trade unions can never be viable vehicles of advance towards socialism in themselves; by their very nature they are tied to capitalism. They can bargain with society but not transform it.'*

It would appear that trade unions on their own cannot achieve this overall political objective. They can at best conscientise and build up solidarity among the working class. The actual job of transforming society evidently belongs to other bodies especially established for this purpose, with whom the trade unions may work in a supportive role. The other problem is that, if a purely socialist system is eventually achieved, trade unions might find themselves in a position where they are redundant as far as their workplace role is concerned because they would no longer have to bargain with employers, although they might then engage in bargaining with the State. Also to be taken into account is the fact that, during the past fifty years, many Western societies have abandoned pure free market and capitalist systems for more 'mixed' systems which, while operating on broadly capitalist principles, incorporate socialist aspects in the form, for example, of the growing welfare function of the State and the breaking down of capitalist class structures. This has led to a change in the overall approach of trade unions. As Salamon states, 'the early political, revolutionary approach displayed by some trade unions has given way to a more conservative approach based on evolution within the existing industrial and political system.'

The above does not signify that trade unions should not have or no longer have political objectives, but merely that the revolutionary objective of trade unions may be difficult to achieve, may lead to their own destruction and may no longer be necessary. Yet trade union members still have a stake in the social and political systems which dominate their lives, and trade unions necessarily have to represent the interests of their members in these spheres. Thus to say that trade unions should not be 'political' would be unrealistic. Trade unions constitute a very potent political force, and most trade unions do engage in political action of some kind or another. They differ only in degree and in the means used to achieve their sociopolitical objectives. Their methods vary according to their own policies and circumstances. Certain trade unions may attain a direct voice in government; others are content merely to lobby governmental and local organisations, while yet others are obliged to engage in direct protest action. Finally and most importantly, the degree of politicisation of trade unions depends largely on the type of system in which they exist. The more inequitable the system (according to the perception of trade union members), the more will their unions be obliged to engage in direct and overt political actions.

METHODS BY WHICH UNIONS ATTEMPT TO ACHIEVE THEIR OBJECTIVES

Before discussing specific methods by which unions attempt to achieve their objectives, it is necessary once again to stress the importance of power in adversarial labour relations and its significance to the union, as representative of one party in the relationship. The achievement of power is, for the union, both an objective and a means by which it can achieve other objectives. It has been said that individual employees gain power by establishing or belonging to a union. Yet the union, too, has to ensure that it can wield power *vis-à-vis* the employer and the State. A union gains power firstly from the solidarity of its members and their willingness to engage in collective action. If membership is individualistic or reluctant to engage in action, the union will lose power. The establishment of power in this respect will depend largely on the morale of the members, on effective leadership and on the involvement of the members with union affairs. Secondly, a union gains power from the depth and extent of its organisation. A poorly organised body, representing only a small number of employees, will wield no power. Thus most unions, except perhaps those representing employees in strategic occupations, have to continue growing but, at the same time, have to improve and deepen their organisation. Thirdly, a union gains power by the skill and expertise of its negotiators, by its ability to evoke sympathetic action from other organisations in the industrial and sociopolitical spheres and, finally, by its ability to influence government and business agencies, by either direct or indirect means.

It is remarkable that the aforegoing discussion on the role of power has led inevitably to the mention of various means by which power, and thus the objectives of the union, may be achieved. This most aptly demonstrates the interrelationship between the achievement of union objectives and the achievement and use of power. The existence or use of power underlies many of the specific methods which unions use to achieve their objectives. These methods, which are interactive, include the following.

Collective Bargaining with Employers

Collective bargaining with employers is the primary function of the union. It is the method by which it attempts to improve the economic position of its members and to regulate their terms and conditions of employment. Bargaining is an ongoing process. It does not end with wage negotiations. A union which actively represents its members will continually be engaged in negotiation of some kind or another.

Collective Action

Collective action is an integral part of collective bargaining, since collective action (in the form of a go-slow, a work-to-rule, a strike or a boycott) is merely a means by which unions show their power and by which they attempt to pressurise the employer into continued negotiation or into adopting a position more favourable to the union. A union need not engage in direct action in all instances of disagreement, but the employer should be aware that the union has the power to engage in such action if it so wishes.

Representation at Company Level

It is necessary for the union continually to be involved in or have knowledge of all actions affecting its members which may occur at the workplace. For this reason unions provide for the election of shop stewards to represent the workplace interests of their fellow employees. Such shop stewards usually have special rights, among which is the right to represent other employees during the conduct of grievance and disciplinary procedures, although, when these procedures reach an advanced stage, union officials may themselves become involved. Shop stewards also transmit information regarding the needs and problems of employees to the union so that union officials may take up such issues with management.

Affiliation with Other Bodies

Unions will attempt to affiliate with other like-minded organisations, both nationally and internationally, in order to increase their bargaining power with employers and with the State. The voice of a federation of unions is more easily heard than that of a lone union, particularly as regards matters affecting all workers. Furthermore, one union can rely on sympathy action from other unions, should it be at issue with a particular employer or a group of employers. Where a union has international affiliates, these affiliates could oblige their own employers to bring pressure to bear on the local employer or could cause economic harm to the local employer.

Collective Bargaining with Government

A union movement which is sufficiently strong can oblige the government to take heed of its demands. In the extreme this is achieved by the threat of a general strike. The purpose of collective bargaining with government is to represent the economic and social interests of union members at the highest level and to obtain concessions in both industrial and sociopolitical legislation. Very few union movements achieve this kind of power without a political vehicle through which they actively participate in government. Other than that, their role is usually representative.

Representation on Local and National Bodies

No local or national authority can afford to ignore the voice of a strong union movement. Therefore, in most Western countries, trade unions will be represented on local and national boards engaged in activities which directly affect the union and its members. Examples of such bodies are manpower, pension and economic planning committees. With sufficient and effective representation on these boards, unions can do much to safeguard the interests of their members.

Representations to Government and Employer Organisations

Unions can take up issues such as unfavourable legislation or general discrimination in industry with government or employer organisations by making direct representations on the issues concerned. In their dealings with government, unions may sometimes use employer organisations such as chambers of commerce and industry as intermediaries. Because these bodies may be in a stronger position with government, the unions may request them to pressurise the government on their behalf.

Political Involvement

In a system where union members are generally dissatisfied with the economic and political *status quo*, unions may seek to bring about a change of government by actively supporting an opposition political party or even forming their own political wing. This occurred in Britain, where the establishment of the Labour Party was a direct result of the trade union movement's perception that it could best represent the interests of its members by voting its own political party into power. However, it should be borne in mind that, where trade unionists are elected into government, they cease to be trade unionists as they would then have a wider constituency and would, of necessity, have to balance the interests of all stakeholders.

Benefit Funds

Unions try to assist their membership by establishing pension, provident and medical aid funds and even housing and education schemes. This happens particularly in countries where employers or the government do not provide sufficient cover. A problem does exist in that some unions overemphasise this function to the detriment of other union functions. Also, a member who participates in any of these schemes is to some extent bound to the union. Thus it may happen that an employee who is dissatisfied with the union and does not take part in its activities retains his membership merely for fear of losing the benefits concerned. On the one hand, control of benefit funds does, through their investment power, give unions greater power — both within the industry and in the economy.

Education and Social Programmes

A union is also responsible for the individual growth of its members, especially those from underprivileged communities. As a result, unions will be actively involved in the establishment of education and training programmes at the place of work, as well as in the social responsibility programme of the organisation. Also, unions may institute their own social and education programmes. These may range from basic programmes on personal hygiene, health, good house-keeping and motherhood to formal lessons and advanced discourses on social and economic developments.

The discussion on union objectives and the methods of achieving these has served to illustrate the complexity of the union function. This function can be performed effectively only by sound organisation and effective leadership.

TRADE UNION STYLES

As explained earlier, trade unions arose out of the perceived unequal treatment of employees and the subsequent realisation that an equalisation of power could be achieved only by combination. The core of a trade union's existence is, therefore, to be found in the representation of the economic and job-related interests of its members within a particular enterprise or industry. However, as the membership, power and influence of unions expanded, so did their objectives, evidenced by those of the British Trade Union Council to which reference was made at the commencement of this chapter. Unions found that they could play a role not only at a particular enterprise but in an entire industry; that they had achieved notable status in their respective communities; that they could control vast funds and that they could influence both economic and political developments. In terms of its circumstances, a union emphasises one or more of these objectives and from this will derive its individual approach and style. Thus union styles vary, leading to the following broad classification.

- **Business Unionism**. This refers to those unions which concentrate on the improvement of wages and working conditions, at either plant or industry level. At the most, such unions will lobby for or provide input as regards proposed labour legislation or comment on economic policy, but they refrain from any significant sociopolitical involvement. In some instances these unions are also described as 'workerist', as opposed to 'populist', in their approach.
- **Community Unionism**. Unions of this school are actively and continuously involved with the communities from which their membership derives, and see their role as protecting the interests of those communities. Thus they have strong representation on local bodies and, where communities are politically divided, they may adopt a political stance.
- **Welfare Unionism**. Certain unions derive their strength and support from the fact that they provide benefits for members in the form of pension and sick funds, funeral benefits and even educational assistance. If these unions are organised on a large scale, they could eventually control national funds and so become entrenched in their positions.
- **'Economically Responsible' Unionism**. This description has been coined to identify those unions which perceive their role as the promoters and protectors of general economic welfare, be this at industry or national level. Such unions would wish to play an active part in the planning and promotion of the industry in which they operate and in national bodies dealing with the economy as a whole.
- **Political Unionism**. In this instance the emphasis falls either on the promotion of a particular party or on general sociopolitical change. The union utilises its power base to support a political party, to lobby influential organisations, or — through mass action — to provide the impetus for political change. Individual unionists who support this approach are sometimes described as 'populists'.

While different approaches have been outlined, it should be remembered that more than one approach could be adopted simultaneously and that the classification rests with the emphasis placed on a particular objective rather than on its adoption to the exclusion of all others. Also, the approach selected by a union, as well as the degree of militancy displayed, will depend on various factors such as the ideological stance of the union, whether unions subscribe to the same ideology as employers and the government, the dominant sociopolitical system, government regulation of labour relations, class inequalities within a particular society, sociopolitical deprivation (or otherwise) of union members, employer attitudes and policies, and economic conditions prevalent at the time. Thus, if most of its members are sociopolitically disadvantaged, the union will necessarily adopt a more overtly political style. Equally, a union whose members subscribe to the same ideology as management and do not view themselves as disadvantaged can afford to concentrate on economic rather than political issues and it would, therefore, become a business union.

One other aspect of union behaviour deserves attention: the degree to which unions are prepared to engage in cooperative relationships with employers. Traditionally, unions view themselves as the adversaries of management, yet collective bargaining — as the main process emanating from the union–management relationship — relies on a certain measure of cooperation. This notwithstanding, most unions would hesitate at the prospect of taking such cooperation further. They fear that cooperation would result in shared responsibility, which would detract from their role as challenger of managerial decisions and actions. Historically, it was essential for unions to adopt strongly adversarial positions, but in advanced labour relationships this may no longer be necessary. However, the position adopted by the union will once again depend on the external influences mentioned in the previous paragraph. Unions do sometimes engage in cooperation in times of economic difficulty, but only if management and unions share a common ideology can any advanced system of cooperation be instituted. Equally, employees should not be economically, socially and politically disadvantaged and management, by its policies and actions, would have to lay the foundations for cooperation. Of course, where unions reject any form of private ownership of the means of production, the question of cooperation becomes completely irrelevant.

THE ORGANISATION AND MANAGEMENT OF TRADE UNIONS

Trade Union Organisation   Trade union organisation varies and will depend on the size, policy, constitution and rules of a particular union. Nevertheless there is, in most unions, a hierarchical form of organisation similar to that found in business undertakings but, unlike business organisations, power is not necessarily vested at the top. The broad base of this hierarchy consists of the general membership, who may, at each plant or business where they have significant representation, elect shop stewards to liaise with management and with the local union body.

Depending on their numbers, such shop stewards may establish plant-based or area-based shop steward committees, which constitute the next level in the organisational hierarchy.

Local Branches

The axis on which trade union organisation revolves is found at the level of the local branch. It is the branch which coordinates trade union activity, actively recruits new members and acts as transmitter of general union policy to local members or, conversely, ensures that suggestions, complaints and requests from local members reach the higher levels of the organisation. A branch is constituted of all the trade union members in a particular area and every branch

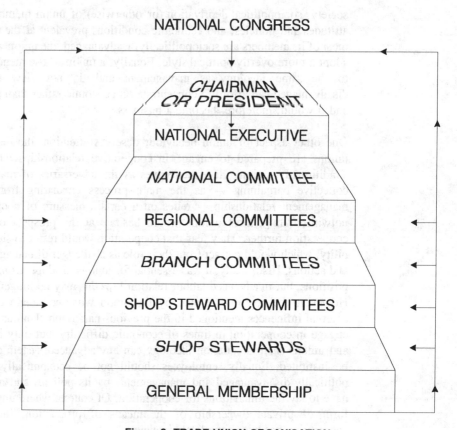

Figure 9: TRADE UNION ORGANISATION

will have its own chairman, secretary and treasurer. The branch committee may consist of shop stewards and elected local members but, if its size and range of activities so warrant, a branch may appoint fulltime officers and fulltime organisers, to be paid from the funds collected by that branch.

Regional Organisation

Most larger unions also find it necessary to establish some kind of regional organisation in the form of a regional committee. This committee will usually consist of representatives from the various branches but may, like the branch committees, have fulltime officers and organisers. The regional committee, in its turn, will act as coordinator of branch activities and as liaison between branches and the national committee or the national executive.

Organisation at National Level

At the apex of the hierarchy is the national committee and the national executive, consisting of the union president or chairman, the vice chairman, general secretary and treasurer. The manner in which these officials are appointed or elected and the powers bestowed on them will depend on the constitution of a particular union. In some instances the members of the national committee and executive come from the ranks of the local or regional committees, while in others they are elected by general congress. It is the task of the national committee and particularly the executive to implement union policy and decisions, to speak and act on behalf of the union and, in general, to ensure that the organisation functions as smoothly as possible.

National Congress
In democratic unionism, policy decisions are taken by the national congress, representing grassroots membership. Congress also elects the executive, and should have the power to hold executive members accountable to the national congress.

The aforegoing description of trade unions presupposes that the organisation develops from the bottom upwards, and not the other way around. There are some organisations were a reverse development occurs, or has occurred, but, because trade unions are grassroots organisations, a top–down structure is regarded as undesirable.

Trade Union Management   The management of a trade union rests with the various executives at branch, regional and national level. Insofar as these committees are constituted of elected trade union members (office bearers) or officials elected or appointed by the members, it can be said that the members manage the union, true to the dictum that 'the members are the union'.

Officials and Organisers
In keeping with this policy, unions may not accord officials or organisers appointed from outside, such as the general secretary, a vote in committee or executive decisions. In such instances the official becomes nothing more than an employee of the union. He may advise elected office bearers and union members, but may make no determinations of his own accord. Furthermore, a typical union constitution will determine that changes in union policy and fundamental decisions may be effected only by a general congress of trade union members, or (in the case of larger unions) a general congress of representatives from each region. The purpose is to ensure that the highest decisionmaking authority remains vested in the members themselves and not in the executive, which is supposed merely to implement the policies established and the decisions taken by general congress.

The Question of Union Democracy
The principle of member management and control is an ideal which may not always be achieved in practice. This is so firstly because unions may be dominated by certain factions or officials who pursue their own interests and not those of the general membership. Secondly, most officials and organisers will influence and, to some extent, control union members merely by virtue of their greater expertise and knowledge and of the fact that union business is their only business. Thirdly, there are many day-to-day decisions which have to be taken by individuals, committees or executives without the opportunity of first obtaining the approval of the general membership — although, in such cases, provision may be made for *post hoc* ratification by the membership. Fourthly, and most importantly, trade union members are sometimes apathetic. Having

once paid their dues, they do not actively participate or take an interest in union affairs, except when a crisis arises. Because of their lack of interest, they allow the few who do participate or the elected officials to act in an undemocratic manner. Finally, individuals appointed to important positions in the union hierarchy will hold substantial power. They are able to influence a vast number of people and, because of their positions, may become public figures. This may result in a 'power complex', where the individual perceives himself as more important than the union or its members. Simplistically phrased, he believes that he is the union or that he runs the union. Consequently, he will jealously guard his position — at the cost, very often, of democracy and the welfare of the general membership. There are, in fact, numerous theorists who believe that unions move in a continual cycle from democracy to oligarchy and back to democracy. Because of the factors mentioned, a union which was originally established on a democratic base may eventually be dominated by a few skilled or powerful individuals. This phase will continue for some time until members become aware of and dissatisfied with the situation, whereupon there will again be an initiative towards democratisation. However, unfortunately and almost inevitably, certain individuals will again achieve dominance, particularly if there is a lack of involvement on the part of members or if the union operates at a highly centralised level.

Despite the problems mentioned, numerous trade unions do attempt to conduct their affairs along democratic lines. It may at times not be feasible for officials to report back to the membership on a continuous basis, but they are, in the final analysis, accountable to their membership. Should these members be dissatisfied, they hold the democratic right to demand the removal of the officials concerned or to vote them out of office at the next election. Moreover, important decisions too pressing to be kept over for the next general congress may be tested by referendum, the most common form of which is the strike ballot. In the same way, most negotiators will not act outside the terms of their mandates without first referring the matter to their general membership. The most effective safeguard against undemocratic action is to be found in the greatest possible involvement of members at all levels of the organisation. For this reason unions which take democracy seriously will attempt to involve shop stewards in negotiations, will report back as often as possible and will ensure that office bearers on the national executive are drawn mostly from membership ranks. Ultimately, the membership as a whole is responsible for the type of government a union has. By exercising their vote responsibly and involving themselves in the affairs of their union, individual members can ensure that their organisation is not run on undemocratic lines.

'Responsible' Leadership

The principle of union democracy may prove a problem to employers who are wont to insist on rapid decisionmaking and that union leaders 'control' their members. A union which insists on continual reportback may not be able to give an immediate decision; and a leader who represents the interests of his members and abides by the majority decision cannot 'control' his members, although he may be able to influence them and to dissuade them from irresponsible actions. Thus the management call for union leaders to act 'responsibly' may contradict the democratic principle on which unions are based.

Administrative Functions

Besides their leadership and representational functions, union office bearers and officials also have an administrative role. They are responsible for recruiting and enrolling new members, ensuring that dues are paid, keeping books of account, running the day-to-day business of the union, submitting the necessary documents and statements to maintain registered status, administering benefit funds on behalf of the union and disseminating information to members. In large organisations, where there is a heavy administrative load, the very real danger exists that office bearers and officials will concentrate on these functions to the detriment of their representative and organisational role. There are unions where the necessary balance has not been maintained, in which case the union has become little more than a slow-moving bureaucracy.

Trade Union Discipline A union constitutes a collective which the individual joins of his own accord. Having once joined, he is subject to the rules and decisions of that collective. Should he disagree, he is free to withdraw his membership, but he may not act in his individual capacity or distance himself from union decisions at will. This applies particularly to office bearers of the union.

All in all, union management is a complex and difficult task and the manner in which it is tackled will vary from union to union. The style of management in a particular union will in the end depend largely on the historical development of that union, its overall ideology, the degree of interest displayed by its members and the particular circumstances in which it is obliged to operate.

TRADE UNIONISM IN THE FUTURE

In certain Western countries trade union membership has decreased in relative terms over the past decade or more. This may be attributed to a number of factors, among which are the increased wellbeing of the working class, the tendency to establish 'mixed' economic and sociopolitical systems and the need for greater cooperation between employers and employees in order to ensure continued economic prosperity.

Trade unions arose out of the necessity to protect employees from exploitation in societies where there was a polarisation between those who owned and those who laboured, where employers held absolute power and where governments were not overly concerned with the general welfare of all people. Their role was essentially antagonistic in that they had to battle, often against great odds, for every concession. In such a climate it was natural that a 'we and they' mentality should develop and that trade unions would fight for concessions for their members with little consideration for the general welfare of the company or even the country as a whole. The post-war years, particularly in Europe, have seen a gradual breaking down of class structures, a more general spread of ownership (also to employees), the introduction of laws protecting workers from exploitation and even, in some countries, laws mandating a degree of joint decisionmaking by employers and employees. Comprehensive welfare schemes, especially in the areas of health, housing and old age pension, have diluted the benefit function of trade unions, and the working class in general has become more prosperous. Moreover, in countries such as the United States, the threat of competition from foreign imports and the danger this poses to the economy have necessitated a joint effort by employers and employees to improve productivity and to make local goods competitive with those from other countries.

Consequently, trade unions may be faced with the dilemma of balancing antagonism with cooperation. In certain countries trade unions have managed to achieve some balance by separating their bargaining function from their cooperative and co-decisionmaking function. This has happened in Germany, where trade unions bargain centrally with employers, but where they also appoint representatives to management supervisory boards and where participation at plant level is in the hands of workers' committees. In other countries, such as Britain, unions still tend to emphasise their bargaining role and to shy away from direct cooperation with management. This is evidenced by the initial resistance of British unions to the principle of co-decisionmaking on management boards. In Britain the growth of employee shareholding in companies may further complicate the task of trade unions. Representing the interests of a member who is both employee and part owner may prove even more difficult than cooperating with and opposing management.

It is not foreseen that the bargaining function of unions will disappear within the near future. Yet, as societies progress, the importance of the bargaining function in relation to the union's other representational functions may greatly diminish. Even if this occurs and even if the importance of trade unions diminishes, the concept of unionism will remain as a deterrent to exploitative practices by employers. Should these re-emerge, aggressive unionism would re-emerge. Also, it could be postulated that unions might lose their impetus at the workplace, but that they may continue to operate at a more centralised level, as power blocs within the sociopolitical dispensation.

THE SHOP STEWARD

The Role of the Shop Steward

A union which wishes to be continually in touch with events on the shop floor and to be permanently represented at the workplace will insist that members at every plant elect shop stewards from amongst their own ranks and that management recognises such shop stewards as the legitimate representatives of the union members in their employ.

Consequently, union–management agreements will provide for the election and recognition of a certain number of shop stewards and for shop steward facilities such as time off, venues for meetings and even the necessary physical facilities. The number of shop stewards elected will depend on the size of the undertaking and the nature of its operation. Shop stewards are elected on a *pro rata* basis — say, one for every fifty union members or, where operations are physically separated, one per department or section.

The shop steward plays a pivotal role in union organisation. He performs his union duties in the course of his employment and is the one official who can directly represent workers' interests towards both management and the union. He also acts as a link between the union and the workers and the union and management.

Figure 10 illustrates the pivotal role played by the shop steward in the communications network. To his fellow employees he is more often than not 'the union' or the person to take their problems to management. To management he also represents 'the union', but he is at the same time one of their employees with whom they may be able to communicate more easily than with another union official and through whom they can transmit ideas and proposals to other employees. To the union he is not only their representative at the workplace, but also an employee who knows what is happening, what other employees are thinking, how they will react and what management is planning.

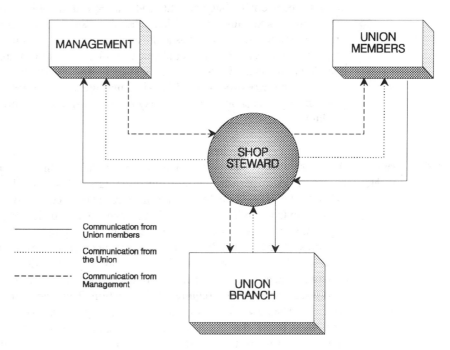

Figure 10: THE ROLE OF THE SHOP STEWARD

Qualities of a Good Shop Steward

If a shop steward is to perform his role effectively, he should have the respect and trust of the union, his fellow employees and management. He should, furthermore, be an effective communicator or be trained to make independent, objective judgments and to reach rapid decisions where necessary. Most importantly, he should be committed, diligent and fair-minded, and he should be knowledgeable in union, employee and even management affairs.

Duties of a Shop Steward

One of the primary functions of a shop steward is to ensure that the relationship between the union and its members is maintained and promoted. For this reason he will be involved in the work of the local union branch, will recruit new members and collect dues, will encourage his fellow employees to participate in branch activities, will advise his co-employees and, in general, keep them informed of union policies and plans. Equally, he will keep the union up to date with developments at the workplace and will inform union officials of problems and complaints that need to be handled at a higher level. In union negotiations with management he will either be a direct participant or serve as liaison between union negotiators and the workforce. Furthermore, he may be selected as delegate to the national congress, in which case he would represent the interests of his fellow workers at the highest level.

It is also the shop steward's task to ensure that workplace relations are maintained. Therefore, at the workplace itself, the shop steward deals with day-to-day issues affecting his constituents. It is his duty to ensure that any arrangement between management and the union is properly implemented, that workers receive negotiated benefits and that agreed procedures are followed by management and employees alike. The shop steward represents his fellow unionists at disciplinary hearings and usually plays an integral role in the conduct of grievance procedures. His constituents will expect him to take their general complaints to supervisors or other managers and to act as their mouthpiece whenever the necessity arises. Likewise, management may relay resolutions or plans through the shop steward or may discuss with him any problems with the workforce.

Shop Steward Rights

A shop steward performs his 'external' union duties in his free time, but he will be called on to perform certain functions during his normal working hours. Whereas he will normally recruit new members, collect dues and address workers in his own time, his job of work may have to be interrupted to bring an urgent matter to the attention of management, to negotiate with management or to represent fellow members during the conduct of grievance and disciplinary procedures. Thus shop stewards are allowed greater flexibility than other employees and will be permitted to leave their posts at short notice if a workplace related matter requires their attention. This may lead to friction with their direct supervisors, who may be loath to give the necessary permission, since they resent the freedom granted to shop stewards and the high-handed manner adopted by individual stewards. Shop stewards, in their turn, need to remember that they fulfil two roles, that of employee and that of shop steward, and that they should first step out of the one before adopting the other. Thus, as employees, they need to ask permission to leave their place of work in order to fulfil their role as shop stewards. However, from the supervisor's side, cognizance should be taken of the employee's need to fulfil this other role and, therefore, permission should not be unreasonably withheld.

Problems also arise with the insistence of some unions that shop stewards be granted time off for training or attending important union congresses. Certain employers are of the opinion that this constitutes union, and not union-management, business and that training should be undertaken and conferences attended outside normal working hours. Nevertheless employers will usually agree to a reasonable amount of time off for these purposes.

The exception rather than the rule are those employers who regard the shop steward as extremely valuable in their communications with employees and the union. Employers who are of this opinion will grant the shop steward extended rights and may agree to appoint fulltime shop stewards or a fulltime coordinating shop steward.

Shop Steward Committees	Usually shop stewards from the same union or even those from different unions in the same enterprise will establish shop steward committees. Joint shop steward committees may be formed for shop stewards in the same area or shop stewards working for the same, geographically spread organisation. The main function of a shop steward committee is that of coordination, but it also serves as a forum where shop stewards can discuss problems and strategies. It is customary for in-house shop steward committees to be granted a certain amount of time per week to hold meetings and discuss plant-related problems.
Shop Steward Power	The power vested in shop stewards depends largely on the type of industrial relations system, the level at which collective bargaining occurs, the policy of the trade union, the historical development of the trade union movement and the shop stewards themselves. In some instances shop stewards wield tremendous power and act relatively independently of union officials, while in others they are allowed to act only as intermediaries between the union and management and the union and its members.

If plant-level organisation is strong, if bargaining takes place at plant level and if numerous other matters are jointly regulated by management and the union, the shop steward gains in importance and power. On the other hand, where agreements are highly centralised and there is little joint regulation at plant level, the shop steward's role may diminish, although he could become increasingly independent of the union and assert his own power base at plant level. There are also those cases where there is a great deal of joint regulation at this level, but where the task of representing worker interests at plant level may be given to a works committee, from which the shop steward may be excluded or where the union may not wield exclusive power. This would greatly weaken his position.

As far as the unions themselves are concerned, there are some which emphasise the role of the shop steward and others to whom he is not as important and to whom he may even post a threat. In South Africa the unions existing between 1950 and 1970 to some extent neglected their shop stewards and it was only with the advent of the so-called 'new' unions in the Seventies that shop steward representation gained increased prominence. In general, trade unions do not favour independent action by shop stewards. Essentially they are expected to act as liaison and should not be proactive or reactive in their own right.

In the final analysis the shop steward's power will depend on his own perception of his position, his loyalty towards the trade union, the degree of support he receives from his constituents and the strength of the trade union itself. If the union is weak, if the shop steward views himself and his fellow employees as constituting 'the union', if he enjoys the full support of his constituents and if he or the members are disenchanted with the union, the shop steward will tend to act without reference to other union officials and may eventually achieve total independence.

Whether a shop steward acts independently or not, he remains an important (if not the most important) conduit of the employer–employee relationship. A shop steward can make or break this relationship.

IN-PLANT UNIONS AND WORKERS' COMMITTEES

A union is in essence a collectivity of employees. If this is so, then any permanently constituted body which represents the interests of employees *vis-à-vis* those of management could perform the functions of a union. An outside body or the interference of officials who are not employees of a particular enterprise is not always necessary. The adoption of this perception would result in support for the establishment of in-plant trade unions or the accordance of bargaining rights to workers' committees, which then constitute in-plant unions. Such bodies are usually granted the right to negotiate on all substantive issues, to participate in procedures and to challenge managerial decisions. If, in addition, they are accorded the freedom to strike and can rely on the support of their constituents, they can effectively perform their task of representing employee interests.

As is to be expected, management would favour these bodies above 'outside' unions which may have hidden agendas, may not be conversant with the company culture and rarely have goals in common with those of management; yet it is this very endorsement by management which lends a stigma to in-plant unions and brands them as 'sweetheart' bodies. It is difficult for a committee or union which has no existence outside the enterprise to assert its independence and to establish its status as equal to that of management at the bargaining table, even if representatives have the necessary expertise, which is very often not the case. Furthermore, trade unions also promote the sociopolitical interests of their membership and constitute a power bloc within society. This would be impossible if employee representation were limited to a particular plant. It may be argued that social and political interests could be promoted by other bodies external to the employer–employee relationship but, even than, some kind of collective employee representation may be necessary to ensure that governmental policies as regards industrial relations and the economic dispensation do not unjustly favour the employer party.

There are, indeed, distinct advantages to in-plant bodies as opposed to unionisation from the outside. Problems may be more speedily resolved. In-plant representatives have a more intimate knowledge of the workplace and its operations, and there is a closer relationship between representatives and their constituents, as well as between representatives and members of management.

Although it could be argued that the aforegoing could apply where there is effective representation by shop stewards, in-plant bodies have the added advantages that outside influence is minimised and that there is less likelihood of power struggles such as those between shop stewards and union organisers. By far the greatest advantage is to be found in the fact that common goals are more readily perceived and that the relationship is more easily converted from an antagonistic to a cooperative basis. In fact, such cooperation should constitute the *raison d'être* of plant bodies in that these bodies should be regarded as the forerunners of increasing and continued participation, rather than a handy means of coopting employees or preventing unionisation from the outside. For this reason, relationships between management and in-plant unions should rest on a foundation of integrative bargaining reliant on trust, good faith and sincerity of intent. If this is absent and if management treats the in-plant body merely as an emasculated union, the entire exercise assumes farcical overtones.

There are also numerous instances where workers' committees are established on a consultative or participative basis and where they may exist side by side with trade union representation, without necessarily excluding trade unions or shop stewards from representation on the committee. Where trade unions are active at the workplace and see themselves as regulating organisational matters, there may be a conflict of interest or, at the least, an overlap between workers' committees and shop steward committees. This is not necessarily bad, but could become a problem where trade unions represent only a proportion of the workforce, where there are divisions amongst employees, where trade unions jealously guard their prerogative as sole representatives of employees, or where they cannot distinguish between their bargaining and participative roles. The situation is exacerbated where there is inherent distrust between unions and management. These factors should be seriously considered in relation to the existing provision for the establishment of workplace forums in South Africa.

EMPLOYERS AND EMPLOYER ORGANISATIONS

MANAGEMENT AS REPRESENTATIVE OF EMPLOYERS

Industrial Relations theory uses the term 'employer' or 'employer representative' as against 'employee' and 'employee representative'. While the word 'employee' is an accurate description of the party involved, the use of the word 'employer' may be misleading in modern circumstances. Nowadays very few business undertakings are owned and managed by a single employer/owner. Generally they are either private or public companies owned by shareholders, headed by a board of directors and run by a management team. The shareholders are the actual employers but, since they take no active part in the day-to-day running of the company's affairs, they are rarely seen as such. Instead the word 'management' is now used synonymously with 'employer'. This in itself an anomaly as most managers are themselves employees. Nevertheless, those in positions of authority in an undertaking are seen by employees as representatives of the employer. They are the concrete manifestation of an unidentifiable group of shareholders, and it is towards and against them that their employees and their representative union will direct their requests and actions.

THE GOALS OF EMPLOYERS

Although there may be a diversity of individual goals and interests, employers and members of management are bound by the common goals of maximising the profit potential of the undertaking, ensuring the future of the enterprise, expanding the market, satisfying customers, utilising resources efficiently and looking after employees. The emphasis placed on the various goals — and especially the place granted to employee care, in relation to the other goals — will vary from company to company and will depend on the management team and the organisational policy, but usually the primary goal remains that of maximising profit potential. It is this which brings management into conflict with employees and unions. Management may care sufficiently for its employees but it is debatable whether it will, in the end effect, put the interests of employees above those of the business. Besides management's emphasis on the profit motive, there is the fact that employers or managements will, in general, insist on their right to manage. Any form of procedural agreement with a union encroaches upon this prerogative and increases the conflict potential between the two parties. Yet most employers are nowadays aware that the profit motive cannot be pursued to the detriment of employees and that managerial prerogative is not absolute. This does not signify that conflict between unions and employers has ceased to exist. The issue now is one of degree rather than principle. Management has to decide how much to grant to employees without damaging the business, and how much power it can relinquish without completely losing control.

ATTITUDE TOWARDS UNIONS

Just as employer policies, styles and structures differ from company to company, so does their treatment of unions. Whereas one company may establish relatively amicable relations with a union, another may persistently oppose unions as a matter of principle. Yet another may attempt to dissuade its employees from unionising by offering better wages, benefits and conditions of service than unionised companies. Although this difference in treatment does exist, there is little doubt that the majority of employers would, if they could, have no unions in their organisation. They would prefer to run their businesses as they see fit, to gain the commitment (if possible) of their employees and even to engage in some form of joint decisionmaking with the employees themselves, provided that this is at the employer's initiative. However, since unions are a fact of life, employers have had to accept them as such and have learnt to live with them, if not in absolute harmony, then at least as peacefully as possible.

EMPLOYER ORGANISATIONS

Types of Employer Organisation Because employers have interests other than the regulation of the employer–employee relationship, employers may belong to various organisations, some of which play no role in industrial relations. So, for example, employers have traditionally established trade organisations for the purpose of promoting and protecting common business interests.

Another form of employer organisation is the chamber of commerce or industry, which will have as members the majority of employers from a certain geographic area. The purpose of a chamber of commerce or industry is to serve as forum and to represent the interests and opinions of businessmen towards government and other sections of the community. A chamber will attempt to cover all facets of business and will, consequently, also deal with manpower matters and industrial relations. Issues and developments in these spheres are discussed at chamber meetings, proposed legislation is reviewed, positions are adopted and, where necessary, representations are made to government and other bodies. The chambers serve as useful representational, liaison and advisory bodies and, in doing so, may succeed in promoting healthier relations; but they do not actively intervene in the employer–employee relationship and do not engage in collective bargaining. The only organisations to do this are those specifically established for the purpose. These are generally known as employers' associations, and are usually constituted on an industry basis. Chambers may, however, be represented on bodies where input is required as regards labour legislation and labour relations policy.

Collective Bargaining Associations

In contrast to the employee, an employer may not need to combine with other employers in order to hold power in the labour relationship. His power is derived from his ability to hire and fire, from the fact that he determines wages and increases and from the authority vested in him. Because he already holds power, he does not have to elicit concessions from his employees. Consequently he will focus on 'collective' labour relations only in reaction to the initiative of his employees or a union. In dealing with an approach from a union, he may decide to negotiate on his own (which he is quite capable of doing) or he may, for various reasons, decide to combine with other employers and establish an employers' association.

There is no doubt that the first employers' associations in Britain were established for the sole purpose of taking a concerted stand against the then emerging trade unions. Employers came together and agreed that they would not recognise trade unions; they lobbied government to impose restrictions on the unions. As trade unions began to establish themselves despite the opposition encountered, employers gradually conceded, but they still found coalitions useful for bargaining purposes and for establishing joint policies. The power gained by coalition and uniformity of action was usually greater than that which an individual employer could exercise in opposition to a union or a number of unions. Employers found that, if they combined to counter union action, they were likely to meet with greater success. As proof of this Green refers to the action of engineering employers from London and Lancashire in 1852, when all employers locked out their tradesmen after the latter had refused to accept an increase in the ratio of unskilled to skilled employees. Since there was no work to be had at any plant, the tradesmen were obliged to accept the new ruling before they could return to their jobs.

Classification of Employers' Associations

Nowadays most employers' associations are established for the purpose of joint collective bargaining. As they are reactive bodies, the type of association formed depends largely on the prevalent collective bargaining level and on the organisation and strategies of the trade union movement. If unions are organised on a national, industrial or occupational basis and bargaining is highly centralised, employers will be represented by a single, national industrial association which will speak for all member employers in the industry or in a number of associated industries. Representation on such a body is on a direct basis. In South Africa the best example of a single national association is the Chamber of Mines. Alternatively, where an industry is geographically spread, employers may form regional associations which may then establish a national federation based on these geographic associations. Bargaining may take place at regional level or may be conducted at national level with participation by delegates from each region. The largest such federation in South Africa is the

Steel & Engineering Industries Federation, which each year engages in prolonged national negotiations. Where industries have varied areas of specialisation, specialised associations may be established, such as those for civil engineering employers in the engineering industry. These may or may not join national federations. Then there are the local organisations, which represent employers from a certain area and which bargain at district and regional level only.

Although employers' associations are generally constituted on industry lines, there are companies with geographically spread operations which may choose to bargain with all unions at company rather than plant level. These companies establish associations composed of representatives from head office or from the various plants. Finally, there are those employers who do not bargain jointly with a union, but who nevertheless form associations for the purpose of establishing joint strategies and policies in their dealings with a particular union or unions. Such associations are usually confined to a specific area or region.

Organisation and Management of Employers' Associations

Employers' associations are constituted by the various employers in an industry, be this on an area, regional or national basis. Membership of an employers' association is voluntary and, as in the case of the union, a particular association may be established by a group of employers, who will then invite other employers to join them. Since employers also gain power in proportion to their representivity, recruitment of new members is one of the functions of the officials, but recruitment is not as active and forceful as in a union.

A national or regional association may have sub-organisations at various levels. The members at each level of the organisation will elect a committee, which in turn elects its own executive. Fulltime officials, such as secretaries, are appointed to run the day-to-day affairs of the association. The ultimate authority and decisionmaking power of an employers' association is vested in the general meeting. Here general policy is established, general directions are given and mandates are granted. In theory the same democratic principles apply as in a union organisation, but in practice most of the decisions are taken and the general business is conducted by the executive committee and by specialist committees elected by the general meeting. A problem encountered in many employers' associations is that large companies tend to dominate these associations. This happens particularly where votes in the general meeting are granted in proportion to the size of an employer's business.

Like unions, employers' associations attempt to maintain democracy within their organisations. Once an employer has chosen to join an association, he is bound by the decision of the majority; but he can use his vote to sway decisions, and can withdraw from the association should he be dissatisfied with its decisions. Also, officials and committees are answerable to the general meeting and, where votes are equitably apportioned, democracy is maintained — provided that, as in a union, the general membership remains involved.

Functions of Employers' Associations

The primary function of an employers' association is to represent the collective interests of employers *vis-à-vis* the union. Employers' associations engage in regular collective bargaining with unions and their main purpose in doing so is to ensure uniformity in wages, conditions of employment and procedures. In negotiating uniform wage structures, they try to prevent 'wage leapfrogging'. This occurs when a union uses an agreement with one employer as a starting point for its agreement with the next employer.

Employers' associations also represent the interests of their members with government and other agencies. Representatives of associations are invited to sit on national boards and other bodies dealing with employer–employee affairs, and associations are among the first to be asked for comment when new labour legislation (or any other legislation which will impact on employers or employees) is proposed. Since they may be in closer contact with unions, employers' associations are sometimes required to bring to the attention of government matters which are of importance to the union and to take a stand on any government action which impacts negatively on the trade union movement. In the past this has occurred in South Africa, where at times the relationship between the government and trade unions did not allow for direct communication.

Besides their representative function, employers' associations and the officials of such associations act as advisers to employers in an industry. They set guidelines for members on matters such as procedures and the general conduct of labour relations, and officials may serve as mediators between a particular employer and a union.

Finally, and very importantly, the combination of employers into associations enables them to establish comprehensive benefit and training funds, which individual employers and especially the smaller employers, would not be able to provide for their employees.

The Future Role of Employers' Associations In countries where there is an increased incidence of plant-level bargaining in preference to centralised negotiations, employers' associations as bargaining bodies are becoming less relevant. Yet they are likely to remain, if only to represent the joint voice of employers *vis-à-vis* the unions and government, to advise members and to provide continued benefits.

CONCLUSION

The collectivisation of workers was brought about by the actions of employers. As the adage would have it, 'Unions are a function of management'. Conversely, employers' organisations arose in reaction to unionisation. It is highly possible that the need for collectivisation may, in time to come, change as the actions of management or the composition of business undergoes modification.

SOURCES

Anderson, P 'The Limits and Possibilities of Trade Union Action' in Blackburn and A Cockburn (Eds) *The Incompatibles*, Penguin, 1967.

Flanders, Allan 'What are Trade Unions For?' in McCarthy, W E J (Ed) *Unions*, Penguin, 1978.

Green, G D *Industrial Relations*, Pitman, 1987.

Salamon, Michael *Industrial Relations Theory and Practice*, Pitman, 1987.

Salamon, Michael 'Individual and Collective Rights and Responsibilities in Creating Wealth' (Paper delivered at Industrial Relations Conference, Johannesburg, March 1990).

Winkler, J T 'The Ghost at the Bargaining Table: Directors and Industrial Relations' in *British Journal of Industrial Relations* Vol XII, No 2, 1974.

SOUTH AFRICAN TRADE UNIONS AND EMPLOYERS' ORGANISATIONS — THE TRIPARTITE RELATIONSHIP

By 1980 the trade union movement included the long-established South African Confederation of Labour Associations and the Trade Union Council of South Africa, as well as the newly formed Federation of South African Trade Unions, the Council of Unions of South Africa and the General Workers' Union. In addition, there were the Cape Town Municipal Workers' Association, the revived Food & Canning Workers' Union and the Black Allied Workers' Union, from which had arisen a new branch, the South African Allied Workers' Union. These bodies, between them, represented the entire political spectrum and ranged from exclusively white organisations to multiracial, nonracial and, finally, exclusively black bodies.

The 1980s saw the rise of more politically involved, community-based unions, of which the South African Allied Workers' Union was a precursor. This, the actions of the State and the formation of the United Democratic Front and the National Forum placed greater pressure on the previously established newer unions to become more politically involved. The rise of so many bodies, including the black consciousness-orientated Azanian Confederation of Trade Unions, also increased the necessity for unity amongst the members of the newer movement. Attempts at creating unity had commenced in 1982, but it was only in November 1985 that a new federation — the congress of South African Trade Unions — was eventually formed. COSATU united the nonracial unions, including those with a community and UDF base, but CUSA and AZACTU had withdrawn from the unity initiative. They later went on to establish the National Council of Trade Unions, which has a distinctly black consciousness bent. In the meantime a new union movement, the United Workers' Union of South Africa, had been established under the auspices of Inkatha. Also at the end of 1986 TUCSA, from which a number of unions had defected, was eventually dissolved.

The demise of TUCSA and the rise of black consciousness and Inkatha unionism were reflective of greater polarisation in South African society. The disintegration of TUCSA swelled the ranks of the independent unions, since most of the ex-TUCSA unions did not initially join other federations. Independent unions now formed a large bloc of unions, but there was little common policy or purpose among these bodies. At the beginning of the 1990s many of these bodies joined the Federation of South African Labour, consisting mostly of white-collar unions.

The federation which is at present in the forefront is COSATU, followed by NACTU, FEDSAL, SACLA and then UWUSA. Realliances may again occur in the future, and a new federation may still be formed.

In February 1990 the then State President announced far-reaching reforms within the sociopolitical system. As may be expected, these greatly changed the preoccupations, attitudes, strategies and expectations of trade unions.

COSATU immediately entered into an alliance with the ANC and SACP, but is still debating the merits and demerits of its position. The federation is intent on maintaining a significant role within the sociopolitical dispensation and a dominant one in the restructuring of the economy. Consequently, many of COSATU's strategies and policies now hinge on its national position, in both the collective bargaining and political spheres, and much energy has been spent in this direction — perhaps to the detriment of work-related issues and grassroots organisation. NACTU, on the other hand, has refused to align itself to a political grouping but remains widely supportive of the PAC and AZAPO. FEDSAL, too, believes that trade unions should not seek alignment with political organisations. All three federations are now represented on NEDLAC, and attempts have been made to bring about some measure of unity.

The legal position of unions still rests on the premise of voluntarism — that is, there is no legal obligation on unions to register. However, the Labour Relations Act of 1995 provides that all rights granted in terms of the Act will be accorded only to registered unions. This places an indirect onus on unions to register. On the other hand, the registration procedure has been greatly simplified, rendering the process almost automatic.

Like unions, employers are granted the right by law to form and register employers' associations for the purpose of collective bargaining. In all but a few respects the same provisions apply to employers' associations as to trade unions. There are a number of large, influential employers' associations in South Africa. These associations have long bargained with unions on industrial councils and were initially antagonistic to the demands of newer unions for plant-level bargaining. Some have become more accommodating and, in addition to their collective bargaining function, many now advise members on industrial relations matters. There are also other (unregistered) employer bodies, such as the Chamber of Mines, which were not established specifically for the purpose of collective bargaining but which have traditionally engaged in centralised bargaining with unions in the industry. Since 1992 the number of registered employers' organisations has actually decreased, perhaps because certain employers no longer perceived an advantage in centralised bargaining. This led to confrontation with unions intent on greater centralisation. The new labour legislation does promote centralised bargaining, and it is expected that employers will have to realign themselves in the future.

Besides collective bargaining bodies, there were in South Africa numerous employer organisations, such as the chambers of commerce and industry and the South African Consultative Committee on Labour Affairs, which represented employer interests and impacted on the conduct of labour relations. These bodies monitored developments in the industrial relations sphere, provided advice to members and, where necessary, made representations to government. Since 1985 employers have increasingly adopted a stance also in the sociopolitical dispensation, leading to the establishment of the South African Business Charter in 1986. Like unions, employer representatives perceived the need to position themselves within a possible new dispensation.

The role of SACCOLA grew in importance after the 1988 amendments to the Labour Relations Act. Union reaction to the amendments obliged SACCOLA to consult with them. These consultations led to the SACCOLA–NACTU–COSATU accord, which was later accepted by the government and which resulted in the scrapping of the most controversial amendments.

With the imminent establishment of NEDLAC, SACCOLA was replaced as principal negotiator for employers by Business South Africa, a more widely representative and mandated body.

NEDLAC epitomises the spirit of cooperation and consultation between business, labour and the government which is being sought within the new sociopolitical dispensation. The first real 'negotiations' which occurred in NEDLAC were those centring in the proposed new labour relations legislation. It was obvious from events during 1995 that different perceptions as to the role of NEDLAC and the interactions of parties within this body do exist, and that a great deal of readjustment is necessary if the corporatist concept is eventually to be successfully implemented.

SOUTH AFRICAN TRADE UNIONS

THE TRADE UNION MOVEMENT AT THE BEGINNING OF THE 1980s

The Overall Position   The development of the various streams of the South African trade union movement since the beginning of this century have been outlined in Chapter 4. As described in that chapter, the all-white and multiracial movement, as it existed in 1980 and as embodied by the South African Confederation of Labour Associations (SACLA) and the Trade Union Council of South Africa (TUCSA) had been established in the 1950s. The nonracial movement, representing mainly black employees, which had been established in the same period under the banner of the South African Congress of Trade Unions (SACTU) had by 1960 disintegrated and it was only at the beginning of the 1970s that the black and nonracial trade union movement re-emerged under the auspices of the various worker aid societies established in Natal, the Transvaal and the Western Cape. By 1978 the Unions formed by the Trade Union Advisory & Coordinating Council (TUACC) in Natal, the Urban Training Project (UTP) and the Industrial Aid Society (IAS) in the Transvaal and the Western Province Workers' Advice Bureau (WPWAB) in the Cape had already made their mark on the South African industrial relations scene, even if they were not yet firmly entrenched. As indicated in Chapter 4, they had introduced a new dimension into South African labour relations by concentrating on strong shop-floor representation and recognition at plant level.

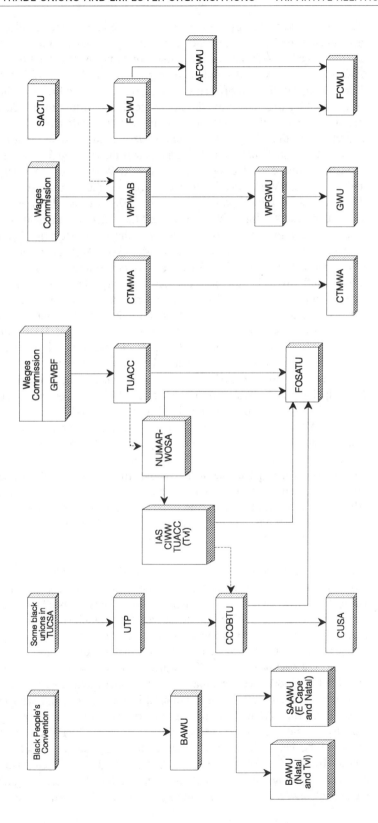

Figure 11: THE EMERGING TRADE UNION MOVEMENT

The unions established by the workers' aid societies to represent black employees had, during the latter part of the 1970s, made various attempts at coordination, coming together with the National Union of Motor & Rubber Workers of South Africa (NUMARWOSA) and other unions in the Consultative Committee of Black Trade Unions, an offspring of the Urban Training Project. The initial idea of establishing one federation did not succeed. According to Friedman, this was mainly because the UTP unions in the Consultative Committee were apprehensive that the TUACC unions were dominated by non-Africans and because of tensions between UTP unions and those belonging to the Council of Industrial Unions of the Witwatersrand (CIUWW), the IAS's successor. (In 1978, the CIUWW was itself succeeded by the Transvaal branch of the TUACC.) Also the WPWAB, which in 1978 became the Western Province General Workers' Union (WPGWU), left the federation talks at an early stage, declaring that the time was not ripe for the establishment of a new body. Nevertheless, the TUACC unions, NUMARWOSA (later to amalgamate with other unions to become NAAWU, the National Automobile & Allied Workers' Union) and two UTP unions, together with large factions of two other UTP unions, in April 1979 established the Federation of South African Trade Unions (FOSATU), the first nonracial trade union federation representing mainly black workers since the demise of SACTU in the early 1960s. Soon afterwards, in 1980, the unions remaining on the Consultative Committee established the Council of Unions of South Africa (CUSA). In addition to these two bodies, there were in existence at the beginning of the decade the nonracial Cape Town Municipal Workers' Association, the Western Province General Workers' Union (which shortly afterwards became the General Workers' Union) and the Food & Canning Workers' Union/African Food & Canning Workers' Union (which had existed since 1941 and had gone into a period of decline, but had been revived in 1977). Furthermore, the Black Allied Workers' Union, founded by black consciousness activist Drake Koka, had split into the Black Allied Workers' Union, still maintaining the black consciousness ideology, and the South African Allied Workers' Union, espousing nonracism and finding its base mainly in the highly politicised East London area. The various developments in the emerging union movement up to 1980 are illustrated in Figure 11.

Sociopolitical Orientation   With the emergence of the new unions, South Africa had once again a union movement reflective of the entire spectrum of South African society and of the various political orientations within the South African constellation. On the right was the exclusivist white union movement, which by then had become reactionary to perceived changes in government policy since the government appeared to be moving away from white exclusivity and dominance. The middle position was occupied by TUCSA which, with its 'separate but equal' policy, might before 1980 have been placed to the left of government policy but which now appeared satisfied with the sociopolitical *status quo* and with promises of gradual reform. To the left of the government was the emerging nonracial movement embodies by FOSATU, the GWU, the CTMWA and the FCWU, while still further to the left was, because of its high degree of politicisation, the South African Allied Workers' Union. CUSA and BAWU, both espousing a type of black consciousness (although of different breeds) were, because of their racial exclusivity, almost as reactionary as the all-white movement.

Trade Union
Policies and
Practices

SACLA

As mentioned in the previous chapter, SACLA was originally established in opposition to the perceived liberalism of the TLC–TUCSA unions. It saw and still sees its role as that of protector and preserver of white supremacy and exclusivity. One of its main functions, therefore, was the preservation of jobs and opportunities for Whites and the prevention of black participation in the industrial relations process. Since many of the unions which later formed SACLA had originated among the previously less privileged sector of the white community, a number of the former SACLA officials and office bearers were dyed-in-the-wool trade unionists and the dominant Mineworkers' Union continued to display a militancy not found in many of the TUCSA unions. Yet, with the advent of the new labour dispensation of 1979 and the evidently more progressive government policies which accompanied it, SACLA was for the first time out of step with the reigning policy in the country. As a result, it suffered a rapid decline in membership during the early 1980s, since many unions saw their future in a move away from white exclusivity; but the core of the SACLA movement remained and bodies such as the Mineworkers' Union and the Iron & Steel *(Yster en Staal)* Workers' Union continued to wield a significant influence in their industries. Later, SACLA was bolstered by growing white reaction to the reforms initiated by the government and, undoubtedly, some of its officials work closely with the Conservative Party and the Afrikaanse Weerstandsbeweging.

TUCSA

At the beginning of the last decade TUCSA was still by far the largest trade union federation in South Africa. As such, it was a much looser federation than FOSATU and could, perhaps, better be classified as a trade union confederation than a federation *per se*.

By 1980 TUCSA unionists had become entrenched in their position as a dominant force in the labour relations sphere and as major spokesmen for the trade union movement. The emergence of the new union movement did, as described in a previous chapter, pose a significant threat to TUCSA. In an effort to maintain their position, TUCSA unions which in the past had opened, closed and then reopened their doors to black African employees made a concerted effort to organise amongst these employees and also to represent their interests in the collective bargaining forum. In many cases they were hampered by regulations necessitating the extension of their registration to include black Africans. This aroused suspicion among prospective black members, who felt that they were being treated as special cases. Moreover, conflicting interests between the different race groups and geographical separations often made it expedient for TUCSA unions to maintain the practice of racially separate branches, adding to the distrust of black employees. This distrust was heightened by the fact that TUCSA unions operated at industrial council level, at that time a strange concept to unskilled and semiskilled black employees. The unions had also not established a sufficient shop-floor presence and numerous officials and office bearers had become well ensconced bureaucrats. Thus, despite their efforts to accommodate the black workforce, the large majority of TUCSA unions gradually started falling behind the newer unions. Even those black workers who, by virtue of closed shop agreements, had automatically become members of TUCSA unions later joined the newer unions and gave their allegiance to these bodies. By late 1982 it had become evident that, unless TUCSA underwent drastic change, it could not possibly survive.

FOSATU

Although numerically not as large as TUCSA, the major force among the emerging unions at that time was the FOSATU alliance. The FOSATU affiliates catered basically for unskilled workers, but they had found it expedient to organise under the banner of industrial unions. At the 1982 FOSATU congress, general secretary Joe Foster spelled out FOSATU's policy of organising strong industry unions which would eventually become a 'national presence'. According to Foster, FOSATU's role was '... to unite these industrial unions into a tight federation that is based on common policy and a sharing of resources'. FOSATU leaders clearly perceived that the power of unions representing unskilled workers lay in their degree of centralisation and the strength of the emerging bodies. Yet, realising the danger of bureaucratisation and alienation inherent in a centralised system, FOSATU insisted on democratic representation from the factory floor in its own unions and was strongly protective of the power of shop stewards and plant-level bargaining, even within a wider system. The increasing strength of FOSATU unions at this level was evidenced by their claim to recognition at 113 factories by the end of 1982. Most FOSATU unions were not opposed in principle to bargaining at regional or industry level, but they had not yet accepted the industrial council system. They realised that, as they grew, a wider system would have to evolve; but they disliked and feared the industrial council system for what they described as its bureaucratic form, its undemocratic structure and the power wielded by established unions in these councils. Furthermore, they were not yet sufficiently organised to wield power in a centralised forum. This position later changed and some unions did join industrial councils.

Another strong FOSATU stand was its insistence on nonracialism. At the time it represented mainly black workers and, according to Freddie Sauls of NAAWU, would have opposed an *en bloc* entrance of Whites into the federation, but it did declare itself prepared to welcome individual white members. Initially the driving force in the FOSATU unions was supplied by white officials and academics. This also changed as black leadership developed and previous officials moved into the background. In its stand on nonracialism, FOSATU — like the General Workers' Union and the South African Allied Workers' Union — to some extent distanced itself from other emerging unions which subscribed to the ideology of black exclusivity. This FOSATU saw as merely another form of racism and nationalism, which did not fall within its ideology of a 'democratic' nonracial sociopolitical system. Although it subscribed to this ideology, FOSATU initially remained aloof from factional political and community issues, to which other nonracial unions such as SAAWU paid a great deal of attention. Instead FOSATU expressed its intention of founding its power base in a 'worker movement', foreseeing that such a movement would eventually wield more sociopolitical power than factional or liberalising political parties or movements. Nevertheless, events such as the detention of trade unionists in the early 1980s, culminating in the death of Dr Neil Aggett, obliged these unions to take a political stand.

The emphasis on a stronger worker movement which had as its eventual aim '... worker participation in and control over production' had strong socialist overtones. Yet FOSATU's stress on work-related issues and on economic goals, and its orientation towards its members rather than community issues, albeit within the wider framework of equalisation in the sociopolitical sphere, placed it more towards the middle of the trade union spectrum and, on the political spectrum, slightly to the left of Progressive Party policy at the time.

During the years which followed the FOSATU unions, most of which were by then registered, continued to grow in strength and to play a dominant role within the new labour dispensation. It was in fact the unions in this federation which provided the major impetus for the later formation of COSATU. Also, with its increased prominence and as a result of circumstances, FOSATU was obliged to play a greater political role. Although, unlike CUSA, it did not affiliate to political bodies such as the UDF, it did join in protests against government actions and was one of the first union bodies to support disinvestment.

The GWU

The GWU shared with FOSATU its insistence on 'nonracialism' and its emphasis on the worker movement, but there were large structural differences between the two bodies. Whereas FOSATU supported a strongly centralised, industry-directed structure and a binding policy on all affiliate unions, the GWU saw itself as a coordinating body for independent workers' committees. Consequently, the General Workers' Union placed great importance on negotiations by and recognition of the workers themselves, with the GWU acting merely in an advisory and supportive capacity. Furthermore, whereas FOSATU had narrowed its scope to workers in certain key industries, the GWU — like SAAWU — was prepared to advise and support any group of workers, be they industrial, agricultural, domestic or clerical. In this it was more truly a worker movement and slotted more readily than the FOSATU affiliates into the definition of a general union. The GWU, more than FOSATU unions, directed itself at and found support in the wider community.

A loose organisation of workers in greatly divergent occupations and industries, gaining recognition as and when the opportunity presents itself, will not have a sufficient power base. This very realisation later led the General Workers' Union to concentrate on organising workers of a certain type throughout the country. Its efforts in this direction came to fruition when, by gaining recognition as representative of stevedores in Durban harbour, it became the first newer union to represent a certain class of workers nationwide.

In the trade union spectrum as it existed at the time, the GWU could be placed slightly to the left of FOSATU. This classification is based on the fact that, although the GWU was more political and more community-orientated than FOSATU, it placed priority on trade union issues and worker mobilisation around these rather than on its antagonism to the sociopolitical dispensation. Furthermore, it consistently refused to affiliate to any political movement, claiming that its task was to represent workers across the spectrum.

The General Workers' Union was originally an unregistered union which operated outside the official system and strongly opposed the government-established industrial relations mechanisms and procedures. As it was difficult for general unions to be registered in terms of the existing law, the GWU might not — even had it wanted to — have been able to operate within the system. It did, however, promote its bargaining power at plant level and proved in 1982 that successful negotiations could take place outside the industrial council system by negotiating wage agreements with two companies, both party to the Metal Industry Industrial Council. Like FOSATU, it revealed itself as a growing force which would formulate its own policies and procedures as circumstances dictated. The GWU later joined the move towards a national federation and disbanded after the formation of COSATU in order to merge with other unions in the COSATU fold.

FCWU/AFCWU

The Food & Canning Workers' Union was the oldest union in the emergent grouping. Together with its sister union, the African Food & Canning Workers' Union, it had a long history of organisation among black and coloured workers in the Western Cape, but after the bannings of the 1960s both unions almost disintegrated. They were revived in 1977 and gradually began to regain their membership. Initially they did not pursue formal recognition, although they sometimes negotiated with employers on conciliation boards to ensure enforceability of agreements. The two unions later amalgamated. By this time they had spread their activities to the Transvaal and the Eastern Cape. In 1980 the FCWU concluded its first recognition agreement, with Fattis & Monis, following the extended boycott of that company's products.

The FCWU was more overtly political than the FOSATU unions and lent its support to the UDF when the organisation was formed; but, like the FOSATU unions and the GWU, it concentrated on concerted organisation. It later amalgamated with other food unions in the COSATU grouping to form the Food & Allied Workers' Union.

SAAWU

Placed to the left in the trade union spectrum and on the ultra-left of the political one, SAAWU largely took the place of the SACTU unions and was similarly subjected to continual interference from government agencies. It certainly proved to be more highly political and more community-orientated than any of the other nonracial movements existing at the time. Although it declared itself as the only truly nonracial movement, the fact that SAAWU found its membership mainly among highly politicised black workers and non-workers in the Eastern Cape gave it the stamp more of a freedom movement than of a trade union proper.

Like the GWU, SAAWU was a loose organisation which recruited workers as and when the need arose. Unlike GWU, however, it did not operate on the system of transferring complete powers to the workers' committee, nor did it attempt to extend its base by organising certain industries nationwide; this despite the fact that SAAWU termed itself a federation and had, theoretically, unions in every sector which it organised. SAAWU's strong community orientation was proved by the fact that it attempted to organise a union of unemployed workers, more as a sign of community and political protest than to exert pressure within the industrial sphere. On an *ad hoc* basis SAAWU did show successes, particularly during its initial organisation in the East London area. Its momentum in this region later fizzled out, but it did show a presence in Natal and in the Transvaal. Part of SAAWU's problem lay in its lack of a concerted policy and in factional conflicts among officials. This was exacerbated by the fact that it did not have the opportunity to build up a leadership cadre, owing to the frequent detention of important SAAWU officials. Despite initial clashes, SAAWU was present at the launching of COSATU, where it merged with other unions. Its members are still playing a role in this organisation.

CUSA

The Council of Unions of South Africa, originating from the Urban Training Project and the Consultative Committee of Black Trade Unions, appeared initially to be more conservative than the other organisations which were emerging at the time. Unions belonging to this body used plant-level committees as a stepping stone towards unionism, but did not initiate militant industrial action to the same extent as the FOSATU unions; nor did they gain as significantly in terms of recognition. On the other hand the Steel, Engineering & Allied Workers' Union, a founding member of CUSA, was one of the first of the newer *genre* to join an industrial council. At a later stage many of the CUSA unions did change their tactics and commenced more rigorous plant-level organisation, showing greater involvement with issues at this level. With this also came increased militancy.

The Council of Unions of South Africa is described as black consciousness-orientated because it always espoused a policy of black leadership, as against the FOSATU unions where Whites initially formed the leadership *cadre*. CUSA's position in this respect may be attributable to the fact that the UTP was established with the specific purpose of encouraging Blacks to run their own unions. This policy became a principled stand among CUSA members, despite the fact that certain white intellectuals played a prominent role in the Urban Training Project and in some CUSA unions. Therefore, CUSA's stand was not one of aggressive black exclusivity and could, instead, be described as Africanist. The federation did declare itself willing to admit Whites, as long as they worked their way up through the ranks. Its stand was also somewhat ambivalent, proved by its later allegiance to both the black consciousness-orientated National Forum and the nonracial United Democratic Front. In this respect, CUSA differed from FOSATU. It was prepared at a much earlier stage to align itself to a political movement even if, by all appearances, it could not quite decide which body deserved its support.

CUSA was for three years involved in the initiative to form a united union movement but later withdrew from the unity talks, seeking allegiance with the black consciousness-orientated Azanian Congress of Trade Unions (AZACTU). These bodies have now united to form the National Council of Trade Unions (NACTU).

When speaking of CUSA, reference should be made to the Commercial Catering & Allied Workers' Union of South Africa (CCAWUSA), which at one stage appeared to be part of this federation. CCAWUSA never joined CUSA, although it may have worked with CUSA unions. It remained independent until the formation of COSATU, and is now a prominent member of this body.

BAWU

The Black Allied Workers' Union did not prove itself to be a significant force on the shop floor, even though (like SAAWU) it later claimed to be a federation and to have unions in every sector it organised. At one stage certain sections of BAWU in Natal appeared to be aligning themselves with the Inkatha movement. By all appearances it remained independent, although some of its members may have gone over to NACTU.

DEVELOPMENTS DURING THE 1980s

The Rise of Community-Based Unions

The early 1980s saw the establishment of unions which found their power not only in shop floor organisation but also in gaining the support of the community. The South African Allied Workers' Union was the forerunner of this movement. It was followed by the Motor Assembly & Component Workers' Union of South Africa (MACWUSA), which was born out of the dissatisfaction of workers at Ford's Cortina plant with the National Automobile & Allied Workers' Union, a FOSATU affiliate. MACWUSA had its base in Port Elizabeth's black townships and notably in the Port Elizabeth Black Civic Organisation (PEBCO). MACWUSA and its sister union, the General Workers' Union of South Africa (GWUSA), used township meetings to organise workers and, like the South African Allied Workers' Union, also concentrated on recruiting the unemployed. These unions adopted a fiercely anti-government stance and, as a matter of principle, refused to register.

The fact that they were organising the same workers led to rivalry between the community-based unions and the older emergent unions, which concentrated on shopfloor issues. This and the question of registration for some time caused a rift in the new union movement. Some acrimony had already arisen between the FOSATU unions and the General Workers' Union over the question of registration. This increased when the General Workers' Union formed a loose alliance with the unregistered South African Allied Workers' Union and the African Food & Canning Workers' Union in the East London area. The GWU later approached MACWUSA, with a view to cooperation, but it was rebuffed by this union's leadership.

According to Friedman, SAAWU and MACWUSA were alike in that they attracted younger, more educated workers. He quotes one critic as charging that SAAWU concentrated on factories where you needed 'matric to get a job'. This was certainly not the case with the GWU, which concentrated on migrant workers — in many respects the least privileged of the black working class. Furthermore, the community-based unions did not emphasise worker leadership to the same extent as the 'older' unions such as the GWU and the FOSATU affiliates. SAAWU and MACWUSA were to some extent dominated by certain fulltime officials, which accounted for SAAWU's problems when key officials were detained.

It was these differences in organisational methods and attitude which, in the early years of the new decade, bedevilled efforts towards unity among the newer unions. The position became even more difficult after the establishment of the United Democratic Front in August 1983. This body immediately concentrated on gaining worker support. Early in 1984, a speaker at a rally in Athlone warned that '... workers will be forced to pursue more militant actions'. In the union movement, divisions arose over the question of affiliation to bodies such as the UDF. While SAAWU, MACWUSA and even CUSA immediately affiliated to the UDF, FOSATU and the GWU remained resolutely independent of any sectoral political affiliation, even if they vigorously supported the objectives of a national resistance movement. Moreover, the establishment of the UDF gave rise to a number of unions, born out of the activities of UDF supporters. These unions, such as the Clothing Workers' Union (CLOWU) and the Retail & Allied Workers' Union (RAWU) in the Cape, had a strong community base and organised on an *ad hoc* basis. Their activities were very much the same as those of a number of general unions, such as the General & Allied Workers' Union and the National Federation of Workers, which had sprung up in different parts of the country. With this branching out of unions representing black employees, it was a wonder that some degree of union unity was eventually achieved.

The Black Consciousness Unions

The black consciousness wing of the trade union movement had already been established in the 1970s by the Black Allied Workers' Union, but this body remained weak. This led the Azanian People's Organisation, established in 1977, to seek the support of the Consultative Committee of Black Trade Unions, from which CUSA later developed. Initially these two bodies cooperated, but it soon became clear to the unions involved that they might, in the process, lose their independence. By 1980 the CCOBATU unions had withdrawn from the alliance, leaving AZAPO without any substantial union support. In 1983 the National Forum was launched with AZAPO as its leading constituent. Soon afterwards, in May 1984, black consciousness-orientated unions launched the Azanian Confederation of Trade Unions (AZACTU). AZACTU disclaimed formal links with AZAPO, but it was clearly the trade union branch of this movement. The unions in this alliance, such as the Insurance & Assurance Workers' Union of South Africa and the Black Allied Mining & Construction Workers' Union, did not have as strong a shopfloor base as the FOSATU unions. Nevertheless, it was evident that the unions in this grouping would form a definite wing in the trade union movement.

Friedman states that AZAPO maintained from the outset that all Blacks were workers. This was questionable, since there were already numerous Blacks in managerial and employer positions. He also alleges that the unions established under the auspices of AZAPO insisted that their leadership should be drawn from worker ranks; yet very often office bearers were workers in industries or services other than those covered by a particular union.

An older union which became a member of this movement was the Media Workers' Association of South Africa (MWASA), an offshoot of the Black Journalists' Union. MWASA also admitted black writers and poets and was, to some extent, a black national movement. This union's allegiance to AZACTU later led to a split between black consciousness members and those supporting a policy of nonracialism and affiliation to the UDF.

Unionisation on the Mines

The unionisation of black African workers was not as immediate and rapid in the mining industry as in the manufacturing sector. This was partly due to the fact that unions could not gain access to hostel dwellers on the mines without the permission of employers. By 1982 mine employers, overtaken by events in other sectors, had started granting limited access to unions representing black and coloured mineworkers. In late 1982 the Council of Unions of South Africa, which had been approached by individuals organising black mineworkers, decided to launch a union in the mining industry. The result was the formation of the National Union of Mineworkers (NUM), with Cyril Ramaphosa as general secretary. The NUM grew rapidly to become, by 1985, the largest union representative of black workers.

Towards Greater Unity

In August 1981 and April 1982 representatives of the then emergent unions came together in Cape Town to discuss trade union unity. Not much was achieved because of basic differences on the question of registration which some unions, such as the GWU, regarded as a route to cooption. However, at the 1982 FOSATU congress its general secretary, Joe Foster, gave impetus to the unity initiative by stating FOSATU's intention of forming a tight federation of like-minded unions. Not long afterwards FOSATU declared itself willing to disband in favour of a new federation. In July 1982 another round of unity talks was held. Here the newer community-based unions, among which were MACWUSA/GWUSA, SAAWU, the Orange–Vaal General Workers' Union and the General & Allied Workers' Union, presented the seven principles which they regarded as the basis for unity. These included:

- non-registration,
- shop floor bargaining,
- nonracialism,
- a binding federal policy,
- worker control,
- participation in community issues, and
- rejection of reactionary national and international bodies.

The talks ended in deadlock, mainly because no agreement could be reached on these principles. Nevertheless, in April 1983 a steering committee was formed to establish the principles for a new federation, but new differences arose on the issue of industrial versus general unionism. The community-based unions and CUSA did not provide the information necessary for demarcation plans, in line with the other unions' idea of establishing strong national industrial unions. At the next meeting, held in March 1984, the South African Allied Workers' Union, the General & Allied Workers' Union and the Municipal & General Workers' Union were granted observer status on the grounds that they were not yet ready to join a new federation as they had not provided the information required for demarcation. These unions refused to accept their new status and withdrew from the talks.

The Formation of COSATU

In the meantime certain CUSA unionists had become concerned at the fact that those involved in the unity initiative had not emphasised black leadership. Also, the unions affiliated to the UDF formed a separate interest group from the core unity unions, such as the FOSATU unions and the GWU, which had persistently refused to align themselves with any political organisation. There was talk at that stage that SACTU would be revived and that the UDF-aligned unions would join this federation. Yet in May 1985 talks between all the unions were reopened for the purpose of discussing a draft constitution. The AZACTU unions which had for the first time been invited to join in the unity movement proposed an antiracist position. Differences regarding the question of nonracialism came to the fore, and AZACTU did not attend subsequent meetings. Shortly afterwards CUSA also withdrew from the unity initiative, stating that it had reservations about '... participating in talks which do not enforce the principle of black leadership'. CUSA's withdrawal resulted in the NUM's disaffiliation from this body, as it wished to be part of the new federation. The withdrawal of AZACTU and CUSA left the unity initiative with the community-based and general unions on the one hand and the industrially based unions on the other. These bodies found common ground in the principle of nonracialism. Furthermore, agreement was finally reached on the principle of industrial unions, with various unions declaring themselves willing to amalgamate in order to establish single industry unions. Other principles accepted were worker control, representation on the basis of paid-up membership and cooperation on a national level. Thus the new federation, the Congress of South African Trade Unions (COSATU), was eventually launched on 30 November 1985. It consisted originally of 449 279 paid-up members in 33 unions, including all previous FOSATU affiliates, the General Workers' Union, the Food & Canning Workers' Union, the Commercial Catering & Allied Workers' Union, the National Union of Mineworkers, the South African Allied Workers' Union, the Motor Assembly & Component Workers' Union of South Africa and nine other UDF affiliates. These unions subsequently merged into single-industry unions and, most recently, their numbers have been swelled by new affiliates.

Inkatha and the Trade Union Movement

The Inkatha movement, established in the mid-1970s, has always been eager to garner trade union support. While there had been links between the Trade Union Advisory & Consultative Committee and the Kwa-Zulu leadership in the early 1970s, the relationship cooled considerably from the middle of that decade onwards. With the formation of Inkatha, Chief Buthelezi invited unions to join the movement, but the trade unions had by now gained in strength and — although many of their members also belonged to Inkatha — they evidently saw no reason to forge closer ties with this movement. Subsequent attempts by Inkatha to gain union support also met with little response. Instead, Buthelezi claimed that from 1979 onwards FOSATU adopted an 'anti-Buthelezi and anti-Inkatha' line. In June 1984, Chief Minister Buthelezi stated that 'because Inkatha has a membership dominated with peasants and workers, we have for a long time felt the urgent need to make its power available to workers'. By then discernible rifts had emerged between Inkatha and the unions operating in Natal, one of the reasons being Chief Buthelezi's opposition to FOSATU's disinvestment stand. Shortly after its inauguration, COSATU expressed strong criticism of Inkatha. Alan Fine, in describing COSATU's stand at the time, states that it was a 'potentially self-damaging move'. According to Fine, it was generally conceded that '... COSATU would have been wiser to consolidate its strength in Natal before taking on what is, after all, an extremely powerful force in that area'. COSATU's acrimony later declined, but it was matched by a counterattack from Chief Buthelezi at the inaugural meeting of the Inkatha-backed federation, the United Workers' Union of South Africa (UWUSA) on May Day 1986.

UWUSA, which had had its origins with a group of dissatisfied FOSATU members in the Richards Bay–Empangeni area, was established with a view to Inkatha's involvement in the worker movement and in opposition to the COSATU unions. In fact, Chief Buthelezi alleged that COSATU had become overinvolved in politics and in its supposed support for the ANC and UDF, thereby neglecting workplace interests. The allegation was hardly justified.

UWUSA claimed at its inauguration to have a membership of 85 000, but it had not at that stage organised at any specific plants.

The Establishment of NACTU

After the withdrawal of the Azanian Confederation of Trade Unions and the Council of Unions of South Africa from the unity initiative, it was evident to most observers that a new black consciousness alliance was in the making. This came to pass when, in October 1986, CUSA and AZACTU merged to form CUSA/AZACTU, later to be known as the National Council of Trade Unions (NACTU). Of the two, CUSA was the stronger on the shop floor, but apparently the AZACTU unions refused to become submerged in the new alliance, putting a question mark on this federation's ability to establish strong industrial unions. The alliance was in many senses an unlikely one, as CUSA was not as extreme in its black exclusivity stand as the AZACTU unions. Moreover, the CUSA unions had traditionally worked within the system, while those in the AZACTU camp had tended not to follow this line. Therefore, some compromise in ideology and strategy still had to occur.

The Demise of TUCSA

The gradual demise of the Trade Union Council of South Africa has already been described in Chapter 4. Despite efforts by individual TUCSA unions to accommodate the black workforce, the organisation eventually proved itself unable to adapt completely to changing circumstances. As time passed, numerous unions which had opened up their ranks to black employees found their membership of TUCSA to be a hindrance rather than an asset. The exit from TUCSA was led by the South African Boilermakers' Society and, by 1984, eight more unions, including the Engineering & Allied Workers' Union, the Motor Industry Combined Workers' Union, the National Union of Distributive & Allied Workers and the South African Wood Workers' Union, had resigned from TUCSA. The Council's membership thereafter declined from 478 420 members in 57 unions in 1983 to 379 620 members in 47 unions in 1984 and to 340 464 members in 45 unions in 1985. The unions which remained formed two groupings: those representing white-collar and supervisory workers, and those representing mainly skilled workers in the textile, leather and garment industries. In 1986 some of the textile and leather unions left TUCSA and at the end of that year the Council was dissolved. The demise of TUCSA did not initially swell the ranks of other federations. While some of the textile unions amalgamated with COSATU's National Union of Textile Workers to form the Amalgamated Clothing & Textile Union of South Africa, most of TUCSA's ex-affiliates remained independent. (AGWUSA later amalgamated with GAWU to form the South African Clothing & Textile Workers' Union, SACTWU.)

FEDSAL

The Federation of South African Labour was revived in 1985 and, by 1993, had 17 affiliates and 270 000 members, of whom 60 000 had joined since 1991. It represents mainly non-manual white workers, but has a black membership of some thirty percent and was recently joined by an all-black union. The biggest unions in FEDSAL are the Association of Municipal Employees of South Africa and the Hospital Personnel Association of South Africa. One large affiliate, the Society of Bank Officials, has now joined COSATU.

The Formation of FITU

During the 1990s a number of the independent unions — many of them former TUCSA affiliates — realised that, unless they formed an official bloc, they would have no say in important national policy decisions. This led to the establishment of the Federation of Independent Trade Unions, seemingly a loose federation of unions amalgamated primarily for the purpose of a united voice at national level. As yet, FITU has not really achieved this objective and does not, for example, have a seat in NEDLAC.

Trade Union Membership

The legitimacy granted to trade unions representing black employees has, as indicated in Chapter 4, resulted in unprecedented union growth over the past ten years. According to the 1990 Report of the Department of Manpower, membership of registered trade unions increased from 808 503 in 1980 to 2 458 712 in 1990. It was estimated that a further 352 000 persons belonged to the 38 known unregistered unions, bringing total trade union membership in 1990 to 2 810 712, or 25,72 percent of the economically active population.

By October 1994 over 2,47 million workers belonged to registered trade unions. Membership of unregistered unions was 510 000, thus bringing total union membership to 2,98 million. However, union density had shrunk to 23,7 percent of the economically active population, indicative of a slowing down in union growth. In fact statistics reveal that, although the number of unions increased from 194 in 1992 to 213 in 1994, actual membership of trade unions decreased from 2 908 933 in 1992 to 2 470 481 in 1994.

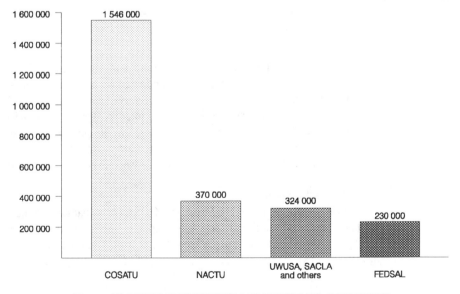

Figure 12: UNION MEMBERSHIP ACCORDING TO AFFILIATION
(Source: Department of Labour, 1994)

Sociopolitical
Orientations

The realliances in the trade union movement and the demise of TUCSA reflect the increasing sociopolitical polarisation in South African society into the white exclusivist camp, the black exclusivist and black national camps and the nonracial movements. These, at present, are the three dominant sociopolitical orientations in South Africa. Ranging in between are the independents, some of which have joined the Federation of South African Labour and the new Federation of Independent Trade Unions.

If developments in the industrial relations sphere are regarded as indicative of developments in society as a whole, then there is a lesson to be found in the disintegration of TUCSA with its 'separate but equal' policy and in the fact that traditional structures and attitudes in this movement could not accommodate the new dispensation which arose with the opening up of the system.

It has become obvious that it is impossible to speak of the South African trade union movement without reference to parallels in the sociopolitical sphere. It is a common fallacy to expect of unions that they should be completely apolitical. This problem was discussed in Chapter 6, where it was pointed out that unions are necessarily political and that they vary only in the degree of their involvement and according to the society in which they operate. In South Africa, with its history of incisive political and social divisions, it would be totally unrealistic to expect unions to operate regardless of political considerations. As stated previously, until the 1990s the union movement had been the only legitimate voice of the disenfranchised section of the population. It was to be expected that this section would use its industrial muscle also to raise political demands and grievances and that emerging political organisations would woo the worker movement because of the powerful base from which it operated. Thus by 1990 the South African trade union movement, despite all protestations to the contrary, still reflected the divisions within the sociopolitical spectrum.

TRADE UNION POLICIES

COSATU

The COSATU Launch

What was notable at the launching of COSATU at the end of 1985 was the fact that it was not the ex-FOSATU unions and their leaders who completely dominated the organisation, as had been feared by many of the other unions. The new president of the federation, Elijah Barayi, was an official of the National Union of Mineworkers, while the Commercial Catering & Allied Workers' Union and the General & Allied Workers' Union were also represented on the executive. Only the first vice president, Chris Dlamini, general secretary Jay Naidoo and the treasurer, Maxwell Xulu, were ex-FOSATU members.

Aims and Objectives

Cyril Ramaphosa of the NUM opened COSATU's inaugural congress by stating that 'workers' political strength depends upon building strong militant organisations at the workplace' and that 'it is also important to draw people into

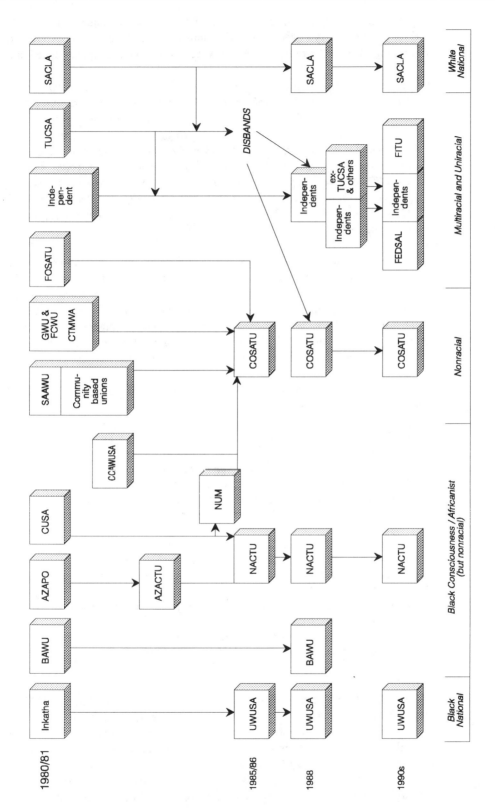

Figure 13: NEW ALLIANCES IN THE TRADE UNION MOVEMENT 1980-1995

a programme for the restructuring of society in order to make sure that the wealth of our society is democratically controlled and shared by its people'. In discussing COSATU's role in the South African situation, Ramaphosa stated that:

'... we have also recognised that industrial issues are political. Workers have long realised when they are paid lower wages that it is a political issue. But what is difficult is how to make the link between economic and political issues ... We all agree that the struggle of workers on the shop floor cannot be separated from the wider struggle for liberation ... Our most urgent task is to develop a unity among workers. We would wish COSATU to give firm political direction for workers ... [but] When we do plunge into political activity, we must make sure that the unions under COSATU have a strong shopfloor base not only to take on employers, but the State as well.'

Thus, from the outset, COSATU set itself a dual economic and political role. In the preamble to its constitution, COSATU established as its main tasks the organising of unorganised workers, the building of effective national industrial unions, the unification of these into a worker-controlled federation, the combatting of divisions among the working class, the encouragement (with other progressive movements) of democratic worker organisation and leadership in all sectors of society and the reinforcement of progressive international contact and solidarity.

The aims and objectives of COSATU, as spelled out at the inaugural congress, were as follows.

- To secure social and economic justice for all workers
- To strive for the building of a united working class movement regardless of 'race', colour, sex or creed
- To encourage all workers to join trade unions and to develop a spirit of solidarity among all workers
- To understand how the economy of the country affects workers and to formulate clear policies as to how the economy would be restructured in the interests of the working class
- To work for a restructuring of the economy which will allow the creation of wealth to be democratically controlled and fairly shared
- To strive for just standards of living, social security and fair conditions of work for all
- To facilitate and coordinate education and training of all workers, so as to further the interests of the working class

Organisational Structure
FOSATU, the GWU, the Food & Canning Workers' Union and, later, COSATU emphasised the principle of trade union democracy, resting on maximum participation by union members, equality of membership and decisionmaking from the bottom upwards. In COSATU unions, workers are represented on all committees. Fulltime paid officials have no vote, and negotiations are supposed to be conducted by shop stewards with the assistance of union officials — although very often this does not happen in practice. The president of a union

should be a shop steward, and each shop steward is accountable to his own constituency. Attempts are made to curb the abuse of authority by officials and to prevent the union being dominated by a minority. These policies are not always easy to implement. In practice, a balance has to be achieved between the power relations in the organisation. As example, Alec Erwin posed the question as to whether the union could be expected to support shopfloor representatives who decided independently to engage in strike action and then requested the union and its resources to back them. There is, furthermore, the problem of ensuring that workers are fit to carry out their responsibilities and that worker control is real. Also, if democracy is practised to the full, workers should have authority over fulltime officials and should be able to hire and fire such officials. According to Erwin, it has been proved that the stronger, better organised unions are the more democratic, and *vice versa*.

COSATU itself is structured on the same principles as the individual unions (see Figure 14). Each committee should have a worker majority and organisation is based on local and regional committees. The unions within COSATU are supposed to be autonomous and only on major issues, such as a collective bargaining campaign, should they be ruled by general COSATU policy.

COSATU Policy

COSATU's inaugural congress adopted policy resolutions related to matters such as the State of Emergency, the homelands policy, the call for 'one man, one vote', disinvestment, the need to combat unemployment and the campaign for a national living wage. Various campaigns were launched in support of these policies and, even though there were strong reservations about the effects and effectiveness of sanctions, COSATU called for 'comprehensive and mandatory sanctions' to bring about more effective pressure on the government of the time. At the same time, COSATU insisted that companies withdrawing from South Africa should first negotiate such withdrawal with COSATU unions.

In line with developments within the country, COSATU's second congress was marked by a greater emphasis on political issues. Among others, Congress resolved to accept the Freedom Charter as a guiding document and to take political action in the interests of the working class, but **not to affiliate with any particular political organisation**. Other resolutions related to matters such as links with international organisations, single-industry unions, the rights of domestic workers, a national Public Works programme, a 40-hour week with a ban on overtime, the establishment of cooperatives and the organisation of the unemployed. COSATU also reiterated its full support of a living wage campaign and the need to protect members from victimisation.

It was decided to launch a special campaign around national demands such as a guaranteed annual income, a living wage, a 40-hour week, the abolition of tax deductions, job security, retrenchment pay of one month's salary for every year of service, six months' maternity leave and increased technical and vocational training for females and youth; the end of the hostel system; the right to decent education and training, and the right to strike and to picket.

It is obvious from the diversity of these resolutions that COSATU, even at that stage, had already committed itself to action on a wide economic and political front. The question was whether the new federation, in which there were internal divisions, had built up a sufficient basis and enough organisational

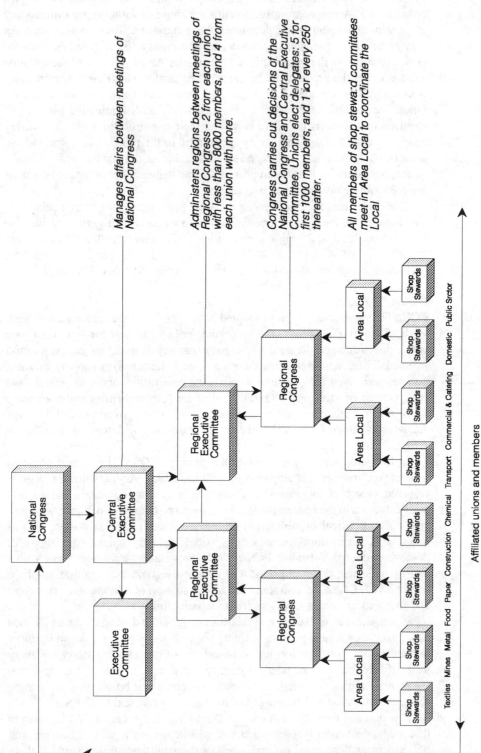

Manages affairs between meetings of National Congress

Administers regions between meetings of Regional Congress - 2 from each union with less than 8000 members, and 4 from each union with more.

Congress carries out decisions of the National Congress and Central Executive Committee. Unions elect delegates: 5 for first 1000 members, and 1 for every 250 thereafter.

All members of shop steward committees meet in Area Local to coordinate the Local

Affiliated unions and members

Textiles Mines Metal Food Paper Construction Chemical Transport Commercial & Catering Domestic Public Sector

Figure 14: COSATU STRUCTURE
(Source: COSATU News, March 1987)

strength to intensify both its economic and political thrust. Furthermore, COSATU's political statements evoked government reaction in the form of restrictions and detentions. This could have damaged the federation's organisational base. Nevertheless COSATU persisted and, while the need for some of the objectives was obviated by political developments, other goals were achieved. Still others, such as the demands for a 40-hour week and one month's *pro rata* severance pay, remain unattained.

Strategies and Actions

COSATU's initial objective of reorganising affiliates into industrial unions within six months proved to be unrealistic. Later, however, significant restructuring occurred so that, by 1990, COSATU had only 14 affiliates as compared with the 33 unions which together launched COSATU. Mergers took place in the metal industry, the commercial and distributive trade, the food industry, the textile industry, the paper and printing industries and in the absorption of the General Workers' Union into other unions. Thus COSATU had built national industrial unions, while there were still competing unions within other federations.

During 1986 and 1987 COSATU launched a number of campaigns, the most successful being the demand for May Day as a paid public holiday. The COSATU unions also continued to make shopfloor gains, despite the hardening attitude of employers towards unions during 1986. Strike action increased, but gains achieved from such action diminished and many of the unions appeared to reassess their strategy in this respect. As the COSATU unions gained in strength, some — such as the National Union of Metalworkers of South Africa — came to play a prominent role on industrial councils, but in many instances they still found themselves at odds with other unions on the councils.

A notable feature during 1986 and 1987 was the increased incidence of worker stayaways, often for the purpose of political protest. According to Fine, the '... tendency to call stayaways indiscriminately was halted by COSATU's failure to mobilise more than a handful of workers on 14 July (1986) in a protest against the state of emergency and the detention of trade unionists'. He maintained that COSATU officials realised the difficulty of mobilising regular mass protests. This was supported by the fact that, in 1988, COSATU, in calling for a protest action against the Labour Relations Amendment Bill and the restrictions on trade unions, left it to the regions, in cooperation with progressive bodies, to decide on the form the action should take.

Unions from various federations, but particularly the COSATU affiliates, brought pressure relating to political issues to bear on employers. It was increasingly expected of employers to use their power and voice in society in order to address issues of importance to the trade union movement. This was evidenced by COSATU's lobbying of individual employers and of the South African Consultative Committee on Labour Affairs (SACCOLA), with regard to the Labour Relations Amendment Act.

1988 proved to be a year of reassessment for COSATU. In May of that year the Central Executive Committee frankly admitted that the federation suffered from numerous weaknesses. These included the need to integrate the structures of merged unions, the weakness of many union structures, failure to implement COSATU campaigns and a lack of financial self-sufficiency, skills and organisational experience in unions. The CEC acknowledged that there were instances of financial maladministration, poor distribution of information and ineffective measures against employer strategies. It was decided that COSATU would continue to decline assistance from the International Confederation of Free Trade Unions but at the same time would promote unity and ensure that delegates obtained mandates and acted in a disciplined manner; and that leaders should not be elected on purely political considerations, but rather that the most capable, disciplined and hardworking members should be elected to regional leadership. Finally, the Committee emphasised the need for a democratic approach to problems and disagreements, and the necessity to seek compromise where there were sharp divisions.

At the special COSATU congress held shortly afterwards, emphasis was placed on the economic problems facing the country and its workers, on health and welfare and particularly on the question of unemployment. Shortly after the congress, COSATU general secretary Jay Naidoo admitted that weaknesses had become clearer and that COSATU needed to look critically at past strategies and to assess which changes should be made. Nevertheless he added that: 'This does not mean that we sit back and do nothing. Nor does it mean that we can only take up factory floor issues'.

Workerist–Populist Debate

Many of the trade unions established during the 1970s deliberately avoided overt involvement with political bodies, firstly because it might anger some members, secondly because it would detract from their shop floor organisation and, thirdly, for fear that, like the SACTU unions, overinvolvement would eventually lead to their disintegration as a union movement. More importantly, they saw their battle as centring on the workers and their economic upliftment, which could later lead to sociopolitical upliftment. They also placed emphasis on democratic structures. Political movements had not arisen out of democratic structures and, according to Friedman, the union leaders were of the opinion that they would not win economic equality if '... the white elite was simply replaced by a black one and the political movements were usually led by members of a small black elite'.

This refusal to align themselves with political movements did not prevent the unions from taking a stand on political issues, as evidenced by FOSATU's reaction to the detention of trade unionists and the death of Neil Aggett in the early 1980s. With the rise of the UDF and the community-based unions, there was increasing pressure on the unions in the older grouping to play a role in political actions organised within the community. This pressure arose not only from competition in the union constellation, but also from the demands of union members who had become active in community organisations. The first indication of greater political mobilisation by the older union grouping came with the campaign against the government's proposed new constitution. Employers were obliged to explain their stand regarding the proposed constitutional changes. Then, at the end of 1984, FOSATU backed a student call for a massive stayaway in the Vaal Triangle. The success of the action proved the strength of the union movement and, as Friedman states, the unions now saw that they would have to play an even greater role in politics. Yet, even at this stage, divisions arose between unionists who emphasised their political role as against those who were still wary of placing union organisation and power behind community demands and of an overemphasis on political issues to the detriment of workplace organisation.

With the formation of COSATU it was accepted that this body would have to play both a political and economic role, but divisions continued to exist concerning the method of intervention and the degree of cooperation with other bodies in the political arena. These divisions were strengthened by the fact that the previous community-based unions were now also members of COSATU. However, the argument no longer centred on the issue of political involvement, but on the 'how' of such involvement. This was evidenced at the 1987 congress, where there were, essentially, three factions: those who urged the adoption of the Freedom Charter and affiliation to the UDF; those who supported the adoption of the Charter and closer links with community organisations and the UDF, but no affiliation; and those who opposed adoption of the Charter, since it would cause division in trade union ranks. The middle group won and, although COSATU pledged itself to disciplined cooperation with the UDF, Jay Naidoo maintained that COSATU would retain its independence from both the UDF and the ANC.

As Maree stated, COSATU is not a political party, but it realised that it had a political responsibility. The workerist–populist debate merely reflected two poles of the same basic commitment. The 'workerist' stand was not an economic one. Rather it reflected concern that overinvolvement in political issues would detract from basic worker interests, cause divisions in the trade union movement or lead to overhasty actions, lacking an organisational base. The greatest fear was possibly that of submergence into organisations which might not be structured on the same democratic principles as the union movement.

The unions, in their turn, played an important role in encouraging democratic practices in community organisations, but, as Friedman warned, the extent of such democracy depended also on government attitudes and the opportunity for open organisation. He stated that:

> 'While unions are never likely to lead political action, they can influence it — and so ensure that the politics of mandate and negotiation take root outside the factories. But mandate and negotiation are fragile: they can flourish only where those with power are willing to talk and those without it have enough hope to want to talk to them'.

Furthermore, Friedman struck a prophetic note in saying that the union emphasis on democratic principles

> '... offers the powerless a chance to change the world themselves, rather than at the behest of charismatic leaders who might later turn against them — and the powerful the prospect of orderly change instead of a violent struggle they must one day lose. For the present, the future of the union's political style will depend on whether those in power allow negotiation and hope to thrive in the townships as it has begun to do in the factories. If they do not, the style which grew in the factories will inevitably perish in the townships.'

As was later proved, COSATU did play a major role in bringing about a new political dispensation. Yet, even within the new sociopolitical *milieu*, the workerist–populist debate continues, albeit in a different form. The issue now is whether COSATU, as a supporter of the majority party in government, should put the interests of the government and society at large above the interests of its members or whether, regardless of the effects, it should promote only the wellbeing of its members — who, after all, constituted a relatively small portion of South African society.

Positions and Stances within the Changed Political Dispensation

The unbanning of various political parties in February 1990 and the numerous subsequent reforms were bound to have a profound effect on the trade union movement and particularly on COSATU as the main player in that movement. Certain observers were of the opinion that the new legitimacy initially granted to the SACP and the ANC would take the pressure off COSATU in the political sphere and allow the trade union federation to concentrate on worker-related issues. Two factors militated against this prediction, however. Firstly, COSATU was by that time a very potent political force and was unlikely to surrender its position on the political stage. Secondly, COSATU had throughout committed itself to improving the position of its members, not only at the workplace but also in society at large. It came as no surprise, despite its previous commitment to non-affiliation, that COSATU formed a broad alliance with the ANC and the SACP with a view to influencing the negotiation process, and that Cyril Ramaphosa, one of the most prominent COSATU officials, soon assumed a leadership position in the ANC.

There is no doubt that its role in the Alliance has strengthened COSATU's position. However, much debate at that time centred in the political implications of this new role. Not unexpectedly, there was criticism of the Alliance from within COSATU ranks. Some union leaders objected to what they perceived as COSATU's 'junior status' in the Alliance and the ANC's failure to consult COSATU before making certain policy decisions. Others feared that a close alliance with the ANC and SACP would endanger COSATU's independence and, in a future dispensation, make it beholden to a political party — despite assurances from ex-COSATU president Baraji that the Alliance was a loose one reflective merely of a shared commitment to the breaking down of apartheid structures, and that each of the Alliance members would remain independent. Added to this was the debate centring in COSATU's position *vis-à-vis* a future democratic government. The question was whether COSATU should entrench its position as the labour wing of the ANC or SACP, requiring any future government to obtain a mandate from the trade union movement before instituting legislation affecting workers; whether it should form its own political party; or whether it should remain independent and concentrate on restructuring industries and the economy by extended centralised and national bargaining.

While some observers believed that certain trade union officials were working within the SACP with a view to changing it to a Labour Party, there were other trade union leaders — notably those from SACTWU ranks — who held the opinion that any form of political allegiance endangered the independence of the trade union movement. In an article on the subject John Copelyn, general secretary of SACTWU, explained that 'what makes the union movement an *independent* one, however, is whether it is prepared to risk the anger of the government in the pursuit of its members' mandate'. Noting that until then COSATU had always been prepared to risk antagonising the government, he posed the question as to whether this willingness to risk antagonism would persist were a labour-supported government to come to power:

> 'Will we say that, now the workers' interests are protected by the people's government, unions should not make the tasks of that government more difficult by pressurising and threatening mass action? Will we support the government in saying that workers must recognise the broader goal and not pursue sectional interests? Will we explain to the members that, no matter what happens, they must not rock the boat because the government is doing its best? ... Or will we remain an **independent** force?

Copelyn went on to warn that, if the trade union movement were to become merely the labour wing of the SACP, the time might come when the union leadership would be held responsible for '... all bad planning, poor laws and all social evils brought about by a post-apartheid government'. The solution suggested by Copelyn was that the trade unions utilise collective bargaining institutions as an independent base from which they could 'constructively influence society'. Negotiations on national industrial councils could be broadened to include also general economic and social issues, while negotiations with bodies such as SACCOLA could deal with matters of general concern to employees and business. According to Copelyn, 'the State would function as an *enabling* institution, enacting in law the agreements reached by organised labour through collective bargaining'. Having warned business that, unless it was prepared to negotiate on a broad front, the union movement would have to revert to political influence, Copelyn ended by noting that:

> 'Historically, socialists have been fixated on the idea that the State is the crucial institution for transforming the quality of life of workers and the oppressed. This fixation resulted in the Eastern European model of socialism. A perspective which gives a substantially greater role to the independent organisations of civil society — such as trade unions — can do two things. Firstly, it holds greater promise of a democratic transformation of society through organisations which depend for their power on the constant involvement of their membership. Secondly, it helps to build an organisation capable of exercising a strong check on the institutions of the State and the exercise of State power.'

A slightly different view was held by NUMSA which, although admitting after a workshop on reconstruction that 'the union movement must have its own policy, irrespective of the policies of organisations such as the SACP and the ANC', concluded that 'there is no prospect for successful restructuring unless the working class has strong influence over State power; unless there is a strong State involved in decisive, coherent planning; and unless the State is democratic and involves the unions'. The workshop participants went on to suggest that:

> 'It might be a good strategy to enter into a "reconstruction accord" or agreement with a political party which is sympathetic to the working class and likely to be the government. The key player would probably be the ANC, but other political organisations would not be excluded. This would

> not be a "social contract" with capital but an agreement between unions,
> civics, rural organisations and progressive political organisations on a
> national development strategy ... After a reconstruction accord had been
> drawn up ... these organisations would have to take the accord to business
> and negotiate an agreement with it.'

The NUMSA members went on to warn that the unions would, however, have
to take care since business was intent on a 'social contract or partnership with
labour' which, in their opinion, should be avoided as employers would want to
restructure 'to maintain profitability', whereas the aim of the unions should be
'an increase in employment; earning a living wage; the production of goods and
services needed by the people; increasing worker power and positioning the
working class for moving towards socialism'.

It appeared likely that COSATU would, for the time being, continue to
operate on both fronts — that is, through the bargaining machinery and by
utilising political clout. That it was not prepared to be ignored, particularly in
matters related to the economy and labour legislation, was obvious from various
actions commencing with its protests against the Labour Relations Amendment
Act of 1988, the ensuing COSATU–NACTU–SACCOLA accord (which was
directly responsible for the scrapping of these amendments in March 1991) and
the November 1991 stayaway in protest at the imposition of Value Added Tax.
In its anti-LRA action COSATU negotiated with business and the government.
That it intended to continue with this strategy was proved by renewed
negotiations with SACCOLA and proposals for additional amendments to the
Labour Relations Act. Furthermore, COSATU agreed for the first time to take
a seat on the National Manpower Commission, but later withdrew from that body
in protest at the government's refusal to extend its activities to include economic
planning. During the nationwide anti-VAT strike, COSATU proved that it could
mobilise a wide range of labour, political, civic, business and welfare bodies and
that it would act as champion of wider societal interests. This strengthened the
federation's position in both the political and industrial relations spheres while,
at the same time, sending a clear message to the government that it could not
introduce new policies without first negotiating these in a tripartite forum
consisting of labour, employers and the State. On the micro-level, individual
COSATU affiliates also took up strong positions in the industries in which they
operated, displaying their intention to play an important part in the future
development of the industries concerned.

Politically, COSATU made its presence felt by the debate on a Workers'
Charter and its constitutional campaign which called for trade union rights and
independence, accountable government, a democratically planned economy and
equality of the sexes. Any new Constitution should, according to COSATU,
allow for the right to picket, the right to organise, freedom from victimisation
or interference with trade unions and a separate labour court, presided over by
union and employer nominees.

At its congress in June 1991 — the first since the political changes of 1990
— COSATU pledged itself to developing a programme for restructuring the
economy which would lead in the short term to a high wage–low cost
dispensation and, in the long term, to socialism. At the same time it was
resolved that a worker bill of rights, to be included in the constitution, should

provide for a multiparty democracy, the right to strike and guaranteed individual and collective rights. The COSATU congress further decided that sanctions would remain until the process of reform proved irreversible, but that a conference would be held to review the question of economic pressure. The suggestion was also made that consideration be given to the replacement of sanctions with an investment code for new investors. Although COSATU reaffirmed its commitment to the COSATU–ANC–SACP alliance, the independence of the trade union movement was restated and reservations were expressed about the manner in which the ANC was handling negotiations. As a result the Central Executive Committee was mandated to explore COSATU's role in negotiations, with certain delegates favouring direct involvement while others suggested that the ANC should obtain mandates from COSATU followed by reportback meetings. Nevertheless, the congress reaffirmed its commitment to negotiations and to the peace process.

Much of the congress was devoted to condemnation of the Nationalist government for its funding of Inkatha and UWUSA. It was further claimed that evidence was available of collusion between Inkatha, UWUSA, government security agents and the business sector. This led to the announcement of a joint campaign between the ANC, the SACP and COSATU commencing with a boycott of white-owned business, but not much was heard of this initiative.

A final issue discussed by congress was the ongoing controversy as to whether COSATU officials could also hold office in political parties. The new president, John Gonomo, occupied leadership positions in both NUMSA and the SACP and the first vice president, Chris Dlamini, a NUMSA official, also held a leadership position in the SACP. Certain union leaders were still fiercely opposed to dual leadership, claiming that persons holding two offices could not do justice to both. However, Congress resolved that only paid fulltime office bearers would be prohibited from occupying positions in political organisations.

Problems with the New Dispensation

COSATU's transition from an anti-government force to the main supporter of the government in power was not an easy one and raised many complex issues and questions in union ranks.

Having made a pact with the ANC, the federation put all its energies into ensuring an ANC victory in the elections. More than twenty leading figures in COSATU were released to stand for parliament, while numerous others later left of their own accord in order to take up new positions which were being offered. This 'brain drain' is still continuing as reforms take place in the civil service.

Both the election campaign and the release of members proved to be a severe drain on COSATU's resources. Officials freely admit that, in the run-up to the elections, shopfloor issues were neglected — although closer contacts with communities did lead to a gain in membership and the revival of some dormant locals. Some of the remaining union leaders were dissatisfied with the fact that top union officials had been released without ensuring their accountability to the union movement. It was wondered whether these ex-unionists would continue to push a labour agenda.

In the immediate post-election period unions have been faced with heightened expectations and militancy at grassroots and, on the other hand, with a government which expects them to curb this militancy in the interests of the country as a whole. From numerous quarters accusations have been thrust at COSATU: that they are supporting a labour elite while ignoring the interests of the poorest and most disadvantaged members of society. This has been countered by the federation's emphasis on its support for the Reconstruction and Development Programme and the argument that it was the workers in COSATU who supported many of the poor and unemployed.

The COSATU leadership is aware of the economic pressures faced by the new government, the need for enhanced global competitiveness and for restructuring of industries, yet the federation maintains that economic prosperity can best be obtained by the promotion of a 'high wage, high skill' policy and by 'huge amounts' being directed at human resource development. Some union leaders have declared themselves willing in the future to sacrifice higher wages, but maintain that they would then demand input into the allocation of surplus resources.

Another freely admitted problem is the growing gap between leaders and members. The most effective local officials have moved up in the ranks, and leaders and organisers have neglected to service their members. This has led one member to accuse the union office of operating 'by remote control', while another has admonished that 'leaders and officials make decisions in their heads, but workers' families feel them in their stomachs'. It is, in fact, argued in the federation that the COSATU unions are 'losing sight of the practices of democracy, accountability and worker control which have been our key pillars'. Even shop stewards have been accused of being less democratic and of following the example of some political leaders who 'do not show much concern for democracy'. Officials are playing a greater role in unions and at them is levelled the accusation that they exert control by deliberately holding back information from members. Workers complain that they are not being kept fully in touch with top-level decisions. On the other hand, leaders are concerned that organisation at local level (and attendance at meetings) is almost non-existent.

Part of the reason for this gap lies with COSATU's concerted drive towards centralisation. It is no coincidence that COSATU publications continually refer to the bureaucratisation of TUCSA and its subsequent demise. A very real danger exists that, if COSATU does not re-establish its grassroots connections, it will go the same way. General secretary Sam Shilowa has warned that workers will no longer, as in the past, join COSATU merely because of its alliance to the resistance movement, but will expect COSATU to safeguard their future interests.

The problems and tensions faced by COSATU have led to continued questioning of the federation's relationship with the ANC and its position within the tripartite alliance. Even before the elections, the South African Railway & Harbour Workers' Union questioned COSATU's canvassing of votes for the ANC, maintaining that in the process it was chasing away members of other political parties. Pointing to the fact that, at the 1992 economic policy conference, COSATU's emphasis on socialism was not well received by the ANC, SARHWU suggested that the federation should not compromise on its independence and should not agree merely to reforming capital, but should aim to 'build socialism on its (capitalism's) ashes'. Likewise NUMSA, in 1994, proposed that COSATU withdraw from the alliance.

There continues to be talk in union ranks of establishing an independent workers' party, by building up the Workers' List Party or by using the SACP as vehicle for such a party. It would, indeed, appear that there is at present a closer allegiance between the top COSATU leadership and the SACP than between the federation and the ANC. Most of COSATU's central executive committee members are also members of the SACP, as are numerous office bearers in the National Union of Mineworkers and the National Union of Metalworkers of South Africa. At a recent SACP conference attended by COSATU delegates and at which the delegates were described as 'the top leadership of the two main socialist organisations', concern was expressed at the development of a small black elite and at the government's perceived intentions to privatise State-owned organisations. It was further stated that 'previously the ANC had a moral vision', but that this could no longer be relied upon. The conference resolved to use 1995 as a year in which to develop a clear alternative to 'neo-liberal free market ideas'.

Notwithstanding the above, COSATU has (at least for the time being) decided to maintain its position in the alliance, even if only to ensure that it continues to wield the necessary influence.

National Congress, 1994

At its national congress in 1994 COSATU delegates again dwelt on the accusation that they constituted a labour elite. The mood was not improved when President Mandela warned delegates that they would have to 'tighten their belts' and went on to say that they should 'think of those who don't have jobs before you demand higher wages'. In reaction, delegates pointed to the fact that directors' salaries and those of unproductive workers usually constituted some sixty percent of wage bills, and that no mention had been made by the President of efforts to stop the gravy train.

Amongst other matters, Congress discussed the need to canvass white and white-collar workers, to establish training schools for trade unionists, to conduct regular forums and to redevelop the locals. It was further decided that unions should embark on a concerted membership drive, that COSATU should open its doors to other federations and that regional congresses should be held once a year. Unions should be urged to become financially independent, should take over some of the activities of the central office and should exercise strict financial management and control.

The question of more equitable gender representation was raised, but evidently remains a controversial issue — as is the treatment of women by some COSATU officials and members.

Much time was devoted to the RDP and the independence of the federation. It was agreed that the support and implementation of the RDP remained a priority and that COSATU should guard against opposing forces which were attempting to 'hijack' the RDP for their own ends. Unions said they would be prepared to sacrifice, as long as the RDP also promoted worker interests. RDP councils should be set up at workplace level, and concrete demands — relating, for example, to affirmative action — should be put forward. It was further suggested that members could contribute directly to the RDP or that they could work on certain holidays without pay, provided that they were involved in the allocation of the funds so generated. COSATU would remain in the tripartite alliance and even try to strengthen it, but there should be 'total independence of parties and government in matters of policy and action'. It was not in the interest of workers to pull out of the alliance at this stage, although the federation's affiliation should be reviewed from time to time. The South African National Civic Organisation should also be brought closer to the alliance in order to coordinate the stronger elements in civil society.

In an attempt to consolidate its shopfloor relations, COSATU endorsed a 'back to basics' strategy. This strategy reaffirmed the necessity for industrial action, a renewed living wage campaign, the continuance of the battle against racism, support for affirmative action and insistence on a greater say in the running of industry and the workplace. Congress bemoaned the fact that workers and unions were not involved in industrial restructuring policies and demanded a share in all economic decisionmaking, whether at national, sectoral or shop level. Although the push towards centralised bargaining would continue, Congress also foresaw that this would be supplemented by bargaining at company and shop level. The State should provide training for shop stewards, as well as social adjustment programmes and social plan funds to support retrenched employees. Employers should be obliged to pay four weeks' wages for every year of service as compensation for retrenchment, to retrain retrenchees and to support job creation programmes. Finally, Congress agreed that it was 'time the law shifts the balance of power to the workers' and that key demands — such as those for a 40-hour week, the phasing out of casual work, the demand for parental rights and a 'living' UIF benefit — should still be pursued.

Developments During 1995

During 1995 COSATU reaffirmed its intention to define its position in the mainstream of the political process together with the ANC, SACP and SANCO. The need to build up a 'strong and vibrant' civil society and for the federation not to isolate itself from the community was reiterated. The federation intends to use its position to build greater political influence, and will suggest the inclusion of civics and students in the alliance.

COSATU sees as one of its main objectives the promotion of democracy at the workplace and the involvement of workers in job evaluation, training, affirmative action, investment, job creation and productivity. Particular attention will be paid to these aspects in State institutions, to reducing the almost 300 job gradings and job categories in the civil service and to realignment of public institutions with the RDP. The federation will challenge inequality, promote rural development, and lobby for anti-trust laws and the development of human resources. It is determined to oppose any wage freezes, cuts in social spending and what is called the 'investment strike' by business.

On the other hand, COSATU will strive for international worker solidarity, particularly in Africa and other developing countries. It also intends to pursue greater union unity, to encourage the amalgamation of unions in the same field and to establish its own investment company to manage pension and provident funds. In brief, the federation intends to engage in 'strategic unionism' and the 'politics of engagement' as the best means of achieving its three principal objectives: namely redistribution, economic growth and economic democracy.

Evaluation

Despite the problems encountered, COSATU's numbers have swollen to almost 1,5 million members in nineteen unions. Some of these unions are due to amalgamate soon, and the federation is intent on eventually establishing an even larger, united trade union federation. It is evident that COSATU refuses to be sidelined and that it sees itself as playing an even more prominent role in the future. Although experienced leaders have been lost to politics and the civil service, there is evidence of greater sophistication in the federation's approach, brought about partly by its new position as alliance partner and the greater security it now enjoys. However, it would appear at times that COSATU expects too much from its partnership with government and reacts somewhat sullenly when it does not get its own way: in spite of the claimed victory in negotiations on the new Labour Relations Act, COSATU leaders still grumble that scabbing has not been completely outlawed, that there is no provision for compulsory centralised bargaining, that retrenchments need not be negotiated and that no strikes over dismissals will be allowed. Furthermore, tensions and differences within the federation as well as within the tripartite alliance cannot be easily talked away; neither can the fact that COSATU unions are losing touch and are sometimes out of kilter with their grassroots membership. This allows for the entry of other smaller and more down-to-earth unions, some of whom have their own political agendas. At the same time, the institution of workplace forums may bring its own problems and tensions.

COSATU has set itself a daunting and complex task and, notwithstanding the confidence espoused by the leadership, may yet have to tread a very rocky path.

NACTU The policy of the National Council of Trade Unions, launched as CUSA/ AZACTU in 1986, was declared to be '... based exclusively on the broad democratic aspirations of the most oppressed and exploited'. The federation also emphasised its belief in 'worker unity based on the material conditions workers are exposed to' and in '... worker control based on antiracism and nonracialism to build a non-exploitative democratic society based on the leadership of the working class'. Although the alliance declared its belief in nonracialism, CUSA had fallen out with the other unity unions over the question of white leadership and the federation remains black consciousness or Africanist orientated by its emphasis on black exclusivity at the one extreme and black worker leadership at the other. Yet, like COSATU, it also adopted the principles of worker control, non-affiliation to political organisations, financial accountability within unions and the autonomy of unions within the framework of the federation. As guidelines for its future policy, NACTU adopted the principles of 'anti-capitalism, anti-imperialism, anti-racism and anti-sexism'.

At NACTU's annual congress in August 1988, it was revealed that the federation's membership had dropped drastically, from an estimated 275 000 in 1987 to just over 150 000. (Afterwards, NACTU membership again increased to 258 068 in 1991.) Also, no significant progress at merging unions operating in the same industry had been made. (NACTU still had five different unions operating in the metal and motor industry.) The congress stressed the need for affiliates to form bigger industrial unions and for the participation of rank-and-file members in union and federal structures. It was further decided that affiliates should become self-funding. Generally, the congress revealed growing divisions between black consciousness and Africanist factions in the federation. The former group stressed black exclusivity, while the latter faction was intent on uniting the oppressed, irrespective of race or colour, although black leadership would predominate. The black consciousness movement can be described as black nationalist, whereas the Africanist movement is more socialist in nature. According to the Africanists, 'the oppressed, exploited and dispossessed are in chains because of the economic interests of those who oppress and exploit us'.

The guiding figure in the federation at that time was Piroshaw Camay, former general secretary of CUSA and later the general secretary of NACTU. James Mndaweni was the president and Patricia de Lille the vice president. All these individuals had strong Africanist leanings.

Besides the question of white participation in leadership positions (a practice which was in any event declining in COSATU), there was not much difference in ideology and policy between COSATU and NACTU, even though organisational structures and everyday practices differed and although old disagreements, dating back to the Consultative Committee of Black Trade Unions and the suspicion that some CUSA unions were too willing to accept the system, could still have existed. Also, the stronger NACTU unions (such as those in the chemical, iron and steel, mining and construction and food industries) were in direct competition with the COSATU unions in the same sectors. This led to inter-union rivalry, which can bedevil industrial relations.

There were indications of reciprocal support between the two movements when NACTU reacted to the restrictions placed on COSATU, which it labelled as an attack on the entire trade union movement. NACTU subsequently challenged the government on issues which, in essence, were very similar to those previously raised by COSATU. Also, both bodies cooperated in opposing amendments to the Labour Relations Act.

In 1989 NACTU called for a Workers' Summit to discuss trade union unity, but later postponed the summit at short notice. COSATU went on to hold the summit without NACTU. Later in the same year, NACTU refused to attend the Conference for a Democratic Future. This led to the resignation of Piroshaw Camay, who claimed that decisions were being made in political and not in union forums.

Despite strong political leanings within NACTU, in 1990 the federation again took a resolution of non-alignment to any political party, stating that, subject to its policies, it would cooperate with all political organisations. At the same time NACTU reaffirmed its commitment to the liberation struggle. It is believed that NACTU's refusal to align itself with any of the major political groupings is partly responsible for the fact that NACTU and COSATU had not yet taken any definite steps towards unity, although NACTU had committed itself to the objective of one federation for the entire country. On the other hand, the political divisions within NACTU itself would make it difficult for the federation to align itself within the spectrum of factionalised and factionalising political parties. The divisions between the black consciousness and Africanist sectors of NACTU did not disappear: different NACTU affiliates still operated in the same sectors, despite previous resolutions to form unified industrial unions and notwithstanding a directive issued in October 1990 that the 23 unions in NACTU should merge within six months to form 14 industrial unions.

NACTU's efforts to merge unions in the same industry continued. By October 1994 three mergers had been successful, and NACTU now had eighteen affiliates with a total membership of 329 000. Mergers were still being attempted in the catering, transport and metal sectors, and the federation aims eventually to have only fourteen affiliates. NACTU's area of growth appears to be in the former homelands, with the Media Workers' Association of South Africa being the fastest-growing union in the NACTU fold.

At the NACTU congress held in 1994, it emerged that NACTU had problems and strategies similar to those of COSATU. Foreign funding was dwindling and affiliates were being urged to become self-sufficient. Most importantly, NACTU had relinquished its insistence on African leadership as it felt that the African working class leadership had been 'sufficiently developed to stand its own ground', and it now also has white members.

Like COSATU, NACTU admits to losing membership through lack of service and non-implementation of worker control. Moreover, the leadership is aware that ideological argument among leaders has demotivated members. The federation believes that capitalism is not delivering, and that it should work towards a socialist system where workers are in control.

Since 1993 NACTU has undertaking structured shop steward training. A number of shop stewards have been put through a one-year part-time course at UNISA, which has also designed a course to help officials and stewards to understand management issues.

NACTU remains unaligned to any political party. It does have links with the PAC and AZAPO, but maintains that it will not promote any particular party.

Perhaps because of their smaller numbers, NACTU unions do appear to be closer to the ground than COSATU affiliates. For example, NACTU has not had much success in establishing regional structures and operates mostly through locals. However, the failure of unions operating in the same sphere to amalgamate is still cause for concern.

FEDSAL   The Federation of South African Labour now constitutes the third significant trade union federation. Together with NACTU and COSATU, it forms the union delegation to NEDLAC. FEDSAL describes itself as a multiracial organisation representative of the 'moderate voice in the labour movement'. Many of its affiliates, such as the Hospital Personnel Association, have been around for many years and most believe in negotiation rather than mass action. The federation has ambivalent opinions on centralised bargaining, and does not support the principle of one union per industry as it believes that too much power might then be concentrated in too few hands. It also sees participation in party political activities as an impediment to the independent functioning of trade unions. However, FEDSAL does support a democratic system which protects individual freedom, and is particularly vociferous on the issue of taxation and wastage by the authorities. It also strongly supports job creation and investment to counter the 'unbelievable rate of unemployment'.

The moderate stance adopted by FEDSAL may eventually prove attractive to workers disillusioned with the more militant unions.

UWUSA   The most divisive factor among the unions representing black employees was the continuing conflict between the United Workers' Union of South Africa and

COSATU. This conflict commenced in Natal and later spread to the Transvaal. Ironically, UWUSA was the first large union movement within the new labour relations dispensation to be formed directly by a political body, despite claims of non-involvement from Inkatha.

In line with the Inkatha policy, UWUSA supported the free enterprise system and opposed sanctions against South Africa. This made it more acceptable to some employers. In fact, COSATU unions did accuse some managements of favouring UWUSA or of using UWUSA to oust COSATU. While some Inkatha members remained loyal to COSATU, there were a number of defections — among which was that of its Natal regional chairman. UWUSA in 1988 claimed a membership of 150 000 and certain factories previously organised by COSATU had been lost to UWUSA. Statistics for 1990 reflected a much more realistic membership figure of 28 706. UWUSA's organisation is not sufficiently strong to present a serious challenge to COSATU, but the ongoing clashes between the two movements provide a reason for continued concern.

The Independents The independent grouping consists, basically, of four streams:

- Those unions which have formed a loose federation in FITU
- A few minor unions which have always retained their independence
- New black unions which have not joined any of the federations
- Unions which resigned from TUCSA or were left without a federation when this body disintegrated, and who did not later become part of either FEDSAL or FITU

SACLA The South African Confederation of Labour Associations, now the oldest federation in existence, may once again play a role as reactionism among certain Whites increases. In the political arena this development was foreshadowed by the installation of the Conservative Party as the official opposition in the previous parliamentary system.

In 1985 the all-white Mineworkers' Union extended its scope of registration to become, in effect, an all-white reactionary general union. The fact that it commenced organisation in other sectors, in opposition to other White-supported unions of a more moderate bent, proved that its intention was not only to maintain white exclusivity, but to muster reactionary white worker power against the perceived progression towards less racially exclusivist practices.

This development was foreseeable, both in the light of the shift in emphasis to the black employee in the labour relations sphere and the white backlash in the political arena; yet, like the divisions in the black worker movement, this extreme polarisation causes further problems for those involved in the conduct of labour relations, unless it is believed that the 'divide and rule' principle places employers in a favourable position.

NEW UNITY MOVES

Since 1990 repeated moves have been made by COSATU to turn into reality its ideal of one federation for the entire country. Rapprochement between COSATU ··

and NACTU has taken place on a regular basis, with NACTU maintaining that it is not averse to the principle of uniting but that it needs first to build up its own organisation. Moreover, NACTU unions appear to be afraid of being swallowed up by larger bodies, and the federation also has reservations about COSATU's affiliation to the ANC and the SACP.

Most recently, COSATU has extended a hand also to FEDSAL which, like NACTU, agrees with the principle of unity but is concerned about COSATU's strong political involvement.

It appears unlikely, therefore, that unity will be achieved within the very near future unless the government or business engages in extreme reactionary behaviour, rendering them the common enemy of all trade unions.

THE WORKERS' CHARTER

The issue of a workers' charter, spelling out the basic rights of trade unions and workers, has often in the past occupied union movements, including the South African Congress of Trade Unions. At the beginning of the 1990s it received renewed attention from both COSATU and NACTU who had collaborated on the drafting of a document to serve as a frame of reference even within a post-apartheid society. Copelyn maintains that this debate about the content of a worker's charter 'shows a developing consensus about union independence' and that 'unions are seeking to protect themselves against laws which offend mass organisations such as the trade union movement, and against laws which undermine the protections afforded to civil society under a Bill of Rights'. Many observers agreed that, by establishing a workers' charter and ensuring its entrenchment in the Constitution, the unions were seeking to avoid the fate suffered by their counterparts in other parts of Africa who were more often than not swallowed up or nullified within socialist systems.

The debate on a workers' charter was initiated within COSATU when it was pointed out by the then Metal & Allied Workers' Union that the Freedom Charter could not be used as a guiding document, mainly because it was 'not a socialist document'. At a subsequent congress in 1989, COSATU resolved to develop a workers' charter but only after the contents of such document had been widely debated by all affiliates and with all members. At a special Workers' Charter Conference held towards the end of 1990, various recommendations as to the contents of a draft workers' charter were made. It was suggested that the rights to stop order facilities, to information at the workplace, to collective bargaining, to education and training for improved literacy and to participation in decisionmaking should be granted to all employees and unions; that employees' organisations should have the entrenched rights to organise, to hold meetings, to publish and disseminate information and to negotiate closed shops; that victimisation of shop stewards should be forbidden by law; and that protection of the right to strike was essential. During strikes unions should be granted the right of access to premises and facilities, no use of scab labour should be allowed, employers should be prevented from using interdicts or other legal actions against strikers, and strike ballots should be held on company premises. Furthermore, consumer boycotts and sympathy strikes should not be prohibited. As regards the control of enterprises, the conference proposed that employees should be entitled to elect managers, should have some control over the production process and should negotiate investments. Contributions were also made to the constitutional debate in the form of proposals that there should be democratic elections and a government based on proportional representation; that a certain number of voters (say 50 000) should be able to petition the State on any issue —including the promulgation, repeal or amendment of a law — and that the State would then have to hold a referendum; that the State President should not hold office for more than two terms; that a Constitutional Court should be established to ensure that legislation conformed with the Bill of Rights; and that there should be broad development towards worker ownership and control of the economy in a socialist state. This would, in terms of the proposals, entail democratic planning of the economy, trade union participation in such planning, redistribution of wealth, land reform and full information on all economic aspects. Within the broader society, trade unions would remain independent but would directly influence State policy, particularly in matters directly affecting trade union members. The question of participation in structures such as the National Manpower Commission and the Unemployment Insurance Fund was also debated.

The debate around the Workers' Charter eventually led to the establishment of a Platform for Workers' Rights (see Annexures). This concern with the rights of workers left no doubt that the union movement (in particular COSATU and NACTU), although supportive of the mass democratic movement, was aware of the dangers inherent in a constitution which did not acknowledge the independence and rights of trade unions. They were, therefore, intent on protecting themselves in advance against any such eventuality.

As demonstrated in Chapter 5, many — but by far not all — of the rights demanded by the unions have, since the transition to a democratic dispensation, been granted either via the Constitution or in the new labour legislation. Although it is to be doubted that the more extreme demands will be met, the union movement will probably continue the campaign for expanded worker rights.

FUTURE DEVELOPMENTS

The impact of trade unions is diminishing throughout the world and, in order to survive, the trade union movement has been obliged to change its stance on many issues. The reasons for this development are to be found in growing unemployment, increasing use of technology, the decreasing need for unskilled and manual labour, the globalisation of markets, more cooperative practices on the part of employers, the convergence of ideological stances and the various social welfare policies adopted by governments. Thus unions have been forced to take greater cognizance of job security and productivity and to relinquish extremely radical and adversarial stances.

In South Africa the union movement was in the past obliged to adopt a radical stance, towards both business and the previous government. Even after the advent of the new dispensation the conditions in South Africa are such that trade unions still have a significant role to play in the upliftment of the working class, but they represent only a small proportion of the previously disadvantaged population. The government for its part is concerned with the upliftment and prosperity of the entire nation and particularly with the poorest of the poor, while business sees its role as delivering the necessary jobs by becoming more competitive and attracting additional investments. The union movement thus has two choices: it can continue in the adversarial mode and protect the interests mainly of its members, or it can decide to cooperate with government and business in the reconstruction of industry and the economy. This will be no easy task as, while union leaders may have the necessary sophistication and insight to engage in cooperation and yet maintain independence, grassroots membership may not understand the union strategy and may turn to other, lesser but more militant, movements. The likelihood of this occurring increases if it is considered that a great deal of suspicion and mistrust still exists between the parties, and particularly between management and workers.

Despite vociferous claims to the contrary, the union movement at the moment is in an unenviable position, beset by pressures and tensions on all sides. If the major federations fail to service their grassroots membership, their eventual demise is inevitable. Yet the dearth of a trained leadership *cadre* and other national concerns force them to concentrate on high-level issues. As it is, it is impossible to predict what the future holds. The situation at present is extremely fluid, and too many variables impact on it. The next few years may see COSATU and the other federations going from strength to strength. On the other hand, we may well see the complete fragmentation of the union movement.

THE LEGAL POSITION

Voluntarism as Regards Registration

In keeping with the principle of voluntarism, trade unions in South Africa have until very recently not been subject to control in that they were not and still are not obliged to register in terms of the Labour Relations Act. Nevertheless, there was indirect encouragement to conform to the provisions of the Act since only registered trade unions were permitted to join industrial councils and, until 1983, only these unions could apply for the establishment of conciliation boards. Furthermore, there was until 1979 a negative prohibition on unions representing black employees, by the exclusion of the latter from the definition of 'employee' in the Labour Relations Act. This meant that a union representing black Africans could not register as representative of such employees. The change of definition in the 1979 amendments to the Labour Relations Act opened up the system of registration to these unions and, since 1983, unregistered unions too were permitted to apply for the establishment of conciliation boards.

In terms of the Labour Relations Act of 1995 all rights accorded to unions in terms of the Act (such as the rights to access, to hold meetings on the employer's premises and to elect shop stewards) will be accorded only to registered unions. This would most certainly encourage all active unions to register: by implication an unregistered union, although it may enter into an agreement with an employer, will have no statutory rights.

The Registration Process

The registration of trade unions and the regulations pertaining to registered unions are contained in Sections 95 to 106 of the Labour Relations Act of 1995. Any trade union **may** apply for registration on the prescribed form, provided that it selects a name which cannot be confused with the name or shortened name of another registered union, that it has adopted a constitution with the required provisions, that it has an address in the Republic and that it is independent. (A trade union will be regarded as independent if it is not under the direct or indirect control of any employer or employers' association and if it is free from any type of influence or interference from an employer or employers' association.) An application for registration must be made on the prescribed form and be accompanied by a copy of the union's constitution and any other information which may be of use to the Registrar in deciding whether the union conforms to the requirements for registration. In terms of Section 96(5), the constitution of a union must contain provisions relating to the following.

- A statement that the union is an association not for gain
- Qualifications for membership
- Conditions under which membership will be denied
- Membership fees, and the method by which these fees will be determined
- Termination of membership
- Cancellation of membership
- Appeals against withdrawal of membership rights, procedures for such appeals and the naming of a body to hear appeals
- The calling of meetings, including the quorum required and the taking of minutes
- The method by which decisions will be taken
- The position of secretary and the duties involved in that position
- Other office bearers, officials and shop stewards and their respective duties
- The procedure by which office bearers and shop stewards will be nominated
- The procedure for the nomination, election and appointment of officials
- The removal of office bearers, officials and shop stewards, procedures for appeals against such removal and the designation of a body by which such appeals can be heard
- The circumstances in which a vote by ballot should be held
- The holding of a vote by ballot before a strike is called
- A prohibition on the disciplining of a member or the cancellation of membership when the member refuses to take part in a strike which has not been subjected to a ballot, or where a majority of persons involved did not vote in favour of a strike
- The deposit and investment of funds
- The application of funds
- The date on which the financial year will end
- Procedures for amendments to the constitution
- Procedures whereby the union can, by resolution, be liquidated

(All the above provisions, except those relating to shop stewards, apply also to the constitutions of employers' organisations.)

On receiving the application, the Industrial Registrar may request additional information in substantiation of the application. He will then consider the information supplied and, if convinced that the applicant conforms to the requirements, will register the union by writing its name into the Register of Unions, furnish the union with a registration certificate and send the union a certified copy of its constitution. Where the Registrar is not convinced that the applicant meets the requirements, he must inform the union in writing of the reasons for his decision and give a union thirty days to meet the requirements. Should the union attempt to conform and the Registrar still not be convinced that it does, he must refuse the registration and inform the union accordingly.

Effect of Registration Registration bestows on the union the status of a juristic person and protects members from obligations and liabilities incurred by the union. A member, office bearer, official or shop steward is not personally responsible for losses suffered by anybody as a result of the actions undertaken by a member, office bearer, official or shop steward on behalf of the union.

Obligations Every registered trade union or employers' organisation is obliged to:

- keep a register of members, listing names and membership fees paid;
- keep proper books of account and records in respect of its income and expenditure, assets and liabilities;
- within six months of the financial year end, prepare annual statements of income and expenditure and an end-of-year balance sheet;
- submit its books of account, records and financial statements to annual audit;
- obtain a written report from the auditor, in which he expresses his opinion as to whether the union has adhered to its constitution as regards financial matters;
- table the financial statements and the auditor's report for inspection by members, and present these documents to a meeting of members or their representatives;
- keep all books of account, substantiating documents, records of membership fees or levies paid by members, income and expenditure statements, balance sheets and auditor's reports, in original or reproduced form, for a period of at least three years;
- keep a register of members;
- keep minutes of meetings for a period of three years;
- retain ballot forms for at least three years from the date on which the ballot was conducted;
- by 31 March each year, supply the Registrar with a certified membership list;
- supply the Registrar, within thirty days of its receipt, with a certified copy of the auditor's report and the financial statements;
- within thirty days of the election of national office bearers, supply the Registrar with the names and work addresses of these office bearers; and
- inform the Registrar within thirty days of any change of address.

Change in Name or Constitution A union may, by resolution, decide to change its name or constitution, but must inform the Registrar accordingly.

Rationale of Registration

The rationale of registration is usually to ensure conformity amongst bodies utilising the industrial relations machinery of a particular country. Registration may also entail some measure of control, the purpose of which should be to protect members from malpractice by officials and to prevent unions being formed by bodies with no serious intent. It could be argued that malpractice by unions or officials should be of no concern to a government, as members are not coerced into joining an association and it is the duty of the members to ensure that proper procedures are followed. On the other hand, it is equally argued that the State has an obligation to protect the public from being misled or misused by certain individuals.

Additional Provisions Regarding Union Administration

Two or more unions may decide to amalgamate and apply to the Registrar for registration.

The Labour Court may order the liquidation of a union if that union has, by resolution, decided to liquidate or if the Registrar or any member of the union has applied to the Court and the Court is convinced that the union, for one reason or another, can no longer exist. Application may also be made to the Labour Court for sequestration in terms of the Insolvency Act, or for the withdrawal of registration from a union which is no longer independent.

Union Federations

A union federation is obliged to furnish the Registrar, within three months of its formation and thereafter by 31 March each year, with the names and addresses of affiliated unions, the number of persons representing each of the affiliates, the names and addresses of its national office bearers and a certified copy of its constitution. Should the federation change a part of the whole of its constitution, the Registrar must be notified within thirty days. Should it be decided by resolution to liquidate the federation, notification of the intended liquidation must reach the Registrar within fourteen days.

Union and Shop Steward Rights

The chapter of the Labour Relations Act which deals with organisational rights provides not only for the election of shop stewards (union representatives) by a majority union or unions (see Chapter 9), but also spells out the rights of shop stewards and union office bearers at the place of work.

In terms of subsections 14(4) and (5) shop stewards are entitled, at the request of an employee, to assist such employee during disciplinary and grievance procedures; to monitor the employer's adherence to the Act and to any binding collective agreements; to report any transgression of the Act or an agreement to the employer, the union and/or a responsible authority; and to perform any other function agreed upon between the union and the employer.

The shop steward is also entitled, subject to reasonable conditions, to take paid time off during working hours to perform his functions or to receive relevant training. An employee who is an office bearer of a representative union or of a federation to which that union belongs may reasonably take leave from his post to perform his functions as office bearer. The employer and the union should agree on the duration of such leave, on the question of payment and on the conditions attached.

EMPLOYERS' ORGANISATIONS

COLLECTIVE BARGAINING ORGANISATIONS

Registration   The Labour Relations Act provides for the formation and registration of employers' associations for the purpose of collective bargaining. The process for the registration of employers' associations is essentially the same as that relating to trade unions (described previously). According to the Department of Labour there were, at the end of 1994, 191 registered employers' associations in existence. Of these, the Steel & Engineering Industries Federation of South Africa, the Master Builders' Association and the Textile Industries Federation were among the most influential. It should be noted that the number of employers' organisations had declined from 271 in 1987 to 237 in 1990, and that the number has now decreased further. During 1994 only two new employers' associations were registered, while seven cancelled their registration — indicative of a lack of interest in centralised bargaining on the part of employers. However, it is expected that, with the renewed drive towards centralised bargaining, the number of employers' associations will increase (see below).

Activities   Employers' associations are established mainly for the purpose of collective bargaining with unions on bargaining councils, but in recent years many of these organisations, some of which have firmly established structures, have acted also as advisors to their members on general industrial relations policy. Initially, approaches by unions for bargaining at plant level were strongly resisted by employers, often upon the advice of the employers' associations. This protectionist stand later mellowed and there was greater accommodation of newer unions and of alternative practices. The developments required no small measure of readjustment by the employers' associations, which, like the established unions, had before 1979 been firmly ensconced in the industrial council system. As a result, there were divisions in employer ranks arising from different attitudes to new developments. Furthermore, employers' associations were later obliged, by the then Minister of Manpower's insistence on wider representivity before extending industrial council agreements, to consult with non-party employers before concluding agreements. Thus the previous dominant influence of these associations diminished. From the mid-1980s, unions which had previously shunned industrial councils began to assume prominent positions on these bodies, bringing to them a significant change in tone and sometimes also demanding additional negotiation at plant level. This and the necessity to consult with non-party employers led employers' associations to question the value of industrial council bargaining. Many now felt they could wield greater power at plant level. This has led to continued friction between the unions and some major employers, once again evidenced by the deadlock in NEDLAC over the proposed new labour legislation, a central issue being the unions' demand for mandatory centralised bargaining. Whether industry or sectoral level bargaining is compulsory or not, it would appear that negotiations will increasingly be conducted at a highly centralised level. This would require the maintenance or establishment of strong national employers' organisations.

Non-Registered Bodies

Another body which is important in the collective bargaining sphere is the **South African Chamber of Mines**. The Chamber is not registered as an employers' association and has other functions than that of collective bargaining, but it has traditionally bargained with mining unions on behalf of employers in the mining industry. Even the National Union of Mineworkers, which originally sought recognition at individual mines, now bargains centrally with the Chamber on behalf of the employees which this union represents.

OTHER EMPLOYER BODIES

Chambers of Business

Other employer bodies which do involve themselves in industrial relations (although they do not engage in bargaining *per se*) included in the past various **chambers of commerce and industry** and the **South African Coordinating Committee on Labour Affairs**. The South African business community is not large in comparison to that of European countries, but it too displays the divisions prevalent in South African society. Despite some efforts at unification, the following bodies still exist.

- Regional chambers of commerce and industry, some of which have now amalgamated and are called chambers of business. Previously the chambers of commerce resorted under the Associated Chambers of Commerce (ASSOCOM) and the chambers of industry under the Federated Chamber of Industries. These bodies amalgamated to form the South African Chamber of Business. The chambers of commerce, industry and business are representative mainly of the English-speaking sector of the business community.
- Regional, Afrikaans-orientated 'sakekamers', under the Afrikaanse Handelsinstituut (AHI)
- Regional associations for black businessmen, coordinated by the National African Federation of Chambers of Commerce (NAFCOC)

The chambers of commerce and industry and the Afrikaanse Handelsinstituut have traditionally had a voice with government as regards labour affairs, and regularly submit comments or make representations relating to developments in this sphere. Although they initially adopted a conservative role as regards the development of the new unions and the demand for plant-level bargaining, bodies such as ASSOCOM and the FCI later commenced encouraging their members to deal with representative unions. Since then manpower matters have become as important as economic issues on the agendas of these bodies and guidelines regarding new developments in the labour field are regularly issued to members.

SACCOLA

The South African Consultative Committee on Labour Affairs, SACCOLA, had its origins in the South African Employers' Committee on International Labour Affairs, established in 1948 to study international labour trends and standards and to participate in the International Labour Organisation. Even after South

Africa resigned from certain ILO committees in 1954 and after its total withdrawal in 1964, SAECILA retained its membership of the International Employers' Organisation in order to have input into ILO investigations on South Africa and to maintain international links.

In 1975 the FCI took over the secretaryship of SAECILA. The name of the committee was changed to SACCOLA, and it was decided that the committee would continue to represent a coordinated employer view on both national and international labour matters. SACCOLA joined forces with the Urban Foundation to establish the SACCOLA Code of Employment Practice, intended as an alternative for the numerous international codes which were at that time being applied. By 1983 pressure against South Africa had mounted to such an extent that SACCOLA was expelled from the International Employers' Organisation. Thereafter it concentrated on domestic developments and on representation of employer interests in this regard, although it also tried to maintain international links.

SACCOLA represented all the major employers' associations, the South African Chamber of Business and numerous large employers on an individual basis. In all, approximately ninety percent of private sector employers were members of SACCOLA. It was not a collective bargaining association, but would consult its members when deciding on major policy issues.

The objectives of SACCOLA were, broadly, as follows.

- To formulate policies in relation to such labour affairs as may be deemed to have a bearing on the interests of employers in South Africa
- To coordinate with national and international employers' organisations
- To make representations on labour affairs to national and international authorities
- To liaise with government as regards labour matters

The South African Coordinating Committee on Labour Affairs was thus, as its name states, an umbrella body, established specifically to coordinate employer inputs and reactions in the labour relations arena. For this reason it was SACCOLA and no other employers' association which became involved with the unions when they demanded changes in the labour relations dispensation. As indicated previously, the unions viewed SACCOLA as the 'national' bargaining body, and some intended to use negotiations with SACCOLA as a forum for making important economic and industrial relations decisions. The functions of SACCOLA have now largely been taken over by Business South Africa.

The SACCOLA- NACTU- COSATU Accord

The 1988 amendments to the Labour Relations Act elicited widespread reaction from the trade union movement, which viewed the amendments as an attempt to clamp down on union activity and to place employers in a more favourable position *vis-à-vis* trade unions. Shortly after the passage of the Act, COSATU launched a countrywide campaign to protest the amendments. Shopfloor protests and demonstrations increased, and a national stayaway was threatened by both COSATU and NACTU. It was in this climate that SACCOLA approached the trade union federations with a view to establishing their main grievances and putting forward the employer viewpoint. Initially meetings were strained and reciprocal threats were frequently uttered. Gradually, however, certain points of agreement as regards suggested changes were reached, resulting in what was generally known as the SACCOLA–NACTU–COSATU accord.

The accord was an historic development. Although SACCOLA had previously enjoyed cordial relationships with the established trade unions, this was the first time that employers and the newer trade unions had, on a national level, reached agreement on aspects of the overall labour dispensation. Certain observers hailed it as the first indication of a 'social contract' relationship between organised labour and employers. This expectation may have been somewhat exaggerated, but what the accord did was to send a signal to the government that, when employers and unions combined, it would have to take heed of their demands. The National Manpower Commission was later invited to send delegates to the talks. Representations were made to the Minister of Manpower and the result was that the government agreed to implement changes, subject to representations from other concerned parties. As it was, the Laboria Minute was signed, the SACCOLA–NACTU–COSATU proposals were implemented almost in their entirety and, in March 1991, all the most controversial amendments promulgated in 1988 were removed from the Labour Relations Act.

Even while negotiations regarding the amendments were in progress, the unions broadened the agenda to include other proposed changes to labour legislation, including proposals that

- all employees be included in the Act,
- provision be made for farm and domestic workers, and
- the situation as regards the Labour Appeal Court be reviewed.

A special working party was established by the State President 'to find ways and means of restoring confidence between the Department of Manpower and the parties to the SACCOLA–COSATU–NACTU accord'. In September 1990 the government agreed to give attention to most of the recommendations made by the working party. Although the unions afterwards complained that the government was dragging its heels in implementing the suggested reforms, the meeting was another significant milestone for SACCOLA and the union movement and, as such, is indicative of a more corporatist approach to labour relations, particularly as regards the drafting of labour legislation.

Business South Africa The problem with SACCOLA was that it was not a representative, mandated body but rather a more informal association of employers. For this reason, business in general at times questioned SACCOLA's right to speak for South African employers. When it became apparent that national consultation and consensus seeking between business and representatives of organised labour would become institutionalised through the National Economic Forum, it was decided to establish a more widely representative body in the form of Business South Africa. It is this body, encompassing also the Afrikaanse Handelsinstituut and NAFCOC, which now represents the employer interests in NEDLAC.

THE RELATIONSHIP BETWEEN EMPLOYERS, UNIONS AND THE STATE

Although the government during the previous decade adopted a predominantly *laissez-faire* approach to the conduct of labour relations, it still played a major role in that it implemented legislation governing the system, sometimes without sufficient consultation with all the major participants and in particular the trade union movement. This was not solely the fault of the government, as NACTU and COSATU had in the past persistently refused to deal with a government which they regarded as 'illegitimate' and to participate in any official bodies such as the National Manpower Commission, the Unemployment Insurance Board and the Pensions Board. The union position in this respect changed with the implementation of political reform. With a new political dispensation in sight, the trade union movement now insisted on the broadest possible consultation — perhaps too broad in the government's opinion, since some acrimony resulted from COSATU's insistence that unions have direct, decisive input also into economic legislation. However, there was agreement as regards labour legislation. The Laboria Minute noted that 'the working party agrees that legislation on labour relations cannot work unless there has been extensive consultation on the legislative framework for the regulation of labour relations'. The same Minute promised that no new labour legislation would be promulgated 'unless considered by the NMC' in restructured form. The problem was that, owing to COSATU's additional demands, difficulties were experienced in restructuring the NMC. Nevertheless, consultation between the government, employees and unions continued.

The National Manpower Commission and the National Economic Forum

The Manpower Commission, provided for by the Labour Relations Amendment Act of 1979, was a standing body intended to review labour requirements, to conduct research and to provide advice to government on labour affairs. As mentioned above, it was only after the signing of the Laboria Minute that the unions representative of black employees agreed to sit on the NMC. Shortly afterwards the National Economic Forum was established with a view to gaining the input also of business and labour as regards proposed economic reforms. Both these bodies were replaced at the beginning of 1995 by the National Economic Development & Labour Council, NEDLAC (see Chapter 5).

CORPORATISM — THE WAY FORWARD?

Definition

Karl von Holdt describes corporatism as 'an institutional framework which incorporates the labour movement in the economic and social decisionmaking of society'. He goes on to state that 'Generally corporatism tends to introduce a more cooperative relation between the three parties (capital, labour and the State) as well as the capacity to negotiate common goals'.

Corporatist policies are usually introduced by governments which have the support of labour but which deem it necessary to promote economic activity by way of free enterprise and which therefore need to take into account also the interests of business.

Problems with Corporatism

In a corporatist system, government obtains input from both labour and capital but retains the right to final decisionmaking. Unions are often not satisfied with this arrangement, demanding instead a form of 'bargained' corporatism by which business and labour negotiate and use power to reach agreement on important issues, and where government often acts merely as a rubber-stamping agency. Thus different perceptions of corporatism may lead to tensions within the corporatist relationship itself, as there are very few governments which would abdicate their right to the final decision.

Those unions which aim eventually to achieve a completely socialist dispensation may view corporatism as the antithesis of this objective. They see it as promoting a partnership with capital, thereby ensuring the acceptance and promotion of a capitalist economic dispensation. On the other hand, it is argued that corporatism constitutes merely a necessary interim or evolutionary stage preceding the final achievement of a socialist state.

In an article written for the *South African Labour Bulletin* in January/February 1993, Von Holdt pointed to the dangers of corporatism for the union movement. He warned that it could only entrench the power of an 'unaccountable bureaucracy' in trade unions, could result in the disintegration of the mass or grassroots base of unions and lead to the alienation of unions from their membership. Also, according to Von Holdt, corporatism 'co-opts labour into accepting the economic perspectives of capital'; it centralises power in the hands of an elite group of trade unionists, businessmen and government officials and 'stabilises capitalist society' by ensuring that 'the labour movement cannot struggle for socialism'.

Von Holdt, while favouring entry into a corporatist relationship, at the time counselled unions actively to promote 'militant strategic unionism' and thereby to avoid the dangers of becoming 'corporatist unions'. This, he argued, they could achieve by developing clear strategies and objectives for national, industrial and workplace interactions; by negotiating from positions of independent strength, by complementing national demands with demands for increased worker power at plant level and by promoting broad coalitions with other popular organisations as well as a reconstruction accord with the ANC. By these means they could, from his perspective, use strategic unionism as a means to achieve the 'radical democratisation and transformation of the social order'.

DEVELOPMENTS IN SOUTH AFRICA

Since the publication of the Laboria Minute and the subsequent formation of the National Economic Forum, it was evident that government, organised business and organised labour were increasingly moving towards a more corporatist approach. This trend culminated in the formation of the National Economic Development & Labour Council with its labour market, trade and industry, public finance and development chambers. However, there are some commentators, like Webster, who believe that NEDLAC is not a typical corporatist institution since it includes not only the parties to the tripartite labour relationship but also another interest group: that representing 'community and development organisations'. These have been included because in South Africa, with its high levels of unemployment, organised labour and business do not represent the majority of the population. Thus corporatism in its 'pure' form could elicit accusations of elitism. Conditions for admission to NEDLAC are quite stringent and thus far only three other bodies have been accepted: the Women's National Coalition, the National Youth Development Forum and the South African National Civics Organisation.

According to Webster, NEDLAC is an attempt to 'go beyond parliament to build a broad social consensus by incorporating the key institutions of civil society in the reconstruction of society'. Whether it will succeed in doing so depends on the willingness of the parties to cast aside factional interests and pursue common goals.

THE REALITY OF CORPORATISM IN SOUTH AFRICA

While corporatism, with its concomitant cooperation and consensus, appears to be the most sensible strategy within the context of reconstruction and development, there are in the South African situation numerous factors which militate against its successful implementation. The still existent racial divisions between capital and labour render it difficult to create a climate of mutual acceptance and trust between the parties, and even between business and government. Moreover, the overt alliance between the ruling political party and the major trade union federation may create, in the ranks of both business and the other trade unions, suspicions of favouritism. In fact, Von Holdt reports that, during negotiations on the new Labour Bill, both NACTU and FEDSAL

> *'... clearly had mixed feelings about COSATU'S alliance with the ANC. On the one hand there was uneasiness that COSATU was meeting alone with the ANC, and might seek to change the labour caucus's position on behalf of the ANC ... On the other hand, COSATU's political alliance with the ANC gave them access to information and a lobbying capacity.'*

That COSATU expected the ANC to promote its interests is proved by a remark appearing in *The Shop Steward*, that 'Comrade Tito Mboweni never forgot on which side of the trenches he was located'. However, at the Witwatersrand Regional Shop Steward Conference, delegates slated the final agreement on the new legislation and called for the dissolution of the political alliance with the ANC. Clearly they had expected more — that the government give in to all their demands.

The somewhat unrealistic expectation at grassroots that the government should endorse all of COSATU's demands tends to compound the problem for the federations negotiators at NEDLAC. While they themselves may be aware of the complexity of the problem and the need for compromise, it is difficult to communicate this to the general membership. Also, COSATU leaders themselves are inclined to engage in militant rhetoric, which does not improve the situation. Added to this is the fact that many COSATU unions and members still see mass action as the means to their ends. They have not yet shifted paradigms into the cooperative and consensual mode, and essentially still view themselves as obtaining what they want by the use of their mass power base. In an article appearing in *The Shop Steward Campaign Bulletin* in February 1995, the COSATU central executive in fact states that it regards NEDLAC as a base to build the power of workers, to redistribute wealth, to rebuild and ensure job security and job creation and to entrench democracy. That COSATU regards NEDLAC essentially as a forum for distributive negotiation is further proved by the fact that COSATU insists that 'decisionmaking in NEDLAC must be made after proper mandating, and we should not break off from decisions not in our favour'. The federation also foresees that it will have to 'mobilise workers behind the demands we put to NEDLAC'.

In line with this perception of demand-based negotiations, COSATU has established its own agenda for NEDLAC which includes the reform of all labour laws, affirmative action, a wages policy, industry restructuring, job creation, social funds and a social plan Act, social clauses in trade agreements, the government budget, privatisation, investment policy, taxation, a new national health system, electricity, housing, rural infrastructure and transport. While most of these issues would, in all likelihood, also constitute the concerns of the other parties and especially of government, true corporatism would require that such an agenda be drawn up jointly by all parties and not put forward as the 'demand' of only one party.

The government itself is walking a tightrope. In a corporatist relationship government would, as Webster states, expect union leaders to deliver restraint, as well as greater productivity from their members. Government would expect to be the leading and guiding party and, indeed, were it not for the timeous intervention of the Minister of Labour, the new labour legislation would probably still be a bone of contention. However, at the same time the government is aware of the trade union movement's capacity for mass mobilisation and of the expectation of delivery from those masses which brought it into power. It does not want to be seen as being on the opposing side to the labour movement, although it now has a far wider constituency and far more complex problems to consider. This perhaps extreme sensitivity of the government to labour's position is best illustrated by the presence of President Mandela and other ANC leaders at the marches protesting the legislation which their own Minister of Labour had introduced — an anomalous situation, to say the least! Admittedly the marches were disguised as demonstrations against the 'intransigent stand' of business, but business did not in the first place introduce the legislation. Furthermore, during the ensuing negotiations between labour, business and the government, there was often great tension between labour and government negotiators as the latter consistently refused to accede to the more extreme demands of the labour caucus.

Within the labour caucus itself there was not always agreement. The smaller federations have interests which differ from those of COSATU, and NACTU especially regarded some of COSATU's proposals as undemocratic. The question is whether COSATU will eventually be able to absorb or co-opt these smaller bodies.

Business, as the third important party in NEDLAC, may also not have comprehended fully the nature of corporatism. Business representatives tended to see themselves as being in a defensive position and 'saving as much as possible' against the 'onslaught' of the labour movement and government. They, in their turn, should have formulated their own vision of the future, based on the

South African reality and taking into account the perspectives of the other parties. Had they done this, they might have been able to adopt a far more proactive stance and have emerged with a better solution.

Evaluation   It is evident from the aforegoing discussion that, in South Africa, the road to true corporatism is fraught with obstacles. All parties are very new at the game, and numerous lessons need still to be learnt. The ANC and COSATU need to delineate their relationship more clearly insofar as concerns areas of cooperation and independence. COSATU in particular needs to reassess its position and actions within the new constellation. As Von Holdt states, 'the driving imperative to attack the legitimacy of the apartheid government has fallen away. The old repertoire of demands, mass action and victories does not match the complexity of relations and outcomes'. Business, too, needs to shift paradigms if it is to partake successfully in cooperative endeavours. Some success has been achieved, and it is generally accepted that there will be differences. In fact, differences dealt with in a constructive manner can lead to more creative solutions.

As NEDLAC director general Jayendra Naidoo has stated, 'NEDLAC was formed as a mechanism for ongoing cooperation and problem solving by social partners'. The Council has now released a discussion document providing 'a framework for social partnership and agreement making in NEDLAC'. It is sincerely hoped that this will not remain merely a document for discussion, and that a more constructive relationship will soon be perceived.

CONCLUSION

Developments in all spheres of labour relations were extremely rapid during the 1980s, and the momentum increased from the beginning of 1990. This was nowhere more evident than in the changing attitudes and stances of employers, unions and the State and in the almost unexpected consultation and consensus among the various participants. Overall, every party — although perhaps pursuing its own agenda — displayed greater pragmatism, as well as a willingness to negotiate and to reach a compromise.

SOURCES

Copelyn, John 'Collective Bargaining: A Base for Transforming Industry' in *South African Labour Bulletin*, Vol. XV no. 6, March 1991.

Erwin, Alec 'The Question of Unity in the Struggle' in *South African Labour Bulletin*, Vol. II no. 1, 1985.

Fine, Alan 'Trends in Organised Labour' in *South African Review 4*, Ravan Press, 1987.

Friedman, Steve *Building Tomorrow Today*, Ravan Press, 1987.

Lewis, John and Randall, Estelle 'Survey: The State of the Unions' in *South African Labour Bulletin*, Vol. II no. 2, 1985.

Maree, Johann (Ed) *The Independent Trade Unions 1974–1984*, Ravan Press, 1987.

South African Labour Bulletin, Vols. XVI, XVII, XVIII and XIX, Umanyano Publications.

The Shop Steward, Umanyano Publications, January 1993–October 1994.

Von Holdt, Karl 'The Dangers of Corporatism' in *South African Labour Bulletin*, Vol. XVII no. 1, March 1995.

Von Holdt, Karl 'The LRA Agreement: Worker Victory or Miserable Compromise?' in *South African Labour Bulletin*, Vol. XIX no. 4, September 1995.

Von Holdt, Karl 'Towards Transforming South African Industry: A Reconstruction Accord between Unions and the ANC' in *South African Labour Bulletin*, Vol. XV no. 6, March 1991.

Webster, Eddie 'NEDLAC: Corporatism of a Special Type' in *South African Labour Bulletin*, Vol. XIX no. 2, May 1995.

Department of Labour *Annual Report 1994*, Government Printer, Pretoria, 1995.

Department of Manpower *Report of the Director General* (annual report), Government Printer, Pretoria, 1994.

'A Shake-up in the Leadership of No. 2', *The Weekly Mail*, 12–18 August 1988.

COSATU 'Forward to the Special Congress', *COSATU News*, May 1988. Separate Campaign Edition, March 1987. Second National Congress Report 1987.

COLLECTIVE
BARGAINING

OVERVIEW

Collective bargaining is the central process emanating from the conduct of the traditional collective labour relationship. Having sought their power in the collectivity and having identified interests and goals divergent from those of the employer, employees, through their unions, will demand from the employer that he establish a bargaining relationship with them so that together they may attempt to resolve their conflicts and regulate their relationship. Such a relationship will be established because there is a common interest between the two parties and to prevent either party from using its coercive power to achieve its own ends. Nevertheless, the threat that a particular party may apply coercive power is always present in the traditional bargaining relationship and serves to pressurise both sides into agreement.

Once a bargaining relationship has been established, the bargaining process will cover a wide range of items, some of them substantive and others procedural in nature. These may be dealt with by various processes, such as distributive or integrative bargaining. Also, bargaining may be conducted in different types of bargaining units and with employers at various levels. Bargaining units and bargaining levels determine bargaining structures, of which there are many forms.

The type of bargaining structures established in a particular industrial relations system will characterise the relationships and interactions within that system and, in turn, are dependent on a number of factors, most of them related to union or employer organisation and strategy. The State, too, may play an important role in determining bargaining structures and in the bargaining relationship in general.

COLLECTIVE BARGAINING AS CENTRAL TO THE LABOUR RELATIONSHIP

Beatrix and Sidney Webb described collective bargaining as '... one method whereby trade unions could maintain and improve their members' terms and conditions of employment.' The description is basically correct, firstly because collective bargaining *is* a union-initiated process. If employees did not form collectives and demand that employers bargain with them, bargaining might never occur. Secondly, the initial purpose of collective bargaining *is* to obtain improved employment conditions for trade union members. On the other hand, the description given by the Webbs may be insufficient, since it fails to highlight the interactive nature of the process, its paradoxical basis and its central position in the conduct of the traditional labour relationship. The collective bargaining process, although it may be union-initiated, is a **two-way process** in which there is traditionally pressure and counterpressure from both sides. Just as the union might wish to elicit concessions from management, so, too, might management wish to gain concessions from the union. To these ends they bargain and eventually reach a compromise. Furthermore, the collective bargaining process is to some extent a cooperative process. It might arise from a conflict of interests and goals and might be essentially antagonistic in nature, but it can take place only because there are **common interests** and its purpose is to contain conflict and even to promote cooperation. Most importantly, in a predominantly adversarial milieu, the process of collective bargaining is the principal method by which employers and their employees as a collective **establish and continue a relationship** which might otherwise prove difficult to maintain. If there were no collective bargaining, there might be no relationship between employers and employees except the individual contractual relationship, which is essentially unbalanced. Collective bargaining constitutes a means by which the two sides can get together, talk about their problems, needs and goals and try to settle their differences. As such, it becomes a valuable instrument towards improved communication.

The definition given by the Webbs also fails to describe the **dynamic nature** of the collective bargaining process, its reliance on the **power of the parties** and its susceptibility to **outside influences**. Collective bargaining is not a 'one off' process nor even a procedure instituted at regular intervals — for example, once a year when wage bargaining takes place. Where there is an established relationship, it is a continuous process of give and take. How much a particular party gives will usually depend on the power of the other, but power is not static. The fulcrum of power continually shifts between the two parties. Also, as with all other aspects of the labour relationship, collective bargaining is subject to external influences in the shape of economic and sociopolitical developments, technological innovation and demographic changes. Because they help to determine the power balance between the parties and lead to issues over which there might be disagreement, these external factors will affect all stages of the collective bargaining process.

In the light of the above, the collective bargaining process may be more comprehensively described as:

> **a process, necessitated by a conflict of needs, interests, goals, values, perceptions and ideologies, but resting on a basic commonality of**

interest, whereby employees/employee collectives and employers/ employer collectives, by the conduct of continued negotiation and the application of pressure and counterpressure, attempt to achieve some balance between the fulfilment of the needs, goals and interests of management on the one hand and employees on the other — the extent to which either party achieves its objectives depending on the nature of the relationship itself, each party's source and use of power, the power balance between them, the organisational and strategic effectiveness of each party, as well as the type of bargaining structure and the prevalent economic, sociopolitical and other conditions.

COMMONALITY, CONFLICT AND POWER IN COLLECTIVE BARGAINING

Commonality as Basis for Bargaining

Bargaining would not take place if there were no point of common interest between employer and employee. If it were not necessary for the parties to work together to produce goods or services and, in the long term, to ensure the future of the enterprise and the economy as a whole, there would be no need for them to come together in order to sort out any differences which they might have; but, because all the parties involved will ultimately benefit from the enterprise and because one needs the other to achieve his own goals, bargaining does take place. Thus commonality of interest and interdependence form the basis of the bargaining relationship in the pluralist system.

Because the commonality of interest is antiposed by a conflict of individual goals, it may happen that the parties (or one of them) do not recognise this commonality. Employees in particular may view themselves as merely doing a job or as being exploited by the employer. They are inclined to emphasise the conflict of interest between the parties and to minimise the commonality. Employers, on their part, may overemphasise the employee's common interests with the employer. They expect him to appreciate the opportunity he has been given, to be loyal to the company and to deliver his best for the good of the undertaking. In the process, employers tend to ignore the fact that employees do have different needs, interests and goals. In general, they prefer to believe that there is little or no basic conflict between employer and employee or, at the very least, that commonality of interests greatly overshadows conflict. Despite this varying emphasis on the role of commonality, both parties must eventually perceive its existence before bargaining can commence.

In certain circumstances commonality of interest may, for both parties, override conflict. This could occur when the general economy of a country or the future of the enterprise is threatened, where employees share in the decisionmaking process or where moral principles dictate the relationship. If this happens, the relationship becomes more cooperative than antagonistic and bargaining, where is does occur, is aimed at promotion of the common good rather than at the settlement of opposing interests.

The Role of Conflict in Collective Bargaining

Conflict as Reason for Bargaining

Just as the parties to the labour relationship would not agree to bargain if there were no common interest, so would there be no necessity for bargaining if no conflict of interests existed. This conflict was briefly described in a previous chapter, where it was pointed out that the parties will have different goals, needs, interests, attitudes, values and perceptions. Since each party will pursue his own goals, in the light of his own interests and values and possibly at the cost of the other party, conflict necessarily arises. Were such conflict allowed to continue, it could reach destructive proportions, which would negatively affect both parties. As Anthony has stated,

> 'There are many circumstances in which any one of the parties to the employment relationship becomes an obstacle to the achievement of the purpose of one of the others. Industrial Relations are especially concerned with those circumstances in which different groups are set upon different courses in the pursuit of which one becomes an obstacle to the other. ... The procedures of Industrial Relations are, for the most part, concerned to protect the parties from inflicting an unacceptable degree of damage upon each other in a relationship which is often hostile.'

Fortunately, if both parties hold sufficient power, it is usually realised that a one-sided pursuit of goals results in continued conflict and that, in view of the commonality of interest, an attempt should be made to contain or handle the conflict in as functional a manner as possible; hence the agreement by parties to engage in a bargaining relationship, to establish procedures to regulate their relationship and to negotiate on issues where disagreement exists.

The agreement to bargain does not negate the presence of conflict; nor is there an attempt to eliminate conflict altogether. It is accepted that conflict exists, and that, if it is handled correctly, it will not assume exaggerated proportions. As mentioned earlier, conflict as such is not necessarily dysfunctional. The modern view holds that a certain amount of conflict will, provided it remains manageable, help to stimulate growth, innovation and change and to bring about improvements in the organisation. In the labour relations sense the conclusion could be drawn that the acceptance of conflict and the agreement to bargain may eventually serve this purpose.

Sources of Conflict

According to Luthans, the most common sources of organisational conflict are the following.

- Scarcity of resources
- Incompatibility of needs, goals and interests
- Different attitudes to work
- Different attitudes, values and perceptions in general
- Shared work activities
- Ambiguity in responsibilities and roles
- Poor or inadequate organisational structure
- Poor communication

Luthans does not apply these sources of conflict specifically to the labour relations situation, but they are equally applicable to this relationship. The most common source of conflict between employers and employees or unions is to be found in arguments concerning the application of scarce resources, the scarcest resource being money. Management not only has a responsibility towards its employees, but also needs to consider the shareholders, to expand and develop the business and to satisfy customers. Consequently, it will apply resources, in the form of available finances, as it sees fit. Management may decide to grant a higher dividend to shareholders, to acquire new machinery or to offer a vast sum for the expertise of a particular individual. This may not meet with the approval of employees and unions, who could be of the opinion that a higher percentage of available money should have been allocated to wage increases. A case in point is the current argument by many South African unions that the profit margins of South African organisations are too high and that companies could afford to pay higher wages at the cost of a cut in profits and a decreased dividend to shareholders. They may also feel that there is too great a divide between the remuneration of the lowest paid workers and that of top management; thus they may demand an increased minimum wage and a freeze on management salaries. The living wage campaign is, besides the implications of exploitation, nothing more than a reflection of union opinion that the financial resources of the enterprise are being unequally distributed.

Closely related to the conflict arising from the scarcity of resources is the fact that employers and employees come into conflict essentially because they have different needs, goals and interests. An employer's primary goal is to raise profit margins and to develop the organisation, whereas the objective of employees is to earn as much as possible for the work which they perform. Furthermore, in order to run his business effectively, an employer needs to be flexible. To achieve such flexibility, he might demand the right to dismiss inefficient workers, to work short time when necessary and to retrench workers in a downward cycle. Employees, on the other hand, insist on job and income security. They wish to be assured that they will retain their jobs and that their incomes will remain stable even in times of economic recession. At the very least, they will demand compensation for the 'unwarranted' loss of their employment. Another source of conflict lies in the fact that, traditionally, employers have believed that they possess the right to exercise full control over employees and that decisionmaking regarding all matters of importance rests entirely in the hands of management. This assumption is being increasingly challenged by employees and unions and even by government legislation. On their part, employees may believe that they have the right to raise demands for shorter working hours, longer leave, sick leave, training programmes and time off on public holidays. These demands will conflict with the employer need to utilise machinery as effectively as possible or to serve the interests of customers at all times. Employees will also insist on absolute guarantees concerning health and safety which an employer, if he is to run a profitable business, may not be able to provide. It is this conflict in needs, interests and goals which underlies most labour relationships and results in issues between employer and employee at the bargaining table.

Underscoring the conflict in goals and interests is the fact that management and employees may have different attitudes to work and different attitudes, values and perceptions in general. Whereas a manager will seek commitment and loyalty from employees and will expect them to work harder for the good of the enterprise, employees may not like to work, may not consider it their duty to produce more effectively and may regard it as their right to change jobs at their pleasure. Equally, an employer could regard competitive basic wages and bonuses for higher productivity as just rewards for the employee's efforts, while the employee himself may desire improved status, job satisfaction or the fulfilment of his social and educational needs. Perceptions and values which individuals acquire in their particular societies will also result in conflict. Employees may view themselves as a disadvantaged class, may not have the same work ethic as the employer or may expect the employer to practise social responsibility according to their perception of this concept. In the extreme, employers and employees may subscribe to completely different economic and sociopolitical ideologies. Whereas an employer might support a capitalist system, employees might believe in the redistribution of wealth and employee control of the means of production. Similarly, an employer might be quite satisfied with the sociopolitical *status quo*, but the employee might regard it with antagonism. Such conflict in ideology will inevitably place greater stress on the employer–employee relationship.

Finally, the very fact that employers and employees have to work together, that the employee is obliged to take instructions from and support the manager, that an employee might not be certain of the role he has to perform or might not be given sufficient authority to perform this role, may increase the conflict potential. Added to this is the possibility that the organisational structure and management style may be of such a nature as to promote conflict and that communication structures may be ineffective. Besides causing its own conflict, ineffective communication will exaggerate conflict arising from other sources. In this respect, the act of bargaining is in itself a means towards more effective communication.

Collective Bargaining as the Hitherto Preferred
Method of Handling Conflict

It has by now been established that, since conflict is inherent particularly in the adversarial labour relationship, it is necessary to be continually aware of its existence and to attempt to handle it in as effective a manner as possible. This applies not only to the collective bargaining relationship, but also to the day-to-day interaction between employer and employee and to particular incidents or developments. Organisational theory teaches that there are various methods of handling conflict. These may be broadly divided into three types: those methods which bring about solutions favourable to neither side (a lose–lose situation), those resulting in solutions favourable to one side but not the other (a win–lose situation), and those resulting in solutions favourable to both sides (a win–win situation). Although the last is the most preferred solution, it is not easy to achieve a win–win situation in practice.

One of the least preferred methods of handling conflict, if it can be termed a method, is that of complete **avoidance** or **withdrawal**. This usually occurs where the conflict is of such a trivial nature that it does not merit intervention or an attempt at a solution, but it may also occur because one party refuses to recognise the existence of conflict. In the labour relations situation, there are individuals, particularly on the employer side, who attempt by all means to avoid conflict situations and especially the basic conflict of interest between employer and employee. This is not advisable, since avoidance will result in a lose–lose situation and the conflict itself does not disappear. It may merely smoulder quietly to reappear in an intensified form on a later occasion. Yet there are occasions also in labour relations when minor incidents are best avoided, particularly if more important issues are at stake, if there is no possible solution or if the disruption caused by addressing the conflict situation is greater than the advantages of its solution.

A method similar to the avoidance of conflict is that of attempting to **smooth over** the problem, either by getting one party to capitulate or by both parties relinquishing their stands. Again this does not solve the problem as far as basic employer–employee conflict is concerned, since the differences will remain, but it could be of use in specific instances where there are other, more important, issues to deal with or where harmony is, at that particular point, of the utmost importance. In the labour relations sphere, employers may attempt to smooth over basic conflicts of interest by using employer-biased propaganda or by adopting a paternalistic, protective attitude towards employees, but this may not help to solve the problem.

A less preferred but still widely used method of resolving conflict, also in the labour relations situation, is that of **dominance** or **suppression**. Positions of authority or the organisational structure are used to put down any sign of conflict. In labour relations, this would entail victimising employees for union membership and dismissing or punishing employees who make demands or who attempt to assert their interests against those of employers. Suppression leads to a win–lose situation and, as in the case of other ill-advised methods, the conflict does not disappear; it merely goes underground.

The resolution of conflict could, in many instances, be effected by applying the **democratic method** or the principle of majority rule. However, when the parties are in strong opposition to one another and the issues are of great importance to them, a majority decision resulting in a win–lose situation may not resolve the problem. It could lead to continued dissatisfaction on the part of the losing party or parties and to a negative aftermath. For these reasons the democratic method cannot be effectively applied to resolve conflict in the employer–employee relationship. Another reason for its non-use is that the parties are numerically unmatched. It could, nevertheless, be employed in specific situations where these factors are irrelevant or where there is total worker participation in the decisionmaking process.

Where conflict cannot be resolved by the parties themselves or where it threatens to become dysfunctional, it may be necessary to make use of **mediation** or **arbitration**. This involves the calling in of a third party either to encourage a settlement between the parties or to decide on such settlement. In labour relations the parties involved usually prefer first to attempt settlement amongst themselves. Consequently, arbitration and mediation are employed as methods of settlement only after other possibilities have been exhausted or when it becomes necessary to obtain an impartial perspective.

The best method of resolving conflict is by **integrative problem-solving**. This approach necessitates a relationship of trust between the parties and, although there may be confrontation, it occurs within the ambits of a common concern to find solutions favourable to both parties. Integrative problem-solving is marked by a free exchange of ideas and is undertaken in an atmosphere of frankness and openness. It is also more easily achieved if there is a **substitution of superordinate goals** for the individual goals of the particular parties. Because the parties would be working towards a common, more important objective, they might more readily shelve their individual objectives or attempt to find joint solutions. In labour relations integrative problem-solving is normally achieved only by parties who have a long, established relationship, by employers and employees suffering common hardship or by parties whose differences in goals, interests and perspectives have narrowed considerably.

A radical means of resolving conflict is by entirely **restructuring the organisation and changing management style**. In labour relations this could entail the granting of increased participation in the decisionmaking function to employees. This might greatly diminish the basic employer–employee conflict; but, unless there was in essence no difference at all between employer and employee, conflict could never be totally eliminated.

The last method of resolving conflict is that most commonly used in the conduct of the labour relationship, namely **individual negotiation** or **collective bargaining**. It has become evident that all the other methods proposed are either ineffective or, where at least one of the parties is unsophisticated and intent on confrontation, not suitable to the particular nature and circumstances of the labour relationship. Collective bargaining is not the ideal method of resolving conflict as it may lead to a win–lose situation and to a negative aftermath. On the other hand it could be argued that, unless power is very unequally distributed, individual parties will lose in one instance but win in another. At the least, the process of bargaining endows the parties with equal status. It also rests on the presuppositions that neither party is completely right or completely wrong, that concessions by either party do not necessarily signify weakness in that party and that, while the individual goals of the parties may be important, the ultimate achievement of these goals should not occur at the cost of disrupting the organisation as a whole. For these reasons collective bargaining, though not ideal, has hitherto served as the most feasible and mutually beneficial method of resolving basic and ongoing conflicts between the parties to the labour relationship.

Stages of Conflict

The handling of conflict requires awareness of its various developmental phases. The first of these is the stage at which **potential for conflict** exists. There are, in all situations, certain conditions which are conducive to the breeding of conflict and, unless circumstances change, these will eventually give rise to an actual conflict situation. In the labour relations context, potential for conflict exists because of the very nature of the labour relationship in a capitalist system. Awareness and acceptance of this potential serves as preparation for the handling defusion and containment of conflict at a later stage.

In the second stage of its development conflict has become concretised, but the parties themselves may not have expressed its existence and it remains latent. It may eventually require a trigger incident to bring the conflict into the open. This is of particular relevance in labour relations where **latent conflict**, centring on the basic employer–employee differences or in general employee dissatisfaction with the *status quo*, manifests itself in a trigger incident arising from a relatively minor problem.

The trigger incident will bring the conflict into the open. Once conflict has become **manifest**, it can be dealt with in a more direct manner. This is the stage at which, in the labour relationship, there is a demand for the establishment of a bargaining relationship.

Finally, there is always an **aftermath to conflict**. Although a particular problem may have been resolved, the general potential for conflict will probably have been heightened by its overt manifestation. In labour relations, not only is there the inherent potential for conflict but this potential may also be heightened after each particular incident. This is especially so if one party perceives itself as having been involved in a win–lose situation.

It would be impossible within the present context to discuss all the intricacies and ramifications of conflict both in general and, specifically, as it manifests itself with regard to the labour relationship. These aspects are covered in greater detail in Chapter 13. Suffice it to say that the existence of conflict is the trigger towards the establishment of a collective bargaining relationship and that the containment of the conflict between employer and employee is the main purpose of the collective bargaining process.

Power as Regulator of the Bargaining Process

While commonality of interest may be the basis of the bargaining relationship and conflict the reason for bargaining, power could be described as its driving force. The parties enter the bargaining relationship because they do have a common interest on the one hand and diverse interests on the other and because, for the common good, they need to regulate the conflict which arises from their diversity of interests. Yet most often neither party, despite the common interest, would enter the relationship if it did not perceive the other as holding equal or almost equal power. Should one party hold all or most of the power, it will usually pursue its own interests to the detriment of the other party. This did happen previously when employers held the greater power and dictated terms and conditions of employment, limited only by the dictates of the labour market, the individual contract of employment or the power of the State in the form of legislation pertaining to minimum conditions of employment. In general, a party will — except in those instances where it is limited by law or where considerations of social responsibility, fairness and morality play a part — be limited in the pursuit of its own interests only by the power or counterforce which the other party can apply. Anthony, in describing one party as an obstacle to the pursuit of self interest by the other, puts it thus:

> 'The force of one kind or another, which can be brought to bear in removing the obstacle, and the force with which the obstacle can resist removal, represents the constraints with which management and unions seek to influence each other's behaviour.'

However, despite all pronouncements about equal power, it may be argued that this remains merely an illusion. There are theorists who believe that equal power is never achieved since, immediately there is some semblance of equality, at least one party will engage in power competition, which spirals as the relative power of the parties increases. Marxists, too, believe that equal power can never be achieved within the capitalist system, since employers will always hold a power edge over employees and unions.

Although, on both employer and employee side, power can assume various forms, the basis of the employer's power is the fact that he provides the employee with the opportunity to work and earn a living, while the employee, on the other hand, holds power because of his ability to withhold his work from the employer. The unequal distribution of power in the individual employer-employee relationship becomes obvious if it is considered that it is easier for the employer to withhold work opportunity from the employee than it is for the employee to withhold his labour from the employer. The employer may not be dependent on the work of one employee for his basic livelihood and, even if he is, he could replace the employee with another worker or with machinery; while the employee, unless he can easily find alternative employment, depends on the employer for his own livelihood and that of his family. Therefore an individual employee may not be in a position to withstand the power of the employer, unless he, the employee, is irreplaceable or difficult to replace. Also, the individual employment contract is asymmetrical in that the common law contractual duties of the employer — namely to pay the employee, to provide safe and healthy working conditions, not to oblige the employee to do work junior to his status and not to contract the services of the employee to another employee — are concrete and do not detract from the power of the employer, while the duties of the employee — particularly the duty to work to the best of his ability and to obey all reasonable instructions — are limitless by implication and render the employee relatively powerless. For these reasons employees have to establish combinations, either informally or in the form of trade unions. A trade union, having behind it the power of the collective employee body and their collective threat of jointly withholding their labour , can more easily counter the power of the employer, thereby placing employees on a more equal footing with the employer. It is usually only a display of joint employee/union power, often in the form of threatened strike action, which obliges the employer to engage in a bargaining relationship with employees.

Thus the threat by employees that they will use their coercive power against the employer underlies the bargaining relationship. The paradox lies in the fact that the purpose of establishing a bargaining relationship is to forecome the use of coercive power by either side, yet the ability of each side to apply coercive power continues to influence the bargaining process. In establishing a bargaining relationship, the parties agree that they will not, if possible, use their muscle against each other, although they may continue to flex such muscle from time to time and may use it if circumstances so require. They will attempt to settle their differences by negotiation but, should negotiations not succeed, each may use his coercive power against the other. Consequently, the freedom to engage in a strike and a lockout are part and parcel of the normal collective bargaining process. Yet unions in general still believe that the right to strike should not be counterposed by the right to lock out. They maintain that the employer's entrenched power is sufficient to counter the coercive power of a strike action by an employee without him (the employer) resorting to a lockout.

Having once established a bargaining relationship, the parties will bring whatever force they can muster to bear on that relationship. Besides their basic coercive power, employers and trade unions will attempt to gain power from other sources. An individual employer may combine with other employers, employers as a body may lobby the government to exert their power in the relationship, or they may use economic and other circumstances against the union. Unions, on the other hand, may attempt to elicit the sympathy of other employees or employers, of other institutions or the community, or they may attempt to gain political power. At any stage during the bargaining process the overall power of each party and its willingness to engage in a demonstration of coercive power will greatly influence the conduct of the negotiation and its substantive outcome in the form of benefits for either side. If, at a particular time, a union wields more overall power, and if it is willing to engage in strike action, then it is more likely to gain concessions from the employer than would otherwise be the case. The same would apply to the employer in the reverse situation. Thus the collective bargaining process relies mainly on a continual power play between the parties and, since the power balance is in a state of continual flux, collective bargaining is an ongoing, dynamic process in which even the rules of the game may change from time to time. Figure 15 illustrates the interplay between commonality, conflict and power in the establishment of the bargaining relationship.

For the sake of clarity of conceptualisation, the role of conflict and power have been emphasised throughout this section, perhaps to the detriment of other forces, such as cooperation and considerations of fairness. There are employers who will engage in a bargaining relationship with employees not because they are obliged to do so by a display of power, but because of their own values and moral convictions or simply because it makes good business sense, and there are others who have managed to minimise areas of conflict between themselves and their employees. Nevertheless, in essence, the traditional bargaining relationship does arise from conflict and it does rely on the use of power and, although the relationship itself may lead to greater cooperation, an element of antagonism will remain.

THE ESTABLISHMENT OF A BARGAINING RELATIONSHIP

**Character-
istics of a
Bargaining
Relationship**
The bargaining relationship may be described as the extension, collectivisation and formalisation of the labour relationship. Prior to the establishment of the bargaining relationship, a formal relationship, regulated by the contract of employment or legislative provisions, does exist between the employer and the individual employee. Also, negotiations might be conducted between the employer and individual employees, but there is no formal relationship between the employer and the **employee collective**, at least not one of the same type as the bargaining relationship. In the absence of a bargaining relationship there might be an informal collective relationship in that the employer may from time to time call his employees together, speak to them and canvass their opinions, or there might be another kind of formal relationship, embodied by a workers' committee or workers' council. The first type of relationship puts no onus on the employer to consult with or heed the opinion of his employees, while the second may not allow employees to use their power to elicit concessions from the employer unless the workers' committee acts also in a bargaining capacity.

The bargaining relationship is marked by the employer's formal agreement to enter into negotiations with his employees or a group of his employees with a view to mutual regulation of their relationship. In agreeing to bargain, the employer acknowledges the power of his employees and their standing as equal

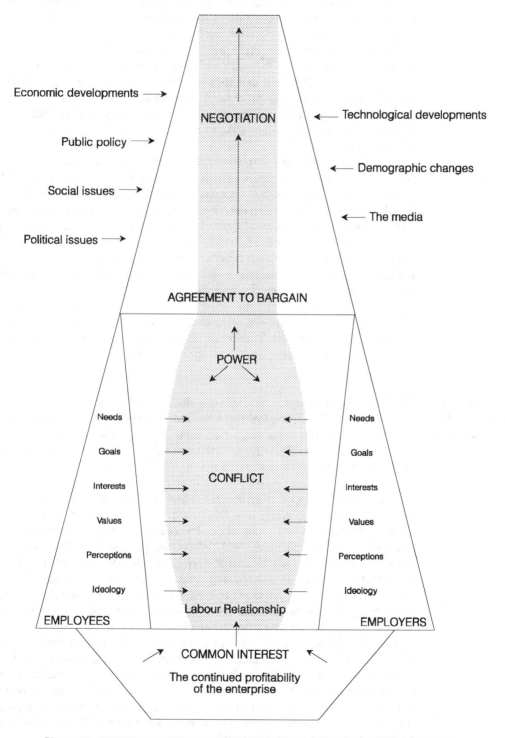

Figure 15: ESTABLISHMENT OF THE COLLECTIVE BARGAINING RELATIONSHIP

negotiating partners. Implicitly he accepts that there is a conflict of interests and he accepts the necessity of containing this conflict through the bargaining process. Moreover, acceptance of the bargaining relationship would, in a voluntary system, imply acceptance of the employees' freedom to strike and the employer's freedom to lock out his employees.

By the establishment of the collective bargaining relationship, the parties agree, in the first place, that each will not pursue his own interests to the exclusion of the other, but that they will interact within the framework of mutually agreed rules and procedures. As Hawkins has stated, 'The rules embodied in collective bargaining procedures represent a voluntary undertaking by employers and trade unions alike to act in accordance with accepted norms of behaviour.'

Most importantly, the bargaining relationship differs from the normal employer–employee relationship in that an outside party, in the form of the union, usually represents the interests of employees. For this reason the bargaining relationship is often described as an employer–union relationship or a relationship between an employers' association and a union and not as an employer–employee relationship, which it essentially is and should remain. The entry of a third party, whether it is in the form of a trade union or an employers' association, greatly formalises the relationship. Such formalisation is necessary but it may, at times, hamper the relationship.

There are instances when the employer agrees to enter into a bargaining relationship with his employees without the presence of a union or where an employer will bargain with a union on an *ad hoc* basis without concluding a formal agreement, but these are the exception rather than the rule.

Agreement to Bargain — The Process of Recognition

The bargaining relationship has been described as a union-initiated relationship. It is uncommon for an employer to approach his employees or a union with a view to establishing a bargaining relationship, although this might happen at a highly centralised level or in a very formalised system. The majority of employers do not regard it as necessary to establish a bargaining relationship with their employees and might even be loath to do so. In certain countries, an employer may be compelled by law to establish a relationship with a representative union, while in others it is left to the union or a group of unions to approach an employer or a group of employers and demand the establishment of a bargaining relationship from them. Where the law has provided a statutory bargaining system, the union demand may be for the formation of a statutory bargaining body, such as a bargaining council. Where no such statutory body exists or where a union prefers not to avail itself of such body, the demand will be for recognition of the union as representative of the employees and as equal bargaining partner. Agreement by the employer or employers to enter into the relationship will lead, in the case of a statutory or formalised body, to the drawing up of a constitution; and, where there is no such body, to a recognition agreement. The constitution of a formal or statutory body on the one hand and a recognition agreement on the other are, therefore, primarily reflective of the agreement by both parties to enter into a bargaining relationship and to attempt to regulate between them matters of concern to both parties. This is, essentially, the meaning of the term 'recognition'.

The formalisation of the relationship requires that the constitution of a statutory body or a recognition agreement should also stipulate the procedures to be adopted in conducting the relationship. For this reason recognition agreements are generally described as procedural agreements. Once a recognition agreement has been concluded or a constitution has been accepted, the parties will proceed to the regulation of other aspects of the employer–employee relationship and to negotiations on substantive issues.

Bargaining within the Relationship   In reality the bargaining process commences with the approach for recognition or with the suggested formation of a bargaining body. Already at this stage the parties assess the strengths and weaknesses of the other side, measure their own potential and attempt to gain advantageous positions. Should an employer or a group of employers prove reluctant to engage in a bargaining relationship, the union may, in the early stages of the relationship, or before that relationship has actually been established, be obliged to engage in a show of strength by staging what is generally known as a 'recognition' strike. If this occurs, bargaining has begun in earnest, as the employer will be obliged to apply counterforce or to engage in negotiations towards the establishing of a bargaining relationship. The establishment of the relationship does not occur overnight. While parties may initially agree that such a relationship is necessary, each will, in setting the parameters for the relationship and establishing the procedures for its conduct, attempt to place himself in the most favourable position. Consequently, a final recognition agreement may be concluded or a final constitution may be agreed upon only after months of negotiation between the parties concerned. This happens particularly where employers adopt a highly constitutionalist approach, requiring every aspect of the relationship to be regulated in minute detail, or where such matters are not already regulated by law.

At this stage the parties have merely formalised the relationship and have not yet begun to negotiate on the real issues, but they will already have engaged in very real collective bargaining. The recognition agreement or constitution establishes the parameters for further negotiation. It sets the stage for consultation, negotiation and even cooperation in respect of those matters which are of mutual interest to the parties concerned.

THE SCOPE AND CONTENT OF COLLECTIVE BARGAINING

The scope of collective bargaining varies from one bargaining relationship to another and from system to system. Bargaining arrangements commence with negotiations concerning the procedures to be adopted in regulating the relationship between the bargaining partners. Consequently, bargaining initially hinges around procedural issues and any bargaining arrangement will, at the least, contain procedures for meetings, arrangements for negotiations and procedures for the settlement of disputes between the parties concerned. Provision will, furthermore, be made for the winding up of the relationship, should either party so desire. Thereafter the main focus of the bargaining relationship is usually economic. The parties agree that they will, at regular intervals or when circumstances require, bargain on substantive issues such as wages and conditions of service. In certain instances bargaining scope extends only to this point, mainly because employers, although willing to cede substantive benefits to employees, are not prepared to concede to joint decisionmaking regarding the procedures used to regulate the employer–employee relationship. Unions, on the other hand, may demand a say in the establishment of grievance, disciplinary and retrenchment procedures and in the procedures adopted to safeguard the health and safety of employees. They may, furthermore, demand to be consulted before new technology is introduced or on any decisions which will directly or indirectly affect employees. Thus agreement will be negotiated also on procedural issues such as these.

In the extreme, political and social issues may be carried into the bargaining arena. Management, on the other hand, besides bargaining on union demands, will raise issues of its own. These may include matters such as productivity, training, salary and wage structures, worker commitment and even a possible decrease in wages in times of financial difficulty. However, because management is the party from whom concessions are mainly elicited, the issues raised by management are normally fewer than those brought to the bargaining table by the union.

The scope of collective bargaining can, in effect, be extended to include all areas of conflict in the labour relationship. Thus there is a direct link between the sources of conflict described in a previous section and the issues raised to the bargaining arena. Table 3 serves to illustrate this point. The range that a particular bargaining relationship will cover, whether it will deal with only substantive or with substantive and procedural issues and the degree of joint decisionmaking to be allowed will be decided by the parties concerned. This in itself forms a bargaining issue. Normally bargaining agreements are intended to cover 'any matter of mutual concern between employer and employee'; yet employers and employees differ in their perception of 'matters of mutual concern'.

BARGAINING STYLES

Distributive Bargaining

This is the most common type of bargaining and that which usually occurs in the traditional labour relations situation. Distributive bargaining takes place when management and the union are in opposing positions and when a gain for one party represents a loss for the other. Because there is antagonism, distributive bargaining items are described as issues. As has been seen, the most prevalent issue between management and the union is economic in nature. Distributive bargaining centring in economic issues would include such items as wages, annual leave, holidays, benefits and bonuses. Besides economic issues, managements and unions also hold conflicting views on the rights and obligations of parties. Consequently, items in this sphere, such as disciplinary, grievance and retrenchment procedures, could become issues in distributive bargaining. On the other hand, should management and the union decide to work together and adopt a common goal regarding these items, they could be subjected to integrative bargaining.

The conduct of distributive bargaining involves the use of power tactics and every other possible strategy by both sides. Since each party strives towards an outcome favourable to itself, it will carefully assess the position, strengths and

SOURCE OF CONFLICT EMPLOYER ORIENTATION vs EMPLOYEE ORIENTATION		ISSUES	TYPE OF ISSUE
Higher profits, Development of business	Higher income	Wages	Substantive
		Hours of work	Substantive
		Holidays	Substantive
		Sick leave	Substantive
		Benefits	Substantive
		Allowances	Substantive
		Bonuses	Substantive
		Productivity	Substantive
Flexibility	Security	Dismissals	Procedural & substantive
		Discipline	Procedural
		Short time	Procedural
		Retrenchment	Procedural & substantive
		Technology	Procedural
		Pensions	Substantive
		Seniority rights	Procedural & substantive
Control	Shared decisionmaking	Grievance handling	Procedural
		Discipline	Procedural
		Consultation	Procedural
		Worker participation	Procedural
		Shop steward rights	Procedural
		Union rights	Procedural
		Committees	Procedural
Worker commitment Productivity	Unconcern Leisure	Premiums	Substantive
		Working hours	Substantive
		Leave	Substantive
		Absenteeism	Procedural & substantive
		Productivity	Procedural & substantive
Profitability	Ensured health and safety	Health and safety procedures	Procedural
		Health and safety committees	Procedural
Competitive salaries	Development Job satisfaction Social needs Status	Training	Procedural
		Productivity bonuses	Procedural & substantive
		Organisation of work	Procedural
		Wage structures	Procedural
		Organisational structure	Procedural
		Job descriptions	Procedural
Concentration on business matters	Concentration on social problems	Housing	Substantive
		Education	Procedural & substantive
		Rehabilitation of alcoholics	Procedural
		Bursaries	Substantive
		Social responsibility	Procedural & substantive
		Equal opportunity	Procedural
		Environment	Procedural & substantive

Table 3: COLLECTIVE BARGAINING ISSUES AND PROBLEMS

weaknesses of its own side and of the other party, in order to gauge just how far it can press its own demands without obliging the other side to engage in the use of overt coercive power in the form of a strike or a lockout or other industrial action. In the extreme, each party will also consider the possibility of allowing the other to apply coercive power and assess, in the light of this, its own ability to withstand it.

Since distributive bargaining constitutes the main activity during negotiations, it will be dealt with in greater detail in Chapter 13.

Integrative Bargaining

Integrative bargaining occurs when both parties have the same preference for a successful outcome or are equally concerned to solve a problem. Whereas in distributive bargaining there is a clear distinction between losses and gains, resulting in a win–lose situation, integrative bargaining strives for a win–win solution. In practice it may happen that either party loses a little, but neither suffers a total loss. Overall, both parties gain. It is a case of granting concessions and gaining concessions, so that both parties move from the *status quo* to a better position.

Because conflict is minimised, items subjected to integrative bargaining are described as problems.

Matters which may be dealt with by integrative bargaining include such items as job security, procedures, promotion, benefits and institutional security. Retrenchment and promotion could be regarded as problems rather than issues. Instead of each side striving to impose its own views, a joint attempt could be made to find the best solution possible. Similarly, benefits should be a matter of mutual concern. Also, management might itself benefit by allowing the union certain rights in the form of access and time to address employees.

There are particular steps to be followed as general guidelines for the conduct of integrative bargaining. In the first place, both parties should recognise and identify the problem. There should be a maximum exchange of information and an attempt to ascertain whether integrative bargaining is, in fact, possible. The next step entails a search for alternatives. These may not be immediately obvious and care should be exercised that the consequences of alternatives are properly researched. Thereafter alternatives should be thoroughly evaluated and compared and minimal as well as optimal solutions should be postulated. Only then should a final course of action be determined.

Certain conditions will facilitate the conduct of integrative bargaining. Both parties should be highly motivated. They should regard the problem as important enough to drop or minimise their differences. There should be free access to information and effective communication between the parties. Integrative bargaining is best conducted in a climate of trust and support, in which participants are encouraged to engage in free expression of their ideas and reservations, where neither party is defensive and where conflict is moderate but sufficient to stimulate problem-solving. The negotiators should be close to each other and meet frequently, perhaps holding preliminary discussions on an informal basis.

Important objectives could be achieved by integrative bargaining. Furthermore, the supplementation of distributive with integrative bargaining may contribute to a better overall bargaining climate. Instead of the parties being in continual opposition, there should be times when they also work together and engage in what is essentially integrative problem-solving.

Attitudinal Structuring

Although this is usually classified as a bargaining style, attitudinal structuring could be better described as a strategy to facilitate bargaining rather than a method of bargaining. It constitutes the efforts on the part of one party to influence the course of negotiations by subtly changing the relationship between the parties and, consequently, their attitudes to one another. The purpose is to replace hostility with friendliness, suspicion with trust and competition with cooperation. It is hoped that the change of attitude engendered will render the second party more amenable to the consideration of the other's demands. Alternatively, attitudinal structuring could create a climate for integrative rather than distributive bargaining on a number of issues and, in this respect, could be regarded as an essential element of the total collective bargaining process.

Intra-Organisational Bargaining

Again this is not an actual collective bargaining style, but it is an important part of the collective bargaining process. On both union and employer side, intra-organisational bargaining has to be conducted and concluded before bargaining with the other side can take place. Intra-organisational bargaining is undertaken by members of the same organisation. Because amongst themselves they may have different needs, goals, interests, values and perceptions, there has to be gradual transmission and adjustment in order to achieve a unified approach or to plan a concerted strategy. Consensus has to be reached regarding objectives, targets and resistance points, areas of concession and items which are regarded as non-negotiable. In doing so, every aspect of the organisation has to be taken into account. It is no use, for example, for a negotiator to set limits to increases without having canvassed the opinion of the financial manager; neither would it benefit a union to enter into negotiations determined to stage a strike if it docs not have the backing of all its members.

Like inter-organisational bargaining, intra-organisational bargaining is not a 'one off' process. It is a process of continual adjustment and readjustment, which takes place both before and during the conduct of negotiations with the other party.

BARGAINING STRUCTURE

The Concept of a Bargaining Structure

The term '**bargaining structure**' encompasses also the concepts of '**bargaining units**' and '**bargaining levels**'. A bargaining unit is composed of the employees who will be covered by an agreement. Since this depends also on whether the union is bargaining with one or more employers, employers are implicitly included in our understanding of bargaining units. Simplistically, the composition of a bargaining unit will determine on behalf of whom and with whom bargaining will take place; also, whether bargaining will be conducted with one union only or with a number of unions and with one employer or a number of employers. Thus, as dictated by the demarcation of the bargaining unit, an agreement can apply to a single group of employees at one plant, to all employees or most of the employees at that plant, to a certain type of employee working at various plants but for the same company, to all or most of the employees of that company, to certain types of workers in an industry or area or to all or most of the employees in that industry or area and, finally, to craftsmen or other specialists across industries. It follows logically from this that the bargaining unit will determine whether negotiations will be conducted with plant-level management, with the head office of a company, with a number of employers in an industry or area, or with employers from different industries. This leads to the establishment of bargaining levels — that is, the decision as to whether bargaining will take place at a decentralised level or at a more centralised level or at different levels where different issues are concerned.

It is obvious from the numerous possible combinations that there are many types of bargaining structures and that the kind of structure established will vary from company to company, from industry to industry and from one industrial relations system to another.

Importance of the Bargaining Structure

The type of bargaining structure established will determine which employees are to be covered by an agreement. Consequently, it also determines who will receive protection from an agreement, especially if such agreement becomes enforceable by statute. It will determine the amount of union influence in a company or industry and the power which both a union and employers can exercise during negotiations. Sometimes a union is able to wield more influence if it bargains at plant level, and at other times it is more powerful if it engages in collective bargaining at company or industry level. Related to this is the fact that the level of bargaining will directly affect the degree of employee participation in decisionmaking at plant level. Where agreements are highly centralised, participation decreases. Equally, bargaining structure affects member participation in decisionmaking. The more centralised bargaining becomes, the less will unions be able to receive a direct input from their membership, unless certain safeguards are instituted. Furthermore, the level of bargaining and the bargaining unit will determine the diversity or homogeneity of interests to be represented and the amount of inter-union or inter-management conflict which will occur. Finally, according to the level of bargaining, bargaining outcomes will be homogeneous or diverse and strike action will be geographically limited or widespread.

Types of Bargaining Structure

Kochan has identified four types of bargaining units or bargaining levels. These include the following.

Narrow Decentralised Units

This type of bargaining unit is established when a union represents the interests of one group of workers at a particular plant or where various unions, each constituting a different bargaining unit, represent the interests of different groups of workers at that plant. A unit of this kind minimises intra-organisational conflict and maximises commonality of interest and worker participation at plant level, but it does so at the risk of strengthening management power, encouraging union rivalry and allowing the employer to apply the 'divide and rule' principle. The effect of strike action is minimised since, except when a union represents strategically important employees, production can continue without the members of a particular union. However, the danger of multiple strikes increases. Furthermore, where an employer has to deal separately with more than one union at a plant, negotiations become time-consuming and the danger of whipsawing exists, or else the employer pays the highest negotiated wage to all employees. Finally, if managerial decisionmaking power is centralised at a higher level than the plant, the union may not be dealing with the real locus of power in the organisation.

Broad Decentralised Units

In this instance all the unions or a number of unions at a particular plant combine to form one bargaining unit. They may bargain as a team or engage in coalition bargaining, whereby each union will retain its independence and may negotiate special conditions for its members or withdraw from an agreement, if it so wishes. Broad decentralised units retain the advantages of narrow decentralised units in that they advance the special interests of workers at that plant and allow for maximum employee participation, but management does not hold the same power as it would wield against a single union representing a particular group of workers. Strike action is likely to be instituted by all or most of the employees at that plant, leading to total loss of production. Nevertheless, if intense inter-union rivalry still exists, the 'divide and rule' principle could also be applied in these circumstances. Because different interests are represented and prolonged intra-organisational bargaining has to be undertaken, negotiations may be lengthy and laborious. Lastly, as in the case of narrow, decentralised units, the unions may not be reaching the real locus of power in the organisation.

Narrow Centralised Units

This type of structure is established when one union or a number of unions representing a particular sector or interest at a company, plant or industry, or in different industries, bargain centrally with the company, with a number of employers from the same industry, or with employers from different industries. Narrow centralised units retain uniformity of interests, but not to the same degree as narrow decentralised units, since unions now have to represent the interests of employees at different plants or different companies. In the process of centralisation, the degree of employee participation at plant level or member participation in actual negotiations may also diminish. Furthermore, the danger exists that agreements reached at centralised level may be undermined by managements at particular plants and, when the bargaining unit is company-centred, the risk of whipsawing from company to company or from agreement to agreement becomes very real. As far as employers are concerned, the problem of having to deal with a number of unions in different bargaining units is not overcome and, if different agreements are concluded with different unions, union rivalry may complicate bargaining or multiple strikes may occur. On the other hand, there may be less direct conflict between individual managements and employees and, if the workers represented do not occupy strategic positions, the effect of strike action is minimised. Also, although strikes may be more widespread, they are likely to occur at less frequent intervals. For both sides there are benefits in that the bargaining process is depersonalised and, in cases where all employers in an industry are involved, the wages of that group of workers are taken out of competition. For the union, additional benefits are gained from the increased possibility of reaching the real decisionmakers in management and the increased prominence of the union or unions involved.

Broad Centralised Units

A broad centralised unit is established when one union or a number of unions representing diverse interests bargain with a number of employers at industry level. This is a very complex structure, the principal advantage of which, for both sides, is the uniformity of wage levels and benefits achieved by a centralised agreement. This means that an employer need not be concerned that wage increases granted will render him less competitive and the union is not faced with an employer who, because of this concern, attempts to keep wages at the lowest possible level. Another advantage is to be found in the fact that, because a number of employers are involved, benefit structures and training programmes can be established which individual employers would not have been able to provide of their own accord. Moreover, negotiations are conducted on a more depersonalised basis and on a more professional level. Consequently, the danger of spontaneous strike action decreases, although strike action, when it does occur, is on a much larger scale. Whether employer or union power increases or decreases with greater centralisation is debatable and depends greatly on the circumstances. A strong union may actually lose strategic power by engaging in centralised negotiations, but it may do so for the sake of other advantages such as wider influence and control in an industry. Likewise, it may be more advantageous for a strong employer to bargain individually with a union. Weaker or smaller employers and unions may gain from the support of others, but they may equally find that wages and conditions negotiated are not favourable to their particular circumstances or, in the case of unions, do not meet the demands of their members. Broad centralised agreements are usually concluded at the cost of worker participation in decisionmaking at plant level and membership participation in the bargaining process, unless separate provisions are made for plant-level participation and the union or employers' association adopts alternative strategies to allow for maximum member participation in negotiations. There is also the increased possibility of inter-union and inter-employer conflict and a greater need for intra-organisational bargaining. As a result, negotiations may be lengthy and cumbersome. This might eventually negate the cost reduction achieved by joint negotiation.

Besides the bargaining structures mentioned, most systems are prone to a form of **pattern bargaining**. Pattern bargaining may be confined to particular industries, may range across industries and may be union-initiated or employer-initiated. It occurs when an agreement or a set of agreements, usually with an important employer, sets a precedent for other agreements. Unions or employers in that industry, or in all industries, follow suit by demanding or offering the same increases, conditions and benefits as were granted by the first employer. This brings about a high degree of uniformity, without the necessity of highly centralised bargaining units. The same happens when employers in a particular industry or area agree informally to establish common parameters during individual negotiations with unions or a union, or when unions agree on the same principle.

The question as to whether centralised bargaining is preferable to decentralised bargaining has been widely debated. As has been seen, both have advantages and disadvantages. Alternatively, an advantage for one party may prove a disadvantage to the other. This is further illustrated in Table 4. Very

CENTRALISED BARGAINING		DECENTRALISED BARGAINING	
Advantages	**Disadvantages**	**Advantages**	**Disadvantages**
Wages out of competition (pro for unions and employers)	Wages may be set at minimum levels (con for union)	Wages differentiated according to particular organisation	Danger of whipsawing (con for employers) Employers afraid to become uncompetitive (con for unions)
Better benefits at less cost		Benefits tailormade for individual needs	Fewer benefits provided
Larger-scale training programmes		Programmes tailormade for specific needs	Less likelihood of large-scale training programmes
Fewer strike actions	Industrial action on a wider scale		Likelihood of spontaneous strikes increases
	Does not diffuse workplace tensions	Diffuses workplace tensions	
Limits power of workplace organisation (management and employees)		Increases power of workplace organisation	Workplace representatives may become too independent of union
	Possibility of democratic decisionmaking in unions and employer organisations decreases	Greater opportunity for democratic decisionmaking	
	Diverse interests represented	Caters for specific needs	
	Greater intra-organisational conflict	Intra-organisational conflict minimised	
	More inflexible	More flexible	
	May smother smaller employer or union	Allows employers and unions to follow their own noses	
Bargainers usually more professional			Bargainers may not be sufficiently experienced
Long-term objectives			Objectives may be short-term
Provides overall, uniform standards and minimum safeguards			May lead to employer playoffs and wage inflation

Table 4: ADVANTAGES AND DISADVANTAGES OF CENTRALISED AND DECENTRALISED BARGAINING

often employers and unions will opt for a two-tier system, where minimum conditions and benefits are negotiated at central level and more particular or improved conditions and procedures are established by plant-level negotiations.

Variables Influencing the Type of Structure Established

The bargaining process is a union-initiated process. Therefore the primary determinant of the bargaining structure will be the organisation, scope of representation and strategy of trade unions. Clegg has stated that '… the power of trade unions lies at that level at which bargaining takes place'. The logical corollary to this is that unions will attempt to bargain at that level where they will wield the most power and that their preferences for a certain level of bargaining at a certain time or in a particular industry will be dictated by circumstances. These circumstances will include the following.

Union Representation
A union strongly representative of employees at a number of plants or companies, but not sufficiently representative in the industry as a whole, may prefer to bargain at plant or company level. Alternatively, a union which is weaker at particular plants but has a fair spread of members throughout the industry may opt for industry-level bargaining.

Union Organisation and Policy
Unions differ in structure and policy. In some organisations power is highly centralised, while others prefer to decentralise and to emphasise member participation in negotiations. Unions of the latter type will choose to bargain also at decentralised level or, where they do engage in centralised negotiations, may insist on shop steward participation in such negotiations or demand that certain issues be negotiated at plant level.

Union Strategy
A union will assess at which level it can wield the most power and influence; whether, for example, strikes staged at plant, company or industry level will be strategically more effective. Herman and Kuhn explain that, where a company markets different products, the union would wish to centralise in order to be able to influence production at all plants simultaneously, thereby preventing the employer from carrying on production at one plant while others are on strike. Union strategy may change from time to time and, consequently, so will the union preference for bargaining at a particular level. Union strategy may also involve the achievement of sociopolitical ends. For example, a union may wish to wield influence when it comes to the restructuring of industries and the establishment of industry policies, as well as general economic policy. If this is so, the union will attempt to gain wider influence by bargaining at a highly centralised, even national, level.

Scope of Union Registration or Recognition
The type of employees which a union, by its registration or the process of recognition, is entitled to represent will determine the bargaining unit it can establish; that is, whether it is entitled to bargain on behalf of all employees in a plant, company or industry, or only for a certain group.

Inter-Union Competition

Where unions are highly competitive, they may refuse to establish a joint bargaining unit, thus obliging the employer to engage in separate negotiations with a number of unions.

Member Preference

The members of a union may express a preference for certain bargaining units and bargaining levels. This preference will have to be taken into account by the union.

Type of Bargaining Issue

Certain issues, such as wages, benefits and training, lend themselves more easily to centralised bargaining, whereas procedural issues and questions regarding workers' participation may be better decided at plant level. Thus the bargaining structure will depend also on the type of issue or problem on the bargaining table, or separate bargaining structures may be developed to deal with issues of different types.

Management Organisation and Policy

The manner in which a particular company is structured and the level at which decisionmaking occurs, may influence the union's preference for a certain level of bargaining. Should management be decentralised, the union may opt for plant-level bargaining, whereas centralised bargaining would be preferred if major decisions can be taken only by top management. Similarly, unions organising the employees of large corporations may choose to bargain on behalf of all corporate employees in one bargaining unit. Where a number of employers have already formed a combination for other reasons, such as trade promotion, the union might find it convenient also to establish a bargaining relationship with the employers as a group.

Economic Factors

The nature of the product and labour markets will play an important role in the union's decision regarding bargaining units and bargaining levels. In the case of strong competition between different employers marketing the same product, the union may prefer to bargain with all employers at a centralised level, since it knows that individual employers will attempt to keep wages as low as possible for fear of becoming uncompetitive in the pricing of their products. Similarly, craft unions in particular may, in order to control the supply of labour, choose to enter into centralised agreements with all employers in an industry.

Government Policy and Legislation

By its legislation a government may impose a bargaining structure on participants, or it may create a preference for a certain type of bargaining forum by making agreements concluded in that forum legally enforceable. Directly or indirectly, government policy and legislation and the guidelines it sets will influence the type of bargaining structure established.

The establishment of a collective bargaining structure has been considered from the perspective of the trade union as the principal initiating agent. In the final analysis, a decision as regards bargaining structure rests with both partners. There are occasions when the initiative is taken by employers. Even if they are not the initiators, employers will generally have some say in the type of structure established. The employer considerations in establishing a bargaining structure are the same as those of unions, although — particularly in respect of strategy and bargaining power — the reverse arguments will apply to employers. Like unions, employers' associations will take into account their representivity, their scope of registration and the preferences of their members. Individual employers will take cognisance of their organisational structure and policy, the type of bargaining issue and the product and labour markets. They, too, will attempt to bargain at the level where they can wield the most power or gain the best strategic advantage. Thus a multi-plant company engaged in the manufacture of different products would prefer decentralised bargaining, since industrial action at a single plant would not affect their overall operations. Finally, like unions, employers are obliged to consider government policy and the use of the statutory machinery.

The variables mentioned are interrelated. No single variable will act as sole determinant of a bargaining structure. In the decisionmaking process of the union and the employers the variables interact; also, each side will be influenced by the stated or implied preference of the other party, by current circumstances and by the totality of legislation governing the bargaining process.

THE ROLE OF THE STATE IN COLLECTIVE BARGAINING

As a third party to the labour relationship, the State, in the form of the government, will usually not play an active role in the collective bargaining process. It may, according to the degree of voluntarism in a particular system, set the parameters for collective bargaining by establishing bargaining institutions, limiting the freedom to a strike or a lockout, demarcating bargaining units or determining the scope of registration of particular unions. On the other hand, it may interfere to a greater extent — for example, by enforcing centralised bargaining. As such, it serves more as an influence on collective bargaining than as a participant in the process. However, the State itself may from time to time engage in bargaining with either or both of the other parties. This occurs when the State desires cooperation on its economic or other policies from the parties concerned, in which case it will trade off advantages, such as tax reductions for both employers and employees or greater decisionmaking participation for employees, against agreements to freeze wages or prices or to maintain levels of employment.

In its role as an employer the State does play an active part in collective bargaining. By its own practices it sets an example to the other parties as far as both procedures and substantive issues are concerned.

CONCLUSION

Collective bargaining demonstrates the dynamic nature of Industrial Relations. The collective bargaining process is conducted by two essentially antagonistic yet cooperative parties, subject to a continual interplay of sometimes contradictory forces and to numerous interacting environmental influences. As such, it constitutes one of the major processes in industrial relations, and *the* major process in traditional labour relationships.

SOURCES

Anthony, P D *The Conduct of Industrial Relations*, Institute of Personnel Management, London, 1980.

Clegg, Hugh *Trade Unionism under Collective Bargaining*, Basil Blackwell, 1976.

Hawkins, K 'The Future of Collective Bargaining' in *Industrial Relations Journal of South Africa*, Vol 1, No 1, 1981.

Herman, Edward E and Kuhn, Alfred *Collective Bargaining and Labour Relations*, Prentice Hall, 1981.

Kochan, Thomas A *Collective Bargaining and Industrial Relations*, Richard D Irwin, 1980.

Luthans, Fred *Organisational Behaviour*, McGraw-Hill, 1986.

Marshall, Alfred *Principles of Economics*, Macmillan, 1920.

Salamon, Michael *Industrial Relations Theory and Practice*, Prentice-Hall, 1987.

9

COLLECTIVE BARGAINING IN SOUTH AFRICA

South African labour relations legislation has, since its inception, protected the right to free collective bargaining, underscored by the right to freedom of association and freedom from victimisation. However, until 1979 only white, coloured and Asian employees were covered by this legislation. Thus black African employees and their unions gained access to bargaining forums and the statutory collective bargaining machinery only after 1979 and, since then, have become dominant parties in the industrial relations sphere.

Our new labour relations legislation re-emphasises the rights outlined above, and further grants unions certain organisational rights which facilitate their entry into collective bargaining relationships. It heeds the union concern for 'free riders' by allowing for the conclusion of agency shop agreements and, perhaps unnecessarily, also for closed shop agreements. Furthermore, all collective agreements are now made binding and enforceable in terms of the Labour Relations Act — a move to be greatly welcomed.

As far as the question of bargaining levels is concerned, this remains ambivalent since the legislation does not, as desired by the union movement, enforce bargaining — either at centralised level or at all. Yet, in a subtle manner, it does promote the establishment of centralised structures and the extension of their agreements to non-parties. This thrust towards centralisation may elicit reaction from employers, and particularly from small business.

The old, centralised industrial council system has been replaced by a system of bargaining councils, to be established also in the service industry and the public service. Bargaining councils will perform the same functions as industrial councils, but their powers and sphere of influence have been extended. In addition, provision is made for statutory councils in situations where the parties are not able to establish fully fledged bargaining councils.

Whether bargaining councils will receive enthusiastic support from employers and smaller unions remains to be seen. Many of the employers and smaller unions may still prefer to regulate their relationships and substantive conditions of service at plant level. This would be achieved through the recognition process and the establishment of a recognition agreement allowing, inter alia, for regular negotiation on substantive issues and matters affecting employees.

Thus the South African collective bargaining system may, despite efforts to the contrary, retain the dualistic character adopted in the early 1980s when the unions now promoting centralised bargaining vehemently opposed the industrial council system and opted for their own system of plant-level recognition. Also, if unions remain active at plant level, tensions are bound to arise between bargaining forums and workplace forums at this level.

Finally, there is the question of the duty to bargain and the duty to do so in good faith. Various Court judgments have in the past pointed in these directions, but the legislation itself does not prescribe such a duty, leaving the matter to dispute and advisory arbitration.

It is certain that the next few years will see numerous developments and readjustments in the collective bargaining structure. In the final analysis the processes and interactions are of so dynamic a nature that, in a mainly voluntary system, the parameters cannot ultimately be dictated by legislation.

THE RIGHT TO FREE COLLECTIVE BARGAINING

As supporter of individualism and of the free market system, South Africa has in the past subscribed in its official industrial relations policy to the principles of voluntarism, freedom of association and free collective bargaining. However, until 1979, these principles were not equally applicable to all sections of the working population. Although no law prohibited black African employees from forming unions and even obliging employers to bargain with them, the official government policy obviously did not favour such practices and the exclusion of Black Africans from the provisions of the Industrial Conciliation Act of 1924 bestowed on them the position of outsiders as regards the officially sanctioned collective bargaining system. This situation changed in 1979. Since then, all employees have had the officially sanctioned right to freedom of association and free collective bargaining. Within the previous sociopolitical dispensation the system remained largely voluntary, with the Government establishing only the parameters, protecting the basic interests of both sides and establishing the machinery for the settlement of disputes.

With the drafting of the new labour relations legislation, no radical shift has occurred. There is no mandatory duty to bargain, although the Labour Relations Act of 1995 does confer rights on unions which will facilitate the establishment of a bargaining relationship with employers. Also it promotes (but does not enforce) centralised bargaining in the now renamed bargaining councils.

FREEDOM OF ASSOCIATION AND FREEDOM FROM VICTIMISATION

In order to engage in effective collective bargaining employees in particular, but also employers in some instances, will join collective organisations.

If power is to be balanced and free collective bargaining is to take place, it is essential that persons should have the freedom to join the organisation of their choice, that no manipulation of membership should occur, that the collective organisations themselves should have free choice and be free from influence, and that members of such organisations or their office bearers should not fear victimisation. For this reason any free collective bargaining system is based on the joint principles of freedom of association and freedom from victimisation.

Freedom of association and freedom from victimisation were guaranteed in the past, but the Labour Relations Act of 1995 stresses the importance of these precepts by providing for protection of these rights immediately at the commencement of the Act (Sections 1 to 10). The contents of these sections have been discussed in detail in the chapter on labour legislation (Chapter 5).

ORGANISATIONAL RIGHTS

As mentioned previously, the Labour Relations Act of 1995 grants unions a number of organisational rights to which there was previously no entitlement. These rights pave the way for the union's entry to the workplace and, therefore, set the preconditions for recruitment of members and for subsequent collective bargaining, whether at plant or industry level. Issues such as access and the holding of meetings, which were previously regarded as 'interests' and were the subject of extended negotiation between employer and union, are now no longer subject to negotiation but to legal prescription.

The Act distinguishes between rights granted to 'representative' unions and those accorded majority unions. However, no threshold for representativeness is established. It is stated merely that a 'representative' union means a 'registered union, or two or more registered unions' acting together, which is sufficiently representative of the employees employed by an employer. While it is understood that the assessment of representativeness may depend on particular circumstances, the lack of certainty in this respect is likely to give rise to confusion and, eventually, to a number of disputes.

The Right to Access
Section 12 of the Labour Relations Act of 1995 grants any office bearer or official of a representative union the right of access to the employer's premises for the purpose of communicating with its members or serving their interests. The union is further given the right, outside working hours, to hold meetings with employees on the premises of the employer, and to conduct ballots among employees. These rights are not absolute in that they are subject to reasonable arrangements with the employer regarding time and place insofar as this is necessary for security purposes and to avoid disruption.

Stop Order Facilities
The employer is obliged, if so requested in writing by an employee, to deduct union dues from the wages of that employee and to pay over to a representative union the amounts so deducted by the 15th day of the following month. The employee may, subject to one month's written notice to the employer and the union (if in the private sector) or three months' notice (if in the public service), withdraw his permission for such deductions, which should then cease at the end of the notice period. The employer must, with each month's payment, supply the union with a statement containing the names of every employee from whom deductions have been made and details of the amounts deducted and paid over, as well as with copies of all notices of withdrawal.

Election of Shop Stewards
In terms of Section 14 of the Act a majority union, or two or more unions which together represent the majority of employees at a workplace, have the right to elect one shop steward (now called a union representative) in any workplace

where ten union members are employed. Should there be between ten and fifty union members, two shop stewards may be elected; thereafter, one additional shop steward may be elected for every fifty members to a maximum of seven shop stewards. Where there are more than 300 members, seven shop stewards are elected for the first 300 members and thereafter one for every additional 100 members to a maximum of ten (600 members). For a membership of between 600 and 1 000 one shop steward is elected for every 200 members in excess of 600, to a maximum of twelve; and where there are more than 1 000 union members one shop steward is elected for every 500 additional members, to a maximum of twenty.

The nomination, election, term of office and removal of a shop steward are to be determined by the union's constitution.

Sections 14(4) and (5) and Section 15 of the Act spell out the rights of shop stewards and union office bearers at the workplace. These include the right to represent co-employees, to monitor the employer's implementation of the Act, to report any transgression of the Act and to take reasonable time off during working hours to perform the duties of a shop steward or to receive training.

Disclosure of Information

Section 16 of the Act determines that a shop steward of a majority union is entitled to all relevant information required for the fulfilment of his duties. Furthermore, an employer engaged in negotiation with a majority union is obliged to furnish the union with all relevant information required by the union for effective consultation or collective bargaining. Should such information be of a confidential nature, the employer must inform the union in writing to this effect. A union cannot demand information which is legally privileged or which an employer cannot furnish without disobeying a Court Order; nor is the employer obliged to give information which, if it is publicised, could cause the employer substantial damage or which is private to a person (unless such person grants permission).

Disputes regarding disclosure may be referred to the Commission for Conciliation, Mediation & Arbitration which will attempt to mediate and, failing an agreement, resort to arbitration. The Commissioner hearing the dispute must first decide whether the information requested is relevant or not. If he finds it to be relevant, he needs to consider the disadvantage which both sides will suffer should the information be disclosed (or not disclosed). Should the Commissioner decide that the information ought to be disclosed, he may determine conditions aimed at limiting the damage. The Commissioner is also charged with considering whether breach of confidentiality had previously occurred in the relationship. Where previous breaches have occurred, the Commissioner may withdraw the right to information at that workplace for a specified period.

This section does not apply to the domestic sector.

Right to Establish Thresholds of Representivity

A majority union or unions at a workplace or a bargaining council may conclude an agreement with the employer in which thresholds of representativeness are specified regarding such rights as access, stop order facilities and time off for trade union officials. Since these are the only rights accorded to non-majority unions, an agreement which sets high thresholds can ensure the presence of only one union and make it difficult for any other union to canvass membership. Such an arrangement could be both advantageous and disadvantageous to the employer: on the one hand it discourages multi-unionism, but on the other may prevent effective representation of all employee interests.

Rights of Unions Party to Bargaining Councils

A union which is party to a bargaining council is accorded the right in terms of Section 19 of the Act to have access, to hold meetings at and request stop order facilities at any workplace within the registered scope of that council, irrespective of whether or not the union is representative at that particular workplace.

Procedure for the Exercise of Organisational Rights

A registered union wishing to exercise any of the rights described above should inform the employer in writing of its intention to do so. Such notice should be accompanied by the certified copy of the union's registration certificate and should specify the workplace in respect of which the union wants to exercise these rights, its level of representativeness and substantiation thereof, as well as the rights which the union wishes to exercise.

The employer is obliged to meet with the union within 30 days of receipt of such notice and to attempt to reach a collective agreement on the manner in which these rights will be exercised. Should no such agreement be reached, either of the parties may refer the dispute to the Commission, which will attempt conciliation. Should conciliation fail, arbitration may be undertaken if either party so requests.

Evaluation

It is obvious that, by providing for these organisational rights, the law has assured the union a presence at the workplace. There can, for example, no longer be any argument as to whether the employer will allow the union to recruit or hold meetings. This should facilitate entry into a bargaining relationship. However, the Act still allows the parties to reach a private agreement relating to organisational rights.

BARGAINING UNITS

The legislation contains no prescription as to bargaining units at plant level. At centralised level the nature and extent of the bargaining unit will, of course, be defined by the scope of registration of the bargaining council.

With organisational rights being granted also to 'representative' unions, it may happen that various bargaining units exist at particular plants. Contrarily, the wiser employer will attempt to establish a joint bargaining unit, particularly where different unions represent the same interests.

CLOSED SHOPS AND AGENCY SHOPS

The Problem

Unions have for long experienced problems with so-called 'free riders'. These are employees who fall within the bargaining unit, but who do not belong to the union negotiating on behalf of that bargaining unit. Since employers find it difficult to pay differentiated wages to employees in the same bargaining unit, increases and improved conditions of service negotiated by the union will be granted also to non-union employees. The union argument is that these persons gain at the expense of other employees who pay union subscriptions, and that they too should be obliged to pay for the services the union renders.

Agency Shops   With a view to this situation, the new labour relations legislation now provides for the establishment of agency shops, subject to agreement between an employer and a majority union. An agency shop agreement does not oblige employees to become union members, but it may provide that non-members who are eligible for union membership are obliged to pay a subscription which does not exceed the amount payable in dues by union members. These subscriptions are paid into a separate fund, administered by the majority union or unions, and are to be used to advance the 'socioeconomic welfare' of all employees. Thus the union could apply the funds to support its bargaining initiatives, but also for more general purposes, such as the establishment of a crèche or recreation facilities at the workplace.

Closed Shops   Over and above the provision for an agency shop, the legislation also contains provision for closed shop agreements between a majority union or unions and an employer or employers' association. Essentially, such an agreement obliges all eligible employees to become members of the majority union. However, the legislation does provide that persons already in employ at the time that a closed shop agreement is concluded, or persons who have conscientious objections, cannot be obliged to join the union. The conditions of an agency shop may then be applied to them.

A union party to a closed shop agreement may, in terms of its constitution, withhold membership from an employee or may terminate his membership for 'fair' reasons, including (but not limited to) behaviour which hampers the collective exercise of trade union rights. This could mean that an employee who refuses to take part in a strike could have his membership terminated. The employer would then be placed in a position where he has to dismiss such employee. In fact, the legislation provides that it is *not* unfair for an employer to dismiss an employee who refuses to join a closed shop union, who has been refused membership of a trade union which is party to a closed shop or whose membership has been terminated by the union. Nevertheless, the Labour Court may find such dismissal to be unfair if the reasons for withholding or terminating membership are found to be unfair.

A closed shop agreement may be concluded only if two thirds of the employers to be covered by it have voted in favour of such agreement. Furthermore, the agreement must stipulate that no portion of the subscriptions should be used to pay for affiliation to a political party or as a contribution to a political party or candidate; nor may the funds be applied for any purpose other than the promotion and protection of the socioeconomic welfare of employees. Closed shop agreements have to be subjected to a vote every three years, or if one third of the employees covered by the agreement so request. Also, a union which is not party to such agreement but which has a significant interest in or representation among the employees concerned can apply to be admitted to the agreement. Should the application be refused, the dispute may be referred to the Commission for Conciliation, Mediation & Arbitration.

Evaluation   While the concept of an agency shop is still defensible, the closed shop has long been the subject of great controversy — the main criticism being that it impinges on the individual's right to freedom of association, guaranteed in terms of both the labour legislation and the Interim Constitution. The criticism is valid, since the enforcement of a closed shop agreement abrogates the employee's freedom of choice. Moreover, there is a strong tendency among closed shop unions to neglect servicing their membership, as the agreement entrenches their position within the organisation or industry. The new Labour Relations Act has attempted to build in some safeguards, but whether these will prove sufficient to counteract the negative aspects of closed shops is to be doubted. Particularly questionable is the clause which specifically allows the employer to dismiss a banished or non-admitted employee. This clause counters entirely the logic of the unfair labour practice provisions.

In general, it is wondered why it was deemed at all necessary to provide for closed shop agreements, since the provision for an agency shop more than adequately addresses union concerns as regards 'free riders'. It can only be surmised that the main objective of unions promoting the concept of the closed shop was to eliminate, as far as possible, the existence and acceptance of other unions within the bargaining unit and, by this somewhat illegitimate means, to maintain or extend their own power base.

ENFORCEABILITY OF AGREEMENTS

Centralised bargaining agreements (previously industrial council agreements) have always been enforceable in terms of the Labour Relations Act. However, recognition and other plant-level agreements were regarded merely as contracts at common law and were, therefore, enforceable by the lengthy processes of the civil courts — although, in some instances, they could be enforced via the unfair labour practice jurisdiction.

The new labour relations legislation makes all collective agreements binding on the parties to the agreement, as well as on employees who are not members of a party union if such employees are identified or bound in the agreement or if the union is a majority union. Moreover, agreements will remain binding for their duration even on a member of a union or employers' association who withdraws or becomes a member during the currency of such agreement. Collective agreements automatically change individual contracts of employment.

Should a dispute arise concerning the interpretation or implementation of a collective agreement and if there is no existent or operative dispute settling agreement between the parties, or if one party has obstructed settlement, such dispute may be submitted to the CCMA for conciliation and, failing settlement, for arbitration. All closed shop and agency shop agreements have to contain a provision for dispute settlement by conciliation followed by arbitration. The parties may choose to have the CCMA conduct such conciliation and arbitration.

The new provision for the enforcement of agreements is to be welcomed, since this constituted a problem area in the past — particularly with regard to agreements concluded outside the statutory bargaining system.

CENTRALISED BARGAINING STRUCTURES: BARGAINING COUNCILS

As frequently mentioned in this text, the new labour relations legislation promotes the use of centralised bargaining structures. In essence it retains the previous industrial councils, now renamed bargaining councils, and extends these also to the public service. Some aspects of councils have been modified, however. Provision has also been made for statutory councils in areas where unions may not be sufficiently representative.

Establishment of a Bargaining Council

A bargaining council may be established by one or more employer party and one or more employee party. In the case of the employee side, the party must be one or more *registered* trade unions, while the employer party can be one or more *registered* employers' associations. The State may also be regarded as the employer party to a bargaining council in a sector or area in which it acts as the employer.

Bargaining councils are, in effect, established when these parties *voluntarily* come together and agree to bargain with each other, but the council will come into existence in the official sense only after the Industrial Registrar has agreed to its registration.

In order to register, a council needs first to have a constitution. Section 30 of the Labour Relations Act of 1995 rules that an industrial council constitution *must*:

- state how representatives on the council and their alternates are to be appointed (half the representatives have to be appointed by the employer party and half by the employee party);
- provide for representation by small and medium enterprises;
- provide rules for the appointment, removal, duties and powers of office bearers and officials;
- state how representatives will vacate their seats;
- state how decisions are to be made;
- provide procedures for the calling and conduct of meetings, including requirements for a quorum and the keeping of minutes;
- provide for the establishment and functioning of committees;
- establish procedures for dealing, by way of arbitration, with disputes regarding the interpretation and implementation of the constitution;
- establish procedures for dealing with disputes between the parties to the council and for dealing with disputes between individual members;
- state under which circumstances additional members will be allowed to join the council;
- state for which purposes funds will be applied;
- state how funds will be deposited and excess funds invested;
- provide for alteration of the constitution and the winding up or liquidation of the council; and
- establish a procedure for granting exemptions from collective agreements (by a party independent of the council).

Once a constitution has been approved by all parties, it is submitted to the Industrial Registrar, together with the prescribed application and any other information which might be of use to the Registrar. The Industrial Registrar publishes in the *Government Gazette* a notice of the application received, and allows time for objections to be lodged. An objection may be lodged on the grounds that the applicant did not comply with the provisions of the Act, that the sector or area applied for is not applicable, or that the applicant is not sufficiently representative. The Registrar then sends the application and objections to NEDLAC, which will delimit the sector or area. Should NEDLAC fail to do so, this task reverts to the Minister.

The Registrar will satisfy himself that the council has complied with all prescribed procedures, that the constitution contains all the prescribed provisions, that no other council is registered for the same scope and that the parties are 'sufficiently representative'. Once the Registrar is thus satisfied, he must register the council and send a registration certificate, together with a certified copy of the council's registered constitution, to the council concerned. The certificate of registration in effect bestows on the parties to the council the right to self-government. They may thenceforward regulate their affairs — and those of others in the industry or area if their agreements are extended — in whatever manner they deem fit, provided that they do not break any laws.

The Functions of Bargaining Councils

The overall functions or duties of industrial councils were set out in Section 23(1) of the Labour Relations Act of 1956. In terms of this section, it was the duty of an industrial council:

> '... within the undertaking, industry, trade or occupation and in the area in respect of which it has been registered, [to] endeavour, by the negotiation of agreements or otherwise, to prevent disputes from arising, and to settle disputes that have arisen or may arise between employers and employers' organisations and employees or trade unions and take such steps as it may think expedient to bring about the regulation or settlement of matters of mutual interest to employers or employers' organisation and employees or trade unions.'

Essentially, this remains also the main function of bargaining councils. As already mentioned in Chapter 5, the Labour Relations Act of 1995 also spells out the following detailed functions and powers.

- To conclude and enforce collective agreements
- To prevent and settle disputes
- To conduct conciliation and arbitration in terms of the Act, or to provide for such conciliation and arbitration
- To establish a fund for the settlement of disputes
- To establish and promote education and training schemes
- To establish and administer pension, provident, medical aid, sick, holiday and unemployment funds
- To make representations to NEDLAC (or an appropriate body) regarding policy or law affecting their industry

- To determine, by collective agreement, issues which for the purposes of a strike or lockout will be regarded as 'issues in dispute'
- To delegate to workplace forums additional matters for consultation

A bargaining council thus has two basic functions: a collective bargaining function and a dispute settlement function. The latter function can apply not only to the parties to the council but to all employers and employees in the sector, industry or area in which a particular industrial council has jurisdiction. This dispute settlement function will be dealt with in an ensuing chapter and, for the present, attention will be focused on the collective bargaining function. The main purpose in the establishment of a bargaining council is to create a forum for collective bargaining although, indirectly, this also achieves the purpose of maintaining labour peace. Through negotiations on the bargaining council the parties will regulate the relationship between them and reach agreement on substantive issues such as wages and working conditions.

As can be seen, the new legislation, by specifically granting bargaining councils powers to establish funds and have an input into policy and law, envisages also a broader degree of operation for these councils as looking after the industries or sectors in which they operate, even to the point of determining matters for consultation with workplace forums in such industries.

Bargaining Council Agreements

Bargaining council agreements are largely substantive agreements dealing with wages and conditions of service, but they may also contain procedural items such as job evaluation and grading systems, retrenchment procedures and even (though not advisably) grievance and disciplinary procedures. Usually the substantive items in the agreements, and particularly wage rates, are renegotiated from year to year or, where the agreement so determines, every two or three years. This is effected by an amendment to the agreement which should then be read in the context of the entire agreement.

In terms of the Labour Relations Act of 1956, industrial councils could deal with certain specified matters, and it is expected that bargaining councils will deal with the same issues. These included the following.

- Minimum rates, average minimum rates and method of calculation
- Wage and salary scales
- Grading systems
- Piecework rates
- Payment of industrial council levies
- Pension, insurance and sick fund contributions
- Limitations or prohibitions on overtime
- Payment of money in lieu of notice
- Prohibitions on deducting from the employee's wages monies other than those specified in the agreement
- Prohibitions on setoff debts
- Regulations regarding time and manner of payment to employees
- Regulations regarding the maximum number of employees in each section, or regarding proportionate distribution of employees
- Prohibitions on piecework

- Prohibitions on the employment of persons under a specified age
- Prohibitions on 'payments in kind'
- Prohibitions on contract work
- Provision for a closed shop

In addition, bargaining council agreements may contain regulations regarding hours of work, maximum working hours per week, payment for overtime and for work on Sundays and public holidays, notice periods for different categories of employees, regulations pertaining to paid public holidays, annual leave, sick leave, layoffs, short time and desertion. Some agreements may contain retrenchment procedures and procedures for dealing with those disputes which do not arise during the course of bargaining council negotiations; but disputes procedures actually belong in the council's constitution and, since the council cannot cater for particular circumstances, retrenchment procedures should be merely guidelines.

It becomes obvious from the above that these agreements deal in detail with the regulation of substantive conditions of employment — so much so that they resemble the Basic Conditions of Employment Act. They are, in fact, basic condition statutes for particular industries and, once gazetted, they supersede the last-mentioned Act. It is also obvious that, because their application is general, they cannot deal with specific issues and circumstances and do not provide (except perhaps by a retrenchment agreement) for any employee share in the decisionmaking function — for example, by the appointment of shop stewards. Furthermore, individual employers, whether or not party to a council, are free to offer their employees improved wage rates and conditions of service.

Extension of Agreements

The parties to a bargaining council are not necessarily representative of all employers and employees in that industry or area. Since one of the main purposes of a centralised bargaining forum is to establish uniformity, the parties will want all employers and employees to be covered by their agreement. This they may do by requesting the Minister of Labour to extend the agreement also to non-parties who fall within the registered scope of the council and by proving to him that one or more unions whose members constitute a majority among the unions which are party to the council, and one or more employers' associations whose members supply employment to the majority of employees employed by party employers, have voted in favour of such extension. The Minister in turn must satisfy himself that the unions on the council are representative of the majority of employees within the registered scope of the council, and that the employer parties employ the majority of employees in the council's registered scope; that the non-parties mentioned in the request fall within the registered scope; that the agreement makes provision for exemptions to be granted by an independent body, that it contains criteria to be applied by this body in granting such exemptions and that the agreement does not discriminate against non-parties. However, despite the requirement that parties should have majority representation, Section 32(4) of the Labour Relations Act of 1995 allows the Minister to extend the agreement to parties which do not have majority representation if he is satisfied that they are 'sufficiently' representative and that failure to extend the agreement will be detrimental to collective bargaining at sectoral level. Since the term 'sufficiently representative' is not defined, this leaves the Minister with a great deal of discretion to promote centralised bargaining arrangements where he deems fit.

The extension of centralised agreements to non-parties has in the past been, and will probably continue to be, a bone of contention. Especially smaller employers argue that this bestows on councils unwarranted powers of control and is contrary to the principle of freedom of association; also that agreements contain provisions and levies with which smaller enterprises can comply only to their own detriment. The original purpose of extending agreements was to prevent the exploitation of non-unionised employees. This presupposed that councils established only minimum-level wages and conditions of service. The Basic Conditions of Employment Act now establishes relatively satisfactory employment conditions, and it is to be doubted that wage levels set by councils (particularly those dominated by large employers) are minimum-level wages. Moreover, councils have now instituted funds and levies of all types which non-party employers and employees may reject as not being in their interests, yet to which they are compelled to contribute. It is wondered whether parties to councils, and the government, have not perhaps lost sight of the actual purpose of these councils, and whether they are not using the system merely to extend their control and influence rather than to protect employees and to promote the industry. If this is the case they may, in the process, be negatively affecting job creation in general.

The above does not constitute an argument for the payment of exploitative 'market-based' wages by non-party employers, but rather a plea for less rigidity and bureaucracy on the part of councils. The new provision for exemptions to be granted by an independent body does, in theory, prevent councils from abusing their power; but, unless bargaining councils demonstrate the ability to look at the rationale and spirit of provisions rather than their letter, the controversy is bound to continue.

Duration of Agreements

The parties themselves will decide on the period for which the agreement will be binding. Usually an agreement is effective for between one and three years, and a new agreement is negotiated before the previous agreement expires. Should the parties decide that they need more time to renegotiate the agreement, they can apply to the Minister for a temporary extension of the existing agreement. Alternatively, they can reach a gentlemen's accord to adhere to the provisions of the expired agreement.

Administration and Policing of Agreements

Most bargaining councils will appoint administrative assistants, the number of assistants depending on the size of the council. The administrative staff is headed by a secretary whose function it is to arrange meetings, take minutes, prepare and submit agreements, supervise the administration of benefit funds and the collection of dues, supervise the accounting function, receive reports from inspectors and generally to deal with any matter which may arise in the day-to-day running of the council's affairs.

The actual overseeing of agreements is left to agents or inspectors, who may be appointed in terms of the Labour Relations Act and who are vested with wide-ranging powers. These agents visit organisations which are subject to the jurisdiction of the council. They ensure that such organisations are registered and that there is compliance with the terms of the bargaining council agreement. Any transgression (particularly the underpayment of wages) is reported to the council, which will attempt to oblige the employer or employee concerned to rectify the situation and, if this fails, will institute criminal proceedings.

Exemptions and Appeals

An independent body designated by the council may grant a particular employer or employee exemption from all or some of the terms of a bargaining council agreement. The applicant is issued with an exemption certificate, which he retains as proof that the exemption has been granted.

Bargaining Councils in the Public Service

The new labour relations legislation makes provision for specific regulations regarding bargaining councils in this sector and for a compulsory Coordinating Bargaining Council for the public sector. This body will concern itself with norms and standards which are applicable throughout the public service, or with matters applicable to two or more sectors. The Coordinating Bargaining Council, or the State President, designates an area of the public service as a sector for which a bargaining council should be established. Moreover, the State President may designate a sector for employees of the State or organs of the State who are not in the public service.

A bargaining council established for a particular public service sector will have sole jurisdiction in that sector as regards matters which are to be subject to negotiations with the State as employer.

Statutory Councils

An entirely new section in the Labour Relations Act of 1995 makes provision for a trade union or unions, en employers' organisation or organisations which represent thirty percent of employees or employers in a sector (industry) or area to apply for the registration of a statutory council. The Registrar will apply basically the same procedure as he would with the application for registration of the bargaining council, except that he measures representativeness in terms of the stated percentage. Should the Registrar be satisfied that the applicant has conformed to all the requirements, he will publish a notice in the *Government Gazette* establishing the statutory council and inviting all registered unions and employers' associations (or any other interested parties) in the sector or area to a meeting, to be presided over by the CCMA, the purpose of which is to reach an agreement regarding representation on the statutory council. Should no agreement be reached, another attempt at a meeting will be made, following which the statutory council will be established with the applicant union or employers' association and other parties which may be allowed, as representatives. Where there is no union or employers' association party, the Minister will appoint representatives of employees or employers, as the case may be, in that industry or area as parties to the statutory council.

Essentially, therefore, a statutory council can be established where there is no majority trade union or employers' organisation presence. This does indeed constitute an unashamed promotion of a more centralised system of representation, the idea evidently being that statutory councils will eventually develop into full-blown bargaining councils.

A statutory council may perform the same dispute settlement functions as a bargaining council, may establish and promote education and training schemes, may establish various funds and may, by its constitution, perform any of the functions of a bargaining council.

A statutory council which is sufficiently representative may apply to the Minister to have its agreements on education, training and funds gazetted as determinations in terms of the Wage Act and, in making such determinations, the Minister may impose a levy on all employers and employees within the registered scope of the statutory council.

The provision for statutory councils opens up the possibility for hitherto unregulated sectors, such as agriculture, to be subjected to 'centralised' agreements or determinations.

Evaluation   As will be seen from a later discussion in this chapter, tension still exists between the institution of centralised as against decentralised bargaining forums. Despite union demands to the contrary, the new government has not made centralised bargaining compulsory, although the Act does promote this bargaining structure. Whether bargaining councils will, as is hoped, be generally accepted and supported (particularly by employers) will depend on their effectiveness and on the dissolution of tensions between the various bargaining levels.

DECENTRALISED BARGAINING STRUCTURES: THE SYSTEM OF PLANT-LEVEL RECOGNITION

Antiposed to the centralised bargaining council system is the system whereby a union gains recognition at a particular plant or undertaking and then bargains on behalf of employees at that plant or undertaking or in a specific bargaining unit.

Previously union efforts at plant-level recognition were often hampered by the employer's refusal to grant access (or permission to hold meetings) to the union. In terms of the organisational rights now accorded to unions by the new labour relations legislation, a union has merely to prove sufficient or majority representation in order to exercise these and other rights. Much of the game-playing which in the past preceded recognition, therefore, may now disappear.

The Nature of Recognition   Although unions are now possessed of prescribed organisational rights, there is as yet no compulsion on the employer to bargain with a particular union. The union still has to approach the employer to demand that it be recognised as the representative of **and bargaining agent for** a particular group of employees. In the final analysis the employer could refuse to enter such bargaining relationship, but this would be difficult if the union already has a presence at the workplace and particularly where a majority union has requested the appointment of shop stewards. Thus the following logical step would be to enter into a formal or informal agreement with the union.

Where such arrangement is formal, it takes the form of a **recognition agreement** whereby management agrees to recognise the union as the collective bargaining agent of employees or a specified group of employees, known as the **bargaining unit**. In establishing such a bargaining unit, the employer should take cognizance of existing bargaining structures and of other unions representing other employees with whom he has to deal or may have to deal in future.

The Recognition Agreement

The recognition agreement will not only confirm that the employer accepts the union as a bargaining agent, but will also stipulate the rules and procedures for the further conduct of the relationship and the parameters within which the relationship will be conducted — that is, the issues and procedures which will be subject to bargaining or joint decisionmaking. In this respect the recognition agreement resembles the constitution of a bargaining council. However, the recognition of a union as representative of employees at plant level is slightly different from a general agreement to bargain, especially if the latter agreement is reached at a more centralised level. Recognition, because it entails closer involvement of the union with the organisation, tends to encompass not only collective bargaining but also a certain measure of joint decisionmaking.

Types of Recognition Agreement

A recognition agreement need not be committed to writing. It could be a verbal agreement between the parties that management recognises the right of the union and its shop stewards to represent employees, that shop stewards will be appointed and that management will negotiate with the union following the presentation of demands. This kind of agreement is made only if there is a high degree of trust between the parties — which, in practice, is very rarely the case. Besides the lack of trust, there is the fact that personalities on both sides change and, with such changes, verbal agreements will disappear. Moreover, a verbal agreement gives rise to too many uncertainties. Consequently, a written agreement is usually preferred.

A written agreement, by Piron's definition, may take the form of a skeletal agreement which merely states principles, or it may be a full agreement, containing detailed procedures and providing for every eventuality. A full procedural agreement has the advantage that it eliminates uncertainty, particularly on the part of managers and shop stewards who have to implement the agreement. Rights and obligations are clearly spelled out. This facilitates administration and litigation, in case of breach of the agreement. However, Piron explains that full procedural agreements do tend to be complicated and legalistic, necessitating training for those involved in their implementation. A detailed, legalistic agreement may create suspicion between the two parties, and any mistake which may have been made in the agreement is more difficult to rectify. A skeletal agreement is more flexible and less conducive to a climate of suspicion, but it could lead to uncertainty and thus to further conflict in the future. Skeletal agreements also presuppose a relationship of trust. Because of the very tentative relationship between unions and employers, the majority of agreements signed in South Africa so far have been full procedural agreements.

Contents of a Full Procedural Agreement

Although no two agreements are exactly alike and parties will tailormake agreements to suit their particular needs, a full procedural agreement will probably contain a combination of the clauses listed below.

Preamble

A preamble is not always necessary and will be worthless if it merely indulges in pleasant-sounding phrases; but a preamble does set the tone for the agreement and the relationship. A good preamble will spell out the objectives of the agreement and the spirit in which these objectives are to be pursued. It will also state basic principles, such as the belief in freedom of association and in management's right to manage, subject only to the terms of the agreement. A statement to the effect that the agreement is binding on both parties — and, if such is the case, that it is legally enforceable — may be contained in the preamble, or it may be inserted at the end of the agreement.

Definitions

This is an important section, as it serves to eliminate uncertainties. Special attention should be paid to the definition of 'employee' or 'eligible employee', since this definition specifies who will be covered by the agreement. For example, should the company not wish foremen to be represented in the bargaining unit, these employees will be specifically excluded from the definition.

Other definitions which require attention are those relating to the company, factory or plant. Particularly, a multiplant company which is concluding an agreement for one plant only should specify that the word 'company' in the agreement refers only to the company as operating at that specific plant.

The rest of the definitions are relatively straightforward and will include a definition of a union, a union member, an accredited union official, a shop steward, a management representative, a dispute, a grievance and access. It is necessary to ensure, before putting a definition into writing, that both parties know exactly what is meant by the definition.

Recognition Clause

This clause commits the act of recognition to writing. It states that the company agrees to recognise the union as representative of and as collective bargaining agent for its members. Here again, it may be necessary to specify the bargaining unit by adding, for example, that collective bargaining shall be undertaken only for those members in a particular employee category or a particular section, or those who resort under the definition of 'employee' or 'eligible employee' in the agreement. However, to simplify matters and forecome continual amendments, many agreements now specify that the bargaining unit will encompass all employee classes where the union has significant representivity. Usually this clause contains the proviso that recognition will be effective only as long as the union remains representative. The proviso is intended to safeguard management if the union loses significant support, but it is not intended to be rigidly enforced when (for example) union membership, due perhaps to cyclical changes, drops by a few percent.

A common union demand is that the union be recognised as sole bargaining agent or sole representative of the employees concerned. The granting of this request will depend on management's industrial relations policy, the nature of the workforce and developments within the trade union movement. Management might wish to bargain with only one representative union, in which case it will readily accede to the demand. On the other hand, it might be held that this impinges on the rights of other employees. Where different factions or interests are present in the bargaining unit, the granting of sole bargaining rights may not be advisable. Also, the new legislation now grants organisational rights to unions which do not have majority representation, making the granting of sole bargaining rights to one union even more problematic — unless, of course, a different threshold of representivity has been agreed upon with a majority union. In any event, it is not advisable to grant a union sole bargaining rights at the company as a whole. Sole bargaining rights should pertain only to employees in the bargaining unit.

Other items which may be dealt with under this clause include matters such as the submission of the union constitution to management before entering into a recognition agreement. While management should not request the union constitution at the first approach, it may be useful for management to have the constitution once a relationship has been established and some degree of trust exists.

Access

Although a union may now have automatic access, this clause will regulate the procedures for union officials to enter company premises. Normally, for reasons of security, access is permitted only with the prior permission of a specified managerial representative, who will accompany the official to his destination in the plant or will arrange for the official to be granted access by responsible persons. Access may be granted on an *ad hoc* basis or provision may be made for regular access at a certain time. It is necessary also to specify the union officials to whom access will be granted.

Demands for access also include requests for the use of facilities, such as notice boards and venues for meetings. In most cases unions are allowed to place notices on company boards, provided that these have been countersigned by a member of management. Certain facilities, such as the use of an office for meetings with shop stewards or use of the canteen for a general meeting, will also be granted.

Check-Off Facilities

This refers to the deduction of union dues from the wages of employees. The law now entitles representative unions to such facilities even before recognition is granted. However, the procedures may well be set out in the agreement. Check-off facilities are granted subject to a signed stop order being received from the employee concerned. The company then pays the collected subscriptions into the union account within fifteen days of the end of the month. Provision should also be made for resignations from the union and changes in subscription rates, and lists should be supplied regularly to the union.

Check-off facilities are useful to unions in that they obviate the need to collect dues from individual members, but unions used to prefer the latter method for the very reason that it necessitated contact between union officials, shop stewards and individual members. From management side, the granting of check-off facilities provides a means of monitoring union support.

Shop Stewards

Although shop stewards are elected by union members, they are, in effect, jointly appointed by the union and management. The number of shop stewards to be appointed is now guided by law. However, the number of shop stewards will also depend on the manner in which the workplace is organised. Eligible employees may form one homogeneous group or be geographically separated into smaller groups. The best practice is to divide eligible employees into constituencies and to assign a certain number of shop stewards to each constituency. Provision should be made for different shifts and some unions may request that a deputy shop steward be appointed so that he may replace a shop steward who is absent from work. Furthermore, management may agree to the appointment of senior shop stewards who will have special privileges and will coordinate the activities of other shop stewards.

Shop steward elections are conducted on company premises and are supervised by the union, but management could demand that a managerial representative be present to monitor the elections. The recognition agreement may set out the conditions under which members will be eligible to vote or to stand for election as a shop steward, as well as the procedures to be followed during the election. Some disagreement exists regarding management's right to co-decision in the termination of a shop steward's functions. Unions maintain that the shop steward is a union appointee and that his conduct is the business of the union. Nevertheless most agreements will contain provisions stating that a shop steward will no longer hold office if he fails to perform his duties, is no longer an eligible employee, resigns from the company or resigns from the union.

The rights and duties of shop stewards and senior shop stewards should be spelled out in the agreement. It ought to be stipulated that a shop steward cannot leave his place of work in any random event and that permission should be obtained from his supervisor, but that shop stewards will be granted reasonable access to their constituents and time off to deal with problems. It is also customary to grant shop stewards permission to hold regular meetings within their normal working hours.

Time off for the training of shop stewards may be requested by the union. Unions regard it as their right to train shop stewards during company time and this is now endorsed by legislation, as is the right of employees who are union officials to take time off to attend to union business, subject to mutual arrangement.

Victimisation

The shop steward clause is generally followed by an undertaking from management that it will not victimise a shop steward for his actions during the performance of his duties as shop steward; for that matter, that it will not victimise any employee because of his union membership.

Negotiation Procedure

The negotiation procedure sets out the parameters for further negotiations, whether these be of a substantive or a procedural nature. Agreement is reached as to the number of negotiators on each side and the number of observers who will be allowed. The procedure for initiating negotiations is also established. It is advisable to stipulate the subject matter of negotiations. A statement that negotiations will be conducted 'on all matters of mutual interest' is too vague, unless clarity has been obtained on 'mutual interests'. Management should rather declare itself willing to negotiate on any matter **directly** affecting the welfare of union members. Furthermore, provision should be made for annual negotiations on substantive issues, such as wages and conditions of service. Again, the contents of such negotiations should be spelled out. In the case of wage negotiations, provision could be made for a minimum number of negotiation meetings, to lessen the possibility of one party not attempting to negotiate at all.

Finally, provision needs to be made for the taking of minutes and the drafting of agreements and for reportback by shop stewards or union officials to members during the course of negotiations. It is best to stipulate that reportbacks during company time will take place only by arrangement with management. Moreover, management should retain the right to inform employees of the developments in negotiations or to issue a joint communiqué with the union.

Dispute Procedure

A dispute procedure is an essential part of the recognition agreement. It will describe the route to be followed if deadlock is reached or an employee grievance cannot be resolved. Some agreements merely stipulate that, in such an event, either party may use the dispute resolution procedure provided in the Labour Relations Act. Most unions and managements prefer first to attempt resolution of the dispute themselves. The dispute procedure will, consequently, provide for declaration of the dispute, in writing, by one party and a response from the other party. The latter should be given sufficient time to respond, whereafter the parties will meet to attempt to settle the dispute. The number of meetings to be held should be stipulated. On average, dispute procedures provide for three meetings and some agreements stipulate that no more than two of these should be held in one day. Continued negotiations in these meetings may not result in agreement. To provide for this possibility, the parties may agree beforehand on the procedures to be followed thereafter or the agreement may merely stipulate that a decision will be made if the dispute meetings end in further deadlock. In some dispute procedures the next step entails mediation and in others the parties agree that any unresolved dispute will be submitted to arbitration. More sophisticated agreements will distinguish between disputes of right and disputes of interest, and will prescribe different settlement procedures for each. Certain newer agreements also contain detailed regulations for picketing by union members. Where no definite step has been agreed upon, the decision is left to the negotiators. Should mediation fail and no arbitration take place, the parties will probably meet again and decide on further steps, or it may be specified in the procedure that either party could then declare an official dispute in terms of the Labour Relations Act.

As with all dispute procedures, that contained in the recognition agreement is intended to promote further negotiation, in the hope of a peaceful settlement.

The Peace Obligation

The peace obligation is a declaration of good faith on both sides. The company undertakes not to lock out its employees at will, and the union that it will generally not encourage its members to engage in strike action or any other form of industrial action. Cognizance is usually taken of the fact that employees may engage in a wildcat strike, without the union's authorisation. Consequently, the recognition agreement could contain the undertaking by management that it will not exercise its common law right to dismiss employees who are striking illegally for a specified period after the commencement of the strike. This period might range from one to three days and even to a week. The union, in turn, undertakes to do all in its power to persuade strikers to return to work pending negotiations on the issue at hand.

Those agreements not providing for arbitration on all matters (which is unlikely) will further stipulate that the peace obligation does not detract from the right of either party to institute lawful industrial action in terms of the Labour Relations Act, if such action is provided for in the dispute procedure.

Duration and Termination of Agreement

This clause stipulates the period for which an agreement may remain in force (usually indefinite) and, more importantly, the conditions under which it will be terminated. The latter conditions include breach of contract or notice by either party. Some agreements state that termination will come about or the agreement will be suspended if union membership drops below a certain percentage. Again, this is merely a safeguard and need not be strictly implemented.

Amendment of Agreement

It is necessary to state under which conditions an agreement will be modified, suspended or cancelled and the procedures to be followed in such an event.

General

This clause may contain any other matter relevant to the agreement.

Domicilia and Notices

The physical address of both the company and the union should be given, and provision needs to be made for notification of change of address.

Signing of the Agreement

The agreement will be signed by an official of the union, entitled in terms of its constitution to contract on its behalf, and by the Managing Director or a member of management with the necessary powers. Signatures must be dated and witnessed.

An example of a full recognition agreement is contained in the Annexures.

The Need for a Recognition Agreement

Some commentators are of the opinion that — now that the law regulates matters such as the right to access, to hold meetings and to appoint shop stewards — there is no longer any necessity to conclude a recognition agreement. However, as indicated earlier, organisational rights do not guarantee recognition and agreement to bargain. Furthermore there are numerous other arrangements which do require attention in the form of an agreement.

Substantive Agreement at Plant Level

Once a recognition agreement has been concluded, the parties will from time to time engage in negotiations on substantive issues. The procedures and the nature of the issues will depend on the terms agreed upon in the recognition document. Such substantive agreements will be similar in form to bargaining council agreements, but may not be quite as detailed as they do not cater for a whole industry.

Other Procedural Agreements

Once recognition has been achieved, numerous other matters may be subject to negotiation between the union and management. These would include training, discipline, grievances, retrenchment, job grading and so forth. Each of these would require a special procedural agreement setting out the steps to be taken.

Evaluation

If the thrust of the Labour Relations Act of 1995 towards a more centralised bargaining system is reflected in practice, then the institution of plant-level bargaining may gradually disappear. This may be supported by the fact that workplace forums might, in future, perform many of the functions of plant-level unions. On the other hand, it could be postulated that the participants in the South African system have not yet reached the stage at which they will accept only centralised bargaining. Accordingly the two bargaining structures are likely to exist side by side for some time to come.

THE DEVELOPMENT OF THE DUAL COLLECTIVE BARGAINING SYSTEM

The Industrial Conciliation Act of 1924 – Establishment of the System

After the promulgation of the Industrial Conciliation Act of 1924 collective bargaining, as central to the conduct of relations between employer and employee, became accepted practice in South African labour relations. The principal aim of the Act was to make provision for institutions to be utilised for the purpose of dispute settlement and collective bargaining. To these ends, the Act provided for the establishment of industrial councils by representative, registered employer and employee bodies.

In the years from 1924 to 1979 industrial councils (being the only officially sanctioned forums for collective bargaining) established themselves as integral to the industrial relations system, and collective bargaining took on a highly centralised, bureaucratic form. Agreements with employers were negotiated mainly by centrally organised unions. These agreements were, in most cases, extended to non-party employers and employees.

By 1980 there were approximately 100 industrial councils and 250 agreements in operation. The fact that less than ten of these councils accounted for more than 80 per cent of workers covered by councils reflects their high degree of centralisation. The councils gradually developed a well-oiled machinery and negotiations ran extremely smoothly, to the satisfaction of both employer and employee bodies. Because black Africans, by their exclusion from the definition of 'employee' in terms of the Act, were not permitted to belong to registered trade unions, a large percentage of the workforce had no representation in this collective bargaining machinery.

The Black
Labour
Relations
Regulation Act
of 1953 and
Subsequent
Amendments
— The System
of Workers'
and Liaison
Committees

The exclusion of black Africans from the definition of 'employee' prior to 1979 did not, as has been seen, preclude the formation of black trade unions.

Black Africans could form trade unions but such unions could not be registered and, although some were initially strong, their power gradually declined. After the passage of the Black Labour Relations Regulation Act of 1953, black Africans could be represented by workers' committees and coordinating workers' committees and, after 1973, also in liaison committees. The function of the committees was to communicate to management the aspirations and wishes of these workers. As indicated in a previous chapter, an anomalous position existed in that black Africans, who had no registered trade union rights, had been granted a form of workers' participation at plant level, a type of representation which had been denied to white and coloured workers. Thus the two basic forms of worker representation had been strictly divided and allotted between the different race groups.

In terms of the 1977 amendment to the Act, black Africans, who had previously been denied the right to strike, were granted the use of a dispute settlement machinery through the system of Labour Committees. These procedures were mainly unused and, as mentioned in Chapter 4, the 1973 Natal strikes proved that African workers could, by their force of numbers, withhold their labour outside the statutory system without suffering any severe official repercussions. Thus the pattern for the future had already been established.

The Industrial
Conciliation
Amendment
Act of 1979 —
The 'New'
Dispensation

The Industrial Conciliation Amendment Act of 1979, together with later amendments, drastically altered the labour relations constellation and, with it, the collective bargaining spectrum in South Africa. The redefinition of the term 'employee' to refer to workers regardless of race gave black Africans the right to form and belong to registered trade unions and thereby to take part in the statutory bargaining machinery, centring on the established industrial councils. It was expected that the emergent black (mainly unskilled) workers and their representative unions would require, accept and enter into the same highly centralised, bureaucratic structures which had served privileged, skilled, non-black workers for so long. The planners of the new dispensation, lulled by the previous era of static and somewhat lopsided labour relations, not only ignored the sociological tenet that changing constellations will inevitably result in modified or new structures, but also disregarded the dynamic nature of a **free** labour relations system. In the words of Flanders:

> 'The fact that industrial activity changes day by day ... means that it cannot be directed, with a sensitive regard for the manifold and diverse interests of those involved, by a regime of strict external law and outside regulation. Fixed codes of rights and obligations, rigid notions of justice and equity, are not applicable to industrial relations.'

No actual attempt was made to force the newer unions into the statutory system by means of the law, but the expectation did exist that they would follow only established practices. The years 1980–1985 proved these expectations to be largely unfounded.

The Two Bargaining Systems

For their own reasons the majority of the then emergent unions, although later willing to register, proved themselves reluctant to enter industrial councils and to make use of the statutory collective bargaining machinery. Instead, they opted for a shadow or non-statutory system of plant-level recognition agreements. Thus, equity under the law notwithstanding, South African labour relations in the sphere of collective bargaining still reflected the dualism of the pre-1979 era, with established unions (representing mostly Whites, Coloureds and Asians) firmly entrenched for the most part in the industrial councils and fully utilising the statutory machinery, and the then emergent unions using non-statutory machinery and still possessing little power of legal enforcement. In fact, some of the newly emerging unions took over, for their own strategic purposes, the functions and character of the pre-1979 workers' committees, but their status as trade unions rendered them more able than the committees to force employers into negotiation.

The rapid growth of plant-level recognition and the fact that recognition agreements were entered into by employers party to industrial councils or covered by an extension of industrial council agreements led to much controversy and the speculation that the industrial council system was disintegrating. Whether this was so or not, it was true that the collective bargaining system and the sole sanction accorded to industrial council negotiations would have to be reviewed. Plant-level negotiation was, at least for the time being, a labour relations reality. To ensure greater industrial peace, this bargaining forum would have to receive greater sanction and status from both employers and the State; nor would the mere decentralisation of existing industrial councils prove an adequate alternative.

The Disputed Status of the Recognition Agreement

The recognition agreement and subsequent plant-level bargaining were not new phenomena, peculiar to South African industrial relations. In Britain, for example, there had already been a proliferation of plant-level recognition agreements. In South Africa conflict between plant-level and industrial council negotiations arose — not over the fact that a recognition agreement had been concluded, but over the substantive issues governed by the recognition agreement. Protagonists of the industrial council system maintained that matters such as wages and strike regulation fell solely into the ambit of the council and that any attempt to negotiate on these at another level was a preemption of industrial council negotiations and of the statutory regulations governing councils. Yet a union enters into a recognition agreement in order to bargain collectively. The most obvious facet of such bargaining is remuneration. Granting recognition without the right to bargain was a decapitation of the recognition process. Furthermore, an employer's main concern when dealing with a union should be the maintenance of labour peace. The statutory machinery was proving ineffective in preventing illegal strikes, and a recognition agreement without a disputes procedure would have brought the employer no nearer to his perceived aim and would have been, at the very least, a futile exercise.

Workers' Committees within the New Constellation

The Labour Relations Amendment Act of 1981 repealed the Black Labour Relations Regulations Act of 1953 and made provision for the establishment of works councils, which would be constituted in the same way as the old liaison committees. These councils did not possess the bargaining powers of the pre-1979 committees. The functions of these councils remained vague and, because emergent unions had to a certain extent amalgamated the functions of workers' committees and plant-level unions, the concept of works councils was implemented in only a very few instances.

Contrasting Attitudes

The Government

From approximately 1982 onwards the government adopted an increasingly *laissez-faire* stance towards the conduct of labour relations. In an address to the Afrikaanse Handelsinstituut in April 1982, the then Minister of Manpower stressed the government's principle of minimal interference in the labour relationship between employer and employee. According to the Minister, the decisive consideration of employers should be '... the importance of maintaining not only short-term but also long-term peaceful labour relations'. While not actively encouraging the new developments, the government did not discourage the signing of recognition agreements between employers and so-called independent unions. It thereby placed the ball firmly in the court of the employers.

The Employers

In his keynote address to the FOSATU Congress in March 1982, FOSATU general secretary Joe Foster stated that the struggle of the worker had too long been mistakenly directed against governmental policies rather than against capital. According to Mr Foster, 'The position was such that learned liberal academics saw in capital the great hope for change, despite the fact that capital and its lackeys were undoubtedly the major beneficiaries of apartheid'. Shortly thereafter the Director General of Manpower stated that employers were '... lagging far behind' the government in respect of the new labour policy. The stage had been set. It was up to employers to utilise it to its fullest potential.

The employer stance was a difficult one to fathom. On the one hand, it would have appeared that employers welcomed their new freedom and accepted the responsibilities entailed in the regulation of their own labour relations.

On the other hand, many employers displayed a great deal of reservation as regards the conclusion of recognition agreements with the then emerging unions. A very large number of employers disapproved of certain substantive issues, such as wages, being negotiated at plant level. There were companies which went ahead and negotiated all important conditions of employment with representative unions, but the majority of employers might well have been accused of lagging behind.

Flanders, in referring to British management, could have been speaking to South African employers when he said that:

> 'The paradox, whose truth managements have found so difficult to accept, is that they can only gain control by sharing it. Cooperation in the workplace cannot be fostered by propaganda and exhortation, by preaching its benefits. Nor does it depend, primarily, though this is an important factor, on improved systems of communication ... Cooperation demands first and foremost the progressive fusing of two systems of unilateral control — which now exist in conjunction and frequently in conflict with each other — into a common system of joint control, based on agreed objectives. Such agreement can only be reached through compromise.'

It may well be contended that initially employers wished to reduce plant-level unions to mere workers' committees without any statutory or even admitted bargaining rights. Furthermore, employers — no longer able to use government policy or the registration issue — started to use the industrial council system against the unions. The position was accurately summed up by Alec Erwin when he said:

> 'All employers seem to have been carefully programmed. Mention negotiation and out will pop the words "Industrial Council".'

To the employers Erwin posed this question:

> 'Do we accept that the unionisation of Black workers will pose the need for some quite dramatic, fundamental changes in both our attitudes and the structures of bargaining of the past, or is it a matter of merely bringing Black workers into the tried and tested procedures which they have regrettably been left out of up to now?'

These statements are underscored by Hawkins who, referring to the British dilemma, states that:

> 'The normative assumptions of the "formal system" were, however, inhibiting the response of many managements to the increasingly important "informal system" of workplace bargaining.'

He went on to warn that:

> 'If, by contrast, management refuses to accept the concept of extended joint regulation and seeks to keep the scope of substantive collective bargaining to a minimum, the outcome may well be a progressive deterioration in the climate of workplace negotiations.'

The Established Trade Unions

In general, the then established trade unions continued to accept and support the industrial council system, in which they were firmly entrenched and where they possessed the power of veto on the entrance of other unions. This opinion is substantiated by an investigation into bargaining methods conducted in 1982, which revealed that the established unions would opt for the sectorisation of existing industrial councils rather than for plant-based bargaining. In the same year Anna Scheepers, then president of the Garment Workers' Union, one of the oldest participants in the established system, while extolling the benefits of the industrial council and exhorting unions to use the system, stated that: 'If the apartheid government disappeared tomorrow, our Labour Relations Act would still have to be retained as an extremely good legal framework for promoting the interests of workers.' However, it remained an open question as to what the attitude of the established unions would be if all emerging unions were to enter the industrial councils and preempt negotiations there. The fact that the Steel, Engineering & Allied Workers' Union, representative mostly of black African employees, had in 1982 become party to the Industrial Council for the Metal

Industry had greatly complicated negotiations in this council and had also led Ben Nicholson, spokesman for the established unions, to accuse employers of pandering to unskilled workers. The clash of needs and interests between unskilled and skilled workers which initially existed could most certainly have hampered progress towards agreement in industrial councils.

The Newer Trade Unions

The reasons for the rejection of the industrial council system by the newer unions were many and varied. Most often heard was the explanation that unions rejected the system on political grounds; that they saw it as symbolic of the apartheid regime. On closer analysis it would appear that, except in the case of extremely politicised unions, the political factor, although it may have affected the unions' judgment, was not the main motive. Registration was conducted at first along racial lines and, as registration was essential for entrance to an industrial council, the two issues might well have been confused; but, as time progressed, registration lost its relevance as a point of issue in the union movement. It cannot be doubted that an affective reaction to the industrial council, as a system from which black African workers had been excluded in the past, did exist, yet even such affective attitudes could have been and were overcome.

The two major reasons for rejection by the newer unions lay in their perception of the 'undemocratic' structure of industrial councils and the danger that entrance to the councils would dilute their power base. The newer, nonracial and black trade union movement placed great emphasis on the democratisation of their structures and the protection of the power of the shop steward. Even where a newer union, such as the National Automobile & Allied Workers' Union, entered an industrial council, it insisted on continual contact and consultation with its shop steward committees. That such democratic consultation becomes extremely difficult, the higher the level of bargaining becomes, is self-evident. Yet, even if consultation with shop floor leaders was not necessary, the fact remained that leaders of established unions had in many cases taken on the character of bureaucrats far removed from their actual union constituents. This was off-putting to the newer unionists, with their emphasis on democratic structures. Also, the threat of power dilution remained. Initially the newer unions, with a few exceptions, were able to organise only at individual plants and it was there that their power lay. They were not sufficiently representative or strong enough to compete with established unions at industry or national level. It was not surprising, therefore, that they demanded to be recognised and to bargain at plant level.

Certain newer unions later extended their power beyond plant level and experienced the concomitant need for a wider bargaining system. Some, such as the National Automobile & Allied Workers' Union and the Steel, Engineering & Allied Workers' Union, joined existing industrial councils in an attempt to try out the system, but both experienced difficulties. Following its dissatisfaction with the outcome of the Metal Industries Industrial Council negotiations, SEAWU started reassessing its position as party to the Council, and deadlock reached in the negotiations of the Industrial Council for the Motor Industry in the Eastern Cape resulted in NAAWU's temporary resignation from that council. NAAWU's dilemma was highlighted by the fact that it could not speak or take responsibility for striking NAAWU workers while the Industrial Council for the

Motor Industry in the Eastern Cape was conducting negotiations. Following the breakdown in industrial council negotiations, motor industry workers again reverted to the demand for plant-level bargaining. This did not necessarily lead to the conclusion that emerging unions were unfit for centralised negotiations, but merely pointed to a need for adaptation on both sides. Soon afterwards the general secretary of the Federation of South African Trade Unions, Joe Foster, admitted the need for a wider system in addition to plant bargaining, adding that 'we must see industry bargaining not as something to be feared but as a logical extension of our present structure and practices'. However, the majority of the emerging unions did not immediately accept the industrial council system as matters stood. They preferred to build their own wider system from the bottom up.

Pros and Cons of the Two Systems   In the early 1980s there was much controversy regarding the advantages and disadvantages of centralised and plant-level bargaining. Both have their advantages (see Chapter 8). Yet, in the South African situation there was at first no basis for such comparison, as both systems were not interchangeable. They catered for different needs in differing circumstances and were established by unions having different interests. At best, they could be used to supplement each other.

The power of the workers represented by the newer unions lay not in their skill but in their numbers, and their organisation rested at plant level. These workers had unique problems such as poor working conditions, low wages, arbitrary dismissals and a lack of job security. In their perception, these problems were urgent and pressing. They required rapid solutions which could not be resolved by industrial councils, of which they were suspicious in any case. To them and their unions, the insistence of management that they seek representation on certain substantive matters only through industrial councils, was a means of entrapping them. At the time Alec Erwin said of the industrial council system: 'It is a product of complex historical developments and, contrary to popular belief, it is not God-given. It is at present a mixture between the powerful and relatively effective and the outright bizarre.' A somewhat extreme view, but perhaps it was necessary to jolt the extremism of some industrial council protagonists.

It was contended, and generally accepted at the time, that adherence to the industrial council system promoted labour peace. Admittedly, the strike weapon was used with increasing readiness by plant-level organisations over the years. The question was, however, whether the involvement of the newer unions in negotiations at industrial council level would in any way have minimised strike action by workers at plants. Since this was unlikely, the cause could have been a defective collective bargaining machinery and a lack of accepted procedures in general, rather than the non-participation of unions in industrial councils. According to Flanders, 'all strikes, whether official or unofficial, are — to adopt the well-known phrase — the continuation of industrial relations by other means'. This was especially true in South Africa, as many of the newer unions were obliged to strike in order to enforce recognition. Again Flanders has the last word when he says: 'If unions are denied recognition by an employer, the strike is the only available sanction'. Therefore, the solution to strike action seemed to lie in the conduct of agreements containing strike and lockout procedures and in the assurance by the union that it would maintain reasonable control of its members. Flanders substantiates this by saying of 'unofficial' strikes that:

> '... in the absence of agreed rules to regulate these relations, it is to be expected that contentious issues will be settled by a trial of strength. As always, the only alternative to the rule of war is the rule of law, and where law cannot be imposed by tyranny, it must be sustained by consent'.

After the introduction of the new labour dispensation in 1979, strike action increased but the incidence of spontaneous, or illegal, strikes slowly diminished as unions settled down to using established procedures.

Acceptance of the Dual Structure

Towards the middle of the 1980s the collective bargaining system moved onto a more even course. Employer resistance to plant-level recognition declined and the number of recognition agreements concluded increased significantly. The 1987 report of the Manpower Commission put the total number of recognition agreements in existence at 322, but unofficial figures put this figure closer to 800.

The industrial council system remained the officially sanctioned and statutorily entrenched system, but the fact of plant-level agreements had been officially admitted. Certain amendments to the Labour Relations Act and other statements issuing from official sources proved that, although recognition agreements did not enjoy the same status at law as industrial council agreements, they had been accepted by the legislators as part of the collective bargaining system in South Africa.

In the meantime, the newer unions also developed towards greater acceptance of and participation in the industrial council system. Those unions with a sufficiently strong power base joined industrial councils in the hope of making the system work for them, though they did not initially neglect their plant-level interests. Others developed their own, more centralised bargaining forums. Also, as they became more sophisticated, these unions used established dispute procedures, involving industrial councils and conciliation boards, to a greater degree. This brought them into closer contact with the industrial council system and, at the same time, necessitated an adjustment of attitude on the part of established unions and employers on industrial councils. On their part, established unions began to pay greater attention to plant-level interests.

Conflict within the System

The participation of newer unions in industrial councils and the greater involvement of established unions at plant level, although a positive development, was not without problems. Whereas previously there had been a strict separation of interests represented at plant level and those represented by the industrial councils, many unions now functioned at both industrial council and plant level and, consequently, appeared to have a choice as to the level at which they would bargain. This would have been acceptable if there were a strict separation of issues negotiated in industrial councils and those resorting under plant-level bargaining, but no such distinction yet existed. The National Union of Metalworkers of South Africa (NUMSA), of which the old Metal & Allied Workers' Union formed the core, upon its entry to the industrial council, insisted that it would retain the right to negotiate wages at plant level with individual employers who, in the union's opinion, could afford to pay more than the industrial council rates. The subsequent refusal of one company to bargain at plant level with NUMSA led to a long legal wrangle.

It could be argued that there is no reason why plant-level wage agreements should not supplement industrial council agreements, but employers hold a different view. They become party to councils mainly to avoid wage leapfrogging or to keep wages out of competition and, if there is no uniformity in wages, there might be no reason for their continued participation in industrial councils and the centralised bargaining system would disintegrate.

Another problem experienced in industrial councils had its origins in trade union divisions. Within the context of the South African situation, different unions on industrial councils represented different, often conflicting, interests. The resultant lack of unity weakened the position of the employee representatives vis-à-vis the employer body and it did happen that some unions on a council accepted an employer offer, while other unions rejected it.

In the situation as it was, four possibilities existed. Industrial council bargaining could remain, but with the proviso that industrial councils merely establish minimum wages and conditions of employment and that the parties be free to improve on these by plant-level agreements. Were this to happen, employers might find some way of agreeing on wage limits and unions might not gain the advantage they expected. Moreover, duplicated bargaining would be time-consuming and costly. Alternatively, industrial councils could cease to function as bargaining forums, in which case bargaining would become increasingly decentralised. Unions which were involved in centralising on an industry basis might find this problematic and inevitably a tendency towards centralisation, either by the reinstitution of industrial councils or by the establishment of some other centralised forum, would develop. The third possibility was that the two systems be used on a supplementary basis and that different issues be subjected to negotiation at different levels. Fourthly, plant-level bargaining could be replaced by a system of worker participation in the undertaking. All the possibilities were viable and possible.

BARGAINING STRUCTURES WITHIN THE PRESENT DISPENSATION

Latest Developments in Bargaining Levels

Of late, some major employers have displayed increasing unwillingness to bargain in industrial (bargaining) councils, claiming a greater tendency towards decentralisation in their own organisations, whereas COSATU, as the largest union federation, is now committed to industry-wide or sectoral bargaining. This is evidenced by COSATU's demand for legislation enforcing centralised bargaining and its expressed intention that, in the future, there should be only eight major sectors.

COSATU's renewed commitment to centralised negotiations should be viewed not only as a logical development phase but also in the light of political developments since the beginning of 1990. The federation is now obliged to become more involved in the economic future of the country. With this in mind, it will seek to extend bargaining in national industrial councils to include also the 'social and economic concerns' of its members. Thus, as suggested at a NUMSA workshop in 1990, industry-level bargaining could deal with issues such as the restructuring of the industry, job security, job creation, skills and training needs, job grading, employee development, benefits, wages and a general wage policy, while 'national negotiations' with joint employer bodies (in NEDLAC, for example) could cover issues such as 'investment priorities for public and private sector investment, investment codes for foreign investment, the role of pension funds in investment; labour market issues such as a framework for training, minimum wages, etc.; international trade controls and incentives, and workers' rights'. In an article on the importance of collective bargaining in the future, John Copelyn, then general secretary of SACTWU, also stated that industry-wide agreements could be utilised for industrial restructuring, while negotiations in these forums 'could fundamentally influence the development of a set of tertiary national education institutions (universities, technikons, etc.), changing the focus and controlling structures of these bodies'. Furthermore, according to Copelyn, centralised negotiations could contribute to the development of a national health plan and the constructive investment of pension fund monies '... to redress the economic deprivation of the former victims of apartheid'. He warned that, if employers did not agree to broaden negotiations at industry level, the unions would have no alternative but to '... tie themselves more closely to the State and to seek to influence society through political developments'. Neither Copelyn nor NUMSA spelled out the ambit of negotiations at plant level. In fact, the NUMSA workshop argued that 'the unions would have to work out what sort of issues they want to negotiate at company and plant level'.

From the above it would seem that the issue of bargaining levels is, for COSATU, closely tied to its overall objective of actively restructuring the economic system. In a later report, COSATU did state that company or plant-level bargaining allowed 'no way of controlling the wages and working conditions of unorganised workers' and 'leaves employers in unorganised companies free to exploit at will'; but the main objection was still that decentralised bargaining made it difficult to build solidarity and did not help to build a 'consciousness of the whole industry', nor did it allow opportunity for restructuring the industry.

In the same report it was pointed out that centralised bargaining did endanger democracy, but that this could be countered by having large numbers of observers at negotiations and by worker leadership in negotiations. Three problems regarding industrial councils were also highlighted: there was no proportional representation, the Minister of Labour could interfere by refusing to gazette agreements, and wages negotiated in industrial councils were often quite low. The former problem was addressed by NUMSA when it requested proportional representation on the National Industrial Council for the Metal Industry where, it said, it had — despite its numerical strength — often been defeated by a coalition of more conservative unions.

The problem of minimum wages was addressed in certain industrial councils where the demand was for the negotiation of 'real' wages. It would seem that unions would forgo their demand for additional plant-level negotiations if employers were to negotiate adequate wage levels in the industrial council. However, as NUMSA admitted, this could occur only where the members of the employer party possessed similar resources — as, for example, in the motor industry.

That unions are determined still to exert influence at plant level is demonstrated by their demand (before the passage of the Labour Relations Act of 1995) that workplace forums be union-based. This may be seen as an effort to maintain dominance at plant level and not be absorbed into a wider participation forum consisting of all employees. The demand substantiates the fear of many employers that workplace forums will become merely alternative bargaining forums.

Not all unions and not all union members are in favour of more centralised negotiations. This was illustrated by the 1990 strike at the Mercedes-Benz factory in East London. Here the employees, believing that they could negotiate better wage levels at the plant, went on strike to demand decentralised negotiations. The union was hard put to settle the dispute and to counter allegations that it was becoming 'bureaucratic'. As bargaining becomes more centralised, problems like this will probably increase. Also, federations such as NACTU and FEDSAL, which are not so strong at industry level, appear to be having problems with COSATU's stand on centralised bargaining.

Employer Responses to the Union Stand

During the deadlock in NEDLAC over the new labour legislation, one of the main issues was the unions' insistence on mandatory centralised bargaining. the employer body declared that, while they were not averse to centralised bargaining, they believed that this was a matter which could not be determined by legislation but should preferably be subject to agreement between the parties. Evidently employers fear that, should centralised bargaining become mandatory, unions may still demand also to bargain at decentralised level in certain instances, thus causing unnecessary duplication. Some employers are also of the opinion that their interests and those of their employees are better served at plant level.

Small to Medium Enterprises

The most vehement reaction to centralised bargaining has come from the ranks of small business, which sees the extension of centralised agreements to non-parties as undemocratic and a negation of the freedom of association. Furthermore, as mentioned earlier, many argue that they are unable to pay the wage rates set by industrial/bargaining councils and that, if they are obliged to do so, they may be put out of business. On the other hand, unions argue that exclusion of small business from such agreements could result in exploitation.

While the union argument is accepted, over-legislation in this respect may well hamper government attempts to encourage small to medium enterprises and thereby to boost the economy and create much-needed jobs.

The Legal Position

It has been stated that the new legislation promotes but does not enforce centralised bargaining supplemented by a system of plant-level participation through workplace forums. Industrial councils have been renamed bargaining councils to provide also for centralised bargaining in the service and public sectors. Like the old industrial councils, bargaining councils may extend their agreements to non-parties. Even where a bargaining council is not sufficiently representative of employers and employees in the industry, the Minister may still approve extension of the agreement if he believes that it will promote the practice of centralised bargaining. Some allowance has been made for small business interests by the stipulation that councils must, in their own constitutions, allow for effective representation by small to medium enterprises and the provision that exemptions will now be approved by an independent body and not, as in the past, by the council itself. However, provision is also made for statutory councils which, although they may not be representative, can apply to have their agreements gazetted as a determination in terms of the Wage Act.

The above leaves no doubt that the legislators favour the concept of a more centralised bargaining system, perhaps because they view it as promoting greater rationalism and labour peace.

Workplace Forums

As a means of compensating for greater centralisation, the legislation now provides for the establishment of workplace forums, to be initiated by majority unions. Where unions still insist on active bargaining at plant level, tension between the bargaining structure and the workplace forum are bound to arise.

Assessment of the Present Position

While the intention of those who promote centralised bargaining is understood, it is wondered whether the players in the system are as yet sophisticated enough for such practices. In systems where bargaining takes place at a highly centralised level (such as Germany, for example), the union movement was relatively united and did not have a history of strong shop-floor representation. In South Africa unions remain divided, and particularly the COSATU and NACTU unions have a history of activity at plant level. Moreover, employees have a heightened awareness of their rights in a democratic system and they may continue to take action at plant level. The unions do not have sufficient resources or trained manpower to operate effectively at both levels (partly the reason for their insistence on centralised negotiations). This creates the possibility of diminished democracy and the real threat of independent action by plant-level representation or disillusionment of members with the union.

Already the news on the ground is that the unions are in disarray and that particularly COSATU unions are losing membership. This is bound to happen as their activities become more centralised and workplace forums more effective. The unions can no longer rely on a 'common enemy', in the form of the ruling class, to unite workers. On the other hand, they may utilise impatience with the failure of the new system to deliver concrete economic benefits as a basis for mobilisation. This will mean increased industrial action, also at centralised level.

Whatever happens, the system — insofar as it concerns bargaining structure — has gone full circle, with the very unions who so vehemently opposed industrial councils now constituting the major proponents of a centralised bargaining system.

THE DUTY TO BARGAIN

It has been mentioned in a number of instances that the institution of collective bargaining in South Africa has, since its inception, been based on the principle of voluntarism. If this is accepted, then no duty to bargain can by law be imposed on the employer or employee party. In these circumstances the issues surrounding the bargaining relationship — including the question of recognition, bargaining units, bargaining levels and bargaining content — would be resolved by a power play between the parties concerned. Where the union held more power, it would be able to oblige the employer to recognise it and to bargain at a particular level; but where the union was weak, the preference of the employer would hold sway. In the extreme, the employer could refuse to bargain with a union which did not hold sufficient power.

However, it has also been noted that a system of complete voluntarism does not exist; that the State, in its efforts to maintain labour peace, will usually establish parameters for the conduct of the relationship, will attempt to create a power balance within the relationship and will protect both parties against exploitation and unfair labour practices. Consequently, it is within these constraints that the freedom to bargain or not will have to be judged.

In South Africa there has been no legal compulsion to bargain with a union, whether or not representative of the majority of employees; but the employer's refusal to do so could in the past constitute an unfair labour practice in terms of the definition contained in the Labour Relations Amendment Act of 1979. This was particularly so in the case of the 1988 definition (afterwards amended), according to which '... any act or omission which unfairly infringes on or impairs the relations between an employer or employee' and '... the unfair, unilateral amendment of terms or conditions of employment' could be regarded as unfair. Even in terms of the 1991 definition, the failure to negotiate could still be regarded as unfair, since it could lead to labour unrest and could 'detrimentally affect' the relationship between employer and employee.

From the above it follows that a fine balance needs to be achieved between the retention of the voluntarist principle and the protection of each party's right to fair treatment. In the past the achievement of this balance was left to the Industrial Court, and its task in this respect was most certainly not an easy one. Initially, the Court shied away from imposing any duty to bargain, but this stance was later modified to the point where there existed an implied duty to bargain on disputes of interest. This did not signify that the employer was obliged to enter into a permanent bargaining relationship with the union concerned but that, where a dispute of interest arose, an employer who refused to bargain with a representative body could well be guilty of an unfair labour practice. This was in line with the Court's view that it should uphold and promote the principal objectives of the Labour Relations Act, one of which is the maintenance of labour peace.

Within the present sociopolitical dispensation, the principle of voluntarism has largely been maintained. The Labour Relations Act of 1995 contains no explicit duty to bargain. This contrasts strongly with the new rights of access and representation granted to trade unions. In the extreme it could lead to a situation where an employer, in terms of the law, allows a union access to employees and permits the appointment of shop stewards, but refuses to engage in a bargaining relationship. This would mean that the union would ultimately have to use coercive power in the form of a strike to enforce bargaining. However, in the absence of the previous wide definition of an unfair labour practice, the legislation does provide that, where a dispute centres in the refusal to bargain, such dispute must be subjected to advisory arbitration. Section 64(2) of the Act describes the refusal to bargain as a refusal to recognise a union as collective bargaining agent, a refusal to agree to the establishment of a bargaining council, a withdrawal of recognition as a bargaining agent, the resignation from a bargaining council or a dispute about appropriate bargaining units, bargaining levels or bargaining subjects. Evidently it is hoped that the parties, particularly the employer party, will heed the pronouncements of the arbitrator. Should they choose not to do so, they may then follow the procedures to a legal strike or lockout.

There is, furthermore, a duty to bargain in good faith. This means that the party concerned should display sincere intention to achieve resolution, that he should make proposals and concessions indicative of good faith, that he should not unilaterally institute changes or use delaying tactics, should not set unreasonable preconditions for bargaining, should not bypass acknowledged bargaining agents, should supply sound arguments for a particular stance, should not suddenly change bargaining conditions, should not unnecessarily withhold information and should never engage in insulting behaviour. Concerning the withholding of information, it is interesting to note that the Labour Relations Act of 1995 makes it compulsory for employers to disclose any information which the union may require for collective bargaining purposes.

Whereas the duty to bargain in certain circumstances and to bargain in good faith may be easily established, much controversy has previously reigned as regards other bargaining issues, particularly the imposition of certain bargaining levels and the choice of bargaining partners. In the past, a number of cases hinged around union demands that employers party to industrial councils should bargain also at plant level. In this respect the Court was hesitant to set any definitive guidelines, but the general stance did appear to be that bargaining at industry level did not preclude plant-level bargaining, and *vice versa*. Where the bargaining level was at issue, consideration would be given to the practical implications and to the circumstances and practices of each party. The Labour Appeal Court, on the other hand, stated that the choice of bargaining levels was a strategic question with which the law should not readily interfere.

On the subject of bargaining partners — and, therefore, bargaining units — much controversy existed. In terms of one decision handed down by the Industrial Court, the employer should bargain with any party, including individuals. Other decisions indicated that the union should have a significant presence, while still others would have it that the employer need bargain only with a majority union. The freedom of association principle does dictate that no employee should be debarred from representation by the body of his choice, yet although an employer may talk to any union concerning the interests of his members, practicalities prohibit him from dealing on a permanent basis with each and every body which claims to represent a particular group of employees. On the other hand, the majoritarian principle is not always democratic, particularly where various interest groups exist and where the majority gained is negligible. In the light of this, the Court's tendency was in the past to promote negotiations with unions which had a stable and substantial presence, or those representing special workplace interests. The new legislation substantiates this line of thinking by granting organisational rights, as the precursors of bargaining, only to unions which are sufficiently representative and, in other sections of the Act, providing that arbitrators should have a view to preventing the proliferation of union representation in a particular plant or industry.

Furthermore, as indicated earlier, the Act allows a majority union and an employer or a bargaining council to conclude an agreement establishing levels of representivity. Effectively, the majority union could then achieve sole bargaining rights. Also, provision is made for the conclusion of closed shop agreements which would, in effect, prevent any other union from claiming sufficient representation at that workplace — unless, of course, there occurs a repeat of the 1980s dilemma, where employees joined the closed shop union and another union. This could indeed present a problem.

One last issue remains: bargaining content. Here it would seem that the old adage that there is nothing which is not negotiable still holds. In essence, any matter of mutual interest between employer and employee may be subject to negotiation. This hardly bodes well for those employers who still rigidly insist on managerial prerogative and cling to what they regard as non-negotiables.

In practice, most bargaining still centres in wages and conditions of service; although, of late, issues such as education and training, as well as job grading, have increasingly come to the fore. It could be argued that the provision for certain matters to be dealt with by workplace forums (and, therefore, to be subject to consultation or co-decisionmaking) would preclude these from being subject also to negotiation. It was certainly the intention of the legislators that a clear distinction should be made between matters subject to collective bargaining and those to be submitted to participatory processes. However, whether such a distinction will occur in practice remains to be seen, particularly since unions may already have these items on their bargaining agendas or may merely use forums for negotiation.

In the absence of any specific provisions regarding the duty to bargain, therefore, it can be expected that numerous disputes will arise around this issue; but perhaps, in the process, some guidelines will be established.

CONCLUSION

It is obvious that, despite attempts at greater rationalisation of collective bargaining, the South African collective bargaining system is still in a state of flux and subject to tensions, not only between employers and unions but also between various unions and between national and plant-level representatives. This situation may be eased or exacerbated by the introduction of workplace forums. As it is, the situation is bound to remain fluid for some time to come.

SOURCES

Clegg, Hugh *Trade Unionism and Collective Bargaining*, Blackwell, 1974.

Copelyn, John 'Collective Bargaining: A Base for Transforming Industry' in *South African Labour Bulletin*, Vol XV No 6, March 1991.

Erwin, Alec in *Industrial Relations Journal of South Africa*, Stellenbosch, Vol. 1. No 3, 1981.

Flanders, A *Collective Bargaining: Prescription for Change*, Faber and Faber, 1967.

Hawkins, K in *Industrial Relations Journal of South Africa*, Stellenbosch, Vol. I No 1, 1981.

Koopman A D, Nasser M E and Nel J *The Corporate Crusaders*, Lexicon, 1987.

Malherbe, A in *Industrial Relations Journal of South Africa*, Stellenbosch, Vol. 2, No 1, 1982.

South African Labour Bulletin, Vols. XVI, XVII, XVIII and XIX, Umanyano Publications.

'Unions must use Industrial Councils', *The Garment Worker*, 23 August 1972.

Labour Relations Act (no. 66 of 1995), *Government Gazette* Vol 366 no.16861, Government Printer, Pretoria, December 1995.

10

LABOUR RELATIONS AT THE WORKPLACE

All too often, labour relationships are viewed merely within the framework of collective bargaining with unions. The labour relationship is an employer–employee relationship. Consequently, whether a union presence exists or not, the practice of sound labour or industrial relations is integral to the managerial function within the enterprise. Moreover, it is a function in which all levels of management, from supervisor upwards, should be involved, since very few managers are not concerned with or responsible for employees. Thus the establishment of a general labour relations policy, in which organisational objectives and labour relations objectives are integrated, is essential for the guidance of management at all levels.

While all managers will be responsible for the conduct of individual and collective labour relations between themselves and their subordinates, the general overseeing of the relationship is the task of the personnel or labour relations manager. He is responsible for the balancing of employer and employee interests, for ensuring that the labour relationship is maintained on an even keel, for advising on negotiations with employee representatives and for the actions and decisions of other members of management, some of whom he will have to persuade into consideration of employee interests. To fulfil these tasks he requires a broad knowledge of all aspects of industrial relations and of the circumstances which can impact on the labour relationship. He needs, furthermore, to be versed in the functioning of the total enterprise. His role is that of diplomat, educator, negotiator, communicator and troubleshooter, a task which, under all circumstances, requires constant attention.

The total personnel function is closely related to the labour relations function. Personnel practices such as recruitment, induction, training and assistance rendered to employees will determine the degree to which the employee is integrated into the organisation, his view of management, his motivation and personal satisfaction. All these factors impact on the labour relationship. Furthermore, the method and consistency of payments could cause satisfaction or dissatisfaction among employees, while the personnel department, in its monitoring of labour turnover and absenteeism, will be able to identify problem areas and prevent conflicts from arising.

Part of the overall function of the personnel department is the establishment of effective communication structures. Although communication is not the cure for all problems, it is essential for the conduct of any relationship. Those involved in communication should be aware of the multitude of barriers which may hamper effective communication or distort the message which is being transmitted. This leads to a continuous search for new and improved methods of communication. Also, within any organisation and particularly as regards the labour relationship, upward and lateral communication is as important as downward communication. There are numerous methods of broadening communications and of ensuring effective two-way communication but, from a labour relations point of view, the suggestions made by the International Labour Organisation require special attention.

One method by which improved communication can be effected is by the institution of workplace committees and by more participative practices at the workplace. Provision for the establishment of workplace forums is a step in that direction.

The effective conduct of the labour relationship also requires uniform procedures as regards the disciplining of employees and the raising of grievances by employees. Ad hoc disciplinary measures and the inability of employees to raise complaints with management result in an unnecessary and unwanted escalation of conflict. Procedures should be known to all employees and managers, and those most closely involved need to be carefully trained in the use and implementation of grievance and disciplinary procedures.

Besides procedures relating to the day-to-day conduct of the labour relationship, there are those which provide for irregular occurrences or eventualities, such as retrenchments or industrial unrest. Job security is an accepted condition of employment. Where such job security is threatened, employees or their representatives need to be informed and involved. Management is under an obligation to search for alternatives before instituting a retrenchment programme and, where retrenchment becomes inevitable, to agree on the criteria to be adopted in selecting retrenchees. Furthermore, some form of compensation, over and above the normal notice pay, ought to be offered. The possibility of industrial action by employees is always present, irrespective of the relationship between an employer and his employees. Therefore management needs to have an overall contingency programme which will provide for concerted, coordinated action, and for the necessary negotiation with employee representatives. Management's aim will be to continue operations if possible but, where this possibility does not exist, to ensure that calm and rationality prevails. Unions, too, may establish their own strike action or lockout contingency plans.

We live in an era of continual change and increasing complexity. Consequently, the relationship and the organisation should never be static but should be continually evolving. It is the task of the personnel/industrial relations manager to see that this does happen.

THE LABOUR RELATIONSHIP AT COMPANY LEVEL

Labour relationships are not established only when employees organise themselves into a collective and demand to bargain with the employer. The labour relationship exists as soon as one person is employed by another. Even in an individual employment relationship, a number of factors will regulate and influence the conduct of both parties. In any undertaking, therefore, notwithstanding its size or the degree of unionisation, sound labour relations practices have to be established. Labour relations begin at the workplace and collective bargaining with unions is merely the outward manifestation of the internal relationship. Employees, although each may stand in an individual relationship to the employer, also form a collective and their individual as well as their collective interests have to be taken into account. Moreover, any action or event at the workplace will affect the labour relationship. Thus there is a need for continual care and the establishment of procedures to avoid discongruent action and to ensure equitable treatment.

LABOUR RELATIONS AS A TOTAL MANAGEMENT FUNCTION

Just as labour relations cannot be confined to collective bargaining with unions, so the labour relations function — and, for that matter, the non-administrative content of personnel management — is not the function solely of the industrial relations or personnel department. Appointees in these departments perform (besides the administrative and planning functions) merely the role of advisers, facilitators and coordinators because, in the final analysis, it is the function of line management to manage, motivate and satisfy those who work under them. Every manager is a 'people' manager and, therefore, also an industrial relations or personnel manager. For this reason the success of an industrial relations or personnel manager may be measured by the degree to which he makes himself redundant; that is, the extent to which the policies, structures, systems and processes instituted and the advice given by him allow other managers, right to supervisory level, to manage their people on their own.

In the light of the above it is obvious that the labour relations function cannot be viewed in isolation; that the policies, structures, systems and processes implemented have to be part of a total management strategy and have to be established in consultation and conjunction with other members of management as well as with consideration of, and representation from, the employees in the undertaking.

THE OBJECTIVES OF MANAGEMENT IN LABOUR RELATIONS

It has been stated above that the management of people is the responsibility of all those appointed in a line function. It follows that all managers, including the top management team, should establish objectives related to the successful management of people in the organisation and to the facilitation and improvement of work relationships. Consequently, no Mission Statement is complete if it does not contain some mention of the employees in the organisation and of the attitude of management towards the work relationship. This sets the framework for strategic planning as regards this facet of the organisation and for individual managers, including the industrial relations appointee, to establish their own objectives and strategies relating to the treatment of employees and the development of the labour relationship. Thus, if the mission statement of the organisation contains a clause to the effect that the organisation is committed to the recognition and development of its employees and to the establishment of a sound working relationship, all managers, within their own spheres of influence, need to decide how best they will give effect to this mission in practice.

Unfortunately, many (or most) managers usually see their objectives as centring only in such matters as profit maximisation, increased productivity and the maintenance of flexibility and control. They would, if they could, have no labour relations objectives at all. However, the growth of employee awareness and action, as well as a new emphasis on the importance of effective human resource utilisation, has led to the realisation (albeit reluctant) that, without the consideration of employees, the other objectives of management may not be achieved. The result is an acceptance of the fact that business objectives have to be integrated with labour relations objectives, and that often business objectives such as profit maximisation may have to be adapted in the face of labour relations realities.

Achieving management consensus on labour relations objectives is not always an easy task. As Anthony explains, there are managers who react irrationally to the realisation that their prerogatives might be limited. Some develop a fixation reaction, either continuing as they did before or adopting a reactionary attitude towards employees. Their individual labour relations objectives become the maintenance of their managerial prerogative and a resistance to any consideration of employee interests. The rational reaction would be to search for means of achieving maximum efficiency within the framework of both business and employee needs. Anthony confirms that a rational reaction would lead to the formulation of one or all of the following objectives.

- To achieve synthesis — that is, to persuade employees that the goals of management and workers are coincidental and that they should work together for the common good
- To achieve cooperation by such methods as attitudinal restructuring, integrative bargaining, improved communication and leadership, joint consultation and the establishment of committees
- To accommodate conflict in a process of tough, but fair, bargaining

It is generally accepted that the first objective, because it ignores the conflict of interests, may have only limited effectiveness and that a combination of the three is the most appropriate.

The type of labour relations objectives established will depend on the attitudes, personalities, values and perceptions of top management and other managerial staff, the present and predicted business environment, the extent to which achievement of these objectives will affect business objectives, the proportion of labour costs to total costs, the nature of the employee body and the nature of representation desired. Because these factors vary from one organisation to another, objectives will differ from company to company.

ESTABLISHMENT OF A LABOUR RELATIONS POLICY

The Need for a Policy

Any company, whether unionised or not, needs to establish a general policy to reflect its objectives in labour relations and in the light of which it will conduct its relationship with its employees. Salamon describes the labour relations policy as a 'management statement issued for the guidance of management'. He explains that it brings consistency in standards and ensures equitable conduct. A labour relations policy, preferably in the form of a written document, clarifies management's industrial relations objectives, established in the light of the overall objectives of the company, confirms the relationship with and interest in employees, indicates how this relationship can be maintained and informs of the practices by which this can be effected. Thus it serves as a framework for managerial behaviour towards employees, results in the establishment of systems and procedures, and is used as a guideline when decisions have to be reached. Also, even in a company which is not yet unionised, it establishes the parameters for the company's treatment of a union.

Unfortunately, many industrial relations policies, although fine sounding, are vague to the point of being meaningless. Because they are regarded by some managers as a public relations exercise, they stress 'goodness' of objectives rather than efficiency and effectiveness. Furthermore, they may serve as a cover-up for the real objectives of management or as an excuse for management's lack of verbalised industrial relations objectives. Only when these objectives have been clarified, with the necessary reference to the company's overall objectives, can an effective industrial relations policy be established.

Establishment of an Effective Policy

A labour relations policy is usually established in a number of stages. In the first stage labour relations objectives are, after consultation with all parties and consideration of all circumstances, generally determined. Thereafter the labour relations objectives are correlated with business objectives to ensure that they do not impede the achievement of overall objectives and are compatible with other systems in the organisation. Once consensus has been achieved, an overall labour relations policy can be formulated.

The next step is to decide by which methods these objectives may best be achieved. This would necessitate a thorough scanning of the environment, consideration of employee representational needs and of structures and procedures generally adopted. It may also entail consultation with representative unions or the employee body, since their non-acceptance of labour relations structures and procedures would render the policy meaningless. Again, consensus has to be achieved among managerial representatives and, this having been done, a detailed final policy may be established. According to Salamon, an effective industrial relations policy will contain the following.

- *'Managerial principles relating, for example, to management's right to manage its business and make operational decisions; its intention not to negotiate under duress or to make concessions without a corresponding gesture from trade unions and its right to communicate directly with its employees on any matter*
- *The relationship between management and employees, including the recognition of the value of employees as an asset of the organisation; their right to represent grievances to management and to join trade unions who may act on their behalf; the basis on which trade unions are to be recognised for collective bargaining and representing their members' interests; and management's desire to develop a climate of mutual acceptance, trust and cooperation within the organisation*
- *The determination of terms and conditions of employment through appropriate, recognised institutions of joint consultation and/or bargaining; the achievement of stable or reducing costs through increased productivity; the maintenance of a fair and equitable payment system which rewards both the value of the job to the organisation and the efficiency of the individual; and the intention to be bound by agreements reached within any recognised collective bargaining machinery*
- *The approach to employment to be adopted in ensuring that the organisation has an adequate level of trained and experienced manpower for its needs consistent with maintaining security of employment for the individual employees (recruitment, training, motivation, promotion and termination of employees)*
- *The role of procedures in resolving problems speedily and in a mutually acceptable manner, in contributing to employee participation and joint decisionmaking and the extent to which third party processes of conciliation and arbitration may be used'*

In short, the labour relations/human resource policy will reveal management's attitude towards employees and will state how management will treat employees and develop the labour relationship.

Finally, it is important to bear in mind that the mere establishment of a labour relations policy is an exercise in futility. The sections which, under prevailing circumstances, are necessary to maintain sound labour relations should be implemented, continually monitored and amended if necessary. The implementation of policy entails the transference of principles into actual practice by, for example, establishing equitable wage and salary scales, job enrichment programmes, communication structures, grievance and disciplinary procedures and organisational development programmes or, if a union becomes representative, engaging in collective bargaining. Different circumstances may warrant the implementation of certain facets of the policy. A labour relations policy is not intended only to cater for current circumstances, but should also serve as a guideline for future behaviour.

THE ROLE OF THE LABOUR RELATIONS MANAGER

If it is the function of every manager to look after his own people and his relationship with them, what then is the role and function of the labour relations manager?

In the first place it should be mentioned that, except in larger organisations, labour relations is usually not a separate function, divorced from the rest of the personnel/human resource function. In most cases it is integrated in the same department, and often in the same job. While the 'personnel' aspect of the job may be divided into personnel administration (record-keeping and wage administration) on the one hand and, on the other, maintenance and development functions such as recruitment, selection, interviewing, job grading, performance appraisal and training, the labour relations aspect is more global. It rests heavily on the successful implementation of the already mentioned personnel aspects, but also engages in negotiation and reformulation of these aspects to meet changing needs. Furthermore, it generally oversees the facilitation and development of the work relationship within the organisation, dealing both with internal stakeholders and with those representing them from the outside, such as unions and community organisations.

The title of Labour Relations (or Personnel) *Manager* is in some respects a misnomer. Although the appointee has the responsibility of overseeing the effective utilisation and treatment of employees and of ensuring harmonious relationships and although (especially in the planning and strategic aspects) his is a management function, he does not *manage* the people of the organisation as such — except, of course, those in his own department. Perhaps the word 'Consultant', now being used by some organisations, would be a preferable designation. Using the title 'Manager' immediately places the labour relations or personnel appointee in a particular camp — as representing the interests of management (and, therefore, the employer) against those of the employees. In fact he should essentially act as middleman between management and employees or their representatives. It could even be argued that the use of the title 'Manager', and the consequent perceptions of employees as regards this position, have hitherto led to the failure of personnel or labour relations managers in fulfilling their most essential tasks: to promote effectively the interests of both employees and the organisation, to facilitate the relationship between various parties and to ensure that change, where required, occurs. Because they are viewed as belonging to the employer camp, they fail to achieve the necessary credibility with all stakeholders in the organisation. Without credibility and trust, facilitation and change become problematic.

It follows that, if a labour relations or personnel appointee is to perform his function effectively, he needs to be a person of great integrity. His value system should be dictated not by the sectarian interests of either the employer, individual managers or employees but by his own beliefs and by his professional and ethical code. In the light of this, he negotiates with all parties in order to bring them closer together. When dealing with any one party he will widen the framework of the discussion by bringing also the perspectives of other stakeholders. Thus, when he finds managers pursuing only the interests of the employer, he will remind them of the interests and perspectives of the other parties in the organisation. Similarly, in his dealings with employees and unions, he will bring the perspectives of management to the fore.

Since conflict underlies the relationship within an adversarial system, the labour relations specialist should himself be an expert at handling such conflict and should train others to do the same. However, he should at the same time be establishing processes and structures aimed at minimising conflict and promoting cooperation and integration. His task is to train and advise his fellow managers (and, if possible, also employees and their representatives) in the use of such procedures and in the implementation of sound and fair practices and interactions. Not only should he forestall problems and crises but, when these do occur, he should also be on hand to guide the other parties to a successful resolution.

As can be seen from the above, the principal roles of the labour relations specialist are those of troubleshooter, facilitator, negotiator, trainer, educator and adviser. His is essentially a staff function, and it is not appropriate to place him in the forefront of substantive negotiations with the union or, for example, to require him to chair disciplinary hearings or to handle problem employees (except in a counselling function). Where other persons in the organisation lack the expertise to perform these functions, it may sometimes be necessary for the industrial relations specialist to do so; but this should be only a temporary role, as his purpose should be to equip others with the necessary expertise so that, in time, he may stand back and adopt the wider perspective of facilitator, counsellor and adviser — to all stakeholders.

The role of the industrial relations expert gains its greatest import in the strategic sphere. He is, in essence, the eyes and ears of the organisation and, therefore, the most important quality is that of awareness. The incumbent will continually monitor the climate, both internal and external. He must know what is happening within all spheres of the organisation and, at the same time, monitor all external developments which can impact on the workplace and on the work relationship. In terms of the knowledge gained he will warn, plan and strategise with the purpose of preparing all stakeholders, avoiding imminent pitfalls and bringing about the necessary changes.

This last aspect is of the utmost importance. In a world in which change has become inevitable, the management of change is one of the primary functions of the industrial relations manager. It is his duty to initiate organisational developments and, in particular, to develop the employer–employee relationship in new and different directions.

THE EFFECT OF THE BASIC PERSONNEL FUNCTION ON LABOUR RELATIONS

Integration with the Labour Relations Function

The labour relations function is integrated with the personnel function and the achievement of a healthy labour relationship within a company will greatly depend on the manner in which the total personnel function is executed. If the personnel function is concerned mainly with shuffling paper and filling in forms, the labour relationship is certain to suffer, for it is the task of personnel management to look after employees, to integrate them into the company and provide them with the opportunity to grow. It has been stated that managers should learn to take care of their own subordinates. Yet line managers also have other duties and do not have the overall perspective of the employee collective which personnel managers should have. It is to the personnel manager that the line manager will turn if he needs to check records or wishes to gain more information about a particular employee, or if he finds that certain employees need growth opportunities. If the necessary information and advice is not forthcoming, the line manager may be unable to care for his employees in the proper manner. Dissatisfaction grows, and labour problems result.

Recruitment and Interviewing

The labour relationship commences when the prospective employee is recruited by the personnel department. Through the interviewer the employee formulates his first image of the company. If this image is negative, he may still take the job, but the negativism will remain and be reflected in his work and his attitude to management. Alternatively, an interviewer could leave incumbents with un-realistic expectations, resulting in future dissatisfaction and, eventually, greater conflict between workers and management. The method of recruitment and selection will also determine the calibre of the workforce and the suitability of an incumbent for the job in hand. This is becoming increasingly important, since it is now accepted that it is the responsibility of the company to find the right person for the job. This responsibility cannot be taken lightly as it will be very difficult, after a period of time has elapsed, to claim that the incumbent is unsuitable for the position and, consequently, to dismiss him. The onus will then be on the employer to do everything possible to render the incumbent more suitable.

Not only does the employer have this onus but he will also, in terms of the Labour Relations Act of 1995, have to prove that he appointed the most suitable person for the job in terms of measurable criteria. This is because the new definition of an unfair labour practice provides that, where discrimination is alleged, an applicant for a position may also be regarded as an employee and may, therefore, allege that he was discriminated against during the selection process. The burden of proof against this allegation will then rest on the employer. Another aspect to consider is that a candidate might possess the proper qualifications, but the interviewer will need to decide whether he would be able to work with others in the department to which he will be assigned. The greater the ability of the personnel department to match incumbents with people as well as jobs, the less will be the likelihood that conflict will arise. The personnel department, therefore, establishes and sets the basis for the relationship.

Induction, Performance Appraisal and Job Enrichment

Once an incumbent commences employment, it is the responsibility of the personnel department to ensure that he becomes integrated into the organisation. Improper induction results in the estrangement of the employee, a situation from which it may be difficult to rescue him in the future. The employee needs to become acquainted with the entire undertaking, not merely his own department. He should be informed of the company policy, its manner of operation and also its rules and procedures. At the same time the personnel function should oversee his induction into his job, taking care that the necessary on-the-job training is conducted. The personnel department's duty does not, however, end there. The progress of the new incumbent should be monitored, as should that of all employees. This may be achieved by performance appraisal, but the purpose of monitoring is not only to measure the employee's performance or his suitability for the job. The objective should also be to determine whether the company and the job suit the employee. Performance appraisal is a communication process. Without feedback from management and employee, performance appraisals will be of little value. Where performance appraisal enhances communication, it results in corrective behaviour on both sides and leads to job enrichment and job satisfaction. It will improve the labour relationship, as might other schemes for job enrichment which, again, should emanate from the personnel department. These could extend to career planning as well as education and training initiatives, both of which are increasingly being placed on union agendas in their negotiations with management.

Wages and Salaries

Wages and salaries and the methods used to establish differentials in this sphere are a continuing source of conflict between employees and management. All too often, personnel managers advise the use of standard wage scales. These may appear impressive on paper, but they could lead to much disgruntlement in practice. A wage structure should be indigenous to the company. While standard scales may be used, their rationale should be carefully studied and it should underscore the company's labour relations policy and objectives. Reasons for differentials should not only be acceptable, but also explicable. Structures should be sufficiently flexible to allow for all eventualities and for the necessary mobility, otherwise dissatisfaction and conflicts are certain to result. Nowadays, rigid job evaluation and compensation systems are becoming less popular and more progressive companies may in future tend to pay the man rather than the job. This is already evidenced in the demand for multiskilling and for broadbanding evaluation techniques which allow for far greater flexibility within job grades.

Even the method of payment and defaults in the payment process may lead to unnecessary disruption. The date of payment most suitable to the employer and to the employees should be considered and unnecessary mistakes or delays avoided. Erroneous or unexplained deductions have been known, in volatile situations, to lead to strike action.

Training

Training — although it may be undertaken in various instances and by different departments — is, overall, the responsibility of the personnel department. Effective training results in more productive workers and in job and personal satisfaction, job enrichment, opportunity for growth and a feeling among employees that the company is interested in their advancement. Training programmes should be geared to the needs of employees, as well as those of the company. A personnel department which cares for employees will assess the needs and capabilities of workers and will institute training programmes geared to this assessment. Training will, moreover, extend to management and managing director level, especially if such training is concerned with information giving, attitudinal structuring and the promotion of stable labour relationships.

Labour Turnover and Absenteeism

One personnel function which is often neglected — or, if not neglected, then underrated — is the monitoring of absenteeism and labour turnover. In labour relations this practice is most important, since high turnover and absence rates are more often than not indicative of poor management or conflicts within the relationship. Also, accurate labour turnover figures lead to better manpower planning and to the avoidance of intermittent retrenchments. It is not sufficient merely to monitor turnover and rates of absence. The reasons for their occurrence have to be established and the problems from which they arise need to be resolved. In this context the exit interview or follow-up questionnaire plays an important role.

Personal, Social and Financial Aspects

Employee care embraces attention to the personal, social and financial problems of individual workers. While good line managers may have established a relationship of confidence with their subordinates, conducive to the raising of problems, it is the function of personnel management to concern itself with the general welfare of employees. Problems at home or in the community, as well as financial troubles, are transferred to the working environment and impact negatively upon it. The personnel department will ensure that welfare schemes are adequate and will establish programmes to meet the most pressing needs of the employee body. These may include education schemes or housing benefits. As the holder of confidential information, the personnel department will also cater for the needs of individual employees. The more the organisation is seen to care for its employees, the greater the opportunity for cooperation rather than conflict.

Communication and Information

Overall, the personnel department facilitates the conduct of the labour relationship by the introduction of effective communication structures and systems. The dissemination of general information is usually a personnel function, as is the establishment of communication bodies, practices and procedures.

Despite the statements to the contrary at the commencement of this chapter, it would appear that the personnel and labour relations functions can never become completely redundant. Individual managers can and should learn the art of personnel and industrial relations management and to this extent personnel and labour relations functions do become redundant, but the overall integration of people within the organisation remains the function of the personnel department.

THE ROLE OF COMMUNICATION IN THE LABOUR RELATIONSHIP

The Importance of Communication

To say that an organisation cannot function without communication has become platitudinal. The truth of the statement is obvious. No relationship can be conducted without communication of one kind or another. However, it is not the fact of communication, but the effectiveness of such communication which is of importance in any relationship; thus also in the labour relationship. It is estimated that the average person — and, therefore, the average manager — spends four fifths of his working life communicating. A manager may well spend most of his working day either receiving communication or communicating information to others, but no fraction of that effort may have contributed to the establishment of a healthier labour relationship. In fact, the major part of the communication process may have had the opposite effect. Thus, when we speak of communication as it relates to the labour relationship, we speak not only of the furnishing of information, which is certainly important, but mostly of the creation of greater understanding between the parties, leading to consideration for the position of the other party. This necessitates a two-way communication process, often not effected in organisations.

A common fallacy among those who have become aware of the importance of communication is to attribute all problems and conflicts arising at the workplace to ineffective communication. The corollary to this is the belief that more effective communication is a panacea for all problems experienced in the labour relationship. These persons give the assurance that, if effective communication channels are established, most problems will disappear. Unfortunately, many of the problems experienced at the workplace are more deeply rooted. They arise from differing attitudes and perceptions, from the organisational structure and the basic conflict of interests and goals between management and employees. Better communication will not solve these problems, but it might alleviate them to some extent. Also, if communication is ineffective or absent, these problems will intensify. Communication is the oil which lubricates the organisational machinery but, if parts of the machine are defective, no amount of lubrication will ensure that it functions properly.

Definition of Communication

Communication is described by Luthans as 'the flow of material information, perceptions and understandings between individuals and between different groups'. It is a means of exchanging behaviours, perceptions and values, of getting others to behave and to feel differently and of creating understanding. It remains the sole method by which people interact and influence one another. Communication can be verbal or non-verbal, written or oral. A parent who sets an example to a child is communicating values and behaviours. A toddler looking at a picture book is receiving communication. It is an ongoing process which, in modern life, may be conducted through the most ordinary or the most technologically sophisticated channels.

The Communication Process

Simplistically described, communication takes place between a communicator (sender or transmitter) on the one hand and a listener/reader/observer (receiver) on the other. The message is transmitted from the sender, who encodes the message in whatever form he finds most suitable, to the receiver, who decodes it and reacts accordingly. Here the first problem arises, since the sender may not encode the message in a form which the receiver is able to decode. He may use words which are not known to the receiver, signals which the latter cannot interpret or show a picture which to him carries meaning, but which is meaningless to the receiver. Translated to the conduct of the labour relationship, these **semantic** and **cognitive** barriers have important implications. A manager who speaks of percentage increases to employees who do not know the concept, or of productivity margins to a shop steward unacquainted with business terminology, is not communicating or is inculcating misconceptions. Thus the sender needs to ascertain that the receiver knows the code or, if he does not, has to educate the receiver towards understanding beforehand. Furthermore, the sender will need to check that the receiver has understood the message correctly. This he can do by obtaining **feedback.** While communicating, he may observe

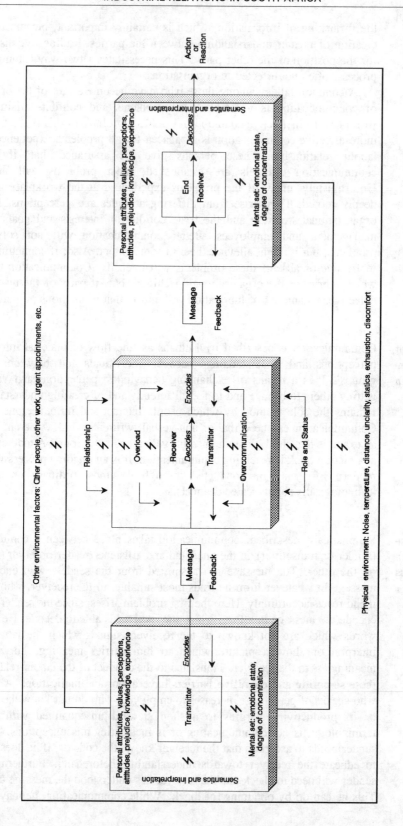

Figure 17: THE COMMUNICATION PROCESS

the reactions of the receiver or, once the message has been transmitted, he may require an answer, action or reaction of some kind.

The process becomes more complicated within a communication chain, since each receiver along the line will have to decode the message and encode it for the next receiver. The possibilities for misunderstandings and **distortions** multiply. In labour relations problems are caused by the fact that, very often, communication between employer and employee takes place through intermediaries, in the form of the union representative, the shop steward, the workers' committee member or a line manager. Direct communication would be preferable but this may not be possible, since an attempt at communicating directly with employees may be viewed as subversion of the authority of the intermediaries concerned. In these cases choosing the most suitable intermediaries — that is, **routing** the message properly and ensuring effective feedback from intermediaries and eventual receivers — will at least provide some proof that the message has been correctly transmitted and received.

In effect, perfect communication is rarely possible. Not only are the problems already discussed always present, but there are also numerous other barriers to effective communication. Both sender and receiver enter the communication situation with a certain **mental set** and within the framework of their own **values, perceptions, experience, knowledge, attributes** and **attitudes**. All of these will affect the manner in which the sender transmits the message and the manner in which the other party receives it. A sender may be impatient, may regard the receiver with disdain or may not himself have understood the content of the communication. Furthermore, he will **filter** that part of the message which is important to him, which coincides with his own values and perceptions and experience, and he will encode the message in the form most familiar to him. The receiver, in turn, may be concentrating on another matter, may not be a good listener in general or may already have prejudged the message or the sender. He, too, will filter the message and select what is most important to him. The blocks which personal attributes, attitudes and mental set and the filtering process can place in the way of effective communication are too numerous for detailed description.

The **relationship** between sender and receiver will further impact on the effectiveness of communication. Persons who are very close are able to communicate with looks and gestures, while strangers need to verbalise communication. A relationship of animosity and suspicion easily results in distorted communication. Equally, **differences in status** will affect communication. A 'boss' communicates differently with an employee and the latter receives him in a different way than if each were communicating with an 'equal'. When communicating with an equal, the boss may find it necessary to give explanations, whereas he wrongly perceives that this is not necessary when speaking to a subordinate. The latter may, in his turn, resent the authority of the superior or, alternatively, overrate the intelligence and capabilities of the sender. This also raises the question of **credibility**. In all communication, but particularly in management–employee communication, credibility is of the utmost importance. Messages from those who do not possess credibility are either ignored or wrongly received. Labour relationships can, particularly in times of crisis, be destroyed by a lack of credibility on the part of the transmitter. Furthermore, if the relationship itself does not have a sound basis, communication may prove ineffective.

Besides semantic, personal and relationship factors, there are also **physical barriers** to communication. Noise, temperature, discomfort, distance and the method of communication may all provide interference, as may the presence of other persons, other communication processes, urgent work waiting to be done or an urgent appointment which has to be kept. Added to the physical factors is the problem that some individuals are inclined to **overcommunicate**. They engage in too much detail, thereby losing the gist of the communication, or they **overload** the content of communication. The human mind is capable of absorbing only a certain amount of information at a time. The average person can concentrate fully for a maximum of twenty minutes. Too much information or communication over too long a period without a break defeats the original purpose. The **timing** of communication is also important. Asking a father for pocket money while he is showering is bound to have an adverse effect.

Communication is an extremely complicated, **transactional process**, subject to a great deal of **interference, filtering** and **distortion**. It is a two-way process and, unless **feedback** occurs, its effectiveness cannot be measured. Even while communication occurs, the receiver may be sending back to the sender certain information which makes the latter change this communication. The total environment as well as the method used and the personal attributes, feelings and experiences of the transmitter or transmitters and receiver or receivers will impact on the communication process. This is graphically illustrated in Figure 17.

Methods of Improving Communication

In the case of the transmitter, the following basic guidelines may be implemented as methods of improving communication.

- **Adjustment to the world of the receiver** — The communicator needs, as far as possible, to be aware of the capabilities, personal attributes, perceptions, values, prejudices and experience of the receiver and to fashion his communication accordingly. The communication should be such that it interests the receiver, or else he may not listen. Also, most individuals prefer active participation in the communication process to passive absorption of information. Thus workshops, discussions and role plays are often more effective than written or verbal information.

- **Creating the correct mental set** — A pastor obliged to bring a tragic message to a family will, by his looks, words and demeanour, prepare his listeners for the news they are to receive. Any listener must be equally prepared for the message to be transmitted, in order that he may concentrate on its content, absorb the most important aspects and react in the desired manner.

- **Follow-up and reinforcement** — Feedback is vital to the communication process, since without it the greatest misconceptions and misunderstandings between individuals may arise. Feedback in the form of a positive answer to the question as to whether a message has been understood is usually not sufficient. All too often receivers are embarrassed to admit that they have not understood the message. Alternatively, they may be impatient and will give a positive answer merely to end the communication process. Other methods of checking on the receiver's understanding have to be devised. Once feedback has been obtained, it might be found that further communication is necessary. The sender follows up with more information and thereby reinforces the original message.

- **Utilisation of different forms of communication** — The method of transmission used should take cognizance of the receiver and of the situation in hand. Storming into a superior's office with an angry complaint may be less effective than a well reasoned, sober statement of the problem in writing. Equally, a written message to a semi-literate person is of little use. Verbal communication may be backed up with a written statement, image or picture. It is nowadays accepted that reception is best when the message is both seen and heard; hence the increased use of audiovisual communication methods.

- **Using direct communication** whenever this is possible and feasible — While in certain situations the position may be such that direct communication is not feasible, it is preferable in most instances. Direct, face-to-face communication places the sender in a closer relationship with the receiver. He is able to judge the receiver's reactions and to obtain instant feedback, in the light of which he may adapt his message or reinforce it. In this respect eye contact is also of importance.

- **Using alternative channels of communication** – Where direct communication is not possible, the channels (that is, the intermediaries or intermediary devices through which the message is transmitted) should be carefully selected. Different channels may be used for the same message, or a second channel may be selected if the first proves ineffective.

- **Regulating the flow of information** — Communication should be such that the important points are highlighted and that only the details necessary to substantiate the main facts are given. Where a great deal of information has to be supplied, it is preferable that it be broken down into different parts to prevent overloading the receiver. However, care should be exercised that the purpose or general content of the information is supplied initially, so that the receiver has some concept of the whole before the parts are fed to him.

- **Avoiding problems of size** — The fewer receivers there are, the greater will be the opportunity for effective communication and purposeful feedback. Too large an audience leads to a dilution of communication by generalisation and increases the possibility of interference.

- **Establishing credibility and trust** – Both credibility and trust enhance communication. Where these are absent, it is preferable to channel communication through persons who are respected and trusted by the receiver.

- **Awareness of barriers** – A communicator who is generally aware of the barriers to communication will attempt to eliminate or avoid as many of these as possible. It needs specifically to be borne in mind that the receivers of communication will not accept any message which conflicts with their own values and beliefs or, at best, will distort or filter the message to fit into their own belief and value systems.

As far as the receiver is concerned, the following techniques apply.

- **Adjustment to the world of the sender** — It is not only the sender who needs to be aware of the personal attributes, attitudes and experience of the receiver. On his part the receiver, too, should interpret the message in the context of the general characteristics of the transmitter; in short, he should attempt to understand the message from the transmitter's point of view.
- **Creating the correct mental set** — The receiver himself needs to ensure that he is in the correct frame of mind to receive the message. The student who enters a classroom engaged in plans for the approaching weekend has not created the correct mental set. Equally, the manager who is planning a business deal is not in a frame of mind conducive to the reception of an employee grievance.
- **Cultivating the art of listening** — One of the greatest problems in communication is the fact that people do not listen. They hear, but they have listened only partly or not at all. Listening requires concentration on the message being transmitted by the communicator. Many individuals who appear to be listening are either wrapped in other thoughts, fantasising or already preparing their responses. Someone who is intent on receiving meaningful communication will train himself to listen attentively and perceptively.
- **Feedback and active contribution** — By providing feedback, the receiver not only assists the communicator but also ensures that he himself has understood the message correctly. Active participation by the receiver stimulates the communicator to enlarge on the content of his communication, thereby improving understanding.

The guidelines are those commonly mentioned as contributing towards more effective communication. They are firstly, interactive; secondly, they should be regarded as pointers, since communication is such a complex art. There are many who have studied the art of communication, but who are still unable to communicate. Equally, an organisation might introduce sophisticated communication systems, yet no real communication between employer and employee occurs. The dynamics and most vital ingredients of communication are not easily transferred into concrete explanations. In the labour relationship in particular, the relationship itself and the process of communication are so enmeshed and interdependent that a separation of the two is usually not possible. Without effective communication the relationship will falter; yet, if the relationship itself is shaky or if suspicion and animosity prevail, the most intensive communications may prove to no avail.

The Purpose of Organisational Communication

Communication takes place within organisations for various reasons. Communication processes are usually initiated to give instructions, to supply information, to obtain permission, to question, to plan and to control, but they should also be used to hear grievances, complaints and demands. More importantly, communication is the means by which all individuals involved in an organisation interact. The communication which occurs in organisations is more often than not of a formal nature; yet informal channels of communication may often prove to be invaluable.

The Effect of Organisational Structure on Communication

The type of communication which occurs within an organisation and the effectiveness of such communication will greatly depend on the manner in which the organisation is structured. The strict, hierarchical organisational design still prevalent in numerous organisations lends itself mainly to command and request communication, filtered through narrowly structured channels. In such a structure a line manager or employee will not communicate on organisational matters with another manager or employee, except through his superior. The latter will, in turn, feed the communication to his superior, a process which continues until a common point is reached from which the communication is filtered downwards to the eventual receiver. In these circumstances communication and action are inevitably delayed and the danger exists that the message becomes distorted while passing through the various intermediaries. As far as employees are concerned, it may lead to lack of involvement and to a sense of futility. The first remedy to this situation is to provide what Fayol calls 'gangplanks' whereby, at the least, lateral communication between various managers and employees can be initiated.

In recent years organisational structures have flattened, although they are still basically hierarchical in nature. 'Gangplanking' is commonplace and management meetings ensure that continued interaction takes place. Yet, where the lower levels of the organisation are concerned, the hierarchial channels remain. This may be necessary in order to maintain the authority structure, but communication could be made more effective if more channels were opened, as occurs in the more democratic organisational design. The authority structures need not necessarily be eliminated, but provision needs to be made for shortcuts and for greater interaction.

An additional problem with the classic organisational design was that it provided mainly for management-initiated communication. Employee-initiated communication was limited to requests for permission. With increasing demands that employees participate actively in the organisation, various channels for upward communication were opened. Some, such as grievance procedures, follow the hierarchical route; others, like hotlines, are more direct. These and representational bodies have contributed to interactive communication, but the formal nature of some procedures, although unavoidable, still has an inhibiting effect.

Types of Organisational Communication

The forms of organisational communication range from written documents, letters, brochures, journals, notices and memoranda to meetings, interviews, training sessions, audiovisual programmes, briefing groups, green areas, team sessions, 'think tanks', annual get-togethers, grievance and disciplinary procedures and interpersonal conversations. Organisational communication may be of a horizontal or a vertical nature. Finally, it may be formal or informal. Formal communication has the value that it is more reliable, can be substantiated, could ensure feedback and maintains the authority structure. However, particularly if it is management initiated, formal communication may be negatively received. By contrast, informal communication is faster, may create a more favourable climate and be met with a more favourable reception, but it could lead to inaccuracy or false rumours and is difficult to control. Thus formal communication remains the preferred method, but informal communication is used to substantiate and supplement formal communication channels.

Employer–Employee Communication

Industrial relations concerns itself with those communication processes which lead to interaction between employees and management. While most managers are accustomed to communicating with employees in order to issue instructions or to provide functional information and while workers may communicate with management to gain permission for certain activities, both parties have until recently remained relatively inexperienced at interactive communication. Where such communication did occur, it was conducted through an outside intermediary in the form of the trade union, and not directly with employees themselves.

The word 'interactive' is indicative of a **sharing** of information, experiences, thoughts, ideas, feelings, perceptions and problems. In the context of the labour relationship this sharing takes place with the purpose of improving the relationship, by promoting knowledge of the organisation and of the other party and mutual understanding. The communication which occurs may be employer-initiated, may stem from the employee or may take the form of joint consultation, the style being adapted to the needs of the parties, the requirements of the organisation and the circumstances in which the communication occurs.

One of the most common methods of interaction between management and employees is that which occurs during negotiations or consultations with shop stewards or workers' committees, but there are numerous other methods by which interactive communication can be promoted. These include:

- Management-initiated information on the organisation, working conditions, employee prospects, organisational changes, immediate and future plans — This information may be supplied in writing, through letters, bulletins, journals, memoranda, etc.; or orally during the conduct of general meetings, briefing groups, induction or training sessions.
- Structures such as work groups and quality circles
- Management explanations of behaviours — for example, when disciplining employees
- Employee-initiated grievances, which are channelled through the grievance procedure

- Systems encouraging employee suggestions and initiatives, such as suggestion boxes and hotlines
- Systems aimed at gauging employee perspectives, such as questionnaires, the adoption of an 'open door' policy or the appointment of an ombudsman
- Committees other than shop steward or workers' committees, such as health and safety or productivity committees
- Company functions and sporting or other activities, aimed at promoting informal communication

The methods mentioned are not mutually exclusive. All or some could be used either simultaneously or on different occasions, to achieve optimal interaction.

What Employees Want to Know and How to Transmit Information

There are organisations where a great deal of communication is initiated but where much of that communication does not interest or is not relevant to employees. Manning, in his book *Communicating for Change*, lists in the following order the subjects which management should communicate.

1. Organisational plans for the future
2. Job advancement opportunities
3. Job-related 'how-to' information
4. Productivity improvement
5. Personnel policies and practices
6. How we're doing versus the competition
7. How jobs fit into the organisation
8. How external events affect a job
9. How profits are used
10. Financial results
11. Advertising and promotional plans
12. Operations outside departments and divisions
13. Organisational stands on current issues
14. Personnel changes and promotions
15. Organisational community involvement
16. Human interest stories about other employees
17. Personal news such as birthdays and anniversaries

While 79,8 percent of employees surveyed wished to know more about organisational plans and 72,5 percent wanted information on job advancement opportunities, only 16 percent were interested in personal news and 21,6 percent in human interest stories. Manning warns that 'to communicate is to share meaning' and that 'hard facts about your organisation sharpen meaning'. It is interesting to note also that, in terms of effectiveness of communication, one-to-one meetings rate highest, followed by small group meetings, large group meetings, telephone conversations, personal notes or letters, impersonal notes and then printed messages such as circulars, newsletters and posters.

ILO
Recommen-
dation
Concerning
Communica-
tion within
the Under
taking

That the International Labour Organisation views communication as important for the promotion of sound labour relations is evidenced by the fact that it was regarded as necessary to issue Recommendation No. 129 of 1967 on this subject. The Recommendation is based on the premise that it is in 'the common interest' of employers and employees to '... recognise the importance of a climate of mutual understanding and confidence within undertakings that is favourable both to the efficiency of the undertaking and to the aspirations of the workers'. The recommendation goes on to state that '... this should be promoted by the rapid dissemination and exchange of information, as complete and objective as possible, relating to the various aspects of the life of the undertaking and to the social conditions of the workers' and to recommend that '... management should, after consultation with workers' representatives, adopt an effective policy of communication with the workers and their representatives'. It is important that the ILO stresses the fact that workers should be consulted before communication structures are established. Not all forms of employer–employee communication would require reference to the employee body, but those aimed at greater cooperation certainly would.

Having stated the initial premises and conditions, the recommendation goes on to provide guidelines for an effective communication policy. These include the following.

- The policy should ensure that '... information is given and that consultation takes place between the parties concerned before decisions on matters of major interest are taken by management', but this with the qualification that information and consultation extend only '... so far as disclosure of information will not cause damage to either party'.
- The method of communication should '... in no way derogate from the freedom of association; they should in no way cause prejudice to the freely chosen workers' representatives or to their organisations', meaning that a demand for communication through a representative body should not be denied even if alternative communication structures have been established. In choosing channels for communication, management should take cognizance of the different functions of supervisors and workers' representatives. (They should not channel communication meant for a representative body through supervisors.)
- Steps should be taken '... to train those concerned in the use of communication methods and to make them, as far as possible, conversant with all the subjects in respect of which communication takes place'. (From this arises the insistence on the training of workers' committee members and shop stewards.)
- Workers' representatives should be afforded the means to communicate information rapidly and completely to the workers concerned.
- A communication system should be designed to ensure 'genuine two-way communication' between 'representatives of management (head of the undertaking, department chief, foreman, etc) and the workers' and between 'the head of the undertaking, the director of personnel or any other representative

of top management and trade union representatives or such other persons as may ... have the task of representing the interests of the workers at the level of the undertaking'. (It is noteworthy that, contrary to common belief, direct communication between management and workers is advised, in addition to commun-ication with a representative body.)

- The communication policy should be '... adapted to the nature of the undertaking concerned, account being taken of its size and of the composition and interests of the work force'.
- The medium of communication and its timing will depend on the circumstances of 'each particular situation, account being taken of national practice'.

The recommendation also specifically states that management should address its communication to representatives or to the workers and that the communication should include, as far as possible, '... all matters of interest to the workers relating to the operation and future prospects of the undertaking and to the present and future situation of the workers, in so far as disclosure of information will not cause damage to the parties'. Specific information which management should give, according to the recommendation, includes information regarding the following.

- General conditions of employment, including engagement, transfer and termination of employees
- Job descriptions and the place of particular jobs within the structure of the undertaking
- Possibilities of training and prospects for advancement within the undertaking
- General working conditions
- Occupational safety and health regulations; instruction for the prevention of accidents and occupational diseases
- Procedures for the examination of grievances as well as the rules and practices governing their operation and the conditions for having recourse to them
- Personnel welfare services
- Social security or social assistance schemes within the undertaking
- The regulation of national security schemes to which the workers are subject
- The general situation of the undertaking and its prospects or plans for its future development
- The explanation of decisions which are likely to affect, directly or indirectly, the situation of workers
- Methods of consultation and discussion and of cooperation between management and its representatives on the one hand and the workers and their representatives on the other

Finally, the communication media recommended include:

- meetings,
- bulletins and personnel policy manuals issued to supervisors,

- mass media, such as house journals and magazines, newsletters, information and induction leaflets, notice boards, annual or financial reports, employee letters, exhibitions, plant visits, films, film strips, radio and television, and
- media allowing workers to submit ideas and suggestions.

Grievance and disciplinary procedures are understood to be included in these but are not specifically mentioned as other ILO recommendations deal with these topics.

A study of the ILO Recommendation provides a sufficiently comprehensive framework for the establishment of interactive communication systems within the undertaking. It is aimed particularly at management, because most communication systems are management-initiated. Also, much of the information to be shared emanates from management and not from the employees. In this respect the role of employees and their representatives is reactive. Information to which they would not otherwise be privy is supplied to them for the formulation of a response. Other than that, employee communication will be concerned mainly with grievances, requests, suggestions and, perhaps, personal or social problems.

Collective Bargaining and Communication

Collective bargaining also provides a forum for communication in that employee demands and employer responses are formulated and, by the interactive process, a compromise is reached. It may well be the most important form of interactive communication between managements and employees but falls outside the scope of this chapter, which is essentially concerned with internal communication structures.

PLANT-LEVEL COMMITTEES

Shop Steward Committees

As soon as more than one shop steward is elected by members of a recognised union, they will form a shop stewards' committee. Such committee will be entitled, in terms of the new Labour Relations Act, to meet regularly during working hours. The shop stewards' committee will also meet with management at regular intervals. At other times it may, as a matter of urgency, arrange *ad hoc* meetings with management or, conversely, management may ask for a meeting with shop stewards to discuss plans or proposals.

Management—shop steward meetings are essentially negotiation and communication forums where any matter of mutual interest, and particularly matters affecting the union members, will be discussed or negotiated. Issues such as proposed changes in working hours or the shift system, retrenchments and redundancies, the use of casual labour or temporary employees, grievances raised by employees, changes in method of payment and other management actions often form part of the agenda at these meetings; but, in essence, shop stewards and management can (and do) discuss any matter relating to the work situation and the employment relationship.

Workers' Committees

In the past, workers at some companies have preferred not to join a union but rather to establish in-house workers' committees to represent their interests.

The concept of workers' committees stemmed from the Black Labour Relations Regulation Act of 1953, which made provision for such committees to be established to represent the interests of black African employees. These committees were intended as a substitute for trade unionism and were largely ineffectual. Thus the black employees and the unions established in the 1970s and 1980s stigmatised them as 'sweetheart' bodies, to be avoided at all costs.

However, during the 1980s a new kind of workers' committee emerged, often established by employees who had become disenchanted with trade union representation, particularly when the trade union concerned acted at a centralised level. The new breed of committee was different in that it often negotiated a recognition agreement which gave representatives the right to negotiate on substantive issues and to initiate strike action. They could, therefore, more rightly be classified as in-plant unions.

Such committees have the advantage that they are not influenced by external agendas and can thus devote all their energy to in-plant matters. Since they control their own finances in instances where constituents pay dues, they are often better trained than shop stewards to perform their representative functions.

On the other hand, they cannot wield any influence outside the plant — that is, in society or the political arena — nor do they receive support from other workers and employee bodies. A great deal of their success depends on the expertise and assertiveness of the elected representatives, since there is no union organiser to advise them or to assert the rights of employees towards management. Also, where constituents do not pay dues, such committees are financially dependent on management, which makes it difficult to bring actions on behalf of members.

In certain instances these committees represent only a specific category of employees, while in others they may represent all types of employee in the entire organisation.

Where workers' committees play an active role in representing employees, they perform essentially the same function as shop steward committees, although they may prove more ready than shop stewards to engage in cooperative efforts with management. Thus, to a large extent, the effectiveness of committees depends on the attitude of management and its acceptance of the representatives' legitimacy.

Workers' Councils

The Labour Relations Amendment Act of 1979 provided for the establishment of workers' councils, to be made up of an equal number of employer and employee representatives, thus essentially promulgating the concept of liaison committees as established under the Black Labour Relations Regulation Act of 1973. Although these councils could deal with any matter of mutual interest between employer and employee, they were seen (even more so than workers' committees) as an attempt to bring black employees into a cooperative fold at a time when new unions were emerging and threatening the absolute prerogative of management. Consequently very few workers' councils have been established, although in some instances councils or forums representing diverse interests or unions within the organisation have been formed. Many, however, have found it difficult to accommodate the diversity of interests and have subsequently disintegrated.

It is foreseen that, with the introduction of workplace forums in terms of the new labour legislation, workers' councils will either undergo a change of name and perhaps of function, or will completely disappear.

Workplace Forums

The Legal Position

The concept of workplace forums has been introduced by the Labour Relations Act of 1995. These forums may be established at the request of a majority union or unions. Their purpose is to promote a cooperative relationship between employees and management through consultation and co-decisionmaking on specific issues. It is hoped that this will promote a more peaceful labour relationship, co-responsibility and, consequently, improved productivity and efficiency.

The Role of the Workplace Forum

In terms of the Labour Relations Act of 1995, a workplace forum should strive to promote the interests of all employees at the workplace, whether they are union members or not, and to improve efficiency at the place of work. It is interesting to note that the term 'employee' is specifically defined in the relevant section of the Act to include all persons employed at the workplace, except senior management staff whose service contract or status gives them the authority to represent the employer in interactions with the workplace forum, to determine policy and take decisions which may lead to conflict with employee representatives at the workplace.

Establishment of a Workplace Forum

A workplace forum may be established in any workplace where more than 100 persons are employed. A workplace is defined in the Act as a place or places where those employed by a particular employer work. Where the employer conducts two or more operations which — in terms of their size, function, operation or organisation — are independent of each other, each activity is regarded as a separate workplace. (This wide and rather ambiguous definition is bound to cause confusion, but the word 'independent' should be regarded as crucial.)

A majority union can apply to the Commission for Conciliation, Mediation & Arbitration for the establishment of a workplace forum. Such application must be accompanied by proof that a copy of the application has been served on the employer concerned.

Once the Commission receives the application, it has to ascertain that there are more than 100 employees at a particular workplace, that the applicant union has majority membership and that another functioning forum, operating in terms of the Act, has not already been established. Thereafter the Commission will appoint a Commissioner, whose role it will be to assist the parties in reaching a collective agreement relating to the establishment of a workplace forum or, if this fails, himself to establish such workplace forum. The Commissioner has to call a meeting between the employer and all registered unions in the workplace — or, at the very least, between the employer and the applicant union — with the purpose of bringing about an agreement. Should an agreement be reached, the role of the Commissioner as regards the establishment of a forum has been completed. However, should no agreement be reached, the Commissioner will once again attempt to bring about agreement. Failing this, he will himself establish a forum, appoint an electoral officer and set a date for the election of the first forum members.

Where an employer conducts independent activities or where his business is geographically spread, he may decide to establish a coordinating workplace forum and subsidiary forums at the different 'branches'.

In the case of the public sector, the Commission does not need to be involved as the relevant Minister has the right, after consultation with the Coordinating Public Service Bargaining Council, to publish a notice in the *Government Gazette* whereby a schedule regulating the establishment of workplace forums in the public service is appended to the Act.

Finally it should be noted that, where a union is recognised by way of a collective agreement as representative of all employees at the workplace, such union may select representatives to the forum solely from its own ranks. The nomination, election and removal from office is then regulated by the constitution of the applicant union. However, the workplace forum so established will be dissolved if the agreement ends or the union concerned no longer has majority representation. This provision would, in practice, mean that shop stewards would have two representational bodies: the shop stewards' committee and the workplace forum.

The Constitution of a Workplace Forum

The Act contains detailed guidelines regarding the various matters to be covered by the constitution of a workplace forum, including the manner in which representatives are to be elected. In this respect it is interesting to note that only a majority union, twenty percent of employees or 100 employees, whichever is the lesser, may nominate representatives for election.

A full outline of the required constitution is contained in the Annexures.

Meetings of Workplace Forums

In setting out the procedures for meetings, the constitution of the forum could provide that:

- the first meeting should be held as soon as possible after elections;
- at such meeting, the members should elect from among their ranks a chairman and deputy chairman;
- a workplace forum should meet whenever necessary, but at least once a month;
- a quorum should constitute the majority of members; and
- a majority decision should be regarded as the decision of the workplace forum.

The new legislation explicitly provides that:

- the workplace forum must hold regular meetings;
- regular meetings must be held between the forum and the employer and that, at such meetings, the employer must report to the forum about his financial and employment situation, the performance of the organisation since the last report and expected short- and long-term performance. Furthermore, he must consult with the forum on any matter arising from the report

which may affect employees at the workplace;
- the workplace forum must at regular intervals hold meetings with employees at the workplace and that, at such meetings, it should report on the forum's activities in general as well as on the matters in respect of which is has engaged in consultation and co-decisionmaking with management;
- tho omployor must call an annual mccting with employees and, at such meeting, present a report of his financial and employment situation, overall performance and future plans and prospects;
- meetings with employees must take place during working hours and without loss of pay by employees, at a time and place agreed upon between the forum and the employer.

Matters Subject to Consultation with Workplace Forums

Except where a collective agreement (in the public service, this refers only to a bargaining council agreement) determines otherwise, a workplace forum is entitled to be consulted on proposals relating to any of the following matters.

- The restructuring of the workplace, including the introduction of new technology and work processes
- Changes in the organisation of work
- Partial or complete plant closure
- Mergers and transfers of property rights, insofar as these affect employees
- The dismissal of employees based on organisational requirements (retrenchments and redundancies)
- Exemptions from agreements or any legal provision
- Job grading
- Criteria for the granting of merit increases or discretionary bonuses
- Education and training
- Export promotion

Besides the matters mentioned above, a bargaining council having jurisdiction may grant workplace forums the right to consultation on additional matters; the employer and majority union(s) may conclude an agreement subjecting additional matters to consultation; or another law may determine that additional matters be subject to consultation. In the public service, no matter may be added, but some may be removed from the list. The union and management may also agree that, notwithstanding existing health and safety legislation, the parties must consult with each other regarding the initiation, promotion, monitoring and revision of health and safety regulations; additionally, that the establishment of a health and safety committee be initiated by a meeting between the workplace forum and management, and that one or more members of the workplace forum be regarded as health and safety representatives in terms of the relevant legislation.

The Nature of Consultation

According to the new legislation, the purpose of consultation is to reach agreement. During the consultation process, the employer must allow forum members to make representations and to offer alternative suggestions. Such suggestions should be carefully considered by the employer. Furthermore, he needs to react concretely to these and, should he not agree with the forum, to furnish reasons for such disagreement.

When no agreement can be reached the employer must, before he implements his plans, follow an agreed procedure aimed at reconciling differences.

It is evident that the Act intends consultation to be taken seriously but that, once procedures have been exhausted, the employer will make the final decision.

Matters Subject to Joint Decisionmaking

Unless otherwise determined by a collective agreement, the employer is obliged to consult with workplace forums and to reach consensus on any proposal relating to:

- disciplinary codes and procedures;
- rules relating to the regulation of conduct (but not to work performance);
- measures aimed at protecting and developing employees disadvantaged by unfair discrimination (affirmative action); and
- changes to rules regulating social benefits which are controlled by the employer.

A newly constituted workplace forum may also request an employer to produce for review already existent criteria for merit increases and discretionary bonuses, disciplinary codes and procedures and measures aimed at regulating conduct (other than performance-related conduct) at the workplace.

Where the employer and majority union(s) agree, additional matters may be subjected to joint decisionmaking, or certain matters may be removed from the list above. Any other law can also grant workplace forums the right to co-decisionmaking on matters other than those listed above.

The Joint Decisionmaking Process

The aim of the joint decisionmaking process is to achieve **consensus**. Essentially this means that all parties should be persuaded that the solution offered is the best possible one. Consensus, therefore, differs from agreement in that agreement often entails compromise and sometimes is reached by majority decision, whereas consensus implies unanimity. Consequently, the joint problem solving approach should be adopted and there should be a search for viable alternatives which are acceptable to everyone.

Consensus is not easily achieved. For this reason the legislation determines that, where consensus is not possible, the employer may submit the matter to arbitration in terms of an agreed procedure or, should there be no procedure, to the Commission for Conciliation, Mediation & Arbitration. The Commission will attempt to conciliate but, if this is unsuccessful, the employer may request that the Commission engage in arbitration. The Act is mute on the steps to be followed should the employer decide not to submit the dispute to arbitration; but, since he may not implement his proposals or procedures until consensus is achieved, it is doubtful that employers will choose this alternative. It would appear preferable for both parties to reach agreement on consensus-achieving mechanisms, such as fact-finding or task groups, and to build these into their own procedures.

Disclosure of Information

One aspect of the new legislation which employers find most problematic is that relating to the disclosure of information, for the purposes of both collective bargaining and participation.

In terms of the Act, employers are obliged to provide the forum with all relevant information, including copies of documents, required by the forum in order to engage effectively in consultation and co decisionmaking. This provision is fairly wide, and it is assumed that the nature of the information to be disclosed will be determined by the matter being subjected to consultation or co-decisionmaking. As indicated in a previous section, the Act does exclude information which is legally privileged, information which the employer is prohibited from disclosing by law or a Court order, information which is so confidential that its disclosure would cause the employer considerable harm, and private personal information concerning an individual employee — unless that employee consents to the disclosure.

While some employers may not be unwilling to disclose information to workplace forums, they are concerned about the degree to which such disclosure will remain confidential. Section 201 of the Act does provide that, where information has been received by an individual acting on behalf of a council, the Industrial Registrar, an accredited agency, the Commission for Conciliation, Mediation & Arbitration or an independent body established to grant exemptions from bargaining council agreements, such individual may be fined or face imprisonment should he breach confidentiality. However, this section specifically excludes individuals who have received information aimed at enabling them to fulfil their functions in terms of the Act and, consequently, does nothing to allay the fears of employers regarding breach of confidentiality by union or forum representation.

It is foreseen that, unless a framework for disclosure, a definition of 'harm' to the employer and strict requirements regarding confidentiality are built into the agreement between the employer and the applicant union(s), numerous demands for disclosure will lead to dispute situations.

Should a dispute regarding disclosure arise, such dispute may be submitted to the CCMA. The party referring the dispute must prove that a copy of the referral has been served on all other parties. The Commission will first try to conciliate; if this fails, any one of the parties may request that the dispute be referred to arbitration.

In dealing with a dispute concerning disclosure, the Commission should first satisfy itself that the information requested is relevant and, should it prove to be so, what harm such disclosure or lack of disclosure could cause to either party. Should the Commissioner find that the balance of prejudice weighs in favour of disclosure, it may order disclosure subject to certain conditions aimed at minimising the potential for harm to the employer. The Commissioner has also to consider past breaches of confidentiality and, should these have occurred, he may for a period determined by him refuse the disclosure of information which, under other circumstances, would have been disclosed. The employer may also declare a dispute centring in breach of confidentiality, and the Commission may then order that the right of the forum to any disclosure be curtailed for a period determined by the arbitrator.

Establishing Workplace Forums

Rationale

As stated previously, the expressed purpose of workplace forums is to promote cooperation and, hopefully, greater efficiency and productivity in the organisation. Whether they will achieve this purpose depends to a large extent on the manner in which they are established and function; the attitudes of unions, other non-unionised employees and management towards the forum; and the degree to which unions can separate their bargaining function from their cooperative function. The latter aspect is of particular importance since, as indicated in a previous section, the activities of unions and shop steward committees at plant level overlap to a large extent with the proposed functions of workplace forums. Workplace forums function more easily and independently where collective bargaining is restricted to centralised level. This is not the case in South Africa, and the situation is exacerbated by the legislators' well motivated (but perhaps unrealistic) insistence that unions play a dominant role in the establishment and functioning of workplace forums — so much so that a forum not applied for by a majority union or unions will have no legal status. This, however, does not exclude an employer who has no significant union presence in his organisation — or, for that matter, employees in that organisation — from initiating the establishment of their own forums, regulated by agreement rather than statute. Such an employer may be well advised to do so; and it may ultimately be found that the latter type of forum is more effective than that regulated by statute.

Delimiting the Workplace or Independent Workplaces

It is as well, even before any initiatives are taken towards the establishment of workplace forums, that agreement be reached on the definition of 'workplace' since, if this is not done, unnecessary disputes are bound to arise regarding the degree of representivity of a union or unions. If, for example, a union which is now representative of a particular bargaining unit applies for the establishment of a workplace forum, it needs to be ascertained whether such union is representative of the workplace as a whole; alternatively, whether such bargaining unit can be described as independent in terms of its size, function or operation and can thus be regarded as a separate workplace. Where the employer has different workplaces or where operations and geographically spread, a decision also needs to be made as to whether the parties will opt for a coordinating workplace forum with various subsidiary forums.

Owing to the existing ambivalence in the definition of 'workplace', the above will not be an easy task and it is foreseen that certainty will be achieved only by guidelines derived from arbitration awards.

The Initiation of a Workplace Forum

Where the establishment of a forum is initiated by a majority union or unions, it is advisable for the employer to reach an agreement with the other party, since this allows him to negotiate certain aspects and functions of the forum and to deviate in some respects from the statutory provisions (see previous discussion). If the employer resists the conclusion of a collective agreement, a workplace forum and the accompanying constitution and procedures will be imposed on him by the Commission for Conciliation, Mediation & Arbitration.

Agreement on Common Values and a Common Purpose

Before the constitution and procedures are agreed upon, it is essential that the parties reach consensus concerning the purpose of the forum and particularly on the values which underlie its establishment. This may require some time since, at present, most employers and employees are still approaching the issue from different perspectives. Also, a clear distinction needs to be made between, on the one hand, the negotiation functions of unions and shop stewards and the matters to be dealt with by negotiation; and, on the other, the consultation and co-decisionmaking functions of the forum and matters to be dealt with by the forum.

Obtaining a Clear Understanding of the Consultation and Co-decisionmaking Process

The parties need to achieve a common understanding of what is meant by these processes and to set in place some framework for consultation and co-decisionmaking procedures. Also, agreement has to be reached on the mechanisms to be utilised in situations where no agreement or consensus can be achieved.

Agreement on the Definition of Senior Management, Occupational Division and the Spread of Representation

Management needs to present its understanding of the organisational situation and the different categories of employees, whereafter the parties should engage in consultation on the management level to be excluded from the workplace forum and on the type of representative spread which would ensure full and equitable inclusivity. At the same time, management will need to designate the senior employees who will represent the employer in dealings with the forum.

Clarification of Confidentiality Provisions

Management needs to share with the other party its concerns regarding disclosure, with the purpose of creating mutual understanding on how a breach of confidentiality on certain issues could affect the entire organisation and, therefore, all stakeholders. At the same time, agreement could be reached regarding the sanctions to be imposed on individuals who have breached confidentiality.

Drawing Up of a Constitution

Many of the aspects mentioned above will eventually form part of the constitution, the contents of which are contained in the Annexures. However, it should be borne in mind that certain provisions regarding the constitution, as outlined in the legislation, may be amended or omitted by agreement between the parties.

Appointment of an Electoral Officer and the Holding of Elections

Once an electoral officer has been appointed in terms of the constitution, nominations should be canvassed and elections held as soon as possible thereafter. The Commission for Conciliation, Mediation & Arbitration may be requested to render assistance in this regard.

It is also important that, before elections are conducted, all employees be briefed on the purpose and function of the forum and the role and duties of forum members, so that informed decisions can be made as regards the nomination of members who will, in the final analysis, be accountable to their constituents.

Once elections have been held, members should be immediately installed and the first meetings between members of the forum, with management and with employees should be held as soon as possible thereafter.

Training of Forum Members
At the forum's first meeting with management, or as soon as possible thereafter, an analysis of training needs ought to be undertaken in order to establish a training programme for members. This can be effected only if the meeting discusses the types of issue to be dealt with in meetings between management and the forum, the processes involved and the nature of the information to be disclosed.

Although some employers may object to the fact that they will have to train forum members, it is in their own interest to do so since unnecessary delays will be avoided and decisions will be of better quality if members are fully equipped to deal with the issues at hand.

Review of Existing Practices and Policies, Goal Setting and Monitoring of Processes
In all likelihood, the members of the forum would wish to review existing policies and practices related to those issues which are to be subject to consultation and joint decisionmaking. In the light of this, the parties can establish objectives for the forum as well as a monitoring procedure intended to check on progress and on the efficacy of the consultation and joint decisionmaking processes.

Developmental Characteristics
Workplace forums, if properly implemented, can be valuable structures for extended communication and cooperation. It is unlikely that most newly established workplace forums will function effectively from the outset. The process of participation is developmental in nature and, as time progresses, it may well be found that the range of issues subject to forum processes is extended — either by agreement or by new provisions in the legislation.

Since the purpose is to develop a new type of relationship at the workplace, the effective functioning and development of workplace forums will depend largely on the sincerity of both parties' intentions and the degree to which each side sees itself as benefiting from the interactions.

Health & Safety Committees

Rationale
Health and safety committees are established for the sole purpose of creating a cooperative structure to attend to this area of joint employer–employee interests. Worker representatives are appointed to such a committee so that, together with management, they may promote healthy and safe working conditions. Although shop stewards and workplace forums will naturally also have an interest in health and safety and may be represented in these matters, the Occupational Health & Safety Act requires that an independent committee, dealing only with health and safety, be established.

Composition of the Committee

Health and safety issues are the concern of both parties to the employment relationship. The employee needs to be assured of health and safety at the workplace and to bring any irregularities to the attention of management. The employer, on the other hand, wishes to reduce the risk of accidents and to encourage employees to take the necessary precautions. Consequently, a committee established to deal with this matter would ideally comprise employee representatives from various workplaces and those management representatives responsible for ensuring safe working conditions. Any other person who has experience or expertise in the field could be coopted by the committee. A number of committees, functioning under a coordinating committee, may also be created.

In many instances trade unions and even workers' committees resent the establishment of separate health and safety committees. The contention is that matters of health and safety should be dealt with by shop stewards or by the workplace forum. In response the counterargument may be raised that health and safety representatives fulfil a unique function at the workplace. Whereas shop stewards represent sectional interests which may be antagonistic to the interests of management, health and safety is a truly common interest. Representatives on these committees, although they may also represent the employee point of view, are expected to police both management and their fellow employees and at all times to cooperate with management in promoting health and safety. This would conflict with the inherently antagonistic and representational role particularly of shop stewards, who might find their positions challenged were they to report irregularities on the part of employees. On the other hand, as indicated in a previous section, the drafters of the new labour relations legislation have seen fit to involve workplace forums, as cooperative bodies, in health and safety matters to the extent where allowance is made for certain workplace forum members to be designated as health and safety representatives. Therefore, a health and safety committee might also have representatives from other structures, as indicated in Figure 18.

Functions of the Committee

It is the function of a health and safety committee to receive regular reports on the various workplaces, to ensure that workplaces are made safe, to initiate action where unsafe conditions prevail and to handle incidents and claims resulting from unhealthy or unsafe conditions. Furthermore, the health and safety committee has a planning and educative task. It should continually search for improved means of ensuring the health and safety of employees and for new methods of training employees in the use of correct procedures and precautions.

Establishing a Committee

It is the function of management to initiate and establish a health and safety committee and to formulate — in consultation with the workplace forum, a representative union or the employees — the criteria by which employee representatives are to be elected or appointed. South African legislation is very specific on this point. Employers are obliged to appoint a safety representative for every workplace or for every 50 persons employed if the operation is engaged in production, and one for every 100 employees if it is an office or retail business. Furthermore, the representative has to be an employee who is acquainted with the workplace. Managers, therefore, have no option but to appoint the necessary representatives and to establish committees.

Once the criteria, whether optional or compulsory, have been established, it will be necessary to educate the workforce in matters of health and safety and on the functions of their representatives. Thereafter the elections or appointments may proceed. It is advisable, after representatives have been decided upon, that they be officially introduced to their fellow employees, with emphasis being placed on the role they will in future fulfil.

In the meantime, management will have selected managerial representatives to the committee, which may then be formally constituted. Meetings ought to be conducted along formal lines and the necessary minutes should be kept.

Health and safety requires ongoing training of both representatives and the employee body. Representatives should be trained in all aspects of health and safety, inspection and reporting procedures, the establishment of communication channels with fellow employees and in the procedures followed at meetings. The employee body needs to be constantly reminded to take the necessary precautions and not to engage in risky activities.

A properly functioning health and safety committee could do much to promote cooperative activity between employer and employee and to assure employees that employers have also their interests at heart.

Other Workplace Committees

Various other committees could be established to deal with areas where cooperation is encouraged. These may include productivity committees, technology, affirmative action and social responsibility committees. Alternatively, these could be constituted as sub-committees of the workplace forum.

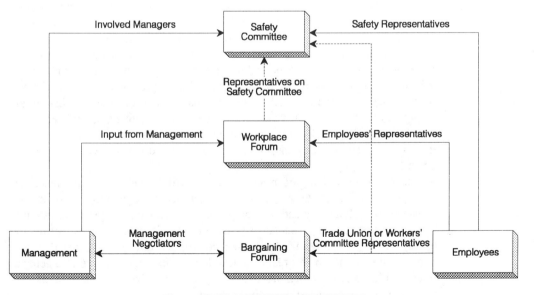

Figure 18: PLANT-LEVEL STRUCTURES

PLANT-LEVEL PROCEDURES

The Need for Procedures

In the aforegoing sections various modes and structures for interaction between management and employees at the workplace have been discussed. The establishment of some of these structures is optional, although advisable, but there are three areas in which formal communication or consultation have become a necessity. Procedures for effective communication and consultation are required to deal with employee grievances, with the disciplining and dismissal of employees and with retrenchments and redundancies. The necessity for dealing in a consistent and proper manner with employee grievances arises not only from the fact that employees have a right to formal channels through which grievances may be expressed, but also from the very real danger that individual grievances may escalate and promote industrial unrest. Discipline, too, cannot be meted out on an *ad hoc* basis or in terms of criteria established by individual line managers. If a consistent policy as regards discipline and dismissal is not adopted and implemented throughout the organisation, allegations of unfair practices may well result. Retrenchment, on the other hand, is not regarded as a normal dismissal. It is generally accepted that employees are entitled to job security and that, in the event of imminent retrenchments, employees or their representatives have the right to be consulted and to question the retrenchments; also that a consistent retrenchment policy and procedure should exist. All in all, the consistency achieved by generally applicable procedures ensures the equal and fair treatment of all employees and prevents overhasty actions or reactions on the part of management.

Establishment of Procedures

Grievance, disciplinary and retrenchment procedures may be negotiated with a union, drafted by management in consultation with union or other employee representatives, or instituted solely by management. Where there is active employee representation at the plant, the latter route is not advisable. In fact, the law now prescribes that, where a workplace forum exists, management is obliged to engage in co-decisionmaking regarding grievance and disciplinary procedures. Unions contend that employee grievances, dismissals and retrenchment resort within their sphere of interest and that they have a right, at the very least, to make an input, even if the procedures are not directly negotiated with them. Whether or not there is union, workers' committee representation or a workplace forum, these procedures need to be established to protect the rights of all employees, both individually and as a collective. It is, furthermore, necessary that those members of line management who will be most closely involved with the implementation of procedures should be consulted when the procedures are drafted.

The exact form of any of these procedures will depend on the circumstances of a particular undertaking, its size, work process, organisational structure, management style and the nature of employee representation. A procedure should be developed to suit a particular organisation. Managements frequently attempt to implement procedures used by other companies, only to find that they are impracticable in their own organisations. Nevertheless, there are certain general rules and guidelines which have to be borne in mind, irrespective of the particular circumstances of an individual undertaking.

The Grievance
Procedure

Definition of a Grievance

Employee grievances are wide-ranging and vary from general dissatisfaction with wages and conditions of service, dissatisfaction regarding promotion or training and complaints about lack of facilities or inadequate equipment to unhappiness on the part of an employee regarding unfair treatment, unreasonable orders, unrealistic expectations and blatant discrimination. Not all of these would resort under a formal grievance procedure. Common grievances regarding wages and conditions of service are usually channelled through a representative union or, where no union exists, through a representative employee body. Individual grievances regarding wages may be aired in personal interviews with management or may be channelled through a workers' body, as may dissatisfaction regarding promotion and training. A workers' committee will also raise issues regarding facilities and equipment.

It is indeed difficult to concretise the type of grievance which would resort under a formal grievance procedure. Usually a formal grievance is initiated when, within the day-to-day work situation of the employee, an incident has occurred or the employee's position is such that he is left with a general feeling of dissatisfaction or a sense of injustice. A supervisor may have consistently discriminated against an employee or group of employees, or may have treated him or them with unnecessary harshness; an employee may have been unjustifiably disciplined or insulted, or he may not have been allowed time off which otherwise would have been common practice. This is the type of issue which will be channelled through the grievance procedure, the rationale being that it requires the formal consideration of management. Moreover, a grievance of this nature is the type of issue which, if unresolved, may lead to a situation of dispute between the company and the employee or group of employees. It is this latter aspect which differentiates a formal grievance from those of a more trivial nature; that is, those not warranting the declaration of a dispute. There are other more serious grievances, such as those related to wages and conditions of service, which could also result in disputes, but these are dealt with by the collective bargaining mechanisms and become demands rather than grievances. Thus a formal grievance may be defined as **a complaint, other than demands formulated by a collective body, which is related to the employee's treatment or position within his daily working routine and which, because it may result in a dispute, warrants the formal attention of management**.

Objectives of a Grievance Procedure

A grievance procedure fulfils the following functions.

- It creates the opportunity for upward communication from employees.
- It ensures that complaints are effectively dealt with by management.
- It creates awareness of employee problems or of problem areas which could be subjected to further investigation.
- It prevents disputes from arising.
- It renders the disciplinary procedure more acceptable, since employees also have a means of objecting to management performance.

- It emphasises management's concern for the wellbeing of employees.

These objectives will be achieved only if the grievance procedure functions effectively and is properly utilised.

The Grievance Procedure in Practice

As indicated at the commencement of this section, there are no prescriptive steps which have to be adhered to at all costs in the establishment of a grievance procedure, but the following general rules apply.

- The employee should be granted the opportunity to bring his grievance, albeit in stages, to the attention of top management.
- He should be permitted representation, if so desired.
- Management, at the various levels, should give careful consideration to the grievance and make genuine attempts to resolve it.
- Time limits should be established for each stage of the procedure.
- The grievance will not be resolved before the employee declares himself satisfied.
- The employee has the right, if the grievance remains unresolved, to declare a dispute.
- Grievances should, wherever possible, be handled by line management, but other staff (in the form of the personnel department) may act in an advisory capacity.

In the light of these guidelines, a grievance procedure might, depending on organisational structure and management style, consist of the following steps (Also illustrated in Figure 19).

Step 1: The employee verbally raises a complaint with his immediate supervisor. The supervisor undertakes to investigate the complaint and to furnish the employee with his opinions and suggestions. If the employee has difficulty in verbalising his grievance he may, at this stage, speak through a representative, but this is usually not necessary.

Step 2: Should the employee find the supervisor's suggestions unacceptable, he lodges — with or without the assistance of a representative — a formal written grievance for the attention of the supervisor or the next level of management (for example, the foreman). The supervisor or foreman, as the case may be, investigates the matter, or reinvestigates it in the case of a supervisor, discusses the matter with the employee and records his findings and recommendations.

Step 3: If, at this stage, the employee remains dissatisfied, the written grievance, together with the report of the supervisor or foreman, is forwarded to the next level of management, in the person of the departmental, section or factory manager. The manager concerned studies the written documents, interviews the employee and gathers all relevant information. On the basis of this, he presents his recommendations or proposed solution to the employee and his representative. The manager is also obliged to report in writing on his investigation, his recommendations and the outcome.

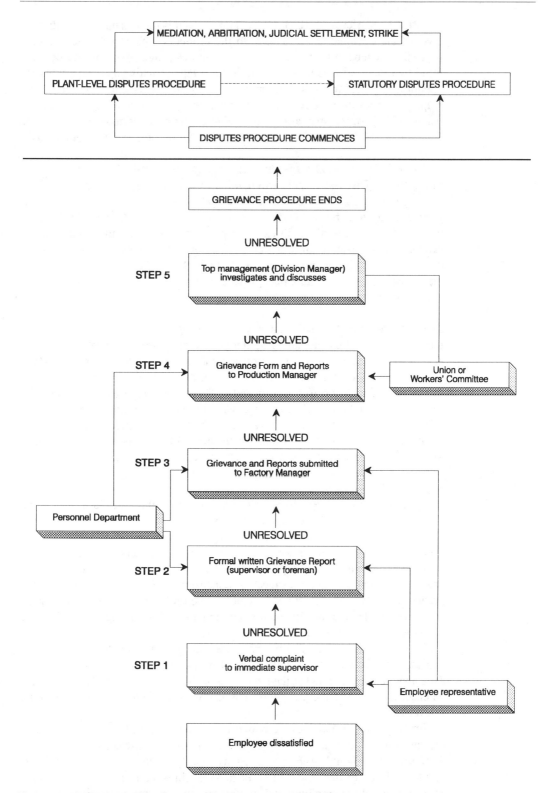

Figure 19: GRIEVANCE PROCEDURE WITHIN A LARGE, HIERARCHICALLY STRUCTURED ORGANISATION

Step 4: A grievance which remains unresolved is then channelled to the next level of management (for example, to the production manager), and the same procedure is repeated but, since at this stage the danger of a dispute becomes more imminent, provision may be made for a representative body — a workers' committee or union — to become involved in discussions relating to the employee grievance. The personnel manager or a senior member of the personnel department may also be invited to sit in on discussions. The personnel department, on the other hand, may already have become involved at an earlier stage.

Step 5: In the final stage the grievance is brought to the attention of top management. Discussions held will involve various management representatives, the employee and his representative or delegates from a representative body. The meetings may now begin to take the form of negotiations. A lack of solution at this, the final, stage will result either in the employee's backing down or in his declaration of a dispute, in which case the issue will be processed either through the plant-level dispute procedure or through the statutory dispute settlement mechanism. Either procedure may provide for mediation or arbitration or judicial adjudication.

The grievance may be resolved at any stage during the procedure. If this occurs, the method of settlement should be noted in writing and the employee should, also in writing, signify his satisfaction with the solution. In a smaller undertaking or one which does not have a steep hierarchical structure, the number of steps in the procedure decreases significantly. The procedure need not necessarily extend to the highest level of management. It could be terminated at Step 3 or 4 if management at this level is regarded as the final authority on issues relating to employee problems. The dispute procedure would then be implemented after this step. (For an example of a grievance procedure, see Annexures.)

Ensuring Effectiveness

If a grievance procedure is to be effective it must, in the first place, be known to all employees in the undertaking, who should be initiated into its use. Consequently, a certain amount of training regarding the grievance procedure needs to be undertaken, either during induction or in other training sessions. Role plays will assist the employee in grasping the procedure. He should be urged to formulate the grievance as concisely as possible, to express his grievance freely and clearly and to consider beforehand what he would regard as an acceptable solution. Instruction and practice in the filling in of grievance forms is also advantageous.

The employee will not feel free to express his grievances unless he is assured that the steps taken by him will not result in his victimisation or intimidation. This may be clearly stated at the beginning of the procedure. Employees should be encouraged to use the procedure, but also warned not to abuse it with trivial grievances.

Employee representatives are bound to become involved in the operation of the grievance procedure. They, too, need to be instructed in its use. Representatives should be advised to listen carefully to the employee's complaint, to sift the facts, to investigate in order to ascertain whether the employee has a case, to counsel the employee and to represent the employee effectively.

Even if the above precautions are taken, the grievance procedure will not be effective unless the members of management who will be involved in the handling of grievances are trained for the task. Line managers, from supervisors upwards, should be completely conversant with all the steps in the grievance procedure and should be trained to listen carefully to the grievance, to clarify any uncertainties, to distinguish fact from opinion, to confirm that understanding is correct and to elicit a suggested solution from the employee. The manager should know how to investigate the grievance, verify the facts, and how to find and promote a solution. He should show sympathy, not be defensive or hostile, but state his own position clearly to the employee.

A grievance procedure will work only if there is a sincere desire on all sides to solve problems. In this respect the personnel department has a duty to monitor the use of the grievance procedure and to advise on possible solutions.

The Disciplinary Code and Procedure

Definition

A disciplinary procedure outlines the formal process adopted whenever an employee breaks the rules of the undertaking or commits any other act which might be in breach of his contract of employment, excluding the type of action to which he is entitled by law. The disciplinary procedure informs on the steps to be taken in the case of transgressions of various kinds, some of which might warrant the dismissal of the employee.

Rationale

Contrary to the opinion of many employees, a disciplinary procedure is not intended merely to ensure that they are properly disciplined. This could be effected without the use of a procedure, but then discipline would be meted out on a random and *ad hoc* basis. It is to prevent this from occurring that procedures are introduced. The use of a disciplinary procedure ensures that all employees are treated in the same manner; that an employee is not disciplined or dismissed at the whim of a manager or supervisor; that he, the employee, is accorded the opportunity of a fair hearing before dismissal occurs; that a transgression of the same kind is treated in the same manner by all managers; that employees have certainty regarding the type of treatment they will receive and that managerial representatives also obtain certainty about their actions and decisions. Lastly, the purpose of a disciplinary procedure is not only to punish, but also to correct the employee. For this reason a follow-up on disciplinary action is essential.

Ground Rules for the Establishment of a Procedure

As in the case of all other procedures at company level, the type of disciplinary procedure established will depend on the nature and structure of the undertaking, but, again, there are a number of ground rules which should be observed. These include the following.

- A disciplinary procedure should be **comprehensive and complete**. It should list all types of transgression which may occur and specify the disciplinary measures to be applied in each case. This presupposes that company rules, prohibiting certain practices and actions, have been established.

- The procedure must be **clear and accessible** to employees. Explanations ought to be worded in simple language which all employees can understand, and the procedure must be known to employees.
- The procedure should conform to the **principles of natural justice**. This means that the incident should be investigated, the punishment should match the offence, an employee must be fully informed of the reason for disciplinary action against him, he must be provided with an opportunity to present his side of the story, he should be allowed a representative, the circumstances should be taken into account and there should be conformity in disciplinary measures.

These rules apply to all disciplinary actions, but particularly to those which may lead to the dismissal of the employee. (A detailed disciplinary procedure is contained in the Annexures.)

A schedule appended to the Labour Relations Act now outlines a Code of Good Practice relating to the discipline and dismissal of employees. The introduction to the Code concedes that each case is unique and digressions from the Code may, in certain instances, be justified; also that, in terms of the number of persons employed, a different approach may be acceptable. The most important principle, according to the Code, is that there should be mutual respect between the parties. The Code further places a premium both on fairness and on the effective operation of a business and states that, although employees need to be protected from arbitrary action, employers are entitled to expect satisfactory conduct and performance from their employees.

Rules of the Company

Before drawing up a disciplinary procedure, a company will need to establish a set of company rules applicable to all employees. The Code of Good Practice now states that every employer must adopt disciplinary rules which establish the requisite norms for the conduct of employees, but does concede that there are some rules and norms which are so well known that they need not be formalised. These rules to some extent concretise the general policy of the company. If rules are not generally applicable to all employees, no uniformity of behaviour among employees and uniformity of action amongst managerial representatives can be expected. Various managers may impose their own rules, or one manager may set greater store on a particular rule than another. Thus it is also necessary for all managerial representatives to be involved in the formulation of rules and for agreement to be reached on the relative importance of different rules.

The rules established in a particular undertaking will depend on the nature of its operation, its organisational structure, the nature of its workforce, the relationship between management and employees and the needs of the company. Smaller organisations may require fewer rules, whereas larger establishments need to cater for every eventuality. Whatever the rules established, it is necessary that they be clearly formulated, that they be ranked in order of importance and communicated to employees. Employees also require certainty as to what they may and may not do. The mere existence of rules does not signify that they are known and accepted by employees, and direct communication with employees in this respect is essential. Usually this is achieved during the induction period.

Categorisation of Transgressions

According to the Code of Good Practice, the Courts support a system of corrective and progressive discipline by which employees can be made aware of the standards expected of them. The disciplinary procedure is based on the categorisation of the transgressions which will be subject to disciplinary action. Transgressions are usually divided into three types, namely transgressions, serious transgressions and transgressions which may result in dismissal. The degree of seriousness attached to each transgression will depend on the undertaking. In certain companies the mere intake of alcohol, no matter what the amount, constitutes a dismissable offence, whereas in others only drunkenness which leads to incapacity would be regarded in such a serious light. Generally, all types of misconduct regarded at common law as reasons for instant dismissal are categorised as very serious offences. The categorisation of offences requires detailed consideration and consultation with all levels of management.

Disciplinary Process

Once the transgressions have been classified, a **disciplinary mould** is established for each. This will state the nature of the action to be initiated if an employee commits a particular transgression. Thus, as illustrated in Figure 20, a transgression which is not of a serious nature would, in all probability, be subject to a verbal warning in the case of a first time offender, a written warning for a second offence, a final warning and then dismissal. The Code of Good Practice advises that formal procedures are not always necessary and that, in the case of less serious transgressions, informal advice and correction will often prove more effective, whereas repeated misconduct will necessitate formal warnings. More serious transgressions or continual misconduct may necessitate a final warning or other sanction, such as the temporary withholding of privileges. In terms of the Code, dismissal should be reserved for very serious transgressions or continued misconduct despite several warnings. In fact the Code states that, in general, it is not acceptable to dismiss an employee for a first offence unless the misconduct is so serious that it renders the continuation of the employment relationship impossible. Although the Code concedes that every incident has to be judged on its merits, it gives as examples of such misconduct gross dishonesty, wilful destruction of property, intentional threats to the health and safety of others, a physical attack on the employer, a co-employee, customer or client, and gross insubordination.

Common Law Reasons for Dismissal

The following acts on the part of the employee have usually been regarded at common law as reason for summary dismissal by the employer. Although nowadays the employee need not necessarily be summarily dismissed, most are still regarded as serious transgressions.

- **Failure or refusal to work** — This does not include participation by the employee in a legal or protected strike, as the Labour Relations Act of 1995 now supersedes the common law by specifically providing that employees who have followed the statutory procedures towards the calling of a legal strike may not be dismissed for breach of contract. On the other hand, employees engaged in an unprotected (illegal) strike may be dismissed subject to certain conditions (see page 369).
- **Deliberate and continued absenteeism** — This does not refer to absenteeism for illness or another valid reason, but rather to an employee who is continually absent and can be proved not to have had a valid reason, or to an employee's absenting himself on purpose when he was expected or instructed to work.
- **Gross negligence** — The negligence must have had severe consequences and it must be proved that these consequences resulted from the wilful negligence of the employee. It is important to note that the extent of the damage is not a measure of the degree of negligence. An employee may have been merely remiss, although he may have caused a great deal of damage. This does not constitute gross negligence. On the other hand, another employee who deliberately neglected his duty will be guilty of gross negligence, even if the damage was not extensive.
- **Serious incompetence** — It is presumed that an employer will, before taking someone into his employ, satisfy himself that the incumbent is able to perform the work he has been employed to do. If he has failed to do so, the incompetence of the employee might be condoned. On the other hand, if the employee has misled the employer into believing that he (the employee) is able to perform the work, the employer would have sufficient reason to dismiss him. A schedule appended to the Labour Relations Act of 1995 specifically outlines a procedure to be followed in the case of incompetence (see page 367).
- **Refusal to carry out orders** — The orders must be reasonable and within the ambit of an employee's normal job. The employee is entitled to disobey an unreasonable order or one not related to his actual work.
- **Repeated unpunctuality** — The latecoming must be of an ongoing and serious nature, and the employee must be given the necessary warnings before dismissal occurs.
- **Incapacity of the employee** — If the employee, by reason of illness or disability, is unable to perform his work, the employer will be entitled to dismiss him. Nowadays such dismissal rarely occurs without the necessary notice and lengthy consideration. A procedure to be followed when dismissing for incapacity is also contained in a schedule to the Labour Relations Act of 1995 (see page 368).
- **Dishonesty in the sphere of work** — This includes stealing, failure to account for funds, fraud, misappropriation of money or goods and the acceptance of bribes.
- **Dishonesty outside the sphere of employment** — An employee who has been convicted of a crime which places serious doubt on

his trustworthiness in or suitability for the position he occupies, may be dismissed.

- **Disloyalty to the employer** — This may take the form of competition with the employer's business, the leaking of confidential information to competitors or any other type of assistance to a competitor. Disloyalty in the form of derisive remarks about the undertaking is not included if this does not directly affect the employer's business or competitiveness.
- **Drunkenness** — Unless the nature of the business is such that no alcohol may be consumed, this must be of such a nature that it results in negligence or incapacity to perform the work in hand.
- **Assault** — Any physical attack on another employee or on a member of management is regarded as sufficient reason for dismissal.
- **Gross insubordination or insolence** — Merely being cheeky towards a manager or supervisor is not sufficient reason for instant dismissal. The transgression must be such that it undermines the authority and position of the superior.

In cases where an employee has been summarily dismissed for any of the above reasons the **onus is on the employer to prove** that the transgression was of such a nature that it warranted dismissal without notice. This is often difficult. For this reason and because common law reasons for instant dismissal may not hold in terms of unfair dismissal provisions, it is preferable not to institute summary dismissal unless the situation leaves no alternative.

Managerial Responsibility
A comprehensive disciplinary procedure will specify the level of management which will be responsible for deciding on the disciplinary measure to be taken. While verbal and first written warnings may be given by the employee's immediate supervisor, it is preferable that final written warnings be issued at a higher level, such as that of production manager, and that a decision regarding dismissal be taken only by those managers vested with this authority (see Figure 20).

Time Limits
Disciplinary action is subject to fixed time limits. This applies both to the period within which any action can be brought and the time allowed for an investigation, or enquiry and appeal. Time limits should preferably be relatively short as disciplinary action should be almost immediate, but — particularly in the case of a serious offence — sufficient time should be allowed for notification of the employee and for the necessary evidence to be collected by both sides.

Warnings
All warnings given, including a formal verbal warning, should be acknowledged by the employee concerned. The employee will append his signature to the warning or to the formal disciplinary report. Where a formal verbal warning has been given, the employee signs an acknowledgement that he has received the warning and that he understands its contents. An employee may refuse to sign a warning, in which case the fact of his refusal should be noted and witnessed.

Warnings are not effective for an indefinite period and usually expire after six to twelve months, so that two transgressions of a similar nature committed within a period of fifteen months would both be classified as first offences and not as a first and second offence. Warnings which have expired cannot be taken into account in a decision as to the guilt of an employee in that they cannot constitute a reason to dismiss or compound the transgression but, when mitigating and aggravating circumstances are considered after the decision as to guilt has been taken, a large number of previous warnings of different kinds could count against the employee since they prove generally poor conduct.

It is sometimes taken for granted that different transgressions cannot be computed within the steps of a disciplinary procedure; that an employee who has been late two weeks in a row and has received a verbal and written warning for these transgressions cannot be given a final written warning instead of the normal verbal warning if, in the next week, he is impudent towards his superior. The problem with this assumption is that, within a period of six months, a particular employee could commit the entire range of first or second level transgressions and still not be subjected to a final warning, whereas another employee who commits the same transgression three or four times in succession may be dismissed. The solution may lie in making the procedure progressive by grouping certain transgressions in the various categories together and clearly indicating that a warning for one of the transgressions so grouped will be regarded as applicable to the other transgressions in the group. (See Disciplinary Procedures in Annexures.)

Investigations and Inquiries

Any transgression allegedly committed by an employee has to be investigated and in each case, no matter how minor the transgression, the employee should be given a chance to explain or bring his side of the story. In some instances this would entail merely calling the employee, or the employee and other employees, into an office and establishing the facts — as would be done, for example, if an employee arrived late for work. In the case of more serious transgressions a detailed investigation may be necessary. Witnesses may have to be found and statements might be taken, although it should be remembered that such statements cannot eventually be presented on their own. They serve merely as corroboration of statements made during a final hearing. If necessary, a preliminary inquiry may be held in order to ascertain whether there is sufficient reason to subject the employee to a final disciplinary hearing. Note that the employee under suspicion is always entitled to know that an investigation is being conducted. He is, in fact, the person with whom the investigation commences.

The Disciplinary Hearing

The *audi alteram partem* principle demands that an employee be always afforded the opportunity to plead his case, no matter what the transgression involved. Even if an employee is merely receiving a verbal warning, he is entitled to state or argue his case and to have a representative if he so desires. This becomes essential where an employee is in danger of being dismissed, or where he might receive another severe sanction such as suspension or a final warning. For this reason a possible dismissal is always preceded by a formal disciplinary hearing.

It is a simple rule of justice that the accuser should not also be the judge. Consequently the disciplinary hearing should, if possible, not be chaired by the manager bringing the case against the employee. The latter should act as the arraigner and another, impartial manager — or a panel of managers — not previously acquainted with the case, should chair the hearing.

The arraigner should ensure that the employee receives written notification of the hearing. Such notification should allow the employee sufficient time to prepare his case, and should:

- clearly **state the reason** for the hearing — that is, what the employee has allegedly done and why this constitutes a breach of the disciplinary code or a breach of contract
- **inform the employee of his rights** to be represented, to have a translator present, to call witnesses, to cross-question managerial witnesses and to present evidence to support his plea.

Once the hearing has been convened, the arraigner presents his case, supported by the necessary evidence, whereafter the employee or his representative is allowed to plead and cross-examine. Only after all the evidence has been heard will the chairman or panel make a decision as to whether or not the employee has committed the alleged transgression and, if so, whether or not it constitutes a severe transgression, but he (they) will not at this stage decide on the sanction to be imposed. Before this can occur, the personal circumstances of the employee and any mitigating or aggravating circumstances have to be taken into account (see *Decision to Dismiss* below).

Having made a decision as to the sanction to be imposed, the chairman will inform the employee and supply clear reasons as to why he has reached that particular decision. He will also inform the employee of his right to lodge an appeal, or to declare a dispute and refer such to the Commission or to a bargaining council within the prescribed time. The decision should then be confirmed to the employee in writing.

The Need for Consistency
A general misapprehension exists that all employees who commit the same transgressions(s) in terms of the disciplinary code should receive the same sanction. If this were so, then it would not be possible to take into account the circumstances of a particular case, the circumstances of the employee and general mitigating or aggravating aspects. Consistency refers to the fact that all employees should be subjected to the same disciplinary mould; that is, they should all receive equal treatment but, according to the particular circumstances, different decisions could be made as to sanctions. However, care should be exercised that clear reasons exist for imposing a particular sanction or otherwise, and that it does not constitute mere favouritism or carelessness on the part of the chairman.

Decision to Dismiss
Nowadays the majority of employers are acquainted with the principles of procedural fairness and rarely default in this respect, yet many employees are still unjustifiably dismissed.

When deciding on a particular sanction, the manager chairing a hearing should take into account all mitigating and aggravating circumstances. Mitigating circumstances could include those surrounding the transgression (for example: provocation, the employee's awareness or knowledge of the rule, past enforcement of the rule, a public penalty already imposed; as well as long service, a clear disciplinary record, previous performance, the employee's personal circumstances and management's contribution to the transgression); whereas a previous poor disciplinary record, betrayal of trust and deliberate intent or deliberate disregard of the disciplinary code could be classed as aggravating circumstances.

In addition, it might be advisable to test the decision by asking the following questions.

- Is the purpose of the sanction to **deter other employees**? Will the proposed sanction do so? Is it in fact necessary to do so? Here the nature of the employer's business has to be taken into account. If, by the nature of the business, it is easy for other employees to do the same thing, then deterrence becomes an important consideration.
- Is it necessary to impose the sanction to **prevent a recurrence** — that is, would the consequences would be serious were the same thing to happen again? This also entails asking oneself whether the employee is likely to do it again, whether it is in character for him to commit such an act. His previous record and performance are, therefore, of importance in this respect.
- Can the employee possibly be rehabilitated without the sanction, or is sanction **necessary to rehabilitate him**?
- Will imposition or non-imposition of the sanction **adversely affect the company**, the employee or other employees?

If aggravating circumstances outweigh mitigating factors and if the answers to some or most of these questions point to the need for imposing a sanction, then that sanction is in all probability well justified.

Appeals and Reviews

The Code of Good Practice referred to earlier does not make mention of the necessity for an appeal or review. It can be accepted that, with the facilitated dispute settlement procedures (see Chapter 14), the legislators may regard it as more feasible that a dismissal which is in contention be referred immediately to the Commission for Conciliation, Mediation & Arbitration or to dispute settlement by the bargaining council having jurisdiction. However, in the past it was accepted that employees had the right to demand that a decision taken against them be submitted to a higher or another authority for reconsideration or review. This applies to all steps of the disciplinary procedure, but appeals or reviews are mostly instituted only in more serious cases, such as those where a final warning or dismissal occurs. Although appeals are more commonplace than reviews, they may be less advisable, since they tend to undermine the authority of the line managers responsible for instituting the sanction on the employee and may cause conflict within management ranks. A factory manager who has decided that an employee should be dismissed might resent a general manager's

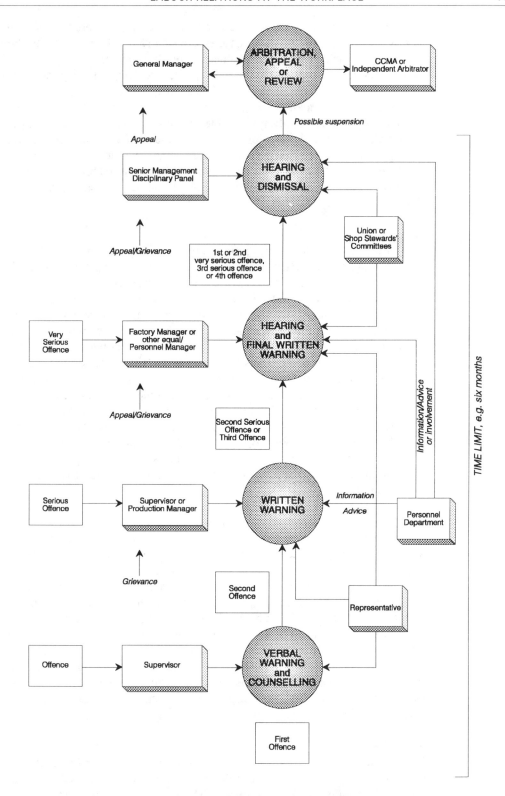

Figure 20: DISCIPLINARY FLOW CHART

decision to the contrary, unless new facts have been uncovered. It could be argued that the possibility of a mistaken decision should be accepted by those involved in implementing a disciplinary procedure and that appeals should, consequently, be accepted. On the other hand, a review, with suggestions and pointers for reconsideration, may equally lead to a change of decision, but it will have maintained the authority of the decision maker. Where reviews or appeals are allowed, they should always be subject to certain conditions and to specified time limits. It is also worth while to bear in mind the ILO directives regarding an appeal: that the body or person to whom an appeal is made should consider the reasons for the decision, the circumstances surrounding it and the justifiability of the decision. It is not intended that the case should be reheard from the beginning.

Sanctions

One of the principles of natural justice is that the punishment meted out should be proportionate to the offence. This raises the question as to the type of sanction which should be imposed in the case of serious or habitual offenders.

The ultimate sanction to be imposed on an employee is his dismissal from the organisation. Warnings, whether verbal or written, are merely indications that this sanction may in future be imposed. Yet sometimes the employer may wish to impose a sanction which is stricter than a final warning but not as severe as a dismissal. In the past there was a measure of uncertainty as to the legality of sanctions such as withdrawal of privileges, fines, suspension without pay or temporary demotion since these contravened either the common law or the Basic Conditions of Employment Act. It now appears that such lesser sanction may be permissible, as the new Labour Relations Act makes mention of sanctions other than dismissal and, in doing so, may overrule both the common law and the Basic Conditions of Employment Act. Nevertheless, it is advisable to negotiate this with the union — or at least to provide specifically for lesser sanctions in the disciplinary code.

The Role of the Personnel Department

The personnel department has a legitimate interest in disciplinary action, and should always be informed when such action is being considered. Final reports on action relating to serious and other transgressions are submitted to the personnel department in its capacity as custodian of employee records. Furthermore, members of the personnel department may attend disciplinary investigations and inquiries in a consultative capacity. It is advisable that actual disciplinary action should be undertaken by line management but, because many line managers do not possess sufficient knowledge of procedures and common disciplinary practices, it is not unusual for the personnel manager to be directly involved in the conduct of disciplinary hearings. Other members of management, particularly those from the same department or section, may also be invited to attend or participate in disciplinary hearings.

Record Keeping

It is essential that all disciplinary actions be recorded on a disciplinary form and on the employee's disciplinary record. Such records will reflect the date of the offence, its nature and the action taken. The reports should be witnessed, and stored for later referral. Records should also be kept of interviews and hearings. In the case of a hearing centring in a very serious offence, it is advisable that the entire proceedings be recorded, either in writing or on a tape, and that these recordings be verified by the parties.

Corrective Measures

Discipline has as a corollary the correction of unacceptable behaviour. While the sanction imposed on the employee may serve as incentive to modify his behaviour, this may not be sufficient. Therefore, it is also the duty of the employee's immediate superior to monitor subsequent performance and behaviour and to provide assistance where necessary. In this respect it is useful to establish review dates, which could coincide with the expiry of a particular warning. More progressive employers will engage in extensive counselling of employees, both when deviant behaviour first becomes noticeable and in the event of subsequent lapses. In fact, numerous disciplinary codes now provide for counselling before any warning is given.

Effectiveness of Procedure

A disciplinary procedure will not be effective unless it is comprehensive, accessible, lucid and conforms to the principles of natural justice and unless the rules have been clearly formulated. Furthermore, a disciplinary procedure has to be made to work. Its mere publication will not ensure its effectiveness. Management representatives in particular need to be trained in the conduct of the procedure. If they are to conduct investigations and hearings successfully, they will need to acquire people-handling and judgmental skills. They should learn to remain calm and neutral, to weigh the relevant facts and reach a reasoned decision. A member of management conducting a hearing should not adopt a prejudiced attitude. He will allow the employee sufficient time to speak. He must be able to supply the necessary explanations in understandable language and to summarise decisions clearly. In short, his demeanour should command respect, yet not lack sympathy. Representatives, too, may have to be trained to assess the employee's position, to collect the necessary evidence and to present the employee's case in a lucid manner, while the employee himself needs to know how the procedure works and what his rights are in terms of the procedure.

A disciplinary procedure which is fairly and consistently implemented can create trust, reliance and good faith in the labour relationship.

The Question of Fairness Aspects of the Code of Good Practice, as these pertain to different reasons for discipline and dismissal, have been discussed in different sections; but essentially any disciplinary action, and especially that which entails a more serious sanction such as dismissal, should be both procedurally and substantively fair.

Substantive Fairness

A disciplinary action will in all probability be regarded as substantively unfair under any of the following conditions.

- The employee was **unaware of the rule** broken by him. An employee cannot be expected to behave correctly if he is not informed of the requirements for correct behaviour.

- There is **no clear reason** for the disciplinary action. Such reason may be established in terms of the law, the contract, the disciplinary code and the expectations and circumstances of the organisation. In terms of the Labour Relations Act of 1995 only three valid reasons for dismissal exist, namely *misconduct or incompetence* on the part of the employee, the *incapacity* of the employee, and *operational requirements* (retrenchment or redundancy).

- The **treatment** of the employee is **inconsistent** with the treatment of other employees who committed the same or an equal offence. This points to the necessity for a generally applicable and consistently implemented procedure.

- Before the imposition of the sanction, there was **no consideration of the special circumstances**, such as mitigating and aggravating factors, length of service and the previous record of the employee.

- There was **insufficient proof** of misconduct. The onus is on the employer to establish, on the balance of probability and on reasonable grounds, that the offence was, in fact, committed. In previous cases the Industrial Court has condoned the action of the employer upon finding that the employer had 'reasonable grounds' for believing that a particular offence had been committed.

- The **sanction was too severe** for the offence which was committed. This is a fairly well-established principle. The employer would have to prove that the misconduct on the part of the employee constituted sufficient reason for the disciplinary action.

- The employee's case has been **prejudged** or the chairman or manager has shown **partiality**. As mentioned previously, the accuser cannot also be the prosecutor and, therefore, especially the decision to dismiss should be made by an impartial third party.

- The expectations of the employer were **unreasonable or unlawful**. An employee could not be disciplined for refusing to work overtime if this could not reasonably or lawfully have been expected of him, or if he refused to lie on behalf of an employer.

- The disciplinary action constitutes **victimisation** of the employee.

- The disciplinary action **contravenes a law, service contract, wage determination or industrial council agreement**.

Procedural Fairness

A disciplinary action would be regarded as procedurally unfair in the following circumstances.

- **The employee was unaware of the nature of his offence.** The employee must be informed, in language which is understandable to him, of the charge against him before any disciplinary inquiry or action is instituted.

- The employee was **not given sufficient warning** where this is required in terms of the disciplinary code or reasonable expectations.

- The employee was **not given the opportunity to state his case.** In this respect, the principle of *audi alteram partem*, or hearing the other side, has been mentioned repeatedly by the Industrial Court. It is for this reason that the conduct of a disciplinary hearing is essential in dismissal cases. Yet the Code of Good Practice also concedes that, in certain circumstances where it cannot reasonably have been expected of an employer to follow these guidelines, certain pre-dismissal procedures may be waived. In cases where the employee *repeatedly* refuses to attend, a hearing may be held *in absentia*, but this would not apply in a case where the employee was unable, for other reasons, to attend a hearing. Also, procedures need not be over-formal, as long as the principles of fairness are maintained.

- The employee has **not been allowed representation.** This is related to the employee's right to state his side of the case. It is taken that an employee may not always be capable of presenting his own case and might need somebody to speak for him, to ensure that he is not intimidated and that proper procedures are followed. In the same light, the employee should be allowed the services of an interpreter and to call witnesses, if necessary. If he is to present his case adequately, he also needs timeous prior notification of a final hearing.

- The employee is **not fully informed of the reason for the decision** given. In dismissal cases the decision, as well as the reason for the decision, should be given to the employee in writing.

- Finally, in terms of the Code of Good Practice, an office bearer or official of a union should not be disciplined unless his union has been notified and the opportunity for consultation has been provided.

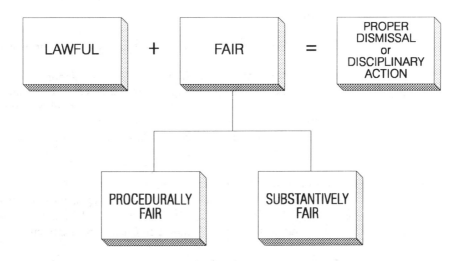

Figure 21: BASIS OF A GOOD I.R. DECISION (by courtesy of Mr Brian Dalton)

A disciplinary action in which all the conditions described have been met would generally be regarded as fair. It needs to be emphasised that the conduct of a procedure leading to dismissal is not prescribed and need not be excessively formal, but that compliance with the general principles is essential.

Disciplinary Checklist

In order to ascertain whether discipline has been fair, the following questions may be asked.

- Is there a **valid reason** for disciplining the employee (e.g. transgression of disciplinary code, material breach of contract or breach of law)?
- Did the employee **know the rule**? Were the rules of the company conveyed to him, and was he acquainted with the disciplinary code?
- Did he receive **sufficient warning**? In the case of a minor offence, were previous valid warnings given? Was he warned, through the disciplinary code, that certain acts might result in severe sanctions?
- Was the existing nature of his **offence explained** to the employee?
- Was there sufficient **proof of misconduct**? On the balance of probability, did the employee commit the transgression? Was the evidence valid and admissible?
- In the case of severe misconduct, was a **proper hearing** held? Was the employee given reasonable notice and sufficient time to prepare? Was he informed of the allegation against him? Was he allowed a representative and interpreter? Was he allowed access to documents and records? Was the presiding officer impartial — did he have no direct interest in the matter? Was the employee given a chance to state his case, allowed to bring witnesses and to cross-question evidence? Was the employee informed of his right to appeal, and were the proceedings recorded and verified?
- Was the sanction imposed **consistent** with that imposed on other employees committing **similar transgressions**, but with due consideration of the particular circumstances?
- Was the employee **informed of the reasons** for imposing the sanction?
- Was the **sanction justified** — did a valid reason exist? Were all mitigating and aggravating circumstances taken into account? Did the sanction match the offence? Was it aimed at deterrence or prevention or rehabilitation? Alternatively, was rehabilitation impossible? Was there no law, contract or agreement preventing the imposition of that sanction?

Dismissing Employees

Definition of Dismissal

At the workplace the ultimate sanction from management's side is the dismissal of an employee. The Labour Relations Act of 1995 now devotes an entire chapter to unfair dismissals. As noted in Chapter 5, dismissal is defined as:

- the termination of the employment contract (either with or without notice);

- the failure to renew a fixed-term contract where a reasonable expectation of renewal was created;
- selective re-employment of employees who were dismissed for the same reason;
- coercion or pressure on an employee which leaves him with no alternative but to resign (constructive dismissal); or
- failure to re-employ an employee who has been on maternity leave or who has been absent because of her confinement.

While the first part of the definition is self-evident, it is interesting to note that an employer cannot end or re-advertise contract appointments at will, and that attention has been paid to the more subtle constructive dismissal.

Automatically Unfair Dismissals

The legislation stipulates that a dismissal will be regarded as automatically unfair if the reason for dismissal is:

- victimisation;
- that the employee engaged or intended to engage in a protected (legal) strike or demonstration;
- that the employee refused or expressed his intention to refuse to perform the work of another employee engaged in a legal strike unless such work is necessary to protect the life, personal safety or health of individuals;
- that the employer wishes to force the employee to agree to a demand related to any matter of mutual interest;
- that the employee took steps or intended to take steps to enforce any right or participate in activities in terms of the Act;
- that the employee is pregnant (or for any other reason related to her pregnancy); or
- that the employer is discriminating against an employee on arbitrary grounds, including (but not limited to) race, gender, sex, ethnic or social origin, colour, sexual orientation, age, disability, religion, conscience, belief, political opinion, culture, language, marital status or family responsibilities. (Such dismissal will not be unfair, however, if the reason is related to the inherent requirements of the job or if an employee has reached pensionable age.)

Special Dismissal Procedures The Code of Good Practice contains specific procedures not only as regards misconduct (which has been extensively discussed above) but also as regards the dismissal of probationary and other employees who have proved to be incompetent at their jobs, the termination of service of employees who have been incapacitated and the dismissal of illegal strikers. These procedures are outlined below.

Dismissal for Poor Work Performance

According to the Code, a new employee may be appointed for a probationary period the length of which will be determined by the nature of his job and the time which the employer needs to ascertain whether or not the employee can perform the job satisfactorily. Where required, an employer must evaluate the employee and provide him with any advice, education, training, counselling or guidance needed to enable the employee to perform competently. Should the employer decide to dismiss the employee during the probationary period, the employee should be afforded the opportunity to be heard and to be represented by a shop steward or another employee. In fact, it is advisable to evaluate the employee at regular intervals, to inform him of the criteria and standards and to warn him beforehand that his performance is not satisfactory.

Where an employee is no longer on probation, the Code specifies that he may not be dismissed for poor work performance unless the employer has undertaken the appropriate evaluation and has provided the employee with the necessary education, training, guidance and counselling. Only if a reasonable time has passed and if the employee still shows no improvement may the employer dismiss him (see Disciplinary Procedure contained in Annexures). Furthermore, the procedures leading to dismissal should include an investigation into the reasons for the employee's incompetence, and the employer should look for alternative solutions before contemplating dismissal. The employee must of course be granted the right to be heard and to be accompanied by a representative. As in the case of probationary employees, it would be advisable that a fair procedure, including the necessary warnings, be followed.

In the case of both probationary and other employees accused of poor performance, the Code specifies that the following factors should be taken into account.

- Whether or not the employee succeeded in achieving the performance standard and, if not:
- Whether he was aware of the standard and it could reasonably be expected of him to be aware of the standard
- Whether he was granted a reasonable opportunity to conform to the required standard
- Whether dismissal is a suitable sanction for his failure to achieve the required performance standards

Dismissal due to Ill Health or Injury

Since incapacity due to ill health or injury may be temporary or permanent, the Code determines that the employer should first establish the extent and degree of incapacity. Where an employee is temporarily incapacitated for a period which (according to the circumstances) would appear to be unreasonably lengthy, the employer must first explore all possible alternatives to dismissal, taking into account the nature of the employee's work, the period of absence, the seriousness of the illness or injury and the possibility of a temporary replacement. Should the incapacity prove permanent, the employer must attempt to accommodate the employee by considering alternatives such as alternative employment or the adaptation of the employee's duties or working conditions.

The Code further specifies that the cause of the illness or injury should be considered and that, where this is found to be related to the employee's work or to the workplace, an additional onus to accommodate the employee rests with the employer. Also, in the case of alcoholism and drug abuse, the employer could first consider counselling and rehabilitation. In all cases the employee has a right to be heard and to be represented.

In deciding whether a dismissal for incapacity is unfair, the following will be taken into account.

- Whether or not the employee is able to perform the job and, if not:
- The extent to which the employee is still capable of work
- The extent to which the employee can be accommodated by adapting his work conditions and/or his duties
- The availability of suitable alternative employment

Dismissal of Unprotected (Illegal) Strikers

The Code clearly states that participation in an illegal strike constitutes misconduct but that, even where employees have not followed the prescribed procedures towards a legal strike, their actions do not automatically warrant dismissal. The fairness of their dismissal within the context of the circumstances surrounding their action still needs to be considered.

In deciding whether the dismissal of illegal strikers is fair or not, the question should be asked whether the transgression of the Act's provisions was a serious one, whether any attempts were made to act in terms of the law, and whether the strike occurred in reaction to an unfair action on the part of the employer.

Before dismissing illegal strikers, the employer must consult with the union representing them, issue an ultimatum which can be clearly understood and which warns of the consequences of disobedience, and grant the employees sufficient time to react to the ultimatum. However, the Code does concede that there are certain circumstances in which the employer cannot reasonably be expected to conform to these requirements and that they may then be waived.

All in all, the Code provides concrete guidelines on a number of previously contentious matters, and thereby at last provides some certainty as regards the procedures to be followed in the instances mentioned.

Disputes Centring in Unfair Dismissals Where an employee alleges that he has been unfairly dismissed and the employer offers as reason for such dismissal the misconduct, incompetence or incapacity of the employee, the dispute may first be referred to the Commission for Conciliation, Mediation & Arbitration or to a bargaining council which has jurisdiction. The same applies where constructive dismissal is alleged. The Commission or bargaining council will attempt to conciliate the dispute. Should conciliation fail the Commission or council must, if the employee so requests, arbitrate on the dispute. (See Chapter 14.)

Where the dismissal was one classified in the Act as automatically unfair, was the result of an illegal strike, resulted from the employees' refusal to join a closed shop union (or from the closed shop union's refusal to accept him as a member), the same initial procedure should be followed; but, in these cases, if conciliation fails, the dispute may be submitted to the Labour Court.

ILO Recom-
mendation
Concerning
the Termin-
ation of
Employment

The unfair dismissal legislation, the activities of the Labour Court or the Commission for Conciliation, Mediation & Arbitration in this respect and determinations made by the Court or the Commission should be measured in terms of international standards applicable to the termination of service. These are to be found in a specific recommendation from the International Labour Organisation, namely **Recommendation (No. 119) concerning Termination of Employment at the Initiative of the Employer (1963)**. Section (2) of this Recommendation states that:

> 'Termination of employment should not take place unless there is a valid reason for such termination connected with the capacity or conduct of the worker or based on the operational requirements of the undertaking, establishment or service.'

The following should not, in terms of the Recommendation, constitute valid reasons for termination.

- Union membership or participation in union activities
- Seeking office, acting as or having acted as worker representative
- The filing, in good faith, of a complaint against an employer for violation of a law or regulation
- Race, colour, sex, marital status, religion, political opinion, national extraction or social origin

As regards the redress available to an employee, the ILO recommends that:

> 'A worker who feels that his employment has been unjustifiably terminated should be entitled to appeal, within reasonable time, against the termination with the assistance, where the worker so requests, of a person representing him, to a body established under a collective agreement or to a neutral body, such as a court, an arbitrator, an arbitration committee or a similar body.'

The ILO further recommends that the body to which the employee appeals should be entitled to **examine the reasons** given for termination, **other circumstances** relevant to the case and the **justification of the termination**, and that it should be empowered, upon finding that the dismissal was **unjustified**, to order the reinstatement of the employee, with payment of unpaid wages where appropriate, to order that he be paid adequate compensation or that the employee be granted such other relief as may be determined.

As regards notice periods, the following is recommended.

- The employee should be given a reasonable period of notice, or compensation in lieu of notice.
- He should be granted time off during his notice period to seek other employment.
- He should receive a certificate from the employer, specifying the dates of engagement and termination. Such certificate should not contain anything unfavourable to the employee.

Provision is made for dismissal without notice in cases of serious misconduct, but it is recommended that instant dismissal for serious misconduct should:

- occur only *'... where the employer cannot, in good faith, be expected to take any other course'*, and
- be taken within reasonable time after the employer became aware of the misconduct.

Further that:

> *'... before a decision to dismiss an employee for serious misconduct becomes finally effective, the worker should be given an opportunity to state his case promptly, with the assistance, where applicable, of a person representing him'.*

It can be taken that the latter recommendation applies to all dismissals, whether with or without the necessary notice. No other specific recommendation regarding procedures to be followed, is given, but it is recommended that '... the question whether employers should consult with workers' representatives before a final decision regarding termination of employment is taken should be left to the laws, regulations, collective agreements, work rules, arbitration awards or court decisions of a particular country.'

The Recommendation does exclude a number of employee categories from its scope. These include:

> *'(a) workers engaged for a specified period of time or a specified task in cases where, owing to the nature of the work to be effected, the employment relationship cannot be of indeterminate duration;*
>
> *(b) workers serving a period of probation determined in advance and of reasonable duration;*
>
> *(c) workers engaged on a casual basis for a short period; and*
>
> *(d) public servants engaged in the administration of the State to the extent only that constitutional provisions preclude the application to them of one or more of the provisions of this Recommendation'*

Unfair Labour Practice

Definition

An unfair labour practice was originally defined in the Labour Relations Amendment Act of 1979 as 'any practice which in the opinion of the industrial court constitutes an unfair labour practice'. This definition was severely criticised for being too wide and was changed in 1980 to the following.

> *'Unfair labour practice means —*
>
> *(a)   any practice or any change in labour practice, other than a strike or a lockout, or any action contemplated in Section 66(1), which has or may have the effect that —*
>
> > *(i)   any employee or class of employee is or may be unfairly affected or that his or their employment opportunities, work security or physical, economic, moral or social welfare is or may be prejudiced or jeopardised thereby;*

(ii)   the business of any employer or class of employers is or may be
        unfairly affected or disrupted thereby;
(iii) labour unrest is or may be created or promoted thereby;
(iv)   the relationship between employer and employee is or may be
        detrimentally affected thereby; or

(b)   any other labour practice or any other change in any labour
        practice which has or may have an effect which is similar or
        related to any effect mentioned in paragraph (a)'.

In 1982 the definition was again amended to eliminate the exclusion of actions
comtemplated in Section 66(1) — the victimisation clause. After that most of
the definition, as quoted, remained in effect.

Even the amended definition was open to wide-ranging interpretation. In
essence, *anything* which *unfairly* affected the welfare of employees, the business
of an employer and the employment relationship or which might create labour
unrest could be regarded as an unfair labour practice. It was left to the Industrial
Court to establish criteria for fairness and it was expected that, in time,
guidelines as to the nature of unfair labour practices would be established. The
Court relied on the cases brought before it. The majority of these cases centred
on ordinary dismissals or retrenchments, but cases alleging the following, among
others, to be unfair labour practices were also brought before the Court.

- Victimisation
- Failure to bargain with a representative union
- Refusal to bargain at plant level
- Dismissals for strike action
- The use of insulting and disparaging terms
- Unilateral implementation of new terms and conditions of
  employment
- Unilateral change in bargaining forum
- Differential and discriminatory terms and conditions of
  employment
- Body searches
- Refusal to work overtime
- Disruptive action by union organisers
- Refusal to grant access to trade union officials

Not all actions were successful. Some failed for technical reasons, while in
others no unfair labour practice was found to have been committed. It should be
borne in mind that the Court adjudicated in the light of the circumstances of each
particular dispute. Consequently, although general guidelines might be
established, no binding precedents were set.

The 1988 amendments to the Labour Relations Act included an extended
definition of the unfair labour practice. Unfair dismissal and retrenchment were
codified in this definition, as well as a number of other practices. These
amendments furnished proof of the legislature's intention to use guidelines
established by the Industrial Court and contingencies encountered in the
day-to-day practice of labour relations as basis for a gradual codification of
unfair labour practices.

In terms of the 1988 amendments, strikes and lockouts were no longer excluded from unfair labour practice jurisdiction. The definition commenced with an attempt to clarify the word 'practice'. Thus an unfair labour practice was generally defined as '... any act or omission which in an unfair manner infringes or impairs the labour relations between an employer and employee'. According to Section (1), such practice could include the following.

- The dismissal of an employee for disciplinary reasons, without furnishing a valid reason and without adopting a 'fair procedure'
- The dismissal of employees for other reasons besides disciplinary action (that is, the retrenchment of employees) unless certain rules had been applied
- Unfair discrimination on the basis of race, sex or creed, except where this was in compliance with a law or wage regulating measure
- The unfair, unilateral suspension of an employee or employees
- The unfair, unilateral amendment of terms or conditions of employment, except where this gave effect to a law or wage regulating measure
- An illegal strike or lockout *(Such actions were evidently included as unfair labour practices to encourage greater use of the statutory dispute settlement machinery.)*
- A second strike or lockout centring on a dispute which, in the aforegoing 12 months, had given rise to a similar action *(The purpose was to prevent repeated strikes over the same issue.)*
- Any strike or lockout involving an employer not directly concerned with the dispute *(This related to sympathy strikes in undertakings not owned by the employer against whom the original dispute was declared, or not forming part of the same company.)*
- The support of, participation in or furtherance of a product or service boycott by a trade union, union federation or any of the office bearers of a union or federation *(The inclusion of this clause meant that no union or office bearer could organise a consumer boycott of any kind whatsoever without risking an unfair labour practice suit. This provision and those relating to sympathy strikes and repetitive strikes evoked sharp reaction from the union movement.)*
- The use of 'unconstitutional, misleading or unfair methods' of recruiting by a trade union, employer's organisation or federation, provided that the refusal to accept a member in terms of a constitution would not be regarded as unfair
- Any act of intimidation of an employer or employee, the purpose of which was to persuade him to agree or not to agree with an action in connection with the employment relationship
- The failure or refusal to abide by the terms of an agreement
- Interference with the freedom of association, including (but not limited to) attempts at preventing an employer from negotiating with employees who were not members of a particular trade union or federation *(The latter provision could be read as a discouragement of the demand for sole bargaining and representational rights.)*

The last section of the amended definition contained the previous definition of an unfair labour practice, with two minor changes.

The proposed amendments to the definition of the unfair labour practice met with a mixed reception. While some observers viewed the extended definition as a step in the right direction, there were those, especially in union ranks, who regarded it as an attempt to undermine union power and to limit the discretion of the Industrial Court.

Following repeated demonstrations against the Labour Relations Amendment Act of 1988 and the ensuing SACCOLA–NACTU–COSATU accord, the Labour Relations Amendment Act of 1991 deleted the detailed codification of an unfair labour practice, which was once again broadly defined as:

'any act or omission other than a strike or lockout which has or may have the effect that —

- *any employee or class of employees is or may be unfairly affected or that his or their employment opportunities or work security is or may be prejudiced or jeopardised thereby;*
- *the business of any employer or class of employers is or may be unfairly affected or disrupted thereby;*
- *labour unrest is or may be created or promoted thereby;*
- *the labour relationship between employer and employee is or may be detrimentally affected thereby'*

The insertion of a new, wider definition did not signify that the specific practices defined as unfair labour practices in terms of the 1988 amendments could no longer be judged as unfair. Any of the practices codified by the 1988 amendments could still be judged as unfair by the Industrial Court — which was as it should be, since many of these had prior to 1988 been proclaimed as unfair by the Court.

The Meaning of Fairness

A general discussion on fairness and the problematique of this concept is contained in Chapter 1. There, the conclusion was reached that an action or behaviour could be considered fair if there was balance between the parties, if both parties received equitable treatment, if there was conformity with universally accepted standards and if consistency was exhibited. It was further pointed out that the Industrial Court applied the test of the reasonable man, particularly as regards the fairness or otherwise of a particular sanction; also that a party had to be *seen* to be acting fairly. However, these are merely pointers to fairness. The concept is so laden with nuances and subjective assessments and its interpretation so dependent on circumstances that it would be virtually impossible to establish delimited standards of fairness. It is possibly for this reason that the Industrial Court was granted discretion in its unfair labour practice jurisdiction and that no absolute precedent was established by Industrial Court decisions.

The lack of concrete standards as regards fairness did lead to much uncertainty and criticism of the Court's decisions, but it might equally be unwise to restrict unfair practices to a few concretised instances of unfairness, as the new legislation proposes.

When the unfair labour practice jurisdiction of the Industrial Court was first implemented, much argument centred on the lawfulness of certain actions. A common proposition was that an action which was lawful was also fair. Consequently it was argued that, if the employer possessed the common law right to dismiss an employee, the dismissal was essentially fair. The Industrial Court repeatedly refuted this assumption and it became accepted that lawfulness is not necessarily equated to fairness; that an action may be lawful, but may still be unfair. The corollary, however, is not true. An action which is unlawful cannot be fair. It is because the Industrial Court concerned itself with fairness, as against lawfulness, that it was described as a court of equity and not a court of law. (In the new Act it is regarded as a court of law.)

Some Guidelines regarding Unfair Labour Practices

Although, as has been stated, no definitive list of unfair labour practices was established, some guidance could be obtained from decisions of the Industrial Court. It became clear, for example, that an employer who dismissed an employee without a fair and valid reason and without following a fair procedure would probably be guilty of an unfair labour practice. It was, however, interesting to note that the Court was loath to reinstate employees permanently if the only default on the employer's part was procedural in nature. Compensation was the preferred mode of redress in these cases.

Also well established was the precept that an employer could not retrench without consultation, without following an agreed procedure and without adopting provable criteria.

Usually the Court would not be prepared to assist an employee who resigned of his own accord, but it would render assistance when it could be proved that the employee's resignation resulted from the employer's conduct. The Court took the view that an act on the part of the employer which forced the employee to resign could be construed as dismissal on the part of the employer.

Even before 1988 a number of cases dealing with racial and sexual discrimination were brought before the Court. The decisions in these cases proved that the Court viewed any kind of discrimination in a very serious light. Equally, inconsistent treatment of employees was usually unfair. In this respect it should be noted that the emphasis was on behaviours. The outcomes in each case might well be different.

The dismissal of employees following strike action was tested on numerous occasions. Some clear guidelines were established in this respect. It is also interesting to note that an employer who dismissed employees for refusing to work in conditions which they *believed* to be unsafe was probably acting unfairly.

Any unilateral action on the part of the employer in circumstances where he could reasonably have been expected to consult with employees or their representatives, including the unilateral transfer of an employee, was likely to be regarded as unfair — if only because this runs in contradiction to the *audi alteram partem* principle. In line with this, a refusal to grant employees adequate representation was essentially unfair.

Failure to negotiate in good faith on a particular issue was usually unfair, as was the reorganisation of work for the sole purpose of ridding the enterprise of certain unwanted employees. Where one employee was declared redundant and another with a similar portfolio employed, the company would be hard pressed to prove that it had acted fairly.

An interesting development during the early 1990s was the attention given to issues surrounding pension funds, the alleged unfair handling of such funds and the manner in which benefits were paid out. However, the Court's jurisdiction in this respect was not fully tested.

Other issues which to a large extent remained untested were the more subtle forms of unfairness such as the retardation of an employee's progress and development, the unfair use of job evaluation and performance appraisal techniques, sexual harassment, the lack of disclosure to and the manipulation of more senior managerial staff and the wilful (though inconspicuous) retardation of work by employees.

The practices mentioned here reflect but a few of the thousands of cases brought before the Industrial Court. In most cases the matter was more complex. However, the above provides a few useful pointers to some of the most blatant and most frequently committed unfair labour practices.

One final point to note was the Court's view of the term 'employee'. According to the definition as then contained in the Labour Relations Act, an employee was 'any person ... employed by or working for any employer and receiving or entitled to receive any remuneration and ... any other person whomsoever who in any manner assists in the carrying on or conducting of the business of an employer'. The Court was obliged to abide by this definition and to regard any person in employ, including a temporary, casual or probationary employee, as entitled to relief in terms of the Act. It was to be expected that the unfair labour practice legislation would be used increasingly as more employees — including those in white-collar and managerial positions — became aware of their rights in terms of the Labour Relations Act.

Unfair Labour Practices in the New Dispensation

Definition

As indicated earlier, unfair dismissals have now been separated from other unfair labour practices and are dealt with in detail by the Act itself. In addition, the Act now provides for so-called **residual unfair labour practices** which, in all likelihood, will later be removed from the Labour Relations Act and resort under an Equity Act. For the time being these are included in a schedule to the Labour Relations Act, and will be enforced in terms of this Act.

The definition of an unfair labour practice as contained in the schedule has been reproduced in Chapter 5. The new definition greatly limits the ambit of unfair labour practices to acts of discrimination, unfair conduct relating to training, promotion, demotion or benefits; unfair suspension or other disciplinary action, and failure to re-employ where an agreement to this effect has been concluded. It is wondered whether this limited definition will stand the parties (and especially employees) in good stead. There are other possible unfair labour practices, such as sexual harassment, actions relating to job evaluation and insulting behaviour which have not been codified. The question will be what action employees subjected to these practices will then be able to take. It appears that the legislators may have become over-enthusiastic in their desire to obtain certainty and clarity as regards unfair labour practices and that some amendments may later be necessary.

As mentioned elsewhere, the discrimination clause also applies to applicants for positions and employers will have to be very careful that, in future, they adopt provable criteria and assessment techniques so that they may be able to counter any allegations of discrimination brought by prospective employees. Provision is made for affirmative action initiatives but again, to avoid allegations of discrimination, the employer will have to prove that he was acting in terms of a policy which, if there is a workplace forum, will have had to be subject to co-decisionmaking by that forum. Other than that, it may be argued that a person of a particular type was appointed because of the inherent requirements of the job; but care should be exercised in this respect as it is all too often merely accepted without due reason that, for example, females are not fit for certain jobs. Also, some employers refuse to employ anyone who does not have a Matriculation certificate, even though the job may not require this qualification. It could be argued that this policy discriminates against those who did not have the opportunity to continue their education.

The provision regarding promotion links in to that relating to applicants, since a promotion is essentially an appointment to a new position. In the past it was difficult for an employee to bring a case alleging that he was unfairly overlooked when it came to promotion as the decision to promote was still regarded mainly as the prerogative of management. Also demotions and refusal to grant benefits, or unequal treatment in this respect, will now come under the spotlight.

Finally, the provision relating to the suspension of an employee or any other disciplinary action (besides dismissal) now opens the door for lesser sanction than dismissal, and also addresses the prejudice which may be caused to an employee who is suspended, even on full pay, pending a disciplinary hearing.

Unfair Labour Practice Disputes

The procedures to be followed in the event of a dispute centring in an alleged unfair labour practice are outlined in Chapter 14. Eventually such disputes may be referred to the Labour Court, which may make any decision including (but not limited to) reinstatement or compensation. It is assumed that, in the spirit of the Act and in line with the provisions relating to unfair dismissals, the Court will not order reinstatement in the case where an action is found merely to be procedurally unfair and that the compensation ordered will not be more than that stipulated for procedurally unfair dismissals.

Retrenchment Procedures

Definition

The retrenchment procedure is that procedure whereby the possibility of a reduction in employment is foreseen and regulated. The procedure establishes principles and practices which, when retrenchments become imminent, will lead to the necessary information being furnished, the necessary consultation taking place and to the use of objective criteria for selection of retrenchees. In all, it will ensure consistent and fair behaviour on the part of the employer.

Retrenchment versus Redundancy

A distinction is made between retrenchment and redundancy in that the former is attributed to cyclical downturns, market losses or other economic factors which oblige the employer to reduce his labour force, whereas redundancy occurs when jobs are lost through reorganisation or the introduction of technology. In the case of retrenchment, the jobs may be reinstated if economic circumstances improve, but when redundancy occurs the loss of jobs is usually permanent. Also, it is believed that more responsibility can be placed on employers for redundancies than for retrenchments and unions may claim greater compensation in the case of redundancies.

Rationale

Previously it was regarded, particularly in South Africa, as the right of management to reduce or enlarge the workforce according to the dictates of production and economic cycles and in terms of business rationale. With the growing emphasis on employee rights, and especially the right to job security, the position has changed; employers can no longer claim that retrenchment or redundancy is entirely a managerial prerogative, nor can these be undertaken on an *ad hoc* basis. The very necessity of retrenchments, particularly those arising from a cyclical downturn, is questioned. Unionists maintain that employers are all too ready to reduce employment levels as a first option in times of economic recession. They argue that there is an obligation on the employer to keep employees in their jobs, since it was those employees who supported him when business was booming. On the macro-level, the necessity for retrenchments is viewed as a direct result of the inadequate workings of the capitalist system. According to Dave Lewis, 'Retrenchments and economic crises are neither an act of God nor part of the natural order — but a direct outcome of the capitalist system itself. Crisis is inherent in the process of capital accumulation, which entails increasing capital intensity, a declining rate of profit and problems of inadequate markets — although theorists may debate the precise mechanisms and relationships'. As far as unions are concerned, employers' reasons for retrenchment, such as falling demand, the need for more effective utilisation of manpower, etc. are no longer acceptable. A company wishing to retrench or to declare workers redundant, for whatever reason, will have to persuade worker representatives that the short- or long-term existence of the undertaking — and, therefore, total employment — is at stake and particularly that the retrenchments are not being considered merely to maintain profit margins or dividends to shareholders.

In South Africa the issue of retrenchment is exacerbated by high unemployment, calculated at approximately 45 percent of the economically active population. Thus retrenchment becomes not only a business issue but also a social one, since it may be regarded as directly contributing to the high crime rate in this country. Nevertheless, if there is no alternative, union and worker representatives will eventually accept the inevitability of retrenchment, as long as it is concluded in a fair and equitable manner. In years to come this may not be the case and the right of an employer to reduce his workforce, either for economic reasons or because of reorganisation and technological innovation, may be increasingly challenged.

ILO Recommendations   The ILO recommendation concerning termination of employment provides specifically for retrenchment procedures by stating firstly that:

> *'Positive steps should be taken by all parties concerned to avert or minimise as far as possible reductions of the workforce by the adoption of*

*appropriate measures, without prejudice to the efficient operation of the
undertaking, establishment or service.'*

Regarding consultation, it is recommended that, when a reduction is
contemplated, consultation with workers' representatives should take place '... **as
early as possible on all appropriate questions'**. Questions suggested for
consultation include:

- measures to avoid the reduction of the workforce
- restriction of overtime
- training and retraining
- transfer between departments
- spreading termination of employment over a certain period
- measures for minimising the effects of reduction on the workers
  concerned
- selection of workers to be affected

On the question of selection of employees for retrenchment, it is recommended
that this should be effected '... *according to precise criteria which ... should be
established, wherever possible, in advance and which should give due weight
both to the interests of the undertaking, establishment or service and to the
interests of the workers'*. Criteria adopted may include the following.

- The need for the efficient operation of the undertaking
- The ability, experience, skill and occupational qualifications of
  individual workers
- Length of service
- Age
- Family situation

It is also recommended that employees who have been retrenched should be
given priority of re-engagement, that such priority of re-engagement may be
limited to a specific period of time, that the wages of employees who are
re-engaged should not be adversely affected, with due regard for the differences
between the previous and new occupations, and that national employment
agencies or other appropriate agencies should be fully utilised in attempts to
place redundant workers in alternative employment.

In the light of the Recommendation as a totality, the rationale of the unfair
labour practice legislation in South Africa — and specifically the codification of
dismissals and retrenchments in the Labour Relations Act of 1995 — becomes
clear.

Fairness in Retrenchments
In terms of the Labour Relations Act of 1995, organisational requirements
(retrenchment and redundancy) will be accepted as valid reasons for dismissal
of employees. However, dismissals resorting under this category will be subject
to certain very strict conditions.

The Act provides for consultation with representative bodies, outlines the
nature of such consultation as well as the type of information to be supplied to

representatives, and sets a minimum standard for retrenchment packages. The various provisions are discussed in greater detail under the relevant sections.

The Need for a Policy

It is of advantage to an undertaking, whether union presence exists or not, to have some kind of retrenchment policy, since it is preferable to have a policy or procedure before the fact than to flounder around for solutions when the reality of retrenchment has to be faced. Many companies which have agreements with unions by now also have agreed retrenchment policies and procedures, but even those which do not have high-level union presence need to consider establishing policies and procedures. These could be solely for the guidance of management or could take the form of public policy, made known to workers or to the workplace forum.

Consultation

Consultation is mentioned as the first step in the retrenchment procedure, although it need not occur at the beginning and will be necessary at various stages of the retrenchment programme. Where plant-level representation exists, consultation (and probably also negotiation) will already occur when general policies and procedures for retrenchment are established. This type of consultation will probably culminate in a general retrenchment agreement, which would facilitate consultation when the need for retrenchment or redundancy actually arises. Worker representatives would want to know in which circumstances the employer would regard retrenchments as necessary. It is also advisable to agree on some mutually acceptable standards or methods by means of which such circumstances may be verified. Consideration will, furthermore, be given to possible alternatives to retrenchments, but the most important issue during this phase would be the negotiation of mutually acceptable criteria for selection of retrenchees and agreement on the exact steps and procedures to be followed in the actual event of retrenchment.

Whether there is a prior retrenchment agreement or not, consultation of some kind or another will occur once retrenchments or cutbacks become imminent. This entails notification to the union or worker representatives that the employer may have to retrench or is actually planning retrenchment. Opinion differs as to the length of notice or the exact timing for this type of consultation. It will depend on the nature of the employer's business and the reason for the reduction — that is, whether the retrenchments are due to economic, organisational or technological changes. Unions maintain that the employer should notify or consult as soon as he becomes aware of the need to retrench. In the case of technological innovation, this may be a year or years in advance, and in other areas may range from six months to two weeks. Generally, two weeks is the minimum acceptable notice period, but acceptance of a shorter period will depend on the particular circumstances.

The new legislation stipulates that, where an employer intends to retrench, or make certain employees redundant, he has to consult with a party determined by a collective agreement or, when no agreement exists, with a workplace forum. In the absence of a workplace forum, he has to consult with all registered unions whose members will be affected by the proposed retrenchments and, if no union represents employees, with the affected employees themselves. (There is some ambiguity here: the section of the Act which deals with workplace forums stipulates that they *must* be consulted on proposed retrenchments. Thus, where there is a collective agreement, both the union and the forum will have to be consulted.)

During such consultation the parties must, in terms of the Act, attempt to reach agreement on suitable measures to avoid retrenchments, to limit (as far as possible) the number of people to be dismissed, to change the timing of dismissals or to soften the effects of the dismissals. They should further agree on the criteria for selection of retrenchees and the retrenchment package. All information necessary for effective consultation must be supplied to the employee representatives. The employer must grant the other party the opportunity to make proposals on any matter subject to consultation. He has to consider and react to these proposals and, should he reject them, furnish reasons for such rejection.

The third and last type of consultation will be devoted mainly to verification of the list of retrenchees and to representations made on behalf of particular employees. The Act stipulates that retrenchees must be selected in accordance with agreed criteria or, where no agreement could be reached, the employer must himself apply fair criteria. If no prior consultation has occurred, worker representatives will in retrospect raise the questions mentioned before. Unless the retrenchees have been selected in continued prior consultation with the union or worker representatives, final verification and acceptance of the list of retrenchees may prove a time-consuming exercise.

The question is increasingly being asked as to whether mere consultation on retrenchments is sufficient. Should the employer not be obliged to negotiate with employees or their representatives regarding proposed retrenchments or redundancies? Till now there has been no onus on the employer to do so, but this does not preclude the possibility of such an obligation in the future.

Disclosure of Information
The new legislation stipulates that the employer must supply relevant information in writing which must include (but is not limited to) the following.

- The reasons for the proposed dismissals
- The alternatives previously considered by the employer and the reasons why such alternatives cannot be utilised
- The number of employees and the employment categories to be affected
- The proposed methods of selection of retrenchees
- Any assistance which the employer proposes to give to retrenched employees
- The possibility of future re-employment of employees now being retrenched

In supplying the reasons for the proposed dismissals, the employer may be asked for further disclosure to substantiate the reasons given. This may amount to proof that the retrenchments are in fact necessary, and may involve the disclosure of financial statements or an independent audit. In terms of the Labour Relations Act of 1995, the same provisions rgarding disclosure as are applicable to unions engaged in collective bargaining apply also in the case of proposed retrenchments or redundancies. If the employer is acting in good faith, disclosure of some kind may prove the best method of convincing representatives that retrenchments really are necessary. However, disclosure of financial information will depend to a large extent on the trust relationship between the parties, on the relevance of such information and on the degree of sophistication of employee representatives.

Consideration of Alternatives

It is accepted practice that alternative measures be considered and implemented before a final decision on retrenchment is made. The first and most obvious of these is natural attrition. Surprisingly, there are organisations which decide to retrench without consideration of labour turnover figures and in some organisations no such figures are available. The possible repercussions of a retrenchment exercise could in many instances be avoided merely by allowing for a period of natural attrition. Yet there are employers who place themselves in the invidious position of retrenching only to find out two months later that they are obliged to increase employment, owing to resignations. Similarly there are those organisations which continue to recruit new employees even when aware that they may in the near future have to consider retrenchment. A ban on recruitment, except in exceptional circumstances where special skills are required, is essential in an organisation needing to retrench part of its workforce, as are bans on the employment of casual labour and on subcontracts. Once provision has been made for natural attrition and the recruitment of new employees and casual labour has been stopped, consideration should be given to the transfer and retraining of existing employees, particularly where an employee's job has become redundant. Unions insist that this alternative be considered, not only within the company itself but also among other companies belonging to the same group. Employers are expected to do everything in their power to find other positions for employees whose positions will become redundant. It should be noted that the law now determines that an employee who has unreasonably refused the offer of a transfer or another position will not be entitled to retrenchment pay.

Other alternatives to retrenchment will involve the employees themselves. These fall under the general heading of a cutback in time worked. They include a ban on overtime, short time, temporary layoffs, cycled unpaid leave or shared time. In South Africa, an important point when considering these alternatives is the fact that, at common law and in terms of the Basic Conditions of Employment Act, no unilateral reduction in contracted wages is permissible unless an applicable wage regulating measure, such as an industrial/bargaining council agreement or wage determination, allows for this. For example, an employer whose basis of contract with his employees is weekly may not merely shorten the working week and reduce payment accordingly, but industrial/bargaining council agreements and wage determinations may provide for some form of short time or temporary layoff. Where an employer falls under the jurisdiction of a council or is subject to a wage determination, he should inform himself of the relevant provisions and, if these are not suitable, apply for the necessary exemption. Where wage regulating measures do not apply, the employer needs to obtain the permission of the employees, which effectively means an agreed change in the contract of employment. Should he not do this, he will not only be breaking the law but may be accused of unilaterally changing terms and conditions of employment. The same considerations apply to extended unpaid annual leave or cycled (rotating) unpaid leave. Unions, particularly those representing migrant workers, have in the past been willing to agree to the latter alternative but, like all the other alternatives in this category, it has proved to be of only short-term use. Short time, layoffs and unpaid leave often precede, but do not completely obviate, the need for final retrenchment. Also, a total ban on overtime, which appears to be an easy alternative, may sometimes not be feasible because of the nature of the company's operations. The operations of the undertaking should be carefully considered before agreeing to ban overtime completely.

The final alternative is to be found in early or voluntary retrenchment or retirement of older employees. This can be offered only if the pension and retrenchment package is such that it makes it viable for the employee concerned. In South Africa, early retirement may be a viable option for higher level employees and for employees of all types who are close to retirement age, but it is not a solution for many unskilled workers. Furthermore, one of the reasons for the unions' insistence on the 'last in, first out (LIFO)' principle is their suspicion that management wishes to rid itself of older workers. Also to be considered is the fact that, unless the pension fund is strong enough to bear additional payments, it will be up to management to make the retirement package more attractive and this may well prove a costly exercise.

Criteria for Selection

The question as to the criteria to be adopted in selecting retrenchees is often one of the most contentious in the retrenchment argument. From the outset, the newer South African unions proposed the adoption of the 'last in, first out' policy. They argue that it rewards length of service and that it is the most easily applicable and objective criterion; furthermore, that it prevents any type of favouritism or discrimination against union members. Yet it could be argued that adoption of the LIFO principle does not always favour unions, whose members are often found to be among the younger employees. Employers, on the other hand, contend that there is no reason that they should not be allowed to retrench less competent employees. To this, union spokesmen reply that retrenchments should not be used for disciplinary purposes. Taking up the employer's reference to 'less competent' workers, they query the fact that previous action was not taken with regard to the incompetence of certain workers. On the other hand, unions will agree to the reservation of the employer's right to retain workers with shorter service than others but with special skills necessary for the continued functioning of the organisation, provided that there is no employee with longer service who would be able to do that job or who could be trained for that purpose. Worker representatives further insist that, besides the LIFO principle, consideration be given to special circumstances such as the fact that a certain employee is the sole breadwinner or has a handicap which would render it difficult for him to find new employment.

Initially, criteria for selection of retrenchees were generally set by the union rather than negotiated with the employer. A one-factor approach, consisting of the primary adoption of the LIFO principle with reference merely to special circumstances raised by the union, was generally demanded. Employers are now gradually persuading worker representatives that a multifaceted approach should be introduced, that the employer also wishes special circumstances to be considered and that an appropriate formula encompassing various criteria, perhaps with different weightings, should be worked out. In South Africa, the adoption of various criteria is supported by the Labour Court judgments, which have not insisted on LIFO as the only criterion but have merely advised that criteria should be agreed upon, that these criteria should be objective and that the selection should be fairly made in accordance with the agreed criteria. Furthermore, the 1988 amendments to the Labour Relations Act of 1956 specified that such criteria might include, but need not be limited to '... the ability, capacity, productivity and conduct of those employees and the operational requirements and needs of the undertaking, industry, trade or occupation of the employer'. The new legislation does not stipulate the criteria to be applied. As indicated previously, it provides merely for consultation on such criteria and for the implementation of agreed or fair criteria. This implies that, where no agreement on the criteria can be achieved, the employer may (after reacting appropriately to the other party's proposals) implement his own criteria, provided that these are fair, provable and consistently applied.

In selecting employees for retrenchment, two points need to be borne in mind. Firstly, contract workers should not be retrenched before the term of their contract expires, unless common law notice of three months is given, the employer is unable to carry on business or a clause in the contract provides for monthly review. Secondly, apprentices may not be retrenched in the normal manner.

Also to be taken into account is the fact that worker representatives refuse to accept the principle that a worker who has been transferred to another department will have his previous service disregarded and, should retrenchments occur in that department, be one of the first out in that department. This policy becomes even more difficult to justify if the work done in the new department requires little or no training and if it is considered that the Act now provides for transfer of service in the case of takeovers and mergers. This leads naturally to the question as to whether, if one department becomes redundant, retrenchments should occur vertically in that department alone or horizontally across departments. It is now accepted that, particularly where the LIFO principle is applied, the selection of retrenchees should be conducted throughout the company — or even within a group of companies — unless circumstances dictate otherwise.

Once the list of retrenchees has been compiled, it is common practice to present this to the union or workers' representatives for scrutiny and for representation as regards exceptional cases.

Retrenchment Pay and the Retrenchment Package

The new legislation stipulates that consultation on the amount of retrenchment pay must take place between the employer and the body representing employees, but at the same time specifies a lower limit of one week's pay for every year of service. However, an employer or group of employers may apply for exemption from this minimum payment by utilising the exemption procedure of the Basic Conditions of Employment Act. Contrarily, the Minister may at any time (but subject to consultation with NEDLAC and the Coordinating Bargaining Council

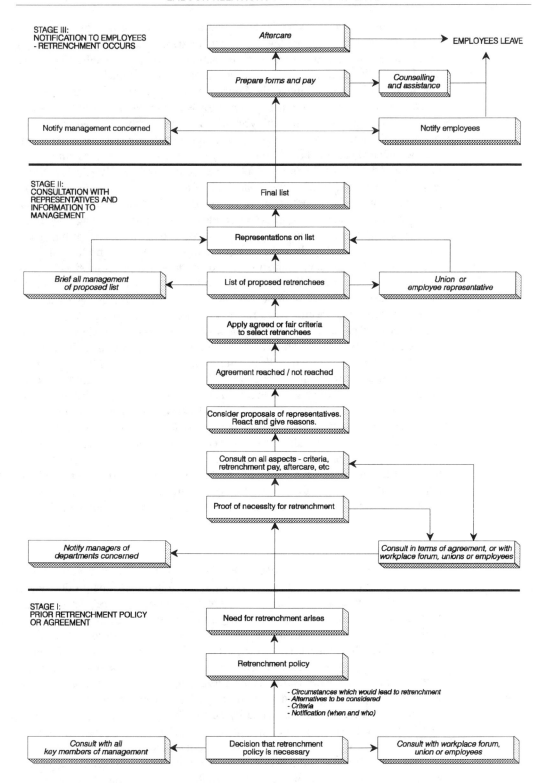

Figure 22: RETRENCHMENT PROGRAMME

for the Public Service) revise the minimum by publishing a new minimum rate in the *Government Gazette*. Should a dispute arise concerning the amount of retrenchment pay, such dispute may be submitted first to conciliation by the CCMA or a bargaining council, and thereafter to arbitration. In dealing with a dispute regarding retrenchment, the Court may investigate the circumstances and determine the amount of retrenchment pay for which the employer will be liable.

As mentioned earlier, an employee who has unreasonably refused transfer or the offer of another job is not entitled to retrenchment pay. On the other hand, retrenchment pay should not be confused with other payments such as notice pay, leave and pension payments to which the employee is lawfully entitled. Some employers agree to add their own contributions to the pension payout or to make provision for added benefits from the pension fund to increase the total retrenchment package. One concern of employers is that management may agree to substantial retrenchment packages and that the employee might soon afterwards be re-employed by the same or another employer. The first, namely re-employment at the same company, would speak of bad planning since, if it is envisaged that reduction will be of a temporary nature, provision should be made for temporary layoffs with limited or no benefits but with the guarantee of re-employment by a specific date. In certain companies, employees are given a choice between permanent retrenchment with the necessary severance pay, and temporary layoffs with a guarantee of re-employment. A few companies have in the past opted for paying retrenchees a limited amount on a monthly basis, either until such time as they can be re-employed or for a specified period. In such cases care should be exercised that repayments do not exceed one third of normal wages, since in South Africa this would debar the worker from receiving unemployment benefits. Also, it may not be prudent policy to have dismissed employees returning at regular intervals to collect payments, particularly if there is little prospect of their re-employment. The second possibility, namely that the employee rapidly finds new employment, should be no concern of his previous employer. Moreover, the likelihood of this occurring could have been established by the employer's own previous attempts to find alternative employment for the worker concerned.

Notification to Employees

The period of notice to employees remains the most contested part of the retrenchment procedure. Employers, to avoid a drop in morale and productivity, usually attempt to delay notification of the actual employees to be retrenched to the last moment. Their reasons for doing so are sound. Yet unions insist that sufficient notice of retrenchment be given to the employees concerned. One of the reasons for this is the very strong psychological effect that summary notice may have on employees. To be out of a job from one day to the next is a severe blow. In response there is the counterargument that rapid severance of a relationship is preferable to a drawn out or gradual parting. Nevertheless, other reasons for sufficient notice are cited by employee representatives, such as the need to allow the retrenchee an opportunity to find alternative employment and the time required to identify cases where particular hardship may result.

It should be noted that the British code on retrenchment advises that as much warning as is 'practicable' should be given to the employees concerned, whereas in South Africa the requirement is that 'reasonable notice' should be given. This allows for a great deal of discretion on the part of the decision taker, but in the past the Industrial Court has indicated that it will order employers who, in its opinion, have given insufficient notice to pay compensation in lieu of notice. Perhaps a compromise could be found by allowing for an additional paid notice period, over and above the normal notice period. This means that the employee is told of his retrenchment shortly before he is due to leave but that he is paid as though he were employed until the end of the month, whereafter his notice period comes into effect. Care should be exercised that, in the payout, a clear distinction is made between 'pay in lieu of notice' and 'retrenchment pay'.

Aftercare

Once retrenchments or redundancies have been effected, it is essential that all the necessary assistance be given to employees in claiming UIF and other benefits. Even if the paperwork has been done before the actual retrenchments, there will invariably be queries and problems. Also, employers should fulfil their promise of assistance in the search for alternative employment. For these reasons it may be necessary, in the case of both partial retrenchment and a complete shutdown and especially in the case of large-scale retrenchments, to set up a temporary aftercare centre, either as part of the personnel department or — and perhaps preferably — completely separated from the employer's other operations.

The Undertaking to Re-employ

Many unions demand that, for a specified period, retrenched employees be given priority should vacancies arise in the future. The procedure requested is that unions concerned be advised of vacancies and that they be given sufficient opportunity to contact retrenchees who could possibly fill such vacancies. The demand for an offer to re-employ is a reasonable one but should be carefully considered, and there should be strict compliance with the offer once it has been made. In at least one Industrial Court case an employer was faced with an unfair labour practice allegation for employing completely new workers in preference to previously retrenched employees. Evidently, he had not foreseen the possibility that he might be obliged to create positions which the retrenched workers could not fill. Consequently, it is essential to phrase the undertaking to re-employ in such terms that the employer will still be able to take on completely new workers with special skills not held by the retrenchees. As retrenchees may often be difficult to trace, a limit should also be set on the time allowed to the union to fill the vacancy with a retrenched employee.

Repercussions

Retrenchment is a delicate and difficult process which needs to be handled with sympathy and circumspection. Those who rush into retrenchments — and particularly those managers who use reorganisation and subsequent redundancies as an excuse to rid themselves of unwanted employees — may find themselves facing serious allegations, as will those companies who engage in bogus sellouts or takeovers merely to avoid a proper retrenchment exercise.

Transfer of Contracts

It has happened in the past that a business is taken over (sometimes merely as a front) and that employees are then regarded as having new contracts. This means that the 'new' employer could then retrench without consideration of length of service. The Labour Relations Act of 1995 attempts to prevent this in a special section referring to transfer of contracts.

The Act probibits the transfer of an employee's contract without his consent. However, it does allow for the contracts of existing employees to be taken over by the new employer where the whole or part of the employer's business is transferred as a going concern to a new owner. The legislation stipulates that in such cases all rights and obligations between the ex-employer and the employees become rights and obligations between the new employer and the employees. Furthermore, anything done by or with regard to the ex-employer will be taken to have been done by the new employer, unless there is an agreement to the contrary. This means that the contract of the employee and his length of service remain intact, and that any agreement between employees and the ex-employer becomes an agreement with the new employer. Thus, if after six months he should decide to retrench certain employees, the new employer will have to take their previous service into consideration and abide by any agreement in respect of retrenchments.

The only exception occurs in the case of insolvency. Where the old employer became insolvent, the contracts are automatically transferred to the new employer; but, in this instance, all rights and obligations as existed at the time of transfer remain the rights and obligations between the ex-employer and the employees. Thus, although the employee's service may be continuous, he may not be able to claim compensation for his full term of service from the new employer — but he might be able to sue the ex-employer for this, especially if there existed an agreement regarding retrenchment pay.

Policy and Procedures for the Handling of Work Stoppages and Strike Action

Rationale

Any management team, irrespective of its relationship with its employees or representative unions, should be prepared for the event that employees or a group of employees stage a work stoppage or strike, as a sign of protest or in support of a demand, particularly where such actions are of a spontaneous or illegal nature. Preparation for this contingency is effected by the establishment of the necessary policy and procedures. The purpose of a contingency plan is:

- to avoid impulsive reaction on the part of management and panic amongst managers or amongst those employees who are not on strike,
- to establish a uniform policy and plan of action and to formulate guidelines for the handling of striking employees,
- to ensure the necessary protection of persons and property,
- to arrange for the continuation of production, or for shutdown or partial shutdown,
- to ensure that a negotiation forum is established, and
- to make the necessary practical or administrative arrangements for the return (or non-return) of striking employees.

Ensuring Preparedness

Certain concrete steps can be taken to ensure that all key managerial personnel have the information they will need immediately a strike or work stoppage occurs, and that coordinated action will be initiated. Coordination requires the prior appointment of one person, in the form of the general manager and/or personnel manager, to whom all others will report and who will act as spokesman for management. Such person will also be charged with the task of dealing with the press. Management should deal honestly with the press, since sensationalism and unguarded statements may lead to an escalation in tension. All other persons should be prohibited from furnishing any statements for public consumption.

The general manager or personnel/industrial relations manager will be assisted by a negotiating committee, appointed beforehand, which will be charged with the function of planning strategy and negotiating with employee representatives. The method of selection of employee representatives should be decided on during the preparatory stage. Management may decide that it will negotiate with shop stewards, union officials, workers' committee members or a number of persons elected by the striking employees. To attempt negotiation with an entire contingent of strikers is usually not feasible. For this reason management should also decide whether or not it will allow strikers to remain on the property and, if so, where they will be allowed to gather and how representatives will be elected.

Practical contingencies need to be foreseen. To these ends a list of persons or institutions such as suppliers, customers and subsidiary agencies who will need to be contacted, and the telephone numbers of each, should be established. Arrangements need to be made for the protection of other employees — for example, by their withdrawal from premises close to the strikers. The necessary security has to be arranged and provision will have to be made for the protection of buildings and property, as well as for the shutting off of machinery. Persons to be held responsible ought to be appointed in each instance. If preparation is made for continuation of production or delivery, this will entail in the first instance the prior establishment of a list of available manpower. The list will describe the skills of each person in the organisation and particularly those at managerial or supervisory level, so that planning and training for redeployment can occur before the event. The manager who will coordinate such redeployment should be specified. The possibility of obtaining additional manpower may also be considered, although this may incense the strikers. Furthermore, the operation of each section needs to be carefully investigated, with the purpose of providing for different or extended shifts or cycles in the event of any irregularity.

Finally, there are administrative details which require attention. These include the issue of notices and ultimatums to striking employees, as well as provision for rapid payout of wages and for new employment or re-employment, should the strike be illegal and dismissals eventually prove unavoidable. The manager responsible must already have devised a plan or made the necessary arrangements.

The Action Plan
The action plan will be drafted beforehand and will include provisions for the following.

- The immediate reporting of a work stoppage or strike action
- Assessment of the extent of the action and the possible cause

- The handling of striking employees
- The evacuation of strikers or their movement to a particular venue
- The shutdown of machinery and equipment and the institution of security measures
- The movement or evacuation of non-striking employees
- The manning of key positions
- Information to outside agencies
- The convening of the negotiating committee
- Communication among managers and between management and non-striking employees
- The keeping of a strike diary
- Communication with the strikers and the appointment of representatives
- The establishment of a negotiation forum
- Notice to striking employees that they will not be paid for the time that they do not work
- Attempts to persuade employees to return to work while negotiations continue
- Prevention of violence and intimidation
- Monitoring of picketing
- Redeployment, continued production and delivery
- Dealings with the media
- The issue of statements to striking employees
- Notification of settlement
- Return to work of employees
- In the case of an illegal strike, ultimatum and notification of dismissals and procedures for payment, employment or re-employment

(A detailed strike contingency plan is included in the Annexures.)

Aftercare

The conflict which gave rise to an action is not necessarily settled when striking employees return to work. Also, as mentioned in Chapter 8, the previous existence of conflict — even where resolution is achieved — leads to a heightened conflict potential. Consequently, the necessary aftercare (which does not signify a pandering to employees) should be instituted. All agreements and promises made must be effected as rapidly as possible and no further recriminations ought to be made. Efforts to improve communication channels and procedures are advisable and the necessary precautions need to be taken to prevent a recurrence of the incident. A follow-up, in the form of a meeting with employee representatives after a cooling-down period has elapsed, might prove valuable.

Effectiveness of the Contingency Plan

Unfortunately, the effectiveness of a contingency plan can be assessed only once an action has occurred. It is never possible to foresee all contingencies and some *ad hoc* action may become necessary. Nevertheless, managerial representatives should be trained in the execution of the plan, possibly by the use of simulation exercises. The existence of a plan does ensure that there is a degree of preparedness, that there is certainty as to the action which should be taken and that cohesion is maintained among members of management.

Unions might equally draw up their own strike action or lockout contingency plan, which will deal with matters such as meetings, strategies, pickets and dissemination of information to strikers.

CONCLUSION

The labour relationship commences at the workplace. Unless proper employee care is undertaken, effective communication channels are established and procedures are introduced which are in line with managerial objectives but which also promote the fair treatment of employees, no amount of negotiation and bargaining will ensure the stability of the employment relationship.

The processes, structures and procedures outlined in this chapter form the basis for sound workplace practices. The chapter is by no means exhaustive: there are numerous other more specialised and informal interactions which help to shape the labour relations climate. Management and employees should at all times be aware that they are constructing and maintaining a relationship, and should act accordingly. Furthermore, personnel/industrial relations practitioners should take care that the relationship does not stagnate, and they should be continuously involved in attempts to develop and improve the relationship.

SOURCES

Anthony, P D *The Conduct of Industrial Relations*, Institute of Personnel Management, London, 1980.

Brassey, Cameron, Cheadle and Olivier *The New Labour Law*, Juta, 1987.

Kochan, Thomas A *Collective Bargaining and Industrial Relations*, Richard D Irwin, 1980.

Luthans, Fred *Organisational Behaviour* (4th ed.), McGraw Hill, 1985.

Manning, Anthony D *Communicating for Change*, Juta, 1987.

Salamon, Michael *Industrial Relations Theory and Practice*, Prentice-Hall, 1987.

Winkler, J T 'The Ghost at the Bargaining Table: Directors and Industrial Relations' in *British Journal of Industrial Relations* Vol XII, No. 2, 1974.

Labour Relations Act (no. 66 of 1995), *Government Gazette* Vol 366 No. 16861, Government Printer, Pretoria, December 1995.

11

BASIC PRINCIPLES OF LABOUR ECONOMICS

Labour Economics is, in itself, an independent field of study. Although the entire field cannot be studied here, it is of importance in the practice of Industrial Relations to be acquainted with the basic principles of Labour Economics, since economic factors wield so great an influence on the conduct of the labour relationship and on the bargaining process in particular.

Central to the study of Labour Economics is the establishment of wage and labour market theory. Early wage theories tended to concentrate on the supply of labour to the market and on methods of regulating this supply while, at the same time, keeping wages at a level which would prove profitable to the entrepreneur. The theory of Market Equilibrium as a means of establishing wage levels was first introduced by Adam Smith, who also foresaw that varying circumstances would result in different types of labour markets.

Another common factor in the earlier theories was a belief in the existence of a fixed wage pool and, consequently, the assumption that any increase in wages for one section of the working population would be at the cost of their fellow employees or at the risk of increasing unemployment. These assumptions were partially refuted by the theory of the Economy of High Wages and the Marginal Productivity theory, but it was not until the late Nineteenth Century that the complexity of the labour market and its susceptibility to numerous factors were fully appreciated.

The labour market is, in terms of modern economic theory, assumed to function in the same manner as other markets, despite the fact that it differs vastly from product and capital markets. Labour market theory is based on the law of supply and demand, but of greater importance to the labour relations specialist are the factors which cause shifts in supply and demand. The elasticity of demand and supply and the theory of marginal productivity should also become familiar concepts. In particular our interest lies in the effect which collective bargaining and wage determinations may have on wage levels and in the results which discriminatory labour practices and labour mobility, or the lack of it, will have as regards both the overall composition of the labour market and the wage levels which are established for different groups.

In all, the subject is of a complex nature, so much so that it can be fully understood and appreciated only after extensive reading.

THE IMPORTANCE OF LABOUR ECONOMICS

The importance of labour economics in modern day life is aptly described by McConnell *et al* when they state that, '... many of the most compelling socioeconomic issues of the day centre upon the labour sector of the economy'. Newspaper headlines regularly cover labour-related issues such as strikes, productivity levels, rising unemployment, wage–price inflation and greater mechanisation, all of which are the concern of labour economists. Also, the major part of national income is distributed in the form of wages. Since wage earners constitute the core of economic activity, it is important to understand how the wage levels are established and the effect of these on the economy in general. This necessitates a study of the wage and labour markets, which display their own particular characteristics, different from those of product and capital markets.

In the industrial relations context, economic aspects and the wage bargaining conducted by unions play an important role in the general conduct of the labour relationship. The level at which wages are set and the bargaining power of each side will be determined, among other things, by general conditions in the labour market and the level of unemployment. In bargaining forums, arguments based on wage theories, the free market principle and levels of inflation are utilised by both sides. An understanding of the rudimentary theories and principles of labour economics is, therefore, necessary for the Labour Relations student as well as the practitioner.

THE NATURE AND SCOPE OF LABOUR ECONOMICS

Whereas, previously, labour economics was highly descriptive and tended to concentrate on such aspects as union activity, the history of the union movement, the effects of collective bargaining and labour law, a change has taken place since the 1960s in that the trend has been to apply macro- and micro-economic theory to activities in the labour sector of the economy. Macro-economics studies the economy as a whole and, in the sphere of labour economics, would concern itself with average wage levels, unemployment levels and average price levels. Micro-economics, on the other hand, is concerned with the functioning of individual labour markets and with wage rates and employment levels in these markets, as well as with the decisions and ability of individuals to participate in the labour market.

In our study of labour economics, macro- and micro-economic aspects are not strictly separated, but are generally integrated to provide a total picture of the labour market.

WAGE AND LABOUR MARKET THEORIES

As industrialisation and commercialisation developed and the concept of a wage earner emerged, it became necessary for the economic thinkers to focus attention on the supply of labour to the market and on methods by which wages could or would be determined. This each did in the light of his own economic philosophy.

The early economic theories, including those on wages, of the **Mercantilists**, **Adam Smith**, **Malthus** and **Marx** have been discussed in Chapter 2. In the early Mercantilist era there were attempts to control wages and prices, but this often resulted only in 'keeping the poor poor'. Smith advocated that wages be set by the market mechanism, although he did realise that the market would not always be perfect, while Malthus proposed the curb of population growth by the payment of bare subsistence wages. Marx, on the other hand, argued that the market-related wage paid to workers allowed for the creation of surplus value. An employee was paid enough to live, but not in proportion to the additional value which he created.

The principle on which most of the early theories were based was that of a fixed **wage fund**. They presupposed that there was a static amount of capital which could be allocated to wages. Wage levels were, in the opinion of these theorists, determinable by dividing the amount of capital that entrepreneurs were prepared to expend on labour by the number of persons seeking employment. Thus, the larger the total amount of persons offering themselves for employment, the lower the wages would be. From this arose the argument that trade unions, seeking to advance wage levels for a certain group of workers, would cause the lowering of other wages, or general unemployment. The same was likely to happen if the State interfered in the market by fixing minimum wage levels.

The wage fund theory was partially refuted by the principle of the **Economy of High Wages**, which postulated that higher wages would increase the productivity of labour, leading to increased capital growth and, therefore, more work opportunity. This led to the abandonment, towards the end of the Nineteenth Century, of the wage fund theory, and to a greater interest in the **Marginal Productivity Theory**. The marginal productivity theory tied the demand for labour — and, consequently, wage levels — to changes in labour productivity. It also led to theories related to the elasticity of demand and to the supposition that, where demand was elastic, excessive wage increases not accompanied by increases in productivity would eventually lead to a shrinkage of the funds available to labour, since employers would attempt to substitute labour by, for example, technology. This theory concentrated on the demand for labour and the relationship between wages and productivity, but it added little knowledge of the way in which the supply of labour was determined. It was only with the advent of more modern economists such as **Alfred Marshall** and, of course, **John Hicks** that it was pointed out that in economics there is an interaction of numerous factors, that demand for labour depends in turn on the supply and the supply price of labour, as well as on the supply of capital; furthermore, that the activities of unions and the practice of collective bargaining may greatly influence the wage levels established.

In modern society there is no set theory for the determination of wage levels. In capitalist systems, wage levels are still broadly related to market trends and traces of the early wage theories are to be found in numerous arguments, but economic systems have become so complex and subject to so great a variety of interacting forces, that a unidimensional approach becomes unworkable. Nevertheless, basic economic concepts relating to supply and demand still underlie our thinking as regards unemployment and the setting of wage levels.

THE FUNCTIONING OF THE LABOUR MARKET

Character-istics of the Labour Market

Although the labour market is, in economic theory, equated to other markets such as capital and product markets, it has its own particular characteristics. Reynolds, Masters and Moser list the following as unique characteristics of the labour market.

- **Multiplicity of Markets** — Reference is usually made to the labour market, but this market is in effect comprised of many different markets, such as those for various skill levels, occupations, age groups, sexes, industries and geographical regions. The various markets are to some extent interchangeable; yet barriers to mobility do exist. It is these barriers which constitute a central concern in labour economics.
- **No Central Clearing House Exists** — Goods may be processed through a central exchange, but there is no such clearing house for employees, who cannot be centrally collected and then apportioned on demand. Thus, when we speak of a certain market in a particular area, the concept is largely theoretical.
- **Workers are not Standardised** — While various applicants might offer themselves for the same position, they will vary in ability, intelligence, motivation, physical characteristics, social behaviour and specific skills. Hence they are not all equally suited for the position. A special concern of labour economics is the development of human capital as a means of broadening the potential labour market.
- **Temporary Nature of the Employment Relationship** — Once a purchaser buys goods for consumption, they become the property of the buyer. This is not so with the employment relationship. Either the employer or employee may decide at any time to terminate the relationship. This leads to greater fluidity and unpredictability in the labour market.
- **Complexity of the Employment Package** — The price paid for labour and the value received may be far higher than the actual wage rate. Employees receive tangible and intangible benefits in the form of pensions, housing, work satisfaction and personal growth. In applying the law of supply and demand to the labour market, these benefits are not taken into account.

When analysing the labour market, and particularly when applying the principles of demand and supply, these factors should be taken into account, but, as Reynolds *et al* confirm, the following assumptions are usually made when applying economic theory to the labour market.

- The wage rate, and nothing else, determines the attractiveness of a particular position.
- All vacancies are filled through the market, and not by internal promotion.
- All workers are the same if they are able to do the same job.
- There is full knowledge among potential employees of job opportunities, wage rates and job characteristics and employers,

likewise, have full knowledge of potential employees.
- The economic motive overrides all others.
- The market is competitive; that there is no restriction or collusion.
- Everything else in the economy remains constant.

The Law of Demand and Supply: A Micro-Economic Analysis

The theory of labour demand and supply is based on the same principles as price theory. The latter theory teaches, firstly, that there is a direct, inverse relationship between price and demand; that **as the price increases, the quantity demanded will decrease.** In the context of the labour market, this means that, as the price of labour (wages) increases, so the quantity of labour demanded will decrease. The Demand Schedule obtained from this premise is illustrated in Figure 23.

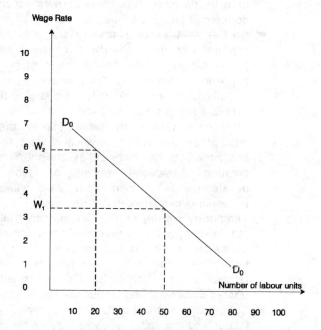

Figure 23: LABOUR DEMAND SCHEDULE

The demand curve slopes upward to the left. According to Figure 23, fifty units of labour would be demanded at a wage rate (price) of R3,00 per hour, but, should the wage rate rise to R6,00 per hour, the quantity demanded would decline to 20 units. The consequences of this on the level of employment are self-evident, a factor which should influence unions during bargaining, but it should be remembered that this is a purist model. It does not take into account factors which cause a shift in the demand curve, nor, as far as unemployment is concerned, growth aspects and the opportunity for alternative employment.

The second principle of price theory is that supply stands in a direct, straightforward relationship to price. The **lower the price, the smaller will be the quantity of goods or services offered to the market**. In terms of labour supply, this means that the number of people prepared to do a certain job will decrease in direct relation to a decrease in the wage level. As a result, the Supply Function illustrated in Figure 24 is obtained.

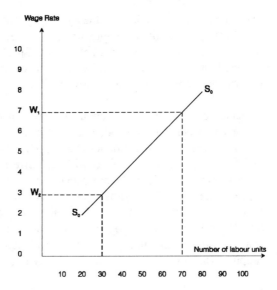

Figure 24: THE SUPPLY FUNCTION OF LABOUR

In terms of Figure 24, seventy workers would offer themselves at a wage of R7,00 per hour while, at a rate of R3,00 per hour, the supply of labour would drop to thirty. This, too, is the simplified theoretical position and factors influencing the supply of labour are not taken into account.

Market Equilibrium   In the perfectly competitive market, **equilibrium** is achieved at the point where the supply curve intersects the demand curve. Equilibrium price and equilibrium quantity of labour demanded and labour supplied are determined by the interaction of market demand and market supply. This is illustrated in Figure 25,

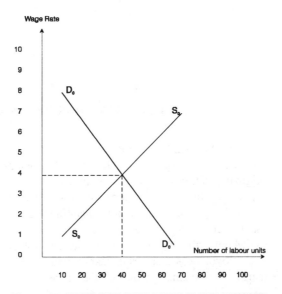

Figure 25: EQUILIBRIUM IN SUPPLY AND DEMAND

where equilibrium would be achieved if 40 people were to be employed at a rate of R4,00 per hour and 40 people offered themselves for employment at this wage rate. This situation arises under conditions of perfect competition, which is rarely achieved in practice. Free market economists, however, believe that there is, nevertheless, always a tendency towards a restoration of equilibrium.

Shifts in Demand

Demand for and supply of labour are not related only to wage levels. Total demand is a **derived** demand, since it depends, *inter alia*, on the demand for goods or services in the product market. Thus an increase in, for example, the demand for goods and services will lead, irrespective of the wage rate, to an increase in the quantity of labour demanded. This occasions a shift in the demand curve to the right of its original position (illustrated by a shift from D_0 to D_1 in Figure 26). If the supply curve remains constant, the consumers of labour (employers) will have to pay more to obtain further quantities of labour. This could entail overtime pay or the offer of higher wages, in order to draw more suppliers (labour units) to the market. Thus a new wage rate (W_2) is established.

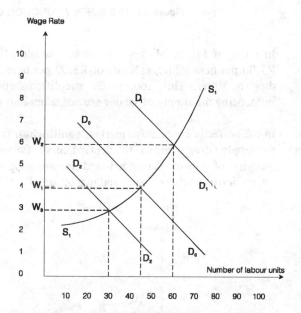

Figure 26: SHIFTS IN THE DEMAND CURVE

On the other hand, if the demand for goods and services suddenly decreases, total demand for labour will decrease. The demand curve shifts to the left of its original position (illustrated by the shift from D_0 to D_2 in Figure 26). If the supply of labour remains constant, this means that the consumers of labour will be able to pay less for smaller quantities of labour. A new wage rate (W_3) is established. This happens because there is greater rivalry among workers, some of whom will be prepared to accept lower wages. It also means that unemployment in that labour market will increase, or that people will leave that market to find employment in other areas.

Shifts in   Shifts may also occur in the supply curve: for example, with emigration,
Supply   immigration or migration. This is very relevant to the South African labour
market and needs a detailed analysis. A shift of the supply curve to the left (S_1
in Figure 27) is occasioned by a general decrease in the supply of labour. Where
demand remains constant, this results in a higher wage rate (W_2) being
established for smaller quantities of labour (an argument similar to that of an
increase in demand). An increase in the supply of labour relative to demand
causes a shift in the supply curve to the right (S_2) and a lower wage rate (W_3)
for higher quantities of labour (see Decrease in Demand).

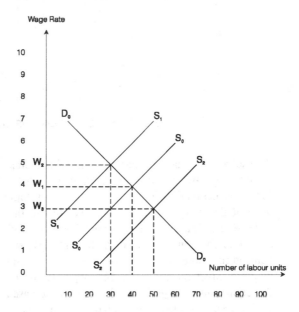

Figure 27: SHIFTS IN THE SUPPLY CURVE

Movement to   According to free market theorists, if all other things remain equal the wage rate
Equilibrium   established by shifting demand and supply will be of a temporary nature since,
as indicated earlier, there is always a tendency towards a restoration of
equilibrium. Thus, if too many employees offer themselves for a particular job
and the supply curve shifts to the right, competition or rivalry will occur
amongst the suppliers of labour. As a result, certain workers will be prepared
to accept lower wages, leading to a decrease in the average price of labour
(wages). Because workers are now prepared to accept lower wages, employers
are prepared to take on more labour. Therefore, there is a gradual move along
the demand curve to a new equilibrium situation, where the price (wage) is lower
than in the perfect equilibrium situation, but higher than it would have been at
the first level of supply — that is, when a situation of oversupply arose, and the
quantity demanded was greater than the original demand but lower than the
actual supply. Similarly, in a situation of excess demand, alternative means of
production may be sought by the employer. If this is not possible, he may offer
a higher wage to attract extra labour units. As a result, more persons will offer

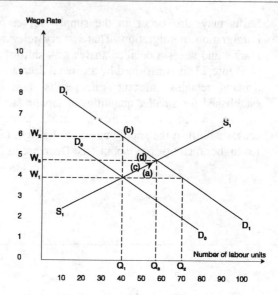

Figure 28: ESTABLISHMENT OF EQUILIBRIUM

themselves for that occupation and, with increased competition, the price of labour drops and a new equilibrium is achieved, where the price is higher than in the perfect equilibrium situation but lower than it would have been at the first level of demand — that is, when the shift in the demand curve arose. This is reflected in Figure 28. If the general demand for labour increases, occasioning a shift in the demand curve to the right (D_0 to D_1), employers are generally demanding more quantities of labour at the same wage rate — (a) on the diagram. Since the additional quantity of labour demanded cannot be obtained at the equilibrium wage (W_1), the rate is increased to W_2 (illustrated by (b) in Figure 28). This attracts more labour to the market, occasioning a movement (c) along the supply curve. Since more employees are prepared to offer themselves, there is increased competition and the wage rate will decrease from its previous high at point (b). A new equilibrium is established, resulting in a new wage (W_3), which is higher than the perfect equilibrium wage but lower than the wage necessitated by the original increased demand. Similarly, the quantity of labour demanded and supplied (Q_3) is higher than the perfect equilibrium quantity (Q_1), but lower than the quantity demanded when the original shortage arose (Q_2).

Factors Leading to a Shift in Demand

Factors mentioned by Fick and High as causing shifts in the demand curve include the following.

- **An Increase in the Number of Employers** — It may happen in a particular industry that a number of new employers enter the market. The demand for labour of a particular type increases. This will cause a shift of the demand curve to the right, leading to the establishment of a higher wage rate for labour.
- **An Increase in the Income of Employers** — If the business of employers suddenly becomes particularly lucrative, resulting in higher profits, or if subsidies were received for the

employment of labour, as happened under South Africa's decentralisation policy, the cost of labour would, in relative terms, become cheaper to the employer. This might result in a shift of the demand curve to the right.

- **Preference for a Certain Type of Employee** — There are occasions when, for various reasons, employers decide that a particular kind of employee is best suited for the job at hand. This may occur in the case where females are found to be defter at executing a certain task, or it could result from an affirmative action programme or from technological developments necessitating the importation of labour. An event of this kind would occasion a shift to the right in the demand for that kind of labour and a shift to the left as regards the rest of the general labour market.

- **The Possibility of Using Alternatives to Labour** — With greater technological development, there is a greater possibility of capital investment in machinery, which would replace labour and, in the long term, prove more cost effective. This will decrease the demand for labour or for a particular type of labour, resulting in a shift of the demand curve to the left and a subsequent decrease in the wage rate.

- **An Increase in the Cost of Labour** — Should the price of labour increase for any reason (such as minimum wage determination, the granting of union wage demands, or the imposition of a payroll tax by government) this may in the longer term lead employers to seek alternatives to labour, thereby occasioning a shift in the demand curve to the left, a situation which will contribute to increased unemployment.

Factors Leading to Shifts in Supply

Shifts in the supply curve will occur for the following reasons.

- **Oversupply or Undersupply of Labour** — If, in general, the market is oversupplied; if there are, for example, too many unskilled workers as a result of immigration by people with poor educational qualifications, the supply curve will be shifted to the right. Conversely, a general shortage of labour — for example, in times of war — will cause a shift of the supply curve to the left.

- **The Amount of Training Needed to Perform a Certain Job** — Training of any kind necessitates expenses, also for the individual undergoing such training. The result is that, as the level and difficulty of training increases, the supply of labour of a particular type decreases. This will occasion a shift to the left in the supply curve and a higher wage rate than the average.

- **Attractiveness of Certain Positions** — Work which has a high public image or offers a great deal of flexibility, such as modelling or public relations, is usually more attractive than other occupations. Unless there are special skills involved, this will result in an influx of persons to that occupation, leading to a shift to the right in the supply curve.

- **Degree of Hardship or Risk Involved** — Occupations which require hard or dirty work or which entail a certain amount of risk are less likely to draw potential employees. This leads to an upward shift in the supply curve relating to that particular occupation. Few applicants offer themselves and wages are higher than the average. A good example is the high wage rate paid to lumberjacks in the Canadian outback or to men prepared to work on oil rigs at sea.

- **Union Activities** — A union, for example by controlling the intake of apprentices, may limit the supply of labour to the market, leading to a shift to the left in the supply curve.
- **Discriminatory Policies** — The reservation, either by law or otherwise, of certain positions for people of a particular race or sex results in a limitation of the supply of labour to those occupations and an oversupply of labour in unreserved occupations. This occasions an upward shift in the supply curve in respect of the reserved occupations and a downward shift in respect of open occupations. Privileged employees will command higher wages, whereas those less fortunate and facing strong competition for jobs have to be satisfied with lower wage rates. Women for many years have suffered this lot, as did black employees in terms of South Africa's policy of racial discrimination.

The factors mentioned contribute towards the creation of an imperfect market. The reasons for these imperfections are numerous, ranging from variables such as economic conditions, educational facilities, demographic influences, government policy, overpopulation, discriminatory practices, union activity, technological development and a lack of labour mobility to personal preferences and the desire for leisure. Some of these problems encountered in the labour market will be discussed in another section, with particular reference to the South African situation.

Elasticity of Demand and Supply

The law of demand and supply postulates that, as the price of labour increases, the quantity of labour demanded will decrease; equally that, as the price decreases, the quantity supplied to the market decreases. Yet there are instances where quantity demanded or supplied is not responsive to price; hence the concepts of elastic and inelastic demand or supply. Where quantity demanded can be rapidly adapted, the demand is elastic, while where quantity demanded cannot easily change the demand is said to be inelastic. The varying positions of elastic and inelastic demand are illustrated in Figure 29.

In Figure 29, the equilibrium wage (We) corresponds with equilibrium quantity demanded (Qe). When wages increase from We to Wn, then there is a change in quantity demanded from:

(a)   Qe to Q_1 where demand is relatively inelastic (D_1)
(b)   Qe to Q_2 with unitary demand (D_2)
(c)   Qe to Q_3 with relatively elastic demand (D_3)

Therefore, one observes a greater sensitivity on the part of the employer to an increase in wages in situations where demand is relatively elastic. The higher wage results in a significant decrease in demand.

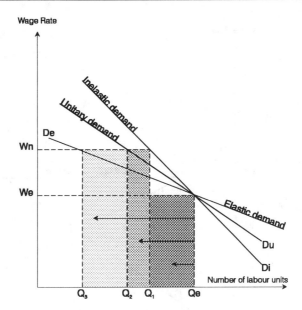

Figure 29: ELASTIC AND INELASTIC DEMAND

In terms of the inelastic demand curve in Figure 29, demand will diminish only slightly, despite a steep increase in wage price. Conversely, in the case of the elastic demand curve, demand decreases rapidly with only a minimal increase in the wage rate.

This is of particular importance as regards levels of employment. Also, as noted in a later chapter, it affects union bargaining power. With an inelastic demand, employment levels remain quite constant, even if a significant increase in wages is demanded by the union. Demand will be more inelastic if labour is essential and irreplaceable, if the employer has to produce a certain number of units at all costs, if labour costs do not constitute a large proportion of total costs and if the supply of capital and other non-labour factors is also constant.

The effect of elastic and inelastic demand on employment levels is best illustrated by observing the effects on employment levels of a wage determination under elastic and inelastic demand conditions, as illustrated in Figure 30.

As can be seen, where the demand for labour was elastic, the higher wage rate imposed led to a drastic decrease in the number of people employed. Where the demand for labour was inelastic, the decrease in employment was insignificant. In absolutely inelastic conditions, the demand curve would be vertical. Thus the imposed minimum wage rate would have no effect on employment levels.

Where the number of labour units supplied changes rapidly with a change in the wage rate, supply is described as elastic. If, on the other hand, the number of units supplied remains relatively constant, the supply is said to be inelastic. Elastic and inelastic supply curves are illustrated in Figure 31.

As seen from the inelastic supply curve (Si), supply decreases only marginally (from Qe to Q_1), despite significant changes in the wage rate from We to W_1. In the elastic supply curve (Se), the quantity supplied will drop rapidly from Qe to Q_3, with minimal changes in the wage per hour.

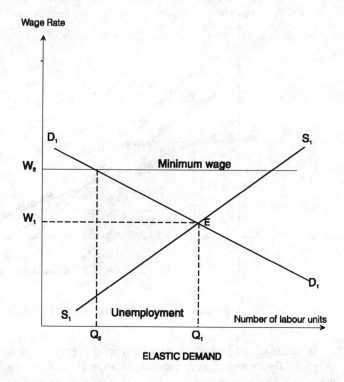

ELASTIC DEMAND

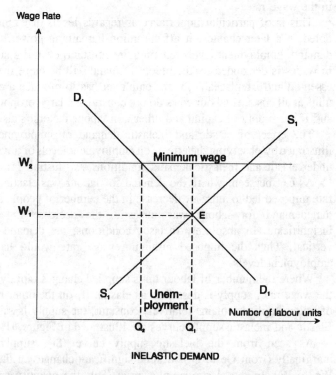

INELASTIC DEMAND

Figure 30: EMPLOYMENT LEVELS AS AFFECTED BY WAGE DETERMINATION IN ELASTIC AND INELASTIC DEMAND CONDITIONS

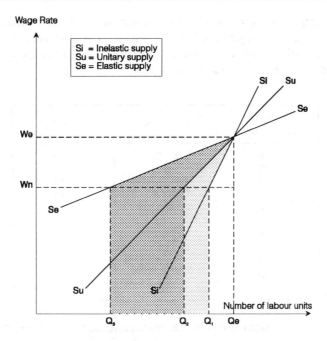

Figure 31: ELASTIC AND INELASTIC SUPPLY

Inelasticity of supply can be caused by a closed labour market, found, for example, in the apprenticeship system. It may also be caused by market discrimination, the immobility of labour or a dearth of training in certain skills. It has an important effect on labour relations in that an inelastic supply can lead to wage fixing, either by employers or unions, whereas an elastic supply leads to more competitive wages.

The degree of elasticity in the demand for and supply of labour constitutes an important consideration in the bargaining situation. Naturally employers will favour circumstances in which demand is elastic but supply remains inelastic. The reverse situation would be favoured by the union.

The Law of Diminishing Returns

The law of diminishing returns postulates that, in any process, a stage is reached at which the input of an additional unit brings a marginally declining return. This can be applied to the use of labour in the production process, to the units of effort or time which will be exerted by an employee to achieve a certain standard of living and to the degree to which a union is prepared to sacrifice employment opportunities for the sake of higher wages.

The Marginal Productivity or Utility of Labour

It is common practice for producers of goods or services to attempt to increase their productive output by increasing labour units — that is, the number of people employed. However, if the other major factor of production, capital, in the form of machinery or available space, remains constant, a stage will in terms of marginal productivity theory be reached where each additional unit of labour will produce marginally less than the previous unit. If a machine or process was designed for operation by three persons or, at the maximum, five persons, then greater total output could be obtained by using seven operators, but each operator after the third will produce marginally less than those before him. This development is illustrated in Table 5.

Number of Labour Units	Total Output	Marginal Output	Average Output per Labour Unit
0	0	–	–
1	12	12	12
2	26	14	13
3	42	16	14
4	57	15	14,25
5	70	13	14
6	80	10	13,3
7	86	6	12,3
8	86	0	10,75
9	84	– 2	9,3
10	81	– 5	8,1

Table 5: TOTAL AND MARGINAL OUTPUT PER LABOUR UNIT

From the table it is obvious that, if only one labour unit is employed, available facilities are completely underutilised. The addition of another labour unit adds substantially to the total output and the marginal output of the second unit (what he contributes to the total output) is higher than that of the first unit (14 *vs* 12). Optimal marginal output is achieved when three units are employed, but it may still be of benefit to employ an additional one or two units, as total production still increases substantially and there is a relatively slighter decline in marginal output and initially a slight increase in the average output per unit. However, any additional employment after the sixth unit requires careful consideration, as total production does not increase to such an extent and there is a substantial difference in the marginal and average output between the sixth and seventh units. The additional value created by the seventh unit is relatively small. At the eighth unit total output remains constant, while marginal output is zero. The addition of the ninth and tenth units results in a negative return. To employ any additional units after the seventh would thus be a foolish practice. The progression, as is developed in the table, is graphically illustrated in Figure 32.

Marginal productivity theory is relevant in labour relations and to general labour market theory, because it firstly sets limits to the number of persons who can be employed without a concurrent growth in capital or in productivity and, secondly, leads to the question as to whether marginal labour employed should not be paid a progressively diminishing rate. In the total labour market, marginal productivity theory underscores the fact that an increase in employment cannot be achieved without the necessary economic growth, increased capital investment or increased production. Moreover, whatever the wage rate, it cannot be expected of an employer to employ more than the optimal number of employees at which output per unit would be maximised, unless additional employees would be prepared to accept a wage decrease in proportion to their decreased marginal utility. Conversely, it could be argued that a limitation on wages does not necessarily lead to substantially higher employment levels since, whatever the wage rate, employers will cease to add additional units of labour once they have maximised productive capacity.

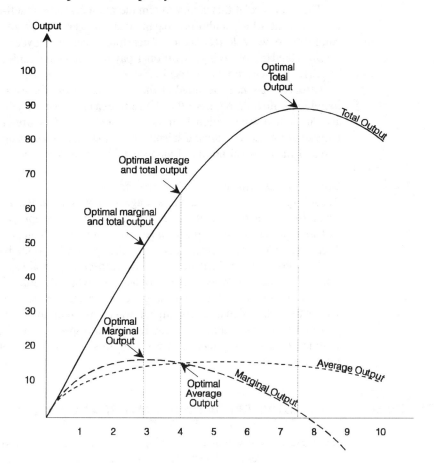

Figure 32: PROGRESSION OF TOTAL MARGINAL AND AVERAGE PRODUCT FUNCTIONS

The Marginal Utility of Income

The Law of Diminishing Returns applies also to individuals in respect of units of effort exerted and time spent on achieving a particular standard of living. Most individuals will reach a stage at which the value they achieve for the additional unit of time or effort is marginally less than that obtained from the preceding units. An employee earning a wage sufficient to provide him with the basic necessities might expend additional time and energy units to achieve an improved standard of living — that is, to buy himself a house and a car and send his children to a better school. Such returns will be highly valued by him but, once he has achieved these objectives, any additional inputs will render only marginal value in the form of a slightly better car or house or better clothes, which are actually not needed by him or his children. Against this he has to offset his preference for leisure or for time spent with his family. The rational employee will attempt to optimise both value achieved and leisure. He will expend sufficient units to provide him with marginally high returns but, as soon as marginal value decreases as against his preference for leisure, he will cease to make additional inputs.

The relevance of this theory to remuneration practices is self-evident. A point is reached at which additional payment no longer acts as an incentive to the employee to work longer hours. Therefore, once employees have achieved a certain standard of living, additional payment may be traded off against an increase in leisure time or a rise in status.

Criticism has been levelled at the marginal utility theory of leisure in that individuals often do not have the choice to expand or shorten their working time and are not always rational. It is suggested that it is preferable to see the individual not as maximising leisure, but rather as maximising his earnings in terms of his personal notion of an acceptable standard of living.

Utility and Disutility of Higher Wages

According to Salamon, a union's wage policy is regarded as '… seeking to maximise satisfaction (utility) in respect of wages and employment'. The union will attempt to reach the highest wage level possible without posing a significant threat to employment levels. This, of course, is subject to the bargaining power of the union. Union behaviour in this respect is not always consistent and researchers such as Mulvey have found that, when demand falls, unions will sacrifice employment to maintain wage levels whereas, when demand rises, they may temper their demands for higher wages in order to promote employment growth. In general, unions are reactive in this respect — that is, they will tend to continue demanding increased wages until such time as a noticeable drop in employment occurs.

THE EFFECT OF COLLECTIVE BARGAINING ON WAGE AND EMPLOYMENT LEVELS

The question as to whether bargaining power has any effect on **real wage levels** remains controversial. There are many theorists who believe that the effect of bargaining on wage levels is minimal, since the wage will always tend to revert to the competitive market price or, alternatively, entrepreneurs will merely raise prices in order to compensate for the higher wage bill. Furthermore, while in certain exceptional cases inelasticity of demand may lead to unions obtaining significantly higher wage levels, general elasticity of demand will prevent wages from increasing disproportionately to the market value. Alternatively, if they do, employment levels might drop. The conclusion that demand for labour is generally elastic arises, according to Dobbs, from the assumptions that the supply of capital is elastic; that, if wages increase, capital invested in wages will shrink; and from the fact that entrepreneurs are able to substitute labour with machinery. Except during boom conditions or where increases are matched with higher productivity, the elasticity of capital and subsequent demand will lead to a decrease in the quantity demanded and in the resultant unemployment.

These arguments are countered by those theorists who maintain that the market wage is not necessarily a 'natural' wage but is determined by the percentage in profit which the entrepreneur wishes to retain for himself and his shareholders. Increased wages need not, therefore, be offset by diminishing capital investment and employment, but rather by decreased profits. Furthermore, there is no real proof that increased wages significantly affect investment. It is also suggested by Dobbs that wage increases, although they may lead to greater unemployment, may profit the working class in general in that, for example, women and younger children may not be obliged to work. Most importantly, wage bargaining raises employees above the exploitation level for, if they remain at that level, they will continue to accept wages below the market rate.

The general conclusion is that, although wage bargaining may not have a significant impact on overall wage levels, it is necessary to prevent exploitation arising from imperfect competition in the labour market and monopolistic practices by employers. With a strong labour movement or free competition, it is unlikely that wages will drop far below subsistence level. On the other hand, the upper limit to which wages are raised by unions may, in the final analysis, depend more on sociopolitical than on purely economic factors.

THE EFFECT OF WAGE DETERMINATION ON WAGE AND EMPLOYMENT LEVELS

Wage determinations can have a two-way effect on wage levels in that they can either establish a minimum rate which is higher than the market rate or limit wage increases to an acceptable level. It is generally held that the imposition of a minimum wage which is above the market rate will lead to a decline in employment levels, as illustrated in the section on supply and demand. However, this need not always be the case, since the manner in which demand will react will depend, firstly, on its degree of elasticity. Secondly, minimum wage regulations have what Reynolds *et al* call a 'shock effect'. Firms which become subject to a minimum wage regulation may be shocked out of organisational inefficiency, resulting in higher production levels and obviating the necessity to reduce employment levels. Similarly, minimum wages may, in some circumstances, offset the monopsomy power of employers, in cases where the entrepreneur is the sole employer of labour.

Wage policies, aimed at limiting increases in wage levels, are usually introduced for the purpose of stabilising the economy and promoting employment. Unless other factors are regulated, the policy may not be successful as a limiting of wage levels may not, as shown in the Marginal Productivity Theory, necessarily be accompanied by higher employment levels. Economic growth or capital investment should, for instance, be stimulated simultaneously if employment is to increase. The theory also presupposes that the supply of labour is adequately trained to fill new jobs which are established.

LABOUR MARKET DISCRIMINATION

Discrimination on the basis of race, sex or creed may take the form of wage discrimination, employment discrimination, occupational or job discrimination and human capital discrimination. In the first instance, discriminatory wages are paid to different types of employees. In the second, fewer persons of a particular type are employed, while in the third certain jobs are not open to all persons and, in the fourth, certain groups suffer because of defective education and training.

There is no doubt that discriminatory practices add to the imperfections of the labour market. They lead to oversupply of labour in certain areas and an undersupply in others. This results in shortages in certain spheres which cannot be filled by the stock of workers from another group. Unemployment levels become unequally distributed since, instead of being spread throughout the total population, there is high unemployment among one group only. This may eventually result in sociopolitical upheaval.

LABOUR MOBILITY

Labour mobility includes both geographic and occupational mobility. The former is influenced by the spread of industry or its concentration in certain areas, by the circumstances of the employee and, in certain countries, by government policy. Occupational mobility usually increases with skill and educational level.

Labour mobility has positive effects in that it stimulates competition and allows for the reallocation of human resources. However, mass migration may have negative side effects in the form of an oversupply of labour in certain areas and coincidental social hardships. Nevertheless, severe external restrictions on labour mobility hamper the functioning of the labour market and prevent the establishment of competitive wage rates.

CONCLUSION

The labour market, perhaps more so than any other market, functions in terms of a set of complex variables. No single variable can be considered in isolation and the application of the theory to the practice would entail a detailed study of the circumstances surrounding a particular labour market.

SOURCES

Dobbs, Maurice *Wages*, James Nisbett & Co, 1966.

Fick, Rod and High, S Hugh *The Theory and Practice of Industrial Relations in South Africa*, Hodder & Stoughton, 1987.

Heilbroner, Robert *The Worldly Philosophers*, Penguin, 1983.

McConnell, C R and Brue, S L *Contemporary Labour Economics*, McGraw Hill, 1986.

Reynolds L G, Masters S H and Moser C H *Labour Economics and Labour Relations*, Prentice-Hall, 1986.

Rowan, Richard L (Ed) *Readings in Labour Economics and Labour Relations*, Richard D Irwin, 1980.

Sadie, J L *Labour Demand and Supply*, Kosmo Publishers, 1980.

Salamon, Michael *Industrial Relations Theory and Practice*, Prentice Hall, 1987.

12

THE SOUTH AFRICAN LABOUR MARKET

In 1987 the then Department of Manpower adopted a policy geared towards the fullest possible utilisation of the country's human resources. To these ends special strategies were adopted, among which were a long-term economic programme, deregulation, privatisation and small business development. This policy has been continued and expanded upon by the present government. However, the concerns which need to be overcome appear almost insurmountable. The main problem is that, while a large pool of labour exists, it cannot be fully utilised since the job opportunities do not exist and, where they do, the unemployed are not sufficiently skilled or educated to fill existing shortages. The present dilemma of the South African labour market is attributable largely to past practices which hampered the achievement of technical and educational qualifications by Blacks, prevented horizonal and upward mobility and led to sanctions and disinvestment.

Unemployment is a thus major problem in the South African labour market. This unemployment used to be mainly of a structural nature, but it has been compounded by cyclical unemployment occasioned by the dragging economic recession. According to reliable sources, unemployment in South Africa now stands at close to 45 percent of the total employable population. From all indications, this figure may increase in the future.

The position in South Africa is anomalous in that, despite the vast supply of human resources, there are significant shortages in certain professional and skilled worker categories. Thus the country suffers from both cyclical and structural unemployment.

The most obvious solution to the problem is to be found in a concerted education and training programme. Furthermore, the entire educational system requires restructuring, so that school leavers are better prepared to occupy positions in business and industry. At tertiary level, emphasis is gradually shifting from purely academic to career-orientated education. This initiative needs to be strengthened. Increased vertical mobility should also be complemented by greater horizontal mobility. Influx control has been lifted but restrictions on the mobility of labour still exist, particularly in the form of inadequate housing and other facilities. Many of these problems, as well as the general problem of unemployment, may in time be addressed by the RDP.

South Africa is at a difficult development stage. If the country is to survive as a relatively prosperous nation, it is imperative that optimal levels of economic growth be achieved. This requires the **full** and **unfettered** development of the South African labour market.

THE OFFICIAL MANPOWER POLICY

According to the 1987 Report of the then Department of Manpower, the manpower policy and objectives of the South African government were summarised as being 'the optimum development, utilisation and conservation of the total labour force.' **Development** of the labour force entails education, training and career counselling. **Manpower utilisation** necessitates the optimal use of the available workforce and, in terms of the Manpower Commission Report of the time, would entail the creation of employment opportunities, the achievement of higher productivity, improved methods of selection, recruitment and placement and the promotion of increased occupational and geographic mobility. **Manpower conservation** involves, according to the Manpower Commission, '... the maintenance of industrial peace, the protection of the psychological and physical welfare of the workforce and the retention of trained workers'.

In order to achieve its stated objectives, the government of the time adopted a manpower philosophy, based on acceptance of the free enterprise and free market mechanism and the principles of maximum self-government, safety, order, stability and consultation with those involved.

Since 1990 special attention has been paid to employment creation. To these ends, the government adopted a **White Paper on a strategy for the creation of job opportunities**, the main features of which were the following.

- A long-term economic development programme
- Plans for deregulation, privatisation and increased competition
- Small business development
- The establishment of a special employment creation programme
- Attention to urbanisation and housing
- The establishment of open trading areas
- The promotion of labour-intensive industry
- Regional and rural development

The new government, elected to office in 1994, has (broadly speaking) not deviated from these principles although, using the Reconstruction & Development Programme as basis, the now renamed Department of Labour has focused particularly on job creation programmes, training (also of the unemployed) and vocational guidance.

LABOUR MARKET PROBLEMS

The present employment situation in South Africa

A combination of past political ills and present economic problems (which are not mutually exclusive) has placed South Africa in an unenviable position as regards employment opportunities. Unofficial estimates place the unemployment level in the region of 45 percent. Job opportunities, which had increased by four percent during the Sixties, grew by only 1,2 percent in the Eighties, while the number of people looking for work during the period increased by 2,3 percent.

In 1991 it was estimated that only seven out of every 100 job seekers entering the labour market during the past five years would find fulltime employment, and that 3,8 million jobs were needed to alleviate the unemployment problem. In the same year, official statistics from the then Department of Manpower placed the number of registered unemployed at 1 212 176 (61 percent) among Blacks, 344 638 (18 percent) among Coloureds, 314 166 among Whites and 102 467 (5 percent) among Asians.

According to the 1994 report of the Department of Labour, the number of registered unemployed persons by the end of that year amounted to 1 050 065, of whom 67 percent were male, 33 percent female and five percent below the age of 21. These figures should not be taken at face value, as the former self-governing territories and TBVC states have not been included, and numerous youngsters do not register as unemployed.

Despite the high unemployment rate, many vacancies still exist in the more skilled job categories. This is especially true in the professional, semiprofessional and technical categories where, according to 1990 statistics, 40 683 vacancies existed. High vacancy levels also existed for apprentices in the motor and other trades, and for certain types of medical personnel.

South Africa is faced with the problem of an economy which cannot accommodate the growing population and with inherent structural imbalances, both of which may to some extent be attributed to the country's sociopolitical history.

Factors Contributing to the Present Situation

As noted earlier, the South African government had in the 1980s pledged itself to '... the optimum development, utilisation, and conservation of the total workforce, irrespective of race, colour or sex'. This policy remains, and special strategies are being adopted towards its implementation. However, the employment situation as it exists does not yet reflect the possible beneficial effects of that resolution but is largely a result of the dichotomy in the labour field prior to 1979 and of the still existent inequality between the different race groups as regards both economic circumstances and educational opportunity, which are important criteria in determining employability. The 'Industrial Colour Bar', operative until 1979 and still operating in indirect ways, effectively relegated the majority of Blacks to the category of unskilled workers and prevented any upward mobility from one category to another. This not only resulted in a lack of facilities and opportunities for the training of black workers but also provided sufficient disincentive for the attainment of any higher educational, professional or technical qualifications. Furthermore, certain regulations adversely affected the development of a black entrepreneurial class, which could have contributed towards employment creation. In the homeland and border industries opportunities did exist, but they were insufficient and accommodated only a small fraction of the black workforce. The position was further exacerbated by the fact that South Africa had a dual economic system consisting, according to Griffiths and Jones, of a modern urban economy on the one hand and the 'traditional rural' one on the other. A large proportion of the unskilled labour force comprised migrant labour which, by its impermanence, counteracted the acquisition of any high level of skill and further negated the necessity for the effective training and promotion of workers. Also, the policy of political and social segregation resulted in unequal opportunity for and unequal quality of education. It is this more than any other factor which accounts for the inability of black workers to fill the existing employment needs of the labour market.

During the past decade there has been a concerted attempt to address these problems and all persons do now enjoy greater mobility, in both the geographical and the educational sense, but more time, supported by affirmative action initiatives, is needed to correct historically created imbalances. Moreover, efforts in this direction were hampered by the depressed state of the economy and the gloomy prospects for the future. Even so, some positive developments did take place. By 1989 the use of non-white persons in high-level positions had increased from 25,5 percent in 1965 to 35,6 percent in 1989. However, if educationists were excluded, the share of non-white persons became only 14,2 percent. The proportion of non-white manpower in middle-level positions increased from 24,8 percent in 1965 to 48,6 percent in 1989, the greatest increase being among mineworkers and transport workers; but white males still constituted the greatest proportion of high-level manpower (44,4 percent), followed by white females at 20 percent. Moreover, in 1994 white mailes still held 96 percent of top jobs. If it is considered that black Africans constitute 67 percent of the economically active population, then the imbalances which still existed become self-evident. Unfortunately, no recent statistics have been made available (owing to a reluctance to base information on race classification), but it can be surmised that the position has improved only marginally since then.

UNEMPLOYMENT

The Nature of Unemploy-ment
Any discussion of employment opportunities necessarily entails the corollary of unemployment. Many and varied definitions of unemployment exist, with some researchers regarding the unemployed as all potential labour without a fixed position, while others concern themselves only with active work seekers who are unable to find jobs. Unemployment statistics should be handled with care and the premise of the researcher should first be established. Sadie defines the unemployed as '... all those who are temporarily or indefinitely laid off without pay and those without a job who are available for employment and are seeking work'. This definition does not take into account the large number of 'underemployed' in South Africa, '... people who work for a few hours a week to eke out an existence and form a large percentage of the economically active population'. The simplified and perhaps the best definition of unemployment is that which describes the unemployed as all those '... who are willing and able to work, but who cannot find work'.

In South Africa, official statistics usually refer only to those persons who have been employed and are now out of work; hence the reference to 'registered' unemployment . Also, statistics often did not include unemployment figures in the former homelands or independent states, or school leavers who are unable to find work. As a result of variations in definitions and criteria, different unemployment figures are provided by various authorities from time to time.

Classification of Unemployment

According to the main reason for its occurrence, unemployment can be broadly divided into four types:

- **Frictional unemployment** — This occurs where existent vacancies on the labour market could be filled by the unemployed, but where these persons, owing either to a lack of information or to dissatisfaction with remuneration offered, withhold their services from the market. Sometimes the communication regarding available positions does not reach the correct unemployed person or information is not widely disseminated. Thus this type of unemployment may be combated mainly by ensuring continual or correct exchange of information and improved vocational guidance..

- **Cyclical unemployment** — Labour employed during peak business cycles becomes redundant during periods of economic recession. This is normally the result of insufficient demand during a recessionary phase. As business activity declines, there is a corresponding decrease in employment levels.

- **Structural unemployment** — In this case employment opportunities may exist, but the available labour does not possess the qualifications or skills necessary to fill the vacancies. This could occur because of basic inadequacies in the labour force or because of technological advancements which render existing skills obsolete. Furthermore, a permanent or lengthy recession may result in structural unemployment. Workers may leave trades suffering from recessionary conditions and not return to these in the future.

- **Seasonal unemployment** — This occurs in jobs which are performed only at certain times of the year; for example, in seasonal fruit picking. Persons employed to do this type of work may remain unemployed for the rest of the year.

Because of its sociopolitical history and the restraints placed on the free operation of the labour market by government intervention, the problem in South Africa used to be mainly one of structural unemployment; but, because the country has been in an adverse economic cycle, the problem is at present exacerbated also by cyclical unemployment. The adverse economic conditions are, in fact, impeding efforts to alleviate the previous and still existent problem of structural unemployment.

Factors Influencing Employment Levels

The level of employment in a particular country depends in general on economic development, the stage of the business cycle and the preceding and existing institutional and legal framework. Furthermore, to balance the quality of supply with demand effectively, the following are necessary.

- The available corps of skilled labour must be so distributed as to meet existing demands in the best way. Optimal distribution of skilled labour depends on the mobility of labour, knowledge of labour market demands, correct vocational guidance and correct vocational selection.

- A sufficient quantity of workers possessing the necessary skills to meet future demands must be timeously trained. To do this necessitates effective planning of training facilities and programmes, in accordance with projected demands.
- Education must be proper and equal, and that education must be aimed towards employability.
- There must be horizontal and vertical mobility of labour, which in turn depends on statutory and administrative regulations, traditional practices, worker preference, wage differentials and the availability of housing.

EDUCATION AND TRAINING

General Level of Education

Griffiths and Jones define education as '... the process by which human capital is created'. They further maintain that '... the stock of human capital is closely related to the rate of economic progress'. If this is kept in mind and if it is taken into account that, in 1988, approximately one third of black Africans had no education whatsoever while two percent had a senior certificate and only 948 had achieved a Bachelor's Degree, then the position in South Africa — where Blacks form the largest proportion of the workforce — becomes disturbing.

The position as it existed was largely the result of social, economic and political discrimination, leading to a dualistic education system in which the quality of education received by Blacks was distinctly inferior to that of Whites. Furthermore, Blacks did not have the same opportunity of, nor were they equally available for, education. Owing to a greater cultural pressure and an increased awareness of the manpower requirements for the future, the past two decades have seen increased spending on black education.

The present government has declared its intention of providing equal education for all race groups and of improving the teacher training in general. It is to be hoped that, with the introduction of compulsory education and a unitary education system for all, the educational level will continue to rise. However, the cutting of expenditure on education and the retrenchment of teachers, which is still ongoing, provides cause for great concern.

Encouraging more pupils to complete their schooling is not in itself sufficient. It will be necessary also to restructure the entire system of education so that the **quality and nature** of education as a whole changes and improves. This is important for both growth and development. The present educational system is not endowing pupils with the necessary skills to handle the real world of work and business.

Education versus Training

As far as the supply of skills to the labour market is concerned, it is not only the educational level of the potential labour force which is of importance. It has been argued that developing countries depend more upon the creation of trained artisans than upon highly educated individuals; yet there is still a tendency among those who engage in tertiary education to follow economically less productive courses, such as Arts degrees, rather than to qualify in technological and business-related fields. This is proved by the fact that, in 1989, only 8 percent of all degrees awarded were for studies in engineering, mathematics, science and computer science; 10,5 percent were for specialisation in health sciences; 16 percent for business, commercial and management sciences; 22,6 percent for social science and 42,7 percent for other disciplines. By comparison, the number of persons enrolling for apprenticeships decreased from 14 500 in 1982 to 9 000 in 1990. In 1993 there were 1 245 fewer apprentices than in 1990 and, in 1995, again 1 245 fewer than in 1993. The government is hoping that the National Training Strategy will help to address this problem. Also, during 1990 only 36 352 students were enrolled at technical colleges, 83 424 at technikons, 50 084 at teacher training colleges and 286 910 at universities. In this respect, this statement by Griffiths and Jones becomes pertinent: 'The growth of the stock of skilled and semiskilled workers through apprenticeships and industrial training courses is potentially the most important factor in the improvement of the quality of human capital in South Africa'.

Previous practices relating to skills training for Blacks rested mainly in a dual scheme, by which prior training was given in State industrial schools in the border areas and in-service training at border industry schools established on industrial premises. These facilities, limited as they were, were not fully utilised by employers and workers. With the lifting of restrictions on training, the State and private enterprise have increased their efforts in the sphere of industrial training. Technikons are being promoted as an alternative to university education and the government has undertaken programmes to train the unemployed. Furthermore, the National Education & Training Strategy has gained momentum, with more industrial and on-the-job training being undertaken. Thus the position, although not ideal, is improving.

Literacy and Adult Basic Education   A major cause for concern is the high level of illiteracy among the South African population. Nowadays the acquisition of most skills depends on an acceptable level of literacy and, most often, on some basic education. Thus all training initiatives and attempts to redress the skills imbalance must commence with literacy training and adult basic education. Fortunately both the private and public sectors, as well as non-governmental organisations, are actively engaged in initiatives towards these ends.

OCCUPATIONAL AND GEOGRAPHICAL MOBILITY

The Importance of Mobility   Griffiths and Jones maintain that it is 'an essential tenet of economic freedom that all workers should be able to sell their services to the highest bidder'. In South Africa, restrictions placed upon Blacks as regards geographic domicile and occupational choice have in the past severely limited this mobility, and with it the right to free choice.

Influx Control   The practice of influx control had its origin in the Black Land Act of 1913 and was further solidified by the Development Trust & Land Act of 1936, the Black (Urban Areas) Consolidation Act of 1945, the Black (Abolition of Passes & Coordination of Documents) Act of 1952 and the Black Labour Act of 1964. The Community Development Act and the Group Areas Act, whereby also Coloureds and Asians were restricted to certain areas, further limited the geographic mobility of labour in general.

While the influx control system was regarded as advantageous in that it prevented overpopulation of the cities and concomitant social problems, it did not solve the question of poverty but merely transferred it from urban to rural areas. Furthermore, its effective implementation required a vast bureaucratic machinery and, therewith, unproductive labour. Because it provided cheap labour to employers, many did not attach importance to the necessity of building up an effective, experienced labour corps.

With the lifting of influx control, the government pledged itself to allow greater mobility of labour, provided that housing and job opportunities exist; yet the problems created by the system, such as lack of opportunity to prepare for the labour market and occupational immobility, will remain for some time to come. Moreover, the previous system resulted in poor urban planning, and one of the greatest problems now facing the government is that of providing sufficient housing, particularly in the urban areas.

The Industrial Colour Bar

The Industrial Colour Bar is defined as '... all those practices that are constraints to black advancement. These constraints come in the form of legal and institutional barriers, social custom, political and economic impediments'. Perhaps the most obvious of these was the institution of job reservation, originally intended to reserve certain skilled positions for persons of certain race groups. Although, officially, only 28 job reservation regulations existed between the years 1965 and 1975, and although in 1975 they affected only 2,3 percent of the total labour force, they were accompanied by unofficial reservation of jobs and employer and social prejudice, which effectively barred the advancement of black, coloured and Asian Africans on the labour market. This, together with the lack of educational and training facilities for these groups, certain closed shop agreements and the fact that black Africans were not regarded as employees and could not form registered trade unions, led to the monopoly of skilled positions by Whites, which in turn resulted in lax work attitudes among Whites, a shortage of skilled workers, artificially inflated wages for Whites and concomitant high labour costs.

With the passage of the Labour Relations Act of 1979, the government committed itself to the elimination of discriminatory labour practices and at the beginning of 1982 the second last job reservation regulation still in existence, namely that pertaining to the employment of Whites only in Cape Town Municipality's traffic police, ambulance services and fire department, was lifted. The only remaining regulation pertained to sampling, surveying and ventilation on the mines, and that was lifted in the mid-1980s. Furthermore, the restrictive effects of many closed shop agreements were minimised by the redefinition of Blacks as employees and by their right to belong to registered trade unions.

Although, legally, most measures restricting the upward and vertical mobility of labour were removed and in many enterprises equality of opportunity became the professed practice, impediments such as social and employer prejudice and restrictions on geographical mobility remained. Furthermore, owing to the heritage of the past, the black labour force was often not sufficiently skilled or qualified to utilise fully the opportunities for upward mobility which might have offered themselves.

Affirmative
Action

During the past few years, the need for affirmative action has been repeatedly emphasised and new job opportunities have been created for persons who were previously disadvantaged, thus addressing to some extent the existent structural imbalances. However, unless these initiatives are supported by concerted education and training programmes, they will prove to be only a stop-gap measure since, ultimately, only education and training will provide previously disadvantaged citizens with the skills necessary to take up their rightful positions in the South African labour market.

For a more detailed discussion of affirmative action, see Chapter 16.

WAGES AND WAGE STRUCTURES

The South
African Wage
Structure

The most controversial aspect of the wage structure in South Africa was the great discrepancy between the incomes of white and black South Africans. The discrepancy can be traced to the **Civilised Labour Policy** which was intended to protect the 'Poor Whites' from competition by black workers. Since then, according to Griffiths and Jones, 'wage policy in South Africa ... has been used to answer political developments ... The changes in direction since 1925 have coincided with either political events and/or industrial unrest.' It is this aspect that differentiates South African wage policy from that of other African countries. Whereas wage policies in the rest of Africa were aimed at specific socioeconomic developments on a broad, undifferentiated scale, irrespective of their overall success, South African wage policy was usually directed at some political or social objective in terms of the country's dominant policy. For this reason it is impossible to study wage policy in South Africa without reference to the social and political dichotomy between the races. The inequalities between black and white wages are the result not only of a historical lack of skill on the part of Blacks but also of discriminatory wage and labour practices, all of which resulted from the political and social dispensation. During the past two decades the wage gap has progressively narrowed and there is no doubt that the real wages of black employees have increased at a far greater rate than those of so-called Whites, Coloureds and Asians. It should, however, be remembered that black employees commenced from a very low base and that numerous workers were still earning lower than subsistence level wages.

The narrowing of the wage gap which has occurred can be attributed largely to the efforts of the newer trade unions and their insistence on the raising of minimum levels, often at the expense of more highly paid employees. Yet during the past year even those unions have had to lower their wage demands in the face of rising unemployment. Within the context of a new sociopolitical dispensation, there has been renewed talk of the imposition of a minimum wage. Unless the employment problem can be alleviated by a greatly improved economy, any attempt to introduce minimum wage legislation might well prove a self-defeating initiative. As it is, enormous gaps still exist between the highest- and lowest-paid persons in most organisations. This provides grounds for ongoing controversy and fuels union demands for higher wages — which may in turn lead to increased unemployment.

THE ECONOMIC SITUATION

No discussion of the labour market can be complete without consideration of the economic situation which, at present, leaves little room for optimism. Over the ten years until 1992 the growth rate averaged between one and two percent, which was in no way sufficient to compensate for population growth and for the increased demands and expectations of all South African citizens. The poor economic performance was, besides global conditions, attributable to continuing disinvestment, sanctions, the cost of maintaining apartheid, violence and social unrest resulting from this, overregulation in some instances, consistently high wage demands, a high strike incidence, a low level of productivity and a very poor work ethic among most South Africans. This resulted in an inflation rate which remained in the two-figure bracket, a poor balance of payments situation, and the continued devaluation of the Rand.

Since 1994 the inflation rate has dropped and there has been a slight improvement in the economy, but this has not been as significant as may have been surmised. Expected investments have not materialised, owing mainly to continuing violence and labour unrest. Moreover, South Africans, long lulled by their isolation, are finding it difficult to compete in world markets.

Any government which wishes to promote the economy through the free market system and which believes that such improvement is the route to job creation will have to take measures to curb violence and labour unrest and to urge South African citizens into a more productivity-orientated mode. On the other hand, there are those who believe that labour market problems will never be alleviated within a capitalistic/free market system and that the government should take more creative steps to control the economy and to provide jobs for its citizens. As it is, the present government appears to favour the free market as a means of promoting economic activity although, at the same time, it may attempt to counter the ills of capitalism and provide increased welfare for its citizens — and in particular for the poor and unemployed.

THE SOCIOPOLITICAL DISPENSATION

Since January 1990 numerous sociopolitical changes have occurred. While normalisation in this sphere will lead in the long run also to a normalisation of the labour market and the eradication of many of the problems which beset it, new problems may be created — particularly if South Africans continue to harbour high and unrealistic expectations.

Various initiatives have been undertaken to alleviate the problem of unemployment. At the beginning of 1991 the government set aside a million Rand for expenditure on the social and economic infrastructure, which was expected to generate 59 000 new jobs; training of the unemployed was ongoing and the Independent Development Fund also planned to spend large amounts on housing, again leading to job creation.

For the 1994/95 financial year, R72,8 million was put aside for the training of unemployed persons, of which R7 008 442 was made available for training in building-related skills. Also in 1992 the NEF (now incorporated into

NEDLAC) established a national job creation programme aimed at labour-based programmes in sectors such as civil engineering.

However, the focus in the new sociopolitical dispensation falls on the objectives of the RDP. In the areas of unemployment, training and the economy, the RDP aims to achieve the following.

- The integration of growth, development, reconstruction and redistribution in a unified programme
- The opening up of previously suppressed economic and human potential in urban and rural areas
- The availability of education and training to all 'from the cradle to the grave'
- An emphasis on affirmative action throughout the RDP
- The focusing of training on the restructuring of industry in order to become globally competitive
- Special attention to development of the youth
- The creation of opportunities for all South Africans to develop to their full potential
- The boosting of production and household income through job creation
- Curbing of the population growth rate by raising the standards of the entire society
- The generation of programmes which will address unemployment and look into local and national development programmes
- The institution of a coordinated public works programme
- The development of knowledge and skills which can be applied to produce high-quality goods and services
- The establishment of a national qualifications framework, integrating all aspects of education and training
- The provision of adult basic education so that all persons may have basic literacy and numeracy skills
- The provision of schooling for all children for at least ten years
- Alignment of the school structure, curriculum and certification with the national qualifications structure
- Establishment of statutory national and provincial teacher, educator and power development centres and an increase in the supply of maths, science and art teachers
- Establishment of a restructured and integrated training system
- The stimulation of industry and agriculture and the establishment of 'a dynamic, integrated economy able to provide higher incomes, reduce excessive dependence on imports and compete on foreign markets'
- Stimulation of both urban and rural development

The RDP has been criticised by some as too Utopian, and many of the objectives outlined above may be difficult to achieve. However, the document does provide insight into the problems facing the South African labour market and the economy, and it does propose some solutions. A critical study of the Reconstruction & Development Programme is, therefore, essential for any student of the South African labour market.

SOLUTIONS

It has become clear from the aforegoing that the inability to provide sufficient job opportunities, together with an oversupply of labour of insufficient quality, are South Africa's most pressing employment problems. To overcome this, it will be necessary not only to revitalise the economy but also to improve the general level of education of the labour force and, especially, to provide greatly increased and improved facilities for training in the skills required by industry. This would entail:

- increased *per capita* expenditure on education and training;
- an open, improved and flexible educational system, with compensatory education programmes where necessary;
- the improvement of training facilities for and the qualifications of teachers and a decrease in the teacher–pupil ratio;
- improved vocational guidance for all;
- a shift of emphasis from education to training, so that a balance of supply is obtained between so-called academic and vocational skills; in particular, the development of business skills to provide a basis for creativity, productivity, inventiveness and efficiency;
- increased attention to the content and extent of courses offered by vocational and technical training institutions so that they match the demands of industry;
- concerted efforts on the part of both the public and private sectors to improve and extend the in-service training of workers;
- incentives to employers and employees to encourage the training of artisans; and
- provision of facilities for adult education, to accommodate illiterate workers and those with an educational achievement below the required level.

The development of a skilled workforce without provision for its optimal allocation and utilisation would be an exercise in futility. It will thus be necessary:

- for the government to institute some form of manpower planning at a national level (this is one of the functions of NEDLAC);
- that accurate projections of future needs be established and training and education be directed towards those needs;
- that labour bureaux and vocational guidance centres be optimally utilised; and
- that private enterprise accurately establish its future requirements before embarking on any programme of manpower training.

Furthermore, in order to utilise the benefits of a free market system fully, the public sector and private enterprise should continue their efforts to remove all discriminatory employment practices.

The long-term objective should be the free mobility of all labour. The thrust to the cities will continue and close attention will have to be given to community development and the provision of housing in the urban areas.

The detrimental effects of an arbitrarily fixed minimum wage have been discussed previously, but the necessity to increase the minimum wage of unskilled workers will remain and it might be advisable for the government to establish guidelines for employers and unions and to encourage responsible action by both parties. Attempts to close the wage gap should continue, but should be directed rather at improving the skill and productivity levels of workers and at closing total income gaps by providing for greater upward mobility among previously disadvantaged employees.

CONCLUSION

Although some of the solutions mentioned have already been implemented, the problems of cyclical and structural unemployment are the most serious and the most difficult to combat. Positive efforts have been and are still being made to overcome the problems of the South African labour market but, if they are to meet with success, sustained economic growth is a prerequisite. In view of this and other circumstances, the enormity of the task becomes self-evident.

SOURCES

Department of Labour *Annual Report 1994*, Government Printer, Pretoria, 1994.

Department of Manpower *Report of the Director General, 1989*, Government Printer, Pretoria, 1990.

Griffiths, H R & Jones *South African Labour Economics*, McGraw Hill, 1980.

Manpower Commission *Annual Report 1989*, Government Printer, Pretoria, 1990.

Sadie, J L *Labour Supply and Demand*, Kosmo Publishers, 1980.

13

NEGOTIATION

Negotiation may be described as the practical implementation of the collective bargaining concept. In the negotiation situation, actual demands have been made or grievances have been raised. An issue exists and the parties meet in order to attempt an equitable resolution. As in all areas of Industrial Relations, the parties will not be operating in isolation but will be subject to numerous external influences. These will play a major role in determining the negotiating power of each party. In its turn, negotiating power, together with the quality and skill of particular negotiators, will influence the eventual outcome of the negotiation process.

In essence, successful negotiation entails the successful handling of conflict, using, if necessary, the power at one's disposal. Thus it is necessary once again to look at the dynamics of conflict and power, this time within the negotiation situation.

In the conduct of traditional labour negotiations, there are certain conventions to which both parties adhere. Negotiations are conducted in a polite and formal manner, even though opposing viewpoints are expressed and although it is accepted that each side can bring to bear all the power it is able to muster.

Where major negotiations of long-term impact are about to occur, careful and detailed preparation is imperative. Such preparation will entail the raising and identification of issues, the appointment of suitable negotiators, the obtaining of mandates, establishment of objectives, preliminary intra-organisational negotiation, the gathering of all relevant information, the setting of targets and fallback positions, deliberations regarding concessions to be made, the establishment of non-negotiable issues, the costing of projected contracts and general planning as to the strategies to be adopted by the negotiators. A lack of planning and foresight could place negotiators in an unfavourable position once actual negotiations commence.

Negotiations vary in length and tone, depending on the nature of the issues and on the stances adopted by the parties. They may be interrupted by withdrawals or by deadlocks on particular issues, but most negotiation sessions can be broadly divided into four stages: the opening phase, which is followed by the body of the negotiations leading to a stage of crisis or near settlement, whereafter there is a closing phase or summing up. In the last stage it is of particular importance that absolute certainty be achieved on agreements reached. In the opening phase and during the body of negotiations, each party will use all methods at its disposal to persuade the other party to relinquish its position. Certain methods used may be of a positive, constructive nature, while others are essentially negative. Whereas the first are referred to as negotiation skills, the second are commonly called *negotiation 'tactics' or manoeuvres. Successful negotiators concentrate on developing skills and avoid manoeuvres.*

In the event of final agreement being reached, it remains only for both parties to ensure that information concerning the agreement is disseminated to all concerned, that the terms of the agreement are correctly implemented and that continual monitoring of the agreement and of practices on either side occurs. Follow-up sessions may have to be held if problems regarding implementation are encountered and the entire agreement may later be renegotiated should a change occur in circumstances or in the power relationship.

This chapter deals mostly with traditional, positional negotiation, which is usually adversarial in nature but is still the most common type of negotiation in the labour relations situation. Ideally there should, as the relation develops, be progress towards more collaborative or cooperative negotiations. These require a different mind set and a sincere effort by both parties to achieve a solution which is satisfactory to all parties.

DEFINING THE CONCEPT

The word 'negotiation' is, more often than not, used interchangeably with collective bargaining. This is understandable, since collective bargaining encompasses the act of negotiation which, in industrial relations terms, means negotiating on behalf of the collective or, alternatively, negotiating by the collective agent on behalf of a particular individual. Nevertheless, in practice, a fine distinction is drawn between negotiation and collective bargaining. The latter is understood to be a more abstract concept and to encompass the wider institutional arrangements for the resolution of conflict between employer and employee, while negotiation may be described as the practical implementation of particular collective bargaining arrangements by the representatives of employers and employees.

Salamon has defined negotiation as '... the interpersonal process used by representatives of management and employees/union, within the various institutional arrangements of collective bargaining, in order to resolve differences and reach agreement'. In distinguishing negotiation from the collective bargaining concept, Salamon characterises negotiation by the following facts.

- 'It is an explicit and deliberate event.
- It is concluded by representatives on behalf of their principals.
- The process is designed to reconcile differences between the parties involved.
- The outcome is dependent, at least in part, on the perceived relative power relationship between the principals.'

The first two are of particular importance in isolating the practice of negotiation. Whereas collective bargaining embraces all the processes, systems and actions employed to resolve collective conflict within the labour relationship, negotiation refers to a meeting of the parties in order to resolve a particular issue or issues. Secondly, while collective bargaining embraces the totality of actors in the labour relationship, negotiation is undertaken by representatives of a particular party or particular parties.

Negotiation, standing in the light of the collective bargaining concept and as traditionally practised, is a process of thrust and parry, give and take. It entails demand, offer and counteroffer, the granting of concessions and the eventual achievement of a compromise solution. It has traditionally been distributive and positional in nature, although some joint problem solving did occur. This means that the parties see themselves as adversaries and each is intent on winning. Essentially, this results in a great deal of game playing. Thus the more progressive trend is to engage in collaborative rather than competitive negotiation and to attempt to gain maximal returns for both parties. However, since most negotiations are still of the adversarial kind, the first part of this chapter will be devoted to positional or distributive negotiation practice.

The issues around which negotiation hinges are as varied as the issues and problems arising from the collective bargaining relationship. Negotiations may be conducted to resolve differences regarding the dismissal of a single employee or the intended retrenchment of a group of employees, or to settle a grievance brought by an individual. Periodically, major negotiations are conducted to determine wage levels and resolve other important issues. Besides these major negotiation sessions, negotiations will be undertaken with every dispute which arises and will have to be instituted or continued should a strike or lockout occur.

THE CONTEXT IN WHICH NEGOTIATION OCCURS

Environmental Factors

Negotiations are greatly influenced by environmental factors in the form of the economy, ideological preferences, sociopolitical developments, public policy and demographic changes. Developments in all these spheres help to determine the **content and progress of negotiation**, the **power balance** between the parties, the **role of government** in the process and the **attitude** adopted by one party towards the other.

Macro-Economic Forces Regulating Negotiation

As Kochan has stated: 'All theories of collective bargaining start with a set of economic variables. The economic constraints, pressures and incentives influence all of the other components of the collective bargaining system.'

Economic factors affecting negotiations may be divided into **macro-governmental policies** and **micro-economic influences**.

Overall Economic Policy
In the macro sphere, a government's overall economic policy will set the stage for collective bargaining and, equally, will determine the importance attached to this process within the totality of a particular industrial relations system. As evidenced from previous discussions, a government adopting the free enterprise system as basis for its economic policy will, in the main, encourage the institution of free collective bargaining related to the laws of demand and supply,

although it may interfere when it perceives trade unions as holding too much power and, consequently, as impeding the free operation of the market. On the other hand, a government with a leaning towards a more planned economy and intent on a redistribution of wealth and the promotion of the working class will either interfere directly in the collective bargaining process by, for example, placing restraints on one or both of the parties, or it will render collective bargaining less relevant by itself engaging in redistribution. It may also legislate employee rights which would otherwise have been achieved only through negotiations.

Monetary Policy

Besides its overall economic ideology, the current **monetary policy** of a particular government will affect the conduct of negotiations. It is this monetary policy which largely determines the rate of economic growth and, with it, inflation and unemployment rates. These in turn affect the expectations of employees and the bargaining power of unions. In times of economic prosperity the expectations of employees will rise. More importantly, labour will be in high demand and unions will have greater bargaining power. This will lead to increased demands by unions and to aggressive negotiation, even though employers are better able to meet union demands than in times of economic recession. The bargaining range will be quite narrow, but because unions hold more power, wage rates will probably show a marked increase. This holds the danger of a rise in unemployment since, with the increase in labour costs, employers may attempt to achieve the same production levels with a smaller workforce or may decide to mechanise. Should this occur, unions may again have to limit demands.

In times of economic adversity and rising unemployment, union bargaining power diminishes. As a result, the demands and expectations of employees may be more realistic and, in the face of common adversity, a more cooperative relationship may evolve at the bargaining table. Yet negotiations are still likely to be lengthy and at times hard fought, since unions might not lower their demands to the extent expected by employers. According to Kochan, studies in the United States have proved that 'unions appear to be more successful in putting a floor on wage increases during recessionary periods so that union employers are less able either to cut wages or to moderate the pace of wage increases during recessions than employers in the non-union sector'.

A high inflation rate or a consistent increase in the Consumer Price Index will inevitably lead to demands for higher wages and for the provision of escalation clauses in agreements. If there is no concomitant increase in productivity and if the government at the same time engages in expansionary economic policies, a still higher inflation rate may result. Prices will increase with the increase in wages, giving rise to a wage–price spiral which may be difficult to break, since employers will expect unions to take the initiative by limiting their demands and unions will expect first to see a decreasing price trend.

Incomes Policy

Should negotiations between employers and unions appear to be contributing to inflation, a government may decide to implement an incomes policy. A government adopting such a policy may either 'jawbone' employers and unions into introducing wage and price limitations by a process of direct negotiation with the parties, or may attempt by guidance or coercion to limit wages and prices. This will affect the negotiation process, as it narrows or completely eliminates the discretion which employers and unions have to set wage levels between them. Very often employers and unions may agree to the limitations imposed in the short term, but sooner or later one or other of the parties will break the pattern. Therefore the conclusion reached by numerous researchers is that, although wage and price limitations may keep wages static or result in minimal increases in the short term, they have no real effect on the general trend in wage increases over a longer period of time.

Fiscal Measures

The last aspect of macro-economic policy affecting the conduct of the collective bargaining process is contained in the fiscal measures or taxation imposed by government. By its fiscal policy a government may redistribute wealth to such an extent that the range for actual bargaining is narrowed. Where there is steep progressive taxation or where added tax benefits are granted to salary and wage earners, employees — particularly those in the lower income group — receive increased nett earnings, obviating the necessity for greater demands on employers. Similarly, company profits and shareholder dividends may be so highly taxed that it becomes feasible to incur expenditure by way of higher labour costs or development programmes for employees. A government may also encourage staff development by granting tax concessions in respect of training programmes, again narrowing the range of issues between employer and employee. This range is further narrowed if the government utilises taxes received to institute welfare programmes and benefit schemes. Problems such as compensation for retrenchment, pension schemes and benefit funds will, as a result, decrease in importance as issues on the bargaining table. Conversely, increased taxation of employees and a lack of government welfare schemes may lead to increased demands by unions and tougher bargaining. Finally, even government regulations pertaining to the collection of tax may intrude on the bargaining relationship. This has happened in South Africa where black employees, who resented the collection of taxes by a government in which they believed they had no say, did raise this issue with employers.

Kochan cites four micro-economic factors as important in the bargaining process. These include the elasticity of demand, labour market competition, product competition and profits shown by a particular enterprise. Marshall originally postulated the theory that **the power of trade unions will increase as the demand for labour becomes more inelastic**. If the demand is inelastic, increases in wages will not result in a reduction of the workforce, and the bargaining power of the union thus remains constant. As mentioned in a previous chapter, inelasticity of demand may be caused by the irreplaceability of labour in a particular process, or it may occur when the demand for the final product will not change, when the supply of other factors of production is static or when labour costs constitute only a small proportion of total costs. If an employer is unable to continue the work process without certain employees or a certain number of employees or if the union has organised workers throughout the market, unions representing those employees hold additional power. If, whatever the circumstances, the product (for example, bread) remains in demand, the union need not be concerned that an increase in wages will affect employment levels. Similarly, if an employer is not able to substitute other factors for labour — in the form, for example, of capital investment in technology — unions gain in strength. Finally, if the cost of labour is relatively low in comparison to the overall costs of production, the employer will more readily absorb increased labour costs than would otherwise be the case. When industry is concentrated and where a number of employers **compete for labour** in a tight market, unions, on the whole, can exercise greater leverage. Conversely, if the **product is highly competitive**, the employer may, particularly if there is no centralised bargaining system, engage in aggressive wage bargaining for fear that increased labour costs will price his product out of the market. The last factor mentioned by Kochan, namely the **level of profit** in an undertaking, may be controversial. However, it is conceivable that an employer showing higher overall profit margins or increased productivity may be more amenable to wage demands than his counterpart who is not in the same position.

The economic factors mentioned are all interactive, not only with one another, but also with other influences on the collective bargaining process. Together they will determine the content and success of bargaining.

Public Policy The government, by its legislative framework and particularly by its industrial legislation, sets the parameters for collective bargaining. It does so by, in the first place, establishing minimum standards as regards substantive conditions of service and by the regulation of such matters as health and safety at the workplace. These minimum standards are used as guidelines for further bargaining by those involved in negotiations. Secondly, a government may guide the collective bargaining process by making provision for statutory bargaining bodies, providing for the statutory enforcement of collective bargaining agreements, establishing a statutory dispute settlement machinery and mediation or arbitration services, limiting the freedom to strike or lock out, enforcing bargaining with a representative union and delimiting bargaining units. Should the statutory machinery provide for centralised bargaining bodies, the employers and unions may be obliged or may prefer to adopt this bargaining structure. Equally, they might be obliged to utilise the statutory dispute settlement machinery or may prefer to do so instead of establishing their own. Thirdly, a government may limit the rights of either party by legislation regarding the organisation and management of unions and employer organisations, by limiting sympathy actions, picketing or boycotts and by the introduction of 'fair' labour practice legislation. By way of example, a government could oblige unions to institute strike ballots; it could legislate for payment of damages in cases of unjustified industrial action and could declare the failure to bargain 'in good faith' an unfair labour practice.

In other cases governmental interference may be more direct. It may take the form of an Incomes Policy or it may extend to intervention in the form of legislated rights for either side, as in the case of compulsory employee profit schemes.

Finally, a government, by its overall policies and legislation, greatly affects the conduct of the bargaining relationship. Should it treat one sector of society as inferior, this spills over into the labour relationship and affects the bargaining power of that group. Also, legislation passed in other spheres may greatly impact on negotiations. This was the case in South Africa where, for years, apartheid legislation complicated the conduct of negotiations.

Political Influences

Strong political divisions within society or a high degree of politicisation in certain groups will eventually be reflected also in the issues raised at the bargaining table and in the attitude of the bargaining partners towards each other. Should the bargaining partners be diametrically opposed in their political viewpoints or should one partner perceive the other as political opposition, bargaining becomes more aggressive and less cooperative. Matters which could otherwise have been dealt with as problems become issues. This has often been the case in South Africa where certain groups viewed themselves as opposed not only to racialism but to 'racial capitalism'. Where politicisation is intense, political issues are added to the bargaining agenda. These may range from demands for the celebration of political holidays to insistence that employers take a political stand on certain issues. In other instances, political divisions in society complicate the bargaining process, as they lead to friction on the shopfloor and the problem of multiunionism. In general, the interplay of political forces, both inside and outside a country — in the form of sanctions and boycotts, for example — will have an effect on economic and social developments. These, in turn, could determine the nature of issues at the bargaining table.

Social Influences

The social influences on the bargaining relationship are many and varied. Primarily, social class divisions between employer and employee, if these are very distinct, could lead to tensions between the bargaining partners and to sensitive areas in the negotiation process. One party may view the other with disdain because of his lack of social manners, while the latter may feel ill at ease in the company of the other or may attempt to compensate for his perceived inequality by abrasive behaviour. On the other hand, group divisions within a community, whether of a social or religious nature, may lead to divisions within employee ranks. This could cause tension at the place of work and further complicate the bargaining process. Moreover, attitudes within a particular society will determine the support or lack of support for unionism. This obviously affects the extent to which collective bargaining is conducted.

In the substantive sphere, problems experienced within particular communities, such as insufficient housing, inadequate child care or other facilities, poor education and lack of or insufficient transport, will make their way to the bargaining table in the form of demands for benefit and other schemes or for social responsibility programmes. An employer could be expected not only to care for his own employees, but also to show some responsibility towards the community from which he draws his labour force.

The Effect of Technological Progress

The effects which technology has on negotiations can be divided into two types. The first relates to the influence of technology on the work process and on the employee who performs that work, and the second to its effect on employment levels.

It is commonly believed that mass production technology alienates the employee from his work, minimises social interaction and, in general, has a dehumanising influence. This results in demands by unions for the humanisation of the work process by, for example, increased job content, whole process tasks, the establishment of work groups and psychological counselling of employees. Demands of this nature become problems or issues at the bargaining table and could be subjected to distributive or integrative bargaining. From the employer point of view, another problem exists in that the monotony of certain work processes may result in a greater propensity amongst employees to undertake strike action, if merely to alleviate the boredom of their daily routine. This may increase the power of unions representing these employees, but it will not promote the effective conduct of negotiation.

The ever present threat of technological development to the job security of employees constitutes a point of constant debate between employers and unions. What is more, technology may be purposely introduced by an employer in order to diminish trade union power. At the very least unions will demand to be consulted on the introduction of new technology and to be assured of compensation, should employees be retrenched. In more sophisticated systems this is followed by the demand for employee retraining or for re-education of employees so that employees themselves are able to man any new machinery which might be introduced.

Technological innovation is a fact of modern life and unions, in the long run, may have to accept this. If they do, technological development will become an item for integrative rather than distributive negotiations.

Demographic Influences

Demographic changes in the composition, average age, predominant gender or average educational level of a workforce and other developments such as greater urbanisation or decentralisation of industry will, according to Kochan, have a direct influence on worker expectations and on employee attitudes towards jobs and unions. This will, in turn, be reflected by changes in union composition and union objectives and, therefore, in bargaining relationships and negotiation issues.

As the workforce on average becomes younger, it could be expected that less emphasis may be placed on job security and more on personal development and that unions will have more militant supporters. Women, too, have become more vociferous in their demands and are particularly sensitive to discriminatory practices. Thus, as the composition of the workforce shifts to include more female employees, it could happen that employees become more militant and that the establishment of women's rights and the solution of problems such as sexual harassment gain prominence as issues in negotiations. Furthermore, a workforce which is, on average, more highly educated will have different priorities to less educated employees and may stress job enrichment and opportunity for leisure rather than increased wages. All these developments will affect the strength and bargaining power of unions. In some instances, union membership may increase, whereas in others it will show a decline. The more rapid the change and the more heterogeneous the membership of a union becomes, the more difficult does it become for the bargaining process to accommodate the various issues raised.

Urbanisation results in greater population density and, consequently, in facilitated organisation for trade unions. Since trade unions are usually more firmly established in the major centres, there are employers who deliberately decentralise their operations in order to avoid unionism. This leads to much rancour between the parties and obliges the trade union to extend its organisation and, perhaps, to spread its manpower too thinly. Furthermore, greater urbanisation will be accompanied by intensified social problems, especially as regards housing. These problems are certain to be brought to the bargaining table.

The demographic variables affecting collective bargaining are numerous, but the practical results of demographic changes are not immediately identifiable, since they constitute long-term shifts. These require detailed research before any concrete assumptions can be made.

The Effect of the Press on Negotiations

The Press, as an opinion-forming medium, has an active influence on negotiations, in both the long and the short term. On the negative side, press involvement can at times detrimentally affect the conduct of actual negotiations and complicate the bargaining relationship.

The Press helps to shape the initial opinions and standpoints of the parties and their attitudes towards other parties. Also, the public as a whole is influenced by the Press and the body public may, by collectivised opinion or the application of pressure, play a role in the negotiation process. Finally, the Press may disproportionately emphasise issues and disputes between the parties or misreport events, thus heightening conflict situations and hampering the progress of negotiations.

As with the economic factors, no single one of the totality of contextual factors exercises sole influence on the collective bargaining process. They are interactive and the effect of any particular factor will depend on the total mix of all the environmental factors impacting on industrial relations and the bargaining relationship.

EFFECTS OF COLLECTIVE NEGOTIATIONS ON THE ENVIRONMENT

Just as environmental influences affect the negotiation process and its outcome, so also does the process itself influence developments in the environment. This is particularly the case in the economic sphere, where agreement on higher wages or other benefits and consequent price increases may largely contribute to inflationary trends in the economy. In respect of public policy, collective agreements reached may be used as guidelines for the State in enacting further legislation. Similarly, repeated, disruptive strike action may necessitate measures limiting the rights of parties.

Socially, the results of collective bargaining are most obvious, especially if parties negotiate social improvement schemes or employers become involved in education and housing problems. Finally, on the negative side, conflicts and problems arising in the negotiation process will be carried out to the wider society and may result in community actions against employers in the form of product boycotts, blacklisting by communities and tensions between various sectors of the community.

VARIABLES INFLUENCING THE NEGOTIATION PROCESS

The conduct and outcome of distributive negotiation, being the practical manifestation of collective bargaining, is ultimately dependent on the power balance between the parties represented. Bargaining power during a particular negotiation depends not only on the parties themselves but also on economic, sociopolitical and other conditions. Furthermore, the degree of success achieved will depend to some extent on the skill of the negotiators, the willingness or perceived willingness of either party to engage in coercive action, the degree of commitment to the reaching of a final agreement, the expectations and needs of both parties, their past relationship, the knowledge that each party has of the other and of prevailing circumstances, and on the amount of trust existing between the negotiators themselves.

There is a tendency among certain practitioners to overstate the importance of negotiating skills, while others completely negate skill as a determinant of negotiating outcome. The variables affecting bargaining power are so numerous and interactive that it would be unwise to rely on the skill of the negotiator as sole determiner of the outcome of negotiation. Yet there is no doubt that a lack of skill — and particularly of experience — could greatly complicate the negotiation process and negatively affect its outcome. The only certainty concerning negotiation is that it is a dynamic, interpersonal process. Although there may be certain generalised preconditions and although generalised guidelines may be followed, there is no set recipe for the conduct of negotiations. A negotiator may be trained to consider preconditions and guidelines and certain skills may be imparted to him, but the real art of negotiation can be acquired only by practice, sensitivity and awareness within the framework of the totality of circumstances in which particular negotiations are being conducted.

CONFLICT AND POWER IN THE NEGOTIATION PROCESS

Sources of Conflict As discussed in Chapter 8, the institution of collective bargaining — and, therefore, the process of negotiation — arises from the need to share scarce resources and from conflicting needs, goals, values, ideologies and perceptions, to which may be added structural imbalances, ambiguities and lack of coordination. The sources of conflict in the labour relationship and the issues which result were described extensively in that chapter. In essence, managers and employees find themselves in conflict for the following reasons.

- Management, while it may believe in paying well, does not want to pay too well; employees believe that, in comparison, they are still getting too little.
- Management likes to be in control and to make all important decisions, but employees continually challenge this managerial 'prerogative'.
- Employees want to be informed on all issues affecting them, while management still closely guards information, often as a source of power.

- Management usually believes that employees do not have the interests of the enterprise at heart; employees equally believe that their interests are not important to management.

- Management may place the interests of the enterprise, of shareholders and executives above those of workers; workers want, at the very least, to receive equal consideration.

- Employees often do not enjoy their work because they cannot develop; management may enjoy work and expect the same enjoyment from employees.

- Management is inclined to view matters only in a company context; employees see work in relation to family and community, and within the sociopolitical framework.

- Both sides, but particularly management, communicate ineffectively and often fail to communicate at all.

These conflicts, if they are not resolved, lead to a lack of trust and cooperation, to a continual challenging of managerial decisions and actions by employees or their unions, continual comparisons and, in general, a 'we' and 'they' approach. It is to ameliorate this situation that negotiations take place.

Methods of Handling Conflict

The various methods of handling conflict as described in Chapter 8 may be divided into two types: the non-confrontational approaches such as avoidance, withdrawal, suppression and soothing; and the confrontational approaches, which would include majority decisionmaking, bargaining or compromise and integrative problem-solving. Although the non-confrontational approaches may be advisable in some instances, negotiation necessarily entails confrontation of conflict — but with the purpose of eventually achieving a compromise. Ideally, a win–win solution should be sought. Unfortunately, the achievement of an integrative climate is not always possible, particularly where relationships are basically adversarial. Consequently numerous issues are still resolved by distributive bargaining, resulting in a win–lose situation.

The Conflict Dynamic

Anstey, in his book *Negotiating Conflict*, provides a process model of conflict in which the sources of conflict are identified as conflict antecedents, but where the degree of conflict arising from these sources depends on what Anstey calls 'moderators' or 'aggravators' which, in turn, will determine the type of behaviour evidenced in conflict situations: whether the parties resort to violent acts, coercion, sabotage and industrial action, whether they engage in negotiation and integrative problem-solving, or whether they resort to the intervention of third parties and litigation to resolve the conflict. Among the aggravators and moderators Anstey mentions such aspects as the aspirations and perceptions of the parties, the history of their relationship, their use of strategies, internal cohesion within constituencies, the acceptance (or not) of the other's legitimacy, the existence of procedures, forums and third party institutions for the regulation of conflict, shared conflict-limiting norms, the 'size' of the grievance or threat, the balance of power between the parties, the existence (or otherwise) of 'cross-cutting group membership', social controls, tolerance and certainty. The extent to which variations of these aggravators or moderators can influence conflict behaviours is self-evident.

Much research has also been conducted on the escalation of conflict, the corollary being that, if escalators can be controlled, the degree of conflict would then be minimised and the negotiation process facilitated. For example, research findings have proved that conflict increases in direct relationship to the number of issues involved. Limiting the issues or settling some issues rapidly, therefore, would serve to de-escalate conflict. Similarly, conflict remains at lower levels when fewer participants are involved, particularly if such participants act in an individual capacity. Where parties form different alliances and collectives, conflict tends to escalate. According to Anstey, conflict is lower when demands are concretised and specific rather than general, 'grandiose' and 'all-encompassing'; and, contrary to the perceptions of many individuals, conflict tends to escalate when resources increase. (This is proved by the fact that negotiations are usually tougher during times of economic prosperity.) Furthermore, the degree of conflict will depend to a large extent on the perceptions of the parties, the relationship between them and the level of communication. Where there is a strong perception of opposition, where the other party is viewed in a negative light, where the relationship is one of hostility and the objective is to inflict as much harm as possible, conflict increases; parties who adopt a non-evaluative stance, who have a more positive relationship and whose objective is mainly to obtain the best deal possible remain at lower conflict levels. Equally — and predictably — conflict escalates where communication is closed and infrequent, and de-escalates in a climate of open and regular communication. One other factor will affect the conflict level: the climate within each organisation. Where there is democratic management and loose controls, conflict is minimised; autocratic leadership, high task orientation and a high degree of mobilisation normally lead to escalation of the conflict potential. In negotiation, the purpose is to minimise the potential for conflict in order to prevent it from reaching destructive proportions. Limiting the issues and the number of participants, concretising demands, engaging in open, continual communication and adopting a positive attitude towards the other party can assist in achieving this objective. Most importantly, negotiators should remember that there is no conflict which cannot be resolved. In fact, studies have estimated that 70 per cent of all conflicts are resolved simply by more effective communication, 20 per cent by negotiation and only about 10 per cent require the active intervention of a third party.

The Use of Power

The role of power in the labour relationship and in the collective bargaining process has been discussed in Chapter 1 and again in Chapter 8. Negotiations are undertaken because both parties perceive the other as holding power.

The power base of management during negotiations rests in its authority, its control of employment, its ability to bestow or withhold rewards and to promote or hamper the development of employees, the possibility of continuing operations without certain employees and its ability to stockpile. Employees, in their turn, derive power from their ability to withhold labour, to disrupt the productive process, to make management lose its market and to disrupt other operations, as well as their ability to 'reward' management by hard work and commitment. During the negotiating process itself, both parties may gain power if they set relatively high aspirations and commit themselves to these, if they have the support of their constituents or principals, if they gain support from the community or, alternatively, can make the other party look bad, if time is on their side, if they are willing to take risks or if they can resort to the law. Most importantly, the knowledge and skill possessed by a particular party will greatly determine its bargaining power.

In utilising his power base to the full a negotiator should, therefore, set high but reasonable targets, create dominance (particularly by displaying knowledge and skill), persuade the other party of his commitment, maintain contact with constituents and principals, demonstrate strength by letting the other know what measures can be taken, point to the benefits of cooperation and the importance of maintaining a favourable image, show that he has contacts outside and that they are willing to support him, see that time is on his side, display a knowledge of the law and act courageously at all times.

In Chapters 1 and 8 it was mentioned that coercive power is that most frequently applied in the labour relationship and that the use of such power forms the basis for the collective bargaining process. However, during the negotiation process, various types of power may be employed in order to enhance the position of one of the parties. Thus **legitimate power** is utilised by ensuring that the chief negotiator is a person who holds a senior position in either management ranks, the union hierarchy or the employee collective. Alternatively, a principal to whom a negotiator refers may be an individual with legitimate power, or recourse may be taken to an outsider who holds legitimate power within society. Within a negotiating team, important issues should be addressed by an individual who holds legitimate power in that sphere. **Reward power** can be utilised on an individual or a collective basis. Individually members of the team may, according to Pienaar and Spoelstra, be rewarded by nods of approval, compliments, praise and even flattery, while a negotiator may point to the collective rewards which can be achieved from agreement. **Coercive power**, on the other hand, is used when negotiators employ threats and bluffs; when they demonstrate displeasure by, for example, walking out of the negotiation session; or when they play on the fears of the other party. One of the best forms of power to utilise in negotiations is **expert power**, which in turn depends on the knowledge and skill of the negotiator. Expertise is demonstrated by creating awareness of a negotiator's experience and background, by citing facts and figures and by the manner in which information is presented and arguments are countered. Expert power can also be enhanced by calling on persons with particular expertise to make presentations during negotiations.

The last form of power listed by French and Raven, namely **referent power**, regarded as the most beneficial form of power, is the one least used in the average negotiation situation. In order to utilise this kind of power, the negotiator would have to be someone with whom the other side could identify, despite their differences. This is why management may sometimes appoint an outside consultant as chief negotiator in the belief that the union team will more easily identify with him than with a member of management. This strategy could backfire since the consultant may also lack credibility with the union, particularly if he identifies too closely with management. Thus an outsider assisting with negotiations should veer towards the role of mediator, rather than that of chief negotiator. However, the use of outsiders is not the only means of utilising referent power. It may also be gained by referring, in argument, to persons with whom the other side can identify or by operating within the context of shared values and beliefs. This, of course, is the ideal negotiating situation.

In addition to the five types of power identified by French and Raven, Pienaar and Spoelstra also suggest another form of power which they describe as 'the power of weakness'. Noting that the countering of power with power can result in an escalation of conflict, they suggest that a party can gain by relinquishing power. Such party will purposely adopt an inferior position or will admit that great damage can be occasioned by the other party's threats; or it will apologise, thereby challenging the other party to carry out its threats. It can be imagined that only the harshest of negotiators will trample on an opponent who so openly admits his weakness, but such harsh negotiators do exist. The admission of weakness, therefore, is at best a risky strategy.

In concluding this section, certain guidelines on the use of power need to be postulated. In order to use power effectively, the user should remember the following points.

- Power is never absolute. It is limited by and relative to the power held by others.
- Power is not static, and power relationships are subject to continual change.
- A balance of power is necessary for effective containment of conflict.
- Power is enhanced if it is based on common ground rather than on differences and coercion.
- Power based on authority should be accompanied by responsibility.
- Power needs to be perceived and accepted by the other party.
- Perceptions of own power should be realistic and the limits of one's power cannot be exceeded, as this leads to loss of self-control.
- The end does not always justify the means.
- Using power in order to achieve more power has negative results.
- Using power defensively may prove harmful to the user.
- The overuse or abuse of power makes a victim of the party against whom the power has been used. Victims can become aggressors.
- A display of power does not always necessitate action.
- Less power is not necessarily bad.
- The use of power always involves costs and risks.
- Power shared is power gained.

Although power is necessary within the context of successful negotiation, power in itself (or even the wrong perception of power) could prove extremely dangerous. Negotiations are not a power game in which the intention of one party is to crush the other completely. The objective is to reach a workable solution — workable in the sense that it is acceptable to both or all the parties involved.

QUALITIES OF A GOOD NEGOTIATOR

Contrary to some beliefs, the best negotiator is not the most forceful or aggressive character in the union or management team, even though evidence of these qualities may sometimes be necessary during the conduct of negotiations. The most important qualities required by a negotiator are sensitivity, tact, discretionary judgment, flexibility, the ability to handle information, the ability to present a persuasive, reasoned argument and the ability to withstand pressure and stress. A good negotiator will be sensitive to the needs, feelings and perceptions of his own team and those of the other side. He will listen carefully and take heed of both what is said and what is not said by the other side. If he is to know more about the other side, its attitudes, position and strategy, he will be obliged to interpret facial expressions, body language, silent interpersonal communications and the myriad of clues which provide the true picture. Diplomacy is essential, since a negotiator who antagonises the other side serves only to harden positions and to decrease the possibility of a compromise. A good negotiator will know when to stand firm and when to concede, when to raise a particular argument and when not, when a change of argument or strategy would be effective and when it would prove disastrous. He should have all the necessary information at hand and be able to use this at the right time in a logical, persuasive argument.

A negotiator intent on winning at all times is not the most effective. A total triumph by one party necessitates the complete defeat of the other. This is bound either to elicit a counterreaction or to lead to heightened conflict at a later stage. The effective negotiator will be flexible and will consider also the other party. He may, and is entitled to, pursue the interests of his own party as single-mindedly as possible and, in the process, to use aggression and threats, but he should do so without totally antagonising the other party and without causing the opposing side to lose face completely. Finally, since there is continual pressure and negotiations are necessarily stressful, the good negotiator will not collapse under stress; rather, he may thrive on it and find it a spur to more intensive thought and action.

To summarise: a good negotiator must plan and think carefully, not be ruffled easily, not become overemotional, be possessed of good verbal skills, have sufficient knowledge, be patient, have earned respect for his integrity, be able to see and use power, have a sense of self-worth, be capable of taking uncertainty, have the desire to achieve, be openminded and brave — and have a sense of humour.

NEGOTIATION CONVENTIONS

The practice of negotiation requires, in the first place, a recognition of the right of each party to state its case, to make proposals and counterproposals and to raise arguments and counterarguments. While the chief negotiator speaks and makes decisions on behalf of his team, this does not negate the right of other team members to speak, either when called upon or at their own request. Also, in properly conducted negotiations both sides acknowledge the need for compromise but, at the same time, each recognises the right of the other to pursue his own targets as aggressively as possible, even to the point of threatened coercive action. Equally, it is realised that each side will carefully guard those items which it regards as non-negotiable.

The art of negotiation relies on gentlemanly behaviour. There is consideration for the other side and correct manners are maintained at all times. It is accepted that no petty harangues will take place and that no personal attacks will be made; also, that negotiators on either side will not lose their tempers. For this reason negotiations normally follow a formal procedural pattern. The chief negotiator on either side is the one to be addressed (if there is no chairman). An agenda is drawn up, minutes are taken, time periods are set and there is an opening and closing address. In more formal negotiations prescribed seating arrangements are maintained and in all negotiations each side has a right to request a caucus or the opportunity to report back to its principals or members.

The question could be raised as to whether less formality would not facilitate settlement. Formality is necessary to maintain the even tenor of negotiations and to prevent arguments from becoming too personalised. This does not preclude negotiators from being friendly, gathering socially, easing tensions with humorous remarks and arranging informal meetings to get to know the other side, thereby enhancing the possibility of settlement; but, during the actual conduct of negotiations, the tone remains formal and polite.

When conducting negotiations, all participants should have equal status. It is accepted that existing agreements will be upheld and that movement will come from both sides. Negotiations should be conducted fairly and in good faith. This means that:

- an offer, once made, cannot be withdrawn,
- verbal offers and agreements are taken as given,
- there should be no denial of something which has been accepted,
- both sides should display willingness to negotiate,
- there can be no outside or informal settlement of a negotiable issue,
- confidential or privileged information may not be abused by either party at a later stage,
- opponents should be left with some credit,
- no trickery should be employed in the final agreement, and
- agreements will be implemented as they stand.

PREPARING FOR NEGOTIATION

Initiating the Negotiation Process
Traditionally the initiative for the institution of the negotiating process has come from the union or employees, either by way of a set of demands or in the form of grievances raised by employees. The reverse could and does also occur. The employer may act as initiator in order to gain certain concessions from, or institute arrangements with, his employees or the union. Whoever the initiator may be, the proposals made by one side are certain to be met with counter-proposals from the other or by an agreement to meet for the purpose of negotiation.

Depending on the nature and extent of the issues, the ensuing negotiation could be conducted at various levels and may be of a very limited or very extensive nature. A grievance raised within a particular department could be dealt with within that department and the negotiations themselves might last no longer than an hour. On the other hand, a demand for the recognition of a union may lead to lengthy negotiations, as will the periodic demand for the renegotiation of wages and conditions of employment. For the present purposes it is assumed that negotiations are of the latter kind.

Selection of Negotlators Any negotiation requires the appointment or selection of the person or persons most suited to conduct the negotiations. The type of issue and the nature of both management and union organisation will determine the type and number of persons appointed. In a small organisation or where a minor issue is involved, one negotiator might suffice; in other instances it might be necessary to appoint a negotiation team. Equally, in a small company, the manager or owner may himself adopt the role of negotiator, while in larger organisations it is regarded as advisable for the managing director to remain in the background, so that he may act as the final authority to whom his negotiators can refer during the negotiation process.

Should a negotiating team be appointed, it will consist of a number of persons, selected on the basis of their expertise or their involvement in the issue at hand. Thus a management negotiating team could consist of the labour relations expert, the production manager, the financial manager, the company secretary and one or two foremen, while the union team may consist of an organiser, the general secretary or president, one or two officials and some shop stewards. The usual practice is to keep the team as small as possible. Too large a negotiating team might encumber negotiations and make it more difficult to reach consensus.

After the negotiating team has been appointed, a chief negotiator will be selected from the ranks of the team members. Conversely, a chief negotiator could be appointed first, whereafter he would select his own team. Such chief negotiator is usually chosen on the basis of his experience, his expertise and his knowledge of both his own organisation and the other party. His task is to coordinate and lead the negotiating team, to get to know the other party, to advise his principals in preparing an objective strategy, to arrange and lead meetings, to continually report back and refer to his principals and, within limits, to reach decisions during negotiations on behalf of his principals. If he is to carry out his task successfully, a chief negotiator will have to establish a sound relationship with his principals, his teammates and the other side. He should have the trust and confidence of all involved and particularly of his principals. Most importantly, the chief negotiator does not dominate or impose his ideas; his is essentially the position of coordinator and skilled expert. The rest of the negotiating team will follow the initiative of the chief negotiator. Some teams may decide to cast each team member in a specific role. One may act the aggressor and another the pacifier, while yet another maintains the position of expert and adviser throughout the negotiations. Although this may prove a good strategic ploy, it is not always necessary, as long as the team coordinates effectively and as long as one team member is designated as listener. This is most important, since negotiators are all too inclined to talk and not to listen. It is necessary that one person, trained in listening and observation skills, refrain from talking and instead sit back to observe innuendoes, subtle gestures and reactions. He is the one who from time to time may call for a caucus in order to inform his teammates of his observations. This person may also act as recorder, but in larger teams it is preferable to appoint another team member to record all important arguments and decisions.

Obtaining a Mandate

Before any preparations for negotiation can commence, the chief negotiator or his negotiating team should obtain an initial mandate from the principals or constituents, whatever the case may be. This will probably not be the final mandate for negotiations, but it will establish a preliminary framework within which planning can take place. On the part of union negotiators this would entail bringing a management demand to their membership or, most often, establishing the needs and demands of their members, while management negotiators will obtain direction from their principals and broadly establish the size of the package which the principals are prepared to offer. However, it needs to be stressed that a mandate is never absolute and that it may change as preparations and negotiations progress.

Setting Objectives

Planning and strategising is usually preceded by the establishment of certain broad objectives and, if possible, calculated guesses as to the objectives of the other party. The objectives are described as 'broad' in the sense that they refer not to targets to be reached during negotiation but rather to the overall objectives of the negotiation process, to the general objectives of management and the union, and to the specific objectives of negotiators.

The overall objective of negotiation is usually to achieve the fairest and most acceptable settlement. There are negotiators who may wish to win at all costs and to crush the other side, but this usually leads to low-value outcomes and often to continued conflict.

This notwithstanding, there are particular circumstances in which the overall objective may be to take a principled stand or to display strength. This usually happens when the other party has, within the history of the relationship, displayed an exaggerated sense of its own power or when too many concessions are perceived to have been made in the past. Whatever the overall objective, it is important that it be clearly defined and that it be kept in mind by the entire negotiating team, since it is this overall goal which will set the tone for the negotiations and which will keep negotiators on course.

The general objective of management is to maximise profit to be used in payment of dividends to shareholders, in reinvestment for growth and in development of the organisation. To achieve this objective management will attempt to minimise labour, capital, operating and maintenance costs. During negotiations, management's main concern will thus be with turnover, profits before and after tax, tax and tax concessions, profit margins, reinvestment, growth, expansion, dividends declared, competitiveness, productivity, market retention, control and cost savings. An appreciation of these concerns by the union can greatly facilitate negotiation and result in better argument. Equally, management should understand and appreciate the union objectives as listed in Chapter 6, and should plan arguments and counterarguments in the light also of these objectives.

Generally speaking, unions want to improve the situation of their members, against the backdrop of continued employment and security, job satisfaction, a happy workforce and acknowledgment of employee rights, while management wants production to continue and improve and the operation to run with as few problems and difficulties as possible. More specifically, all negotiators, whether on management or union side, will want to feel good about themselves once the negotiations have been concluded; they would like to receive praise from their principals or constituents, would wish to be seen as kind, reasonable, honest and fair, would not want to be regarded as 'suckers' and would like to be listened to and to receive good explanations. Understanding these general and specific objectives leads to better strategising and to more reasonable behaviours during negotiations.

One overall objective of negotiation remains, and that is the desire of both parties to maintain and, if possible, improve their relationship. Whatever their individual and separate lines and aspirations, the parties undertake negotiations principally as a means of ensuring the continuity of the relationship. Unfortunately, this is all too often forgotten during the actual conduct of the negotiation process.

Identifying the Issues

Once demands have been posted or proposals and counterproposals have been made, the negotiating team will, as one of its first tasks, attempt to identify the issues to be subjected to negotiation. This is necessary, as not all the issues may be immediately recognisable. In certain cases demands or proposals are couched in misleading language, or one demand raises another issue. It is also important that issues be listed in order of priority and that the possibility be considered of converting certain issues to problems, leading to their being subjected to integrative, rather than distributive, bargaining. The list of issues established at this early stage may later be amended and priorities may change, both after intra-organisational bargaining has occurred and after the initial encounter with the other side.

Intra-Organisational Negotiation

In a previous chapter it was explained that collective bargaining or negotiation with the other side will always be preceded by intra-organisational negotiation, the main purpose being the adoption of a common stand. Furthermore, such intra-organisational negotiation will continue as long as the negotiations themselves last. During intra-organisational negotiation a compromise between the goals of various entities is reached, unrealistic expectations are toned down and a coordinated strategy is adopted. The task of formulating a joint strategy or position will fall mainly on the shoulders of the chief negotiator. In order to achieve the necessary coordination he will have to identify the issues, establish the needs of all concerned (particularly those of his own and the opposing organisation), gather as much information as possible and negotiate with his own team, his principals and other concerned persons within the organisation. Only once consensus has been achieved can the actual planning of negotiations commence. To enter negotiations with a team which is uncoordinated and not in agreement, or without the support of principals, is to court disaster.

Information Gathering

In both the preparation for and the actual conduct of negotiations, information may prove the key to success. A negotiating team should, before it enters the negotiation situation, have all the necessary information at its disposal. This includes information relating to current conditions, its own organisation and the other side. Comprehensive information leads to realistic goal setting, good strategic planning and persuasive argument and counterargument during the conduct of negotiations. As such, it can greatly facilitate negotiations and lead to high-value outcomes.

Current Economic Conditions

The influence of environmental factors on collective bargaining and, therefore, on negotiations has been discussed in a preceding section. Economic, social and political conditions will influence the conduct of negotiations and the bargaining power of each party. Negotiators should know whether prevalent economic developments will favour the other party and whether social or political conditions could play a role in the negotiation process or lead to the exertion of pressure.

In wage negotiations, economic conditions are of particular importance. Thus negotiators need to take cognizance of inflation levels, cost of living indices, levels of economic activity, business cycles, industry trends, economic forecasts, unemployment levels and the general position of the labour market. On the micro level, current trends in wages and prices are often used as a criteria for the formulation of demands and counteroffers, as are wages negotiated in related undertakings, household and minimum subsistence levels, wage determinations and the outcome of arbitration awards. The following statistical indicators are most frequently used during substantive negotiations.

- **Consumer Price Index (CPI)**. This reflects the increased price of goods and services used by an average family, and is calculated by taking approximately 600 consumer goods and services, weighting them in terms of importance, establishing a base year and then calculating the percentage increase from month to month and from year to year. It is used to calculate the inflation rate and to adjust prices and wages, but there are certain inherent problems with this statistic in that the household used is imaginary and the basket of goods is therefore not always typical. Also, it does not take into account direct taxation. In dealing with lower level income groups, it is often advisable to supplement this statistic with the food price index, which may be more relevant.
- **Inflation Rate**. The inflation rate is wider and more general than the CPI, and can therefore be lower. In essence it shows by how much money has devalued over a certain period, and is calculated by taking all prices into account and expressing increases on a percentage basis. It is usually calculated on a month-by-month and year-by-year basis, expressed as a twelve-month moving average.
- **Producer Price Index (PPI)**. Previously called the Wholesale Price Index, this shows the increased price of a representative basket of goods, including capital and intermediate goods. It reveals the increase in the price of imported goods more effectively, and is often used by management to prove an escalation in capital and production expenses.
- **Gross Domestic Product (GDP)**. This statistic reflects the total price of goods and services produced in a country, but does not include unrecorded and non-market activity. It is used to measure the degree of economic activity in a country from one year to

another and to compare this with that of other countries.
- *Per Capita* Income. Income *per capita* refers to the average income per person, and is calculated by dividing the total income by the number of people. It is used to compare earnings with those in other countries and to measure economic progress, but the problem is that it does not say how income is distributed.
- Real Wages. The real wage lag constitutes the loss suffered when prices rise without a concomitant rise in wages. Thus, if the inflation rate is 15 per cent per annum, a wage of R100 in January will amount to a real wage of R85 by December.
- Minimum Subsistence Level and Household Subsistence Level (MSL and HSL). The first determines how much a family of a certain size (usually five or six) needs just to survive, and the second how much they need to subsist reasonably. It is calculated by taking the price of an average basket of goods — but, again, the problem is that the basket is arbitrary and does not allow for any other expenditure except necessities. Nowadays MSLs and HSLs are mostly discredited, with unions preferring to use a 'living wage' as the basic criterion.

Organisational Position

No negotiator can enter into a negotiation situation without full knowledge of the organisation he represents. He should, in the first place, be continually aware of organisational needs for profit, control, stability and expansion. Furthermore, he should have knowledge of the organisation's present position as regards profitability, its plans for the future and the ratio of labour costs to total costs. A negotiator will know, in broad detail, about the operation of each department, he will be acquainted with the production process and aware of the management styles adopted in every department so that he does not make commitments which, in practice, prove to be unrealistic or out of line with general policy. He will also need to engage in continued intra-organisational communication. Intra-organisational negotiation does not end when negotiations with the other side begin. Since negotiations will lead to changed perspectives and expectations, it is necessary for the chief negotiator always to refer back to his colleagues and principals and to seek adjustments on their part.

Knowledge of one's own organisation entails knowledge of related undertakings, particularly those which are in close competition. A very real dilemma in industrial relations is that competition for product markets may limit the possibility of cooperation between companies in the industrial relations sphere. Secretiveness regarding labour relations policy and agreements may place one company in a favourable position *vis-à-vis* other organisations, but it also allows a union to play one organisation off against the other.

From the union side, the union negotiator also has to be fully informed about the organisation he represents and about its competitors. However, in union circles it is not necessary to stress this point as emphatically, since a union is established for the sole purpose of representing the interests of its members, mainly by the process of collective bargaining; in the case of managerial negotiators, negotiation is one of their many tasks.

Knowledge of the Other Side

This facet of information gathering is most often overlooked, especially by management negotiators. From the management side, it is essential to study the union, to know its policy, strategy and past history, to be aware of its successes and failures, its proneness to strike action, its affiliations, the support it may receive and its present position and intentions. The union, in its turn, will study the company, its managerial style, the industry within which it operates and its past history. It will try to learn as much as possible about the company's internal and external organisation, about the work process, profitability levels, wage structures and labour costs. More sophisticated unions will obtain much information from the annual reports of a company and its competitors, or they may request that the company's books be opened for inspection by union officials.

As the relationship develops, much of the information mentioned will become past knowledge, but continual monitoring of developments and the updating of information relating to the other side remains imperative.

Testing the Water Before entering into more detailed preparation for negotiation, it is advisable first to test the water. This entails finding out more about the other side's intentions and objectives, establishing how committed they are to their demands, how much support they have and how they should react to certain proposals. Such initial probing can take place by asking casual questions, holding informal talks and making parallel remarks. It could also be aimed at preconditioning the other side by de-optimising their expectations as regards certain demands or issues.

Delimiting the Area of Negotiation ### Establishing the Bargaining Range

If negotiation is to be of a distributive nature, it will be necessary for each party to establish what it wants to achieve, what it is likely to achieve, to what extent it is prepared to concede and what the other side will want to achieve. This is done by setting upper and lower limits (essentially optimistic and pessimistic projections) for each issue, particularly those of a substantive nature, and thereby gaining some insight into a probable or realistic outcome.

Before upper and lower limits can be established, it will be necessary to establish a possible bargaining range; otherwise the upper and lower limits of one party may be entirely unrealistic and there may be no commonality at all with the limits set by the other party. This will result in both sides having to go back to the planning stage before actual negotiations can commence. The bargaining range is established by studying demands and proposals in the light of current circumstances, knowledge of the other party, general trends in industrial relations and past experience of negotiations or of the other party. Furthermore, the bargaining range will be widely delimited by what is generally known as the area of interdependence.

The area of interdependence is that range — say, in wages — within which it is worth each party's while to try to maintain the relationship; in essence, to continue negotiating. The outer limits of this area are set by the points at which either party would terminate a potentially advantageous relationship. For example, employees might be unwilling to continue working for the undertaking if the wage rate is set at lower than R10,00 per hour while, if the employer is forced to pay more than R20,00 per hour, he might look for alternatives such as giving up the operation, mechanising, or moving to another area where labour is cheaper. Thus, principally, the area of interdependence establishes or limits the bargaining range and can be illustrated as follows.

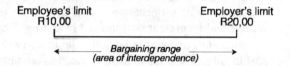

In practice, these limits may be pushed even lower in the case of employees and higher in the case of employers. An employee's decision that it is not worth his while to continue in employment might be affected by his lack of mobility, his limited knowledge of the labour market, the decentralised nature of the market, his experience in a particular type of work, the fact that he may lose benefits or seniority rights, his skill level and the rate of unemployment. The company, on the other hand, may go beyond its upper limit after considering such factors as the high cost of replacement, the cost of severance and of moving. The employer's upper limit, or whether he will go beyond his upper limit, will also depend on the union's control of the labour market. Should the union control the entire market, the employer may have no option but to agree to union demands, but he may eventually decide to mechanise, in which case the union will have gained in the short term and lost in the long term. It is generally believed that high or higher upper limits will be established where demand is inelastic, where there is a national rather than a local product market, where the operations of the employer are of a large scale, where multiunit companies are involved, where it is not easy to relocate and where the products are of a diverse nature. There is a belief that in some industries there is no upper limit at all, although there are usually restraints on the union in the form of alternative options for management.

The area of interdependence will further be affected by what is known as **mutually created gain**. Negotiation is not merely a divisive process. It creates additional value and mutual benefit. In the long term it will lead to trust and confidence between the parties. They may form a unique combination, which provides social satisfaction for both. In addition to mutually created gain, there are **subjective utilities and disutilities** to consider. Although a union may have higher wages as its main objective, it will also consider the subjective disutility of enforcing its demands at all costs, as this may lead to problems in later negotiations and even to a drop in employment. In the same way the employer who may not want to pay higher wages might consider the subjective utility of having a happier and more satisfied workforce and a favourable image in the industry.

The area of interdependence cannot be rigidly established. There are many factors which would influence employees to accept less than their limit and employers to offer more than their limit. In practice, a skilled negotiator will not attempt to push an opponent to these limits, as it greatly endangers the relationship. Also, a negotiator will always set his own limits slightly lower or higher, depending on whether he is on management or union side, than the limits of the party he represents. This is done because he would lose credibility with his party and might even lose his job if he negotiates around their outer limits. The position is thus as follows.

Employee's limit
R10,00

Employer's limit
R20,00

Union Negotiator limit
R12,50

Management Negotiator limit
R17,50

Resistance and Target Points

All the considerations outlined above are not separate steps but form part of an integrated process, the purpose of which is to establish target and resistance points. From these the settlement range will eventually be obtained.

According to Walton and McKersie, targets are based on the highest estimate of what is needed or possible, the most optimistic assumptions regarding the probability of success and the most favourable assessment of the negotiator's bargaining skill, while resistance points are based on the lowest estimate of what is needed or possible, the most pessimistic assumptions regarding the possibility of success and the least favourable assessment of the negotiator's bargaining skill. Resistance points are also those at which a union would go on strike and management would stage a lockout.

Target and resistance points of both parties will be established within the perceived bargaining range. Thus, if the two are brought together, the following will result.

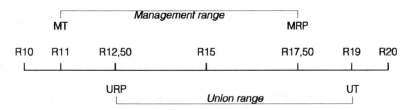

Management range

MT   MRP

R10   R11   R12,50   R15   R17,50   R19   R20

URP   UT

Union range

Settlement Range: The settlement range constitutes the area between the resistance points of both parties. A positive settlement range (one in which there is a likelihood of agreement) is achieved if the Union's resistance point is lower than management's resistance point. This may be illustrated as follows.

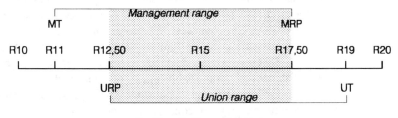

Management range

MT   MRP

R10   R11   R12,50   R15   R17,50   R19   R20

URP   UT

Union range

Positive Settlement Range

Negative settlement range (one where there is little likelihood of agreement) is obtained when the union resistance point is higher than management's resistance point, as in the following example.

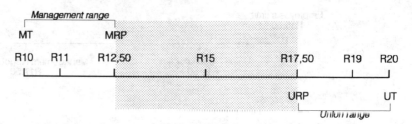

Negative Settlement Range

In order to estimate the range of settlement it will be necessary to make a calculated guess as to the target and resistance points of the other party. This is done by studying the demands of that party, drawing from past experience and other agreements reached, and by estimating the benefits and costs of agreement as against the benefits and costs of disagreement to both parties. It is obvious that, as actual negotiation progresses and more information is obtained, perceptions of the settlement range may have to be adapted. Nevertheless, it is useful to project the settlement range before entering into negotiations, as it assists in the establishment and modification of the party's own targets and is indicative of the type of strategy which will have to be adopted. If the projected settlement range is negative, preliminary efforts will have to be directed towards establishing a more positive zone for negotiation. This may be effected if the party modifies its own resistance and target points or it may be achieved by placing subtle pressure for modification on the other party.

Calculation of Utilities and Disutilities
In attempting to establish realistic upper and lower levels, it is useful to calculate, or to attempt to calculate, the costs and benefits of non-settlement for both sides. Representatives should estimate what they will gain and what they will lose if settlement is not reached at a certain point. Equally, they need to project the benefits and costs which the other side might incur. Benefits and costs relating to one negotiation issue may then be offset against those derived from another issue.

The costs which management could incur by not settling could include losses suffered as a result of a strike, a go-slow or a work-to-rule, a decline in productivity, lack of involvement by employees, loss of time, loss of market segment, a poor public image, lack of credibility in the community, high labour turnover, the consequences of legal action, a breakdown in the relationship, tougher bargaining in the future and the eventual loss of face when forced to settle. Benefits would include savings incurred by not conceding, the establishment or non-establishment of precedents, less administration, time gained for reassessment, opportunity to use stockpiles or to reduce staff, face-saving and readier concessions from the other side in the future. By not conceding employees may lose wages, service and benefits. They may, in the long term, lose more than they gain by weathering the storm, and may face tougher bargaining the next time around. They too are threatened by a breakdown in the relationship. They may eventually lose face, and negotiators might find themselves without support. By not conceding they may eventually obtain a better deal and will establish a precedent and a power base for the future. They will start off from a more advantageous position during the next round of negotiations, may have increased solidarity and greater commitment. They too could save face in the long run or give themselves time to work out a better deal.

Bargaining power is calculated by weighing the other party's costs of disagreeing against benefits derived. Should the one party's costs be greater than his benefits and the other party's benefits greater than his cost, the second party will have more power. Bargaining power could also be calculated by assessing the cost of settlement to the other party. Should the cost to management of a certain settlement be disproportionately high in relation to the benefits derived, it becomes unlikely that management would readily agree to such settlement. Union bargaining power consequently decreases. If, in addition to this, industrial action would affect the union more adversely than management, then the union is obviously in a poor bargaining position. In such an event it would be advisable for the union to set a lower upper limit. The same example would apply to management in the reverse position.

The Contract Zone

The contract zone is that area within the settlement range which will be delimited as the final area of negotiation. The area in which the contract zone is established will depend on the skill of the negotiators on each side and the power of the parties. In the example of a positive settlement range given previously, the contract zone will probably be between R12,50 and R15,00 if management has more skill and power. Conversely, it will be between R15,00 and R17,50 if union negotiators are more skilful and can exert more pressure.

It may be asked whether preliminary establishment of bargaining and settlement ranges is necessary and whether it would not be advisable for each side to make as realistic an assessment as possible and to establish a contract zone forthwith. This is usually not possible, firstly because perceptions of reality are established gradually and may change during negotiations. Secondly, the contract zone established depends to some extent on the actual conduct of negotiations. Thirdly, the act of distributive negotiation is in itself a ritual. Too realistic an assessment of the situation or a very narrow settlement range may leave one or both sides feeling that they really did not negotiate or were not able to trade off a concession on one issue against an advantage on another.

Costing of Contracts

Especially where substantive issues are concerned, it is necessary for management to cost out the projected contracts, both at the most pessimistic level and from a realistic perspective. In the example of a positive settlement range already given, management would need to calculate the increase in labour costs should a wage of R17,50 as against, say, R12,50 per hour be negotiated. Similar costing would have to be undertaken where negotiations hinge around extended leave benefits, fringe benefits, pensions, training and other matters of this kind. In undertaking this exercise, it is advisable not only to cost out individual items but also to draw up various alternative packages and to cost these accordingly. The costing of individual factors and of the total contract leads to considerations regarding affordability, the possibility of trading off one benefit against another and to the possibility of staggered increases. Moreover, total contract costs constitute a powerful argument in persuading the other party to lower its demands or to raise its offer.

Strategic Planning

Once targets and resistance points have been established, strategic planning for negotiations can proceed, taking into account the possible settlement range, the cost of the contract, the bargaining strength of each party, the utilities and disutilities of agreement versus disagreement or industrial action, previous knowledge of the other party, the position of the organisation and current conditions. During the strategic planning stage negotiators will decide which issues to address first, which arguments should be raised, in which instances concessions can be made and which issues or targets will be termed non-negotiable. It is useful at this stage to appoint one of the negotiating team as devil's advocate, or to test arguments on an 'outsider'. This may lead to modification of positions and arguments. One or both parties may decide to insert so-called red herrings among the bargaining issues. These are demands which are not seriously intended, but which can be used as trade-offs on more important issues. At this stage negotiators will plan the initial approach to the other side, the tone to be adopted, the role of the various negotiators and the probable progress of negotiations. Possible industrial action is another aspect which requires close attention. All major negotiations should be preceded by contingency planning for a strike by employees or a lockout by employers.

Timing, too, is of the utmost importance. In management's case it might be strategically expedient to negotiate when there is a downturn in production, when employees want a rapid settlement and when management has all the time in the world. This of course would not be beneficial to the union. Equally, unions would not wish to negotiate when management is busy and can therefore prolong negotiations, nor do they favour negotiation at the beginning of the financial year or when an annual increase date is imminent.

Finally, in order to put their plans into concrete form, negotiators may choose to draw up a negotiation planning sheet. This will list the issues, the bargaining parameters, the projected costs, the areas of concession and matters which are non-negotiable. A planning sheet of this kind provides all members of the negotiating team with the necessary information for reference purposes during the actual conduct of negotiations. (See Annexures for example of planning sheet.)

Administrative Arrangements

Physical and administrative arrangements for the conduct of negotiations are usually made in collaboration with the other party. These arrangements include the drawing up of an agenda, agreement on a suitable venue, the settling of dates and times for the conduct of meetings, a decision regarding a suitable chairman and arrangements for minutes to be taken. The format of negotiation is agreed upon (if necessary) by the parties, and agreement is reached on procedures to be followed in the event of deadlock between the parties.

Other matters which require attention are seating arrangements, the order of speaking, the use of experts, the handling of interruptions, the use of tape recorders, security, the nature and format of public announcements, arrangements for eating and rest times, length of caucuses and whether or not team changes will be allowed. Most of these need not be discussed beforehand, but should receive attention before the actual negotiations commence.

THE CONDUCT OF NEGOTIATIONS

Development of the Negotiation Process

The negotiation process commences with an opening encounter, which sets the climate for negotiations and is usually of a formal nature. After the rules have been established and the agenda has been formulated, each party attempts by various tactics to establish the position of the other side, without itself revealing too much. It may become necessary even at this stage for the parties to reassess their positions and strategies in the light of what they have learnt from the other party.

The opening encounter is followed by the actual body of negotiation, a period of argument and counterargument during which both parties will engage in hard bargaining in an attempt to modify the perceptions of the other and to initiate movement towards their own targets. Concessions will be given and taken, pressure will be applied, joint problem-solving may occur and the commitment of either party to its position is revealed. From time to time, one or the other party may request a caucus to reassess its position or to engage in further planning. Generally, negotiation procedure becomes less formalised and more interpersonal during this stage, and chief negotiators may arrange informal meetings to facilitate agreement. Negotiators will keep their principals or members continually informed and may periodically request the adjournment of negotiations to allow the opportunity for feedback or consultation.

From here negotiations will gradually move to a stage of crisis, where pressure is increased in an attempt to extract more concessions. Sanctions are more seriously considered, impasses are frequent and deadlock may eventually be reached. Before this occurs, the parties may search seriously for alternatives and the bargaining range will have narrowed down considerably.

In the final stage or closing encounter, agreement may have been reached on some issues but not on others. It is essential that the decisions taken be carefully summarised and recorded, since they will form the basis of the ensuing written agreement and any incorrect wording or misconceptions may give rise to disputes in the future. Once a written agreement has been drawn up, it should be studied and signed by both parties — but only after each has ensured that his understanding of the provisions is correct. On issues where agreement has not yet been reached, both sides will start pushing for closure.

The closing encounter necessitates the use of tact, since some aspersions may have been cast and because one party may feel that it has conceded too much. Care should be exercised to create a proper climate for the continuation of the relationship and the joint implementation of the agreement.

Negotiations do not always proceed smoothly. Most often they are marked by withdrawal or the threat of withdrawal, or they may be interrupted by industrial action. These may bring an end to the negotiation process but, most commonly, negotiations are resumed after reassessment by each side.

Opening and Establishing Climate

The opening phase of negotiations has a great impact on the rest of the proceedings, as it is during this stage that the climate for the entire negotiation is established. Such climate may be natural and relaxed, polite but cordial, cooperative or brisk and businesslike. One party may take the initiative in establishing the climate which he deems suitable, or he may want to see how the other party intends to approach the negotiations. Usually both parties will attempt to establish a positive framework for the negotiations and emphasise common ground, or point to mutual gain to be achieved from the negotiations. At the same time, each will be assessing the other's attitude and position and a great deal of careful listening takes place.

Establishing Positions

During the initial stages of negotiation, much time is devoted to establishing one's own position and attempting to discover the real position of the other party. Skilled negotiators will attempt from the outset to establish a position of dominance. This they do by making a very firm offer or demand and displaying great commitment. Although one very strong reason for adopting a particular stance may be proffered, it is not necessary at this stage to engage in any real argument. In fact, attempts at lengthy argument might weaken a negotiator's stand since it may appear to be apologist by nature.

The opening offer or demand could be disproportionately low or high, or it could be more realistic. The proponents of an exaggerated opening bid argue that it allows more room for manoeuvring, but it is also dangerous in that it could be summarily rejected, could harden attitudes and detract from the credibility of the negotiator. Another suggested policy is to follow up an extreme opening bid with a more realistic one which, although still low or high, will then be more acceptable to the other side. This could prove useful but could still detract from the credibility of the negotiator, particularly if he has already displayed firm commitment to his initial offer/demand. He would then have to find a very good reason for changing his stance so rapidly. The best approach is probably to set high but realistic targets and to negotiate around these for some time.

Feeling Out the Opponent

While confirming his own position, the negotiator tries to establish the degree of commitment on the other side. For this reason it is advisable not to talk too much during the initial stages of a negotiation session. Karas suggests that the good negotiator will attempt to discover more about the other side by asking leading or loaded questions, eliciting responses from persons other than the chief negotiator in the opposing team, suggesting that they are not well briefed, trying to ascertain hard and soft lines, noting reactions to statements and questions and, above all, listening to what the other party is saying. Concentrated listening can occur if the negotiator does not become distracted or try to formulate his own responses while the other party is speaking. He should refrain from interrupting, should not jump to conclusions nor allow his personal opinion of the other party to influence him, and should not merely discard what he does not like. It may from time to time become necessary to ask for clarification; moreover, the skilled negotiator will not attempt to remember everything he hears, but will rather note down important points made by the other side.

The other party will at the same time be attempting to establish the negotiator's position. consequently, he should be careful that he himself does not give too much away. According to Karas, he does so by deferring questions from the other party — for example, by asking for clarification, deflecting the question, providing ambiguous or selective answers or breaking down the question. The secret is to gain time to think and to avoid intuitive answers or too many explanations.

Argument and Counter-argument

Once initial positions have been accepted (and perhaps modified), each party will engage in concerted argument and counterargument in an attempt to persuade the other party to move away from his position. Arguments constitute the core of the negotiation process and should be carefully prepared. Also, it is preferable to bring one strong argument than a range of weaker ones, and not all arguments supporting a particular point of view should be proffered from the beginning.

In order to sway the other party to his point of view, the negotiator will require all the persuasive communication skills he can muster. In this regard, it is important to remember that the beginning and the end of a message are of the utmost importance. The negotiator should first express his point of view, then supply the reason and follow this up with a summary or reiteration of his stance. He will also be more persuasive if, from the outset, he takes into account different points of view and provides counterarguments, thus forestalling the argument from the other side. Arguments should be brief and to the point, conclusions should be clearly stated and the message can be repeated as often as possible, perhaps by different members of the negotiating team. Sound argument requires sound knowledge and, if the chief negotiator himself is not in possession of such knowledge, he should defer to another member of the team or, if allowed, use the services of an expert. Points of view may be backed up by illustrations, statistics or written communications.

In presenting his case, the negotiator should aim at persuading the other party that he will benefit from agreement. This can be done by pointing to the disadvantages if he does not agree, and even by *subtle* threats and bluffs. He should try to find common ground, emphasise this, attempt to make his stance sound as reasonable as possible and even appeal to the emotions of the other party. A skilled negotiator, being aware of his own side's strengths and weaknesses, will purposely play upon his strengths and make light of weaknesses, at the same time emphasising the weaknesses of the other party.

When negotiations revolve around a multitude of issues, it is preferable to commence with an issue which is easier to settle and, if possible, to link easier issues with more difficult ones. Commencing with easily settled issues creates a more favourable climate, but it may also not be wise to leave more difficult issues to the very end.

The attention devoted to the presentation of the negotiator's own argument should be equalled by that devoted to the countering of the opponent's argument. The negotiator adopts a critical stance, in that he questions the assumptions, statements of fact and conclusions of the other side. He will challenge inconsistencies, take note of omissions and point to emotionally biased argument. It is usually not advisable to reject the argument of the other party immediately, but the negotiator could question the speaker's credibility, point to the consequences of the proposals, enlarge on the other party's weaknesses and suggest he revise his case. One good method, suggested by Pienaar and based on the Bales' Interaction Process Analysis, is to disagree but at the same time to request clarification and to ascertain whether that is truly the opinion of the speaker. The negotiator then requests his opponent to justify his opinion, whereafter he supplies his own information, opinions and suggestions in rapid succession, ending with a solution and requesting agreement from the other party. This type of advice-giving is often successful, but requires some degree of aggression and can be viewed as manipulative by the other side. However, it can be conducted on a more mutually acceptable basis if exploration of possibilities is undertaken by both sides and the other party is not precipitated into agreement.

During the entire process of argument and counterargument, the skilled negotiator will continually seek clarification from the other side. He will also, from time, summarise his own and the opponent's point of view, thus ensuring that there is mutual understanding while at the same time measuring progress.

Displaying Commitment

In order to gain the necessary dominance, a negotiator should from the outset display commitment to his position. However, this commitment should not be rigid, particularly during the initial stage of negotiations. A negotiator who enters the process with a 'take it or leave it' attitude opens himself to accusations of bad faith. Instead, he should persuade the other party that he sincerely believes his offer/demand to be fair and that only very sound argument from the other side will convince him to change his stance. Thus he allows himself room to manoeuvre and precludes loss of face when he is eventually obliged to move. As he moves nearer to his resistance point his commitment should, of course, become firmer; but he should never be absolutely inflexible unless he has decided that he is prepared to weather the consequences.

Granting Concessions

It is expected that, during the negotiation process, both sides will make concessions; but a trade-off of concessions on a one-for-one basis is not always necessary or advisable. The skilled negotiator will not commence granting concessions until he has the full picture and has felt out the opponent; that is, unless he has purposely opened with an exaggerated offer or demand and intends to make a large initial concession in order to bring movement. Usually concessions are granted slowly, commencing with concessions on smaller issues and moving gradually to larger ones. Initial unwillingness to grant concessions signals commitment and firmness, but care should be exercised that positions do not become hardened. Furthermore, concessions on particular items may be larger at the beginning and become smaller as negotiators move closer to each other, although a larger concession may be made towards the end to signify a final offer.

The manner, rate and sequence in which concessions are to be granted should be broadly planned beforehand, but they should not follow a pattern and adaptations may have to be made in the light of the concessions granted by the other side. Also, negotiators may intentionally grant concessions which actually mean nothing. Where they grant real concessions, they will make the other side feel that these have been hard earned. A good tactic is to link concessions to previous ones, and to indicate that a concession is now expected in return. In some instances, a concession from the other side may not be accepted immediately. The negotiator will indicate that it is insufficient and suggest that it be revised.

The number, type and rate of concessions will eventually depend on bargaining power and the good negotiator will make concessions only if forced to do so or if he wishes to bring about movement, yet he should remain flexible, always bearing in mind the golden rule of concessions according to Karas: not to give too much too soon, too much too late or too little too late.

Caucusing Periodic caucuses are necessary in order to reassess, replan or consider a concession made by the other side, but they are also a sound bargaining tactic. The temporary withdrawal of one party allows the other time for consideration, particularly during moments of heightened tension. Parties may become uncertain and decide to move from previously held positions.

The chief negotiator will be the one to request a caucus, but there should be prearranged signals by which any member of the team can indicate that a caucus is necessary. Usually the party hosting the negotiations leaves the room, unless other provisions have been made. The approximate duration of caucuses should be agreed by both parties and, where extensions are required, it is good form to request these of the other party.

Impasses Impasses may be reached at any point during hard bargaining. These are not deadlocks, in that both sides may still be prepared to move, but neither wants to move first. It is left to the skilled negotiator to bring about new movement, preferably by the other side. This he may do by changing from a competitive to a cooperative mode, or by changing the shape of his own package. On the other hand, he might let the other side know that they cannot afford to remain where they are, he might suggest a change in their package and encourage them to move by indicating that, if they do, he might also move. Karas also suggests that he could limit issues, summarise developments and point to areas requiring movement, suggest that both move together by making a concession linked to one from the other side, or suggest that both refer back to their principals or constituents. If his purpose is to get the other side to move, he should try to provide them with the necessary face-savers. Where tension is high, it might be advisable to move to another agenda item for the time being, to call for a caucus, to introduce a red herring or to use humour. Usually impasses arise because one or both sides become overcommitted. If this is the case, the negotiator should search for a means whereby the other party can graciously move from his overcommitted position.

Final Offers or Demands Once the parties approach the expected contract zone, final offers or demands are put on the table with the purpose of achieving a settlement which is as near to the negotiator's target as possible. Karas suggests that, when making final offers or demands, a negotiator should have considered these carefully and should present them in such a manner that the other party is convinced of their seriousness. The offer/demand should be clear and firm, should be precisely phrased, but can be linked to alternatives and time spans, leaving the negotiator time to manoeuvre. It is advisable not to expect an immediate reaction, but rather to allow the other party time to think. This is generally achieved by timing final offers and demands to coincide with the end of a particular negotiation session.

When countering final offers or demands from the other side, the negotiator should never accept immediately and should not overreact, although he may, as a strategic move, show anger or even stage a walkout. By listening carefully, he will convince the opponent that he is taking the matter seriously; yet he will attempt also to provide his opponent with room to manoeuvre by, for example, changing the subject, providing alternatives or possible solutions, warning him of the consequences and helping him to save face if he changes his position. In essence, final offers are not always final.

Threats and Bluffs
A threat serves as a reminder that the one party can initiate sanctions against the other, or that a particular stand may hold unpleasant consequences for either or both sides. A bluff, on the other hand, is a threat which that party has no intention of carrying out or is unable to carry out and, as such, should be handled circumspectly as the other side may call the bluff, leading to loss of face for the initiator. Threats, too, should be carefully planned and should not be of a spontaneous or idle nature. The other party should be convinced that the threat will, in fact, be executed. Karas suggests that negotiators should gradually raise the level of threats and should set an example by putting minor threats into action. He also warns that the severity of the threat should match that of the issue. Threatening severe sanction on a minor issue opens the negotiator to ridicule. Furthermore, according to Karas, threats should be implied rather than spoken, mild rather than enormous, rational rather than emotional.

One of the best methods of countering a threat is to oblige the other party to articulate it. Very often he will hesitate to do so as he is then committed to carrying out the threat. The negotiator could also pretend that the threat is harmless, or that he has not heard it at all. Alternatively, he could face the threat head on and prove to the opponent that its execution will in fact harm both parties.

Deadlock
Deadlock is reached when neither party is prepared to move any further. Both are prepared to declare a dispute and to risk sanctions from the other side. Many negotiators fear deadlock situations. Karas explains that a situation of deadlock leaves negotiators frustrated, uncertain and with a feeling that they have failed in their task. However, deadlocks merely test the strength and commitment of the parties. They serve to soften positions and to initiate new movement. This is proved by the fact that most dispute procedures provide for renewed negotiation. Yet deadlocks are unpleasant. They usually result in more antagonistic behaviour and may lead to the imposition of a final sanction.

Sanctions
In union–management negotiations the ultimate sanction is a strike or a lockout, but less severe sanctions may be instituted during the course of negotiations. These range from a display of antagonism to temporary walkouts from negotiations, demonstrations, bad publicity, work-to-rules, go-slows and overtime bans. Sanctions are applied in escalating order, according to the severity of the situation.

Closure
Whether or not deadlocks have been declared, most negotiations will reach a stage where one or both parties realise that they are close to an agreement. One method of nudging the other party towards a final settlement is to agree in principle but to ask for something in addition, or to set certain conditions. The negotiator could also attempt to lure the other party into settlement by offering a deal, granting minor concessions or engaging in flattery. Alternatively, he could assume that agreement has been reached and start noting down the details

or summarising the main points. Where the other party continues to hold back, he could express surprise at the fact that a settlement cannot be reached under the circumstances, could point to the dangers or costs of not settling; or he could threaten to withdraw all other concessions if a final agreement is not reached (this only if he has made the concessions conditional on a final settlement). Although within this situation the negotiator should be assertive, even a little aggressive, he should not talk too much and should display a positive attitude.

NEGOTIATION MANOEUVRES

In the aforegoing section, discussion hinged around the art of negotiation. It is necessary also to mention the tactics which some negotiators, intent on gaining the upper hand, may apply. Many of these are negative by nature and, while they may prove useful in the short term, do not necessarily guarantee high-value outcomes.

Deadlines Certain broad time limits for negotiations should be established. However, the skilled negotiator will not be coerced into meeting narrow deadlines, since these create unnecessary pressure and, in the urgency of the moment, negotiators sometimes concede too readily, only to regret their actions once the agreement has been signed.

Limited Authority A negotiator may, when faced with a difficult decision, hide behind the excuse that he does not have the necessary authority to make that decision. While all negotiators will from time to time refer back to their principals or constituents, they should have decisionmaking power within the parameters of their mandate. The best way to deal with an opponent who continues to plead limited authority is to request him to obtain a wider mandate or to have himself replaced by someone capable of making the necessary decisions.

Statistics and Averages Statistics do serve a purpose in that they may support an argument or point of view, but there are negotiators who will attempt to overwhelm the other party with statistical information and with averages which may have no meaning at all. Those subjected to this overuse should remember the adage that 'There are lies, lies, lies ... and statistics'; also that statistics may be interpreted in many ways and that, for every statistic, there is often another which proves the opposite.

'Funny Money' Closely associated with the abusers of statistics are those who play around with figures to prove their arguments. By juggling figures they attempt to show losses and gains which actually do not exist in practice — much like the wife who tells her husband that she has saved him R500 by paying half price for a dress which originally cost R1 000.

Body Language During negotiations the skilled negotiator will closely observe also the subtle, non-verbal communication from the other side. Much is revealed by looks, body movements, posture and gestures. He should, however, be aware that an equally skilled opponent may purposely be misleading him. He may feign boredom by drumming his fingers or a pencil on the desk, try to appear confident and dominant by leaning back with his hands in his lapels, or assume an indifferent attitude by placing his feet on the desk and staring out of the window. It is best not to pay too much attention to such actions, or to make a statement which shocks the other out of his assumed stance.

Shock Tactics and Irritants A negotiator may attempt to put the other party off his stride by doing or saying something which he knows will shock the opponent, or by irritating behaviour. In the process of recovering from the shock or distraction, the opponent may readily concede on an issue, because he is not concentrating fully on the matter at hand.

Fatigue One tactic often used is to continue negotiating until the other party virtually drops from fatigue and, in his desire to end the negotiations, readily comes to an agreement.

Change of Pace Negotiations usually proceed at a relatively even pace but a negotiator may, at a certain point, speed up the process in an attempt to rush the other party into settlement.

Deliberate Errors Particularly when summarising the other party's argument or the points of agreement, a negotiator may deliberately commit an error. If the other party does not listen carefully, he may agree that the summary is correct, thus weakening his own position.

Changing Negotiators A change of negotiators may take place with the purpose of gaining time, since the new negotiator is not up to date with developments during negotiations and a great deal of backtracking has to occur. It is also disturbing for the other party suddenly to have to deal with a new person. There should be an agreement that no changes will be made without the consent of both parties.

The 'Bad Cop, Good Cop' Syndrome Here, one member of the team purposely acts in an aggressive manner and harangues the other side. When a crisis is reached, another member of the team steps in with a much kindlier approach. The other party is usually more willing to deal with the second negotiator, who then commences from an advantageous position.

Addressing the Weakest Member Where a negotiator is unable to elicit sufficient information from the other side or where he is of the opinion that there is some disagreement in the other team, he may attempt to elicit comments or answers — or even agreement — from the weakest member of the other team. Alternatively, he may harangue this person in the hope of breaking him down.

The Defence–Attack Spiral Certain negotiators deliberately initiate attacks on the other party, hoping that he will react defensively. This leads to a defence–attack spiral which detracts from the real issues. A skilled negotiator will absorb such emotional attacks and wait for the right moment to make his own, more rational, counterattacks.

Acted Emotions Many negotiators are also very good actors and can act out emotions such as frustration, anger, disappointment and sadness at will. It is best to allow emotional outbursts, whether acted or not, to subside and not to react intuitively to these.

Killing with Kindness There are negotiators who treat their opponents with such kindness that it is difficult for these persons to oppose or argue with them. The purpose is to change enemies to allies, thereby weakening the stand of the other side.

Interruptions Interruptions can prove very useful, particularly when negotiations are progressing unfavourably for one's own side or when a party needs time to reconsider but does not wish to request a caucus. Experienced negotiators will determine beforehand that no interruptions should occur.

Red Herrings or Straw Issues Here the negotiator deliberately introduces one or more issues which are of no real importance to him but on which he spends an inordinate amount of time. This often distracts the other party from the more important aspects of the negotiations.

As mentioned at the commencement, many of the manoeuvres described have negative effects and they should, therefore, be used with care.

PROFILE OF A SUCCESSFUL NEGOTIATOR

From 1968 onwards, Neil Rackham of the Huthwaite Research Group conducted various studies with the purpose of identifying the attributes of successful negotiators. His observations proved the following.

- When planning for negotiations, skilled negotiators considered a wider range of options and outcomes than those who were less skilled.
- While all negotiators tended to concentrate on conflict areas, skilled negotiators gave far more attention to areas of possible cooperation than did the average negotiator.
- Both skilled and less skilled negotiators tended to concentrate on short-term objectives, but successful negotiators did pay more (twice as much) attention to long-term objectives.
- Skilled negotiators established upper and lower limits during their planning sessions, whereas those less skilled tended to plan around a fixed point.
- Less skilled negotiators established rigid sequences beforehand, whereas the skilled negotiators were more flexible in this respect.
- More successful negotiators seemed to avoid irritating expressions such as 'unfair', 'unreasonable', 'uncaring', etc.
- Skilled negotiators did not make immediate counterproposals as frequently as those who were less skilled.
- Average negotiators engaged in defence–attack spirals on a much more frequent basis than skilled negotiators.
- Skilled negotiators usually warned the other party of the kind of statement they were going to make — for example, by saying that they intended to make an offer; but less skilled negotiators

tended to say 'I disagree' more often than their skilled colleagues who, instead, would commence with reasons and explanations.
- More successful negotiators frequently tested understanding and summarised their own and the other party's arguments.
- Skilled negotiators questioned the other party far more frequently than did their less skilled colleagues.
- While average negotiators tended to concentrate on facts and figures, more successful negotiators frequently explained how they felt about the other side and its arguments.
- Skilled negotiators backed up their arguments with an average of 1,8 reasons, whereas those who were less skilled used an average of three reasons per argument.

Finally, it was found that more than two thirds of the successful negotiators spent time after the negotiations reviewing what had happened and thus learning from experience, while less than half of the average negotiators had acquired this habit. Perhaps this, more than anything else, accounts for the high rate of success experienced by the first group in comparison to the second.

COLLABORATIVE NEGOTIATIONS

As mentioned earlier in this chapter, the traditional approach to negotiation is adversarial in nature. Each party adopts a particular position, which it guards at all costs. The objective of these negotiators is to urge the other party to move as far as possible towards their position, and to concede as little as possible. This results in an extremely narrow approach to negotiation — along a straight line between the position of one party and that of the other, with much game-playing and posturing in between. There is no consideration of alternative solutions, and each strives to gain as much as possible at the expense of the other. Personalities and egos become involved and, very often, the outcome relies on a contest of wills rather than on the realities of the situation.

The description given may be extreme, as most negotiations will involve some attempt also at collaboration; but it serves as typification of the dominant aspects of positional or adversarial negotiation. A more fully collaborative or integrative approach to negotiation would, of course, be preferable and would lead to outcomes which are of greater value for both parties. However, for such collaboration to exist, certain preconditions are required. Some of these have been mentioned in the section on Integrative Bargaining in Chapter 8 and are outlined in detail below.

Preconditions for Collaborative Negotiations

If parties are to engage in collaborative negotiations, each should in the first place recognise the legitimacy of the other party. Each should display respect for the other's needs and interests, approach the negotiations openly and honestly, and be willing to share information and to work towards a solution. In fact, the parties should believe that together they can and will find the best possible solution.

Collaborative negotiations further require that, although there may be different goals and perspectives and although these are respected, common interests predominate. For this to happen, both parties should be accorded equal value and status. One party should not be pleading with or demanding from the other. This means that, in an organisational setting, both management and employees should view themselves as joint stakeholders and the organisation as their point of common interest. Parties will have to share their needs, interests and fears, which in turn necessitates a trust relationship. Such trust is built by engendering psychological closeness, by openness and honesty, by emphasising similarities and interdependence and by displaying positive attitudes — including a desire to cooperate. Power differentials are minimised; in fact, the use of power is to be avoided and, instead of arguing positions, negotiators focus on problems.

Since collaborative negotiation does not rely on positioning and, therefore, on absolute mandates, negotiators have to be trusted by their constituents and be given far greater flexibility and decisionmaking powers than would be granted in an adversarial situation. Therefore, not only the negotiators but also the different constituents have to trust each other. Clearly such a relationship cannot be built up overnight and will be supported by a history of collaboration and goodwill in other areas. Also, it is easier to build a relationship of this kind in a decentralised situation where parties continually work closely together.

Finally, and as always, the successful establishment of a collaborative relationship will depend on continual clear and accurate communication and the furnishing of all relevant information by all the parties concerned.

Initiating Collaborative Negotiations

Collaborative negotiations may commence with a statement of positions; but, instead of concentrating on positions, concessions and demands, the parties explore the needs, interests and concerns behind these positions. In other worlds, the problems have to be separated from the positions, and also from the negotiators themselves. In most cases it is preferable not to state positions at all, but rather for both parties to put their concerns and objectives on the table. These are then placed in organisational context and explored within the framework of prevailing circumstances. However, before this can be done it might be necessary to sideline hardliners in each group and to establish the correct climate by levelling conferences, pre-meetings and training in problem-solving skills. This last is of particular importance since, once concerns have been placed on the table and depersonalised, the parties basically adopt a problem-solving mode.

Steps in Problem Solving

Anstey advises that, in order to engage in effective problem solving, both parties should in the first place jointly define the problem (or problems) and separate this from their own solutions. Issues need to be clarified, goals and obstacles identified. Thereafter, criteria for acceptable solutions need to be agreed upon. This is followed by a search for as many alternative solutions as possible. These are evaluated and narrowed down to the most viable. Finally, both parties need to reach agreement on the total solution.

Evaluation

The collaborative mode is a complex process to which the very sketchy outline above does not do justice. It requires far more detailed study and continued building of the relationship by both parties. In some instances, the parties may not be capable of this on their own and a facilitator may be required during the initial stages. Also, both parties may be reluctant to relinquish power positions. The negation of power (and particularly of coercive power) in negotiations requires a definite paradigm shift, which may not be easy to achieve.

THE OUTCOME OF NEGOTIATION

The Conclusion of Collective Agreements

The purpose of collective bargaining is to reach agreement. Minutes are kept during the conduct of negotiation meetings and, once agreement has been reached, a formal agreement is drawn up and signed by both parties.

Types of agreement

The first type of agreement to be reached between the parties to the bargaining relationship is the agreement to bargain. Thus the recognition agreement or the constitution of a bargaining association, both of which contain basic procedures for the conduct of the bargaining relationship and for the settlement of possible disputes, form the cornerstone of the relationship.

This type of agreement is followed by the conclusion of various agreements or one agreement covering procedural or substantive issues negotiated between the parties. Since certain substantive conditions of employment may be subject to further negotiation at regular intervals, it is preferable that these be contained in a separate agreement. Wages in particular are subject to continual amendment and that is why, in certain bargaining relationships, a main agreement might cover basic procedures dealing with grievances, discipline, layoffs, retrenchment and consultation on technological innovation, as well as basic substantive conditions of employment such as hours of work, benefits and holiday pay, while another agreement will cover wages and other substantive conditions which may change from time to time. Alternatively, the main agreement could merely be amended after each negotiation session, or wages could constitute a schedule attached to the main agreement.

The form and content of agreements vary from one relationship to another and, more broadly, from one industrial relations system to another.

Subject-Related Agreements

Besides the recognition agreement and substantive wage agreements negotiated from time to time, a union with a strong plant-level presence may wish to become involved in health and safety issues, or to negotiate agreements covering certain eventualities, such as retrenchment and the introduction of new technology. In South Africa the question of retrenchment in particular has received attention during the past five years. Also, the employer, if he wishes to introduce changes in the organisation and desires the cooperation of the union and his employees, may enter into an agreement with the union. One such agreement is the productivity agreement. While retrenchment agreements have become a common feature of collective bargaining in South Africa, new technology and productivity agreements are still relatively rare.

Health and Safety Agreements

The type of health and safety agreement concluded with a union will depend on management's own health and safety policy, on other plant-level structures (see Chapter 10) and on the degree of representation accorded to the union as regards these issues. Where no other arrangement exists, the union takes over the function of monitoring managerial practices in this respect.

A health and safety agreement with a union will cover the following.

- The election and appointment of health and safety representatives
- Duties, functions and rights of representatives
- The establishment of health and safety committees
- Joint union–management meetings on health and safety
- The right of the union to declare a dispute if health and safety is endangered
- The appointment of independent persons to verify or contradict allegations in respect of health and safety
- Permission for doctors and health or safety experts appointed by the union to inspect premises or conduct research into health and safety aspects pertaining to the organisation

Where other plant-level health and safety structures already exist, the health and safety agreement will not provide for the election of representatives, but it may allow for shop stewards to have an input on health and safety committees. Otherwise, the agreement would be basically the same.

The Retrenchment Agreement
The question of retrenchment has been discussed in detail in Chapter 10. Unions concluding a retrenchment agreement will wish to ensure that all the steps outlined in that chapter will be followed. Consequently, a retrenchment agreement will contain some or all of the following.

- Provision for prior notice to the union — This is usually set within certain time parameters
- Arrangements for proof of the necessity to retrench — The union may require financial information or an independent audit
- Arrangements for consideration of alternatives to retrenchment — The most viable alternatives will already be mentioned in the retrenchment agreement
- The criteria to be used in selecting retrenchees — The union may insist on using the 'last in, first out' (LIFO) principle, but a range of criteria could be adopted
- Provision for circumstances under which management may retain employees with special skills
- Arrangements for actual selection of employees to be retrenched — This may be undertaken in conjunction with the union, or management may draw up a list to be submitted to the union for approval
- Arrangements for actual notification of the employees concerned — The union may agree not to inform employees of impending retrenchments until the preliminary selections have been made
- Provision for special cases, that is, cases where retrenchment would cause severe hardship, to be brought to the attention of management
- Arrangements for the employer to assist employees in finding new

jobs
- Details as regards the retrenchment package — These include the criteria on which *ex gratia* payments are to be based and may include provision for payment of the employer's contributions to the employee's pension fund
- Arrangements for the retraining of retrenched employees — In some cases employers offer to assist the employee, financially or otherwise, in training himself for another job
- Arrangements for aftercare — The employer may agree to establish an advisory service which retrenched employees could use for a certain period after their retrenchment
- The undertaking to re-employ retrenchees, should vacancies occur which they are capable of filling — This undertaking should not be indefinite and should lapse after a period of one or two years. Moreover, the union should be given a specific time after notification of a vacancy to find incumbents for the job

Where retrenchments have become unavoidable, employers and unions face a common problem. Thus, although there may be much acrimony and although, in matters such as the criteria for selection, distributive bargaining may occur, the retrenchment agreement will usually be concluded by integrative bargaining.

Productivity Agreements

Productivity bargaining has been described as a means of introducing change by consent. It involves the better utilisation of labour, but with the proviso that the income from the additional output is shared by the employees concerned. It is *not* a method by which employers can compensate for higher wages by gaining additional productive output from employees. Nevertheless, it could be introduced as an alternative to substantial increases, again with the proviso that employees share in the profits made. According to Salamon, productivity bargaining is more popular and more acceptable in times of full employment and expanding demand and not in times of general recession.

Productivity bargaining is an extremely complicated process and each agreement is tailormade to suit the needs of a particular company and its employees. Basically, it entails the reorganisation of work and the offer of various packages to the employees. It may also involve the introduction of job flexibility (horizontally, vertically and geographically), time flexibility, changes in payment structures, and the introduction of work groups. Much will depend on the manner in which the package is introduced to the union and, should an agreement be reached, it will be implemented in stages. A productivity agreement requires a change of attitude on the part of employees and perhaps major organisational changes. Therefore, it needs careful planning and its negotiation is a time-consuming process.

Productivity agreements are reflective of joint interests and a shared commitment. Consequently, they will be successfully negotiated only where a developed relationship exists, where there is strong plant-level representation and where management style has changed from the autocratic to the more participative. A high level of trust needs to be established and there should be frequent communication, both between management and union representatives and between management and employees. Historically, management will have to have paid affordable rather than market-related wages and should be prepared for increasing disclosure. A productivity agreement is essentially a step towards a more participative system and will, therefore, have to be bolstered by other participative practices. Productivity or performance agreements which are negotiated merely to serve management's need for increased production are, more often than not, doomed from the start.

New Technology Agreements

The introduction of new technology presents a very real threat to trade unions, as it may lead to redundancies and weaken the trade union base. Contrarily, unions also argue that technology leads to improved productivity and that employees should be rewarded accordingly. However, in most cases where new technology is introduced, unions are obliged to adopt a defensive, rather than an offensive, attitude. Therefore, technology agreements usually hinge on the need for consultation before decisions in this respect are taken and the need for compensation of employees, and not on increased wages.

Salamon refers to the following guidelines issued by the British Trade Union Council with regard to the introduction of new technology.

- Full trade union involvement and agreement before new technology is introduced
- Inter-union collaboration where appropriate
- Access to all relevant information and regular consultation on company plans
- Commitment to expand output/services and no redundancies or, if not possible, planned redeployment and/or improved redundancy payments
- Training, at full earnings, for those affected by new technology
- Reduction in basic working hours and systematic overtime
- Avoidance of disruption to existing pay structures/relativities, maintenance or improvement of income levels, movement towards single status (harmonisation)
- Ensuring that computer-based information is not used for work performance measurement
- Establishment of joint management–union arrangements to monitor and review progress

A technology agreement may centre on some or all of these issues. Technology agreements are relatively new in South Africa. So far, unions have insisted mainly on information and consultation, but it can be expected that in the future they may demand greater joint control.

IMPLEMENTATION AND MONITORING OF AGREEMENTS

Monitoring Agreements Once an agreement has been reached and signed by both parties, it will be necessary to obtain all-round commitment to its successful implementation. The enforceability of agreements has already been discussed in the chapter on collective bargaining. Legal enforcement of an agreement or the declaration of a dispute becomes necessary only when one of the parties has acted in bad faith.

Where good faith exists, the concern is more with monitoring the agreement to see that it works. Consequently, follow-up meetings may take place in order to discuss problems which have occurred, or to renegotiate decisions which have proved unimplementable in practice.

It is the task of the chief negotiator on each side to ensure that the members of his organisation are acquainted with the terms of the agreement and that they adhere to these. The employer has the duty to inform members of management of the agreement and to train managers and supervisors in its implementation. The union, on the other hand, should furnish accurate information to its members and urge acceptance of the terms agreed upon. Management, too, may play some part in disseminating information to employees.

Both sides, through their appointed agents, will monitor the implementation of the agreement by the other side and, should any breach occur, will raise this immediately with those responsible for implementation. Since the breach may be merely the result of an oversight, the common practice is to engage in discussions before declaring a dispute. Should a dispute occur, the agreed or prescribed procedures are normally followed.

In practice, and especially in large-scale agreements, it is the union which does most of the monitoring through its agents and shop stewards, since management's breach of contract is more easily disguised than the same action on the part of the union.

A collective agreement is subject to continued modification. If conditions change or there is a shift in the bargaining power of the parties, an agreement will be renegotiated.

Enforceability of Agreements

In a voluntary system the bargaining relationship is, essentially, a relationship of trust and its successful conduct will depend largely on the commitment of both parties. Consequently, it could be argued that the breach of an agreement constitutes a breakdown in the relationship and that legal enforceability in this instance becomes irrelevant. Nevertheless there are particular instances where legal recourse may be necessary, as in the case where a member of an employers' association fails to abide by negotiated wage rates and conditions of employment or where one of the parties fails to follow agreed procedures for the settlement of disputes. Thus the legal enforceability of agreements is of importance to the parties concerned.

In certain countries provision is made for the statutory enforcement of collective agreements. In South Africa, the new labour relations legislation has now provided for the enforceability of all collective agreements. Where agreements are not granted statutory status, a collective agreement between employer and employee, if properly drawn up, achieves the status of a contract in terms of Common Law. Any breach of the agreement may then be addressed by a civil action against the offending party. The problem with civil actions is that such actions are usually both lengthy and costly, but in times of crisis relief may be sought in the form of an interdict. This usually spurs the offender into complying with the terms of an agreement. For example, a union which is in breach of an agreement and against which an interdict is issued to desist from strike action will reconsider before continuing the action, since it may thereby incur costs and run the risk of having to meet a claim brought against it for damages. The same applies to employers in the reverse situation.

Withdrawal from an Agreement

Once an agreement other than a recognition agreement has become effective, the parties are bound to abide by its terms and conditions and cannot in good faith withdraw from the agreement unless its continued implementation becomes impossible. However, most recognition agreements or bargaining association constitutions will provide for the withdrawal of either party from the relationship after due notice has been given to the other party or parties. Even then, permission to withdraw may be subject to the provision that the withdrawing party abides by the terms of current agreements until such time as these expire. The purpose is to ensure the stability and continuity of agreements, but it is realised that, if the principle of voluntarism holds, the parties cannot be coerced into a permanent relationship. The Labour Relations Act of 1995 does provide that the withdrawal from a bargaining relationship may be regarded as a refusal to bargain and may thus be subject to advisory arbitration; but, if this fails, either party may ultimately revert to industrial action. Therefore, in the final analysis, the parties may use coercive power to attempt to oblige each other to maintain the relationship. This is in line with the voluntarist principle.

Disputes and Industrial Action as Part of the Process Towards Agreement

Where voluntarism predominates and where the freedom to strike is recognised, disputes and industrial action form an integral part of the collective bargaining process. Negotiation does not always end in agreement. Alternatively, while agreement may eventually be reached, the process could be marked by repeated disputes and actions along the way. The reason for this is self-explanatory. At times of complete disagreement between the parties, the coercive power of each party is again brought into play. Employers attempt to oblige acceptance of their terms by withholding the opportunity for work, while employees will attempt to achieve the same ends by the joint withholding of their labour from the employer or by otherwise damaging the business of the employer. Thus industrial action in the form of lockouts, strikes, go-slows, work-to-rules and product boycotts are part of the collective bargaining process. They are not intended to put an end to negotiation, although, in the extreme, they may. Their purpose is to serve as pressure tactics in the negotiation process. Figure 38 illustrates the development of the negotiation process from the inception of the relationship to the point of agreement, via the display of coercive power.

CONCLUSION

The art of negotiation is not easily acquired, although there are rare individuals who appear instinctively to adapt their behaviour to the negotiation situation. In general, the conduct of a negotiation session requires a great deal of knowledge, hard work, preparation and practice and the outcome of a particular negotiation session is never certain until the final agreement has been signed. It is impossible within the context of this book to devote full and detailed attention to the actual practice of negotiation. Individuals who are interested should refer to texts dealing specifically with this subject, such as those by Anstey, Pienaar and Spoelstra, and Karas.

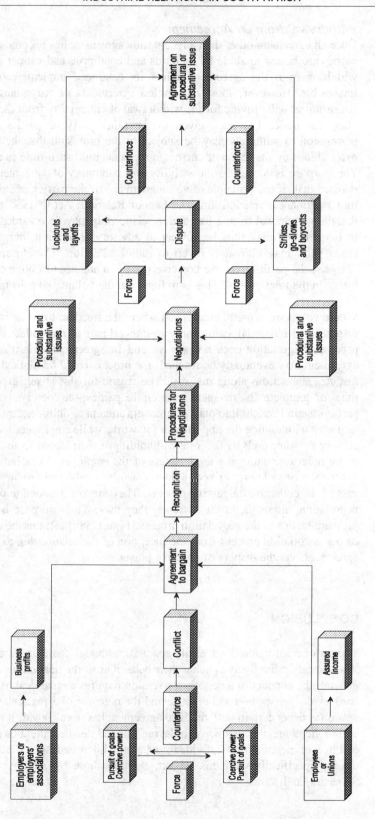

Figure 38: DEVELOPMENT OF THE NEGOTIATION PROCESS

SOURCES

Anstey, Mark *Negotiating Conflict*, Juta, 1991.

Anthony, P D *The Conduct of Industrial Relations*, Institute of Personnel Management, London, 1977.

Atkinson, G *The Effective Negotiator*, Quest Research Publications, 1975.

Green, G D *Industrial Relations*, Pitman, 1987.

Herman, E Edward and Alfred Kuhn *Collective Bargaining and Labour Relations*, Prentice-Hall, 1981.

Karas, C L *The Negotiating Game*, Thomas Y Cromwell, 1970.

Kochan, Thomas A *Collective Bargaining and Industrial Relations*, Richard D Irwin, 1980.

Pienaar, Wynand and Manie Spoelstra *Negotiation*, Juta, 1991.

Salamon, Michael *Industrial Relations Theory and Practice*, Prentice-Hall, 1987.

Scott, Bill *The Skills of Negotiating*, Gower, 1982.

Walton R E and McKersie R B *A Behavioral Theory of Labour Negotiations*, McGraw-Hill, 1965.

Woods, S J *Negotiation Skills*, S J Woods and Associates (Private training document).

14

DISPUTE SETTLEMENT AND LABOUR ACTION

Negotiations do not always end in agreement and, even where agreement is eventually achieved, fundamental disagreements may have occurred along the way. These disagreements give rise to a situation in which the parties are said to be in dispute.

Two kinds of labour dispute exist, namely disputes of right and disputes of interest. Disputes of right do not arise from and are not usually subject to negotiation. Rights are entrenched in law or agreement, and any dispute regarding their institution is subject to arbitration or legal adjudication. Collective conflict in the labour relations situation manifests itself mainly in disputes of interest. Disputes of interest can usually not be settled by legal determination. Consequently, other methods of dispute settlement have to be established.

When disputes of interest arise, the conflict is of such a nature that it cannot be resolved in the normal negotiation forum. Alternatively, there may have been a refusal by either side to attempt negotiation in any form. The immediate reaction in situations of this kind could be that either party resorts to the use of coercive power, in the form of a strike or a lockout. However, since industrial action is detrimental to both parties and to the relationship, it is advisable to attempt settlement by other means before reverting to the use of coercive power; hence the institution and use of dispute settlement procedures.

Dispute settlement procedures may be agreed upon between the parties themselves, or the necessary machinery for the settlement of disputes might be provided by the State. The State's main concern is to protect the public interest and to promote economic activity by the maintenance of industrial peace. The procedures it introduces will, therefore, be aimed at minimising or eradicating the use of industrial action or, at the very least, obliging the parties to cool off before any action is instituted. Controversy exists as to the extent to which the State can oblige the parties to use the legislated machinery, as well as the extent to which it can prohibit or limit strike action. The degree of compulsion and limitation varies from one system to another.

Conciliation, mediation and arbitration have come to be regarded as the best methods of settling labour disputes. Both conciliation and mediation promote the continuation of the negotiation process and the eventual settlement of the dispute by the parties themselves. In arbitration, on the other hand, a determination is made by a third party. There is no possibility of further negotiation but, equally, the use of industrial action is also precluded. The type of dispute settlement procedure chosen and the methods preferred will depend on the needs of the parties and those of a particular industrial relations system.

Despite the use of dispute settlement procedures, industrial action can and does occur. Sometimes it may occur before procedures are utilised and at others after the procedures have been exhausted. A free industrial relations system will not provide for compulsory arbitration of all disputes and will entrench the right to industrial action, and particularly to a strike or a lockout.

Strikes constitute the most obvious form of industrial action. They demonstrate the ultimate power that employee collectives can exert over employers in an otherwise unequal relationship. For this reason the employer action of dismissing striking employees is a thorny issue in labour relations.

The reasons for strike action are many and varied. There are also various circumstances which will lead to the increased incidence of strike action in certain undertakings, industries or areas. These need careful attention, with a view, perhaps, to the minimising of industrial unrest. Also, the institution of strike action involves costs and benefits. These should be considered before strikes are undertaken or before management decides to withstand a strike, rather than to concede to union demands. Equally, both sides should be prepared to handle a strike effectively, so that the least possible loss is entailed.

Besides strike action, employees may engage in other actions aimed at pressurising employers, such as go-slows, boycotts, overtime bans, a work-to-rule or the exertion of external pressure. Management, on its part, could institute a lockout of employees. Whatever action is taken, it cannot be lighthearted and it should, preferably, constitute a last resort.

South Africa has, since the passage of the Industrial Conciliation Act in 1924, had an official dispute settlement machinery aimed at the promotion of collective bargaining and the maintenance of industrial peace. However, this machinery was geared mainly towards the settlement of collective disputes, and it was only after the unfair labour practice concept and the Industrial Court were introduced in the 1979 and subsequent amendments to the Labour Relations Act that the settlement of individual disputes received increased attention. The unfair labour practice legislation also focused attention on the fairness of labour relations practices rather than on their lawfulness. Actions brought in terms of this legislation have had a profound effect on labour practices and, in particular, on procedures leading to the dismissal and retrenchment of employees.

Disputes between employers and employees could be divided into four types: those occurring in essential services, which were eventually subject to compulsory arbitration; 'ordinary' disputes arising at plant level on the one hand and at industrial council level on the other where, if the dispute remained unresolved, the parties could eventually institute a legal strike or lockout; and unfair labour practice disputes, which could eventually be referred to the Industrial Court for a final determination. All disputes had to be processed through an industrial council or conciliation board, the purpose being that negotiation should continue within these institutions. In the case of an alleged unfair labour practice, either party could apply for a temporary Status Quo

Order, to be effective until such time as the dispute was finally resolved. The Act also provided for voluntary mediation and arbitration, should the parties to a dispute agree to these processes.

The Industrial Court came to play an important role in South African labour relations and, although it had various functions, its activities centred mainly on the hearing of Status Quo applications and on making final determinations in unresolved unfair labour practice disputes. It was left to the Court to establish measures of fairness and although, as a court of equity, it did not establish binding precedents, it developed a number of guidelines as regards fair labour practices. Mainly as a result of decisions reached by the Court, various unfair labour practices were codified in the 1988 amendments to the Labour Relations Act. The definition, while retaining its wide core, was greatly extended in the 1988 amendments. In particular, the dismissal of employees without a valid reason and without following fair procedures and the retrenchment of employees without consultation, a proper procedure or objective criteria for selection were classified as unfair labour practices. Although the 1988 definition was later deleted and a broad definition put in its place, the Industrial Court was still entitled to rule that those practices codified by the 1988 amendments constituted unfair labour practices.

The new Labour Relations Act of 1995 has maintained the essential voluntarism of the dispute settlement machinery by providing the freedom to submit disputes to conciliation or mediation and arbitration or, in certain instances, to the Labour Court. A new body, in the form of the Commission for Conciliation, Mediation & Arbitration, has been established to take much of the load previously carried by the Industrial Court. Furthermore, bargaining councils and independent agencies may now be accredited as mediators and arbitrators by the CCMA. In terms of the statute, disputes of right may be submitted first to conciliation or mediation, and thereafter either to arbitration or to adjudication by the Labour Court. This Court replaces the Industrial Court and is now a court of law with the status of a provincial division of the Supreme Court. It is seen as the ultimate decisionmaker on all labour relations matters. Another welcome change is the removal of the two layers of appeal and the granting of ultimate appeal rights to the Labour Appeal Court, which will have the same status as the Appellate Division of the Supreme Court and will be manned by judges from the Labour Court.

The new Act sets out detailed procedures for different types of rights disputes. It further separates unfair dismissals from other unfair labour practices. With some exceptions, unfair dismissals now go to arbitration rather than to the Labour Court. In certain instances, modified procedures are instituted for the public sector. Disputes of interest may also be submitted first to conciliation or mediation. If this fails, parties may choose voluntary arbitration or engage in industrial action.

A very important change is the granting of the right to strike, without fear of dismissal, to employees who have followed statutory procedures. This is supplemented by the right to engage in secondary actions, to form picket lines and to engage in protest actions or stayaways.

Since 1980 the incidence of strike action in South Africa has increased at a steady rate, owing mainly to the rise of unions representing black employees and the plant-related activities of these unions. Initially most of the strikes were illegal, but there has in recent years been a growing tendency to use the official procedures. In the early 1980s strikes occurred most frequently in the manufacturing sector, but industrial action later spread to the mining industry and to the public and service sectors. Massive strikes of long duration in these sectors accounted for the rise in man-days lost and for the lengthier average duration of strike actions. The majority of strikes are supposedly instituted for economic reasons; yet dismissals and conditions of service also feature as reasons for strike action. Of significance is the large number of strikes where the cause is apparently unknown.

So far, the dispute settlement machinery has stood the participants to the labour relationship in good stead. As relationships between employers and unions have matured, arrangements have been made for private settlement of disputes of right — for example, by reverting to private arbitration — as an alternative to the use of the official machinery. This would greatly alleviate the heavy burden which rests on the CCMA and the Labour Court.

LABOUR DISPUTES

THE NATURE AND SCOPE OF A LABOUR DISPUTE

The definition of a labour dispute varies from country to country, but most definitions have in common their limitation of a labour dispute to a dispute between an employer and his employees or their union. Furthermore, the subject matter of a labour dispute is usually limited to those matters which could be regulated jointly by the employer and his employees.

For the present purposes, a labour dispute may be defined as **a continued disagreement between employers and employees or their unions as regards any matter of common interest, any work-related factor affecting their relationship or any processes and structures established to maintain such relationship.** Thus disputes may arise from failure to agree to the establishment of a relationship, disagreement regarding procedures to be adopted, failure to agree on terms and conditions of employment, failure to abide by the terms of an agreement, negation of the rights of either side, poor treatment of one party by the other, or any other action or occurrence which would negatively influence the relationship.

In the definition given the word 'continued' is of importance. The mere raising of a demand or a grievance, which also entails disagreement, does not signify the existence of a labour dispute. A dispute will arise only if there is no final agreement on a demand or if a grievance is not settled in a manner satisfactory to both parties.

In certain instances disputes may be declared without any prior negotiation having occurred but, generally, a dispute is declared only after attempts at negotiation have failed. As such, a dispute or the declaration of a dispute is integral to the collective bargaining or negotiation process. Disputes may be followed by legal action or by a strike, or they may lead to the use of the agreed or established dispute settlement machinery. In the case of the latter option, and probably also during a strike, the process of negotiation will usually continue. Thus disputes may be both preceded and followed by negotiation.

TYPES OF LABOUR DISPUTE

Disputes of Right

A right is that to which a party is entitled by law, by contract, by agreement or by established practice. In the labour relationship, rights are ensured by common law, by labour legislation, by the contract of employment, by legally enforceable agreements and by customary practices at the place of work.

Disputes of right do not initially centre in negotiations. The achievement of rights may be effected by negotiation but, once a right has been established, its transgression constitutes an offence.

Disputes of right will centre in issues of the following kind.

- The failure of one party to abide by the contract of employment
- Failure to implement legally determined conditions and procedures, such as minimum working hours and prescribed notice periods
- Failure to implement the terms of a legally enforceable agreement
- The non-implementation of an arbitration award or wage determination
- The transgression of any other legal determination, such as the prohibition of victimisation or interference with the freedom of association
- Transgression of the common law
- A unilateral change in accepted or customary practices
- Codified unfair dismissals and unfair labour practices

Although attempts may be made to settle disputes arising from these issues by negotiation and other methods before — and even after — an official dispute has been declared, the final recourse is to judicial adjudication or arbitration.

Disputes of Interest

An interest is that to which a party is not yet entitled but to which he would like to become entitled. Whether he achieves his objective or not will depend on whether he can persuade the other party to grant the concessions sought. Thus interests are subject to negotiation. Once agreement has been reached, the interest sought may become a right. An employee who has the right by law to two weeks' leave per year may not be satisfied with this minimum provision. His interest is to be granted annual leave of four weeks. To achieve these ends he would engage, or ask his union to engage, in negotiations with the employer. Should the employer eventually agree and should the new terms be written into a contract of employment or a legally enforceable collective agreement, the interest will have become a right. Disputes of interest arise when no agreement on demands or grievances can be achieved.

The issues which lead to disputes of interest are essentially those listed in Chapter 8 as issues and problems in collective bargaining. Any matter causing conflict between employer and employee and not regulated by law, agreement or custom can give rise to a dispute of interest.

Since it is difficult to regulate any relationship entirely by legal provision and since a conflict of interests is continually present in the labour relationship, disputes of interest constitute a more dynamic aspect of labour relations than disputes of right, and their settlement requires the establishment of procedures outside the normal legal machinery. In all developed industrial relations systems, conciliation, mediation and arbitration have come to be regarded as the most effective methods of attempting to settle labour disputes. Conciliation entails the bringing together of the parties in a new forum, where they are urged to continue negotiation and to attempt settlement. In the case of mediation, a third party acts as go-between to the parties and, by supplying new perspectives and arguments, attempts to achieve a settlement; whereas, in arbitration, the third party takes over the role of adjudicator and imposes on the disputing parties what he regards as a fair settlement.

THE USE OF DISPUTE SETTLEMENT PROCEDURES

It is an accepted fact that, even in relationships of long standing and even after protracted negotiations, disputes do arise and rights are sometimes abrogated. The existence of a dispute of interest does not signify that the possibilities for negotiation have been exhausted. The parties might have been trapped in a defence–attack spiral; they might be so intent on achieving their own objectives or so emotionally prejudiced that perspectives have been distorted. For the time being, no agreement seems possible. The necessity arises for new approaches to be formulated and new perspectives to be gained, and for negotiations to be resumed in a more serious or more favourable climate. Alternatively, if conflict has reached the stage where further negotiation between the parties is virtually impossible, it may be necessary for a third party to negotiate or to take a decision on their behalf. Where a dispute of right is involved, the eventual decision is usually left to a third party.

Dispute settlement is undertaken essentially because the parties have a common interest in continuing the relationship. Should no settlement be reached, the relationship would terminate. Also, in the majority of cases, neither party really wishes to use its ultimate power in the form of industrial action, or to institute legal action. Thus, where a strike, lockout or legal action is threatened, the parties may first resort to an agreed method of dispute settlement in order to maintain the relationship and industrial peace. In rare instances settlement is not achieved, but the ultimate aim of dispute settlement procedures remains the continuation of negotiations towards a settlement or the final imposition of a settlement by another party, bringing about the restoration of industrial peace.

ESTABLISHING A DISPUTE SETTLEMENT PROCEDURE

Employers and employees or their unions may decide among themselves on a procedure to be followed in the event of a dispute arising. Such procedures could specify the following.

- The manner in which a dispute is to be declared — This includes notice to the other party and a specification as to whether or not the declaration should be in writing.
- Time limits for replying to the allegations or claims of the first party
- Arrangements for negotiation meetings to attempt settlement
- Time limits for negotiation — A procedure may specify that, if negotiation does not result in settlement within a period of two weeks, the parties may take recourse to other measures.
- Other methods of dispute settlement, such as mediation or arbitration, which will be used by the parties
- Whether a differentiation will be made between disputes of right and disputes of interest, and whether different settlement procedures will be used in each case
- Whether or not there will be final recourse to the dispute settlement machinery established by the government or to legal action
- Whether or not the right to a strike or a lockout is admitted and, if it is admitted (or legally allowed), the limitations set and safeguards provided. Also, an employer may agree not to dismiss illegal strikers before a specified period has elapsed, or a union may undertake to remove illegally striking employees from the premises of an employer

(For an example of an in-plant disputes procedure, see the recognition agreement in the Annexures.)

The dispute settlement processes established by private agreement may be described as private, plant-level or bargaining-level procedures. Such procedures are particularly popular where a system of plant-level recognition of unions exists. Should there be no private procedure, either party may resort immediately to the use of procedures established by government for the settlement of labour disputes.

PROCEDURES ESTABLISHED BY LEGISLATION

The Role of the State in Labour Disputes

The State has a legitimate interest in the conduct and settlement of labour disputes. As protector of the public interest and as promoter of a sound economic system, the main objective of the State as regards labour disputes is to maintain industrial peace. To these ends it will encourage negotiation and attempt to extend this process, even after a dispute has arisen, by the provision of a disputes procedure. Such procedure will be aimed at conciliation and the reaching of a compromise between the parties. The State may also impose limits on the freedom to strike or, in certain instances, prohibit strike action by the imposition of compulsory arbitration.

In order to facilitate the settlement of labour disputes, the State might provide special labour courts to deal with disputes of right arising from the labour relationship. This is done because labour legislation and collective agreements constitute a particular field of expertise with which all legal adjudicators may not be totally conversant. The State may also establish its own conciliation, mediation or arbitration services (such as the Arbitration, Conciliation and Advisory Service — ACAS — in Britain) to promote the settlement of disputes of interest between the parties concerned. The promotion of fair employment practices and, thereby, the indirect assurance of industrial peace is another area of interest to the State. Depending on the legislative position regarding these practices, the State could provide special courts or industrial tribunals to adjudicate on or arbitrate disputes arising from alleged unfair practices.

The type of dispute settlement procedure established and the services provided in a particular country will depend on its historical development, the development of its industrial relations system, the sociopolitical orientation of the government, the nature and organisation of the trade union movement and current circumstances. In some systems strike action may be completely prohibited, while others may allow for strike action only after certain compulsory procedures have been followed. In certain systems conciliation or mediation is a compulsory step in the dispute settlement process, while in others it is merely a voluntary option. Legislation may provide for compulsory arbitration on certain issues and in respect of certain employee groups. Also, detailed regulations may exist for the calling of a strike or the imposition of a lockout. The possibilities and variations are numerous and, even within a particular system, dispute settlement procedures are frequently amended in the light of the latest developments.

Voluntarism and Compulsion in the Establishment of Legislated Procedures

Controversy exists regarding the degree to which the State could compel the other participants in the labour relationship to use the machinery established by legislation and, even where such machinery is not compulsory, the degree to which it should contain compulsory elements, such as a prohibition on or limitation of the freedom to strike or a compulsion to use mediation and arbitration services. It could be argued that, in a system geared to voluntarism, no compulsion should exist but that procedures should merely be provided for use by employers and employees or unions, should they so wish. Obviously, the State could and would encourage such use. Nevertheless there is in most systems an element of compulsion, the degree of which varies from one system to another. At the very least, the State may indirectly compel or encourage use of the legal machinery by declaring actions such as strikes which occur outside the legislated process as illegal, or by providing for the statutory enforcement of arbitration awards and agreements reached within the legal machinery. It is believed that such agreements will be perceived as having a superior status to others and that this will encourage participants to use the legislated machinery.

The greatest degree of compulsion exists where the freedom to strike is not recognised, in respect of either all employees or certain types of employee. There is a general tendency not to grant this freedom to employees in essential services, by the imposition of compulsory arbitration on employers and employees in these sectors. The argument is that, in the public interest, essential services have to be maintained at all costs. Yet this necessarily detracts from the bargaining power of employees in those services and could place them in an invidious position *vis-à-vis* the employer. In the final analysis, absolute compulsion may not be possible. Even in a system providing for compulsory arbitration of all disputes, the parties might still attempt to settle their differences by other means and strike action could, despite prohibitions, still occur.

The Parties to a Labour Dispute

It appears self-evident that the parties to a labour dispute will be an employer or employers' organisation on the one hand and employees or their union on the other. Essentially this is correct since, if a relationship exists, any dispute which arises will involve the parties concerned. Nevertheless, in many instances only certain employers, employees or unions are permitted to declare a legal dispute and to utilise the legislated dispute settlement machinery. In several countries the right to declare a legal dispute rests only with registered employer bodies or unions, while in others only recognised bargaining partners are entitled to use the legislated machinery. The problem arising from such restrictions is that parties who have no access to the official machinery may use their own, sometimes unorthodox, methods of settling disputes, or they may resort immediately to industrial action. Consequently, it is advisable that all parties who could be involved in a dispute are granted access to the official machinery.

METHODS OF DISPUTE SETTLEMENT

Conciliation

The dictionary defines conciliation as the act of procuring goodwill or inducing a friendly feeling. In the settlement of labour disputes, conciliation does entail the procuring of renewed goodwill. This is done by establishing a forum in which parties who are in conflict or have failed to reach agreement can come together once again and attempt to settle their differences. Conciliation may be effected by the agency of a third party or the State, and a third party may or may not be present during the conciliation process. However, should a third party be present, he will take no active part in the negotiation process, although he may act as chairman during the conduct of meetings.

Essentially, conciliation entails the continuation of negotiation between the two parties; but, in this instance, the negotiations form part of the dispute settlement procedure and failure to conciliate may lead to industrial action or to further steps in the dispute settlement process.

The advantage of conciliation is that it extends the negotiation process and allows for settlement between the parties, without the interference of external agents. Where a procedure requires that conciliation be attempted before industrial action can be undertaken, time is allowed for both parties to cool off, to approach each other in a friendlier manner and seriously to attempt settlement before engaging in an action which might eventually destroy the relationship. In practice, most third parties engaging in conciliation do mediate to some extent — that is, they more creatively try to bring the parties together. The distinction between the two processes, therefore, has become somewhat blurred.

Mediation   *Definition*

Mediation may be described as the active intervention of a third party, or third parties, for the purpose of inducing settlement. Mediation also involves an attempt at conciliation, but, in this instance, a third party, in the person of the mediator, is present at and pivotal to the conciliation process. The mediator plays an active part in the process in that he attempts by all means possible to bring about a settlement. To these ends he advises both sides, acts as intermediary and suggests possible solutions. However, in contrast to arbitration, a mediator acts only in an advisory and conciliatory capacity. He has no decisionmaking powers and cannot impose a settlement on either party.

Purpose of Mediation

Mediation is intended to facilitate negotiation. Situations arise in which participants to the labour relationship are incapable of continuing negotiations on their own or where, because of the inexperience of the negotiators, no progress can be made. The introduction of a neutral person, especially if he is an experienced negotiator, could serve to diffuse tensions and to induce progress towards a settlement. In particular, mediation serves to narrow the gap in the settlement range. Because a mediator does not belong to the opposing party, each party will more easily reveal its actual resistance point or fallback position to him. Consequently his estimation of the settlement range might differ from that established by the participants, and he could persuade one party to move closer to the other within that range. Also, a mediator might more easily elicit concessions from either party, thus promoting a trade-off and a possible settlement. As an outsider who is not directly involved in the conflict between the two parties and as an individual with wider knowledge, he imposes reason and brings new perspectives to the dispute.

Appointment of a Mediator

A mediator may be appointed by the parties themselves or be supplied by governmental or other agencies. In a number of countries the State provides official mediation services, but this does not preclude the operation of independent mediation services.

If the parties themselves appoint a single mediator, such person must meet with the approval of both sides and his neutrality should be beyond question. In the event of a sufficiently neutral person not being available or if the parties are not able to agree, it is common practice for each side to appoint a mediator of its own choice. Each mediator will meet with his side, whereafter the two mediators will come together and attempt, with reference to their principals, to formulate a possible settlement.

Characteristics of a Good Mediator

An effective mediator will have, in essence, the same qualities as a good negotiator, but he should possess these qualities to a greater degree than the ordinary negotiator. Preferably, he should have a proven record of success in negotiations.

A mediator, if he is to be successful, has in the first place to elicit the trust, acceptance and cooperation of both parties or of the party he represents. The parties will accept him only if he has sufficient credibility and if they are assured that he can be entrusted with confidential matters.

Intelligence, discernment and practicality are essential qualities in mediation. A mediator should be able to identify problems and offer workable solutions. To do this he needs to be knowledgeable in all matters related to the negotiations. He should be acquainted with the organisational structures, strategies and attitudes of both parties, have up to date knowledge of labour legislation and of collective agreements or determinations and be conversant with the latest developments in the economic, sociopolitical and technological spheres.

Finally, a mediator should be able to exercise tact and diplomacy. He should be sensitive to nuances, have the necessary powers of persuasion, be an effective communicator and be of strong character, since he may need to nudge the participants aggressively towards an agreement.

In practice, an individual of such high calibre is not easily found, but, even though a mediator may not possess all the characteristics described, he should possess some of them, as the success of the mediation process will depend partly on the qualities of the mediator selected.

The Mediation Process

Kochan has broadly divided the mediation process into the following stages.

Stage 1: Introduction and Establishment of Credibility — During this stage the mediator plays a more passive role than at any other time during the mediation process. His main task is to gain the trust and acceptance of the parties. They should believe that he will be capable of assisting them and that he is a person on whom they can rely at all times. An experienced mediator will leave most of the talking to the disputing parties, but will listen attentively and ask probing questions. His primary objectives will be to diagnose the causes of the dispute, to identify the issues in order of priority, to pinpoint the obstacles to a possible settlement and to gain an impression of the attitudinal climate and the distribution of power between the parties. Once his position is entrenched and he has sufficient background knowledge, the mediator will attempt to persuade the parties to resume negotiations, or he could attempt to steer negotiations in a different direction. This could occur after he has supplied them with a different perspective or after he has removed some of the obstacles to continued negotiation.

Stage Two: Steering the Negotiation Process — In the second stage the mediator intervenes more actively in the negotiation process. He will offer advice to the parties and attempt to establish the actual resistance point of each party and to discover areas in which compromise could be reached. The mediator will encourage the putting forward of proposals and counterproposals and, should a solution be probable, will gently urge the parties towards its acceptance. He may, if a solution appears to be close at hand, become more aggressive and in this manner exert pressure on the participants, but his use of aggression should be based on careful timing and a correct estimate of the willingness of each party to move towards settlement. A mediator who becomes aggressive at the wrong time may antagonise one or both of the parties and thereby lose much of the ground already gained. At the worst, he could face total rejection.

Stage Three: Movement Towards a Final Settlement — An experienced mediator will know when to exert pressure towards final settlement of the dispute. During this phase he would, most probably, conduct intensive negotiations with both parties in an attempt to persuade them to face reality and adjust their positions. He may also become more forceful and aggressive than at any other stage but, again, timing and the interspersion of forcefulness with diplomacy are of the utmost importance. It frequently happens that only the diehards prove an obstacle to final settlement. A useful advantage is gained if the mediator succeeds in obtaining the support of professional negotiators in subduing militants within their own ranks. During the final stages the mediator may himself suggest or draft proposals for a settlement. However, care should be exercised that he is not identified too closely with such proposals, since their rejection may lead to rejection of the mediator himself. In the event of a final settlement being reached, the negotiator remains to assist the parties in the drafting of an agreement and to ensure that both sides are satisfied with the terms and conditions of the agreement.

The process of mediation, more so than negotiation, is dynamic and finely tuned. A mediator has of necessity to be extremely flexible and inventive. Also, he needs to be continually on his guard against interference by his own values. He should ensure that he does not attempt to impose on the parties the settlement which he regards as correct, but rather that he finds one which is acceptable to both parties; preferably that, under his guidance, the parties themselves formulate a favourable settlement.

The Effectiveness of Mediation

It is difficult to establish whether mediation is generally effective or not, since it is impossible in many instances to establish whether a settlement would in any event have been achieved, irrespective of the presence or absence of a mediator. Mediation ultimately depends on the concurrence of the participants and the most a mediator can achieve is to advise or persuade them towards agreement. Nevertheless, it is generally assumed that mediation does facilitate agreement and that it is particularly effective in disputes where, owing mostly to lack of experience, negotiators have overcommitted themselves to a particular stand, as well as in disputes where the impasse is the result of strong intra-organisational conflicts, or where interpersonal hostility between members of the opposing parties is the major reason for the continuation of conflict. Furthermore, mediation is facilitated — and thus more effective — if the parties are strongly motivated to attempt settlement, if external pressures are being placed on the participants to end the dispute, if industrial action is threatened or if the pressure of other commitments prompts a settlement of the existing dispute.

Mediation has proved a less successful method of dispute settlement where conflict has reached a high level of intensity and where matters of principle are at stake. Also, positive settlement range disputes, and disputes centring on procedures or issues such as dismissals, tend to lend themselves more easily to mediation than disputes arising from a negative settlement range or from economic issues, especially where there is inability to pay on the one side and high expectations in the face of eroded wages on the other. Ultimately, successful mediation depends as much on the commitment of both parties to a peaceful settlement as on the skills of the mediator.

Arbitration *Definition*

Arbitration entails the appointment of a third party to act as adjudicator in a dispute and to decide on the terms of settlement. Arbitration differs from conciliation and mediation in that it does not promote the continuation of collective bargaining. In arbitration a third party actively intervenes in the dispute and takes over the role of decisionmaker. The arbitrator listens to and investigates the demands and counterdemands on both sides, and decides on a final settlement. The parties may submit their individual proposals for a settlement to the arbitrator, but the final decision is his. Moreover, whatever settlement the arbitrator imposes will become binding on the parties concerned.

Types of Arbitration

In distinguishing between the different types of arbitration, the first differentiation to be made is between **judicial arbitration** (or rights) and **interest arbitration**. Judicial arbitration is conducted in disputes of right and is undertaken by courts of law or other judiciary bodies. Alternatively, rights arbitration may be undertaken by appointed arbitrators or tribunals. Interest arbitration centres on the issues raised in the collective bargaining forum. It can be conducted by government arbitration bodies or by government-appointed arbitrators. Alternatively, the parties themselves may appoint an arbitrator or they might decide to make use of an independent arbitration service. Besides the difference between judicial and interest arbitration, Kochan distinguishes between compulsory and voluntary arbitration, conventional and final offer arbitration (the latter being package- or issue-related), and between arbitration conducted by a single arbitrator or by a panel of arbitrators.

Conventional arbitration leaves the arbitrator free to impose the settlement of his choice, while in final offer arbitration (also termed pendulum arbitration), the arbitrator studies the final offers of each party and selects one of the proposals for final settlement. Pendulum arbitration may be based on the total package offered by each party, or it could be based on the offers made by the various parties as regards each issue. In issue-by-issue arbitration, the arbitrator may select the final offer of the union on one issue and that of the employer on the other. Pendulum arbitration has the advantage that the parties, knowing that extreme demands would be immediately rejected by the arbitrator, are inclined to modify their proposals and to assess the situation more realistically.

The final question as regards arbitration is whether the parties will accept determination by one arbitrator or whether they would prefer the decision to be made by an arbitrator and an assessor from each side, or by a panel of arbitrators. Should their choice be a panel of arbitrators, such panel might consist of a number of neutral persons. Alternatively, the panel could be chaired by a neutral person, assisted by two or more arbitrators who are selected on a parity basis by each side. It is, in general, preferable to limit the number of arbitrators. Too large a number may result in negotiations eventually having to be conducted also on the arbitration panel.

The Effectiveness of Arbitration

That arbitration is effective in the settlement of disputes is self-evident. Once an arbitration award has been made, the parties are obliged, either by law or by a gentlemen's agreement, to discontinue their dispute and to abide by the terms of the settlement. However, it is not as self-evident that arbitration succeeds in resolving conflict, since one or both parties might be dissatisfied with the settlement and, while they may adhere to the terms of the settlement, the continued conflict may manifest itself in other ways. Furthermore, arbitration may be regarded as a poor option in the overall philosophy of interest dispute settlement, because it does not extend the negotiation process and takes the decisionmaking power out of the hands of the parties involved. In some instances it is viewed as favouring the employer or the employees, resulting in further dissatisfaction or conflict.

Arbitration, particularly in interest disputes, can be subjected to overuse, or what is commonly called the 'narcotic effect'. Parties who have frequently taken disputes to arbitration tend later on to use it as a first, rather than a last, resort. In the event of a dispute arising, no negotiation is attempted and the issue is immediately subjected to arbitration. Alternatively, arbitration may have a 'half-life' effect in that the parties become disenchanted with the outcome of arbitration and resort to other means of settlement. Also, arbitration tends to detract from the credibility of negotiators, particularly those acting on behalf of the union. Negotiators are viewed as having abrogated their power to the arbitrator and may, in the process, lose their standing with their members or their principals.

Despite its obvious disadvantages, arbitration is a popular method of dispute settlement, particularly if, in the case of a dispute of interest, the objective is to avoid industrial action at all costs. In many instances participants accept the decisions of a credible third party who has been endowed with special powers more readily than they would a proposal of settlement from the other party or a mediator. As such, the arbitration process can be rendered more effective by providing for pendulum arbitration on an offer-by-offer basis, rather than for independent decisionmaking by the arbitrator. Also, a tripartite panel of arbitrators may produce a more balanced decision than a single individual. Generally, voluntary arbitration is more effective than that of a compulsory nature. Parties who elect to go to arbitration show greater commitment to a settlement and are able to exercise greater control over the arbitrator.

A recent development is the option of mediation–arbitration instead of decisionmaking arbitration. In the former case, the arbitrator will initially perform the function of a mediator. Before attempting arbitration, he urges the parties towards settlement and he will conduct arbitration only if the parties themselves fail to reach an agreement. However, there may be complications entailed in this process as a mediator, having gained the confidence of the parties, is privy to more and different information than that which would be given to an arbitrator who judges only in terms of the facts of the case. Consequently, it might not be advisable that the same individual conducts both mediation and arbitration of a particular dispute. Alternatively, he could first reach a decision as arbitrator, but not disclose this to the parties, and then go over to mediation in an attempt to persuade them into a voluntary settlement of their own. This would then be known as arbitration–mediation.

Arbitration has many disadvantages, particularly as regards its ineffectiveness in extending the negotiation process, but it is most definitely a viable alternative to strike action. Arbitration is particularly effective where conflict has reached unmanageable proportions and where the parties are strong enough to resist allegations of surrendering their roles as negotiators.

Appeals Against Arbitration Awards

Because one party may remain dissatisfied with the decision of an arbitrator because the possibility of bias cannot be excluded, it has been suggested that provision should be made for appeals against awards made by private arbitrators. Since this already happens in the case of judicial arbitration, there appears to be no reason that private arbitrations should not also be subject to appeal.

The Use of the Various Dispute Settlement Processes

A particular dispute settlement procedure may encompass all or none of the methods of dispute settlement discussed. Alternatively, certain dispute settlement processes may be used on a selective basis. The method of settlement most favoured will depend on the ideological orientation within a system and on the emphasis placed on the avoidance of industrial action. The more the emphasis is placed on the maintenance of industrial peace, the greater will be the tendency to introduce compulsory arbitration or to provide the parties with options which might preclude the use of industrial action. The only problem is that any method of settlement other than conciliation tends to take the initiative out of the hands of the actual participants.

DISPUTE SETTLEMENT IN SOUTH AFRICA

RATIONALE OF THE DISPUTE SETTLEMENT MACHINERY

The Position before 1979

The official South African dispute settlement machinery, which was introduced by the Industrial Conciliation Act of 1924, was based on the principle of voluntarism: that the State should provide only a framework for the settlement of disputes; that the parties to the labour relationship should be encouraged, but not obliged, to use the officially established machinery; and that no solution or determination regarding the dispute should be imposed upon them but, instead, that they should attempt resolution amongst themselves or, if efforts in this direction failed, be legally permitted to engage in industrial action. Thus the Industrial Conciliation Act and subsequent amendments provided for disputes between employers or their representatives and employees or their representatives to be processed through the conciliation machinery before any legal industrial action could be instituted. Parties declaring an official dispute had to refer the dispute to an industrial council or, where no council had jurisdiction, to apply for a conciliation board. Subsequent meetings within or under the auspices of industrial councils and meetings between the parties on conciliation boards would, it was believed, in most instances lead to a resolution of the dispute. In order to allow sufficient opportunity for 'cooling off' and conciliation, the parties were allowed a period of thirty days to attempt settlement of the dispute, whereafter they were entitled to institute a legal strike or a lockout. The fact that legal industrial action could be initiated only if the official machinery had been used did constitute an indirect compulsion to use this machinery but, other than that, the use of the system was entirely voluntary, as was the particular method of resolution used. As far as 'ordinary' disputes are concerned, these conditions still pertain.

Provision was also made in the legislation for the options of mediation and arbitration and, in 1956, for the establishment of an Industrial Tribunal. These options were provided as alternatives to strike action in cases where the parties were unable to settle disputes among themselves, but again no compulsion to use these options existed.

One exception to this rule of complete or almost complete voluntarism existed. Employers and employees in so-called 'essential services', as circumscribed in the Industrial Conciliation Act, were not entitled to engage in industrial action. This was accomplished by providing that unsettled disputes in these services had to be submitted, in terms of Section 46 of the Act, to compulsory arbitration. Employers whose services were designated as 'essential' in terms of Section 46(1)(a) included:

'(a)   any local authority; or
(b)   any employer ... who within the area of a local authority provides light, power, water, sanitation, passenger transportation or a fire extinguishing service;
(c)   any employer to whom the provision of this section has been applied in terms of subsection (7)'.

Subsection (7) provided that the Minister of Manpower, at his discretion and upon publication of a notice in the *Government Gazette*, could advise of his intention to declare as essential services any of the following activities.

'(i)   the supply, distribution, processing, canning or preserving of any perishable foodstuffs; or
(ii)   the supply or distribution of petrol or other fuels for use by local authorities or other employers in connection with the provision of any service referred to in paragraph (b) of subsection (1)'

Thus essential services were fairly wide-ranging. The purported reason for the prohibition on industrial action in these services was that any interruption of service would occasion too great a hardship on society at large, that a dispute in these services extended beyond the realms of the employment relationship and that society, therefore, had the right to intervene. Nevertheless, the bargaining power of employees in these services was greatly curtailed by the limitation imposed on their freedom to strike. Also teachers, as well as employees in health and medical services and in the public service, were not allowed to strike as they were not included under the Act.

The dispute settlement machinery, as it existed, was obviously aimed at the settlement of collective disputes. In effect, because industrial councils were the official bargaining bodies, most disputes were declared in these councils so that the process was considerably shortened. Disputes started in, and were not referred to, councils; from there they led to either mediation, arbitration or industrial action. Individual disputes could be processed through an industrial council or conciliation board and then submitted to arbitration or mediation, but this was unlikely to occur, particularly since a single employee or a group of

employees applying for a conciliation board had to act through a union of which
he or they were members in good standing. Moreover, the final sanction in the
machinery was industrial action, in which a single employee could not engage.
The opinion of the legislators was apparently that individual disputes were not
amenable to conciliation and that such disputes, where they arose, were disputes
of right, centring in a breach of the contract of employment, interference with
the freedom of association or victimisation, all of which could be dealt with by
the ordinary courts or, later, by the Industrial Tribunal.

Thus there was no real provision for the processing of individual disputes in
the Act, with one exception. This exception was contained in Section 43, which
provided that an employee who had been dismissed or suspended or who had
been notified of the intention to dismiss or suspend him, or whose conditions of
employment had been unilaterally changed and who regarded this as unjustified,
could apply to the Minister of Manpower for temporary relief in the form of
reinstatement or the maintenance of the *status quo*, until such time as the dispute
between him and the employer had been settled; with the proviso that the period
of relief would not exceed 90 days. Section 43 was rarely used in the pre-1979
era, probably because employees, whether they were reinstated or not, had little
chance of eventually resolving the dispute with the employer to their advantage.
It was only after 1982, when another provision relating to unfair labour practice
disputes was added, that this section gained prominence.

The dispute settlement machinery, as it existed until 1979, had all the
characteristics of a system based on a belief in the freedom of association, free
collective bargaining, the freedom (but not the right) to strike and minimal
interference in the employer–employee relationship; yet with sufficient provision
for the promotion of labour peace. As such, it could not really be faulted, except
with regard to the lack of provision for individual disputes. However, the fact
remained that vast numbers of South African employees and their trade unions
had no access to the official machinery. Domestic and agricultural workers and
public servants were excluded from the ambit of the Act, and all black African
employees, who were excluded by the definition of 'employee', were not entitled
to use the official dispute settlement machinery. Furthermore, only registered
unions were entitled to join industrial councils or to apply for conciliation
boards. Thus the unions representing black employees could not function on
conciliation bodies. As indicated in Chapter 8, a different machinery had been
established during the Seventies for black African employees, but this was so
cumbersome that it was rarely used.

**Changes
Implemented
from 1979
Onwards**

In 1979 the position as regards black African employees changed, although
public servants, educationists, domestic and agricultural workers were still
excluded from the Act. Yet it was not until 1983 that unregistered unions too
were permitted to apply for conciliation boards.

After 1979 other important changes were introduced. The basic machinery
as it existed before 1979 was maintained, but was supplemented by the definition
of an unfair labour practice, the establishment of the Industrial Court, the
insertion of unfair labour practice disputes in Section 43 (Status Quo Orders) and
the provision for arbitration of unfair labour practice disputes by the Industrial
Court.

The changes introduced provided, in the first place, a viable alternative to industrial action. Before 1979 the parties had little option, if a dispute remained unresolved, but to engage in strike action or to let the matter rest. They could, it is true, have chosen to go to arbitration; but, although an arbitrator might impose a settlement, the findings of an arbitrator — and even an industrial tribunal — had little impact on the general behaviour of the parties concerned. Arbitrations were, in any event, mostly concerned with substantive issues such as wages, and not with the behaviour of the parties towards each other. After 1979 the wide definition of an unfair labour practice allowed the parties to channel all manner of disputes which might otherwise have ended in industrial action to the Industrial Court via the unfair labour practice provision. The Industrial Court, when deciding on unfair labour practice disputes, was in essence conducting arbitration in terms of Section 49 of the Labour Relations Act of 1956. However, because it had the status of a court, the findings of this body had a much greater impact than those of an ordinary arbitrator. Although the Court emphasised that it took into account the particular circumstances of every case, repeated findings on certain issues led to the establishment of guidelines as regards fair labour practices. This brought a completely new dimension to South African industrial relations. Issues which were previously subject only to the bargaining process (if they were subjected to that at all) and which could, if bargaining broke down, be resolved only by conciliation or, ultimately, a show of strength by either party could now be submitted for adjudication by a court, whose findings would serve as a warning to other parties involved in the labour relationship. Thus the introduction of the unfair labour practice definition did serve to establish rights where no rights appeared to exist before, the most important of these being the right to fair treatment and to protection from unfair dismissals.

A second aspect of the post-1979 amendments was that individual employees now had a more permanent and potent form of redress in the use of the unfair labour practice provision and the final submission of their pleas to the Industrial Court. Also, the widening of Section 43 disputes to include unfair labour practices and the fact that the Industrial Court, and not the Minister of Manpower, would now hear Status Quo applications allowed this Section to be used more effectively.

Implications of the Changes Introduced

The concept of an unfair labour practice, the establishment of the Industrial Court and the extension of the Status Quo provision were indicative of greater interference by the State in the labour relationship.

Previously the only mandatory clauses in the Labour Relations Act were those relating to freedom of association, victimisation and legal industrial action. Employers and employees, limited only by the minimum protection afforded by other legislation, could bargain or not bargain and generally treat each other as they pleased as long as there was no breach of the common law contract. The new legislation, by contrast, provided for the **practices** of both parties to the labour relationship to be checked and balanced by another authority. Whether intended for this purpose or not, the introduction of the unfair labour practice established the machinery whereby the relationship between employer and employee could be continually monitored and whereby any imbalance of power between the parties could be rectified. Employees, and particularly individual employees, traditionally hold less power than the employer. Even where employees are organised into a collective, they may still, if their collective is not sufficiently strong or well organised and if their right to bargain or engage in industrial action is circumscribed, hold far less power than the employer and, as a result, be unable to address issues. Furthermore, in South Africa, the position of the black employee had always been even weaker than that of other employees. In the light of the above, it was quite logical that the machinery established by the introduction of the unfair labour practice concept was utilised more by employees and their representatives, and particularly by trade unions representing black employees, than by employers; this despite the fact that the definition of the unfair labour practice was very even-handed and favoured neither the employer nor the employee. It is not that the legislation or the Industrial Court had been biased towards employees, but rather that employees — and particularly black employees and their representatives — had in their view greater injustices to address and, therefore, more reason for bringing unfair practices to the attention of the court.

Martin Brassey, in his discussion of the unfair labour practice jurisdiction of the Industrial Court, refuted the argument that the legislation was introduced to grant greater protection to employees. He stated:

> 'There is no room for arguing ... that the legislator intended the unfair labour practice jurisdiction to confer a benefit or advantage on one or other side. More specifically, it is not the function of the judiciary to improve the lot of employees; nor is it its function to redress the bargaining imbalance that is said to exist between them and their employers and from which they are said to suffer.'

The argument is correct, particularly if fairness is measured in terms of commercial rationale. Nevertheless, it can be contended that, irrespective of the legislature's intentions, the machinery created was of such a nature that it bestowed on its users greater power to address unilateral practices. These practices had previously remained unchecked, for the simple reason that the parties concerned did not have sufficient industrial power to address them and were given no rights in respect of such practices in the then existent legislation. In this manner the legislation served to allow for the redress of the power imbalance. Moreover, it could very well be argued that, if employers found that the disproportionately greater power or perceived greater power of employees and unions led to unilateral action on the part of the latter, they (the employers) might use the unfair labour practice machinery for the very same purpose — to redress the power imbalance. The mistake of employers, in fact, was that they appeared unaware of the even-handedness of the legislation and were all too inclined to brand the Industrial Court as employee-biased.

That there was a tendency to greater interference in the conduct of the labour relationship and to curbing unfettered action which might be based only on the power principle was proved by the amendments to the Labour Relations Act introduced in 1988. These amendments provided for an extended definition of the unfair labour practice. The previous wide definition had been retained, but certain specific unfair labour practices were added to the definition. These included the dismissal of an employee without a valid and fair reason; the retrenchment of employees without following proper procedures; the unfair or unilateral suspension of employees; unfair or unilateral changes in conditions of employment; unfair discrimination on the basis of sex, race and creed; unfair recruitment methods by a union or employers' organisation; intimidation, boycotts and sympathy strikes. This meant that it was no longer entirely at the discretion of the Industrial Court to decide whether one of the practices mentioned constituted an unfair labour practice in terms of the older, main definition. Such practices had to be judged unfair, although in some instances discretion was still allowed in the interpretation of the word 'fair'. In addition to these amendments, another provided that the indemnity of unions in the case of breach of contract was no longer absolute, while yet others extended the powers and enhance the status of the Industrial Court. Although, in the main, it still subscribed to the principle of voluntarism, the government was obviously of the opinion that greater regulation was required in the sphere of labour relations. This was in line with trends in European countries, especially in Britain.

This codification of unfair labour practices was regarded as too prescriptive, and the legislation was viewed as interference on behalf of employers to the detriment of unions. The most controversial amendments were subsequently scrapped, but the government did not revert to a completely *laissez-faire* stance. Instead of unilaterally interfering and prescribing, or interfering on behalf of one party, it now admitted that labour legislation could be effectively implemented only if it is acceptable to all the parties involved.

THE DISPUTE SETTLEMENT MACHINERY AS IT EXISTED UNTIL 1995

The Ambit of the Machinery The dispute settlement machinery, as it existed until 1995, is illustrated in Figure 34. The Labour Relations Act contained no definition of a dispute but, from the definition of the unfair labour practice, it could be concluded that a labour dispute would include any dispute between employers or their representatives and employees or their representatives and would centre on any issue which directly or indirectly affected the relationship between employer and employee. Thus, although the parties to a labour dispute were limited to employers and employees or their respective representatives, the subject matter of disputes was not circumscribed and could include a large variety of issues.

All disputes between employer and employee might first be dealt with by a procedure agreed upon by the parties (see previous section and Annexures) and then, if resolution could not be achieved, channelled through the official machinery. Essentially, four types of dispute could be distinguished. These included disputes of interest in essential services, disputes in industrial councils, ordinary interest disputes and unfair labour practice disputes. Disputes in essential services could be channelled through in-plant procedures and thereafter referred to a conciliation board or industrial council for conciliation. Where conciliation could not be achieved, the parties could opt for mediation; but ultimately these disputes had to be submitted to compulsory arbitration. Industrial council disputes would be dealt with in terms of the procedure contained in the constitution of the council, whereafter mediation or arbitration could be called for. If mediation failed, the parties could then engage in legal industrial action. Ordinary disputes of interest followed the same course as those in essential services, except that mediation was not compulsory and the parties could, if all else failed, elect to institute industrial action. As far as unfair labour practice disputes were concerned, these could also initially be channelled through in-plant procedures and then referred to a conciliation board or to an industrial council having jurisdiction. However, if conciliation by these bodies failed, the parties (if they did not opt for mediation or voluntary arbitration) could refer the dispute to the Industrial Court for a final determination. Since the granting of a final determination could take a long time, further provision was made for Status Quo Orders. These were temporary orders, effective until such time as the dispute was settled or a final determination was made. Thus, particularly employees who had been dismissed were granted interim relief as the Court could order that they be reinstated, sometimes retrospectively, until finalisation of the dispute was achieved.

The Industrial Court

The Industrial Court was established on the recommendation of the Wiehahn Commission, which had envisaged that the Court would hear cases related to 'undesirable employment practices', unfair dismissal, unfair treatment and other grievances and that it would also be able to adjudicate on the legality of industrial action undertaken by the parties to the labour relationship. The reason given for the establishment of such a court was that labour matters required a special type of adjudication and that the officers presiding should have knowledge of labour relations. Essentially, the intention was that the Industrial Court would replace the then existent Industrial Tribunal established by the Labour Relations Act of 1956, but that, as a court of law, it would have more wide-ranging powers and would be able to establish a body of case law, to be used as precedent in labour cases.

The government accepted nearly all the Commission's recommendations concerning the Industrial Court, but did not initially give them full effect. The Labour Relations Amendment Act of 1979 which followed did provide for the establishment of an industrial court, but this did not have the status of a superior court and was not given the power to adjudicate on legal matters such as strikes, lockouts and statutory agreements. The result was that the Industrial Court, once it had been established, found itself pronouncing mainly on matters related to the unfair labour practice. It gained the reputation of a quasi-judicial body, permitted to use wide discretionary powers in its interpretation and application of the unfair labour practice definition. The 1988 amendments to the Labour Relations Act attempted partly to remedy this situation.

The work of the Industrial Court was concerned mainly with applications for Status Quo Orders and with referrals for final determination of unfair labour practice disputes, both of which increased steadily from 1983 onwards. According to the 1994 report of the Department of Labour, 8 400 cases were referred to the Court during that year, in comparison to 6 699 in 1993. Of the 1994 cases, 6 614 were applications from individuals alleging unfair dismissal, 1 199 were related to group dismissals and 208 of the disputes had resulted from staff reductions. By October 1994, 5 033 cases had not yet been finalised and it was estimated that the Court had a backlog of some eight months.

Until 1988, the Labour Relations Act did not provide for appeals against the decisions of the Industrial Court. Since the Industrial Court was regarded as an inferior court, however, the decisions of this court could be reviewed by the

Supreme Court. Furthermore, there was a right to appeal regarding the court of law function of the Industrial Court, and the Court itself could reserve for a decision by the Appellate Division any question of law arising out of the Court's proceedings. Appeals which were lodged, therefore, centred mainly on technical problems such as the right of the court to pronounce on certain matters or to make certain orders.

The 1988 amendments to the Act provided for the establishment of a Labour Appeal Court, to be headed by a judge of the Supreme Court, assisted by two assessors having '... experience of the administration of justice or skill in any matter which may be considered by the Court'. Appeals might be lodged regarding not only questions of law but also final determinations (Section 46(9)) and orders as to costs made by the Industrial Court. Appeals against the decision of the Labour Appeal Court, in turn, could be made to the Appellate Division of the Supreme Court.

From its inception the Labour Appeal Court was the subject of continued controversy. Unions regarded it as employer-biased and criticism was also levelled at the attitude of judges and assessors, the latter more often than not being advocates whose usual work was to represent employers. So widespread was the dissatisfaction with the Court that general agreement was reached by employers, labour and government officials on suggested changes. These included the suggestion that the Labour Appeal Court should have the same status as the Supreme Court, that judges should be selected for their knowledge of labour law and their sensitivity in this area; but that additional members of the Appeal Court, who might also be lawyers, should be drawn from two panels nominated respectively by employers and unions and that these 'wingpersons' should have the power to outvote the professional judges. All were in agreement that the system of double appeal should be removed, that procedures should be expedited and the number of appeals limited.

DISPUTE SETTLEMENT IN TERMS OF THE LABOUR RELATIONS ACT OF 1995

Rationale The new labour relations legislation has retained most of the dispute settlement mechanisms of the previous dispensation. It has, however, attempted both to speed up dispute settlement and to relieve the Industrial Court (now renamed the Labour Court) of much of its burden by separating unfair dismissals from other unfair labour practices and by subjecting most of these to mediation and arbitration by the Commission for Conciliation, Mediation & Arbitration or by accredited bargaining councils or their agents.

The CCMA is an entirely new body, established both to help settle disputes and to assist in the conduct of labour relations, especially as regards workplace forums. In one sense it replaces the system of conciliation boards, which are now defunct. The law will also no longer allow for Status Quo applications, which to some measure were duplicated by final determinations and which may no longer be necessary if disputes (particularly those regarding dismissals) can be rapidly settled by arbitration. However, Section 64(4) of the new Act does provide a watered-down version of the Status Quo Order by allowing employees who refer a dispute regarding unilateral changes to terms and conditions of employment to the Commission or a bargaining council to request the employer to reinstate

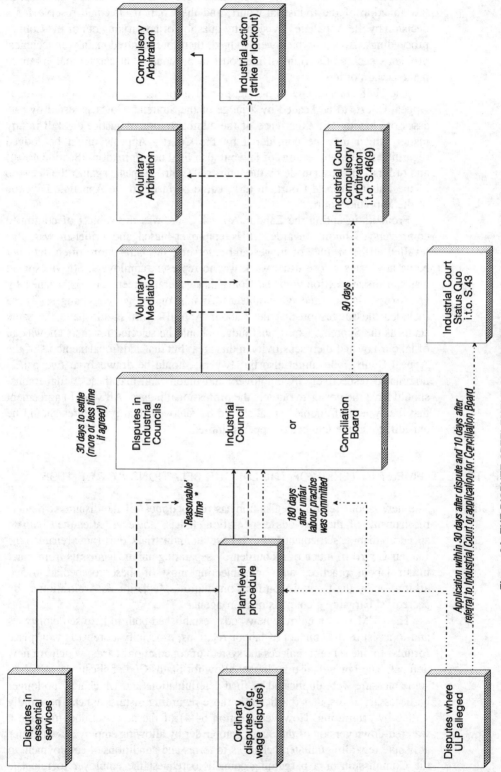

Figure 34: THE DISPUTE SETTLEMENT MACHINERY AS IT EXISTED UNTIL 1995

onditions. Should the employer fail to do so within a period of 48 hours, employees may engage in a strike action without having followed the established procedures.

A broad definition of an unfair labour practice remains but this has, besides the very clear directions regarding unfair dismissals, been supplemented with a number of specified unfair labour practices (see below). The Industrial Court will now be renamed the Labour Court and will have superior status, and its decisions will be subject to only one level of appeal: the Labour Appeal Court.

One long needed change is the clear distinction between disputes of right and disputes of interest and the provision that economic weapons (in the form, for example, of a strike) may not legally be used in disputes of right. Previously this was not the case and employees would, for example, engage in strike action regarding the dismissal of a colleague, notwithstanding that they had recourse to legal adjudication.

All in all, the new legislation does give clearer direction, especially as regards unfair dismissal, and disputes of right will probably be more speedily resolved. It is only to be hoped that the CCMA does not become as overburdened as the former Industrial Court, and that sufficient other competent agencies and individuals can be accredited as arbitrators, thereby relieving the CCMA of some of the load which is bound to fall on it.

Types of Dispute and Means of Settlement

The new legislation distinguishes between many different types of dispute, but essentially all disputes of right may be submitted first to conciliation by either the CCMA, a bargaining council or its accredited agent and thereafter to arbitration by one of the above or, in certain instances, to a final determination by the Labour Court. Disputes of interest too may be submitted first to conciliation by one of the bodies mentioned above; but after that the parties are free, except in essential services, to go to voluntary arbitration or to engage in legal industrial action in the form of a strike or a lockout. The Act interprets 'conciliation' to include fact finding, mediation and even advisory arbitration.

The procedures to be followed in specific types of dispute are outlined below. It should be remembered that certain disputes may be referred to the Commission only if there is no bargaining council which has jurisdiction; further that, in all cases when a dispute is referred to the Commission or to a bargaining council, the applicant will have to prove that he has served a copy of the application on the respondent.

Disputes Arising from Interference with the Freedom of Association

Such disputes may be referred first for conciliation by the CCMA or a bargaining council having jurisdiction and, if they remain unresolved, to the Labour Court for final determination (see Figure 35).

Where victimisation or interference with the freedom of association is alleged, the applicant has to prove that a certain action (for example, dismissal) has been taken against him. The employer will then have to prove that he did not interfere with the freedom of association of the employee, or that he did not victimise him. Thus he will have to show other good reasons for his action or for his treatment of the employee.

Disputes Centring in the Organisational Rights of Trade Unions

Where a union informs the employer that it wishes to exercise its organisational rights in terms of the Act, a meeting has to be held within a period of thirty days with the purpose of establishing an agreement between the parties. Should no such agreement be reached, the union may follow the route to a legal strike — that is, it may refer the dispute to mediation by the CCMA or a bargaining council and, if mediation is unsuccessful, engage in strike action provided the necessary notice has been given. On the other hand, the union may choose not to engage in industrial action but instead to submit the dispute to arbitration by the Commission. The Commission must make a determination within a period of fourteen days (see Figure 36). Where the union has elected to go on strike, it may not for a period of twelve months thereafter refer the dispute to arbitration. It is foreseen that disputes centring in organisational rights will arise from issues relating to the definition of 'workplace', the representativeness of the trade union and the manner in which organisational rights are to be implemented.

The Act provides that, where the Commission has to arbitrate on the representativeness of a union, it should try to avoid multiplicity of trade union representation, to encourage 'a system of a representative union' at a workplace and to minimise the financial and administrative burden placed on an employer who has to deal with more than one trade union. The commissioner should also consider the nature of the workplace, the type of organisational rights being requested, the type of sector in which the employer operates and the history of organisation at that workplace. Furthermore a commissioner may, on his own initiative or at the request of the employer, cancel the organisational rights of another union already operating at the workplace if he is of the opinion that that union is no longer representative.

Disputes Regarding the Interpretation or Implementation of Collective Agreements

Every collective agreement (except an agency shop or closed shop agreement) must provide for a procedure by which disputes regarding the interpretation or implementation of the agreement can be resolved. Such procedure should provide for conciliation as a first step, followed by arbitration. Where there is no disputes procedure in the agreement, where the procedure is not yet effective or where one party blocks the use of the procedure, either of the parties may refer the dispute to the Commission (see Figure 37). The Commission will attempt mediation and, should this fail, either party may request that the Commission engage in arbitration.

The same procedure will apply in the case of agency shop and closed shop agreements, except that any person bound by an arbitration award relating to the administration and application of funds obtained under an agency shop or closed shop agreement may appeal to the Labour Court against such award (see Figure 38).

A different procedure, however, applies where an employee has been dismissed because of his refusal to join a closed shop union or the cancellation of his union membership. This aspect is dealt with later in the chapter.

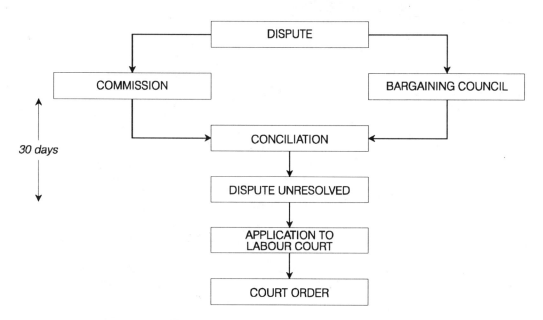

Figure 35: FREEDOM OF ASSOCIATION

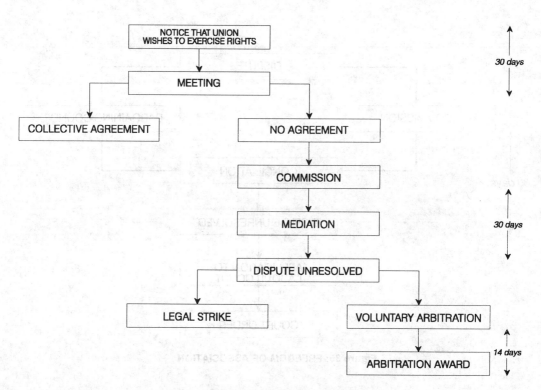

Figure 36: ORGANISATIONAL RIGHTS

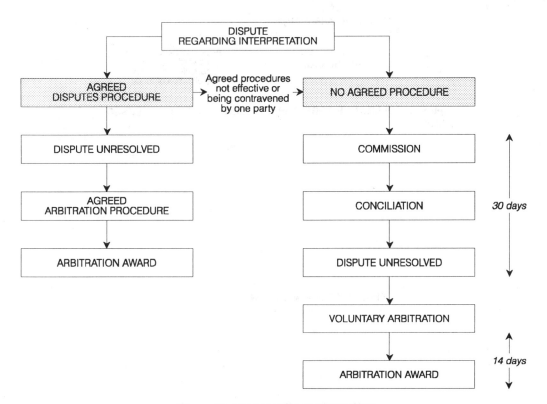

Figure 37: COLLECTIVE AGREEMENTS

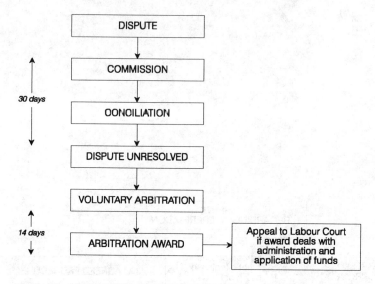

Figure 38: COLLECTIVE AGREEMENTS (AGENCY SHOP AND CLOSED SHOP)

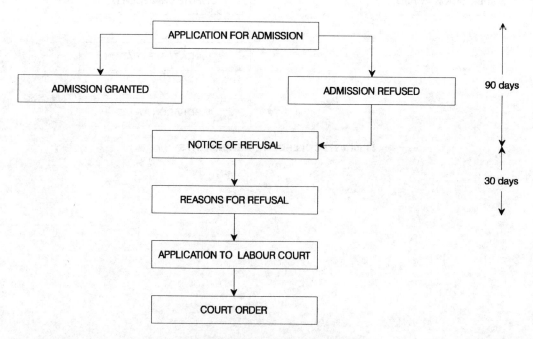

Figure 39: BARGAINING COUNCILS

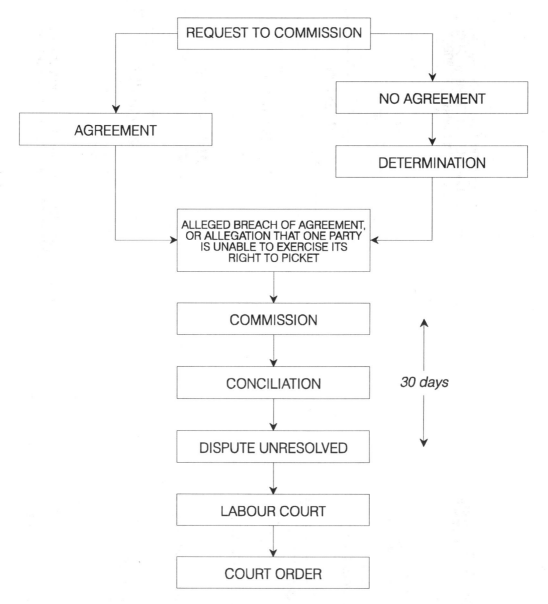

Figure 40: PICKETING

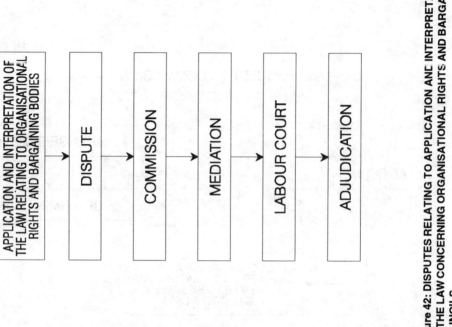

Figure 42: DISPUTES RELATING TO APPLICATION AND INTERPRETATION OF THE LAW CONCERNING ORGANISATIONAL RIGHTS AND BARGAINING COUNCILS

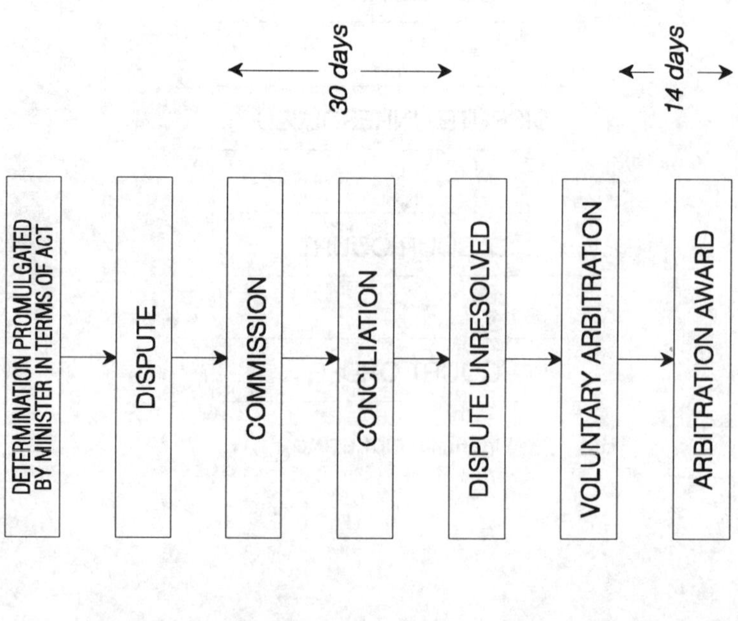

APPLICATION AND INTERPRETATION OF THE LAW RELATING TO ORGANISATIONAL RIGHTS AND BARGAINING BODIES → DISPUTE → COMMISSION → MEDIATION → LABOUR COURT → ADJUDICATION

Figure 41: DETERMINATIONS BY STATUTORY COUNCILS

DETERMINATION PROMULGATED BY MINISTER IN TERMS OF ACT → DISPUTE → COMMISSION → CONCILIATION → DISPUTE UNRESOLVED → VOLUNTARY ARBITRATION → ARBITRATION AWARD

30 days

14 days

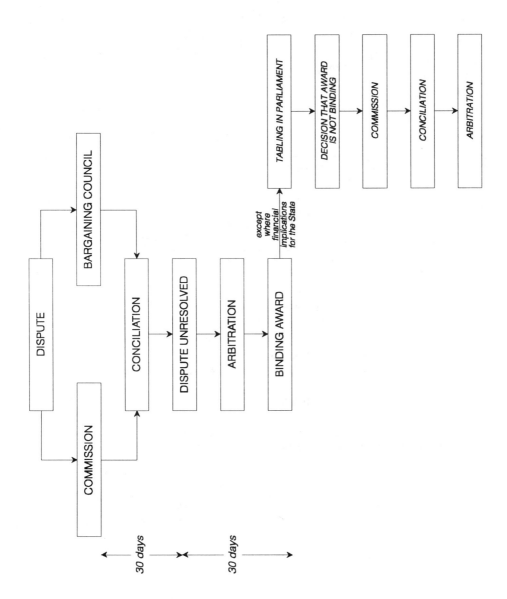

Figure 43: ESSENTIAL SERVICES – DISPUTES OF INTEREST

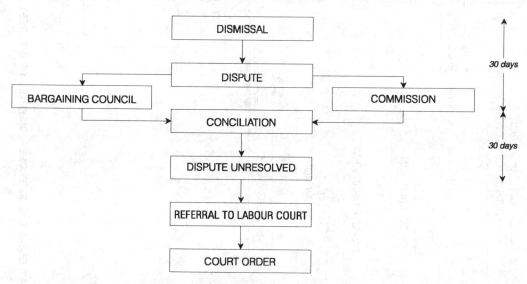

Figure 44: AUTOMATICALLY UNFAIR DISMISSALS and DISMISSALS RELATING TO RETRENCHMENTS, CLOSED SHOP MEMBERSHIP or PARTICIPATION IN AN ILLEGAL STRIKE

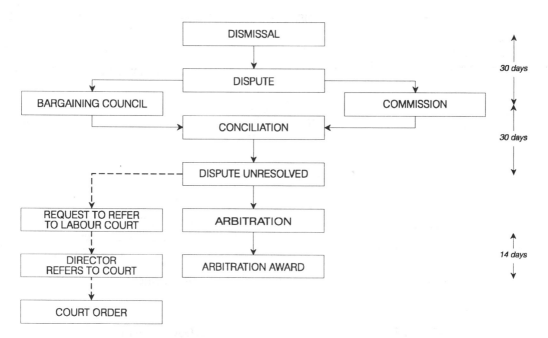

Figure 45: UNFAIR DISMISSAL (MISCONDUCT, INCOMPETENCE AND INCAPACITY)

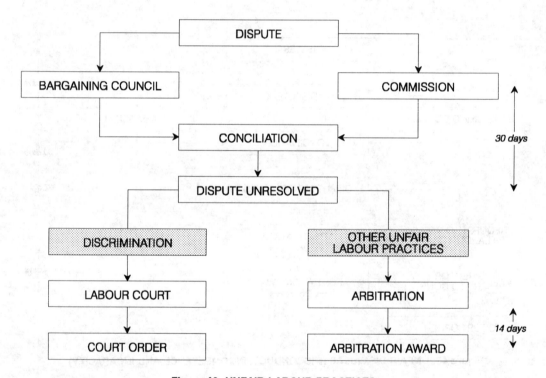

Figure 46: UNFAIR LABOUR PRACTICES

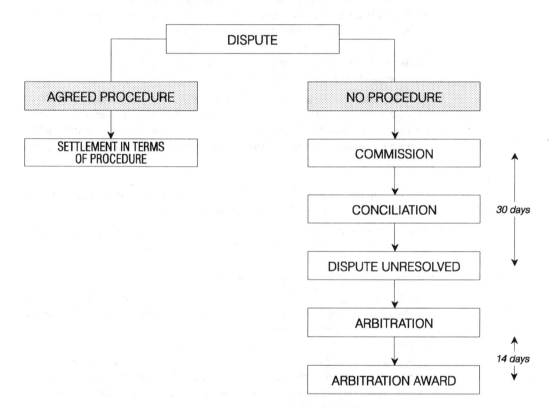

Figure 47: WORKPLACE FORUMS

Disputes Arising from the Refusal to Admit a Party or Parties to Membership of a Bargaining Council

Any registered union or employers' association may apply in writing to be admitted as party to a bargaining council.

The application should set out details regarding the applicant's representativeness, the reasons why the applicant should be admitted to the council and any other relevant information in support of the application. The council then has ninety days in which to decide whether or not to grant admission. Should it refuse admission, it must within the next thirty days supply reasons for such refusal. The applicant union or employers' association may then apply to the Labour Court for an order granting it admission to the council. The Court may admit the applicant to the council, amend the constitution of the council or make any other order which it deems fit. (See Figure 39).

Disputes Relating to Determinations Made by the Minister at the Request of a Statutory Council

When a dispute arises concerning the interpretation of a determination made on behalf of a statutory council via the Wage Act, any party may refer the dispute in writing to the CCMA. The Commission will attempt conciliation and, failing this, either party may request that the Commission arbitrate on the dispute. (See Figure 41).

Disputes Centring in the Interpretation and Implementation of the Act as it Relates to Organisational Rights and Bargaining Bodies

Such disputes may be referred first to the CCMA for conciliation and thereafter to the Labour Court for legal adjudication (see Figure 42).

Disputes Involving Picketing Agreements

Unions and employers should come to some agreement regarding the rules applicable to picketing. If they so wish, they can request the CCMA to assist them in reaching such agreement; where no agreement is reached, the Commission will make the necessary determination. Should one of the parties thereafter allege interference with its right to engage in picketing or that the picketing agreement or determination has been breached, the dispute may be referred to the Commission which will engage first in conciliation, whereafter either party may refer the dispute to the Labour Court. (See Figure 40.)

Disputes of Interest in Essential Services

When a dispute of interest occurs between parties in a designated essential service, such dispute may be referred to a bargaining council having jurisdiction or, where no council exists, to the Commission. The council or Commission will attempt to mediate the dispute but, if no resolution is achieved, either party may request that it be subjected to arbitration by the Commission or the council (see Figure 43). Arbitration must be conducted within a period of thirty days. If the arbitration award involves the State and has financial implications for the State, the Minister may table the award in Parliament and Parliament may then decide that the award should not be binding, in which case the dispute is referred to the Commission for conciliation and, should this fail, eventual arbitration.

To allow time for the Minister to table an award, arbitration awards which affect the State become binding fourteen days after the granting of an award, or fourteen days after the tabling of such award in Parliament.

Disputes Arising from Automatically Unfair Dismissals or Dismissals Centring in Retrenchments, Participation in an Illegal Strike or Refusal to Join a Closed Shop Union or Refusal of Membership by a Closed Shop Union

Certain dismissals (such as those involving victimisation, participation in a legal strike or protest action, the refusal to do the work of a co-worker who is on strike, an attempt by the employer to coerce employees into accepting certain conditions, the employee's exercising or declaring his intention to exercise any right in terms of the Act, the pregnancy of an employee, or discrimination) are regarded as automatically unfair (see Chapter 10).

Disputes centring in such dismissals, as well as disputes relating to dismissals arising from retrenchments, participation in an illegal strike or non-membership of a closed shop union, may — like all other dismissal disputes — first be referred to a bargaining council having jurisdiction, or to the CCMA where no bargaining council exists. Referral has to take place within a period of thirty days from the date of dismissal, but an extension can be condoned by the council or Commission, which will attempt to conciliate. Should mediation fail or if thirty days have elapsed since the referral, the employee may refer the dispute to the Labour Court for adjudication. (See Figure 44.)

Disputes Relating to Other Unfair Dismissals (Misconduct, Incompetence and Incapacity)

Disputes relating to the abovementioned dismissals must also, within a period of thirty days from the date of dismissal (or a longer period if condoned), be referred to a bargaining council or, in the absence of a bargaining council, to the CCMA. Either body will attempt to resolve the dispute by conciliation. Should this fail or if a period of thirty days since the referral of the dispute has elapsed, the Commission or the council, at the request of the employee and within 14 days, will arbitrate on the dispute if the employee alleges that the dismissal was for one of the above reasons, if he alleges constructive dismissal or if he does not know what the reason was for his dismissal. (See Figure 45.)

However, if one of the parties so requests, the Director of the Commission may refer the dispute to the Labour Court. This he will do only after considering the reasons for the dismissal, whether a question of law has arisen, the complexity of the dispute, the existence of conflicting arbitration awards and the public interest. A decision by the Director to refer the dispute is final and binding.

In any actions involving an alleged unfair dismissal, the employee merely has to prove that the dismissal occurred. The onus will then fall on the employer to prove that the dismissal was fair. The Labour Court or an arbitrator may order the employer to reinstate the employee with effect from the date of dismissal, to re-employ him in the same or a similar position from any date following the dismissal, or to pay compensation to the dismissed employee. The first option should be to reinstate the employee — unless the employee does not wish to be reinstated or re-employed, the continuation of the relationship has become impossible, it cannot reasonably be expected of the employer to do so or the dismissal is unfair merely because the employer did not follow a fair procedure.

Where a dismissal is automatically unfair or resulted from unfair retrenchment or redundancy, the Labour Court can make any order which it deems fit. Where a dismissal was procedurally unfair, the amount of compensation should be equal to the remuneration which the employee would have earned from the date of dismissal to the date of the arbitration award or adjudication by the Court (excluding unnecessary delays by the employee in bringing the action). If the dismissal is found to be unfair because it was not related to the employee's misconduct, incompetence or incapacity or to the employer's organisational requirements, compensation should be fair and reasonable but should not be less than that outlined for procedural unfairness or more than twelve months' salary or wages. In the case of an automatically unfair dismissal, compensation may not exceed 24 months' salary or wages.

Unfair Labour Practice Disputes

Where an unfair labour practice (see later section) is alleged, any party may refer the dispute to a bargaining council having jurisdiction or, failing this, to the CCMA. Either body will attempt to conciliate the dispute. Should the dispute remain unresolved it will, if it involves discrimination and therefore is automatically unfair, be referred to the Labour Court. In the case of any other unfair labour practice codified in the Schedule to the Act, the dispute may be referred to the Commission for arbitration (see Figure 46). The Labour Court may order reinstatement or compensation, while the Commission may make any reasonable award.

Disputes Involving Workplace Forums (Implementation of Provisions Relating to Workplace Forums, Joint Decisionmaking and Disclosure)

Any dispute relating to the establishment and functioning of workplace forums, co-decisionmaking with forums and the disclosure of information to forum members may, in the absence of an agreed procedure relating to disputes on that particular issue, be referred to the Commission for conciliation and, should this fail, to arbitration. (See Figure 47.)

DISPUTE SETTLING MECHANISMS

Conciliation If a dispute is submitted to conciliation by the Commission, the commissioner appointed to undertake conciliation should attempt to achieve a resolution within a period of thirty days from the date of referral. However, the parties may agree that a longer period is necessary. The commissioner sets out the procedures to be followed which, as mentioned previously, could include mediation, fact finding (providing detailed, concrete information on issues subject to dispute) or advisory arbitration. In the case of essential services the parties have the option, within seven days of referral, to agree on the commissioner to be appointed and on the procedure to be followed. The Commission may also offer to conciliate in disputes which have not been referred to it.

A party to mediation proceedings may represent himself or be represented by a co-employee or by a member, official or office bearer of his union or employers' association and, if the party is a juristic person, by a director or employee.

At the end of the thirty-day period or whatever longer period may have been agreed upon, the commissioner must issue a certificate declaring that the dispute has been resolved or that it remains unresolved. A copy of this certificate must be served on both parties, while the original is handed to the Commission.

It can be surmised that the same rules will, broadly, apply to mediation under the auspices of a bargaining council or its accredited agents.

Arbitration   The Commission is bound to undertake arbitration if the law provides for it and when requested to do so by one of the parties. The arbitration may be undertaken by the same commissioner who engaged in conciliation and mediation of the dispute but, as explained in an earlier section, this might prove problematic. The Act provides, therefore, that any party may object to the appointment of the same commissioner. In fact parties may, by agreement, express their preference for certain commissioners by providing a list of not more than five names within 48 hours after the issue of a certificate stating that mediation has failed. (In the case of a dispute in essential services, they have seven days to name the commissioner of their choice.) In certain cases the parties may apply to the Director of the Commission for the appointment of a senior commissioner to undertake arbitration. The Director may decide to do so after having considered the questions of law arising out of the dispute, the complexity of the dispute, the existence of conflicting arbitration awards relevant to the dispute, and the public interest. An arbitrator may also, at any stage (but with the consent of the parties), cease arbitration and engage in conciliation.

During arbitration proceedings the parties are entitled to offer testimony, to call witnesses, to cross-examine the witnesses of the other party and to direct closing argument to the commissioner. Parties may represent themselves, or may be represented by a legal practitioner, by a co-employee or by a member, official or office bearer of the union or employers' association; or, if the party is a legal person, by a director or employee. However, where the dispute arises from an unfair dismissal centring in the conduct, competence or capacity of the employee, a party may be represented by a legal practitioner only if all the other parties agree or if the commissioner deems it necessary after considering such matters as the complexity of the dispute and the comparative expertise of the opposing parties and their representatives in handling the dispute. Where an applicant party is not present for the proceedings, the commissioner may cancel the arbitration. On the other hand, if the respondent does not attend, the commissioner may conduct the arbitration *in absentia* or may postpone the arbitration to a later date.

In considering the dispute, the arbitrator is obliged to take into consideration any relevant code of practice published in terms of the Act, or any code issued by NEDLAC. The commissioner has the power to subpoena any person who might be able to provide information regarding the dispute or who might be in possession of a book, document or object relevant to the dispute. He is further entitled to call in or subpoena experts, to interrogate any person who has been subpoenaed and, with the necessary authorisation, to enter any premises, to take possession of any book, document or object and to keep such for a reasonable time. The Commission may charge any individual with contempt and refer the case to the Labour Court if such individual does not heed a subpoena, appears initially but then absents himself from the proceedings, refuses to take an oath or confirm his testimony, refuses to answer any question fully, fails to hand over a relevant book, document or object, deliberately obstructs the work of the Commission, insults, derogates or humiliates the commissioner, unfavourably affects or influences proceedings, unfairly anticipates the findings of the commissioner, openly disrupts the arbitration proceedings or misbehaves in any other way or commits any other action or omission which, in a court of law, would be regarded as contemptuous.

Once the arbitration has been finalised, the commissioner has fourteen days to make an award. (If the dispute involves an essential service interest, he has thirty days from the time of referral, or whatever longer period may be agreed upon.) The award must briefly state the reasons for the decision. Copies of the award must be served on all parties, while the original must be lodged with the Labour Court. The commissioner is empowered to make any award in terms of the Act, including (but not limited to) a declaratory order and an award giving effect to a collective agreement or to the provisions and main objectives of the Act. However, no order as to costs may be made unless a party or its representative acted in a frivolous or obstructive manner by continuing or defending the dispute during arbitration or by his actions during the proceedings. This notwithstanding, arbitration fees can be collected from an employer where it is found that a dismissal was procedurally unfair.

There are circumstances in which the Act provides that a dispute be referred to the Labour Court but where the parties may conclude an agreement allowing them to submit the dispute to arbitration under the auspices of the Commission instead. Unless it specifically provides otherwise, such arbitration agreement may be terminated only with the consent of all parties; but a party to the agreement may at any time apply to the Labour Court to set aside the agreement. If one of the parties has submitted to the Labour Court an issue which has been earmarked for arbitration, the other party may apply to the Court to have its proceedings set aside or, with the agreement of all parties, may allow the Court to continue with arbitration — in which case the Court proceedings will be governed by the rules relating to arbitration.

An arbitration award is final and binding and, unless it is the result of advisory arbitration, can be made an Order of the Labour Court.

Appeals Against Arbitration Awards Usually no appeals may be made against arbitration decisions but a party to a dispute may, within six weeks of receiving a copy of the award, request that the Labour Court review the award. Where corruption is cited as reason for the request, the applicant has six weeks from the date on which the corruption was discovered.

Reviews may be requested only where it is alleged that the arbitration was defective because the commissioner was guilty of misconduct regarding his duties as an arbitrator, because the commissioner committed a gross irregularity or exceeded his authority or because an award was improperly obtained.

The Labour Court may suspend the award pending its decision and may, finally, set the award aside by settling the dispute in a manner which it deems fit or by issuing an Order setting out the procedure to be followed in order to resolve the dispute.

Also, as seen in an earlier section, parties subject to an award pertaining to the application of funds for an agency shop or closed shop agreement may appeal to the Court against such award. Furthermore, Section 151(1)(g) does grant the Court the power to review the performance of any function performed under the Act, on any grounds permissible in law. It could, then, review the function of an arbitrator.

Private Procedures

The parties to the labour relationship may at any time agree on their own dispute settlement mechanisms, which would usually provide for mediation as a first step and, in disputes of right, for eventual arbitration. Such mediation and arbitration may be undertaken by private agencies or may be assigned to the CCMA — but, in such case, the parties will have to pay the Commission.

The Commission for Conciliation, Mediation & Arbitration

The legislation provides that the Commission for Conciliation, Mediation & Arbitration be independent of the State, any political party, union, employer, employers' association or federation of unions or employers' associations.

As explained in Chapter 5, the functions of the CCMA are to attempt, by conciliation or mediation, to resolve any dispute referred to it in terms of the Act, to arbitrate on disputes referred to it, to provide assistance with the establishment of workplace forums, and to compile and publish information and statistics concerning its activities. Furthermore the Commission may, if so requested:

- provide advice regarding procedures in terms of the Act,
- assist any party to a dispute in obtaining legal advice, assistance or representation,
- offer to conciliate in a dispute not referred to it,
- accredit bargaining councils and private agencies,
- conduct, supervise or scrutinise elections for a union or employers' association,
- publish guidelines regarding any matter regulated by the Act, and
- conduct and publish research concerning any matter related to its work and regarding sexual harassment.

Also, if requested, the Commission may provide advice and training to any party regarding the conclusion of collective agreements, workplace forums, the prevention of disputes and grievances, disciplinary procedures, procedures relating to dismissal, restructuring of the workplace or a programme for affirmative action.

The Commission will be managed by a controlling body consisting of a chairman and such other members as are nominated by NEDLAC and appointed for three years, as well as an appointed Director (who may not vote at meetings). The NEDLAC nominations comprise one independent person as chairman, three persons proposed by labour, three by employers and three by the State.

It is the task of the controlling body to appoint as many commissioners and senior commissioners as it deems necessary on a temporary or permanent basis and to establish a code of conduct for commissioners. It may also establish committees consisting of a member of the controlling body, the Director, a commissioner, a member of staff and one other person.

The Commission will initially be financed from the State coffers and thereafter from monies appropriated by Parliament, fees payable to it, donations received and income earned. It may charge fees for the conduct or supervision of an election or for providing advice to any party or parties. Rates will be set by the controlling body and published in the *Government Gazette*.

The controlling body may contract with any person to perform work for the Commission. Such person is subject to the requirement of independence as applicable to the Commission itself.

Accredited Bargaining Councils and Private Agencies

A bargaining council or private agency may apply to the controlling body of the CCMA to be accredited as mediators and arbitrators. However, accreditation will exclude from the jurisdiction of councils and private agencies disputes centring in disclosure of information to unions, organisational rights, the interpretation and application of collective bargaining agreements, agency shop and closed shop agreements, statutory agreements, cancellation of a council's registration, demarcation, picketing, co-decisionmaking, information to be given to workplace forums and the interpretation of the provisions relating to workplace forums. Essentially, then, these bodies will be dealing with disputes of interest and disputes relating to dismissals and the freedom of association.

The controlling body will consider whether the services provided by the council or private agency meet the standards of the Commission, whether the applicant is able to fulfil its duties effectively, whether the person appointed to perform mediation or arbitration will be independent and capable of performing these functions, whether an acceptable code of conduct and disciplinary procedure exist, whether the applicant is broadly representative of South African society and whether the fees charged to clients are reasonable.

Should the controlling body decide to accredit a council or agency, it will enter its name in a register of accredited agencies and furnish the applicant with an accreditation certificate. Once accredited, the council or agency may apply to the controlling body for a subsidy intended to assist it in performing its accredited functions or in training persons to perform these functions.

The Labour Court

Composition and Status of the Court

The Industrial Court is replaced by the Labour Court, which will be a court of law and which, as regards the matters within its jurisdiction, will have the same powers as a provincial division of the Supreme Court. It will also be a court of record. The Court thus gains greater status and effectiveness than the previously existing Industrial Court. It will consist of a Judge President, an Assistant Judge President and as many judges as the Minister of Labour, acting on the advice of NEDLAC and in consultation with the Minister of Justice and the Judge President, may determine. The Judge President and Assistant Judge President must be judges of the Supreme Court who have experience and expertise in labour law. Labour Court judges must also be judges of the Supreme Court, must have worked as legal practitioners for ten years before their appointment and must be knowledgeable, experienced and expert in the field of labour law.

Functions of the Labour Court

As described in Chapter 5, the Labour Court may issue any appropriate order, including the following.

- The granting of urgent interim relief
- An interdict
- An Order providing for an action to be carried out which will help remedy an injustice or give effect to the main objectives of the Act
- A declaratory Order
- An Order for compensation
- An Order for damages
- An Order for costs

The Court may further order implementation of any provision of the Act, declare any accord or arbitration award to be an Order of the Court, request the CCMA to conduct an investigation or to report to the Court, settle a dispute between a member and a union or employers' association regarding the implementation of the latter's constitution, review any action or omission related to a provision of the Act, review (on legally justifiable grounds) any action of the State as employer, hear an appeal against a health and safety inspector in terms of the Occupational Health & Safety Act and perform any activities necessitated by the Labour Relations Act or any other Act.

Labour Court Proceedings and Representation of Parties

All proceedings of the Labour Court must be conducted in open court, but the Court may exclude the public or specific persons from proceedings in any circumstances where a provincial division of the Supreme Court would be entitled to such exclusion.

A party to the proceedings may represent himself or be represented by a co-employee; by a member, official or office bearer of his union or employers' association; or, if the party is a juristic person, by a director or employee.

A decision, sentence or order of the Labour Court has a same force at law as that of the Supreme Court. It may be changed only by the Labour Court itself or by the Labour Appeal Court.

Evaluation

The decision of the legislators was evidently to separate the Labour Court from involvement in the more customary or day-to-day labour disputes and to assign to it only the more complex or extraordinary disputes which may be beyond the powers of the CCMA. By giving the Court the status of a provincial division of the Supreme Court and making it a court of record, the legislation has also added more weight to the decision of the Labour Court. It is further evident that the intention is to extend the Court's function beyond dispute settlement (most of which will now fall to the Commission) and to cast it more in the role of ultimate overseer and judge on labour matters.

The Labour Appeal Court A party subject to a decision of the Labour Court may apply to the Court for leave to appeal against such decision. Should permission to appeal be granted, the party requesting such permission must lodge an appeal within twenty-one days of the date on which leave to appeal was granted.

The Labour Appeal Court is a court of law and equity and will have the same status as the Appellate Division of the Supreme Court. It will be the highest court of appeal against any decision made by the Labour Court, and will comprise the Judge President and Assistant Judge President of the Labour Court as well as three judges from the same court. Appeals will be heard by any three judges from the panel as designated by the Judge President, except that a judge who heard the case which is subject to appeal may not act as chairman during the appeal.

The same rules as regards proceedings and representation in the Labour Court also apply to the Labour Appeal Court. Any decision to which two of the three judges agree will be regarded as a decision of the Labour Appeal Court. During proceedings the Court may hear further evidence, which may be oral or given by way of affidavit, and it may decide to refer the case back to the Labour Court for the hearing of further evidence. After deliberation the Appeal Court may decide to confirm or amend the decision of the Labour Court, or to reject the decision and to give another decision which it deems appropriate.

In exceptional circumstances the Judge President of the Labour Court may decide that a case referred to it should be heard by the Labour Appeal Court as a court of first instance, in which case the Labour Appeal Court is empowered to make any decision which could have been made by the Labour Court.

The scrapping of the two levels of appeal as they existed in the past is to be welcomed. Also, it appears beneficial that the Labour Appeal Court will be constituted from judges involved in the Labour Court. This may obviate the widely differing approaches which in some instances were displayed by the Industrial Court and the old Labour Appeal Court.

Evaluation of Dispute Settlement Provisions

The use of the dispute settlement mechanisms provided for in the Act remains largely voluntary. The parties or a party may, in most cases, decide to refer the dispute to the Commission, a council or accredited agent but may equally decide, even in a dismissal dispute, to follow other agreed procedures. This removes much of the duplication which occurred previously, and the speedy resolution of most disputes by the Commission or other body will certainly render dispute settlement more cost-effective for the parties involved. On the other hand, it places a greater financial burden on the State and it is doubtful whether sufficient persons with the necessary expertise can be found to handle the workload which will most certainly fall to the Commission. Also, the outlining of a specific procedure for every dispute may prove confusing; but clarification is obtained if it is remembered that all disputes first have to be submitted to conciliation. This is usually undertaken by the CCMA but, in the case of freedom of association disputes, interest disputes, dismissal disputes, illegal strikes and unfair labour practices, conciliation will be undertaken by a bargaining council if one has jurisdiction. If conciliation fails, matters relating to freedom of association, admission to bargaining councils, the interpretation of the law regarding organisational rights, bargaining bodies, picketing, automatically unfair dismissals, retrenchments, dismissals for illegal strikes and dismissals resulting from non-membership of a closed shop union will go to the Labour Court. The

Commission,or a council where it has mediated a dispute, will arbitrate on the remaining issues.

INDUSTRIAL ACTION

THE USE OF SANCTIONS IN INDUSTRIAL RELATIONS

During the conduct of the labour relationship, sanctions, in the form of an action of one kind or another, may be imposed by either party. The purpose is to express disagreement with the goals, intentions or actions of the other side, or to persuade the other side to relinquish its position in negotiations and to move closer to that of the party imposing the sanction. Sanctions may be of an individual or collective nature. An employer imposes individual sanctions when he disciplines or dismisses an employee, and collective sanctions when he introduces unilateral rules or conditions relating to his employees. In the negotiation situation, collective sanctions are imposed by the employer's mass dismissal of employees, by a decision to close his undertaking or by the action of locking out employees. Employees, in their turn, may impose individual sanctions by repeated absenteeism, by resigning from their positions, or by industrial sabotage. Collective sanctions by employees and unions may take the form of a strike action, a go-slow, a work-to-rule, a ban on overtime and community or international pressure. Since a particular employee's opportunity for and benefit from individual sanction is less than that of the individual employer, employees and unions engage in the imposition of collective sanctions more readily than would an individual employer. Consequently, strike action is frequently viewed as the main form of collective sanction.

In the process and conduct of the labour relationship and particularly in the negotiation situation, the threat or use of collective sanctions is an accepted method of pressurising the other party into making concessions or into adopting a position more favourable to the opponent.

STRIKE ACTION

Definition of a
Strike

A strike may be defined as a **temporary, collective withholding of labour, its objective being to stop production and thereby to oblige the employer to take cognizance of the demands of employees.**

The fact that a strike is of a temporary nature is of importance. Employees engaged in strike action do not intend permanently to withhold their labour from the employer but merely to oblige him into negotiation or, where negotiations are already under way or deadlock has been reached, to persuade him to adopt a different stance regarding the demands of his employees.

The Freedom
to Strike

The question as to whether employees should at all times be entitled to undertake strike action is much debated in industrial relations circles. Certain theorists and practitioners hold that strike action should be outlawed, as it is a disruption of normal labour relations. This faction argues that conflict should be contained within the other labour relations processes and that the occurrence of strike action is indicative of a breakdown in these procedures. By contrast, there are those who argue that strike action is an integral part of the labour relations process and a legitimate means of expressing conflict or of exerting pressure. In the opinion of the latter group, the occurrence of strike action does not indicate that procedures or negotiations have collapsed — merely that they are being redirected. It is maintained that the freedom to strike, as a last resort and as a final display of power, cannot be denied to employees who, otherwise, would be in an unequal power relationship with the employer. This is the view which is generally accepted in Western society. Therefore the freedom to strike, within certain parameters, is legitimised in most Western industrial relations systems. The parameters mentioned may include the imposition of cooling-off periods before strike action can be initiated, requirements regarding the holding of ballots, liability for damages caused, or a prohibition on sympathy or 'political' strikes. The limitations vary from one society to the next, depending on the sociopolitical inclination of and the degree of interference by a particular government. Conversely, a government may place no or very few limitations on strike action and may further entrench the freedom to strike by granting unions legal immunity during the course of strike actions or by prohibiting employers from dismissing striking employees.

Where the State has imposed certain limitations on strike action, a differentiation occurs between legal and illegal strikes. Legal strikes are those which are instituted within the parameters of government legislation, whereas employees engaged in illegal strike action do not follow the legislated procedures and regulations.

The parameters imposed by government may not be the only limitations which exist. In certain instances individual employers and their employees, or their union, may privately agree to establish their own strike procedures and parameters. These need not be the same as those established by government. A differentiation then occurs between official and unofficial strikes — that is, between those actions instituted according to agreed procedures and those occurring outside the agreed parameters.

The setting of parameters, by either the government or employers, acknowledges the freedom of employees to engage in strike action. Yet employees may take this freedom upon themselves without the approval of government or union officials. Ultimately, no legislation and no criminal sanctions can entirely preclude a large collective of employees from jointly withholding their labour. Employees who engage in strike action outside the parameters of the law or in complete contradiction to the law may have little chance of legal recourse, should the employer initiate counteraction against them, but this does not negate their ability, or even their right, to engage in such action.

The Question of Dismissal — The Right to Strike

The dismissal of striking workers by employers and the question as to whether employers are entitled to engage in this form of redress constitute another subject for debate. The main argument pertaining to the dismissal of strikers is that, even though the freedom to strike may be entrenched in law, the employer still holds the right at common law to dismiss employees who engage in strike action since, by refusing to work, they have effectively breached their individual contracts of employment. The problems related to this assumption are numerous. In the first instance, some differentiation needs to be made between individual and collective contracts. The question is whether employees pursuing a collective demand in terms of a collective contract can also be viewed or treated as individuals.

Another more important point is that the arbitrary dismissal of strikers effectively ends the negotiation process. If the view is adopted that strike action is part of the negotiation process and a legitimate means of exerting pressure, then the dismissal of strikers defeats the purpose of the exercise. This argument is supported by the fact that strike action is defined as a temporary, and not a permanent, withholding of labour. A further argument is that the ability of employers to dismiss striking workers may result in a permanently unequal power balance in the labour relationship. Those who believe the relationship, as determined by the contract of employment, to be essentially unequal maintain that the employer, by exercising the threat of dismissal, is depriving employees of their main source of power, namely their ability to withhold their labour on a temporary basis. Also, it is not as though the employee who engages in strike action does not already suffer a loss. Unless he receives strike pay from the union, he loses his earnings for the duration of the strike. In this light his dismissal is regarded as unnecessary punishment.

On the other hand, it could be argued that the employer has as much right to withhold the opportunity to work as the employee has to withhold his labour. This is so, but the principle is that the withholding should be of a temporary and not a permanent nature. The corollary of the right to strike is, therefore, said to be the right to a lockout and not the right to dismissal. Both sides suffer losses from a strike or a lockout but, in the case of a dismissal, it is the employee who suffers the major loss. Yet there are those who would argue that the right to strike should not be balanced with the right to lock out. It is contended that the employer already holds sufficient power, merely from his control function and by his traditional prerogative; that he is the party who makes the decisions and responds to employee demands. However, there are instances where the employer cannot act unilaterally and has to demand the consent of the employees. If they refuse to consent, then his only recourse may be to pressurise them by a lockout. This is the true purpose of a lockout, and lockouts should not be allowed merely as a reaction to a strike.

A very valid argument from the employer side regarding the question of dismissal is that the term of a strike action may not be circumscribed, that he cannot indefinitely halt the operation of his business or make do with temporary labour. Consequently, it is proposed that employers should at some stage have the right to dismiss strikers and to engage a new workforce. It is contended that, just as the right of instant dismissal may disturb the power balance between the parties, so too will the right of unions to engage in indefinite strike action result in an unequal power relationship.

The dilemma has been solved in different ways within various industrial relations systems. In certain instances employers are prohibited from dismissing striking employees, while in others dismissal is permitted only after a specified time period has elapsed. In other countries no prohibition is placed on the right of employers to dismiss strikers, but employees so dismissed may have recourse to the unfair labour practice machinery. If it can be proved that an employer, in dismissing strikers, acted in bad faith and made no attempt to negotiate a settlement, the court or tribunal adjudicating on the matter might order the reinstatement of the employees concerned.

Private agreements between a particular employer or group of employers and a union or a number of unions may make specific arrangements for the dismissal of strikers. Such arrangements usually include the provision that the employer(s) will not dismiss strikers for a specified period. This allows time for negotiations to be conducted, but it still grants the employer(s) the ultimate right to end the contract of employment, should negotiations prove to no avail and should the employees still refuse to return to work.

There is no doubt that, where dismissal of strikers is not prohibited by law, employers use dismissals or the threat of dismissal as a negotiation tactic. They hope thereby to weaken the union's resolve and to oblige a settlement more favourable to themselves. In many instances, employers do not intend the dismissal to be of a permanent nature. This leads to the problem of the reinstatement of strikers and to the question as to whether selective reinstatement is a permissible or fair practice. In Britain it has been argued that selective reinstatement is not permissible, since the dismissal was directed at the collective and no distinction should, consequently, be made when reappointing employees. This principle has now been entrenched in British law.

Reasons for Strike Action
In discussing the reasons for strike action, a distinction should immediately be made between the overall purpose of strike action and the actual cause of a particular action. Employees engage in strike action for the following purposes.

- To demonstrate general or particular dissatisfaction with management
- To demonstrate collective strength
- To pressurise management into compromising on a particular issue or issues
- To strengthen a union's position or reputation
- To display solidarity with other employees

Employees dissatisfied with a particular occurrence at the workplace, or generally antagonistic to management rules or practices, may stage a spontaneous walkout in order to display their dissatisfaction. Where management has proved reluctant to recognise employees as bargaining partners or is slow in granting concessions during negotiations, employees may engage in a show of strength. This serves as a demonstration of their collective power and as a warning of what might happen should management not accept the union as a bargaining partner or fail to move from its position during negotiations. Although both a display of dissatisfaction and a show of strength are methods of exerting pressure on management, they are essentially demonstrations and not specifically negotiation tactics. The direct pitting of the strength of one party against that of the other occurs with a strike following a deadlock in negotiations. The sole purpose of this type of action is to hold out on the other party until a concession is made or a compromise is reached. On the other hand, where unions are in the process of development or are building up their power base, strike action might be undertaken merely to enhance the image of the union and to extend its area of influence. Such actions usually have very little to do with the particular employer, even though, overtly, an issue related to the undertaking or industry is given as the reason for the strike action. Finally, certain employees might resort to strike action to show solidarity with workers in the same or in other undertakings, and not because they themselves have a quarrel with their management.

The actual triggers or causes of particular strike actions are numerous and interactive. In effect, the causes of strike actions range as widely as the reasons for conflict in the labour relationship. Consequently, the causes of strike action will encompass such issues as wages and working conditions, benefits, training schemes, dismissals, retrenchment, unfair treatment, insulting treatment by superiors, lack of safety precautions, refusal by an employer to recognise a union and a lack of participative management. More often than not strikes appear to be caused by economic issues, disciplinary actions or dismissals. Yet a particular action may have been attributed to one of these causes mainly because they are more easily recognisable or understandable. In the meantime there may be other, more important, underlying causes. Consequently, managements should not accept the supposed cause of a strike at face value, but should attempt to discover the real issues and deal with these during negotiations with the union or employees.

Classification of Strikes The classification of strikes is directly related to the general purposes of strike action.

Demonstration strikes
This refers to those actions intended primarily to display dissatisfaction, as a preliminary to negotiation or to further negotiation.

Recognition strikes
These are actions in which it is intended, by a show of strength, to make management recognise the employees' right to representation or to closer consideration of their demands.

Procedural strikes
This type of strike occurs after procedures or negotiations have been exhausted or are thought to have been exhausted. As no agreement has been reached, a deadlock situation has arisen. In these circumstances, strike action may be seen as a 'last resort' attempt to break the deadlock and to reinstitute negotiations under different presuppositions.

Strategic strikes
These are strikes instituted to consolidate the union's position at a particular plant or in a particular industry or area. They are, in part, a show of strength and are not caused by immediate grievances or demands.

Sympathy or solidarity strikes
It often happens that other employees at a plant, at other plants belonging to the same company, in other organisations in the same industry or area, or belonging to the same union or federation, institute strike action to display solidarity with

a group of striking employees. These sympathy strikers have no issue with their own employers, but their purpose is to pressurise the employer against whom the original action was launched. By engaging in sympathy action, strikers may persuade their own employers to place pressure for settlement on the 'offending' employer. Sympathy actions could extend nationally and internationally, particularly where multinational employers are involved.

Strikes may also be classified in terms of their extent. Thus a certain action may be described as a **plant-level** strike, an **industry strike**, a **company-wide strike** or a **general strike**. Actions of the latter type would involve all employees, and demands made would be more political in nature. This leads to the question as to whether such actions are strikes in the real sense of the word, since strike action is essentially directed at gaining concessions from a particular employer. Thus general strikes, although they take the form of a stayaway from work, could be more readily termed political actions, their main purpose being to obtain political or other concessions from government. Yet, because they are intended also to urge employers to place pressure on government, they could be regarded as employment-related. The same arguments which apply to general strikes, apply to more localised **political strikes**.

A final classification of strike actions arises from their degree of 'legitimacy' within the system. Where legal provisions for strike action exist, there is a classification into **legal** and **illegal** strikes. Where employer–employee/union provisions for strike action exist, a particular strike may be described as **constitutional** or **unconstitutional** and **procedural** or **spontaneous**. The last differentiation of this kind is that between actions authorised by the union and those undertaken by employees without deferring to their union; hence the division into **union-authorised** and **wildcat** strikes.

The type of classification used will ultimately depend on the nature and purpose of the analysis being undertaken.

Factors Contributing to the Incidence and Continuation of Strikes	Although every strike is, in essence, a unique occurrence, certain general problems can be discerned by studying strike actions in different countries over a number of years. One such pattern is the propensity to strike action induced by certain circumstances. The isolation of factors contributing to a higher propensity to strike activity does not necessarily mean that, where these factors are not present, strikes will not occur — merely that strikes are likely to occur more easily and more frequently where these circumstances do exist. Factors usually regarded as contributing to strike-proneness or as influencing the incidence of strike action include the following.

Shifts in the Business Cycle

It is generally believed that unions will more readily engage in strike action during a period of economic growth than during a recession. With an upward movement of the business cycle, labour is in increased demand. Employers become intent on reaching higher production targets, and any interference with the production process will impact more seriously on employers than at a time of declining economic activity. Also, as labour becomes scarcer, employers are unable easily to replace or substitute striking employees. In these circumstances the union can afford to strike, and even an action of short duration will have a major impact on the business of the employer. During a recession, when jobs are in high demand and the employer may have produced more than he can sell, the position could be reversed. The employer is more willing or ready to sustain strike action and may even welcome the temporary closure of his plant.

This is the theoretical situation. In practice it could happen that the decrease in strike action during a recession is not as marked as might be expected. One of the reasons is that employees might still harbour the high expectations which were nurtured during a period of economic prosperity. These expectations might be carried some distance into a recession. Furthermore, employees might be obliged to use all means at their disposal to preserve their positions and wage levels, even to the point of strike action. A very important consideration is the fact that employers, who might more readily agree to employee demands during times of economic prosperity, tend to dig in their heels once the economy starts declining. Consequently, it has been found that, although there may be a decrease in the frequency of strikes during a recession, the actions which do occur are often of a longer duration.

Homogeneous Work Groups
Kerr and Siegel, who conducted detailed research on strike propensity, found that strikes are more likely to occur where employees come from the same community and particularly if such communities are themselves homogeneous and isolated from others. Thus miners who work together and live in the same community, separated from other communities, will more readily engage in strike action than manufacturing workers who are drawn from different, geographically spread communities. Homogeneity of the work group and its reflection in the community not only results in greater solidarity amongst the workforce but also facilitates union organisation. The relevance of this to South Africa, with its migrant labour system and its previous political isolation of certain communities, is self-evident.

Community Support
Closely related to the previous factor is the influence of community support. Such support sustains strikers in their action and increases the pressure on employers for the settlement of disputes.

Industry Location
Business concerns situated close to other concerns, particularly those of the same kind, are more susceptible to industrial action than would otherwise be the case. News travels rapidly along the employee grapevine, and it is easier for unions to organise employees who are in a geographically closed area. Proximity to the actual communities by whom labour is provided further increases the likelihood of action. Industry location is one of the main reasons why the Vaal Triangle and the Durban–Pietermaritzburg areas have shown higher strike frequency than other areas in South Africa.

The Nature of the Work Process
Unpleasant, monotonous work lends itself more easily to strike action than work of a lighter or more interesting nature. Hard work may, in the first place, draw more militant workers. Furthermore, where work is dirty or hard or has become

so mechanised that it is boring, employees may engage in strike action merely to gain temporary relief.

Organisation for Industrial Relations

Where employers are reluctant to recognise unions or to concede to any union demands and where relationships remain fragile, strike action is more likely to occur. There also tends to be a greater incidence of strike action if bargaining takes place on a decentralised rather than a centralised level, although centralised actions, when they do occur, are on a larger scale. Certain theorists believe that strike action increases as relationships become more formalised. This is not necessarily so, since formalised relationships lead to the institution of procedures for dispute settlement and negotiation, which are not present in non-formalised relationships. Such procedures tend to minimise the possibility of strike action, although strikes which do occur may be longer in duration.

The Strength of the Union Movement

A strong union, which has organised effectively and is assured of the support of its members, will more easily engage in strike action than its weaker counterpart. On the other hand, unions in the process of growth may, despite relatively weak positions, stage strategic strike actions to create awareness of their existence, but these strikes are usually shortlived as the union does not have the organisational resources for sustained action. Generally, union strength — more so than weakness — will contribute to the incidence of strike action. This is particularly so if a union has built up sufficient resources to pay strike funds during the course of an action.

Inter-Union Rivalry

Multiunionism and the subsequent heightened inter-union rivalry is likely to lead to an escalation in strike action by all the unions involved.

Government Attitudes and Legislation

Where a government has imposed severe limitations on strike action or has provided an effective dispute settlement machinery, the incidence of strikes may decrease. The converse also holds, in that a complete absence of parameters or limitations will increase the likelihood of strikes occurring. Furthermore, too severe a limitation on action may lead to general dissatisfaction and to a sudden increase in strike action, against the expected trend.

Company Size

Studies have proved that larger organisations tend to be more strike-prone than their smaller counterparts. This is attributed mainly to the fact that large undertakings have cumbersome organisational structures, leading to insufficient communication between employees and managers. Also, large organisations lend themselves more easily to depersonalisation of the employee, encouraging him to act as one of a collective.

Profitability and Costs

Companies which are highly profitable may suffer a greater incidence of industrial action, since employees may view themselves as receiving proportionately too small a share of the wealth generated. On the other end of the scale are organisations which operate on a very narrow margin. Their continual emphasis on cost saving may lead to heightened dissatisfaction on the part of the workforce. The least affected appear to be the companies with profits in the middle regions.

Worker-Related Factors

The profile of a particular workforce is important in assessing the propensity to strike action. Older workers are more inclined to avoid strike action, for fear of loss of position and benefits. Equally, the employee who the sole breadwinner of his family may be less inclined to engage in industrial action, whereby the livelihood of his family is threatened. Despite claims to the contrary, there is no proof that females are less inclined to strike than males. The propensity of female employees to strike action would depend on their position within the household. Should they be the sole breadwinners, they might well be less willing than men in a similar position to engage in an action which might endanger their positions and their livelihoods. In general, employees who are materially deprived and have little to lose or who see themselves as completely disadvantaged in society will more readily engage in strike action than their more privileged counterparts. The personal factors involved in propensity to strike action are numerous, and whether a particular factor will be of importance will depend on the totality of other factors.

Public Opinion and the Influence of the Press

Where the press and the public support actions undertaken by unions, the propensity for strikes increases. A sympathetic public and press strengthens the resolve of strikers and their action may even be assisted by the exertion of pressure on employers.

High-Profile Employers

Employers who have a prominent public image will be more frequently subjected to industrial action, since actions against such employers are highly publicised and add to the union's standing.

The factors discussed are interactive. In isolation not one will have a profound effect, but the presence of a number of strike-conducive factors would lead to a general increase in the incidence of strike action or to a lengthening of actions where they do occur.

The Cost of Strike Actions   Strike action is never undertaken without a loss to both sides. In contemplating possible strike action, both unions and employers need to consider the losses they would suffer against the gains to be achieved by holding out on a settlement. To the employees or their union, strike action will entail a loss of wages or a drain on the financial resources of the union. The union might lose institutional security, in the form of loss of members who might take other jobs or by the eventual disenchantment of union members. The goodwill of the employer may diminish and the union's public image may suffer, since it could be viewed as irresponsible or as ignoring the public interest. As for the employer, he will lose operating profits in the short term and the company's market position in the longer term. There may be damage to the plant and equipment, caused by standstill or sabotage. Individual negotiators may lose their standing with top management or shareholders, since they may be seen to have handled the problem badly. The goodwill of employees may be lost, leading to low morale, low productivity, resistance to change and antagonism, and there may be a loss of public image. No company likes to be seen as being at odds with its employees.

Nevertheless, certain gains may be achieved by making a stand. It adds to the credibility of the side making such a stand, lending credence to threats which may otherwise be regarded as idle. It also serves as a warning for the future. As far as the union is concerned, it may lead to greater solidarity amongst members, who will feel that they are fighting for a common cause. Management, on the other hand, may welcome a break in production.

As mentioned in the discussion on negotiations, these costs and benefits have to be offset so that each side may achieve a more realistic perception of its own and the opponent's position. Furthermore, individual costs and benefits need to be looked at against the background of the economy in general, the state of the labour market, the collective bargaining structure, social and political pressures which could be brought to bear and, in the case of the employer, the level of fixed costs, pending orders and the possibility of stockpiling or continuing operations with administrative staff only.

Handling Strike Action

Both employers and unions need to plan for and handle strike action as effectively as possible.

As far as the union is concerned, its primary task is to maintain the morale of the workforce, to ensure that strikers are effectively looked after so that material considerations do not oblige a return to work, and to undertake talks towards the settlement of a strike action or towards the recommencement of negotiations with management. The union will also attempt to elicit as much sympathy action as possible and to exert pressure through other agencies. Publicity is important. This it will gain through pamphlets and the press and also by picketing, where this action is legally permissible. Finally, the union will attempt, as far as is legally possible, to prevent the replacement of striking workers with scab labour. In this respect, careful control has to be exercised, since attempts to prevent scabbing may develop into actual intimidation.

Management, on its part, will attempt to minimise the effects of a strike and to effect a return to work by negotiation with representatives of the striking workers. (For a full strike contingency plan, consult the Annexures.)

A strike action, being the visible manifestation of conflict between the employer and his employees, is a traumatic experience. Nevertheless, if it is handled with calm and from a rational perspective, it can — and usually does — end in a settlement satisfactory to both sides.

Issues Related to Strike Action

Picketing

Picketing has traditionally been regarded as a peaceful method by which striking workers can publicise their action and encourage others to join them. Picketers occupy positions in front of or at the entrance to the place of work, publicise their strike by placards, try to persuade other workers not to cross the picket line and suppliers or customers not to enter the premises. Problems do arise, however, where large numbers of picketers become militant, disturb the peace and attempt forcibly to prevent entry to particular premises. In many cases this results in unpleasant clashes between picketers and police. Also, picketers tend to spread their activities to head offices, other plants belonging to the same organisation, suppliers and allied undertakings. The problems encountered have led to picketing being outlawed in some countries and severely restricted or regulated in others. (An example of a picketing agreement is contained in the in-plant dispute procedure which is included in the Annexures.)

The Role of the Police

The police have no role to play in strikes. It is not their task to act on behalf of management and to disperse strikers or to force employees to return to work. The police may act only as protectors of the public interest. Thus they may act if strikers cause a public disturbance or pose a physical threat to any person or persons, but their duty towards striking employees is, in this respect, the same as towards the general public.

The Problem of Intimidation

Strikes are dependent on solidarity amongst employees. Consequently, it is accepted that strikers will attempt by all means possible to persuade other employees to join their action. The problem is that, in certain instances, strikers do not limit their actions to verbal persuasion, but extend them to include threats and physical assault. It would appear that, while many trade union members emphasise the freedom of association principle, they do not respect its corollary, which is the freedom to disassociate. Management too has its own methods of attempting to intimidate striking employees. Both unions and employers need to guard against intimidation of any kind and, where it does occur, to treat it as a serious or criminal offence.

OTHER EMPLOYEE ACTIONS

Go-Slow Actions A go-slow is a method of withholding labour and affecting production, without actually bringing operations to a standstill. For employees it holds the advantages that they do not lose their wages as easily and that it is more difficult for management to take action against them. Also, since employees are still manning their positions, they cannot be replaced by temporary labour. Go-slows have the same effect as full-scale strikes in that they bring the dissatisfaction or demands of employees to the attention of management, which may lead to the institution of negotiations.

Managements may treat a go-slow in the same manner as a strike and may issue the same warnings which would have been issued had a strike occurred. Where productive work can be accurately measured, the possibility exists that pay may be decreased for below average production.

Overtime Bans A ban on overtime may have an effect similar to a go-slow in that it influences the production levels of the undertaking, especially where the organisation relies on the extension or completion of the work process. It differs from a go-slow in that, in undertakings where there is no agreement to work overtime or where overtime is voluntary, refusing to work overtime is a more legitimate employee action. Where overtime is regulated by contract or agreement, a ban on overtime definitely constitutes a strike action and would be subject to the same consequences. In the case of a legitimate ban, there is often no scope for recourse by the employer. Bans on overtime may be directly linked to employee grievances that wages are kept deliberately low and that overtime is used as a means of enticing employees to supplement their incomes.

The Work-To-Rule

This is a popular action, especially among employees who perform tasks on their own initiative and who produce or do more than they are strictly required to do. The institution of a work-to-rule leads to employees adhering to set hours of work and doing only what they are ordered to do or what they have to do in terms of their contracts of employment. Professional and skilled employees, in particular, can greatly affect the productivity or services of an organisation by instituting an action of this kind.

Product and Service Boycotts

A boycott is an attempt to stop consumers from buying a product marketed by a particular undertaking or from using a service provided by the employer. It is a means of exerting pressure on an employer and affecting the profitability of his undertaking, without direct action being taken by employees. A boycott requires extensive publicity, organisation and persuasion of the consumers in the marketplace. It is best effected where workers, or other members of the public who would be sympathetic to the cause, constitute a significant proportion of such consumers. Also, boycotts are more successful where a company markets one or two well-known products rather than a diversity of lesser-known goods.

Product and service boycotts are normally instituted only after other industrial action has failed. In many instances the employees involved in the original dispute may already have been dismissed. The union continues the dispute with the employer on behalf of these employees and, because its members have been dismissed, the union does not need to concern itself with the adverse effects a boycott may have on the profitability of the undertaking.

Because of the degree of organisation involved, boycotts are not easily undertaken. They are large-scale and serious actions and, as such, constitute a last resort. Their intention is either to punish an employer for past actions or to oblige him to return to the *status quo* as it existed before he took action against his employees. In South Africa the most widely publicised boycotts have been the red meat boycott, the Wilson-Rowntree boycott, the Colgate and Simba Chips boycotts and the boycott of Fattis & Monis' Products.

External Pressures

Employees who are at issue with their employers may attempt to extend their influence by eliciting the sympathy of other employees and employers, suppliers, consumers, the public at large, community leaders and national or international organisations. These persons or organisations are persuaded to interfere in the negotiations or to exert whatever pressure they can bring to bear on the employer concerned. Where the external pressures are numerous and varied or where the person or organisation exerting the pressure is of importance to the employer, this form of action may prove quite effective.

LOCKOUTS BY THE EMPLOYER

The employee's freedom to strike may be balanced by the employer's freedom to a lockout. Just as employees may decide to engage in strike action should their demands not be met by an employer, so the employer may temporarily withhold employment from his employees if they do not agree to his demands or to a settlement proposed by him. In practice, lockouts occur far less frequently than strikes, firstly because employers are more reactive than proactive and, secondly, because an employer has far more to lose, in total, by closing down his operations than an individual employee loses by engaging in strike action. In cases where lockouts are instituted, there is often confusion as to whether the employer locked out employees or they initiated a strike action. This happens because an employer may lock out his employees in reaction to a protest by them. Lockouts may not be undertaken easily, but, when they are instituted, they bring the reciprocal power of the employer to the attention of the employee.

ASSESSMENT OF INDUSTRIAL ACTION

To the public at large and to some students of the subject, industrial action constitutes the most important and most sensational aspect of industrial relations. While industrial action is important, it needs to be carefully handled. It is only part of a web of interrelated processes and should preferably constitute the last resort following a period of protracted negotiation.

STRIKES AND LOCKOUTS IN SOUTH AFRICA

The Legal Position   Strike and lockout action is not, except in essential services, forbidden in South African labour legislation but, in terms of the Labour Relations Act, strikes and lockouts may occur only if the prescribed dispute settlement machinery has been used. This does not mean that so-called spontaneous strikes do not occur. They have and still do occur very frequently, but are then termed to be 'illegal' strikes, as compared to the 'legal' strikes which occur after use of the official dispute settlement machinery.

The legislation is even-handed in that it allows employers and employees the same rights to industrial action for the purpose of pressing a demand. The employer is as entitled to lock out employees as the latter are to go on strike — provided, of course, that in both cases the dispute settlement procedures have been followed.

Definitions   The new Labour Relations Act defines a **strike** as the **partial** or **complete collective** refusal to work, or the **retardation** or **obstruction** of work, by persons who are or were in the employ of the **same employer or different employers**, with a view to settling a grievance or resolving a dispute relating to **any matter of mutual interest** to the employer and the employee, and includes the refusal to work overtime, whether such overtime is compulsory or voluntary.

A strike, therefore, need not necessarily take the form of a complete refusal to work and can include a go-slow or sit-in. Furthermore, the refusal to work overtime can constitute a strike action. Since confusion may exist as to the question of voluntary overtime, it is taken that this refers to non-contractual but customary overtime or to a situation in which employees have agreed to work overtime for a period and then use a ban on such overtime to pressurise the employer. Where employees have traditionally worked overtime (although they are not obliged to do so in terms of their contract) and then refuse to do so, this refusal may be regarded as a strike. On the other hand, it seems improbable that an employer can suddenly request employees to work overtime and then describe their refusal as a strike.

A **lockout** is defined as the action by the employer of locking out employees from the workplace, with the **purpose of obliging employees to comply with any demand** relating to any **matter of mutual interest** between the employer and employees, **regardless** of whether the employer in the process **breaches the contracts of employment** of the employees.

From the provisions of the Act it could be deduced that, before an employer can lock out, he would have to make a legitimate demand of his employees. This could be taken as denying the employer the right to lock out in reaction to a strike. Should the employer wish to lock out, he would have to make the demand, negotiate with employees or their representatives, reach deadlock, declare a dispute and follow the relevant dispute settlement procedure. He could not merely 'latch on' to a dispute and dispute settlement process initiated by employees or the union. There is, however, a lack of clarity in the Act regarding this matter as other parts of the statute mention a lockout in reaction to a strike. This could refer to an illegal strike, but even then the employer would have to make a demand of the employees (such as a plea to return to work) before he could legitimately lock them out. As it is, a lockout in reaction to a strike does appear somewhat futile.

It should also be noted that the definition protects the employer from legal action for breach of contract. This is reciprocal to the employees' newly instituted right to strike whereby an employee cannot be dismissed for breach of contract should be participate in a legal strike (see below).

Prohibitions on Strike Action

Strikes are prohibited where —

- the parties are bound by a collective agreement prohibiting such action as regards the issue in dispute,
- an agreement obliges the parties to take the issue to arbitration,
- the issue in dispute *may*, in terms of the Act, be taken to arbitration or to the Labour Court,
- the parties are engaged in an essential or maintenance service, or
- the parties are bound by an arbitration award, a collective agreement or a determination for a statutory council made in terms of the Wage Act, unless a period of twelve months has expired since the award, agreement or determination came into effect.

The law on strikes where a matter is subject to arbitration excludes strikes in most disputes of right. However, the Act does provide that strikes can be initiated in disputes relating to organisational rights, even though these could be subjected to arbitration. The legislators have thus decided that, when an employer refuses to grant such rights, the union (if it prefers to do so) may still resort to the use of power in order to force the granting of organisational rights. Should the union elect to follow this route it may not, for a period of twelve months following notification of the strike, submit the issue in dispute to arbitration. Other than the above, the Act also makes provision for the parties to conclude their own agreements outlawing strikes or particular issues which may not be covered by statute.

Essential Services

Essential services include any service the interruption of which may endanger the lives, personal health or safety of the entire population or a part of the population, as well as the parliamentary service and the South African Police. Any disputes in these sectors, whether they constitute disputes of right or of interest, cannot be settled by the use of economic power (see section on Dispute Settlement Procedures). The only alternative, therefore, is to use mediation and arbitration or legal adjudication. It is obvious that any medical or emergency service, such as firefighting, would be classified as an essential service. Persons involved with the supply of water to the general public may also be regarded as involved in an essential service, while the interruption of rubbish collection over a long period may eventually render this, too, an essential service.

The law provides for the establishment of an Essential Services Committee by the Minister, in consultation with NEDLAC. It will be the task of this committee to decide which services should be designated 'essential services', after hearing representations from concerned parties. The committee may also endorse any collective agreement providing for the maintenance of **minimum services** which are then classified as essential services as regards that employer and his employees. However, the disputes procedure applicable to essential services in general will not apply to such minimum services. It is taken that the agreement between the parties will provide for suitable dispute settlement and that employees in a minimum service who engage in strike action could be interdicted by the employer.

Maintenance services are described in the Act as services the interruption of which would result in physical and material damage to plant or machinery. Should there be no collective agreement as regards a maintenance service, the employer may apply to the Essential Services Committee to have the whole or part of his operation declared as a maintenance service. A copy of such application must be served on all interested parties. The law states that, if his operation or a part thereof has been declared a maintenance service, the employer may not during the course of a protected (legal) strike employ substitute (scab) labour. Since employees may not engage in a legal strike if the entire operation has been declared a maintenance service, it can be taken that this provision relates only to operations where a part thereof has been declared to be a maintenance service or to instances where staff not engaged in the actual operation go on strike.

Strike and Lockout Procedures

Employees are granted the right to strike and employers the right to lock out if the dispute has been referred to a bargaining council having jurisdiction or to the Commission and a period of thirty days (or whatever long period the parties may have agreed upon) has elapsed since the referral of the dispute. A party which intends to strike or lock out must give the other party to the dispute at least 48 hours' notice of its intention to undertake industrial action. In the case where the State is the employer, the notice period is extended to seven days. Where the issue in dispute centres in a refusal to bargain, the dispute must have been submitted to advisory arbitration and an award containing a pronouncement on the issue must have been made. The refusal to bargain includes the refusal to recognise a union or to agree to the establishment of a bargaining council, the cancellation of recognition, the resignation of a party from a bargaining council or a dispute relating to appropriate bargaining units and levels or bargaining content.

The procedures outline above need not be followed when a dispute arises in a bargaining council and that council has acted in terms of its constitution, where a collective agreement determines the disputes procedure to be used, where employees strike in reaction to an illegal lockout or an employer locks out in reaction to an illegal strike, and where employees have brought an action regarding unilateral changes in terms and conditions of service and the employer refuses, within 48 hours of the action being brought, to reinstate the terms and conditions which existed before the changes were made. Thus particularly the last two items provide for immediate strikes and lockouts in certain circumstances.

Scab Labour
During consultation on the proposed new legislation, the use of scab or substitute labour by employers during the course of a legal strike was a contentious issue between employer and employee representatives in NEDLAC. Despite vehement opposition from the unions, the Act does not prohibit the employment of replacement labour. Also, as mentioned above, scab labour cannot be employed in designated maintenance services, nor can an employer take in substitute labour during a lockout unless such lockout is in reaction to an illegal strike.

Picketing
Unions may authorise picket lines in support of a legal strike or in protest against any lockout. Such picket lines may be formed in any public place outside the premises of the employer or, with the permission of the employer, on the actual premises. Permission for picketing on the premises may not be unreasonably withheld. It is advisable for employers and worker representatives to establish rules regarding picketing. In the absence of such agreement the CCMA, at the request of either party, will attempt to bring about an agreement and, should these attempts fail, will itself establish picketing rules for the organisation. Such rules may include the right to picket on the premises if the Commission is of the opinion that permission to do so is being unreasonably withheld.

INDEMNITY, LIABILITY AND DISMISSAL OF STRIKERS

Protection from Dismissal
The dismissal of legal strikers has long been the subject of controversy. In terms of the previous legislation, employers could dismiss strikers despite the fact that they had conformed to all statutory provisions. This happened because the sections relating to strike action were negative rather than empowering, in the sense that they merely outlined the conditions under which employees *could not* engage in a legal strike. Furthermore, the Labour Relations Act of 1956 did not

specifically overrule the common law contract. Thus no inherent right to strike was granted, and employees could be dismissed for breach of contract.

The new legislation specifically provides for a 'protected' or legal strike, described as a strike which complies with the provisions of the Act. Moreover, it is explicitly stated that an employee cannot be guilty of delict or breach of contract if engaged in a protected strike and that an employer may not dismiss an employee for participation in or any action in furtherance of a protected strike. Employees are thereby granted the right to strike indefinitely, without fear of dismissal. In addition, no civil legal action may be brought against an employee or employer for participation in or any action in furtherance of a legal strike or lockout, nor will the transgression of any provision of the Basic Conditions of Employment Act or the Wage Act in this respect be regarded as an offence. Failure by the union or employer's association to hold a ballot before a strike or lockout cannot constitute sufficient reason for an action against such union or employers' association, or render the strike or lockout illegal.

This last point contradicts other sections of the Act which oblige unions and employers' associations to provide for a ballot prior to a strike or lockout. In fact, in a certain sense is renders these sections unnecessary since, despite their existence, a strike or lockout may be instituted without holding a ballot. The reason for this anomaly may lie in the fact that employers previously attempted to subvert or delay strike action by technical arguments relating to ballots. The legislators probably have in mind that ballots would still be held by organisations in order to conform to their constitutions and satisfy members, but that the other party will not be able to cause unnecessary delays by questioning such ballots.

An employer is not obliged to pay employees engaged in a protected strike but, where remuneration includes payment in kind (such as accommodation, the provision of food or other basics), he is obliged to continue providing these if the employee so requests. Upon termination of the strike he may recoup the costs by instituting a civil action in the Labour Court.

Finally, despite prohibitions on dismissals and civil action for participation in a strike, the employer is not prevented from either action if the dismissal or civil suit is related to the employee's actions or behaviour during the course of the strike and if this constitutes sufficient reason for dismissal, if any action is a transgression of the law, or if the dismissal is related to the operational requirements of the organisation. This means that the employer may still subject the employee to a disciplinary hearing for misconduct during a strike action; also, that the employer may finally dismiss strikers on the grounds that operational requirements necessitate such dismissals. However, if the employer chose the latter route, he would essentially be engaging in retrenchments and would have to follow the retrenchment procedure as outlined in Chapter 10.

It is expected that the unlimited right to strike now granted to employees will raise a number of problems. Theoretically, employees could strike for a year or more and then return to work. The employer may, in the meantime, have had to survive with substitute labour, which is in itself not satisfactory. Moreover, these employees will have become semi-permanent and he will then have to dismiss them. This would be a difficult situation. It may be argued that the employer could, upon finding the strike to be interminable and the union recalcitrant, advance 'operational requirements' as reason for proposed dismissals. Operational requirements are defined as those based on the 'economic, technological, structural or similar needs of the employer'. Thus the employer might argue that the strike is causing economic hardship. However, economic hardship would be a reason for reducing the labour force, and it may happen that the employer would then have to implement the procedures for retrenchment. Also, this would mean that he could dismiss some of the strikers, but he would not be able to replace them. As it is, the terminology and the definition are vague to the point of being meaningless or, at best, capable of various interpretations. The idea is, of course, that the dispute should be settled as soon as possible; but, where a union is being deliberately obstructive, this may not be achievable.

Illegal or Unprotected Strikes
     The Act grants the Labour Court sole jurisdiction as regards illegal strikes and lockouts, and allows it to grant urgent interdicts prohibiting such actions. The procedures to be followed and the considerations of the Court are outlined hereunder.

Where a party engages or intends to engage in a strike or lockout which is illegal in terms of the Act, the other party may apply to the Labour Court for an

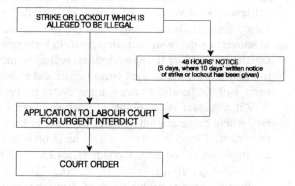

Figure 48: STRIKES AND LOCKOUTS NOT IN CONFORMITY WITH THE ACT

urgent interdict. (See Figure 48.) However, the applicant must give the respondent 48 hours' notice of his intention to apply for such interdict, although the Court may condone shorter notice if the applicant has informed the other party in writing of his intention to lodge an application, if the respondent has a reasonable opportunity to be heard and if there are sound reasons for allowing a shorter notice period. Where notice of the intention to strike or lock out has been given ten days in advance, the applicant for an interdict has to give at least five days' notice of his intentions. However, notice periods are not applicable in the case of an essential or maintenance service.

In granting the interdict, the Labour Court may make an order prohibiting someone from taking part in or promoting an illegal strike or lockout. Furthermore, it may order compensation for any losses suffered after it has considered efforts made to conform to the provisions of the Act and the extent of such efforts, whether the strike or lockout was preplanned and was in reaction to an unfair practice by the other party. The Court also has to take into account the duration of the action, the financial position of each party and the promotion of orderly collective bargaining.

An employer has the right to dismiss illegal strikers. However, the correct procedures still have to be followed. These are discussed in Chapter 10.

Secondary or Sympathy Strikes

In the past, legislation has tried to outlaw or circumscribe sympathy strikes. The new legislation grants employees the right to engage in sympathy strikes subject to the same prohibitions as those applicable to legal strikes and to a notice period of seven days. Furthermore, the nature and extent of the sympathy strike should be reasonable as far as its possible effect on the business of the original employer is concerned.

Despite the right to a sympathy strike, an employer whose employees are engaged in a sympathy action may, after having followed the procedures described in the previous section, apply to the Labour Court for an urgent interdict prohibiting such strike action. The Court or any party to the action may then request the CCMA to investigate the extent to which the sympathy action will have any effect on the first employer.

The law appears to accept that a secondary action, to be legitimate, must be instituted for the purpose of exerting pressure on the first employer to change his position and that it should not be undertaken merely to express solidarity with other strikers.

Protest Actions

Much argument has revolved around the question as to whether protest actions (and, therefore, the absence from work of employees engaged in such action or stayaway) should constitute a labour relations action. It was argued that, since essentially many of these actions did not really involve employers but were aimed at other agencies, employees had no legitimate right to absent themselves from work for these purposes. However, the new legislation does provide for legal (and, therefore, protected) protests or stayaways the purpose of which is to **promote the socioeconomic interests of workers in general**. No definition of 'socioeconomic interests' is given, but the term can be taken to include such matters as actions against the imposition of certain taxes, protests at cuts in government spending or actions relating to the provision of housing.

Employees engaged in protest actions will be accorded the same protection as legal strikers, provided that the action has been instituted by a registered trade union or federation, that the union or federation has sent a notice by registered mail to NEDLAC stating the reason for and nature of the proposed action and that it has, at least fourteen days before the commencement of such action, given notice to NEDLAC of its intention to continue with the action.

When the procedures outlined have not been followed, the Labour Court will have sole jurisdiction to grant an order prohibiting a person or persons from taking part in or taking any action in furtherance of such protest. The Court may also issue a declaratory order taking into account the nature and duration of the protest, the steps taken by the union or federation to minimise the unfavourable effects of such action and the behaviour of those participating in the protest action. Any employee who acts in contempt of an order of the Labour Court in respect of a protest action loses the protection granted by the law.

The habit of stayaways originated in the previous sociopolitical dispensation. It is to be hoped that the rights now granted in this respect will not be abused within the new order.

Evaluation of Strike Legislation

The legislators have declared themselves to be actively engaged in the promotion of labour peace, and to these ends have instituted rapid dispute settlement procedures and institutions for greater cooperation between employers and employees. Nevertheless, they realise that absolute labour peace cannot be achieved and that some conflicts will eventually result in the flexing of economic muscle. This they have attempted to minimise by allowing legal strikes only in disputes of interest and by suggesting that the parties might agree on other matters to be subjected to arbitration rather than eventual industrial action.

Some would argue that the granting of the right to strike will encourage unions and employees to engage in such actions since employees need no longer fear the loss of their jobs. However, it should be realised that employees will still lose income, which many can ill afford, and that by protracted action they may endanger the continued operation of the organisation, thereby eventually endangering also their own jobs. Nevertheless, the granting of an unlimited right to strike and particularly the legitimisation of socioeconomic protests within the labour relations situation still provide cause for concern, especially in the volatile labour relations climate still existing in this country and with a view to the unsatisfactory economic situation.

Strike Statistics

Frequency

During the ten years until 1990 the number of strikes per year increased steadily, with only a slight drop in 1983 and 1985, owing to recessionary conditions. Statistics published by the Department of Manpower revealed that 948 strikes occurred during 1990, compared with 101 in 1979, 342 in 1981, 469 in 1984, 793 in 1986, 1 148 in 1987, 1 025 in 1988 and 855 in 1989. Man-days lost per strike rose from 678 000 in 1985, 1 309 000 in 1986, 5 825 000 in 1987 and

Year	Strikes and Work Stoppages	Employees Involved
1972	71	9 224
1973	370	98 378
1974	384	59 244
1975	274	23 323
1976	245	28 013
1977	90	15 304
1978	106	14 160
1979	101	22 803
1980	207	61 785
1981	342	92 842
1982	394	141 571
1983	336	64 469
1984	469	181 942
1985	389	239 816
1986	793	424 390
1987	1 148	591 421
1988	1 025	161 679
1989	855	177 712
1990	948	350 938

Table 6: STRIKES AND WORK STOPPAGES IN SOUTH AFRICA, 1972–1990
(Source: Department of Manpower)

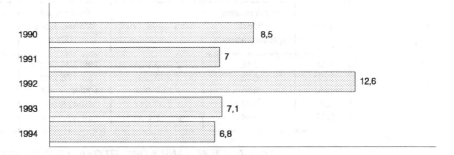

Figure 49: AVERAGE DURATION OF STRIKES 1990-1994
(Source: Department of Labour)

914 380 in 1988 to 1 238 686 in 1989 and 2 973 921 in 1990, while average
duration of strikes increased from 2,8 days in 1980 to 9,9 days in 1987. In 1988,
1989 and 1990 the average duration was 5,6, 7,0 and 8,5 days respectively. As
can be seen from the figures, a peak was reached in 1987, whereafter there was
a drop in 1988 and 1989; but 1990 again showed a steady increase.

On the other hand, a significant drop in strike activity was noted in 1991
which, being the year indicative of radical sociopolitical change, may be
described as the Year of Expectations. Employees, like others in this country,
were adopting a 'wait and see' attitude. From 1992 onwards strike actions again
increased, with only very slight decreases in 1993 and 1994. This can be
ascribed firstly to the perceived need of unions to display their power base within
the changing political circumstances and, of late, to higher expectations and the
perceived lack of any significant change at grassroots level. Overall, the number

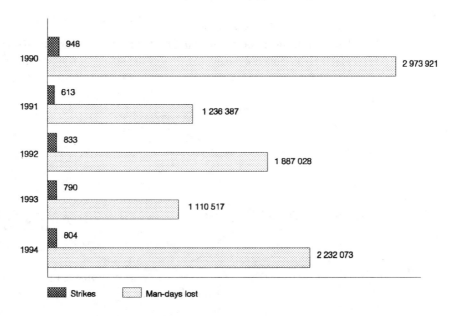

Figure 50: MAN-DAYS LOST PER SECTOR (1994)
(Source: Department of Labour)

Year	Strikes and Work Stoppages	Man-days Lost	Estimated Wages Lost (R)	Workers Involved
1990	948	2 973 921	109 720 398	350 938
1991	613	1 236 381	59 176 463	175 683
1992	883	1 887 028	102 525 755	149 556
1993	790	1 110 517	46 475 331	166 927
1994	804	2 232 073	148 487 876	326 549

Table 7: STRIKES AND WORK STOPPAGES 1990–1994
(Source: Department of Labour)

of man-days lost did not show any significant decrease from the previous decade.

The greatest loss occurred in the manufacturing sector, followed by the mining, trade and accommodation sectors and, thereafter, local authorities and services. The average duration of strikes ranged from a high of 12,6 days in 1992 to 7 days in 1991, compared to the previous 99 days in 1987 and 3,1 days in 1986. While before 1979 South Africa had, in comparison with other countries, a low strike-proneness, it is now regarded as a country with a high strike intensity and, although by 1986 it did not yet match countries such as Italy and the United Kingdom, it was close in intensity to the United States of America. The higher incidence of strike action is attributable mainly to the rise of unions representing black employees, the greater militancy of these unions and their actions at plant level. Noteworthy, though, is the fact that, whereas until 1985 almost all strikes were illegal, there is now a greater tendency, also amongst these unions, to engage in legal industrial action.

Reasons for Strike Action
The reason most commonly furnished for strike action is a demand for higher wages. It is thus not surprising that in the statistics wages should feature as the reason for the majority of strikes which occurred during 1994 (see Figure 52),

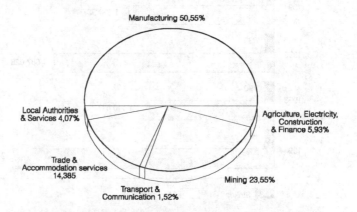

Figure 51: MAN-DAYS LOST PER SECTOR, 1994
(Source: Department of Labour)

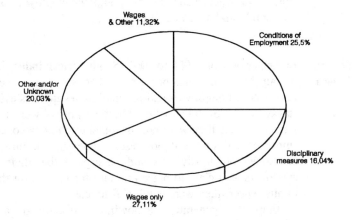

Figure 52: REASONS FOR STRIKES (1994)
(Source: Department of Labour)

although strikes over conditions of service and those for unknown reasons feature as prominently. Strikes hinging on wages or unknown causes are often indicative of generalised dissatisfaction. By comparison, other causes such as wages linked with other matters and disciplinary measures are all apparently of similar importance.

Although wages have always featured prominently as a reason for strike action, there were discernible trends in demands by employees since 1980. During 1982 and 1983 numerous strikes were initiated because of the unwillingness of employers to recognise unions at plant level. Once recognition had become more customary, the unions shifted their attention to a demand for a higher minimum wage. This occurred at the beginning of 1983. However, at the end of that year unions were caught by the recession. The result was a general decrease in strike incidence, but an increase in industrial court actions and a greater focus on retrenchments and dismissals. The latter continued for a while to feature as a reason for strike action but, later, strikes related to dismissals and disciplinary measures appeared to be on the decrease, mostly as a result of improved procedures at plant level. In the meantime, employees have seen their real earnings gradually eroding and wage-related strikes are again on the increase. In future, strikes centring in dismissals and other rights issues should definitely decrease, as legal strikes may no longer be instituted regarding such matters.

Secondary Industrial Action

Product or consumer boycotts have, in the past, been used by unions as a method of obliging employers to reconsider their stand. These boycotts have been instituted only after strike action had proved of no avail and after employers concerned had dismissed striking workers. Some actions, such as the boycott of Fattis & Monis' products in the late 1970s and the Henkel boycott in 1982, had the desired effect, while others such as the boycott of red meat in the Cape and the lengthy boycott of Wilson Rowntree products met with limited or no success. Boycotts, if they are to be successful, require extensive organisation, a wide sphere of influence and solidarity amongst employees. Hence they are instituted only rarely and always as a last resort.

Protest Actions In the period from 1988 to 1991, South African industrial relations were marked by an increasing number of worker stayaways, centring in the political grievances of employees and economic grievances as evidenced by the anti-VAT stayaway in November 1991. These stayaways were not included in the strike statistics, since they were not instituted to oblige a concession from a particular employer and thus did not resort under the definition of a strike. Yet, as mentioned previously, it could be argued that their purpose was to oblige employers as a class to place pressure for change on the government and that, in this aspect, they were employer-directed.

Employers generally did not initiate disciplinary action against employees who heeded the call for a stayaway, although a policy of 'no work, no pay' was usually adopted. There were later indications that the employer attitude towards such actions was hardening and that employees who engaged in stayaway action might run a greater risk of dismissal. (Perhaps this is the reason for the legitimisation of such actions in the new labour relations dispensation.) Many employees, on their part, are beginning to doubt the practicality of repeatedly losing wages during such actions.

CONCLUSION

As noted earlier, the new labour relations legislation has, with a few exceptions, not instituted radical changes to the nature of settlement, although it has provided for more explicit and speedier procedures, thereby bringing about more certainty (but also more interference) and the hope of achieving greater labour peace. Whether the expectations of the legislators will be realisable in practice is, at present, solely a matter for speculation.

SOURCES

Brassey, Cameron, Cheadle and Olivier *The New Labour Law*, Juta & Co Ltd, 1987.

Department of Labour *1994 Annual Report*, Government Printer, Pretoria, 1995.

Department of Manpower *Report of the Director General*, Government Printer, Pretoria, 1990.

Green, G D *Industrial Relations*, Pitman, 1987.

Herman, E Edward and Alfred Kuhn *Collective Bargaining and Labour Relations*, Prentice-Hall, 1981.

Kerr, C and A Siegel (Eds) 'The Inner Industry Propensity to Strike', in A Kornhauser *et al*: *Industrial Conflict*, McGraw-Hill, 1954.

Kochan, Thomas *Collective Bargaining and Industrial Relations*, Richard D Irwin, 1980.

Manpower Commission *Annual Report,* Government Printer, Pretoria, 1990.
Salamon, Michael *Industrial Relations Theory and Practice*, Prentice-Hall, 1987.
Thompson, Clive and Paul Benjamin *De Kock's Industrial Laws of South Africa*, Juta & Co Ltd, 1991.

Labour Relations Act (no. 66 of 1995), *Government Gazette* Vol 366 No. 16861, Government Printer, Pretoria, December 1995.

15

INDUSTRIAL DEMOCRACY AND WORKERS' PARTICIPATION

The institution of free collective bargaining places emphasis on the conflict of interests in the labour relationship and allows each party to pursue his self-interest, limited only by the coercive power of the other party. The concepts of industrial democracy and workers' participation, on the other hand, emphasise the need for cooperation between employer and employee and for an employee share in the decisionmaking processes of management. The introduction of more participative systems is a relatively new development and stems from shifting patterns in sociopolitical and economic ideologies, changing value systems and changes in the ownership structure of industrial enterprises. Many societies have moved beyond the support of pure individualism. Industrial activity is regarded also as a social activity, in which employers and employees hold an equal interest and in which employees should have an equal say.

Industrial democracy, in the sense of government for the people by the people, could be achieved only by a system of worker self-management. This interpretation of industrial democracy is, for various reasons, not prevalent in Western societies, most of which still endorse private ownership of the means of production. Instead, efforts towards greater industrial democracy are geared mostly towards certain participative practices.

Participation entails the involvement of the worker in as many facets of his work life as possible. This may occur either directly or indirectly, through elected worker representatives. Systems of participation vary and, while some are merely consultative in nature, others offer the employee a substantial say in the decisionmaking process.

Managements and unions have their own particular reasons for supporting participative programmes. Whereas management may see participation as a means of obtaining greater commitment and cooperation from the workforce, unions view it as a means of extending employee influence and control at the workplace. Perhaps for this reason unions do not greatly favour share participation schemes, which may bring financial rewards for employees and may induce greater commitment on their part, but which do not immediately extend worker control. Both parties may also have certain reservations regarding participation. Managements may object to participation because it delays decisionmaking, takes control out of the hands of the employer and may prioritise employee goals as against the goals of the organisation. Unions, on their part, encounter many practical problems in demarcating areas for participation from those subjected to collective bargaining. Furthermore, they may find it difficult to reconcile their role as challenger of managerial decisions with that of joint decisionmaker. Certain unions take a principled stand against participation because it is used as an alternative to actual worker management.

The introduction of a participation scheme is a slow process and requires the commitment of all concerned. Also, managements which attempt to introduce participation schemes without consulting employees or recognised unions may find that they are unsuccessful. Should a scheme be introduced, it is advisable that the parameters be clearly delimited, but it is as well to remember that participation in one sphere is likely to lead to demands for further participative practices.

In certain countries worker participation and joint decisionmaking schemes are entrenched in law. The degree of compulsion depends largely on sociopolitical influences, government policy and the influence of the trade union movement. In South Africa participation has until now not been prevalent and has never been legally enforced. With the new labour relations legislation this position has changed. Provision has been made for workplace forums, to be initiated by a majority union or unions. These forums, once initiated, will have statutory rights to information and to consultation or co-decisionmaking on certain issues. The concept of forums has had a mixed reception from employers and unions and, because of the provisions governing their implementation and the historically induced industrial relations situation, numerous problems may arise before they prove to be effective. Nevertheless, they provide for the first time a platform for cooperation as opposed to continual confrontation.

For their own part, certain employers have attempted programmes aimed at greater workplace cooperation. Some of these have had limited success, while others have failed mainly because they were only task-related. Cooperatives initiated by unions and other parties have also had mixed success, as have share ownership schemes.

In all, cooperation in the sphere of South African labour relations is still in its infancy and numerous obstacles need to be overcome if this is to become the dominant mode.

THE LABOUR RELATIONSHIP AS A SOCIAL PARTNERSHIP

It has been stated in previous discussions that, while conflict is inherent in the labour relationship, attempts at the containment of conflict are made and the relationship is maintained only because there is a commonality of interest between the employer and his employees. Despite the existence of both commonality and conflict, traditional labour relations structures and systems have been geared mainly to the institutionalisation and containment of conflict by the process of collective bargaining. In collective bargaining trade unions and employers perceive themselves primarily as antagonists, each being intent on achieving his own objectives and on granting as few concessions as possible to the other party. The point of departure is management's traditional prerogative to manage and to make decisions regarding the enterprise and its employees. Trade unions have traditionally not attempted to take over or share this prerogative. They have attempted merely to challenge it and, by collective bargaining, to limit the absolutism of managerial authority.

Until the 1950s free collective bargaining was, with a few exceptions, the focal point of most Western industrial relations systems. During the past thirty to forty years, a gradual shift of focus has occurred, particularly in Western European society. This change has been occasioned firstly by the fact that free collective bargaining, which has as concomitant the freedom to strike, involves high social and economic costs and leads to a polarisation between capital and labour. Secondly, very few undertakings still belong to single entrepreneurs. This change towards more diffused ownership has made it more difficult to distinguish the employer–owner as a separate entity. Thirdly, and more importantly, sociopolitical values and ideologies have changed and, in the economic sphere, support for what might be termed 'raw' capitalism and the absolute rule of the market principle has been mellowed by considerations of social justice and egalitarianism and by the greater interference of governments as protectors of social interest. Whereas, previously, industrial activity was judged mainly from the point of view of employer interests, it has now come to be judged also on the degree to which it promotes the interests and wellbeing of employees. Furthermore, it has been generally accepted that government, including industrial government, cannot take place without the consent of those who are governed, that decisions cannot be taken without involving those who will be affected by the decisions and, finally, that employers have not only an economic responsibility, but also a social responsibility.

The shift in sociopolitical values has found its reflection in the attitudes of employees who now expect to find greater personal satisfaction and meaningfulness in their work. Also, being generally better educated, employees question the absolutism of managerial authority and the managerial right to sole decisionmaking, limited only by concessions granted during the process of collective bargaining. Employees themselves have become more aware and more knowledgeable and aspirations have increased. This has been accompanied by a greater concern for people in society and in the world of business. As a result of the sociopolitical and economic transition and changes in individual values and attitudes, the labour relationship has come to be viewed not merely as an economic relationship in which one party is the author of decisions and the other the executor of such decisions, but more as a socioeconomic partnership where both parties have equal rights, where the decisionmaking process is shared between managers and employees or their representatives, and where profits are distributed on a more egalitarian basis. This has led to demands for the widening of industrial democracy, in the form of increased employee participation, both in the decisionmaking process and in the profits of the undertaking.

THE PRINCIPLES AND PRACTICE OF INDUSTRIAL DEMOCRACY

Political democracy is interpreted to encompass, in its basic form, the principles of equal rights and of government for the people by the people. Such government may occur either on a representational basis or, in small communities, by direct participation of the people in all the decisionmaking processes of a particular society. Both these practices usually lead to government by the majority, which in itself is not necessarily democratic.

If this concept of democracy is transferred to the industrial situation, then industrial democracy encompasses not only equal rights for all involved in the industrial process, but also the government of the industrial process by all concerned or by their elected representatives. Since employees constitute a majority, by head count, in the industrial situation, this would entail government of employees by employees. Industrial democracy in this, its absolute sense, is practised only where a cooperative of workers or worker–managers control the enterprise, as was the case in Yugoslavia. Even there, the workers were ultimately under the control of the State.

Industrial democracy in its ultimate form is not practised in any Western society, although successful individual attempts at cooperative enterprises have been undertaken in particular situations. The introduction of this form of industrial democracy would entail, at present, a significant shift in sociopolitical and economic ideology. Western societies, in essence, still support the principle of private ownership, even if such ownership has been diluted by corporate shareholding. Added to this is the belief that the success of business undertakings depends on professional management. There is also the argument that the principles of political democracy cannot be directly transferred to economic or industrial activity; that, besides the personifiable factors of production, labour and entrepreneurship, the inanimate factors — land and capital — have to be taken into account when apportioning votes in the industrial system. Since it is the entrepreneur who supplies land and capital, his vote should, in terms of this argument, be weighted on the basis of value added and relative input. If this were done, the employer would be entitled to a vote which is, at the very least, equal to that of his employees and management (as representing the employer) would, at the minimum, have an equal say in the government of the enterprise. Consequently, democracy at the place of work would perhaps (if private ownership remains) be better implemented under the guiding principles of 'equal rights, equal value and an equal say' than under the strictly majoritarian principle.

PRINCIPLES OF WORKERS' PARTICIPATION

Workers' participation entails the involvement of the employee in the organisation and planning of the work process, in the establishment of procedures and future processes, in the decisionmaking function at various levels and in the management and policymaking bodies of the undertaking. As such, it can take various forms and could range from mere information sharing and consultation to joint decisionmaking and shared ownership. Workers' participation is actually intended to promote the extension of industrial democracy in the enterprise, in the form of joint government by employees. Thus only those forms of participation where employees share in decisions or are able to influence the actions of management will be regarded as relevant in the present context.

TRADE UNION REPRESENTATION *versus* WORKERS' PARTICIPATION

It could be argued that industrial democracy is best practised by the institutionalisation of free collective bargaining, in that bargaining limits the authority and prerogative of management and allows for the representation of employee interests as against those of management. In similar vein, it could be proposed that trade union representation is an indirect form of workers' participation, particularly since, by the process of collective bargaining, trade unions and employees engage in joint regulation of workplace-related affairs and may jointly solve problems which arise. In practice, it is preferable to distinguish between the two concepts, since the following differences do exist.

- Trade union representation usually places emphasis on the employer–employee conflict, whereas workers' participation tends to promote cooperation, although elements of both conflict and cooperation exist in both practices.
- Trade union representation rests on the bargaining relationship, while workers' participation is based on consensus and the perception of a social and economic partnership.
- A system of workers' participation in the decisionmaking function presupposes that the right of employees to share in the decisionmaking process is accepted. By contrast, collective bargaining recognises the right of the employer to manage and to take important decisions; in collective bargaining, decisions are not shared from the outset, but are challenged once they have been taken or are tempered by consideration of union power.

Salamon has summed up these differences by defining workers' participation as a ' philosophy or style of organisational management which recognises the need and rights of employees, individually or collectively, to be involved with management in areas of the organisation's decisionmaking beyond that normally covered by collective bargaining.'

In many developed systems participation and collective bargaining are supplementary processes. While free collective bargaining continues, participation is instituted to extend employee influence and to deal with aspects which were either omitted in the collective bargaining process or are not suited to collective bargaining.

The differentiation between the collective bargaining function and the participation function does not signify that trade unions and their office bearers cannot be involved in workers' participation schemes. In the majority of systems where participation has been introduced, trade unions have played an important, sometimes dominant, role. Also, the shop steward, being involved as he is in workplace affairs, may act in both a collective bargaining and a participative capacity. Nevertheless, where unions are involved in participation, their emphasis has necessarily to shift from conflict to cooperation, even though they may still represent the interests of their members *vis-à-vis* those of employers. Furthermore, if unions participate at the higher decisionmaking levels, a certain amount of joint responsibility is involved. This has placed unions in a dilemma in terms of their traditional role as antagonists and challengers of managerial decisions.

LEVELS OF PARTICIPATION

Participation may be instituted at various levels of the organisation, largely depending on whether it is task-centred or power-centred, whether it is aimed at participative work practices or at power sharing. If it is instituted from a task-centred approach, participation will be restricted to the lower levels of the undertaking and will encompass mainly the joint organisation and planning of the work process. Power-centred participation entails the involvement of the employee in decisionmaking related to his section, department, plant or the entire undertaking. Industrial democracy can be extended only by the introduction of power-centred participation. Usually the degree of employee share in decisionmaking increases as the level of power-centred participation rises. On the other hand, far-reaching democracy will not be introduced if power is shared only at the highest levels and if there is no task-centred participation.

FORMS OF WORKERS' PARTICIPATION

Direct and Indirect Participation

Before describing the different types of workers' participation, it is necessary to distinguish between direct and indirect forms of participation. In direct participation, the employees themselves are involved in the activity or process; in the case of indirect participation, their involvement occurs through the agency of elected representatives. Decisionmaking, except at the very lowest levels or in very small undertakings, might be too time-consuming if it involved the direct participation of all employees. It follows that meaningful participation takes place mainly by the indirect method and that direct participation is mostly task-centred by nature. It is also interesting to note that employers who favour an individualist approach will attempt to introduce only direct forms of participation. If it is accepted that power-centred participation is achieved by the indirect method, then it may be concluded that such employers wish to engage in participation only to improve task performance and that they do not wish to share power with employees as a collective.

Information Sharing

By information sharing is meant the dissemination of information or communication from management to employees and from employees to various levels of management. Information sharing can be effected by the use of bulletins, notices, house journals, policy statements, briefing sessions, 'hands-on' sessions, discussion groups, informal gatherings and also by the effective utilisation of suggestion boxes, hotlines, open door policies, works committees and grievance procedures. It is generally believed that the continual two-way flow of information alleviates the fear of the unknown on the part of employees and leads to greater acceptance, involvement and commitment. Although any form of participation most definitely rests on full and continuous sharing of information, mere information sharing is not a participation method in the true sense as it does not in any measurable or concrete form extend the employee's sphere of influence. Even though management might, at its discretion, take heed of the suggestions or grievances of employees, final decisionmaking power and authority may still be vested solely in the hands of the employer. Yet in numerous enterprises this is the only type of participative interaction achieved.

Independent Work Organisation

The concept of shared or independent work organisation arose from the need to alleviate the frustration and alienation caused by the fragmentation of modern work processes. The purpose is to motivate the employee to become involved in his tasks, to gain satisfaction from his work and, thereby, to become more productive. The most common methods of achieving these aims are job enrichment, job enlargement and job rotation, all of which may occur if the workforce is divided into independent work groups. These groups are provided with the necessary material and equipment with which to execute their jobs and are left to decide for themselves how the work is to be done, by whom each task will be performed, who is to lead the group and how long each task will take. An incentive may be added in the form of a bonus for increased productivity or a share of the profits made from additional units. Alternatively, employees might be given a budget of their own, with any excess profits being allocated to them. There is no doubt that the independent work group structure, if properly implemented, could increase employee satisfaction. It encourages individual responsibility and discretion, lends itself to immediate feedback, gives the employee the feeling of having made a significant contribution to the total process and allows for the necessary social interaction. In some instances managers and supervisors may fear a loss of control and authority, but this need not be the case, particularly if leadership by management is effective and regular meetings are conducted.

The independent work group does allow the employee a certain measure of control over his working environment, but participation, if it is restricted to this activity, remains at a relatively low level.

Plant-Level Committees or Councils

The use of plant-level committees or councils constitutes one of the most popular forms of employee participation, but many such committees are not truly participative. Plant-level committees may take many forms, some of which are the following.

Liaison Committees

Liaison committees consist equally of management and employee representatives and are essentially consultative in nature. They are intended to promote interaction between management and employees but, since management has a 50 per cent vote on these committees, it is unlikely that any decision not favoured by management would be taken by a committee of this kind. This greatly limits the influence that employees on such committees could exercise in the organisation.

The type of issues dealt with by a liaison committee will be determined by its constitution and could range from simple physical and hygiene-related matters to conditions of work, workplace procedures and future organisational plans. The higher the level of the issues involved, the greater will be the effectiveness of the committee; but, even so, managerial representatives on these committees are under no obligation to agree to the requests or demands of the employee representatives. This detracts from the effectiveness of liaison committees as participative structures. Yet liaison committees do serve some purpose. At the least, employees are granted the opportunity of bringing their interests to the attention of management. At the best, they are consulted on matters of importance to them and to the company.

Workers' Committees

Workers' committees are comprised solely or mainly of representatives elected by employees. Decisions taken by these committees are, therefore, likely to be more unanimous and more influential than those of liaison committees. As in the case of a liaison committee, the range of issues covered by a workers' committee is determined by its constitution. Thus its scope could be unlimited, but, also like a liaison committee, there is no onus on management to take cognisance of the suggestions, decisions and demands of such a committee; again limiting its sphere of influence. On the other hand, there are instances where the agreement between management and employees, or the law itself, obliges management to consult with these committees before taking decisions on certain major issues. A decision on the part of management in the face of objections from the workers' committee might then have legal implications. In these instances committees perform a more truly participative function. Workers' committees which have the support of the entire workforce could also exert a certain amount of pressure on management. Furthermore, employees soon perceive whether committees are merely puppet organisations or not, and they will treat these committees accordingly.

Ultimately, the effectiveness of workers' committees and liaison committees depends on management's true commitment to participative practices and the perceptions employee representatives hold of their roles. If management has instituted the committee system merely as a whitewashing operation and if employee representatives view themselves as second-rate participants, these committees are bound to fail; but, where there is true commitment to participation, consultation and cooperation, committees can prove very effective.

Although committees could raise wage and other demands, particularly where there is no union presence, and although they may exert subtle pressure, committees are usually not collective bargaining agents. If they were to engage in extensive collective bargaining, they would change their status to that of plant-level unions (see Chapters 7 and 10).

Safety Committees

Management and employers may decide among themselves to form any other kind of specifically designated committee. The most prevalent type of committee so formed is that which deals with matters of health and safety. It is generally accepted that health and safety is a very real concern for all employees and that they are entitled to be represented either on safety committees or worker committees established specifically to deal with this issue. In many societies the law regulates the establishment of safety committees and prescribes the powers of worker representatives. In some instances worker representatives act merely in a consultative capacity, while in others they have extensive decisionmaking powers (see Chapter 10).

Shop Steward Committees

Although shop stewards are the trade union appointees at a plant, they are also the elected representatives of a majority of employees. Where there is strong shop steward presence, management tends to consult with the shop stewards' committee before taking any major decisions affecting employees, if only to prevent repercussions from the union. If plant-level bargaining is prevalent, shop stewards will be engaged in collective bargaining, but they will also present employees' grievances and problems to management for discussion and joint problem-solving. Thus they tend to act in a dual capacity as collective bargaining and participative agents, and they could resent the institution of other participative structures in the face of their own organisation. Should ancillary participative structures be established, the areas of operation of shop stewards and, for example, workers' committee representatives or safety representatives will have to be clearly delimited. It usually happens that there is also a strong shop steward presence in these participative bodies.

Comanagement by Workers

In very few instances in Western society does participation extend to comanagement of the undertaking. Ironically, participation is granted — and, in some countries, legally entrenched — on supervisory boards or boards of directors, but the actual management or day-to-day conduct of the undertaking is entrusted only to professional managers. In a few isolated undertakings management allows joint decisionmaking by elected employee representatives, but even here there is usually not parity in numbers and the amount of shared decisions is limited. Were full comanagement to be introduced, employee representatives would share in decisions of all kinds, such as the decision to dismiss or discipline another employee or a manager, to extend or curtail operations or to cut back on wages. In those instances where comanagement is practised, employee representatives share in some, but not all, of these decisions.

The dearth of shared decisionmaking at managerial level speaks of a general resistance among employers to this final encroachment on managerial prerogative. This resistance could be echoed by unions, who may fear the joint responsibility, possible role conflict and cooption of employees involved in such a system.

Joint Decision-making on Supervisory Boards

The principle of joint decisionmaking by employees on supervisory boards or boards of directors is common practice in a number of Western European countries and is supported by a draft directive to this effect issued by the EEC in 1972. The policy allows for employee–directors, elected by employees or trade unions, to be appointed to supervisory boards or boards of directors. These boards decide on general policy for the enterprise and its management team, but usually do not function in an executive capacity; that is, they are not involved in the actual day-to-day running of the enterprise.

In countries where there is no two-tier board structure in the form of a supervisory board and a management board and where one board fulfils both the policymaking and executive functions, there is a general resistance to the appointment of worker–directors (see Chapter 4). It is feared that, if worker–directors are involved also in the management function, there will be continual confrontation between employee and managerial representatives and that urgent decisions may be delayed. The general feeling is that, while it may be all right to involve employees in long-term decisions and the establishment of overall company policy, they lack the expertise to function at management level and would dilute the authority function of management.

Representation on supervisory boards is very rarely on an equity basis. Most commonly, employee representatives constitute one third of the board, the other two thirds being made up of directors elected by the shareholders. Alternatively, the remaining directorial seats could be divided between shareholder–directors and independent experts.

The appointment of worker–directors to supervisory boards does bring about employee participation at the highest decisionmaking level of the enterprise. A more balanced perspective is achieved and more equitable decisions may be taken, since worker–directors are able to represent the interests of employees at this level and to put forward alternatives to managerial proposals. In essence, such worker–directors share in controlling and supervising the functions and policies of management. However, the fact that parity representation is not granted begs the question as to the degree of influence which can be exercised by worker–directors. It also reflects the belief that, if disagreement exists, the final decision should rest with the shareholders or, at the least, with shareholders and appointed experts.

There is no doubt that joint decisionmaking at supervisory board level, as it is practised, may greatly extend the influence of employees in the undertaking, but it does not grant them an equal say or an active part in the day-to-day conduct of the undertaking's affairs. It is, in fact, questionable whether some trade unions would desire this kind of coresponsibility. Both the question of parity representation and that of actual comanagement are very hotly debated topics.

Profit-Sharing Schemes   The introduction of profit-sharing schemes shifts the emphasis from a share in the decisionmaking and work process to a share in the financial rewards earned by employers and employees while engaged in economic activity. Profit-sharing schemes provide for a fixed proportion of company profits to be paid to all employees, either individually or to a fund established for the benefit of the employees. Schemes of this nature are intended to bring about a fairer distribution of wealth. They may also act as incentive to employees to cut costs and increase productivity and could result in greater cooperation, arising from the perception of mutually created gain. However, unless profit sharing is accompanied by other participative practices, the employee does not gain greater control over his working life and participation, in the decisionmaking sense, is not achieved.

Share Ownership Schemes   Share ownership schemes are intended to counter the employer–employee dichotomy by making employees also the owners of industrial property or, more specifically, part owners of the company for which they work. It could be said that share ownership schemes are the capitalist answer to the more socialistically conceived cooperatives. If carried to the full, share ownership schemes would eventually allow employees to become their own employers.

Under share ownership schemes employees are encouraged to buy shares or are granted shares in the company. Usually there is a prohibition on the sale of such shares for a predetermined number of years. It is believed that, even more than in the case of profit sharing, share ownership encourages commitment to the enterprise and eradicates employer–employee conflict. It is also argued that the position of shareholder allows the employee to participate in decisionmaking at the highest level. He may, theoretically, become a member of the board of directors.

In practice, employees have not proved to be as enthusiastic about share ownership as might have been expected. One reason for this is the fact that share ownership does not bring about immediate concrete results, in the form of an improved standard of living. Thus, particularly where employees perceive themselves as economically deprived, the preference may be for direct economic rewards rather than for intangible investments. Proof of this may be found in the fact that, very often in the past, shares issued have been sold by employees almost immediately after restrictions on sales were lifted. Another reason for non-acceptance is the inability of employees to perceive in share ownership any increased opportunity for employee participation in decisions or for the control of the work situation. Most employees do not see that, by attending shareholders' meetings, they could influence the decisions which affect their working lives. This is especially so if employees hold only a minority of the total shares. Even if they attended shareholders' meetings, their opinions would not hold much sway. Thirdly, employees may not accept shareholder schemes because they view these as a promotion of the capitalist system and as contrary to their ideological beliefs. The counterargument to this standpoint would be that shareholding promotes shared ownership in the same way as cooperatives. Nevertheless, even if they accept this argument, employees still reject share ownership because it does not require the same labour input from all those who hold shares in the company. Consequently, shareholding schemes are likely to succeed only where employees subscribe to the same ideologies as employers, or where share ownership occurs through the collective.

Cooperative Enterprises

Cooperative, worker-managed enterprises have long been the ideal of the socialist worker movement. This ideal appeared to have reached fruition in the State-run collectives established by Marxist governments, but economically most of these ended in failure, as proved by the gradual reversion to systems of private ownership within these societies during the past decade. However, it should be pointed out that, in most of these countries, true cooperatives (that is, organisations owned and managed by 'employees') did not exist. Governments established themselves as owners of the tools of production and coordinators, planners and distributors of the fruits of production and, more often than not, technocrats or party leaders were in charge of running the organisation. No wonder, then, that employees were often no better (and, very often, worse) off than in capitalist systems and that the practice of Taylorism in its traditional form was much in evidence in these systems. Consequently, those who still strongly support the cooperative ideal attribute their failure in these systems to the dominant role of the State and to the corruption practised by bureaucrats and technocrats placed in positions of power. Others would argue that the dearth of free market competition is largely responsible for the collapse of these systems.

Cooperatives have been established also in capitalist-orientated societies, including South Africa, and some successes have been registered; but in market systems cooperatives generally suffer from a shortage of initial funding. Consequently, they remain small and peripheral, unable to compete on any significant scale with larger enterprises. Added to these problems of scale are other organisational shortcomings, such as a lack of skilled manpower, the absence of business acumen, little or no training directed particularly at cooperatives and difficulties experienced in establishing a democratic ethos. Yet there are theorists who believe these obstacles to be transient and who continue to perceive cooperatives as the only and ultimate vehicle towards the achievement of absolute workplace democracy.

REASONS FOR INTRODUCING AND SUPPORTING PARTICIPATION

The underlying reasons for the increased emphasis on participative systems have already been discussed in the introduction to this chapter. Over and above these general changes in sociopolitical and economic ideology and in value systems, there are particular reasons which employers and unions have for supporting participative programmes.

Employers, in general, see participation as a means of overcoming basic employer–employee conflict and as a step towards cooperation and coalition between employers and employees or trade unions. Furthermore, there is a perceived economic advantage, in that cooperation is seen as bringing about greater commitment and involvement on the part of employees and, thereby, greater motivation and higher productivity.

Employees, and particularly unions, view participation as an extension of employee influence at the workplace, as a means of power sharing and even as a step towards eventual control of the productive system. Participation is also perceived as providing greater protection to employees by the extension of the representational function. The objective of unions in this respect is not necessarily the institution of a cooperative effort, but rather an intensified offensive on the prerogative of management.

The parties to the labour relationship thus approach participation from different angles which may, in turn, give rise to conflict. The best to be hoped for is that a point of compromise can be reached between the two approaches. Also, attention should be drawn to the words of Salamon. He points out that employers still approach any development of workplace relationships from a one-sided perspective and within the framework of ultimate managerial authority, while unions protect the collectivist ethic at all costs. Salamon goes on to contend that true development will occur only if both individualism and collectivism are promoted and if the relationship is ultimately based on the concept of an equal partnership.

THE DISADVANTAGES OF PARTICIPATION

With the introduction of any type of participative scheme it is management which will relinquish some of its traditional prerogative. Yet very often the disadvantages of participation are more strongly emphasised by unions than by management.

Managements most frequently object to participation on the grounds that shared decisionmaking leads to lack of control, that it is a time-consuming process and that, as a result, managerial efficiency may be detrimentally affected. The counterargument to this is that, while participation may lead to temporary or marginal inefficiency, it may result in higher quality, more generally accepted decisions and to increased efficiency and productivity in the long term, but not all managers agree with this argument. Furthermore, if the time spent on achieving consensus is balanced against time wasted on resolving unnecessary conflicts and the disruption caused by industrial action, it may very well be found that participation is not as time-consuming as originally imagined.

Another very important managerial problem is that employees may not have the same objectives as management and that, particularly where employees share in higher level decisions, such employees place their preference for economic benefits and for leisure above the long-term interests of the company. Employees fail thereby to perceive that they themselves may be disadvantaged in the long term. The extent to which this occurs will, of course, depend on the level of commitment of employees and on the degree to which they are trained to make responsible decisions. This latter point is a further source of managerial objection, namely that it is regarded as the responsibility of the employer to equip the employee with the skills which will allow him to participate effectively in the decisions of management.

On the union side there are those unions which argue that participation should be extended at all levels, but that emphasis should be placed on the representation of employee interests, as against those of the employer, rather than on cooperation. This amounts to nothing more than the extension of collective bargaining to all levels of the organisation. The argument is used as a solution to the fears often expressed by some unions that joint responsibility and accountability for decisions will dilute the union's traditional role as challenger of managerial decisions. This conflict between cooperation and antagonism is the greatest dilemma faced by unions, especially where participation at higher decisionmaking levels is introduced. A union which was party to one decision by management might find it very difficult to oppose management in other areas. Cooperation, in general, detracts from the union's role as the antagonist.

The opinion of certain unions is that participation constitutes nothing more than a management ploy to coopt employees, to detract from the challenge of the union and to encourage employees towards greater productivity. Those unions which adopt the radical perspective will resist participation on the grounds that it does not change the capitalist system, but leads to the cooption of employees within the existing framework. Trade unions are particularly suspicious of direct employee participation which is not balanced by any form of indirect or representational participation. In direct participation employees are treated as individuals and commonality of interests, as well as the combined power of employees, is diluted. The direct forms of participation are also those which might encourage commitment and higher productivity, but which do not greatly increase the amount of influence employees are able to wield in the undertaking.

On the more practical level, unions may fear that the introduction of participation schemes will eradicate the traditional boundaries between unions and that the inclusion of non-unionised employees in such schemes will dilute union power. There is, furthermore, the problem of the role conflict which might be experienced by shop stewards who participate at the higher decisionmaking levels, as well as the problem of exact demarcation between participative issues and collective bargaining issues and the problem as to whether trade unions or employees in general should elect representatives to participate in decisionmaking at the higher levels.

Participation, as an industrial relations process, is still in its fledgling stages and, as is being proved in Europe, many more problems may be experienced before a system of participation acceptable to both parties becomes common practice.

IMPLEMENTING A PARTICIPATION SCHEME

Salamon offers some useful guidelines regarding the implementation of participation within an undertaking. He points out that management is inclined to believe that its concept of participation is the only correct one while, in reality, the employer's perception of participatory practices may be extremely limited and may not coincide with that of employees or the union. Consequently, management-initiated participation schemes are frequently doomed to failure. Preferably management should approach participation without any preconceptions and, before developing a participation scheme, should consult with employees or their unions so that a joint strategy may be formulated.

The next step would be to gain both employee and managerial commitment to consultation and shared decisionmaking. Participation should be not merely a boardroom policy but an overall managerial strategy, and should be instituted from the bottom upward as well as from the top downward. Most importantly, participation will fail if all managers are not committed to the process, since individual managers will subvert the efforts of others. This is particularly so where supervisors and junior managers view participation as a threat to their positions and authority. These individuals should be actively involved in the scheme and also in higher managerial level decisions.

The introduction of participation may be more difficult where there is a strong union presence. If this is the case, participation should not be viewed as an alternative to unionism and collective bargaining, but as a complementary process. Therefore, unions and shop stewards have to be involved in plans for greater participation, but not to the exclusion of non-unionised employees.

Participation schemes cannot be introduced without the necessary training. Both managerial and employee representatives need to be trained in the utilisation of participative structures and methods. Employees in particular will have to be given extensive information on the operation of the enterprise. They will need to gain the necessary knowledge and confidence to conduct meetings and to question and evaluate managerial plans and decisions. Both parties will have to learn to approach each other in completely new ways.

It is advisable also that a participation agreement be drawn up between management and employees or the union. Guidelines issued by the British Institute of Management suggest that such agreements should cover the following.

- 'The objectives of the participative system and the principles underlying it
- The range of subjects appropriate to the participative system
- The structure and constitution of any participative institutions which are established, e.g. participation committees or councils
- The terms of reference, method of selection and period of tenure of employee–directors, if such appointments are agreed, and their relationship to employee representatives on the participation committees or council
- Confidentiality of information, where appropriate
- Method of selection of employee representatives
- The role of managers and how their interests as employers are to be represented
- The facilities for employee representatives to carry out their role, and particularly to report back to their constituents
- Training of managers and employee representatives in participative practices'

It is obvious that the introduction of a participation scheme is a long-term process and that participation can most certainly not be effected overnight. There has to be gradual adjustment and a change in the perspectives of both parties. Also, participation is a developing process. Participation in one area will lead to demands for its extension to other areas. Salamon suggests that no limits should be set. Management should accept that, once a participation scheme has been introduced, there is no area which might not, in future, be open to cooperative decisionmaking.

The route towards democratisation will necessarily vary from company to company, as each has its own unique business and unique set of employees. There are no recipes or ideal examples; neither should one slavishly follow the practices of other countries. Democratisation is a process which may necessitate that one pulls the organisation apart from time to time and then puts it together again in a new and improved format. Failures and frustrations and backsliding are unavoidable but, as long as there is progress and one learns along the way, the process will eventually succeed. Also, although there exists no universal formula for democratisation, there are nevertheless seven structural pillars without which the process cannot possibly succeed. These are:

- Integrity
- Trust
- Transparency
- Accountability
- Co-responsibility
- Commitment to the organisation and to change
- Continual, meaningful communication

These seven prerequisites are, in fact, intersupportive — should any one be absent, the entire process will collapse. At the same time it should be emphasised that democratisation is not a one-sided process. All participants, whether from the ranks of management or employees, should carry joint responsibility for the process and for its eventual success.

In the 'hands-on' sphere, three areas will require attention: the industrial relations climate; managerial practices and organisational structures; and, finally, employee attitudes and actions.

THE ROLE OF THE STATE IN PARTICIPATION PRACTICES

The extent to which the State will play a role in the introduction of participation schemes will depend on the extent of its commitment to the promotion of employee interests and on its notion of social justice. Where the State views itself as a more active participant in the labour relationship and where it has committed itself to social justice and the promotion of employee interests in the industrial sphere, it may introduce compulsory participation at various levels, as has happened in countries such as Germany and Sweden, and now appears to be happening in South Africa. The action of the State in this respect will also depend on the influence of the trade union movement and its views on participation. In other instances, where the State is not committed to such an extent or where the trade union movement is divided on the advantages of participation, it has been left to the parties to make their own decisions on the implementation of participative schemes, although certain guidelines or directives might be provided by the State. This is, at present, the position in a number of Western European societies.

WORKERS' PARTICIPATION IN SOUTH AFRICA

The Position in South Africa

Workers' participation, as it is practised in Western Europe, has thus far not been prevalent in South African industrial relations. Unions have in the past concentrated and still concentrate mainly on the collective bargaining function, rather than on participative practices. Historically, the concept of workers' participation was introduced by the Black Labour Relations Regulation Act of 1953 but, as has been seen, the purpose of the workers' committees established was to grant black employees some form of representation as an alternative to unionism and not to bring about improved consultation or a greater share by employees in the decisionmaking process. Ironically white, coloured and Asian employees, whose unions bargained at industrial council level and who would have needed involvement and consultation at the workplace, were not until 1981 granted the statutory right to establish plant-level works councils. The newer unions who thenceforward dominated the labour scene had little need for committee participation, as they were already involved at the workplace by the system of recognition agreements. Of late, the concept of participation has received much attention in government, management and union circles. This has led to the provision for workplace forums in terms of the Labour Relations Act of 1995 (see Chapter 10 and discussion below). It would appear that, albeit in a limited way, the new government is intent on giving employees more say by introducing greater participation at the workplace in the hope of engendering greater cooperation and, hopefully, improved productivity and greater labour peace.

Workplace Forums

The legislation as it pertains to workplace forums has already been discussed in Chapter 10. In future, employers who employ 100 or more persons, if so requested by a majority union, will have to establish forums and engage in consultation and joint decisionmaking on certain matters. The Act limits consultation with forums to matters such as restructuring, organisational changes, retrenchments, job grading, education criteria and merit bonuses, while co-decisionmaking will be undertaken only as regards disciplinary codes and procedures, codes of conduct, affirmative action and changes to benefit schemes. However, as previously stated, participation is a process which gains a momentum of its own and it can be foreseen that the issues subject to consultation and co-decisionmaking will gradually increase, either by agreement between the parties or by law. Furthermore the rights to information granted to unions, shop stewards and forum representatives may, in the future, extend workplace democracy.

The provision for workplace forums has met with a mixed reception from both employers and labour. Employers are, quite naturally, fearful of its implications, citing delayed decisionmaking and possible abuse of information as their main concerns. Many employers are also dissatisfied at the fact that forums can be established only upon the initiative of a majority union or unions. In recent years a number of employers have on their own initiated efforts towards greater cooperation at the workplace, albeit often in a limited and production-orientated form. These employers, non-unionised employees and even minority unions might wish to establish forums, but such forums would have no status in terms of the Labour Relations Act. This should not prevent them from establishing forums and from setting their own ground rules for participation. However, given the history of workplace committees, the fear does exist that employers would merely use such forums as a method of 'control by other means'.

It is as a result of this fear and, perhaps, from a desire to appease and reassure the labour movement that the legislators have seen fit to limit the provision for forums to the union initiative. In doing so, they have inadvertently expressed the opinion that, despite recent developments, the majority of South African employees are not capable of asserting themselves and their rights in an organisational context; alternatively, that employees who are unionised are not sophisticated enough to make a significant contribution on their own, that they may be swamped in forums by non-unionised (mostly white-collar) employees and that they therefore need the union to support them. Whether this is the case is arguable, particularly if one takes into account the successful workplace committees which do exist in some organisations and which sometimes achieve greater gains and a greater say in the organisation than groups belonging to an external union. Many employees may lack education, but a lack of education is not synonymous with a lack of intelligence and opinion. It could be alleged that both unions and the legislators have underestimated South African employees and that, had they not done so, they would have provided all employees with legislated rights to participation and to the necessary education and training (possibly even by the State) which would assist representatives in fulfilling their roles and prevent employers from using forums as instruments of co-option. On the other hand, if they were of the opinion that employees were not yet capable of effective representation on workplace forums, then the provisions should never have been instituted as they would be bound to failure or subject to misuse by either employers or unions.

As it is, the suspicion has been created that the decision to assign the establishment of forums to majority unions was a 'political' decision, rather than a rational one based on the effectiveness or otherwise of such union-initiated forums at the workplace. This suspicion is strengthened if it is considered that the German model (from which the legislators have drawn) does not accord the union the same role in workers' councils as does the South African legislation. If indeed this suspicion is warranted, then, by being political and not rational, the legislators may eventually prove themselves responsible for most of the perceived problems with workplace forums, although the existing and historical labour relations realities will also affect the success or otherwise of such forums.

The South African labour relations reality does merit consideration. The German system of workplace participation was established in a virtual void, following World War II. Consequently a system could be designed without consideration of fixed practices and structures. Furthermore, the German working class (meaning all persons who are employed by others) was not fraught with historical divisions as in South Africa. Trade unionism, on the other hand, had a relatively long history and both employers and employees were not averse to engaging in highly centralised bargaining, leaving the regulation of affairs at a particular workplace to a body representative of all employees. In South Africa, historical divisions among employees still impact on work relations and on the willingness of all employees to pull in one direction. The unions which now dominate have a relatively brief history, the greater part of which centred in workplace organisation, and the move towards centralised bargaining is not only relatively recent but also a matter of contention between employers and employees. Added to this is the still existent distrust between employees and unions on the one hand and employers or their representatives on the other. The tag of 'racial capitalism' still adheres. In these circumstances a paradigm shift to a cooperative system embracing all employees, although desirable, will not materialise immediately and will require the abandonment of positioning and posturing on all sides. Also, the unions would have to surrender what they regard as their central position at the workplace, and satisfy themselves with regulating wages and other important general aspects from a centralised level. This the major unions — given their history and concern for grassroots involvement — are loath to do, as are the smaller unions who have no real interest in centralised bargaining structures and wish to continue operating at workplace level. Even were these problems to be solved, the issue of employee divisions might remain; although, if all employees are represented in the same forum, the process of reconciliation might be facilitated.

In the light of the above, it is not surprising that union reaction to the concept of workplace forums has been ambivalent. On the one hand they see the provisions of the Act as extending employee rights and influence at the workplace and providing unions with information they were hitherto not entitled. On the other hand, they are concerned that the introduction of workplace forums may eventually weaken union organisation and undermine shop steward representation at the workplace, despite the fact that forums will be union-initiated and that the majority union(s) will be entitled to attend all forum meetings. Also, they rightly foresee problems arising with the existence at the workplace of two separate structures in the shape of the shop stewards' committee and the workplace forum. Unions argue that numerous items scheduled to be subject to consultation and co-decisionmaking by forums have in the past been part of the union agenda. Moreover, they could ultimately engage in a show of strength related to demands centring in these issues. Where these matters are subject to joint decisionmaking, this will no longer be possible. (This also reveals that unions still view the use of economic power as the ultimate means of enforcing demands of whatever nature.)

Because of the latter concerns, there are those in the labour movement who would favour consultation but not co-decisionmaking. Not only does joint decisionmaking preclude the right to strike, but it also places joint responsibility on the participants and prevents an eventual challenge from the unions. It would appear that this lies at the root of the unions' problem with workplace forums. As with NEDLAC, they still view themselves as having to take a position *vis-à-vis* employers and even the State, and as enforcing these demands by mass action. (It has even been suggested in one instance that unions which were not satisfied with existing bargaining arrangements should request the establishment of workplace forums and then use these forums for collective bargaining purposes!) Until such time as unions are able to distinguish between bargaining and participation, until both sides cease to revert to the use of coercive power whenever disagreement arises and until a clear distinction is drawn between aspects to be dealt with by bargaining structures and those to be the subject of consultation and co-decisionmaking, a great deal of confusion is bound to exist as regards the functioning of forums, leading to numerous disputes concerning this issue.

As far as the unions are concerned, an ideological issue also exists in that participation in forums could from one perspective be viewed as acceptance of and co-option into the capitalist system while, from the other, it could form a useful base for achieving the eventual socialist ideal of worker control. At present both opinions exist within the labour movement. It is, however, to be hoped that fundamentalists in the union movement do not hijack the unions to serve their own ends rather than those of the employees to whom the unions belong.

At the time of writing, workplace forums have not yet been born and are merely a twinkle in the eye of the legislators. The concept itself is commendable but it could be argued that, given the South African labour relations and sociopolitical scenario, the twinkle is perhaps premature. However desirable, relationships cannot be regulated and enforced by legislation; neither is it possible to satisfy all parties at all times. Nevertheless, the law has been brave in establishing the concept as a possibility and an idea which may bear seed but which might, like the unfair labour practice concept, develop a shape and form of its own — a shape which might, ultimately, be quite different from that envisaged by its originators. Whatever the end result, workplace forums will prove successful only if employers, employees and unions are willing and able to make the necessary paradigm shifts and to learn to trust and be trusted, the one by the other. There is no doubt that, in many respects, the future of labour relations and economic prosperity in South Africa depends on their ability to do just this.

Other Initiatives in More Participative Systems

By 1985 a number of major South African enterprises had become aware of the ills and problems resulting from continued adversarial labour relations. In an effort to improve the relationship and to gain the commitment of employees these companies, together with others which had not been unionised but were progressive by nature, began to implement participative strategies. The strategies vary from quality circles, green areas, 'shared value' and 'relationship by objective' programmes to extensive direct and indirect representation, such as that practised at Volkswagen South Africa. Not all can claim unqualified success, but those which appear to have been most successful are the programmes which recognise the individual as well as the collective and where decisionmaking is shared also at the highest levels of the enterprise. Unfortunately many of the programmes were aimed not at changing the power dynamics within organisations, but mainly at task-related participation. Unions, too, have attempted to establish more democratic business organisations by the promotion of cooperative enterprises. These, likewise, have experienced problems.

As stated so often in this text, the introduction of participative structures is a lengthy and cumulative process. Most business enterprises and unions in this country have taken only the first tentative steps.

Share Ownership Schemes

The continuing conflict in the industrial relations and the sociopolitical spheres in South Africa led to a search for a means of overcoming worker resistance to 'racial capitalism'. Certain companies claimed to have found an answer, or at least a partial answer, in the establishment of employee ownership schemes. These schemes provide for the issue of shares in the company to employees, either by way of a bonus or by means of a loan to the employee, enabling him to buy the shares. It was believed that common ownership would promote participation, result in higher productivity and lead to greater responsibility. Moreover the schemes might, in the view of their proponents, make the free enterprise system more acceptable to the previously disenfranchised workforce and lead to a more equitable distribution of wealth, without sacrificing the capitalist philosophy.

There has been in South Africa a far greater dichotomy between capital and labour than in other Western societies. A polarisation occurred, which may not be erased merely by the issue of capital to employees. The argument that share ownership will enhance appreciation of the free market system is also somewhat idealistic. Share ownership is, even for those raised in a capitalist culture, a nebulous concept. Small shareholders, which employees participating in schemes are, usually do not perceive themselves as having decisionmaking powers or any real influence in the company. The financial rewards from shares might bring temporary relief, but it is doubtful that workers see the financial benefits as reward for the shared commitment of management and labour or that, as a result, they embrace the free market system. There is, furthermore, the unfortunate but incontrovertible fact that especially black workers have for a long time suffered harsh treatment and loss of human dignity at the workplace. The emphasis remains on the assertion of their rights and dignity in this sphere. Thus any financial scheme introduced without coordinate or enhanced rights at the workplace may prove unsuccessful.

When share ownership schemes were first introduced, many unions expressed strong reservations. However, this stance has since mellowed and, while they will not accept share ownership as an alternative to a greater say in workplace affairs, they may view it as an additional benefit. Also, unions themselves are now engaging in investment. This is effected either by communal union investment funds or through investments made by individuals; but, where unions do invest in enterprises, they insist that such enterprises should have proved themselves to be 'responsible' employers.

The acceptance by unions of the fact that they, too, can benefit from shareholding is indicative of a far greater acceptance of the capitalist system and of a move away from an ideologically fundamentalist approach.

CONCLUSION

The concept of industrial democracy is one of the most relevant contemporary industrial relations issues. The shift towards corporate ownership, the convergence of socialist and capitalist principles in society and the questioning of traditional institutions and values has made it necessary to reassess the roles of the employer and employees in the enterprise. It seems unlikely that, if the present trend continues, the absolute authority of management and its right to sole decisionmaking will ever again be unquestioningly accepted. Differences in perceptions as to the depth and breadth of industrial democracy will continue to exist and will be a point of contention between employees, unions and management and among individual unions. Nevertheless, some form of compromise between collective bargaining and cooperation, between management's desire to manage effectively and the employee's desire to be party to decisions affecting him and, finally, between the capitalist–individualistorientation of most employers and the socialist–collectivistideologies of numerous employees will, inevitably, have to be achieved.

SOURCES

Anstey, Mark (Ed) *Worker Participation*, Juta, 1990.

Benjamin, Paul 'Reforming Labour' in *South African Labour Bulletin* Vol. 19 no. 2, Umanyano Publications, May 1995.

Hunt, E and Sherman, Howard J *Economics: An Introduction to Traditional and Radical Views*, Harper & Row, 1978.

Koopman, A D, Nasser, M E and Nel, J *The Corporate Crusaders*, Lexicon, 1987.

Maller, Judy *Conflict and Cooperation*, Ravan Press, 1992.

Pasic, N Giozdavic, S and Radevic, M *Workers Management in Yugoslavia*, International Labour Office, 1982.

Salamon, Michael *Industrial Relations Theory and Practice*, Prentice-Hall, 1987.

The Shop Steward, April/May 1995.

Von Holdt, Karl 'Workplace Forums: Undermining Unions?' in *South African Labour Bulletin* Vol. 9 no. 6, Umanyano Publications, December 1995.

'Minister Encourages Employers to Talk to Unions', *The Argus*, 20 April 1982.
'A Slice of the Wealth Cake', *The Argus*, 18 July 1987.
'ESOPS — More than just a fable on the table in US planning for SA', *The Argus*, 20 October 1987.
'Cashbuild assured of a free rein', *The Sunday Times*, 5 October 1991.

16

ORGANISATIONAL CHANGE AND ORGANISATIONAL DEVELOPMENT

Chapter Fifteen emphasised the need for the institution of democratic practices at the workplace. Because organisations have traditionally been autocratic, democratisation involves change — but it is not the only aspect of change. To keep in step with a rapidly changing world, organisations (and especially South African businesses) have to engage in constant reassessment of all facets of the undertaking.

Organisational theory reveals that, since the commencement of the twentieth century, there have been various approaches to the management of men at work. Unfortunately most of these, such as 'scientific management' and even the 'human relations school' were aimed at keeping employees 'happy' so that they would become more productive. Also the various management or organisational styles outlined by Purcell do not, in the ultimate analysis, respect the equal value and worth of employees and their collective. Salamon states that, unless this happens, true change does not occur.

The change process itself is slow and painstaking. It is often discouraging, as results are not immediately visible. This frustrates most employers and also employees, making the former turn to 'quick fixes' which usually prove to no avail. Organisational change requires, in the first place, a change of heart by all participants and therewith a change in organisational culture. Following this, all stakeholders need to be continually involved in what may prove to be a dynamic and never-ending process.

In South Africa there is another imperative for change: the need to redress imbalances in employee demographics. Regrettably, many affirmative action initiatives hitherto undertaken have been largely cosmetic in nature, benefiting neither the incumbents nor the organisations. It is necessary to realise that affirmative action is not a one-off initiative, but a process which requires strategic planning.

It is self-evident that, as organisations develop and as increasing emphasis is placed on the development of the employer–employee relationship, so the task of the industrial relations specialist will move away from mere negotiation and the institution of IR structures and procedures. Instead, it could be postulated that, in the future, industrial relations as we know it will disappear to make way for organisational development.

THE NEED FOR CHANGE

In South Africa 'change' has become the buzzword of the 1990s and indeed, in the sociopolitical sphere, the country has seen breathtaking change within the past five years. However, even in this arena the process has merely begun. All other things being equal, it will be driven by its own impetus and accelerate over the next ten to twenty years, for South Africa has much catching up to do. This applies not only to the sociopolitical arena but even more so to the economy and to organisational development. Having been isolated — and, in a sense, protected — for so many years, South African organisations now find themselves out of step with new global practices, some initiated as far back as the 1950s. Thus South African business has to change and, although this may seem to be paradoxical, has to change *fast* if it is to survive at all. At the very least, there has to be a rapid change of heart and of perspective.

The inevitability of extended change stems not only from the renewed concern with more democratic practices evidenced in the 'new' South Africa, but also from the global social change which has occurred, albeit imperceptibly, since the end of the 19th century and particularly during the past fifty years. As we stand on the threshold of the 21st century, we often fail to realise that the 20th century has seen phenomenal social change — so much so that the social historian, Baraclough, believes that we are at the commencement of an entirely new era in history. If it is considered that an historical era spans a period of some 100 to 500 years, Baraclough's assertion becomes at the same time both daunting and tremendously exciting.

The global picture has been emphasised since it is essential that we view workplace developments — and particularly democratisation — within this broader context of global change. Should we fail to do so, the very real danger exists that we will be blinkered by changes in our own microcosm, so that organisational change (if it occurs) will be narrowly directed only towards meeting local sociopolitical, economic and legal demands. This will leave us, in twenty to fifty years' time, wondering what happened and where we went wrong. In short, South African managers should place their focus beyond immediate contingencies and circumstances, become proactive rather than reactive, and undergo a radical paradigm shift. If not, all efforts at becoming winning organisations are bound to fail.

Of importance in this context are the symptoms isolated by Baraclough as evidence of the perceived global shift. In particular he mentions the transition from nationalism to globalism, the already evident social and ideological convergence, the rise of mass democracy as a challenge to traditional liberalism, and the removal of class distinctions. Translated to the micro level of business, this signifies a shift to global competition and world-class organisations, a marked change in the ideological orientation of business, a growing necessity for democratisation at the workplace and the removal of status differentiation within the organisation. Thus the demands now facing South African organisations are not merely the whim of a new government (which might change its stance or be replaced), but they are the natural outflow of a historical force leading us in a completely new direction.

In line with this global shift, there is also a perceivable change in the nature and composition of the workforce. Employees now have higher education and skill levels or, in the South African context, are aspiring thereto. There is a far greater awareness of rights, and employees are increasingly demonstrating a strong concern for democracy, ethical and transparent management and social responsibility.

The question is whether management, and particularly South African management, is reacting effectively and proactively to these societal and demographic changes. Certainly, most South African organisations are speaking 'global', but the degree to which they will succeed in becoming world-class organisations will ultimately depend on their ability, or readiness, to change in the remaining aspects isolated by Baraclough. Unfortunately, we cannot be too optimistic. As yet, there is no perceivable shift in the ideological framework of business which, in general, still equates the free market system with raw capitalism, although (of necessity rather than conviction) organisations have been forced to engage in some measure of social responsibility. This strong ideological bias not only hampers change, but also precludes the other essential shifts, namely from pseudo-liberal management to democratisation and from status-linked control to the removal of unnecessary distinctions. Furthermore, it prevents management from recognising the changing employee demographies and empowering employees.

That a shift in ideology away from classical capitalism and liberalism is necessary to achieve true democratisation (and, incidentally, enhanced business performance) was proved by Ricardo Semler, a Brazilian who achieved phenomenal business success by tearing up the rule book and radically shifting paradigms. In countering accusations that his organisational policy is socialistic, Semler says:

> 'In restructuring Semco, we've picked the best from many systems. From capitalism we take the ideas of **personal freedom**, **individualism** and **competition**. From the theory, not the practice, of socialism, we have learned to **control greed** and to **share information and power**.'

The above reveals the essence of a true convergence philosophy. For capitalism to remain acceptable, capitalism must be capitalism for all. To achieve this, it is necessary to curb the over-avariciousness of some owners and managers, to pursue transparency in all our dealings and, most importantly, to relinquish management's (and sometimes also the union's) monopolistic hold on power. It is no coincidence that any attempt to restructure capitalism will inevitably evoke the need to restructure power relationships and that this is also the first step towards democratisation. Monopolistic power underscores unacceptable capitalist practices; conversely, power sharing and empowerment constitute the very essence of democracy. To quote the words of British Labour politician, Tony Benn:

> 'If democracy means anything, it means the establishment of institutions in which an **individual** can **influence his own destiny** by having **some share of control** over his material and human environment.'

It may be argued that most of the major South African organisations are already undergoing change and that serious attempts are being made to involve employees. This may be true. However, a more in-depth study will probably reveal that the change, if any, is either cosmetic in nature or of the 'quick fix' variety (the latter aimed solely at improving productivity and not underscored by the necessary paradigm shift, which would entail also a restructuring of power relationships). Thus South African organisations 'dabble' in total equality programmes, quality circles, teambuilding, profit sharing and incentive schemes, green areas, the reorganisation of work and improved communication structures. While all these programmes are commendable — and, indeed, necessary — they are merely tools in the process towards democratisation. Unless supported by a complete cultural change, at the root of which lie the concepts of power sharing and empowerment, they are doomed to failure.

Nevertheless, it should not be concluded that enhanced productivity should not constitute a reason for change; but rather that, if increased productivity remains the sole *raison d'être* for change and if management is not committed to the democratisation process in itself, either from a sense of history, morality or conviction, the goal of improved productivity will not be achieved. Where management merely adopts the semblance of change or goes about change in a limited and piecemeal fashion in order to achieve its own ends, employees will sooner or later realise that they are being tricked, that the 'Great New Plan' is intended only to make them (the employees) work harder and that the benefits derived are not commensurate with their involvement and effort; in short, that, even if minor changes have occurred at the lower levels, traditional management structures and power hierarchies have remained intact — that nothing has really changed and that they themselves remain powerless. It is, therefore, not surprising that those of socialist and Marxist orientation describe this cosmetic shift in management approach as a move from 'direct control' to 'control by other means'; or, as Salamon would have it, from the coercion of employees to their ultimate seduction.

There is no doubt that South African managers are, at the very least, aware of the need for change; but, much like the previous government, they would prefer to bring about change without relinquishing or sharing power. It is this which eventually renders them powerless — powerless to effect real and lasting change and, thereby, finally to overcome the chronic problem of non-productivity, more aptly described as the wilful restriction of output by employees, for it can be very strongly argued that perceptions of inequity and powerlessness constitute the crux of the productivity dilemma; conversely, that only by democratisation and empowerment will organisations attain that seemingly Utopian state where employees give more, rather than less, than is required of them. The success of organisations which have trodden the road to democratisation forms a case in point.

Unfortunately, to many employers and managers the restructuring of power relationships carries connotations of complete capitulation. They thus resist democratisation, saying that, if they have to go that route, they may as well lie down and let the workers rule. This is a common, but misguided, reaction. As Semler puts it:

> '... *worker involvement doesn't mean that bosses lose power. What we do strip away is the blind irrational authoritarianism that diminishes productivity. We're thrilled that our workers are self-governing and self-*

managing. It means that they care about their jobs and about their company, and that is good for all of us.'

What is needed, therefore, is to replace 'power over ...' with 'power to ...'. In the true sense of democracy, management needs to give employees some say over their own destiny, both in the narrow confines of their particular jobs and on a broader company level. At the same time managers should not hide behind democratisation as an excuse to relinquish their leadership roles. A leaderless organisation is not democratic but anarchic.

At present our labour relations practices rest on traditional pluralism and the institutionalisation of conflict which, it could be argued, empowers management and the union but leaves the employee essentially powerless. Management reacts only to the collective power of the union, while employees themselves remain unable to chart their own destinies. The relationship centres in and is ruled by collective bargaining, the collective withholding of labour, mechanistically implemented procedures and adherence to the letter of the law or the agreement. Unions entrench themselves as challengers of managerial decisions and prerogative, but rarely attempt to share decisions and power and, with it, responsibility. While these approaches may have served our purposes in the past and while conflicts will certainly continue in the future, the time has come for both management and union to shift their emphasis from conflict and 'power over ...' to cooperation, co-responsibility and 'power to ...'.

Understandably, many unions have until very recently resisted all attempts at cooperation, viewing them as nothing more than co-option, both because they distrusted management (and particularly *white* management) and because they too could not conceive of a paradigm other than that to which they had become accustomed. South African managers, on the other hand, may have only themselves to blame since they rarely entered into an equal partnership with unions and employees and frequently used cooperative processes (or, alternatively, concentration on individuals) as a means of undermining the collective. Simultaneously, they expected all traces of conflict to disappear.

It has become obvious that, true to the spirit of institutionalisation by which our industrial relations system has hitherto been governed, management's approach to both unions and employees has, until very recently, lacked any depth or dimension. In order to succeed it will in future become necessary for organisational leaders to engage in what Hickman and Silva call 'complexity management'. This approach rests on the assumption that the management of people and organisations is multilayered and multidimensional; that relationships, processes and structures are not cast in stone but are essentially dynamic and interchangeable in nature. Furthermore, it requires that management becomes proactive rather than reactive; that it recognises the individual and the collective; and that it moves from controlling people through the exercise of reward or coercive power to managing relationships through exerting influence over people (referent power). Also, whereas previously managers concentrated only on making money, they will now have to look also to its equitable distribution and, whereas business in the past seemed to care very little for morality, the business of business will in future get done only if governed by a strong ethical and moral code, applicable to all involved in the organisation. In short, managers need to redefine their role, to become more effective and to develop, with people, ways of becoming more productive and efficient, sharing rewards as they go along. They have, of necessity, to create space wherein employees can grow; to encourage openness and transparency; to share the good and the bad, the dreams and the disappointments. The manager of the future will welcome different views and suggestions, encourage innovation and growth and will never rely only on formal negotiations to regulate relationships. He will resist the temptation to confuse democracy with capitulation of his duty to manage (or, rather, to lead); nor will he be engaged in a continual search for recipes or 'quick fixes' — there are none. Most importantly, he will realise that the process of change and democratisation is lengthy, complex, arduous and ongoing.

As stated previously, the responsibility for change does not rest solely with management. Employees, too, need to undergo a drastic change in perspective and attitude. They need to realise that they are responsible for their own quality of life. This necessitates that they commit themselves to excellence and give value for money. The employee of the future, like the future manager, will need to shift his focus from the immediate and short to the longer term, and will himself become proactive. He will need to engage in continuous self-improvement and to develop the confidence and skill to take the initiative. To do this, he will also have to discard previous attitudes and prejudices and learn to trust anew.

On all sides there is a need to remove the shackles of the 'old era' — both globally and locally, to renounce our reliance on traditional approaches to organisational management and to march into the 21st century from an entirely different direction.

ORGANISATIONAL DEVELOPMENT IN HISTORICAL PERSPECTIVE: TRADITIONAL APPROACHES TO MAN MANAGEMENT

In organisational theory, change is not a new concept. Throughout the 20th century there has been a gradual shirf in thinking on organisational design and the management of man at work. Whereas for the first fifty years changes occurred at a relatively slow pace, the last have of the century has seen change gain its own impetus — to the point where change is now 'the only constant'.

As indicated in a previous chapter, the first two decades of the Twentieth Century saw the evolution of business enterprises from single, owner-managed undertakings to large, very complex and often monopolistic corporations. At the same time, employee resistance to managerial control was increasing. This was particularly so in the case of craft workers, who were possessed of the necessary skill and knowledge to do the job required and who, in that respect, possessed more power than management; but resistance was also prevalent amongst the semiskilled and unskilled, most of whom now belonged to labour unions. In these circumstances it became necessary for managers to regain control of the workplace and, in their attempts to do so, they turned to the newly established behavioural sciences. Thus Industrial Psychology, Industrial Sociology and Management and Organisational Science entered the place of work. Later, as working man demanded more meaning and fulfilment in his work life, the emphasis shifted from direct control to more innovative strategies, but these remained broadly based on the work of the behavioural and organisational scientists.

The Industrial Psychologists and the Development of 'Scientific Management'

Early industrial psychologists viewed man as an essentially biological creature whose actions are determined mainly by hereditary and environmental influences. Having accepted this premise, they suggested that working man could best be 'managed' firstly by promoting the positive aspects and controlling the negative side of his hereditary makeup and, secondly, by organising his environment in such a manner as to promote efficiency and productivity. In the extreme this school of thought assumed that man was by nature more readily influenced by personal, particularly financial, gain, that his emotions sometimes interfered with the pursuit of this self-interest and that he was fundamentally lazy and lacking in self-discipline. Thus the task of management was to encourage man's desire for financial gain, using this as an incentive to ensure improved performance, to try to eliminate the effects of his emotions during this process, to counteract his innate laziness and lack of discipline by strict control and supervision and, finally, to organise the worker's environment in such a way as to ensure maximum productivity.

One of the most influential of the early theorists was F.W. Taylor, who developed the theory of 'Scientific Management'. Initially Taylor's intentions were honourable. He suggested that, by sound practices, management might increase the amount of surplus available and that both parties could then share in the rewards. To these ends he proposed that the best way of performing a task should be scientifically determined. This led to the rise of time and motion studies, production planning, cost analysis and task specialisation. Jobs were broken down into the smallest components possible; wages and bonuses were linked to output; every aspect of work was closely controlled and supervised; and much attention was placed on the physical organisation of work as well as on environmental aspects such as lighting and heating. Furthermore, much use was made of the then newly developed psychological testing methods, particularly when it came to selecting 'the right man for the right job'.

Early Industrial Psychology and the often misapplied theories of Scientific Management reduced working man to an automaton, greedy for personal gain. Although it focused on the individual rather than the group, it paid no attention to the individual needs of employees other than the supposedly all-pervasive need for financial gain. Like so many of the earlier theories, the approach was essentially paternalist and autocratic and ignored — or at least tried to ignore — both the social needs and collective power of workers. It is no wonder that the Scientific Management approach was generally rejected by working man, as evidenced in the case referred to by Thompson, where workers in government arsenals in the United States for more than thirty years resisted the introduction of the stopwatch and the bonus system. Later, behavioural scientists and management alike openly criticised the harshness of this approach, yet it can be postulated that the basic tenets of Scientific Management still influence organisational thinking to this day, that they have to some extent been tacitly accepted by workers and their unions and that they are intermittently revived in neo-scientific incentive schemes and some forms of productivity agreement.

Welfare Capitalism

In their quest to promote worker loyalty and productivity, management turned also to the more paternalist personnel practices and the provision of non-job benefits such as pensions, medical aid and housing subsidies. Hickman and Silva, referring to Loren Baritz's *The Servants of Power*, note his observation that '... management during this period took care of workers in the hope that they would reciprocate with appreciation, loyalty and harder and more efficient work'. They point out that 'Welfare plans covered virtually every aspect of the worker's life, from the moment he or she was hired by a centralised and "scientific" employment department to his retirement with subsequent pension benefits'.

The provision of benefits often coincided with the establishment of in-house committees and grievance procedures to facilitate problem solution and, as such, these attempts may be seen as the forerunners of the Human Relations Approach to man management.

The Bureaucratic Approach

Max Weber, the chief proponent of this approach, believed the bureaucratic form of organisation with its hierarchy of offices, each with a specified function and a mapped out career structure, to be the ideal form of industrial organisation, since it supplanted the discretion of individual managers with a complex and comprehensive system of rules and procedures. This type of 'passionless organisation' would be more efficient than any other organisational structure and would eliminate the propensity to irrational personal emotions and feelings.

It should be noted that the bureaucratic approach did not supplant the Scientific Management school but rather supplemented it in that, as Hickman and Silva note, it coupled '... impersonal standards, rules and procedures with careful specialisation and division of labour'. Each job was narrowly defined and measured by adequate performance. A strict hierarchical structure existed and promotion occurred in terms of rules and mechanistic assessment.

Supporters of the bureaucratic approach may have believed in 'looking after' employees but, again, theirs was essentially a paternalist attitude where the interests of the individual were subordinate to those of the enterprise and management always knew better. At best, employees were indoctrinated to strive towards and adhere to the company's goals and rules. Like the Scientific Management school and the early Human Relations school, it attempted to control the individual in the enterprise. There was no emphasis on individual growth and a total negation of both individual and collective worker rights; yet bureaucratic principles, like Taylorism, still influence management thinking on the labour relationship.

The Human Relations School

Whereas the Industrial Psychologists placed emphasis on the worker as an individual striving for personal gain, the Industrial Sociologists stressed the importance of the work group, group norms and group interaction. Ironically this school of thought arose from the work of Industrial Psychologists such as Elton Mayo who, while engaged in the Hawthorne experiments concerning the effects of physical and psychological factors on productivity, gradually came to the realisation that attention had to be paid also to the worker as a human and social being. Industrial problems came to be seen as human problems requiring human solutions. The answer, according to this school of thought, lay in nurturing good interpersonal relations and promoting the enterprise as a social subgroup rather than as a conglomerate of individuals. Emphasis was placed on extensive counselling of employees, although little was done to allay employee frustrations.

Also, attempts were made to replace informal subgroups with organisational groupings. A satisfied worker, who enjoyed being part of the workgroup and of the organisation and over whom only moderate control was exercised, would also be a more productive worker; thus the satisfaction of the worker's social needs would have as concomitant the achievement of organisational goals. Supporters of this approach were greatly influenced by the work of Chester Barnard, who advocated that management should rationally define and set the goals of the organisation and then gain commitment from employees. This led to numerous motivational studies which attempted to discover non-economic incentives for worker performance. Analysis of numerous questionnaires eventually led researchers to isolate 'fair treatment' as one such incentive. Yet, despite all these efforts, hostility between management and workers continued.

Like the Industrial Psychologists, the Industrial Sociologists believed that the interests and goals of management and those of employees could be compatible. While trade unions were not ignored or outrightly opposed, it was believed that they were only functional when they cooperated with management for the 'common good'.

The Human Relations School, as it came to be known, later fell into disrepute, but it has enjoyed a revival of interest and support, evidenced by the popularity of teamwork as a means of improving relationships and productivity at the workplace. This school of thought cannot be completely ignored or discarded, as social relationships at work and identification with the work group are important factors in the work situation. However, the improvement of human relations should not be seen as a panacea for all work-related problems, nor as a substitute for the legitimate representation of employee interests at the workplace.

Neo-Humanism: Emphasis on Interactions and the Needs of Employees

Since the 1950s organisations have been overrun with various theories on the improvement of work relations, most of which developed from the older schools of thought and particularly the Human Relations school, but with one difference: that the interests and needs of individual workers or groups of workers were now also considered. One of the first theorists to make an impact in this respect was Philip Selznick with his theory of institutional leadership. He proposed that management who exercised positive leadership could influence employees to the advantage of the enterprise. This led to a surge in the popularity of management training, organisational development programmes and the oft-abused practice of sensitivity training. His work was supplemented by that of neo-humanists such as Herzberg, Likert and particularly MacGregor, with his 'X and Y theory'. MacGregor reprimanded management for its traditional view of workers as lazy and incompetent and pointed out that authoritarian management would never achieve the most beneficial results. As a consequence, managers began to concentrate on job enrichment and job enlargement programmes; work environments were redesigned and concepts such as job autonomy, teamwork, group decisionmaking, participatory management and decentralisation of power gained great popularity. Japanese practices in the form of quality circles and productivity programmes were later added, fitting naturally into the new environment — an environment now dominated by the need for a mutually acceptable company culture, based on the principles of quality, innovation and excellence.

Critical
Evaluation

It is evident that even the most modern thinking on the management of man at work accepts the directive role of management and adopts an intrinsically employer-orientated perspective. This forms the basis of criticism by radical thinkers, who view all efforts — including the most progressive thinking on the subject — as an extension of managerial control and as the negation of collective worker power. Yet these critics themselves do not offer viable alternative solutions and do admit that progress has been made in the recognition of the worth of employees and their input. There has thus been evolutionary, if not revolutionary, change in attitudes to and the nature of the labour relationship. In essence, tension between proponents of evolutionary organisational development and their critics centres in the emphasis which might be placed on the individual as against the collective. Although there is as yet no foreseeable solution to this tension, some suggestions are offered by Hickman and Silva who, at the end of *The Future 500*, state that:

> '*To strike the right balance, the complexity manager should champion individuality and collective culture at the same time. We think this will be one of the most pervasive paradoxes of the Twenty-first Century ... As constant agents of change, complexity managers must place moral nobility (responsible leadership) where it belongs, with each individual employee.*
> '*As with so many other dimensions of the future, management of the individual depends more on a new mind-set than on a specific set of skills or tools. While the early entrepreneurs looked down from on high at their organisations and their people, and the professional managers assumed a similar perspective, and while the culture builders of recent years have climbed a long way off the throne to work with their people as colleagues, complexity managers should actually look up at their people. This does not mean that they will fear the power of individuals and their group relationships, nor does it mean that they will abandon their leadership roles, but it does mean that they will treat people with the deepest respect, trust and integrity. This goes far beyond "executive ethics" or "corporate responsibility", because it is the basic principle from which ethics and moral responsibility derive ...*'

THE SPECTRUM OF EMPLOYER–EMPLOYEE RELATIONS: VARIATIONS IN ORGANISATIONAL STYLE

The development of organisations depends to a large extent on the style adopted by management and which, in combination with employee attitudes, ultimately determines the style or culture of the undertaking.

In Chapter 2 the three basic approaches to employer–employee relationships were outlined: the unitary, pluralist and radical. It is obvious that few or no managements would adopt a radical perspective, but that both managers and employees could adopt either a unitary or a pluralist approach. Different combinations of these approaches would thus produce different employer–employee relations and, consequently different organisational styles.

Fox's Spectrum of Employer–Employee Relations

Fox, using unitary and pluralist approaches, later developed a spectrum of employer–employee relationships which could evolve from the adoption of a particular approach by one or the other or both the parties. In terms of Fox's model, five types of relationships could be identified:

- The 'traditional' relationship, in which both parties adopt a unitary perspective. Employees believe that they should promote the aims of the organisation, often at their own cost, and that management really does know best. Despite the rise of unionism, many such relationships still exist.
- The 'sophisticated–modern' relationship, in which both parties adopt a pluralist perspective. They believe that conflict can be handled constructively within the context of an ultimate common goal.
- The 'sophisticated–paternalistic' relationship where management, having been conscientised to industrial relations realities, attempts to establish systems and processes to control conflict, but where employees still adopt a unitary approach and do not assert themselves in relation to management.
- Relationships marked by 'classical conflict and continuous challenge'. Here management persists in adopting a unitary approach, whereas employees view the relationship from a pluralist perspective. They thus attempt to assert their interests in opposition to those of a management which persistently refuses to acknowledge such demands.
- The last, which Fox describes as the 'standard modern' relationship, is characterised by a great deal of ambivalence on both sides. Management has taken cognisance of the pluralist approach but still adopts a mainly unitarist perspective, while employees may intermittently stand up for their rights, but generally continues to believe that it is not wise to 'rock the boat'.

Fox's work was later built upon by Sissons and Purcell, who used his classification to identify various management styles.

The style adopted by a particular party is determined also by other aspects of the perceptual framework such as the ideological basis, trade union interventions and government stances. All of these will influence the type of managerial and organisational style which eventually prevails within the individual enterprise.

The best known work concerning the manner in which management approaches the labour relationship was undertaken by Purcell and Sissons who, enlarging on the work of Fox as regards basic approaches to the labour relationship, originally identified five types of organisational style:

- **The traditional style.** This is attributed to those managers who adopt a unitary approach, openly exploit employees and are overtly antagonistic to any form of unionism. When obliged to deal with unions, they try at all costs to win and constantly resort to the law in their efforts to do so.

- **The sophisticated paternalistic style.** This style is also unitary by nature but is marked by paternalism, which leads managers of this school to emphasise the positive motivation of employees and to attempt to gain employee commitment by good human resource policies. Attention is paid to the individual employee, although teamwork and responsibility to the group are also encouraged.
- **The sophisticated modern style.** Here a pluralist approach is adopted. Management accepts the collective power and collective rights of employees and subscribes to the belief that conflict between the two parties can best be contained by the institutionalisation of collective bargaining and by establishing procedures to regulate behaviours within the relationship. Sophisticated modernism may take two directions. It may be highly constitutionalist in that management will attempt to conduct all aspects of the relationship by regulation and try to define clearly the rights of each party, or it may be loosely consultative. In the latter instance, management does not adhere to a pre-established area of prerogative and it may move gradually to joint regulation and to more frequent consultation.
- **The standard modern style.** This has no clearly defined characteristic since it is pragmatic and reactive by nature. Management approach will be largely dependent on the circumstances and particularly on factors such as sociopolitical developments and union strategies.

Purcell later enlarged the above classification on a two-dimensional basis, using the varying individualist and collectivist orientations of management as the bases. On the individualist axis, managements can be judged by the extent to which their policies endorse the rights of individuals and especially on the extent to which they focus on the development of individual capabilities, while the collectivist dimension reflects managerial attitudes towards collective representation; that is, whether the collective rights of employees are rejected or whether they are accepted and even promoted. On each axis three categories were identified.

On the **individualist axis** are those employers who:

- regard employees merely as another factor of production, to be used and discarded according to the dictates of the market; who exercise strict negative control over such employees and to whom the profit motive is paramount
- adopt a paternalistic attitude towards employees, whom they see as incontrovertibly cast in the role of subordinates in need of gentle regulation and care by means of welfare systems or social responsibility programmes
- acknowledge the importance of employees as a valuable resource, engage in extensive internal training and development programmes, attempt to gain employee commitment by improved communication and involvement, and measure individual worth by regular performance appraisal.

On the **collectivist axis** are those who:

- are outrightly antagonistic to any form of employee collectivity
- view the relationship as basically adversarial, engaging in hard bargaining with employee collectives
- attempt also to gain cooperation from employee collectives by discussing plans and decisions with such collectives and bringing about adaptations as a result of employee inputs.

If the individualist and collectivist dimensions are juxtaposed, a grid is formed as illustrated in Table 8. Within this grid Purcell identified six possible management styles:

- **The traditional style** (autocratic unitarism), marked by low individualism and no collectivism. All other aspects of the organisation are subordinate to management's desire to maximise profits. In the light of this, labour costs are kept as low or as near to market rates as possible. Employees have no sense of job security, and are not recognised as individuals. At the same time, any form of collectivism is actively discouraged. Management style is authoritarian, and conflict or disagreement is vehemently suppressed.
- **The paternalist style** (autocratic paternalism), characterised by moderate individualism and no collectivism. This style is in many ways a more genteel version of the traditional approach. The company 'cares for' the employee, but he is expected to know his place within a strictly hierarchical and bureaucratic structure where there is little upward mobility. Communication and positive motivation are encouraged and the premise is adopted that unions are unnecessary since the company looks after its employees. Where unionisation does appear likely, management will attempt to counter this by promoting a sweetheart union or in-company representation.
- **The sophisticated human relations style** (sophisticated, paternalistic unitarism), where there is high individualism but no collectivism. Here, unions are actively avoided by the promotion and development of the individual and by sophisticated human resource management. Employees are paid higher than average wages and given extensive benefits, and large amounts of money are spent on training and development. There is greater emphasis on employee involvement and communication, and internal bodies may be established for this purpose. Also, companies of this kind become actively involved in community development and social responsibility programmes.
- **Bargained constitutionalism** (constitutional pluralism), marked by low individualism and medium to high collectivism. Managers who adopt this style accept and deal with unions as a matter of expedience; that is, with the ultimate aim of containing conflict and maintaining managerial control. There is agreement to bargain on substantive and a narrow range of procedural issues, but such agreements are marked by the insistence on management's 'right to manage' and any encroachment on this prerogative is strongly resisted. Unions are fairly treated as long as they remain within

EMPLOYEES AS
RESOURCE

		Sophisticated human relations		Sophisticated consultative
I **N** **D** **I** **V** **I** **D** **U** **A** **L** **I** **S** **T**	Emphasis on employee development	Sophisticated human relations		Sophisticated consultative
	Paternalist approach	Traditional Paternalist		Modern paternalist
	Workers as factors of production	Traditional	Bargained constitutional	
EMPLOYEES AS COMMODITY		No collectivism (unitary)	Adversarial collectivism	Cooperation

C O L L E C T I V I S T

Table 8: MANAGEMENT GRID (PURCELL)

the limits of the constitutionally established relationship, and dealings with representative unions are regarded as necessary only in so far as these ensure that discipline and order is maintained and labour unrest is prevented.

- **The modern paternalist style** (paternalistic pluralism), where there is moderate individualism and high collectivism. Here there is a concerted attempt, as Purcell puts it, to build 'constructive' relationships by involving the employee collective in consultation. Consultative structures such as briefing groups are set up throughout the organisation, where matters dealt with include everyday operational issues as well as the objectives of the business and management's plans for change. However, the style is still essentially paternalistic in that management shares its plans with the employees in order to gain collective commitment or collective employee reaction.

- **The sophisticated consultative style** (sophisticated pluralism), marked by high individualism and high collectivism. This style develops from sophisticated paternalism, but here management tries to share all aspects of organisational planning with trade unions and employees, and is receptive to their inputs while still reserving the right to make the final decision. Recognition of the collective does not, however, preclude management from involving employees as individuals and gaining their commitment to organisational goals by teambuilding, quality circles, profit sharing and share ownership schemes.

Strictly to categorise any form of human behaviour — and that on a two-dimensional scale — is well nigh impossible. Consequently, Purcell's managerial styles should not be regarded as absolute or mutually exclusive. Also, it would seem that, as circumstances (in the form of trade union activity and strategy, government legislation and other aspects of the sociopolitical milieu) change, management will develop by an evolutionary process through the different styles. It should, furthermore, be asked whether the sophisticated consultative style would really constitute the epitome of such development. Salamon points out that the Purcell model is limited in that it approaches both individualism and collectivism from a managerial perspective and within the framework of management's ultimate authority. Thus the individualist dimension is based on management's beliefs regarding the extent to which they should meet the needs of employees. As Salamon remarks, 'There appears to be no concern to identify the extent of the employee's "right" to express views or, more importantly, to modify and influence management decisions, even as an individual employee.' Collectivism, on the other hand, is assessed in terms of the degree to which management grants legitimacy to collective structures whereas, according to Salamon, 'The ultimate extreme of this dimension must surely, therefore, be an acceptance of the right of employees through trade unions or other institutional arrangements within the organisation (such as Works Councils), both to share responsibility for decisionmaking on an equal partnership basis and to pursue their interests, as defined by them, in that shared decisionmaking process'. Salamon concludes that '… both axes in reality equate to a spectrum from "coercion" to "seduction" of employees to management perspectives and values' and that 'There appears to be no place within the model for genuine pluralism or partnership between management and employees'. He suggests that attention should be focused on the interaction between management styles (which, he says, could favour individualism or 'suborned' collectivism), union style (usually in favour of collectivism but allowing for a decree of individualism) and 'the Government's expectations of organisational style'. If this is done and if, according to Salamon, the issue is approached from '… a genuine acceptance of pluralism, the legitimate right of both management and employees to pursue their interests and the need for the reconciliation of these differing interests', the logical solution is a style which supports equal partnership in that management's right to manage is antiposed by the employee's right to associate and to exercise power by withholding his labour, his right to engage in co-decisionmaking with management as regards the division of wealth, to decide jointly with management on all organisational issues, to develop collective representational systems and to receive full information. He further suggests that both management and the union would then have the right to initiate and contribute to change, the responsibility to consider initiatives from the other party and '… the responsibility to establish an industrial relations system which recognises both conflict and cooperation, which seeks to achieve mutually acceptable settlements (compromise) and which recognises mutual dependence'. Salamon sums up this approach when he says that:

'… it is only through the existence of a genuine equal partnership that we can realistically consider the development of individualism in terms of enhancing the individual's contribution to the organisation, rewarding *individuals on the basis of their attributes and abilities and, above all, meeting the individual's personal needs for satisfying work, a sense of commitment and identification with the organisation, etc. To seek to develop individualism in the absence of a genuine equal partnership suggests the intention to seduce the employees to management values and undermine, if not abolish, the collectivity. But even then, with a genuine equal collective partnership and an increased sense of individual commitment, we must realise that whilst the individual and the union may be prepared to cooperate in developing the efficiency of the organisation, this does not mean that they must, or will, always and automatically accept management's view of the world — they still have the right to analyse and to seek to influence the situation from what they regard as their perspectives and interest.'*

From the above it is evident that the ideal organisational style has not yet been achieved or even conceptualised. However, there is progressive development through the spectrum of organisational styles, and perhaps this is all that can be hoped for — that, by initiating change, we move continually forward. Should this not, ultimately, be the purpose of organisational development?

THE IMPLEMENTATION OF A CHANGE PROCESS

Whereas an awareness of the need for change and acceptance of its prerequisites constitute the foundation of a change initiative, the change process itself is the most complex and least documented. This perhaps explains why, despite the realisation of the need for change, so little change actually occurs. The task would be simplified were we able to clear the slate completely and commence, so to speak, on virgin territory. In extreme cases or where change is brought about by revolution, this is what occurs. On the other hand, the process of evolutionary change requires that we operate within existing structures and bring about change from within. It does not rest on a single initiative or set of initiatives, but constitutes a continuous, dynamic interaction which will take years to climax. It is often discouraging as, in isolation, developments may be imperceptible. Furthermore, it is not a smooth process since a frequent reversion to the security of old habits is unavoidable (thus the need for periodic reassessment); neither can a step-by-step guide be provided. All aspects of the process are interrelated and the exact format will differ from one institution to another because the variables are never the same.

In organisations which are not proactive, change (or the awareness of the need for change) usually arises from trigger incidents or circumstances. These may be internal in the form of a drop in morale and productivity, employee or customer dissatisfaction (which, in its extreme form, may end in revolt), union initiatives, a change in leadership or new financial hardships and budgetary constraints. Alternatively, external factors such as a change in the sociopolitical dispensation, fresh economic initiatives, changed educational and training policy, a shift in employee or customer demographics and increased competition may serve as triggers for change. Most of these triggers do at present exist in organisations. The emphasis on competence, rather than paper qualifications, has obliged organisations to take a new look at employment practices. As previously stated, the rise of mass democracy has engendered among employees an awareness of their rights and a demand for greater organisational democracy and transparency. This demand must be met if organisational health and progress are to be achieved. Changing population and employee demographies are placing increased pressure on organisations to re-evaluate their practices, and the growing demand for diverse education and training will necessitate far greater flexibility in the application of the workforce. Economic constraints will oblige institutions to become more entrepreneurial in their approach and to search for new ways of creating income rather than expending their energy on preserving and administering income. Organisations which previously each had their own established niche in the market will now be competing in a freer market and will have to reposition themselves within the changed constellation. Finally, the changed sociopolitical situation and subsequent legislation will place new pressures and demands on organisations.

As a first step in the change process, the chief executive officer of the organisation has to become aware of the need for change. However, simple awareness is not enough; nor should change be initiated simply as a 'politically expedient' move. The head of the organisation must himself believe in and be totally committed to the change process. Unfortunately, in most instances CEOs merely pay lip service to the principle. This is easily perceived by other stakeholders, who either relapse into apathy or eventually engage in revolt, as evidenced by the recent spate of strike actions.

Taken that the CEO is committed, he then needs to conscientise others who still hold positions of authority — to make them aware of this need. Transformation workshops, encompassing also interaction and correct sensitivity training, are usually required at this stage as the greatest resistance is bound to come from those in positions of power, particularly where such positions were attained by politicking rather than competence. During this process the CEO should closely observe the reactions and progress of these persons, for he will eventually exclude from any participation in the change initiative those who display extreme or fundamentalist positions or a constant resistance to change. Their presence during ensuing efforts would merely impede the process.

In the second stage, the initiative goes public, commencing with a sincere expression of intent by management, followed by an *indaba* of all internal stakeholder representatives, supported by similar *indabas* at all other levels. The purpose is to build support, commitment and trust, but this cannot be done before the organisation and all participants take a clear and honest look at themselves and admit to past mistakes. This would entail employees and existing management engaging in open exchange and clearly identifying areas of dissatisfaction with either the organisation, other stakeholders or the production process. Since long-existent conflicts are likely to emerge, it may (particularly where the level of distrust and authoritarianism is high) be advisable to engage the services of a facilitator who will assist in depersonalising issues and translating them into problems. The expectations of stakeholders should also be verbalised. This type of interchange requires that positions of equality be established, that previous powerholders relinquish positions or assumptions of power and control and that an atmosphere is created in which all views are accepted and valued. All parties should display a willingness to move from existent paradigms and attitudinal stances, to enter into new relationship patterns and to accept responsibility for the change process. This is to some extent a cathartic process. Certain problems may be minimised or eliminated merely by their verbalisation or by the changed interactions; major problems, however, will have to be addressed. This should be done within the framework of what is real and possible (reality testing) and should preferably be undertaken by representative committees whose duty it will be to remove existent obstacles, such as unnecessary regulations and bureaucratic controls, in order to facilitate future change processes.

During this phase it is essential that the principles of **democracy**, **transparency** and **accountability** be clearly established as basis for any future interactions. All too often CEOs hide behind the bland assumption that these are 'processes' the implementation of which will occur over time. It needs to be clearly established that, although systems to ensure the application of these principles may indeed need to evolve, they are not processes but fundamentals in the light of which all future actions will be judged and without which **trust**, the remaining fundamental, cannot be engendered — thus dooming all future initiatives to 'half life' or to absolute failure.

Admittedly the process as described above is not without its obstacles, arising from all participants. While management may cling doggedly to power and resort to existing systems of control and regulations as a camouflage, employees may not initially be capable of handling their newly established roles and may at first pursue only their own objectives. They may have been dulled into apathy or scepticism by previous practices or past disastrous attempts at change, and may not have the long-term interests of the organisation at heart. These obstacles should be openly addressed and unpacked, and strategies for overcoming them must be put in place. This clearly illustrates the complexity of every stage of the change process and the need for continued communication and workshopping. One *indaba* will not suffice. The position should be reassessed on an ongoing basis, but care should be exercised that participants do not become bogged down in old conflicts. Once these have been verbalised and addressed, a shift to a more positive direction — that is, the fulfilment of expectations and the initiation of concrete change — becomes essential.

Only once a basic cultural shift has occurred can further initiatives towards transformation be undertaken. The first stage of this phase would entail a thorough scanning of the environment and of the organisation's position *vis-à-vis* that environment. Are we placing emphasis on the most relevant areas? In which needs of business and industry will new needs arise? What changes have occurred in the general population and what is the educational, social and experiential profile of this population? What external policy frameworks are being developed or are likely to be developed? Are our systems and structures suited to the new demands? Which technologies are available to facilitate our task? What is being done in South Africa and elsewhere in the world? On which financial resources could we possibly draw? What changes are likely to occur? How can we best position ourselves within the existing and future environment?

Such scanning will provide the organisation with a broad framework for establishing its mission and objectives, but no specific objectives can yet be established as the second part of the exercise — the audit of existing and potential internal resources — still has to be undertaken. This would entail a thorough assessment of the financial, material and human resources of the organisation, and constitutes the reality check which will counteract the setting of unrealistic objectives. However, it may equally create awareness of hitherto untapped resources or, at the very least, lead to the formulation of short-term strategies aimed at expanding or improving the resources: for example, retraining or development of the human resource potential, or renewed attempts to create financial resources.

It is accepted that, in line with the new culture, the above steps will have been undertaken in conjunction with representatives of all stakeholders. The next stage would then commence with the joint establishment of a vision and mission for the organisation and the setting of realistic yet ambitious objectives. In this respect the multilayered nature of organisational objectives is of importance. A thorough environmental scan and a meaningful vision and mission will lead to the setting of objectives aimed at both effectiveness and efficiency. Once these broad organisational objectives (sometimes supplemented by more specific objectives) have been established, short- and long-term strategies aimed specifically at their achievement need to be set in place.

Having established a new mission and vision and having framed the necessary objectives and strategies, the organisation needs to involve all participants also at the micro level for, unless they 'buy in', all efforts will have been in vain. Units need to be encouraged to formulate their own vision, mission, objectives and strategies. Management also needs to contract with employees for concrete change and to display a willingness to embrace new paradigms and experiment with new structures and procedures. The competencies necessary for the successful implementation of strategies need to be identified, functional units or teams need to be created, responsibilities should be reassessed and reassigned and new leadership styles and forms implemented. **Functionality** and **expertise**, and not status or administrative ability, become the dominant criteria. This may well entail 'pulling the entire organisation apart and putting it together again'. The present trend of sending existing managers on leadership courses before the organisation has been restructured is an exercise in futility — akin to placing a plaster on a bullet wound before removing the bullet.

In existing organisations the change process will probably commence with a decentralisation and delegation of power, decisionmaking and responsibility to the lowest level possible. This may entail that each section or department becomes an independent profit centre, that administrative functions are decentralised as far as possible and that the overall structure of the organisation is considerably flattened, with the superstructure consisting only of one or two general coordinators. Policies need to be jointly formulated, and each centre should be allowed maximum flexibility and autonomy within the framework of the overall objectives and policies of the organisation. Existing boards should be restructured to include other stakeholders and should function as management boards, their main task being the effective functioning of the total organisation and not the formulation of regulations or the rubberstamping of documents. Within this constellation, the human resource function moves away from its traditionally administrative role and becomes the main instrument for facilitation and organisational development. It should also be mentioned that, in very large organisations, decentralisation should reach the stage where different sectors become fully autonomous.

At micro level (that is, within the various departments), participants should be encouraged to share responsibility and decisionmaking and to engage in self direction, self motivation and self control. Also at this level, therefore, new structures and processes have to be established, layers have to be eliminated and participants have to be equipped and supported to play their new roles. Continued employee development as well as teambuilding and leadership training are a necessity. Training activities need to be jointly re-evaluated and support systems established which encourage employees to take responsibility for their own development and which engender a general culture of continuous development. Close liaison with customers becomes an imperative, as does assessment of both individual and group performance in terms of jointly established competencies and criteria. Employees should be encouraged to look for and to grasp at new opportunities and to bring about innovation on a regular basis. The role of the leader at this and other levels becomes that of facilitator, coordinator and supporter — the creator of opportunities for employees and the organisation. At the same time, he represents his department or section at the broader management level, thus having an impact on developments in the organisation as a whole.

As mentioned initially, the change process is dynamic and indefinite. It will take years before the phases outlined above have been fully instituted and, even while the process is continuing, frequent reassessment is essential. Participants at all levels need to workshop frequently, to assess where they are and where they are going and to identify dysfunctional aspects. If necessary, they may have to backtrack and go in a different direction. This is all part and parcel of the process and, even where all the phases have been implemented, new horizons and challenges will already have emerged. This will necessitate that we move forward again by repeating the process — but, hopefully, now at a more advanced level.

Organisational development, like all human activity, is a multilayered and dynamic process the end of which is never in sight. Indeed it can never be, since we would then have achieved Utopia which is not achievable in this world; yet the fact of its unattainability should never prevent participants from trying — to progress is always to strive and, in the striving, to come a little closer to the ideal.

AFFIRMATIVE ACTION

In the South African context the need for change embraces also the necessity to redress imbalances within the organisational composition brought about by previous sociopolitical designs. Thus affirmative action becomes essentially a change initiative.

Rationale All South African organisations may in future have to prove that they have developed an affirmative action policy and to demonstrate their progress in achieving affirmative action objectives.

The need for affirmative action arises from historical disadvantages brought about by the apartheid system, by male dominance in business and society, the lack of consideration for the disabled and prejudice against individuals who hold convictions, orientations or beliefs contrary to those of dominant groupings. The purpose of affirmative action is thus to ensure not only that such persons are no longer subjected to discrimination but that past imbalances arising from discrimination, male dominance and prejudice are eliminated. The need for such correction becomes obvious when it is considered that, as late as 1994, white males (constituting just over six percent of the population) occupied more than 96 percent of top positions. In fact, in the light of these statistics, affirmative action is not merely a sociopolitical necessity but also makes good business sense — organisations seem to have been drawing leaders and specialists from a very limited pool of resources.

The Nature of Affirmative Action

The term 'affirmative action' refers to the *purposeful* and *planned* placement or development of competent or potentially competent persons in or to positions from which they were debarred in the past, in an attempt to redress past disadvantages and to render the workforce *more representative* of the population, on either local or national level. Consequently, affirmative action has numerous facets. It entails, firstly, the search for persons with known competencies or potential to fill positions worthy of their ability; secondly, the training and development of previously disadvantaged persons so that they may in future possess greater mobility; and, thirdly, a continuous monitoring and adaptation of the demographic spread at all levels of the organisation. Most importantly, affirmative action constitutes an *active intervention*. In this aspect it differs from 'equal opportunity'. The latter refers merely to a policy of 'fairness' (the granting of equal access to all persons) whereas, in the case of affirmative action, organisations have to *ensure access* — or even limited preferential access — to disadvantaged groups, and/or prepare persons in these groups for accelerated development.

To argue that affirmative action can be replaced by a simple policy relating to equal opportunity is, therefore, a fallacy. Equal opportunity can be fair only if all contestants commence from the same starting line. Where some have been barred from opportunities in the past, they may have to be given faster running shoes; alternatively, those already in the lead may have to be handicapped to some extent. However, affirmative action can have only a limited lifespan. Sooner or later (probably when present school entrants leave school), the previously disadvantaged should have caught up. At that stage, a switchover must occur towards an equal opportunity policy.

Problems with Affirmative Action

Most of the controversies and problems surrounding affirmative action arise not from the principle as such but from the manner in which affirmative action is implemented. Wrong implementation occurs because organisations see affirmative action as a political imperative with which they have to comply, and not as a business objective which needs to be sustainable within the framework of the organisational objectives in total — one of which would be to have as effective and competent a workforce as possible. Consequently, persons are appointed in 'affirmative action positions' or imposed on the organisation merely to window-dress or to fill quotas, usually without due consideration of their suitability for the position or the possibility of support and development. Such arbitrary appointments leave other employees dissatisfied and are unfair to the appointees themselves, since they are either placed in meaningless positions or cannot handle their specified tasks, thus perpetuating the myth that affirmative action appointees are 'no good'. Unless affirmative action is tied to valid selection procedures which test relevant competencies or potential and are accompanied, where necessary, by a developmental programme, the myth becomes a reality.

Another problem with affirmative action, especially where higher level jobs are concerned, is the fact that the available pool of previously disadvantaged persons able to fulfil the requirements is extremely small. For example, in organisations where a need has been identified for greater representation of Africans at managerial level and where one of the requirements is a tertiary qualification, the selectors are most certain to encounter problems. 1994 statistics show that just over one percent of the black African population is possessed of a tertiary qualification. The result is that there develops a small, highly sought after group of elite candidates who, as has already been proved, are continually 'poached' by one organisation from another. Thus only this elite group advances, while the rest of the black African population remains where it was before.

For proof of this one need only look at America where, after twenty or more years of affirmative action, it is now admitted that the process has failed — and where inner-city ghettoes are populated by groups who still have not been advantaged by affirmative action. The problem here is, firstly, that employers are looking for 'ready made products' instead of the possibility of developing persons upward in the organisation; and, secondly, that too great an emphasis is being placed on quotas and paper qualifications instead of identifying competencies, experience levels and potential. It also points to education and training, both inside and outside the organisation, as the cornerstone of affirmative action programmes. Whereas many organisations concentrate affirmative action initiatives only on certain areas (and particularly in top, highly prominent positions), the greater part of affirmative action should concentrate on career planning, training and development or support for external education and training programmes.

The most prevalent accusation directed at affirmative action initiatives is that they constitute reverse discrimination. Especially employees who have given long service and were expecting promotion are dissatisfied when an affirmative action appointee, usually from the outside, is given the position which they believe they deserved. Again, affirmative action will become unfair and discriminatory only if a previously disadvantaged person is appointed 'at all costs' and without granting other persons the opportunity to compete. Discrimination occurs only when one party is intentionally disadvantaged. This would happen if an applicant or employee (other than an affirmative action candidate) who is competent to do the job is deliberately disregarded. All candidates have to be granted the opportunity to compete and to be assessed in terms of pre-established criteria; but an additional weighting, which should not be disproportionate to the other criteria, can be placed on affirmative action aspects. By this means the affirmative action candidate is given a slight, but not unreasonable, edge over the other candidates. It ensures relative fairness and also satisfies the employer's need to appoint competent persons.

If the process above is to operate effectively, the use of appropriate selection techniques and suitable test or assessment material becomes imperative.

Groups Targeted for Affirmative Action

If the organisation is to become more representative of the population, then ideally all previously disadvantaged groups should be targeted for affirmative action. For this planners need to be acquainted with the demographic spread of the economically active or potentially economically active population, and to compare this to their internal demographies — both in the organisation as a whole and in different job categories.

One question which occurs is whether the term 'population' should refer to the population as a whole, or merely to the area or province in which the organisation operates. This is a difficult problem, as the demographies in many areas have been artificially established by influx control and other policies. However, it would seem most logical to base representivity on the area from which the organisation draws its workforce and custom. Influx control laws are no longer operative and, as areas become freer, demographies will change. This would entail parallel changes in the objectives of the organisation as regards representation. Affirmative action is a dynamic process, and should not be relegated to a static policy.

Another controversial aspect is the argument raised by some regarding relative disadvantage. It is contended that some groups were in the past more disadvantaged than others. This may be true in society at large, but should not play a prominent role in affirmative action since, if certain previously disadvantaged persons have been more 'advantaged' in the organisation, this will be revealed in the demographies of that organisation and the policies implemented will be adapted accordingly.

The question of relative representivity is one of the central themes of affirmative action. Unfortunately, numerous organisations are implementing affirmative action policies which favour only a narrow grouping of the total spread of previously disadvantaged persons. This is bound to cause dissatisfaction. On the other hand, demographies should provide only a guideline since effectiveness remains an important criterion for selection. Thus, particularly in the interim developmental period, no organisation can be expected to be a mirror image of the society in which it operates. In fact, a brief look at other countries seems to indicate that such Utopian ideals have not yet been achieved elsewhere — even in those countries with longstanding affirmative action initiatives.

Implementing an Affirmative Action Programme

Establishing an Affirmative Action Policy and Strategy

It is an unfortunate fact that most affirmative action policies come in the form of directives from the Board or top management, and are usually thrust on the personnel department as its sole responsibility.

The new labour relations legislation determines that affirmative action should be subject to joint decisionmaking by management and the workplace forum. This notwithstanding, an affirmative action strategy is a change strategy and, as such, should be developed like any other change policy — that is, in collaboration with all other stakeholders in the organisation. A representative group which includes the union and other employee representatives (see requirements as outlined in the section on workplace forums) should be brought together to establish affirmative action objectives and policies and to plan the necessary strategies. This may prove to be a slow process, since different groupings will strive to protect their own interests, which may be in conflict with affirmative action objectives. Thus, extensive information and a sharing of values and perceptions is necessary at this stage. Understanding needs to be displayed for the fears of many existing stakeholders and, where possible, the necessary assurances should be given. Most importantly, no group should see themselves as permanently excluded from opportunities and development, even if some concessions and sacrifices may have to be made in the short term. Furthermore, all participants should be provided with information regarding the prospects of the organisation, manpower planning and the existing demographies.

During this stage the group should come to an agreement regarding the following.

- Their understanding of affirmative action
- Their understanding of the term 'representative'
- The affirmative action objectives to be adopted by the organisation, and an overall strategy for achieving such objectives
- Proposed time frames for the achievement of objectives (This is important, since one of the objectives should be to reach a stage where affirmative action can be replaced with an equal opportunity policy.)
- The manner in which candidates for positions are to be canvassed and selected
- The possibility of developing persons within the organisation (education and training)
- Integration of appointees into the organisation
- Monitoring and performance appraisal systems applicable to all employees
- Support systems for persons whose performance does not meet requirements
- The possibility that some candidates may eventually have to be dismissed, and the procedures to be adopted in such cases
- Support to be given to training and education initiatives outside the organisation
- Sensitisation of other employees to affirmative action initiatives, programmes to change attitudes and, in some instances, to address persons or groups who sabotage affirmative action initiatives
- Information to customers or clients on affirmative action initiatives, and the canvassing of support for such initiatives

Involvement of all Employees

Once a policy and strategy have been agreed upon, these should be shared with every employee in the organisation — possibly via the different stakeholders on the committee. Affirmative action initiatives which are implemented without proper consultation cause distrust and fear, leading either to disregard of the initiative or, at worst, to constant sabotage.

This, too, is not an easy process and has to be approached with great sensitivity. Existing employees need to be given all relevant information, to understand the objectives and their business logic, and to receive the necessary assurances regarding their own job security. Numerous workshops, sensitisation sessions and interactions may be necessary at this stage. If this is not done, employees will deliberately withhold information and assistance from new incumbents, or isolate them within the organisation.

Only after it has the assurance of general acceptance should management go ahead with its affirmative action strategy.

Selection and Appointment of New Incumbents

The starting point for appointments is the existing and future manpower plan of the organisation. If a position is vacant, the demography in that job category should be studied, in conjunction with the demography of the organisation as a whole. It may then be decided to give preference to a person from a previously disadvantaged group for appointment to this position. However, this can never be an absolute imperative, since someone from that grouping with the necessary competencies and experience may not be available to fill the position. Thus the inherent requirements of the job remain central to the selection procedure, and require careful consideration. In the light both of the fact that certain groups were disadvantaged as regards education and of the fact that educational qualifications are not necessarily indicative of competence, these should not constitute the primary criteria as was the case in the past. Selectors have to identify the competency requirements of the job and to establish methods whereby such competencies can be tested or assessed. Here the personnel department plays an important role. It is an unfortunate fact that most traditional tests are now proving unsuitable and that insufficient efforts are being directed at developing effective selection programmes.

Once criteria have been established and assessment techniques developed, it is necessary to attach a weighting to each criterion. This is where affirmative action candidates can be given an edge, by adding membership of a previously disadvantaged group as a criterion and applying a special, proportionate weighting to this. Should the demographies have proved that particular groups are less represented in the organisation or job category, the weighting given (for example) to black females could be heavier than that assigned to white females.

In canvassing candidates for the position it is necessary that advertisements list the competencies and experience level required, and that such advertisements reach as wide an audience as possible. Selectors may actively canvass persons whom they may regard as possible incumbents, but it is not advisable to engage in 'poaching' from other organisations as this merely sustains the elitism of the already employed. It is preferable to approach persons who may not yet be filling a position at a particular level but who display the potential to grow into the job.

All interviews should follow the same pattern, with due regard to (but not over-compensation for) differences in personal experience, culture, language, etc. The total 'scores' obtained by candidates in tests, assessments and interviews serve as guidelines to identify the best candidates. Once this has been done, the selection panel discusses the merits and demerits of each case, being in mind the 'fit' into the organisation and affirmative action objectives. An affirmative action candidate who may score slightly less than another candidate, but who also has displayed the potential to develop into the position, would then in all probability be appointed over the other candidate who may, at this stage, be slightly better, but not that much better. It should never happen that a mediocre or poor affirmative action candidate is appointed in preference to an outstanding person who was not previously disadvantaged or was previously less disadvantaged. This would be detrimental both to the organisation and to the appointee, who will not be able to prove himself worthy of the position.

If the availability of suitable affirmative action candidates is considered, it would seem that the focal point of affirmative action need not necessarily be the higher level jobs in the organisation. This does not indicate the concerted efforts should not be made to change the demographies at these levels, nor that a supposed lack of candidates should blandly be used as an excuse; but that organisations should not concentrate merely on such appointments. Unfortunately numerous organisations, intent on displaying their 'political correctness', do just that — to the detriment of affirmative action in general. Their efforts should be equally directed at future manpower requirements and to developing persons from both inside and outside the organisation so that they may eventually fill positions which are bound to be vacated or created.

The developmental aspect of affirmative action is complex. Manpower needs have to be established, and persons with potential identified or appointed. Thereafter a suitable programme has to be developed for these persons. Various problems may arise: for example, persons identified may eventually prove unsuitable, or other employees may be unhappy at not being granted the same opportunity. Therefore, if possible, developmental programmes should be instituted for as wide a group of employees as possible, together with new appointees, and it should be made clear that eventual promotion will be dependent on competencies achieved.

Integrating Appointees into the Organisation

All new incumbents (and not only affirmative action appointees) should be properly integrated by way of an effective induction programme. However, in the case of affirmative action candidates, there may be circumstances which dictate that their integration be monitored. This should be done in a sensitive and careful manner, as the purpose is not to treat those candidates differently or specially but, at the same time, to ensure that unnecessary stumbling blocks to their integration are removed. If affirmative action candidates have been properly selected, they will more than likely accomplish their own integration; but it may happen that others in the organisation put obstacles in their way. It is unfortunately so that the historical divisions in South African society have left many persons with a deficient sense of self worth. Consequently, quiet counselling and training in self assertion may be necessary, especially where younger candidates are involved.

Monitoring and Performance Appraisal

All new employees, whether appointed in terms of an affirmative action policy or not, may be placed on probation and their performance monitored on an ongoing basis. The new Labour Relations Act outlines a procedure for this, as already discussed in a previous Chapter. All such employees need to be informed of the standards required and given regular feedback as regards their performance. Should they not meet expectations, they should be given the necessary assistance and training. The same would apply to employees who are no longer on probation, although here the monitoring takes the form of regular, interactive performance appraisals. Any employee who, having been given all the assistance and training required, still does not perform satisfactorily may eventually be dismissed.

Career Planning and Career Development

In all organisations, one facet of manpower planning is succession planning and career development. If this is properly done, it offers an ideal route for developing previously disadvantaged persons from both inside and outside the organisation to fill more important positions in the future.

As mentioned earlier, these efforts should embrace as wide a spectrum of persons as possible. To select one or two people and groom them for a future position may prove unsatisfactory. The training provided should be both general and specific, so that candidates who are not eventually selected for the targeted positions may apply for other positions. This is a long-term strategy but, if the country is to develop a pool of trained manpower, probably constitutes the most important aspect of affirmative action.

Support to Education and Training Initiatives

Education and training is, given the massive backlog in this sphere, the only guarantee of the success of affirmative action initiatives and, in fact, of increased economic prosperity. It becomes, therefore, the responsibility not only of the government but of the entire nation and of the business community. South Africa cannot function without effective human resources, and it cannot continue to draw such resources from a limited pool of educated and trained employees. No wonder that the World Competitiveness Report rates South Africa 48th out of 48 countries in terms of the effective use of human resources, particularly if it is revealed that South African companies spend one percent or less of their income on training. Besides the promotion of training and development, business needs to support adult literacy and education programmes, to become actively involved with training institutions and to provide them with input and support.

In measuring an organisation's progress in the sphere of affirmative action, its efforts in respect of education and training should at this stage weigh as heavily as, or even more heavily than, the representativeness of its workforce.

Customer Information and Sensitisation

Business needs to make its affirmative action policy known to its customers and clientele, not for the purpose of canvassing kudos but to gain support and understanding, particularly when certain employees are being developed into positions. Customers also need to know that management will not tolerate any abusive or discriminatory behaviour towards an employee.

Continued Sensitisation of Existing Employees

All too often, affirmative action initiatives are undermined by other staff members who treat new appointees with distrust and, at times, contempt. A paternalistic calling aside of other employees to caution them serves only to emphasise supposed 'differences'. Instead, it is necessary at every opportunity to bring employees into contact with one another, on both business and social level, and to create appreciation of 'sameness' as well as understanding for perceived differences in perspectives and approach.

As mentioned earlier, affirmative action is a dynamic process. Policies, strategies and progress should be constantly reviewed and, if necessary, adapted in terms of changing circumstances and demands.

THE ROLE OF THE INDUSTRIAL RELATIONS CONSULTANT IN ORGANISATIONAL DEVELOPMENT

It has become evident that more progressive organisational styles centre in the continual development of the relations between employers and employees or unions. Since this is the main task of the industrial relations specialist, it follows that he will be closely involved with and, in fact, mostly responsible for organisational development initiatives. It could be surmised that, as the relationship develops with a concurrent move away from adversarialism and mechanistic procedures and systems, organisational development will supplant traditional industrial relations as the focal point of the IR practitioner's experience.

CONCLUSION

Organisations have undergone progressive development throughout the twentieth century. Whereas first change was relatively slow it has, during the latter half of this century, greatly accelerated in pace. Thus we live in a world where, as Johnson puts it, '... the once reliable constants have now become galloping variables' where the only constant is change, and in a country where over the past five years radical changes have been implemented; yet many of our organisations and individuals who hold positions of power still display a resistance to change and, consequently, lag behind. Unless they too are willing to undergo a paradigm shift, they might find themselves increasingly anachronised in a world which has passed them by.

SOURCES

Anderson, Alan H *Effective Labour Relations*, Blackwell Business, 1994.

Baraclough, Geoffrey *Contemporary History*, Penguin, 1990.

Bendix, R *Max Weber: An Intellectual Portrait*, Doubleday & Company, 1960.

Bennis, Warren G *Changing Organisations*, McGraw Hill, 1966.

Fox, A 'Industrial Sociology and Industrial Relations'. Royal Commission Research Paper no. 3, 1966.

Hickman, Craig R and Michael A Silva *The Future 500*, Allen & Unwin, 1973.

Hyman, R *Industrial Relations: A Marxist Introduction*, Macmillan, 1975.

Likert, R *New Patterns of Management*, McGraw Hill, 1961.

Purcell, J *Good Industrial Relations*, Macmillan, 1983.

Purcell, J 'Mapping Management Styles in Employee Relations' in *Journal of Management Studies*, 1987.

Salamon, Michael 'Individual and Collective Rights and Responsibilities in Creating Wealth'. Paper delivered at Industrial Relations Conference, Johannesburg, March 1990.

Salamon, Michael *Industrial Relations Theory and Practice*, Prentice Hall, 1987.

Schumpeter, E F *Small is Beautiful*, Abacus, 1994.

Semler, Ricardo *Maverick*, Arrow, 1994.

Thompson, Paul *The Nature of Work*, Macmillan Education Ltd., 1986

17

INDUSTRIAL RELATIONS IN THE FUTURE

WORLD TRENDS

Society and industry have come a long way since the early years of industrialisation and the then dominant practice of unadulterated capitalism. The industrial practices prevalent at the end of the Nineteenth and the beginning of the Twentieth Century and the undeniably intense conflict between the capitalist owner and his employees were mainly responsible for the institution of industrial relations systems, the growth of trade unionism and the engagement of the latter in aggressive collective bargaining. While collective bargaining has remained a core institution of industrial relations practice in Western society, this practice has been matured and extended to include principles of social justice, welfare, co-ownership, democratic workplace organisation, cooperation, social responsibility and organisational change. Society no longer allows the owner or manager unfettered power and sole decisionmaking at the place of work, and no longer relies only on the collective power of employees to counter the employer. Moreover, it is generally accepted that the employer/manager manages only by the consent of the managed; also, that society at large — and, therefore, each individual member — has a stake in all economic and industrial activity. This trend is not necessarily indicative of a development towards unadulterated communitarianism or to a centrally planned economy, but it does rely on greater cooperation between employers, employees/trade unions and the State and does render the State a more active partner in the labour relationship. Alternatively, where minimal State involvement exists, it might necessitate increased share ownership by the man in the street and the promotion of democratic practices at the workplace.

In every modern, developed society attempts are at present being made to chart a new course for the future: a course which will eliminate the disadvantages of unfettered capitalist accumulation, but which will also avoid the undoubted ills of a centrally planned economy and of total communitarianism. Each society is, in its own manner, attempting to balance the interests and freedom of the individual with the interests of society at large. Likewise, in every industrial relations system, efforts are continuing towards a balancing of the owner/manager's right to pursue the profit motive and to make decisions to this effect and the employee's right to a share in those profits and those decisions. At the workplace a balance is being sought between the promotion and development of the individual and attention to the interests of the collective.

Greater cooperation among the parties to the labour relationship has become a necessity, but this does not render trade unionism and collective bargaining irrelevant. To some extent, increased acceptance of the rights of employees, including their right to a fair wage, has rendered aggressive collective bargaining unnecessary. The trade union is no longer solely the antagonist of management. Unions also play a cooperative and social role, but trade unions may continue to represent the interests of employees towards management, as well as the State, and to bargain with both in respect of these interests. Thus, although there may well be a shift in emphasis from conflict to cooperation and although trade union membership may well decrease as antagonism diminishes, trade unionism as an institution will remain, to guard over the interests of the employee party. Should either of the other parties infringe too greatly upon these interests, trade unions will again be obliged to adopt their role as antagonists. Consequently, trade unionism and collective bargaining will not disappear, but they may decline in prominence and the incidence of strike action may diminish. Trade unionism, around which industrial relations revolved, is essentially a function of management. The worse the management, the more likelihood there will be of a flourishing trade union movement. Hopefully the time will come, both in organisations and in society, when the vast divide between the haves and the have nots, between employers and employees will disappear and all concerned can get on with the job of developing the organisation.

SOUTH AFRICA

South Africa, by world standards, is a young country. This applies particularly to its industrial relations dispensation as it is only during the past fifteen years that all employees have had equal rights within the sphere of industrial activity. During the first half of the Eighties, the major unions within the South African constellation were engaged mostly in aggressive action aimed at consolidating their position and establishing elementary employee rights. Thus they were concerned with what in other countries may be regarded as the most basic issues such as wages, job security and fair treatment. It was only after 1985 that more advanced matters in the form of health and safety and maternity benefits found their way onto union agendas, but among the unions representing black employees the question of a living wage and the treatment received by their members at the workplace remained dominant problems.

There were at this stage definite indications of greater maturity, enhanced by a greater willingness to use established structures, to place relationships on a regulated basis and to participate in more centralised negotiation forums. Also, social welfare issues related to matters such as housing, pensions and education were receiving more attention. Yet, in general, the role of trade unions — and especially that of the newer unions — was reminiscent of early trade unionism in Europe and America. Similarly, the reaction of employers was often anachronistic.

In view of the relative immaturity of the system and the lack of an all-pervasive ideology, it could hardly be expected of trade unions and management to adopt a cooperative rather than aggressive approach in the industrial relations situation. The best that could be hoped for was that they would regulate their relationships so as not to allow too much damage by either side. This, indeed, they did.

From the beginning of the 1990s South Africans of all persuasions were faced with the prospect of a future dispensation which would differ vastly from that experienced during the aforegoing one hundred. Within this context all the major players in the industrial relations system — employers, trade unions and the State — had to take a quantum leap, to reassess their objectives, attitudes and approaches and to replan their strategies. Both employers and government realised that unilateral and biased action of any kind was bound to elicit continued reaction and, in the end, to result in failure. Unions, on the other hand, now had the hope that their members would benefit from a future social and economic dispensation. Consequently they too proved more willing to cooperate with management, and even with the government of the time, in shaping that dispensation; in fact, it appeared that they would insist on playing a major role, especially where the economic system was concerned. Since then a change of government has occurred and all parties have again had to readjust themselves with a view to their changing roles in the new sociopolitical dispensation.

World trends, the necessity to compete in global markets and particular South African realities will, in the future, dictate the nature and pace of change. In order to survive, South African business will have to change and the only viable direction seems to be one aimed at an industrial, social and economic partnership with employees. Still existent autocratic styles of management, the jealous guardianship of managerial prerogative, the unwillingness to deal openly and honestly with employers and the misappropriation of rewards into the hands of a select few will continue to cause unnecessary conflicts, retarding productivity and reducing effectiveness, eventually with disastrous effects. South African managers must learn to rely on expertise rather than on authority, on respect rather than status, and to acknowledge both the individual and collective worth of employees, since only if they do this can they hope for a favourable development of the labour relationship.

On their part, employees will have to accept the responsibility that a partnership of this nature places on them. Like management, employees will need to develop a new work ethic and a far more caring attitude within the work situation. This may prove problematic as many employees now harbour unreasonably high expectations while, owing to historical circumstances, the general level of education is unusually low. Thus training and the upgrading of education will become the most important social responsibility of business and government.

At present, South African trade unions face a number of critical choices. The union movement is revealing chinks in its armour, but is determined to play a dominant role in the shaping of a future sociopolitical and economic dispensation. Until 1994 the essence of the union movement's existence was to be found in its protection of the rights of its members in the face of a perceived onslaught by both management and the State. The question is whether unions will continue to wield as much power and to play as dominant a role in a situation where management engages in partnership with employees and where the State promotes their interests on a hitherto unprecedented basis. In these circumstances unions will not gain power purely from opposition but will be obliged to adopt a more cooperative role and, in fact, to operate on a more centralised level as a social and industrial force. However, centralisation in itself holds the danger of estrangement from grassroots support and, therefore, a loss of power. Equally, alignment to a political party as a means of maintaining influence may result in a loss of independence and, consequently, the inability to claim representation of workers of all persuasions. If unions are to maintain and enhance their influence, they will need to continue operating at both grassroots and centralised levels and, in doing so, to cooperate with management and the government but to maintain their essential identity as the protectors of employee interests. This could occur within the sphere of social and industrial planning. The gravest danger for the union movement lies in its absorption into a factional political party in which it is dominated by interests other than those of the members it claims to represent.

Any government which took office within a democratic South African state would initially be expected to legislate in favour of employees. This was so because those who were previously disenfranchised still regarded themselves as exploited within the work situation. The degree to which a government interferes in the labour relationship depends on the dominant ideology, the influence of trade unions and the demands of economic reality. It now appears to be accepted that — at least for the foreseeable future — a mixed economic system will prevail and private ownership will continue, but that this will be offset by a greater balancing of power between employer and employee and the legislating of new rights for employees, as has already been proved by the Labour Relations Act of 1995.

At present, the South African labour relations system is extremely volatile, with all parties not yet sure of their positions and the stances to be adopted. If the government has its way, there will be increased cooperation and greater labour peace. However, it could happen that the trade union movement increasingly distances itself from the government and engages in more militant action and even forms different alliances in order to reinforce its power base. Alternatively, other newer or less well established unions may gain ground at grassroots level. At the same time economic realities might induce both government and employers to adopt a harder line. Whatever happens, it is to be hoped that economic rationality rather than ideological fundamentalism will eventually predominate.

The aforegoing constitutes merely a calculated guess on the basis of present trends, which may be redirected or reversed from year to year and even from day to day. To lay claim to omniscience regarding the future is in normal circumstances foolhardy and, in the present South African situation, downright presumptuous.

ANNEXURES

COSATU PLATFORM ON WORKER RIGHTS
adopted by COSATU Special Congress 10–12 September 1993

1. Introduction COSATU has been built on traditions of strong shopfloor structures, a militant and active membership and a broad development perspective as a social movement.

Over the past decade, the trade unions have fought for increased influence in decisionmaking processes. This we have started to achieve:

- at workplace level through recognition agreements, collective bargaining and a powerful shop stewards' movement;
- at an industry level through national bargaining and industrial policy forums;
- at a macro level through negotiations in the National Economic Forum, National Housing Forum, National Electricity Forum and the National Manpower Commission.

Democracy brings new opportunities as well as new challenges and struggles to take forward our demands. For workers to benefit from the installation of a new democratic government, the following is required.

- A strong trade union movement protecting workers and fighting for social equality
- A growing economy, characterised by efficient production, high wages and high employment
- A government which has the capacity to implement our Reconstruction and Development Programme
- Increased participation by organised workers in decisionmaking at shopfloor, industry and national level

2. Platform of Workers' Rights Our starting point is the demands generated in the Workers' Charter Campaign. Many of the demands in the draft Workers' Charter have not yet been entrenched in law and many of our existing rights are not satisfactorily entrenched in the legislation. They are dependent on agreements with employers, the discretion of the courts and the goodwill of the Minister of Manpower.

To achieve the opportunities of democracy, the platform of workers' rights listed on the following pages must be implemented by a new democratic government.

2.1 Basic Organising Rights
All workers should have the right to:

2.1.1 join trade unions and organise;
2.1.2 bargain collectively;
2.1.3 strike and picket, on all social and economic matters;

2.1.4 enter into union security agreements, including closed and agency shops;

2.1.5 gain access to information from companies and the government.

2.2 Collective Bargaining

We need a system of collective bargaining which gives workers a key say in industry decisionmaking and where unions are fully involved in designing and overseeing changes at workplace and industry levels. Only if this happens will workers be committed to ensuring that companies operate efficiently or productively.

A new framework should include the following.

2.2.1 *Centralised bargaining* to promote equity for workers and increased trade union participation in decisionmaking.

There should be industry bargaining forums responsible for negotiating:

- industry restructuring for growth and development;
- wages, working conditions, training and grading.

Agreements negotiated in such industry forums should be extended through legislation to all workplaces in that industry.

2.2.2 The *National Economic Forum* needs to consider macro-economic issues including the broad principles of industry restructuring and how industries relate to each other.

2.2.3 *Company or plant-level negotiations* to ensure work reorganisation, based on a nationally negotiated framework.

2.2.4 *Government* should play an active role in facilitating the above through *legislative and administrative reform.*

2.3 Workplace Empowerment

To ensure that democratisation reaches workers, at a factory level there needs to be:

2.3.1 an obligation on employers to negotiate substantial changes about production matters or workplace organisation with workers;

2.3.2 facilities for organisation and communication with workers on economic and industrial restructuring issues;

2.3.3 shop stewards' rights to attend union meetings and training without loss of pay and to address workers.

2.4 Human Resources Development

Education and training of all workers is the key to ensuring the successful implementation of workplace and industrial restructuring. On the basis of our 1991 Congress Resolution on adult basic education, education and training, our human resource development programme should have the following main objectives.

- To remove discriminatory practices built on racial and/or gender bias

- To improve workers' wages and reduce the disparity between low-skilled and high-skilled workers
- To enable workers to advance along career paths within the company, industrially and nationally
- To enable workers to intervene more decisively in the production process
- To ensure that an integrated system of education and training is linked to economic and labour market planning

To achieve these objectives:

2.4.1 *Barriers* that restrict workers' access to education and training *should be removed*. There should be a right to paid education and training leave.

2.4.2 The *quality of workers' education and training should be improved* by developing, for example, a system of nationally recognised certificates. Workers will then be able to transfer their skills between different employers and in all parts of the country as well as undertake further training.

2.4.3 The benefits of education and training should *result in better rewards* for workers through linking training to grading and pay.

2.4.4 *Trade union education should be promoted* in school curricula, on publicly funded radio and TV, etc.

2.5 National, Industry-based Provident Funds

All workers should have a right to pension or provident funds. To improve benefits to workers and increase effective worker control over investment decisions we want national, industry-based provident funds. Employers must be compelled to contribute to pension and provident funds.

3. Achieving our Platform of Workers' Rights

This platform must be achieved through agreement with the ANC, prior to the elections as part of a Reconstruction Accord. This will include ensuring that the above rights are entrenched in international law, in the Constitution and in legislation in the following way.

3.1 International Law

The new government must *sign international labour law conventions* of the ILO concerning freedom of association, collective bargaining, workplace representation and the other conventions dealing with fundamental rights.

3.2 The Bill of Rights

3.2.1 The Bill of Rights must *guarantee the right of workers* to:

- join trade unions;
- conclude union security agreements and bargain collectively on all social and economic issues that affect workers
- strike on all social, economic and political issues;
- gain access to information from employers and the government.

3.3   The Constitution: Ensuring a Central Role for Trade Unions and Civil Society

The new constitution and laws should ensure that civil society, including trade unions, is able to be actively involved in public policymaking. At a national and industry level we want to ensure that workers are able to influence the policies of business and government.

This should occur by:

3.3.1   Promoting the *establishment and strengthening of tripartite and multilateral forums* where trade unions and other representative organisations can participate in democratic public policymaking. This shall include the involvement of trade unions in negotiations concerning restructuring international trade agreements, international loans, etc.

3.3.2   *Restructuring of the Department of Manpower* and institutions which fall in its jurisdiction such as the Unemployment Insurance Board, Workmen's Compensation Board and the health and safety regulatory structures.

3.3.3   *Restructuring of the National Manpower Commission* to be a place where trade unions and other representative organisations can participate in the formulation of labour market policy for all workers in all sectors. The NMC must be responsible to Parliament.

3.3.4   Providing in the Constitution for the *calling of a referendum* by citizens to overturn unpopular laws or to ensure that certain laws get passed.

3.3.5   Providing in the Constitution for a Constitutional Court which will include trade union or labour specialists, jurists who have been selected in consultation with trade unions.

3.3.6   *Public funding of programmes undertaken by trade unions* and other independent institutions in civil society. There should be a requirement that the State and employers provide funding for the education and training of workers and shop stewards.

3.3.7   Providing legislation so that workers have a say over how their *pension and provident funds* are invested.

3.4   Labour Legislation

New labour legislation must provide for the following.

3.4.1   There must be *one single statute* governing labour relations for all workers throughout the economy.

3.4.2   There must be laws that *set basic conditions of employment* such as the Basic Conditions of Employment Act, wage determinations under the Wage Act, health and safety laws, etc. These must apply to all sectors of the economy and must allow workers to be centrally involved in determining minimum standards at the workplace and in their industries.

3.4.3   Employers will be *obliged to negotiate* with workers on any substantial changes at the factory or industry level, e.g. on retrenchments, industrial restructuring or training.

3.4.4   Provision should be made in legislation to *put into place centralised bargaining arrangements* in each industry.

3.4.5   The industrial courts system will be restructured so that workers who have complaints against employers should be able to have these disputes resolved in a cheap, accessible and speedy manner. Tripartite institutions should have a say in determining appointments to the Industrial and labour appeal courts.

Moved: SACTWU
Seconded: NUMSA
Approved unanimously

(Source: SA Labour Bulletin *Vol.17 No.5)*

DRAFT WORKERS' CHARTER OF THE SOUTH AFRICAN COMMUNIST PARTY

Preamble

We, the working people of South Africa, the main producers of our country's wealth, declare:

that as workers, we are daily robbed of a rightful share of the fruits of our labour;

that as black workers we are subjected to even more intense exploitation by a system of capitalism which uses national domination to keep the wages low and profits high;

that, as part of the black oppressed whose forebears were conquered by force of arms, we continue to suffer all the social, political, economic and cultural deprivation of a colonised people;

that the most urgent task facing us as workers and as part of the black oppressed is to use our organised strength both at the point of production and among our communities to put an end to the racial tyranny and to help bring about a united, nonracial, non-sexist democratic South Africa based on one person, one vote as broadly defined in the Freedom Charter;

that we see the winning of such a nonracial democracy as part of a continuous process of creating conditions for the building of a socialist society which will be in the interest of all our people; a society free of exploitation of person by person, which along can complete the liberation objectives in all spheres of life;

that we are the most vital social constituent of the broad liberation movement in which we play a part both as individuals and through our trade unions and political organisations. We stand ready to work together with all other classes and groups genuinely committed to nonracial democracy, at the same time safeguarding our class independence and our right to propagate and mobilise for a socialist future; and

that we extend a hand of friendship to our white class of brothers and sisters whose long time interests lie in the unity of all labour — black and white

in order to ensure:

that victory in the national liberation movement is not hijacked by a new exploiting class of whatever colour;

that the immediate interests of the working people are fully safeguarded in the post-apartheid state; and

that we are not prevented from asserting our democratic right to win the majority of the people for a socialist future.

We, the working people, adopt this charter (as an elaboration of the Freedom Charter) and pledge ourselves to strive together, using our organised strength, to guarantee its implementation.

Ownership and Control of Economy

The commanding heights of the economy shall be placed under the ownership and overall control of the State acting on behalf of the people. Such control shall not be exercised in an overcentralised and commandist way, and must ensure active participation in the planning and running of the enterprises by workers at the point of production and through their trade unions.

Economic policy shall aim to generate the resources needed to correct the economic imbalances imposed by race domination, and bring about wealth redistribution for the benefit of the people as a whole. More particularly, steps shall be taken to do away with the white monopoly of ownership and managerial control.

Participation in the State sector by domestic or foreign private capital, where judged necessary, shall not give such capital a controlling share and all enterprises, whether State-owned or private, shall be compelled to safeguard the interests of the workers and the nation as a whole. The continued operation of market forces in the functioning of the economy shall not prevent State intervention in areas relating to the people's basic needs.

In the period after the defeat of the race tyranny, the fundamental perspective of working class political and trade union organisation shall be able to work for creation of the economic and social conditions making a steady advance towards a democratic socialist society.

The Right and Duty to Work and to a Living Wage

Every adult person has a right and duty to work and to receive remuneration according to his or her contribution. The new state shall, as a matter of priority, work to create economic conditions in which jobs are available to all. Until this is achieved that State shall ensure that social support is provided for the unemployed and members of their family.

All managerial and administrative posts and other jobs shall be opened to every qualified citizen irrespective of race, colour, sex or religion. The equal right of access to jobs managerial and administrative shall be subject to positive measures necessary to correct the imbalances inherited from the era of race discrimination. Public and private institutions shall have a duty to provide facilities for training and opportunities to apply the acquired skills.

The State, in consultation with the trade unions, shall adopt and enforce a minimum wage.

Child labour and all forms of forced and semi-forced labour shall be prohibited.

Special attention shall be paid to redressing the oppressive situation involved in farm work, domestic service and those trapped in the so-called homelands.

The Right to Organisation and Struggle

There shall be no restriction on the right of workers to organise themselves into political parties or trade unions. Trade union organisation shall be based on the principles of 'one industry, one union' and 'one country, one federation'.

Trade unions and their federation shall be completely independent, answerable only to the decisions of their members or affiliates, democratically arrived at. No political party, State organ or enterprise, whether public, private or mixed, shall directly or indirectly interfere with such independence.

The State shall ensure that trade unions, as the key mass organisation of the organised working class, are given the opportunity to participate at all levels of economic planning and implementation.

All workers, in every sector of the economy, shall have the right, through their trade unions, to engage freely in collective bargaining and to use the strike weapon.

All legislation dealing with procedures for collective bargaining, including any limitation on the right to strike in exceptional cases, shall require the consent of the majority in the trade union movement.

In the case of all other labour legislation there shall be prior consultation with the trade union movement, whose views on such proposed legislation should be timeously tabled in Parliament.

The Right to Media Access

Steps shall be taken to break the existing media monopoly by big business and the State and to ensure effective workers' access to all sections of the media.

The Right to Family Life and Social Facilities

All legislation and labour practices which prevent or interfere with the right of families to live together shall be outlawed. Migrant labour shall be phased out or, in cases where it is unavoidable, provision shall be made for family accommodation during any period of service exceeding three months.

The State shall aim to make adequate accommodation and children's schools available to all workers and their families close to their place of work. All enterprises shall help to create local or regional facilities for the workforce as well as crèches and primary health care facilities.

No parent, male or female, shall be disadvantaged or disabled from any form of employment by virtue of his or her duty to help rear children and, where necessary, this shall be ensured by the creation of special facilities including provision for paid maternity and paternity leave.

The Right to Health and Safety

Conditions of work shall not threaten the health, safety and wellbeing of the workforce or of the community at large, or create serious ecological risks.

All workers shall have the right to paid annual leave and sick leave.

Those injured at work shall receive proper compensation for themselves and their families.

Provision shall be made for rehabilitation of all disabled workers including, where necessary, the provision of alternative employment.

The Right to Security in Old Age

All workers shall be entitled to an adequate pension or retirement, provided either by the State or relevant enterprises.

The Rights of Women Workers

The State shall aim to integrate all women workers as full and equal participants in the economy.

Any form of discrimination against women workers in regard to job allocation, wages, working conditions, training, benefits, etc. shall be prohibited.

Positive steps shall be taken to help the discrimination suffered by women both in the workplace and at home. Opportunities shall be created to enable women to acquire skill for employment outside the home.

It shall be the duty of the State, trade unions, workers, political parties and all other mass and social organisations to ensure effective women's participation at leadership, management and other levels to take measures, including educational campaigns to combat all forms of male chauvinism both in the home and outside.

We declare that the above immediate and long-term objectives are in the best interests of all the working people and of society as a whole, and as individuals and as a part of the organised working class we pledge to struggle, side by side, for their full implementation.

DRAFT WORKERS' CHARTER OF THE
SOUTH AFRICAN CONGRESS OF TRADE UNIONS

Preamble   We, the workers of South Africa, declare that the future of the people of South Africa lies in the hands of the workers. It is only the working class, in alliance with other progressive-minded sections of our community, who can build a happy life for all South Africans, a life free from unemployment, insecurity and poverty, free from racial hatred and oppression, a life of vast opportunity for all our people.

The working class can only succeed in this great and noble endeavour if it itself is united and strong, if it is conscious of its inspiring responsibility.

The workers of South Africa need a united trade union federation in which all sections of the working class can play their part unhindered by prejudice or racial discrimination. Only such a truly united federation can serve effectively the interests of the workers, both our immediate interests of higher wages and better working conditions, and our ultimate objective of complete emancipation from national oppression and economic exploitation.

There can be no peace in our country or in the world until all forms of racial discrimination, oppression and exploitation are completely abolished.

We, the workers of South Africa, resolve to protect the interests of all workers with our guiding motto: AN INJURY TO ONE IS AN INJURY TO ALL!

All workers shall have the right to work.
a) The most fundamental right of every worker is the right to work.
b) In a free and united democratic nonracial South Africa, every worker shall be guaranteed the right to work.

All workers shall have the right to:
a) form and join trade unions of their own choice,
b) organise trade unions on the basis of 'one industry, one union',
c) organise all unorganised workers,
d) work towards unification of all democratic trade unions into one national federation,
e) oppose victimisation, harassment, bannings, banishment and imprisonment of trade unionists and workers,
f) reject all forms of representation which are not in conformity with the principles of democracy.

All workers shall have the right to freedom of movement, assembly and speech. Passes shall be abolished and all pass laws shall be repealed. All workers shall receive equal treatment at the workplace and before any court of law.

All workers shall have the right to live with their families in decent housing near their place of work.
a) The State shall provide workers with accommodation, recreational facilities, crèches, nursery schools and playgrounds for our children.
b) All racist legislation restricting the right of our people to live where they

choose like influx control and Group Areas shall be abolished.

There shall be equal opportunities for all workers.
Workers shall not be discriminated against on the basis of race, class, colour, sex or religion. All forms of education and training shall be free and compulsory for all.

Workers shall have the unconditional right to strike in support of their demands.
There are irreconcilable contradictions between capital and labour, therefore workers shall have the right to withdraw their labour to win their demands.

Workers shall be paid a wage which enables him/her to satisfy the minimum needs of the family.
a) Discrimination in wages on the basis of colour and sex shall be abolished.
b) All workers shall be paid a living wage.
c) A national minimum wage (NMW) enforced by law shall be established, linked to the rate of inflation.
d) The national minimum wage shall take into account the need to cover rent, electricity and water, upkeep of the home, food and clothing, transport and entertainment.

Workers shall have the right to:
a) free medical care,
b) three weeks' sick leave per annum on full pay
c) four weeks' annual leave on full pay
d) Women workers shall be guaranteed the right to return to their jobs at the same rate of pay after maternity leave.

There shall be a maximum eight-hour working day.
a) In order to ensure full employment, a maximum of eight hours per day shall be worked, i.e. a basic forty hours per week.
b) Overtime must be banned and the working day shortened.
c) Shift work shall be shortened/abolished.
d) Where workers are involved in strenuous work, a six-hour day shall be worked, i.e. thirty hours per week. This shall ensure adequate time for rest and leisure, giving workers the opportunity to develop their talents and skills unrelated to their specific jobs. This will encourage all-round development of the worker.

Unemployed workers shall be the responsibility of the State.
a) Unemployed workers shall be entitled to unemployment benefits, which will take into account all the basic needs of the worker and his/her family.
b) Unemployed workers shall be the responsibility of the State and will be fully supported.

All workers shall be eligible for retirement with full pension.
a) Pensioners shall be the responsibility of the State.
b) Male workers shall be eligible to pension at the age of 60. Those doing strenuous work shall be eligible for pension at 55.

   c) Female workers shall be eligible for pension at 55.

Health and safety shall be guaranteed.
a) A 'health and safety at work' charter should be evolved to guarantee the wellbeing and safety of workers.
b) Families of those injured at work and the injured workers themselves shall be fully compensated.

Women workers shall have the right to participate in all sectors of the economy without discrimination.
a) Women workers shall enjoy full rights as equal participants in the economy of our country.
b) Women workers shall be guaranteed their jobs back after maternity leave at the same or higher rate of pay.
c) Childcare shall be available for the children of working parents.
d) Women shall have the right to train for any job they wish to.

All racist labour legislation shall be outlawed, including the racist Labour Relations Amendment Act.
All restrictive racist labour legislation shall be abolished such as influx control and the Group Areas Act.

All workers shall have full political rights.
a) All workers shall have the right to vote without any qualification and to stand as candidates for all institutions which make laws that govern the people in a united people's state.
b) Workers shall have greater control over and share in the wealth they produce.
c) All workers and people shall have a universal franchise in south Africa.
d) The working class, the peasantry, the revolutionary intelligentsia, progressive youth and women shall fight side by side until South Africa is free from national oppression and economic exploitation.

AN INJURY TO ONE IS AN INJURY TO ALL.

SOUTH AFRICAN BUSINESS CHARTER
OF SOCIAL, ECONOMIC AND POLITICAL RIGHTS (1986)

Preamble Whereas we, members of organised commerce and industry and of business generally in South Africa;

Mindful of our important role in promoting human rights and the dignity of man, and in acknowledging the concomitant obligations on and duties of everyone to respect the rights and freedoms of others;

Accepting our responsibility to strive for economic growth, wealth creation and the generation of work opportunities in an environment that encourages entrepreneurial endeavour, and constantly mindful of the dignity of all people;

Willing to contribute to the processes of ongoing reform and to create the necessary conditions of peace, stability and prosperity for all South Africans on the foundations of democracy;

Recognising the need for South Africa to take up its rightful place in the international community as a land of justice, equal rights and opportunities and to fulfil its duties in the community of free and peace-seeking nations, and with a deep sense of patriotism for our country;

agree upon and support the following rights and principles,

Part I: Social and Cultural Rights and Principles

1. All human beings are born free and equal in dignity and rights.

2. Everyone has the right to respect for his private and family life; and the widest possible protection and assistance should be accorded to the family, which is the natural and fundamental group in society.

3. Everyone has the right to freedom of thought, conscience, and religion; this right includes the freedom to change his religion or belief, and the freedom alone or in community with others and in public or in private, to manifest his religion or belief in worship, teaching, practice and observance.

4. Everyone has the right to equal educational opportunities, and in the exercise of any functions which the State or private institutions assume in relation to education and to teaching, the State shall respect the rights of parents to ensure such education and teaching in conformity with their own religious and philosophical convictions.

5. (1) All ethnic, religious, linguistic and other cultural groups have equal rights.

(2) Everyone has the right freely to participate in the cultural life of the nation, to enjoy the arts and to share in scientific advancement and its benefits.

(3) Persons belonging to ethnic, religious or linguistic minorities shall not be denied the right to enjoy their own culture, to profess and practice their own religion or to use their own language.

Part II: Economic Rights and Principles

6. (1) Everyone has the right to own property, alone as well as in association with others, including communal ownership as found in traditional communities.

(2) No one shall be deprived of his property without due process of law.

7. Everyone has the right to the rewards of his endeavours, and this right shall be subject only to such limitations as are prescribed by law and are necessary in a democratic society in the public interest and in the promotion of the public weal and wellbeing.

8. (1) Everyone has the right freely to employ labour and to own or manage a business in accordance with the rights and principles set out in this Charter.

(2) Everyone has the right to work and to free choice of employment.

(3) Everyone, without discrimination, has the right to equal pay for equal work.

(4) Everyone who works has the right to fair remuneration.

(5) Everyone has the right to form or join trade unions, or commercial, industrial or other associations of his choice for the furtherance or protection of his economic interests; however, no one may be compelled to join such a union or association.

9. The people may, themselves for their own ends or through the institutions of democratic government, freely dispose of their natural wealth and resources without any prejudice to any obligations arising out of international economic cooperation, based upon the principle of mutual benefit and international law; in no case may a person be deprived of his own means of subsistence.

Part III: Civil and Political Rights and Principles

10. Every human being has the right to recognition as a person before the law.

11. Everyone is equal before the law, and is entitled to equal protection of the law without any discrimination on the basis of race, colour, language, sex, religion, ethnic or social origin, age, property, birth, political or other opinion, or economic or other status.

12. (1) Everyone has the right to life, liberty and security of person.

(2) No one shall be arbitrarily deprived of these rights.

(3) No one shall be deprived of his liberty merely on the grounds of inability to fulfil a contractual obligation.

13. No one shall be subjected to arbitrary arrest, detention or exile, and everyone shall be entitled to a fair and public hearing by an independent and impartial tribunal in the determination of his rights and of any obligations and of any criminal charges against him.

14. No one shall be subjected to torture or to cruel, inhuman or degrading treatment or punishment.

15. No one shall be held in slavery or servitude, and no one shall be required to perform forced or compulsory labour.

16. (1) Everyone has the right to freedom of movement and residence within the borders of the state.

(2) Everyone has the freedom to leave the country and, if having the right of permanent residence, to return.

17. (1) Everyone has the right to freedom of opinion and expression; this right includes freedom to hold opinions without interference and to seek, receive and impart information and ideas through any media, regardless of frontiers.

(2) Any advocacy of national, racial or religious hatred that constitutes incitement to discrimination, hostility or violence shall be prohibited by law.

18. Everyone has the right to freedom of association and freedom of peaceful assembly.

19. (1) Everyone born in South Africa or the independent or national states, or naturalised in accordance with law, has the right to South African citizenship.

(2) Every citizen has the right to take part in public affairs, directly or through freely chosen representatives.

(3) Everyone has the right of equal access to the public service.

(4) Due regard being given to the protection of the rights of minorities, the will of the people is the basis of the authority of the government, and this will shall be expressed by way of periodic and genuine elections which shall be by universal suffrage and shall be held by secret vote or by equivalent free voting procedures.

20. The institutions of democratic government, and in particular the separation of State powers, the independent of the judiciary and the supremacy of the legal system, the freedom of the press and the free formation of political parties shall be the foundations of South African statehood.

21. The State shall not be above the law but shall be, through decentralisation and devolution of State powers, close to the people and responsive to their needs.

22. (1) South Africa, as a sovereign state, shall respect the rights and independence of all nations and shall strive to maintain world peace and the settlement of all international disputes by negotiation, not war.

(2) The right of other peoples to independence and self- government shall be recognised and shall be the basis of close cooperation.

Part IV: Personal and Public Responsibilities

23. Everyone is entitled to all the rights and freedoms identified in this Charter, without distinction of any kind such as race, colour, language, sex, religion, political or other opinion, ethnic or social origin, age, property, birth or economic or other status.

24. Everyone's exercise of his rights and freedoms shall be subject to such limitations as are determined by law solely for the purpose of securing due recognition and respect for the rights and freedoms of others, and for meeting the just requirements of morality, public order and the general welfare in a democratic society.

25. (1) Nothing in this Charter shall be interpreted as a denial of the right and duty of the State to compel any person or group to desist in any activity or to refrain from any act aimed at the abrogation of any of the rights and freedoms of others as set forth herein.

(2) In times of public emergency which threatens the life of the nation or the democratic institutions of the State, or when individuals or groups act or plan to act in a manner aimed at the abrogation or destruction of any of the rights and freedoms of others as identified herein, the State may take such measures to the extent strictly required to meet the exigencies of the situation; provided that such measures are consistent with the laws which provide for such emergency powers, as well as with other obligations under international law; and further provided that they do not involve unlawful discrimination.

We therefore undertake to promote, propagate and implement the abovementioned rights and principles by:

1. Urging all members of industry, commerce and business generally to adhere to these rights and principles

2. Influencing government and all political parties and groups to abide by the abovementioned rights and principles and in this respect assuming an active role to scrutinise all discriminatory laws, measures and practices

3. Working towards the termination of turmoil, unrest and conditions of emergency

4. Striving for the release of political prisoners as defined in the context of the Charter

5. Exploring means of supporting social, economic and political debate and constitutional negotiation towards the realisation of the abovementioned rights and principles

6. Supporting education and training programmes as well as social and welfare schemes

7. Undertaking measures to abolish racial discrimination and injustice within business organisations

8. Launching programmes for better public understanding of human rights and freedoms

9. Aiming at peace and stability in the southern African region

10. Seeking international understanding and cooperation

CONSTITUTION OF A WORKPLACE FORUM

The constitution of the workplace forum will guide its functioning and *must* contain the following.

- **A formula for establishing the number of constituencies** in the workplace. Schedule 2 to the Act suggests that, where there are 100–200 employees, five forum representatives should be elected; for 201–600 employees there should be eight members; for 601–1 000 employees, ten members; and for more than 1 000 employees, one additional member for every additional 500 employees, to a maximum of twenty members.
- **A formula for the spread of constituencies** in such a manner that the employee spread of the organisation is represented. It is suggested that this be done proportionately: for example, if six members have to be elected for 300 employees, of whom 200 are manual workers, 50 are clerical employees and 50 are managerial, supervisory and technical employees, the ratio would be 4:1:1.
- A provision for the **direct election of members of the forum by the employees** at the workplace. It is suggested that every election should be conducted by an electoral officer appointed by agreement between the employer and the representative union and that, where no such agreement can be reached, the Commission for Conciliation, Mediation & Arbitration should be approached to appoint an electoral officer. The constitution should set out the **duties of the electoral officer.**
- A provision that the **election of members** to a workplace forum be held **every two years**
- A provision that, **where another union achieves majority representation, it may**, within 21 months of the previous election, **call for another election**
- The **procedure and methods** by which **elections by ballot** are to be held. For example, the constitution can specify that, within a certain period before the election, the electoral officer should establish a list of all employees in the workplace and call for nominations. It may further be determined by the constitution that members of forums may be re-elected, that the electoral officer should (within a prescribed period) determine whether the nominees qualify for election, that he should publish a list of candidates and compile a ballot paper with the names of nominees in alphabetical order, and that voting should be by secret ballot.
- A provision to the effect that **any employee, including a previous or serving member of a forum, may be nominated** by a registered union having members at the workplace, or by 20 percent of all employees, or 100 employees — whichever is the lesser.
- A clause stating that **every employee is entitled to vote** by secret ballot during working hours and at the workplace of the employer
- A provision that **every employee is entitled to a number of votes equal to the number of members to be elected**, and that he may

bring out one or more of those votes in favour of any candidate

- A section relating to the **term of office** of members of the workplace forum and the **vacating of office** by any member. For example, the constitution could state that a member may at any time resign from the forum by giving written notice and that he *should* vacate his office when his resignation comes into effect, if he is promoted to senior management status, if he is transferred from the workplace, if his services have been terminated or in terms of a determination made by a Commissioner.

- A section relating to the circumstances in which and the method by which a **member may be removed from office**, including the **right of a representative union to remove a union member** who has been elected to office. For example, this section could also state that, where 20 percent of employees petition for the removal of a forum member on the grounds of gross neglect of duty, such petition will be subject to arbitration by the Commission for Mediation, Conciliation & Arbitration.

- A process whereby **vacancies on the forum can be filled**, as well as **procedures for the holding of a by-election**

- A section relating to the **holding of meetings** by the workplace forum (see section on meetings)

- A provision that the employer must give the electoral officer **reasonable time off during working hours** to prepare for elections

- A provision that the employer shall give members of the workplace forum **reasonable paid time off during working hours** to fulfil their forum functions and to receive training related to these functions

- The requirement that the **employer** will take any steps which could reasonably be expected of him to **assist the electoral officer** with elections

- The requirement that the **employer provide** the workplace forum with the **facilities** necessary to perform its function. Such facilities could include monies, necessities and materials required for elections, administrative and secretarial facilities, a room for meetings and access to a telephone.

- A provision for **fulltime members** of workplace forums at workplaces employing more than 1 000 employees. In terms of the Act, fulltime representatives should be paid an amount equal to that earned immediately before their appointment as representatives. Should such a person cease to be a fulltime representative, the employer must reinstate him in his previous position or offer him any promotion post to which he would have advanced.

- A provision that the **forum may invite any expert** to attend its meetings, including meetings with management, and that such expert will have the **right of access to all information** to which the forum is entitled

- A provision that the officials or **office bearers of a majority union may attend meetings of the forum**, including meetings with management

- Allowance for a majority union and the employer to **amend the forum's constitution** by mutual agreement

The constitution *may*, further, contain:

- a procedure providing for **mediation** in matters where consensus cannot be reached;
- a provision for a **coordinating workplace forum** and subsidiary forums. For example, if the employer has operations which are independent of each other, he can provide for a coordinating workplace forum to deal with matters affecting all workplaces and for subsidiary forums dealing with 'local' issues. The same can be done where a workplace is geographically spread; and
- **provisions which deviate from those in the Act** relating to the holding of meetings, consultation, co-decisionmaking, disclosure of information, inspection of documents, confidentiality and fulltime members of workplace forums.

GRIEVANCE PROCEDURE

1. General

1.1 An employee may lodge a grievance without any prejudice or fear of victimisation.

1.2 Grievances should be raised with Management as soon as possible, in order that they may be speedily resolved.

1.3 The duty to resolve grievances will be vested in line Management.

1.4 The Grievance Procedure will not be used by employees for the purpose of:
- (a) amending any provisions of any agreement between the parties;
- (b) amending any substantive condition of employment for any category of employee, e.g. wages, leave, bonuses, etc.

2. Stages of Procedure

Stage I
- (a) The employee will first raise his grievance verbally with his direct superior, in order that it may be quickly resolved.
- (b) If the grievance is not settled within 2 days of first being raised, a written grievance form has to be completed and handed in to the Personnel Department.
- (c) Upon receipt the Personnel Department will send a copy to the Departmental Manager.

Stage II
- (a) If the grievance remains unresolved 2 days after the date on which the Departmental Manger received the copy, he will arrange a meeting with the parties concerned.
- (b) At this meeting, the aggrieved worker, his Shop Steward, if requested, the foreman and a member of the personnel department will be present. (c) Two days will be given to resolve the matter; if it is not resolved, the grievance will be referred to Stage III.

Stage III
- (a) The employee will present a copy of the grievance form to the Production Manager.
- (b) Within a week of receiving a copy of the grievance, the Production Manager or his nominee will call a meeting of all parties concerned. A union representative may be present, if so requested by the employee.
- (c) The Production Manger will propose a final settlement of the grievance within 3 full working days as from the date of the meeting contemplated under (b).
- (d) In the event of the worker and/or his representative being unable or unwilling to accept the settlement as proposed by the Factory Manager, the matter may be pursued in terms of the agreed Dispute Procedure.

GRIEVANCE FORM

Date: . . . .

Name of Employee: . . . .   Clock No: . . . .

Department: . . . .   Shift: . . . .

Foreman: . . . .   Shop Steward: . . . .

Date on which Grievance Occurred: . . . .   Shop Steward No: . . . .

Employee's Grievance: (Short description, only facts to be noted)

. . . .

. . . .

. . . .

. . . .

Settlement Desired:

. . . .

. . . .

. . . .

. . . .

Foreman's Comment:

. . . .

. . . .

. . . .

. . . .

Signed: . . . .   Signed: . . . .
                     Employee   Foreman

Date Received by Personnel Dept: . . . .   Signed: . . . .

Department Manager's Comment:

. . . .

. . . .

. . . .

. . . .

Production Manager's Comment:

. . . .

. . . ., ...

. . . .

. . . .

Date: . . . . Signed: . . . .

Settlement Agreed Upon:

. . . .

. . . .

. . . .

. . . .

Signed: . . . .   Date: . . . .
Employee

Signed: . . . .   Date: . . . .
Shop Steward

Signed: . . . .   Date: . . . .
for Company

Returned to Personnel Dept: . . . .   Signature . . . .

DISCIPLINARY CODE AND PROCEDURE

Purpose of Disciplinary Code
1. To ensure fair and equal treatment of all employees
2. To encourage timely corrective action in the event where an employee's behaviour or performance proves to be unsatisfactory or unacceptable.
3. To ensure that all the principles of natural justice are applied before an employee is dismissed

Principles
1. This code shall be equally applicable to all employees, including supervisors and managers.
2. It is the responsibility of all employees to maintain discipline at all times.
3. An employee subject to action in terms of the Disciplinary Code shall at all times be entitled to representation by a fellow employee of his own choice or by a union official.
4. Any person who is not satisfied with disciplinary action taken against him will be entitled to invoke the relevant steps of the Grievance Procedure.
5. The Disciplinary Code will not be applied for the purpose of intimidation or victimisation.

Categorisation of Transgressions and Actions to be Taken

Category A
If an employee commits a transgression in this category, the following steps will be taken.

1st transgression in this category	: Reprimand
2nd transgression in this category	: Formal verbal warning
3rd transgression in this category	: 1st written warning
4th transgression in this category	: 2nd written warning
5th transgression in this category	: Final written warning
6th transgression in this category	: Disciplinary hearing and possible dismissal

The following will be regarded as transgressions in Category A.

- Repeated latecoming (i.e. initially for coming late without an acceptable reason more than twice in one week, twice in two consecutive weeks or three times in a month, and thereafter in each case of unexcused latecoming)
- Repeated absenteeism without an acceptable reason
- Leaving before closing time
- Arriving late at workstation
- Not clocking in
- Absence from workstation for less than an hour without reason or permission (non-key position)
- Sleeping at workstation
- Failure to carry out routine instructions
- Not wearing protective clothing when provided

- Disregard of safety rules
- First and subsequent proof of inadequate performance
- Disrespect towards superiors, subordinates or colleagues
- Engaging in horseplay
- Minor and unintentional damage to property
- Carelessness (i.e. neglect of a minor nature)

Category B

For transgressions in this category the steps outlined hereunder will be taken (except that, where an employee has already committed more than three transgressions in Category A, he will start at the corresponding stage in this category).

1st transgression in this category	: 1st written warning
2nd transgression in this category	: 2nd written warning
3rd transgression in this category	: Final written warning
4th transgression in this category	: Disciplinary hearing and possible dismissal

The following will be regarded as transgressions in Category B.

- Absence from workstation for less than an hour without reason or permission (key position)
- Absence from workstation for more than one hour but less than two without reason or permission (non-key position)
- Absence after permission refused
- Leaving premises without permission (non-key position)
- Not notifying superior of expected absence in time (i.e. at least three hours before start of afternoon or evening shift, or one hour after commencement of morning shift)
- Sleeping elsewhere than at workstation while on duty (non-key position)
- Sleeping at workstation (key position)
- Not obeying important instructions (non-key position)
- Not obeying routine instructions (key position)
- Refusal to obey security regulations
- Insolence
- Disorderly behaviour (swearing, or behaving in an unacceptable manner)
- Negligence of a relatively serious nature
- Major but unintentional damage to property
- Possession or wrongful use of company property (but without the intention to misappropriate)
- Falsifying or withholding information
- Unauthorised possession of intoxicating liquor or drugs

Category C

Transgressions in this category are regarded as very serious in nature and will be subject to the following actions.

1st transgression in this category : Final written warning
2nd transgression in this category : Disciplinary hearing and possible dismissal

The following will be regarded as transgressions in Category C.

- Absence from workstation for more than two hours without reason or permission (non-key position)
- Absence from workstation for more than one hour but less than two hours without reason or permission (key position)
- Leaving premises without permission (key position)
- Absent from work for three days without notification or reason
- Not obeying important instructions (key position)
- Endangering premises, self or others by ignoring safety regulations
- Insubordination
- Fighting
- Threatening violence
- Intimidating fellow employees
- Sexual harassment
- Discrimination on the basis of race or sex
- Making remarks which cause racial tension
- Not major but intentional damage to property
- Deliberate and unauthorised possession of company property (seemingly with intention to misappropriate)
- Blatant untruths or deliberately giving false information
- Disclosure of confidential information
- Unauthorised intake of intoxicating liquor or drugs on the premises
- Continued, serious incompetence or inadequate performance (only if a period of six months after first indication of incompetence and following repeated efforts at corrective action)

Category D

The transgressions in this category are so serious in nature that the company will have to consider whether the transgressor can remain in his job or in the employ of the company. The following actions may therefore be taken.

- A hearing pending dismissal with notice, or
- A hearing pending summary dismissal

The following will be regarded as transgressions in Category D.

- Absence of more than three days without reason or permission
- Deliberate disregard of safety rules resulting in actual serious damage to persons or property
- Assault with intent to do serious bodily harm
- Sexual assault of any kind
- Major and intentional damage to property

- Gross negligence
- Misappropriation of property
- Disclosure of strictly confidential information
- Competing with the business of the employer
- Intoxication resulting in inability to perform duties or absolutely unacceptable behaviour

Final Warnings

An employee who is on a final written warning for any offence, whether it be in category A, B or C, and who then commits another offence (except one in category A) may then be subject to a Disciplinary Hearing pending dismissal.

Duration of Warnings

Warnings will be valid for the following periods.

All ordinary warnings in Category A	: 3 months
All ordinary warnings in Category B	: 3 months
All final warnings in Categories A and B	: 4 months
All warnings in Category C	: 6 months

Warnings will expire after the prescribed period (that is, the next step cannot be taken if another transgression is committed after three months in the case of Category A and B offences, six months in the case of Category C offences and four months in the case of other final warnings), but the warnings will stand as part of the employee's Disciplinary Record.

Alternatives to Dismissal

The union representatives have agreed that the company may consider the following as alternatives to dismissal.

- A period of suspension without pay
- Demotion to a position paid at a lesser rate for a period of six months

In the case of a Category D transgression, it may be decided during an appeal that, in the light of particular circumstances, an employee should be given a final written warning instead of being dismissed. The same conditions as for Category C offences will then apply.

Counselling

As discipline is aimed at correction, prevention and rehabilitation rather than punishment, all disciplinary action will be followed by counselling from the relevant supervisor or department head. Note should be taken of employees who improve their conduct.

Responsibility for Disciplinary Action

1. The responsibility for taking disciplinary action rests with supervisory staff and members of management.
2. When initiating disciplinary actions, supervisors and managers will adhere to the agreed Disciplinary Code and Procedure and will act consistently at all times.
3. First and second written warnings and verbal warnings may be issued by the employee's immediate supervisor. Final warnings and hearings pending dismissal are the responsibility of the relevant department head.

Department heads will check the disciplinary records of all employees in their departments on a regular basis.

Taking Disciplinary Action

1. Formal verbal warnings and all written warnings will be issued in a formal manner and recorded.
2. The employee concerned will sign the record to acknowledge:
   (a) that he has received such warning, and
   (b) that he accepts it.
3. Where the employee does not accept the warning given, this fact may be recorded but he will sign to indicate that he has received the warning.
4. Where an employee refuses to sign a warning (i.e. to indicate that he has received it), the supervisor or manager may call witnesses to testify to this fact.
5. In the case of a final warning, a formal letter will be issued, warning the employee that he is in danger of being dismissed if he commits another transgression.
6. All warnings and a hearing pending dismissal may be preceded by an informal or formal inquiry to establish the facts of the case, during which period statements may be taken from various parties.
7. Any employee who is of the opinion that a warning issued to him was not justified may lodge a complaint by invoking the relevant steps of the Grievance Procedure.

Hearing Pending Dismissal

1. No employee may be dismissed without being granted a formal hearing, unless circumstances such as the employee either absconding or being unwilling to return to work render this impossible.
2. Where an employee is in receipt of a valid final warning and commits another transgression, or where an employee commits a Category D transgression, the head of department should be immediately informed.
3. The head of department will inform the employee of his position.
4. The head of department may then conduct a formal or informal inquiry to establish the facts of the case and take the necessary statements.
5. Thereafter, the employee will be given due notice (of at least 48 hours) that a hearing to establish whether he is guilty of the transgression will be conducted by the company.
6. Such notice should be in writing and should stipulate the reason for the hearing, the exact date and time of the hearing. It should also inform the employee of his rights during the hearing: his right to an interpreter, his right to select a representative of his own choice from within the company, to state his own case or to let is be stated for him, and his right to call any witnesses or produce any evidence which will substantiate his case.
7. If, after an inquiry, it is felt that the employee should not remain on the premises, he may be suspended on full pay pending a formal Disciplinary Hearing.
8. In order to prepare for the hearing, the employee and his representative will be given reasonable access to documents and information which might be of relevance to the matter in hand.
9. Hearings will be conducted by a panel consisting of members of management, who will select their own chairman. The member of

management involved with the matter will not form part of the panel, but will act as arraigner.

10. Arraigners should adhere to the matter in hand and should produce all the evidence collected by them. The employee or his representative will be allowed to cross-question such evidence.

11. The employee and his representative should be given every opportunity to bring the employee's side of the story.

12. Having heard all evidence and argument the panel will adjourn to consider a final decision, bearing in mind that it should be proved that, on the balance of probability, the employee committed the transgression.

13. Thereafter the panel will decide on the sanction to be imposed, in the light of the fact that any sanction should be aimed at rehabilitation, deterrence or prevention. (The union has requested that the decision concerning the sanction be based only on the case in hand, and not on any other circumstance.)

14. Upon reconvening the hearing, the chairman will inform the employee of the decision taken, the reasons for such decision and the sanction to be imposed. Such information will subsequently be substantiated by a written notification.

15. An employee subject to a decision to dismiss or to a final written warning may, within the prescribed time, appeal against such decision or warning.

Appeals Against Final Warnings or Decisions to Dismiss

1. An employee who feels that a disciplinary hearing has not been properly conducted, that all evidence has not been taken into account or that certain mitigating circumstances exist may lodge an appeal with the General Manager.

2. Such appeal should be made direct to the General Manager within a period of 72 hours after the decision to dismiss or to issue a final warning. It should be in writing and should explain the reason for the appeal being lodged (see above).

3. For the purpose of lodging an appeal, the employee or his representative will be granted reasonable access to the employee's employment records and/or any other relevant information.

4. The General Manager has 72 hours in which to consider the appeal.

5. The General Manager will study the minutes of the disciplinary hearing and the employee's employment record, and will thereafter hold a meeting with the employee, his representative and the chairman of the disciplinary panel in order to hear further evidence and argument. He will also consider the interests of the employee, other employees and the company.

6. Should the General Manager be of the opinion that sufficient mitigating circumstances exist for questioning the decision to dismiss or to issue a final written warning, he will instruct that the disciplinary hearing be reopened within 48 hours.

7. Alternatively, the General Manager may be of the opinion that there are sufficient mitigating circumstances. In this case, he himself will rescind the previous decision and issue a new decision.

8. Should the employee feel that the decision taken is still unfair or unjustified, he may within 48 hours request that a meeting be held between the General Manager, himself and his representative, a union official or other adviser and the chairman of the disciplinary panel.

9. If, after this, the employee remains dissatisfied, he may within thirty days declare a dispute, whereafter the steps stipulated in the agreed Disputes Procedure will come into effect.

Time Limits

1. No disciplinary action may be initiated more than seven days after the occurrence of the transgression which gave rise to the action.
2. An employee wishing to lodge a grievance against a disciplinary action should do so no later than 48 hours after the time at which such action was taken.
3. An employee wishing to appeal against a decision to dismiss or to issue a final written warning must do so within 72 hours of the time at which the decision was taken.
4. The General Manager has 72 hours in which to consider an appeal.
5. An employee wishing to request a meeting subsequent to an unsuccessful appeal should do so within 72 hours.
6. Any employee wishing to declare a dispute in terms of the Disputes Procedure should do so within thirty days of the dispute having arisen.

General

The Disciplinary Code and Procedure, together with the Rules of the Company, will be made available to all employees.

The Code will not be applied frivolously, nor should it be treated in a frivolous manner by employees or managers.

REPORT: DISCIPLINARY INCIDENT

Employee's name: . . . .   Department: . . . .

Supervisor: . . . .   Position. . . . .

Nature of Transgression:

. . . .

. . . .

. . . .

. . . .

Signature of Arraigner . . . .

Date: . . . .   Time: . . . .   Witnesses:

Action Taken:

. . . .

. . . .

. . . .

. . . .

Signature of person
Date: . . . .   initiating action: . . . .

Employee's Reaction:

. . . .

. . . .

. . . .

. . . .

. . . .

Signature of Employee   Signature of Initiator

WARNING: BREACH OF DISCIPLINARY CODE

To: . . . .   Department: . . . .

This letter serves as a . . . . written warning that you have breached the disciplinary
code by . . . .

. . . .

. . . .   on . . . .

Should you commit another breach of the Code within the next . . . . months, we shall
have no option but to invoke the next step of the Disciplinary Procedure as outlined in the
Disciplinary Code.

We regret that this action had to be taken and sincerely hope that your future conduct will
make it unnecessary for us to take further action.

If you feel, however, that this warning is not justified, you have the right to invoke the relevant
steps of the Grievance Procedure.

Yours faithfully

Position: . . . .   Date: . . . .

I, ...   hereby acknowledge that I have understood
the contents of this letter and that I hereby accept/reject the warning given to me.

. . . .   Witness: . . . .
Signature of Employee

Date: . . . .

FINAL WRITTEN WARNING

Mr/Mrs . . . .

. . . .

. . . .

Dear . . . .

FINAL WRITTEN WARNING IN TERMS OF DISCIPLINARY CODE

It has come to our notice that during the past . . . . months/on . . . .
you breached the Disciplinary Code by . . . .

. . . .

. . . .

The company regards these actions/this action in an extremely serious light. If there is no
discipline at . . . .   the company itself will fail and if we were
to take no action against you, it would be unfair to your fellow employees. This letter therefore
serves as **final warning** that you will face a disciplinary hearing pending dismissal should you,
within the next . . . . months, again commit a serious breach of the Disciplinary Code.

We regret that this action was necessary and sincerely hope that no further steps will be
required.

Should you, on your part, feel that this warning is unjustified, you may invoke the Grievance
Procedure or lodge an appeal against the action with the General Manager.

Yours faithfully

Position: . . . .   Date . . . .

I, ...   hereby acknowledge that I have understood
the contents of this letter and that I hereby accept/reject the warning given to me.

. . . .   Witness: . . . .
Signature of Employee

Date: . . . .

DISCIPLINARY RECORD CARD

DATE	TRANSGRESSION	ACTION TAKEN	RESPONSIBLE MANAGER	FOLLOW-UP

ABBREVIATED NEGOTIATION PLANNING SHEET

ISSUES	PRIORITY	NEGOTIABLE / NOT NEGOTIABLE	COMMON GROUND
: : : : : :	: : :	: : : : : : : : : : : :	: : : : : : : : : : : :

ISSUES	WOULD LIKE TO	MAY HAVE TO	LIKELY TO	THEIR LIKELY RANGE
: : : : : :	: : : : : :	: : : : : :	: : : : : :	: : : : : :

MOTIVATIONS

ISSUES	ARGUMENT	POSSIBLE COUNTERARGUMENT
: : : : : :	: : : : : : : : : : : :	: : : : : : : : : : : :

BARGAINING POWER

THEIRS	OURS

STRATEGY

POSSIBLE PACKAGES

HANDLING A WORK STOPPAGE

GUIDELINES FOR USE BY GENERAL MANAGER'S COMMITTEE ONLY

It is this company's policy to resolve problems at the lowest organisational level when they occur. To these ends and to ensure that all employees are treated fairly, we have introduced effective grievance and disciplinary procedures. However, notwithstanding these preventative measures, work stoppages may still occur.

The following is really a broad plan of action intended as a guide in the event of a work stoppage. The model comprises four basic elements:

A. Preparation
B. Guidelines for handling work stoppage
C. Options
D. Follow-up

A. Preparation	1.1	Inform the General Manager and Personnel Manager	*All Managers*
	1.2	Advise the Chief Executive, the Human Resources Director and other General Managers	*General Manager*
	2.	Ensure that the following documentation is at hand (see attached):	*Operations Manager*
	2.1	List of telephone numbers for key personnel	
	2.2	Telephone number of local traffic police	
	2.3	Telephone number of ambulance service/hospital	
	2.4	Telephone number of fire brigade	
	2.5	Telephone numbers of all main suppliers	
	2.6	Telephone numbers of all main customers	
	2.7	Telephone number of Department of Labour	
	2.8	Telephone numbers of local employers' association, chamber of industries and industrial relations attorneys	
	3.	Appoint a negotiating panel consisting of the General Manager and the General Manager's committee	*General Manager*
	4.	Make arrangements for availability of funds and for wages for all employees in the event of the termination of their employment. *(Applies only to illegal strike)*	*General Manager with responsible person*
		Ensure that:	
	4.1	sufficient personnel is available	
	4.2	sufficient funds are obtainable at short notice	
	4.3	there is adequate security for the wage personnel	

4.4   the paying out operation can be completed in less than eight hours

4.5   alternative arrangements are made for wages completion; and

4.6   payment of wages takes place near the gate.

B. Guidelines for Handling Work Stoppage

1. Establish the nature and causes.   *General Manager's committee*

1.1   Endeavour to identify the true leaders or representatives of the strikers and establish the nature of the issue/dispute — e.g. is it a wage issue, a grievance, the recognition of a trade union, and so on?

1.2   Establish scope/area of the stoppage and the real causes. Note that the apparent cause is not always the real cause as this may be difficult to articulate.

1.3   At this stage one's main objective is to gather data. One should, therefore, not react to statements or demands, or make any early concessions.

1.4   Show concern for employees' grievances and undertake to investigate their complaints and to discuss them, if possible, on resumption of work by the employees.

2. Convening of panel: *General Manager*

2.1   The panel should assemble as soon as possible under the coordination and control of the General Manager. Their initial function is to decide on the strategy.

2.2   Inform the Department of Labour, but ask the official to refrain from intervention as management has the situation under control and can resolve the problem without their assistance. (*Note* that this is a legal requirement.)

2.3   Inform the employers' association and the chamber of industries of the situation.

2.4   Keep as many personal notes as possible — remember, once the strike is over, you will want to have all the facts at hand. It is also important to record or diarise events as they occur, but one should separate the facts from personal interpretations.   *General Manager's committee*

3. Open dialogue with representatives of strikers:

Whenever possible, maintain the recognised channels of communication — the elected shop stewards. Call a meeting of the shop stewards and, if it is apparent that the real leaders of the strikers are not union members, augment the shop stewards' committee with a few nominees to be appointed by strikers. If strikers reject the shop stewards, they should be asked to elect four or   *Operations Manager* five spokesmen. Every endeavour should be made to open a channel of communication with the strikers. Avoid communication with the mob.

4. Take precautions:

4.1 Put into effect your plan for the manning of key areas including buildings, plant, vehicles, petrol, stores, etc. This plan would be part of the crisis control action plan.

4.2 Begin the shutdown procedure for plant, steam and electricity and/or the continued operation of key plant. Advise major suppliers to discontinue deliveries and inform the major customers in the event that you cannot deliver key stock.

4.3 If the situation is very tense and violence imminent, take all other employees off the property and allow them to go home. (One might have to consider providing transport.)

4.4 It is in the company's best interest to cooperate fully with the Press and to provide them with factual information to ensure factual reporting and to avoid adverse publicity. All enquiries should be referred to the Chief Executive or his delegate and staff should be instructed to refrain from passing an opinion, even if requested to do so by a reporter. Delegate a senior person to sit with the switchboard operator to prevent any leaks of the stoppage.

Operations Manager

5. Selection of Strategy:

5.1 Reduce the dispute to one clear and concrete issue and identify the real cause.

5.2 Advise strikers that their not being at work means that they will not be paid for that time.

5.3 Keep your options open and flexible at this stage. Endeavour to preserve relationships.

5.4 Be prepared to talk and negotiate with representatives of the strikers. (The more you talk to them, the more chance you have of reaching a solution.)

5.5 Explain your side of the issue.

General Manager

6. Take action:

6.1 Be positive and definite throughout the strike. The strikers must be left in no doubt that what management says, it will do.

6.2 Do not give the impression to the strikers that management is panicking. Act calmly but firmly at all times. Keep it low-key and avoid a confrontation.

6.3 Communicate your decision with the representatives of the strikers and allow a short time for strikers to reach a decision. If at all possible, allow for 'face saving'.

Options There are three main options the negotiating panel can take:

1. Sitting it out
2. Terminating employment *(only if the strike is illegal)*
3. Making concessions

(Note: Other options or a combination of options may exist — management judgment here is very important.)

1. Sit it out:

1.1 This allows a cooling-off period and opportunity for management to take stock. If a principle is at stake, how important is that principle?

1.2 Increase the pressure on the strikers by emphasising possible loss of service benefits. Repeat your offer and allow time for them to consider: if there seems no way of breaking the deadlock, advise the workers that —

The management considers your action as a strike. As from ...[time]..., anyone who has not returned to work will not be paid.

One should allow at least half an hour from the time of issue of this statement to the time for work to be resumed.

1.3 Assess the strikers' ability to hold out, and consider the possibility and effects of consumer action.

1.4 Is the solution within one's power? If not, one can only sit it out.

2. Terminating the Strikers *(Illegal strikes):*

2.1 Terminate workers as a last resort. Remember that, when workers strike, they are not saying that they wish to terminate their contracts with the company. It is, in fact, an endeavour to draw attention to a serious grievance and to have it resolved. Termination of service does not resolve their grievances, and it invariably engenders public, media and (possibly) consumer support for the strikers.

General Manager

2.2 Termination changes the nature of the dispute, for the issue then becomes one of the reinstatement of workers. It also leads to a confrontation situation, which seldom does either party any good.

2.3 Do not resort to termination too early in the process of resolving the dispute; nor should such a decision be conveyed when strikers are emotionally charged, as is sometimes the case.

2.4 Give strikers an ultimatum: either return to work, or face dismissal — and sufficient time to make a decision.

3. Concession:

3.1 Consider the long-term consequences and the costs of conceding. Will it cost more to agree or to disagree?

3.2 Is the grievance legitimate and justified, and was management at fault? If so, it would probably be in the company's interest to concede rather than to try to bluff one's way out of the situation.

3.3 If the issue is one of recognition of a trade union and the union is able to prove representivity, it would be advisable to agree to negotiate the terms of such recognition on condition that the strikers return to work.

D. Follow-up Action

1. Understanding:

Ensure that whatever action management promised is implemented in every detail and with a minimum of delay. If a full investigation was agreed to, the findings thereon, together with management's proposed action, should be communicated to all employees through the usual channels and the communication should be reinforced by using, for example, notice boards and weekly departmental meetings.

General Manager

2. Work Relationships:

Work should be resumed as soon as possible and first-line supervision should be asked to use considerable tact, bearing in mind that employees will be dissatisfied, resentful, antagonistic and uncooperative for a while. Care should be taken to avoid incidents which spark off a recurrence of disturbances.

General Manager

3. Communication:

If it was agreed to negotiate with the employees, it is advisable to allow a 'cooling off' period before commencing discussions with either nominated spokesmen or the workplace forum. This, however, will be dependent to a large extent on objective judgment of the situation at any particular time, and management must not be seen to be dragging its heels on this aspect of agreement.

If the shop stewards were rejected during the strike,

Operations Manager

endeavour to re-establish their credibility (or that of some other representative body) as the official channel of communication as soon as possible.

Meet with representatives of other employees not involved in the strike to put them fully in the picture regarding management's actions and proposed actions.

RECOGNITION AGREEMENT

1. Preamble   1.1   The objective of this Agreement is the regulation of the relationship between the parties.

1.2   The maintenance of a harmonious working relationship is desired by both parties. This requires their cooperation and good faith, which is essential for the successful running of the Company.

1.3   A spirit of mutual respect should therefore prevail in all dealings between the parties.

1.4   Both parties will seek reasonable and satisfactory solutions to disputes which may arise between them, and will develop procedures which assist in avoiding disputes.

1.5   Both parties endorse the principle of freedom of association and accordingly recognise the right of employees to belong to the union of their choice or to refrain from union membership.

1.6   Both parties to this agreement are bound by its terms and conditions, which shall be enforceable by law.

1.7   The Union recognises the rights and responsibilities of managing the Company's establishment, as vested in management, who shall at all times be solely responsible therefor.

2. Definitions   2.1   **Access** means the right of accredited officials to visit the factory, to consult with members, provided that such activities shall not be conducted in such a manner as to disrupt production and always subject to the provisions of this Agreement.

2.2   **Accredited Union Official** means a fulltime employee or office bearer of the Union's office, or a Shop Steward of the Company, who is nominated by the Union to represent it. The Company shall have a written record of all accredited Union officials.

2.3   **Act** means the Labour Relations Act (No. 28 of 1956), as amended from time to time.

2.4   **Company** means the company as operating at . . . .

2.5   **Dispute** means any matter which is declared a dispute by written notice from one party to the other in terms of clause 9 of this Agreement.

2.6   **Eligible Employee** means a Company employee, employed from time to time at the factory in job categories which are remunerated on a weekly basis, as opposed to a monthly basis.

2.7   **Factory** means the Company's factory at . . . .

2.8   **Grievance** means a dissatisfaction or feeling of injustice affecting an employee which arises out of his particular conditions of work or employment, or the employment relationship.

2.9   **Management Representative** means a person nominated by the Company to represent it in its dealings with the Union.

2.10   **Member** means any eligible employee who is a member in good standing of the Union in terms of its constitution.

2.11   **Shop Steward** means an employee appointed to represent the Union.

2.12 **Union** means the . . . .
as constituted according to its constitution, lodged with the Industrial
Registrar in terms of the Act.

3. Recognition The Company recognises the Union as the collective bargaining representative
of its members, within the agreed bargaining unit, subject to the provisions of
this agreement and provided further that the Union shall have and maintain a
minimum membership in excess of 50 percent of all eligible employees at the
factory.

4. Access: 4.1 The Company agrees to grant accredited Union officials reasonable access
Officials   to meet members during members' own time. The Company will provide
adequate facilities where Union business may be conducted without
disruption of the Company's operation.

4.2 The Union will give the Company reasonable notice of any intended visits
and will be advised of the available venue on such date.

4.3 The accredited officials will have to comply with the security
arrangements in force from time to time.

4.4 Visits of other Union officials will not be unreasonably withheld; provided
that the names of such officials, their function and the purpose of such
visit is made known.

5. Notice The Company shall allow the Union the use of Company notice boards for the
Boards display of notices by the Union, provided that such notices shall have been
submitted to and approved by the Company, prior to display, and the Company
agrees that it shall not unreasonably withhold such consent.

6. Checkoff 6.1 The Company undertakes to deduct current Union subscriptions from the
Facilities   wages of members and to remit the amounts so deducted to the Union by
the 15th day of the ensuing month, together with a schedule of the names
and clock numbers of the members.

6.2 The employee shall authorise such deduction in writing, as per Annexure
A.

6.3 The Company shall not be responsible for collecting subscriptions which
are in arrears, save where such arrears arise through the failure or refusal
of the Company to deduct.

6.4 Such authority to deduct shall be terminable by the worker resigning from
the Union. The Union undertakes to notify the Company of any such
resignations within 14 days of the Union's receipt thereof.

6.5 Should subscriptions be increased, the Company requires not less than 14
days' notice to effect such change.

6.6 The Company undertakes to provide the above facilities free of charge.

7. Shop 7.1 **Recognition of Shop Stewards**
Stewards   The Company agrees to recognise Shop Stewards at its premises to
represent employees who are members of the Union and to make
representations on their behalf, in accordance with law and the terms of
this agreement.

7.2 **Nominations and Elections of Shop Stewards**

| 7.2.1 | The Constituencies for Shop Stewards are specified in Annexure B. Changes to these Constituencies shall be determined by mutual agreement. |

7.2.1   The Constituencies for Shop Stewards are specified in Annexure B. Changes to these Constituencies shall be determined by mutual agreement.

7.2.2   Nominations and elections for Shop Stewards will be by secret ballot on the Company's premises.

7.2.3   The members for election must be employed in the Constituency for which they are nominated.

7.2.4   The Union agrees that management may be present to observe the process of nomination and election and to verify the outcome of the elections.

7.2.5   The Union shall, within 7 days of completion of the election, notify the Company in writing of the names of the Shop Stewards and the Constituencies which they will represent.

7.2.6   On election, Shop Stewards will complete a declaration form (Annexure C).

7.3   Termination of Shop Steward's Office
A Shop Steward shall cease to hold office:

7.3.1   on expiry of his two year term of office, but he may make himself available for reelection.

7.3.2   on his resignation or termination of employment with the Company.

7.3.3   on his resignation as Shop Steward.

7.3.4   on his transfer at his own request to any other department or section of the factory outside his Constituency.

7.3.5   on his appointment to a category of work where he is no longer considered an eligible employee.

7.3.6   on his resignation from the Union.

7.3.7   should he not carry out his duties as laid down in this Agreement (see also Annexure C).

7.3.8   on closure or discontinuation of a section or department or shift, whereby his Constituency ceases to exist.

7.4   In case of termination other than by the demise of a constituency, a by-election must be held within 30 days.

7.5   Rights and Duties of Shop Stewards

7.5.1   Management undertakes to discuss with Shop Stewards any matters relating to the terms and conditions of employment.

7.5.2   The Union accepts that those Shop Stewards or Senior Shop Stewards elected are considered to be normal employees, bound by rules and regulations prevailing from time to time in the factory. Their rights should be exercised as laid down in this Agreement and any other Agreement entered into by the parties.

7.5.3   Shop Stewards have the right to bring to the notice of their direct superior in their Constituency any matter concerning a member.

7.5.4   Shop Stewards shall carry out their duties without unreasonably or unnecessarily interfering with or disrupting their own or another employee's work.

7.5.5   The Company agrees to recognise two Senior Shop Stewards, who will be appointed through election from the Shop Stewards' Committee. The Senior Shop Stewards shall have reasonable access to all Constituencies, provided they first obtain the consent of the respective departmental managers.

7.5.6   The Company agrees that for the purpose of carrying out their duties, Shop Stewards and accredited Union officials may meet once a month on Company premises. Such meeting shall not exceed two hours of Company time.

7.5.7   Shop Stewards shall be permitted to meet amongst themselves and with members within their departments in their own time.

7.6   **Victimisation**

The Company undertakes that no Shop Steward shall be victimised as a result of his exercising his right as a Shop Steward in good faith and in pursuance of his duties as a Shop Steward in accordance with this Agreement; neither will the Company victimise any employee by virtue of his union membership.

8. Negotiation Procedure

8.1   The parties agree to the creation of a negotiating committee, which shall consist of not more than five (5) representatives of each party. However the parties agree that up to two Company employees from either side, other than members of the negotiating committee, may attend negotiation meetings as observers.

8.2   The negotiating committee shall be convened as soon as practicable, on the written request of either party, to discuss matters directly affecting employees. The subjects to be discussed at the meeting should be presented in the form of an agenda. Any agreement arrived at shall be reduced to writing, signed by the parties and thereafter binding on the parties.

8.3   Official minutes will be taken at all meetings between the parties and posted on the Company notice boards. These minutes will be confirmed by the parties at the following meeting.

8.4   The negotiating committees shall meet as often as the parties agree to be necessary for the resolution of their differences or matters of mutual concern.

8.5   In cases where the negotiating committee should reach deadlock, the steps as prescribed in section 9 hereafter shall apply.

8.6   If necessary, the Company will allow the union to report back to members on urgent matters during working time.

9. Dispute Procedure

9.1   In the event of failure to reach agreement at any of the meetings held in terms of clause 8 of this Agreement, either the Company or the Union may, on provision of five working days' notice, invoke the dispute procedure. At the time of invoking the dispute procedure, the party invoking the procedure must provide written notice of the nature and content of the dispute, as well as the settlement proposed.

9.2   Within five working days of such notice being received, the receiving party shall respond in writing to the allegation contained in the statement of dispute and, furthermore, shall set out that party's position in regard to the desired settlement as well as its own settlement proposal.

9.3 Within fifteen working days of the date of the written response, the parties shall meet on at least two occasions in order to resolve the dispute.

9.4 The parties may at any stage agree to refer the dispute to mediation. If, after three meetings, the parties cannot agree on a mediator, the Independent Mediation Service will be approached to appoint a mediator of its own choosing. The cost of mediation will be shared by the parties.

9.5.1 If, after fifteen working days, the dispute remains unresolved and if the dispute is a dispute of interest, then either party may institute the statutory procedures towards the institution of a legal strike or a legal lockout.

9.5.2 The company agrees to allow ten strikers to assemble at and around the main entrance during working hours for the purpose of picketing, provided that these persons:

(a) take up fixed positions and do not depart from such positions;

(b) do not hinder access to and exit from the premises;

(c) do not engage in violent or disorderly behaviour and do not damage company property.

9.6 If the dispute is one of right and if after 15 working days it remains unresolved, the dispute will, upon agreement,

9.6.1 be submitted to arbitration by a private arbitrator selected by both parties, or

9.6.2 be submitted to arbitration by the Committee for Conciliation, Mediation & Arbitration, or

9.6.3 be referred to the Labour Court, after the necessary steps have been followed.

10. Duration of Agreement This Agreement shall come into operation on the date of execution hereof, and shall remain in force for an indefinite period from such date unless:

10.1 one party terminates it by giving the other (6) six months' prior notice in writing to that effect, or

10.2 if a party breaches a material term of this Agreement, the innocent party shall be entitled to terminate the Agreement, provided that the innocent party shall first afford the other party three weeks (from date of notice) in which to satisfactorily remedy the breach, or

10.3 in the event of the membership of the Union dropping below 50% of eligible employees and the Company giving the Union written notice calling on it to improve its representation within 30 days. In the event of Union membership at the factory not being in excess of 50% upon expiration of the period of notice, the rights and facilities contemplated in this Agreement shall cease to apply until such time as the Union satisfies the Company that its membership has increased to above 50% of the eligible employees at the factory.

11. General 11.1 This Agreement constitutes the entire Recognition Agreement between the Company and the Union and shall supersede any previous Agreements between the parties.

11.2.1 No term of this Agreement shall be suspended, modified, cancelled or otherwise varied, except by means of a further written Agreement, signed by the parties. The parties may, by common consent, renegotiate any part of this Agreement.

11.2.2 Should the parties fail to reach agreement on any proposed amendment, the *status quo* shall remain.

11.3 The Union will provide the Company with a copy of its Constitution and shall advise the Company within 14 days of any amendments thereto.

11.4 The parties agree that, in the event of any legal proceedings arising between them, such proceedings shall be brought in a court having jurisdiction in respect of the area in which the factory is situated.

11.5 The Company's Personnel Department will provide the liaison function between the two parties.

12. Domicilia and Notices

12.1 For the purpose of this Agreement, including the giving of notices and the serving of legal process, the Company and the Union choose domicilium citandi et executandi ('domicilium') as follows:

The Company at . . . .

The Union at . . . .

12.2 The Company or the Union may at any time change its address by notice in writing, provided that the new domicilium is or includes a physical address within the Republic of South Africa at which process can be served. It shall become effective upon receipt of such notice.

DATED at . . . . this . . . . . . day of . . . .

AS WITNESSES:

1. . . . .
                                           for THE UNION
2. . . . .   in his capacity as . . . .
                                           of the union, he being duly authorised to sign
                                           this agreement on behalf of the union by a
                                           resolution of the National Executive Committee
                                           passed on the . . . . . day of . . . .

DATED at . . . . this . . . . . . day of . . . .

AS WITNESSES:

1. . . . .
                                           for THE COMPANY
2. . . . .   in his capacity as Managing Director, he being
                                           duly authorised to sign this agreement on behalf
                                           of the company by a resolution of the board of
                                           directors passed on the . . . . . day of . . . . .

STOP ORDER FORM

ANNEXURE A

The Secretary

Messrs . . . .   *(Name and address of employer)*

. . . .

. . . .

Dear Sir

(Name of union) . . . .

I, *(full names)* . . . .   *(clock no.)* . . . .

being a member of the abovementioned trade union, hereby request you to deduct an amount of 40c per week or such other amount as may be determined according to the union constitution from time to time, from my remuneration in respect of subscriptions payable to that trade union. I hereby revoke any previous authorisation for deductions in respect of any other union. I undertake to give four weeks' notice of resignation to the union before revoking this authorisation.

Yours faithfully

. . . .   Witness (1) . . . .
(Signature of employee)
                                        Witness (2) . . . .

For Official Use

I certify that the abovementioned person is a member of the . . . . and that his weekly membership fee is 40 cents.

. . . .   Date: . . . .
Secretary

CONSTITUENCIES FOR SHOP STEWARDS ELECTION

ANNEXURE B

1. Cutting	Total : 4 shop stewards
2. Machining	Total : 4 shop stewards
3. Workshop, Stores, Cleaners, Security	Total : 2 shop stewards
4. Finishing, Despatch	Total : 1 shop steward

Total number of shop stewards : 11

SHOP STEWARDS' DECLARATION

ANNEXURE C

As agreed between the . . . . and

. . . . as partners to the agreement

which brought me to office, I, ... ,

shop steward in the constituency of . . . . ,

hereby agree to carry out my duties as shop steward in conformity with the provisions of all agreements made between the two parties mentioned above.

DATED at . . . . this . . . . . . day of . . . .

. . . .
Shop Steward

. . . .
Witness (union)

. . . .
Witness (company)

ABBREVIATIONS

ACAS . . . . Arbitration Conciliation Advisory Service
AFL–CIO . . . . American Federation of Labour–Congress of Industrial Organisations
AFCWU . . . . African Food & Canning Workers' Union
AHI . . . . Afrikaanse Handelsinstituut
ANC . . . . African National Congress
ASSOCOM . . . . Associated Chambers of Commerce
AZACTU . . . . Azanian Congress of Trade Unions
AZAPO . . . . Azanian People's Orgnisation
BAWU . . . . Black Allied Workers' Union
CCATU . . . . Coordinating Committee of African Trade Unions
CCAWUSA . . . . Commercial Catering & Allied Workers' Union of South Africa
CCMA . . . . Commission for Conciliation, Mediation & Arbitration
CCOBTU . . . . Consultative Committee of Black Trade Unions
CEC . . . . Central Executive Committee (COSATU)
CIUWW . . . . Council of Industrial Unions of the Witwatersrand
CLOWU . . . . Clothing Workers' Union
CTMWA . . . . Cape Town Municipal Workers' Association
CNETU . . . . Council of Non-European Trade Unions
COSATU . . . . Congress of South African Trade Unions
CUSA . . . . Council of Unions of South Africa
EEC . . . . European Economic Community
FCI . . . . Federated Chamber of Industries
FNETU . . . . Federation of Non-European Trade Unions
FOFATUSA . . . . Federation of Free African Trade Unions of South Africa
FOSATU . . . . Federation of South African Trade Unions
GAWU . . . . General & Allied Workers' Union
GFWBF . . . . General Factory Workers' Benefit Fund
GWU . . . . General Workers' Union
GWUSA . . . . General Workers' Union of South Africa
IAS . . . . Industrial Aid Society
ICWU . . . . Industrial & Commercial Workers' Union
ILO . . . . International Labour Organisation
IWA . . . . Industrial Workers of Africa
JCATU . . . . Joint Committee of African Trade Unions
LIFO . . . . Last in, first out
MACWUSA . . . . Motor Assembly & Component Workers' Union of South Africa
MICWU . . . . Motor Industry Combined Workers' Union
MWASA . . . . Media Workers' Association of South Africa
MWU . . . . Mineworkers' Union
NAAWU . . . . National Automobile & Allied Workers' Union
NACTU . . . . National Council of Trade Unions
NAFCOC . . . . National African Federation of Chambers of Commerce
NASRAIEU . . . . National Sugar Refining & Allied Industries Employees' Union
NEDLAC . . . . National Economic Development & Labour Council
NF . . . . National Forum

NFW . . . . National Federation of Workers
NUDAW . . . . National Union of Distributive & Allied Workers
NUM . . . . National Union of Mineworkers
NUMARWOSA . . . . National Union of Motor & Rubber Workers of South Africa
NUMSA . . . . National Union of Metalworkers of South Africa
PAC . . . . Pan African Congress
PEDCO . . . . Port Elizabeth Black Civic Organisation
RAWU . . . . Retail & Allied Workers' Union
RDP . . . . Reconstruction & Development Programme
SAAWU . . . . South African Allied Workers' Union
SABS . . . . South African Boilermakers' Society
SACCOLA . . . . South African Coordinating Committee on Labour Affairs
SACLA . . . . South African Confederation of Labour Associations
SACTU . . . . South African Congress of Trade Unions
SACP . . . . South African Communist Party
SAFTU . . . . South African Federation of Trade Unions
SALDRU . . . . South African Labour Development & Research Unit
SANCO . . . . South African National Civic Organisation
SARHWU . . . . South African Railway & Harbour Workers' Union
SATUC . . . . South African Trade Union Council
SEAWU . . . . Steel, Engineering & Allied Workers' Union
TLC . . . . Trades & Labour Council
TUACC . . . . Trade Union Advisory & Coordinating Council
TUC . . . . Trade Union Congress (Britain)
 . . . . Trade Union Council (South Africa)
TUCSA . . . . Trade Union Council of South Africa
UDF . . . . United Democratic Front
UNISA . . . . University of South Africa
UTP . . . . Urban Training Project
UWUSA . . . . United Workers' Union of South Africa
WPGWU . . . . Western Province General Workers' Union
WPWAB . . . . Western Province Workers' Advice Bureau

E

X

Y